Julia Margaret Cameron

The Colonial Shadows of Victorian Photography

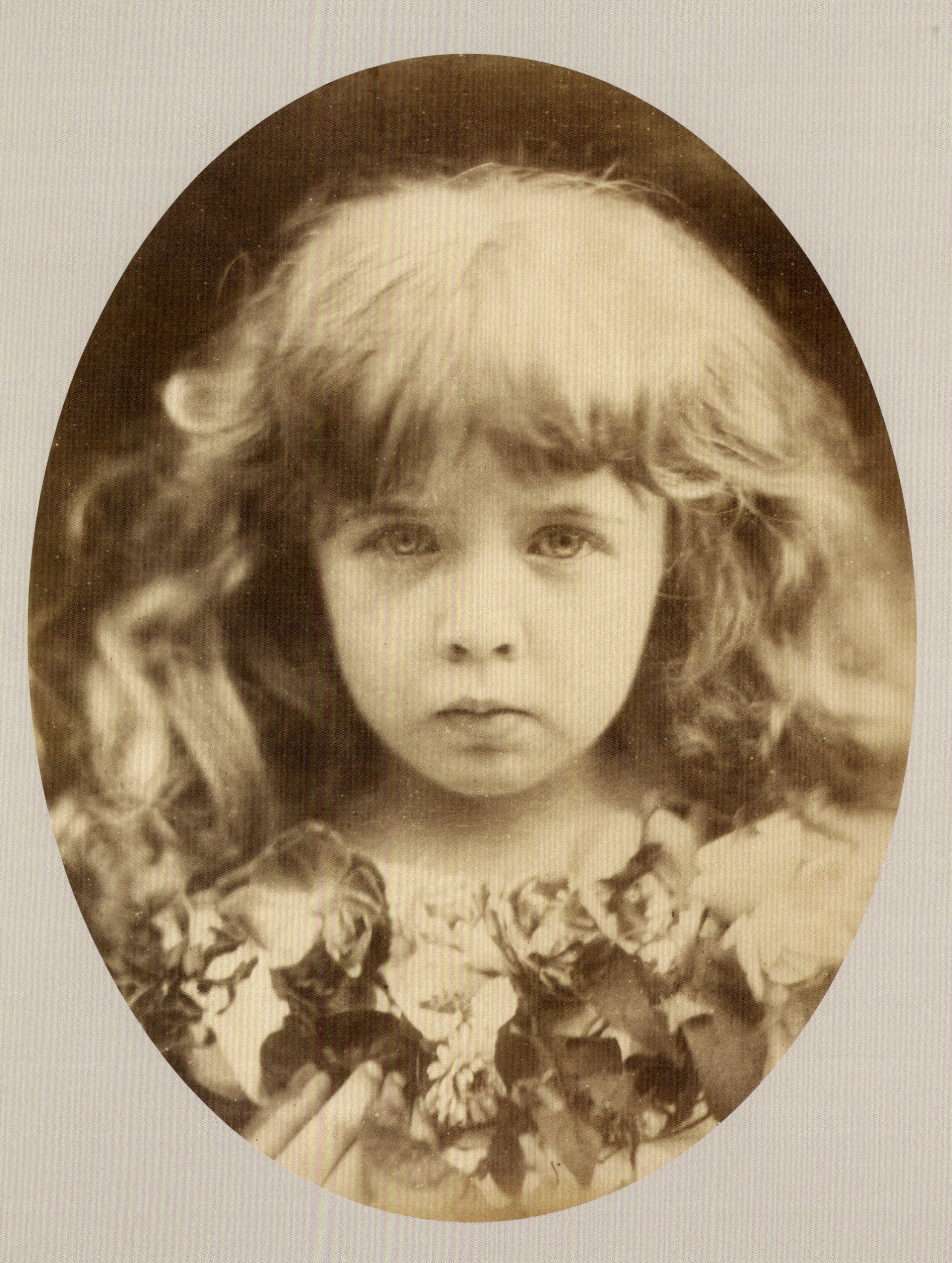

Jeff Rosen

Julia Margaret Cameron

The Colonial Shadows of Victorian Photography

Paul Mellon Centre for Studies in British Art

Distributed by Yale University Press
New Haven and London

First published in 2024 by the
Paul Mellon Centre for Studies in British Art
16 Bedford Square, London, WC1B 3JA
paul-mellon-centre.ac.uk

ISBN 978-1-913107-42-0 HB
Library of Congress Control Number: 2023951058

British Library Cataloguing-in-Publication Data
A catalogue record for this book is available from the British Library

Designed by Robert Dalrymple
Origination by Evergreen Colour Management Ltd
Printed in China through World Print Ltd

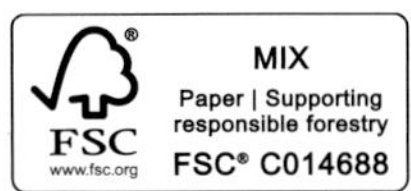

Frontispiece: Julia Margaret Cameron, *Untitled* (portrait of Margie Thackeray), *c.*1868 (see fig. 39).

Contents

Note to the Reader

Two clarifications follow. The first pertains to the historical terminology of 1857. In May of that year, Indian men conscripted to serve in the East India Company's armies, known as sepoys, revolted against British officers who commanded their regiments. This uprising ignited a rebellion that spread throughout the Indian subcontinent. By the end of 1858, bloody reprisals had suppressed the insurrection, and Queen Victoria had dissolved the East India Company, absorbing India as a British colony. In Britain, the rebellion and the war that followed were referred to as a 'mutiny'. This term referred to military insubordination, but also to feelings of social and psychological betrayal and unprovoked defiance. Julia Margaret Cameron, along with her circle of artistic friends, expatriate administrators of the Company, and much of the British press, used the term to describe the conflict. In *Julia Margaret Cameron: The Colonial Shadows of Victorian Photography*, I retain this use only when quoting from primary source documents to reflect the writer's state of mind. Otherwise, I refer to these events as the Indian Uprising, or as the rebellion, revolt or insurrection.

The second point of clarification concerns specific titles and other references to Cameron's photographs in the text. Because she regarded photographs as works of fine art, Cameron copyrighted her imagery and gave her prints evocative titles. Her titles help us identify these subjects, especially literary and allegorical subjects. Occasionally, they also refer to specific events in British colonial history that might be obscure today. The book draws upon these titles to identify specific photographs and to demonstrate how Cameron embedded in her imagery explicit references to the imperial project of which she was a part. It also refers to Cameron's handwritten inscriptions – sometimes made in the letter of a print (on the mount beneath the photograph) or on its reverse side – which provide additional evidence of her efforts to write history by visualizing complex historical narratives in photography.

Therefore, to clarify pictorial references in the text, this book draws upon the *catalogue raisonné* of Cameron's photographs produced by the J. Paul Getty Museum in 2003, edited by Julian Cox and Colin Ford. The digital version, *Julia Margaret Cameron: The Complete Photographs*, is available at: https://www.getty.edu/publications/virtuallibrary/0892366818.html. Citations of specific photographs in this volume, whether the print or the web-based version, use the convention '(Cox/Ford no.)'. This study also analyses the volume of ninety-two photographs that Cameron gave in 1867 to her friend and mentor Sir John Herschel, a collection known as the Herschel Album. Citations of images in this album, which Colin Ford reproduced in facsimile as *The Cameron Collection* (London: National Portrait Gallery, 1975), use the convention '(HA-no.)'. As an example, Cameron's photograph *Iago: Study from an Italian*, which she titled and registered for copyright protection on 4 July 1867, is referred to by its number in the *catalogue raisonné* (Cox/Ford 634) and by its plate number in the Herschel Album (HA-69).

Prologue

Arthur's First Wound
by William Makepeace Thackeray

Published in *The Times*, 11 February 1858, p. 10

Historians have told
How the Spartan boys, of old,
Were trained to hard endurance and the banishing of fear;
And how Spartan mothers gave
The broad shield of the brave,
Saying, 'Let it guard thy breast, or be thy bier!'

But to win the Warrior's meed,
Our English boys have need
Of no precursive trial to lift their courage high;
The red blood in their veins
Each daring spirit trains,
And the motto of their race is, 'Do or die!'

It seems but yesterday
A fragile darling lay,
His cheek rose-flushed with fever, and breathing with a moan;
While the father bent above
With a look of pitying love,
And the tiny hand clasped close within his own.

A fragile child no more
On far India's troubled shore, –
'Gainst wild revolt and massacre our English Arthur strives.
Charge! is the given word,
And he fearless draws his sword,
While around him fall a hecatomb of lives.

Now, God be with the right!
Teach the slender hands to smite,
As when Israel's champion shepherd foiled the huge Goliath's thrust;
Where our young sons make their stand –
The Davids of our land –
Let the Giant of Revolt bite the dust!

Upon that dreary field
Where they fight who will not yield,
And where the only conquered are those the foe hath slain,
Protect them, holy Heaven!
By the bitter war-cry given
Of our women and our children in their pain!

Arthur! thou bear'st the name
Of that warrior dear to Fame,
Who, after all his battles, so calmly sank to sleep, –
With the dint of faded scars
From the old triumphant wars, –
In the hush of love and Walmer's castled keep.

A nation mourned that day!
I saw the proud array, –
I saw the sable catafalque that darkly moved along, –
And the battle charger go,
With his drooping crest bent low,
Riderless amid the funeral throng!

I heard the muffled drum;
I saw the millions come;
Nor were there wanting earnest tears for true remembrance shed;
With a pang of solemn grief
The People mourned their chief,
For Arthur, Duke of Wellington, was dead!

Arthur, may'st thou, like him,
Live till faded eyes are dim,
That with youth's impetuous sparkle watch the battle chances now,
And thy first wound only be
The first leaf from that tree
Whose fabled laurel binds the victor's brow.

May thy name – which now is known
To loving friends alone –
Be one thy country yet shall link with many a famous fight;
And old men give this praise –
'His first wound was in those days
When rebel India crouched to Britain's might!'

THOMAS NEWCOME.[1]

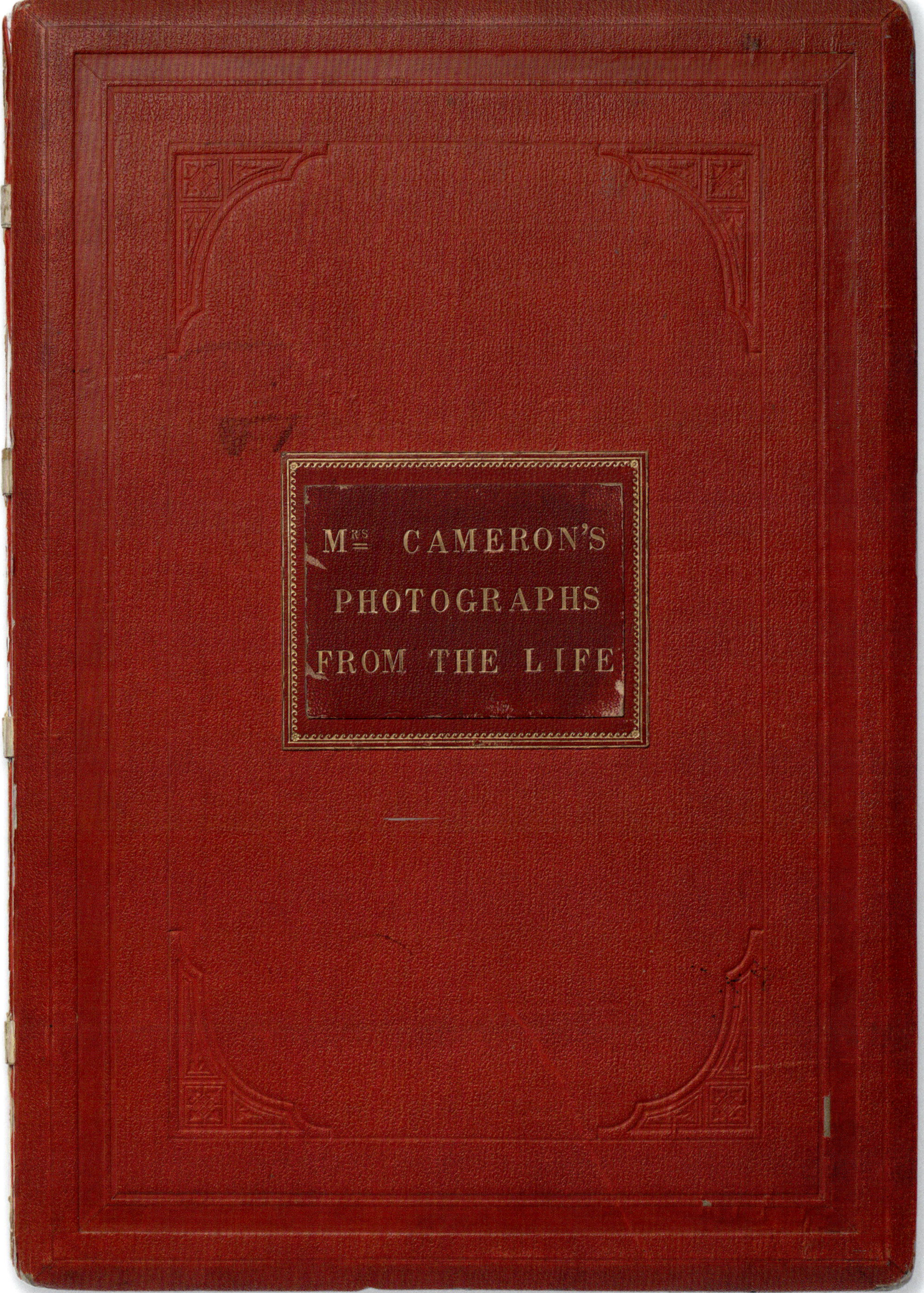

Mrs CAMERON'S
PHOTOGRAPHS
FROM THE LIFE

Introduction
Narrating History

1 *Mrs. Cameron's Photographs from the Life*, 1864–9; assembled 1869; 47.8 × 33.5 × 4.7 cm.

The Museum of Fine Arts, Houston, 2021.282.1-.75. Photograph © The Museum of Fine Arts, Houston: Will Michels.

PHOTOGRAPHIC ALBUMS

In 2018, London's *Guardian* newspaper announced a public appeal to raise funds to keep an album of Julia Margaret Cameron's photographs in England, cautioning readers that the photographs could end up leaving the country, 'unless a buyer with £3.7m can be found'.[1] To prevent an immediate sale, the UK arts minister even placed the album on a temporary export restraint.[2] This collection drive echoed an almost identical plea of more than thirty years earlier: back in 1975, *Creative Camera* called upon the British nation 'to raise funds £52,000 ($130,000) to save' another of Cameron's photographic albums, not from possible destruction, but to prevent that album from leaving England and 'going to a private collector in America'.[3] Setting aside the unmistakable increase in monetary value associated with Cameron's photographs, these two dates bookend the modern period when this Victorian photographer moved from relative obscurity to widespread popular acclaim. As if to greet Cameron's installation into the nation's pantheon of great artists, Kate Middleton, then Duchess of Cambridge, spoke glowingly about her photographs at the opening of the National Portrait Gallery's 2018 exhibition *Victorian Giants: The Birth of Art Photography*.[4] Cameron was central to this story about photography breaking new ground and staking claim to the rarefied world of fine art.

The 1975 fund-raising drive was ultimately successful and the Herschel Album, a volume of photographs that Cameron originally dedicated to her friend the astronomer Sir John Herschel, was welcomed into the collection of a national museum. The 2018 appeal failed, however, and Cameron's album, a collection of photographs she had assembled for her daughter Julia Hay (Cameron) Norman – known affectionately as Juley – left England for the Museum of Fine Arts, Houston (fig. 1).[5] In spite of this disappointment, the sale only cemented the widespread view that photography was now recognized as a legitimate fine art medium, one with a unique history and patrimony, and of evident national value. Indeed, since 1975, numerous publications had ascribed to photographs like Cameron's significant aesthetic and historical importance that merited serious academic study and enthusiastic collection by fine arts museums.[6]

Photography's historiography consequently found in Cameron a person of many parts: a ground-breaking artist, one of the first to take the medium seriously as a form of artistic expression *and* achieve critical acclaim for her efforts, a trailblazing portraitist who made extraordinary celebrity headshots of the great men of her time, a sensitive and devout mother whose imagery embraced the close bower of family, and a woman who led a remarkable life of personal religious devotion. Cameron was remembered as Sir John Herschel's dear friend and as Alfred, Lord Tennyson's devoted neighbour. She was rediscovered as a friend of the Pre-Raphaelite Brotherhood and revived as a prophetic artistic influence on her great-niece Virginia Woolf. In addition, she was revered for her intuitive artistic style by the pictorialist Peter Henry Emerson, and was recalled as a historical favourite of Alfred Stieglitz, who mounted Cameron's first American exhibition as a photographic pioneer, devoting an entire issue of *Camera Work* in 1913 to her photographs.[7] With every new discovery and sale, every historical monograph and fine arts gallery exhibition, new life was breathed into Cameron's unique aesthetic claim on photographic history.

These historical studies have contextualized Cameron's photographs in many important ways. They have situated her imagery in relation to the work of others, especially artists, who also adopted the medium in its early days. They have identified most of her portrait subjects, not only the well-known luminaries of Victorian letters and science but also names of household maids, neighbourhood children, and others from her Freshwater village on the Isle of Wight. They have recognized her aesthetic uniqueness and her formal contributions to photographic printmaking. They have examined her imagery in relation to its literary, typological, and allegorical referents. And they have considered the impact of her religious convictions, motherly devotions, feminist sentiments, personal friendships, as well as her artistic independence, self-reliance, purposefulness, and self-consciousness in relation to the meanings and impact of her work on contemporaries.

These diverse lines of inquiry and analysis have also added immeasurably to our understanding of Cameron's work, and photographic history has certainly embraced her many contributions. But these studies have also largely compartmentalized her imagery, separating portraits of prominent cultural figures, for example, from imagery of family members or neighbourhood children, a sometimes-useful taxonomy for collectors but a potential divide that threatens to obscure relationships across categories. Classification schemes also tend to acquire an authority of their own and may overlook multiple or overlapping ways in which Cameron's contemporaries first perceived or later came to understand her work. In addition, traditional fine art categories tend to isolate works, often unintentionally, into separate genres. Or they may neglect how an artist's photographs intersected with historical and cultural conflicts, especially the colliding global forces of colonialism, political history, and nationalism that transfixed Britain in the mid-nineteenth century. And yet, Julia Margaret Cameron emerged as a photographer precisely in this historical context, absorbed by the greatest political threat Britain ever faced to its imperial ambitions, the momentous anti-colonial rebellion of 1857, known as the Mutiny in Britain and as the Uprising in India.[8] As we shall see, Cameron was enmeshed in a circle of family and friends in London who, like her, were former residents in India, many of them governing officials and military officers attached to the East India Company. In the summer of 1857, Cameron and her family were shaken awake by news of the unrest, riveted by worries for family members in India left vulnerable by the conflict, and rattled by thoughts of a bloody war abroad that provoked feelings of panic and anxiety. From the comfort of Little Holland House, Cameron was also embraced by a confederation of visual artists, critics, and literary figures who created and shared works of art that responded to the conflict. Like Julia Margaret, they were consumed by the shock, disbelief, and grief in the national mood that reacted in unison to these calamitous events.

This book makes the case that Julia Margaret Cameron was shaped personally by these historical forces and argues that the legacy of the war in India infused her sense of national identity and informed both her artistic practice and the narrative choices of her photography. As a result, when Cameron emerged as a photographer, it was in relation to the imperial project of which she was a part. The Herschel Album is instrumental to this story: by examining how Cameron was enmeshed within an extended circle of family and friends that was saturated by representations of Britain's cultural dominance, especially in relation to India, I establish that her early photographic activities – especially her construction of gift albums for members of her circle and other examples containing her earliest photographic imagery – were shaped by a discourse of British colonial superiority and driven by her strong desire to contribute to that historical narrative.[9]

When framed as a 'mutiny story', the history of the Indian Uprising is inseparable from Cameron's own biography: in Victorian England and in Cameron's own circle, this term was used to describe the rebellion in limited terms, confining the insurrection to a handful of discontented and resentful Indian soldiers (whom the British called sepoys) who revolted against their British officers in the East India Company's army. But the rebellion that began in May 1857 in Meerut spread quickly across the territory, leading many observers, both local and international, to characterize the conflict in India as the first great anti-colonial revolt, a crisis borne over the breakdown of governance and military rule. In short, the insurrection in India was a determined and tenacious effort to expel the British from the subcontinent entirely.[10] And yet, when Cameron and her family used the word Mutiny to describe the conflict at the heart of this study, they simultaneously objectified the symbolic bond yoking together British colonists and 'their dark reflection, the shadow of the colonized man'.[11] As we shall see, the long shadow that framed the relationship between Britain and India after 1857 was discussed repeatedly in terms of betrayal, unfaithfulness, and disloyalty. These words echo throughout Cameron's own letters of the time, just as they informed the political writings of her husband, Charles Hay Cameron. But the fallout of the betrayal at the origin of the insurrection tells only one part of the story, as the expanding discourse Cameron and her circle told themselves in the war's aftermath was expressed in a rhetoric of humiliation, expiation, and atonement. But only for so long: in 1858, once Britain subsumed India as a Crown colony and Queen Victoria established herself as Empress, 'God's forgiveness' and 'Britain's humiliation' quickly became discarded afterthoughts, and the Indian revolt became reimagined as only a temporary setback in the long story of Britain's glorious imperial heritage.

But for Julia Margaret Cameron and her family, the shadow of the Indian Uprising was not remote or abstract: it arrived literally on Cameron's family's doorstep in Kensington. This was the cosmopolitan home of Sara and Thoby Prinsep, Julia Margaret's sister and brother-in-law, known as Little Holland House. During the 1850s, the two sisters presided over weekly cultural salons, filling Little Holland House with music-filled evenings and lively discussions about art and politics. Attendees heard classical performances by Charles Hallé on piano, Joseph Joachim on violin, Alfredo Piatti on cello, and the great baritone, Manuel García. This portrait of cultural serenity and bourgeois calm prevailed until it was shattered one day in the hot summer of 1857. As recalled by the Pre-Raphaelite painter William Holman Hunt, 'suddenly news came of the outbreak of the Mutiny', and 'a cloud of fear spread over the house'.[12] The 'cloud of fear' was trained on the uncertain welfare of Arthur Prinsep, Sara's seventeen-year-old son and Julia Margaret's dear nephew, who only the year before had enlisted in the East India Company's Bengali army division. On 20 October 1856, the young man was commissioned a cadet and assigned to the 4th European Light Cavalry. In January 1857, he was promoted to lieutenant and then called into action from a regimental base in Lucknow.[13] If young Arthur faced mortal peril from sepoys stationed to his own garrison, as the Little Holland House company soon learned was likely, he would face even greater danger as a willing participant in Britain's larger punitive response to the Indian insurrection, a journey that would take him physically from the Lucknow fort to the Kashmiri gate in Delhi as a violent accomplice in the symbolic battlefield of colonial retribution, as Britain brutally punished India for having dared to be disloyal.

The cacophony of history is often a product of multiple narratives and overlapping discourses and does not easily lend itself to monographic studies of visual representations, iconography, or historical knowledge in isolation from each other. Rather than sequester Cameron's photographs by creating new boxes or detach the Uprising in India as an isolated and remote historical episode, my interest in this book is to locate how Cameron positioned her photography at the intersection where visual art converged with multiple and sometimes overlapping or even competing historical narratives. For Cameron, as we shall see, these narratives intersected with the activities of family and friends; they were embedded in the shifting discourses that defined national identity; and they were confronted by an unstable imperial landscape, one brought into stark crisis in the aftershock of the rebellion in India. The Herschel Album presents a sterling example of this convergence of art and history in the aftermath of such crisis, a visual imprint of Cameron's historical imagination. Many historians believe Cameron's photographs from this album form a canon of their own, chiefly because they represent the seminal collection of her finest prints. Assembled by the artist as a presentation album to Sir John Herschel, her friend and mentor, she chose each photograph as an expression of both her personal devotion to him and her unbridled enthusiasm for the medium. Consequently, as a historical document, the Herschel Album exhibits essential markers of Cameron's unique authorship, especially because she titled each image and wrote a Table of Contents to the volume. Between the album's two covers, these photographs have been conceived as a privileged and an unparalleled interpretive space shared by the two friends, one that exemplifies their shared understanding of history and love of photography.

Cameron originally presented the volume to Herschel in 1864, her first year as a photographer. But in recognition of her growing success and pride in freshly created work, she asked for the volume's return so that she could expand it by increasing the number of photographs. In 1867, she rededicated the new album. Historians agree that the 1867 collection contains her most valued portraits of eminent cultural figures as well as Herschel's own favourite examples of the allegorical photographs she called 'fancy subjects'.[14] In short, we may consider this album a microcosm of Cameron's achievements in photography, one that contains vestiges of the formal legacy of the imperial mindset that helped give it shape. For example, by examining the Herschel Album we have access to Cameron's earliest experiments in photography arising from her work in 1863 alongside Oscar Gustave Rejlander and their shared outing in Freshwater during which they posed Cameron's housemaids outside her water well. The volume contains numerous portraits, including those of Tennyson, Thomas Carlyle, and William Holman Hunt, the artist who first witnessed how the 1857 Uprising in India affected Cameron and her extended family. The Herschel Album also helps to provide context for Cameron's early experimentation in the medium, in which she explored unanticipated narrative forms of storytelling, taking us back to her early practice of compiling prints and assembling albums as gifts for others. As Patrizia Di Bello has demonstrated, photographic albums, rather than individual prints made for public exhibition, 'were the most common forms for storing, displaying, and circulating photographic prints in the nineteenth century, for artists and amateurs alike'.[15] And in the Herschel Album, especially if we centre attention on two of its most iconic allegorical photographs – the first and the last in the album – we may find latent evidence that Cameron embedded her claims to Britain's imperial past in relation to India. By examining the material qualities of the photographs she produced, we are able to re-evaluate those images, and the album as a whole, in relation to Cameron's efforts to use the medium as an act of historical narration.

The conflict in India incubated its own rhetorical trappings in the British press, framing the event in relation to ideas of 'mutiny and loyalty', 'betrayal and atonement', and 'sovereignty and nationhood'. Consequently, these terms emerged as part of a new imperial vocabulary for British imperialism by providing daily reminders of the war abroad. This discourse informed a wide array of narrative forms that directly affected Cameron and her circle: these included news accounts of the war that she consumed and private letters sent by those caught up in the conflict. The same language informed poems and literary fiction created by Cameron's friends to help them process the implications of the imperial war. Tracts of political economy generated by her husband, Charles, and brother-in-law, Thoby Prinsep, actively reimagined the new world order in these terms in the aftermath of the rebellion as they worked to influence British public policy as well as the future governance of the new Crown colony. As we shall see, Cameron embedded these rival value oppositions in photographs she assembled in the Herschel Album because they embodied these contrasting emblems of national identity, gave visibility to the conflicted public reaction to the insurrection, and expressed her own unique, contemporary artistic and narrative interpretation of the historical event.

ARTISTIC BEGINNINGS

In 1874, Cameron herself complicated how biographers would later characterize this period when she began writing an autobiographical narrative to author her own legacy. She designated 1864, when she turned forty-nine years old, as the date of her 'first success' in photography. Now the stuff of legend, burnished by autobiography, Cameron described her own artistic birth like a flash of creative genius ('*from the first moment I handled my lens*') after receiving a camera from her daughter, who said, 'It may amuse you, Mother, to try to photograph during your solitude at Freshwater'.[16] Treated as a kind of spiritual annunciation, these providential beginnings naturally focus our attention on the years *after* Christmas-time in 1863, when Cameron received her propitious gift. Only in May 1864 did Cameron begin the practice of registering her prints for copyright protection.[17] Cameron's home on the Isle of Wight has also been regarded as idyllic. Consequently, because her family, friends, and neighbours in Freshwater were among her first subjects, her first witnesses, and the first attentive audience for her photography, their influence has naturally been considered primary, their encouragement essential, and their reactions crucial to understanding Cameron's motivations, inspirations, and development as an independent visual artist.

And *before* 1864? Even though Julia Margaret Pattle was born in Calcutta[18] to an official of the East India Company and married Charles Hay Cameron, also a colonial governmental official, Cameron's many biographers have relegated her colonial past to colourful background material, there to be overlooked or dismissed entirely, as if time spent in colonial governmental service was a family's vocational choice much like any other, concluding that the impact upon her worldview was small, barely significant.[19] One writer, so intent to marginalize the colonial context, portrayed Charles Cameron's 'convalescent cruise in the Indian Ocean' as if it were a pedestrian, enjoyable diversion, while another downplayed the arduous sea voyage between Southampton and Calcutta, a trip that Julia Margaret made many times as a child and young adult, as 'slow and tedious' but nevertheless quite pleasant, much like a tourist's leisurely excursion.[20] Both ignored the fact that sea travel was costly and inherently dangerous: Julia Margaret's mother died at sea, as did her oldest sister Adeline, while other relatives, the Pictets, survived the wreck of the *SS Colombo* in 1862.

As a result, Cameron's upbringing, her marriage to a governing official of the Company who was engaged in writing the legal framework of both Ceylon and India, even her immediate personal reaction to news of the 1857 Uprising, have been explained away or minimized, considered unremarkable examples of an otherwise glamorous family of origin. About the rebellion in India, for example, we are told, 'The Pattle clan took the news hard. Julia Margaret was depressed and literally fell ill as the terrible news spread over all England'.[21] But we are not told *why*, exactly, Cameron was affected dramatically in this way when she consumed news of the events in India, as she lived in England, far from the violence of the insurrection. We have no insight into the distraught feelings she experienced and whether these passed quickly, persisted, or recurred sometime later. We are in the dark about how she coped with those feelings or with whom she might have commiserated when she experienced that distress. Aside from 'taking the news hard', we might ask: What precisely was *at stake* for the Pattle clan and for Cameron's circle of Indian expatriates upon learning news of the rebellion in India? How and why did the rebellion there disrupt their life in England? What news from the colony produced such anxiety and emotional pain, and how did the family process that grief? Did news of the insurrection recall experiences from Cameron's earlier years in India that unsettled or disturbed her understanding of the family's relationship to its colonial past? And how did Cameron's close network of family and friends in Little Holland House respond to this crisis, the most grave and all-consuming anti-colonial war in the nation's history?

The circle that gathered at Little Holland House is key, as Julia Margaret Cameron carefully crafted a persona of theatrical elegance behind its walls, one that elevated refined culture and downplayed political intrigue, much as she expunged her early years in India from the autobiographical account of her passion for photography. One expects everyone present in their orbit to have swooned like Anne Thackeray, who chronicled how the Pattle sisters theatrically 'float[ed] into the room with sweeping robes and falling folds' to greet visitors to Little Holland House.[22] Memoirs like these have left the impression that theirs was a charmed life undisturbed by worldly events, passionately and unreservedly devoted to the pursuit of fine art. Consequently, historians have understood the years between 1848, when the Camerons left India for London, and the start of Julia Margaret's photography in 1864, in relation to the influential artistic and literary men in her circle. These included William Makepeace Thackeray, with whom she rekindled an earlier friendship dating to her adolescent years in France; Henry Taylor, who authored the dramatic poem *Philip van Artevelte*, whom she met in 1850; Alfred Tennyson, the nation's Poet Laureate, to whom she was introduced in 1853 and with whom she formed sociable ties to his friends William Henry and Jane Brookfield; and the painter George Frederic Watts; as well as other exceptional artists and writers who gathered as part of the cultural salon at Holland Park. Consequently, Cameron's artistic backstory has evaded mention of the Indian Uprising as if it were a remote historical episode, irrelevant to Cameron's artistic formation and inconsequential to her family and friends, many of whom were artists, authors, and former officials who once governed the colony. Cameron's awareness of world events or political views has likewise been subordinated to her creative ambitions, working from the premise that her avowed interest in fine art dominated her friendship with the literary and artistic men of her time, just as Charles Cameron's publication of a small pamphlet on the sublime in art has been taken as a reflection of his cultured aesthetic sensibilities and genial compatibility with Julia Margaret.[23] The unmistakable implication is that Cameron's circle provided unmatched artistic guidance but also were remarkably free of social or political concern.

Also central to this story is Cameron's long friendship with Sir John Herschel, whom Julia Margaret and her husband Charles first met in Cape Town in 1837. Cameron credited Herschel with introducing her to photography when the medium itself was brand new, writing to him in 1864, 'I remember gratefully that the very first information I ever had of Photography in its Infant Life of Talbotype & Daguerreotype was in a letter I received from you in Calcutta'.[24] From the time that Herschel introduced her to the new medium until 1864, Julia Margaret moved from avid collector of photographs to ardent producer of new imagery, although in her autobiography she maintained that photography came over her abruptly, like a spiritual conversion. But as early as 1857, she began to construct albums into which she pasted her own photographs, mixing these prints with imagery created by others, like those produced by her brother-in-law, Earl Somers. These early albums differ from the Herschel and Norman Albums discussed above, not only because the two later albums were made *after* 1864, but because they contain Cameron's handwritten title pages and have preserved her organization. Consequently, the Herschel and Norman Albums possess an aura of integrity, authenticity, and authorial intention by virtue of having preserved the handiwork of the artist in the actual construction of the album. The so-called Mia Album, which Julia Margaret gave to her sister Maria Jackson in 1863 (but which contains later work, from 1869), and the Overstone Album, which Cameron gave to her benefactor in 1865, also preserve these same elements.[25]

Less well known, however, are earlier albums that the artist assembled and presented as gifts: to George Frederic Watts, called the 'Signor 1857' Album; to Sibella Norman, her daughter's mother-in-law, dated 1859; the album she gave to Henry Petty Fitzmaurice, 3rd Lord Lansdowne, also dated 1859; and the so-called 'Somers-Cocks Album', which Cameron inscribed to her sister Virginia Somers in 1863.[26] In general, because they were assembled over time and often contained loose pages that their owners could fill in later with additional works of art, including drawings, prints, and photographs, historians have no way to retrieve the photographer's original purpose or intentions and even less understanding of how they were read or used by their owners.[27] Moreover, these albums typically contained a mixture of original albumen prints and photographic reproductions; original drawings by artists, like Watts and Rossetti; and other graphic works, like *cartes-de-visite* or loose prints. Other albums from this era that have been disassembled in modern times also fit this pattern well: one belongs to the descendants of Cameron's sister, Sophia Dalrymple, but is no longer contained in one volume and cannot be dated securely. Nevertheless, that collection contains many of the same images that appear in the diverse volumes noted above.

These unfinished, fragmented, or disassembled albums are valuable to the present study because they contain photographs that predate 1864 and because their contents suggest intriguing connections between the photographer and the albums' recipients that offer insights about the political and social world they inhabited. They suggest a working method that is little studied and not wholly understood, one that corresponds broadly to collecting activities that were practised by Victorian women of means and the tactile enjoyment of manipulating fragmented bits of visual imagery.[28] They are a part of Cameron's artistic beginnings but are not analysed here to offer for them new claims of authorship, artistic intention, or authenticity. Rather, these albums provide a record of a shared discourse between the photographer and her recipients, a tangible trace of associations that grew over time: they are artefacts of that relationship which, I shall argue, also contain an embedded ideology of empire. Moreover, Cameron's 'photographic albums' are not limited to photographic prints alone, but rather contain a wide range of popular graphic art and original works on paper. Because some pieces were mass-produced and others were unique, one-of-a-kind works, they offer historians a useful index of a collector's shifting interests and attention. Importantly, these albums also present artworks *in media res*, as they include unfinished sketches, photographic studies, severely cropped fragments, and duplicate photographs in various sizes and dimensions. Consequently, these portable collections conserve visual ephemera. Presented without a Table of Contents and assembled over time, they possess the historical value of unfinished narratives.[29] In this regard, the Henry Taylor Album (conserved today by the Bodleian Library) fits this pattern well, as this volume was also constructed over many years. Although it was not assembled by Cameron and she did not present the album to Taylor as a gift, this artefact reflects a shared understanding about its contents, as Taylor himself appears to have appended the titles of photographs in his own hand, sometimes producing an ongoing index on a separate page, at other times noting a title in the signature of a print.

PHOTOGRAPHIC STORYTELLING

In the chapters that follow, I present evidence that Cameron and her circle avidly consumed news of the Indian Uprising and expressed British concern for the prompt restitution of its imperial authority. The war in India captivated their political attention and influenced their creative work for years to come. For Cameron, this influence shaped her earliest photographic albums. Literary scholars of this era have demonstrated that traumatic after-effects of the war pervaded Victorian literary texts, including personal memoires, gothic and romantic tales, stories of geographic exploration, and novels of everyday life, and that imperial themes rooted in Britain's colonial expansion recurred for years in the form of allegorical projections of civility against barbarism, good versus evil, justice and morality against injustice and depravity.[30] Since 1978, when Edward Said's influential volume *Orientalism* was first published,[31] numerous studies have examined ways that Western artists stereotyped colonial subjects, but only recently have historians examined the aftermath of the rebellion itself in analyses of works of visual art produced in Victorian England.[32]

Because photographers were burdened by the technological constraints of the medium, studies of Victorian photographs have principally examined works produced in the documentary mode. In India especially, these images accrued value for their normalized worldview and practical, utilitarian applications, as Christopher Pinney has written, helping to shape what he called a 'colonial habitus'.[33] Consequently, photographers saw the colonial world through a kind of surveyor's viewpoint, depicting traces of British infiltration in the environment like the railroad, army, telegraph, and civil service, as evidence of expanding colonial authority. Together, these pictorial constraints meant that British photographers in India privileged indexical records; they could depict sites of war, but only long after the battlefield action had ceased.[34] But in England, photographers like Julia Margaret Cameron began using photography in novel and unanticipated ways, creating visual allegories to represented British national identity. Cameron was not constrained by the technical limits or social conventions of her colonial counterparts. Rather, she learned about photography in relation to the complex archive of visual art and graphic ephemera that stands as a legacy of this period, a pictorial melange that includes cartoons in *Punch* and line drawings from the *Illustrated London News*, printed lithographs depicting the heroism of British soldiers and reproductive engravings of topical paintings exhibited in the Royal Academy, memorial sculptures displayed in the International Exhibition and grand commissions erected in the public square. This study returns Cameron's earliest photographs to this broader cultural space and to the larger discursive context that was united by a shared narrative about the constructive role and moral justice of British imperialism.

My approach here is to re-examine Cameron's photography as a form of *narrative history writing* and, as a result, to recentre the question of artistic influence from the 'fine art tradition' to the impact of colonialism. Today, we value Cameron as one of photography's earliest and greatest visual storytellers. Yet when the medium was new, photography did not fit smoothly alongside other forms of narrative expression, chiefly because the camera's frame appeared to bracket off small sections of the world and then re-present those fragments in disjointed and often unexplained ways. Nevertheless, the camera's chief value to many people was the fact that it represented reality convincingly. Looking back on those early years, John Szarkowski wrote that photographers could only 'isolate *the fragment*, document it, and by so doing claim for it some special significance, a meaning which went beyond simple description' (my emphasis).[35] During Cameron's time, essayists like Lady Elizabeth Eastlake expressed a similar view, using terms that despaired of what she termed photography's 'factual' limitations. Lady Eastlake essentially argued the medium contained no capacity to express artistic sentiment or tell stories, and she was especially dubious about any claims photographers might make to assign figurative meaning, like allegorical symbols, to photographic imagery.[36] But over time, perceptions changed, and photographs did acquire broad social value for their apparent realism and truthfulness, their ability to capture exquisite detail, and their judicious isolation and manipulation of symbolic form.[37] When Cameron adopted the camera as a creative tool, she disregarded Eastlake's concerns as irrelevant, if she ever read them: to Cameron, photographs were no different from the literary and visual arts that for centuries had used notable stories to explore the human condition, to interpret the present and to understand the past. Photographic storytelling became Cameron's mission, a tale she told repeatedly throughout her years as a photographer, a legend that informed the perspective of her great-niece, Virginia Woolf, who wrote Cameron's biography in 1926.[38]

Woolf was transfixed by Cameron's approach to visual representation, how she deliberately combined fictional elements and symbolic references in her imagery, how she purposefully created narrative gaps that left some hidden meaning unstated or ambiguous. Woolf wanted to identify those processes by which Cameron inventively created such narrative openings in photography, recognizing this as her signal achievement. To accomplish this goal, she wrote, Cameron had to manipulate the medium sufficiently in order 'to overcome realism'. In using this term, Woolf meant that Cameron worked to obscure those invisible ties that directly bind photographs to their subjects, what today's theorists would call photography's 'indexical value'.[39] How did she accomplish this? First, Woolf observed that Cameron purposefully undermined the naturalism of the camera's lens 'by diminishing just in the least degree the precision of focus', and secondly, that she dressed up her sitters in fanciful costumes to introduce story and symbolism: 'Boatmen were turned into King Arthur; village girls into Queen Guinevere. Tennyson was wrapped in rugs: Sir Henry Taylor was crowned with tinsel'.[40] Theatre and props were therefore put to the high purpose of allegorical representation, an approach that allowed her to initiate and control the narrative structure of her imagery. Consequently, Cameron made the process of interpreting her photographs one of recognizing – or decoding – visual symbols and external references. Sometimes these were found in literary sources, at other times in contemporary political debates. Simple ingredients, indeed: by using deliberate, selective focus to disrupt the expectations of realism and by adopting the conventional language of pictorial art by means of allegorical storytelling and visual iconography, Cameron was able to forge a novel direction in her approach to the medium.[41]

We see that Woolf perceived *how* Cameron overcame the realism of the camera-based image, but did she understand *to what end* Cameron struggled to compose her image, to find the right models, to contend with the harsh chemistry? What stories did Woolf believe Cameron was trying to tell? She left the answer to Roger Fry, who described the photographer's achievements in relation to *historical narration*. Cameron wanted to represent the history of her time, Fry insisted, describing her achievement in photography as capturing 'the transmission of a period'. According to Fry, Cameron's goal was to use the medium to define and convey 'an historical presence' within each image, an apt phrase that captures Hayden White's interest in the way historians use stories to explain the past, a key insight into the way he framed his understanding of the historical imagination.[42] My own interest in Cameron lies precisely here, in trying to understand her unique achievement in using photographs to narrate contemporary history, not through what we might call ordinary documentary means, but by using visual symbols, allegory, and iconography that contained, as Fry insisted, '*an historical presence*' because of its deliberate creative approach to narration.

'Historians were not hobbyists on the sidelines', writes Priya Satia, 'but the very makers of history', a key principle that informs her recent book, *Time's Monster*.[43] Satia argues that the essential interconnections of those who held powerful colonial administrative positions, like the intimate members of Cameron's family and the expatriate friends who comprised her social milieu, 'mutually reinforced' their shared understanding of contemporary history and politics, especially in relation to the levers of power that sustained colonialism. When those structures were threatened, as they were so dramatically during the 1857 Indian Uprising, Cameron's circle huddled ever closer to provide reciprocal support and encouragement. Satia argues that these influential men (and they were almost always men) did so by articulating and recirculating the prevailing symbols of 'historical thinking and power' about British imperialism in the narratives they created. That is, by means of their formal publications and the artistic works they produced during this period, this group 'formed themselves into a canon in dialogue with one another'.[44] But because narration is always provisional and subject to revision over time, writes Satia, historical storytelling consequently seeks new ways 'to discover a meaningful narrative structure – that rational principle – behind events that seem (and are) chaotic and contingent'.[45]

Satia's analysis that historical narration is made by 'the very makers of history' echoes Homi Bhabha's assertion that historians shape narrative *process* as much as narrative *structure* in the writing of history, chiefly because control of the narrative has always been the primary means by which historians frame how events are interpreted. Narrative control must always be provisional, according to Bhabha, because the diverse and competing forms of narration that are undertaken by artists and writers are initially created as rough sketches or outlines. He writes,

> To encounter the nation *as it is written* displays a temporality of culture and social consciousness more in tune with the partial, overdetermined process by which textual meaning is produced. [Original emphasis][46]

In other words, an ephemeral and ambivalent quality characterizes the various discursive forms that take shape when historical narratives are written. As a result, our present-day interpretation of those historical narratives requires context and perspective, which is to say,

> meanings may be partial because they are *in media res*; and history may be half-made because it is in the process of being made; and the image of cultural authority may be ambivalent because it is caught, uncertainly, in the act of 'composing' its powerful image.[47]

In acknowledging that historical narration is often half-made, formed using imagery that may be indistinct or caught in the very act of its own formation, authors and artists may be able to recognize that their own narratives embody such cultural power. For example, Thackeray recognized his own privileged position in this regard in the poem that serves as the Prologue to this book, 'Arthur's First Wound', because when he composed this verse and read it before a gathering at Little Holland House, those assembled did not know how grave were Arthur Prinsep's wounds or if he would even recover from them. Indeed, the outcome of the war itself was still undecided. Nevertheless, Thackeray described the conflict as if Britain's victory over its rebellious Indian colony was all but foretold, a settled narrative of Britain's imperial sacrifice and triumphant nationalism. Reciting his tale in the form a patriotic fable, Thackeray blended historical events of the nation's past together with contemporary history. After reciting the poem before Julia Margaret Cameron's inner circle at Little Holland House, he then published it on 11 February 1858 in the London *Times*, the nation's daily newspaper of record.

In publishing a paean to an imperial war whose success had not yet even been determined, Thackeray contributed to the act of writing history. He followed the same model established earlier by Tennyson, whose poem 'The Charge of the Light Brigade' appeared amid the Crimean war, before that conflict, too, had even been decided. The 'Light Brigade' was published on 9 December 1854 in the *Examiner*. Like Tennyson's homage to the nameless 'six hundred' invoked in his poem, Thackeray did not personally identify the 'Arthur' of his verse. Rather, Thackeray portrayed his 'Arthur' as an anonymous everyman, a willing conscript who was swept up by the heroic imagination, by the charmed stories that shape historical writing. Consequently, Thackeray's Arthur is a fabricated myth, as enigmatic and as heroic as Malory's King Arthur; a civil statesman as patriotic and brave as Arthur Wellesley, the Duke of Wellington; but also a gentle, kind, and humane soul, as compassionate as Tennyson's friend Arthur Hallam, whose untimely death the poet lamented in his tribute 'In Memoriam'. At the same time, by invoking these legendary examples of righteous conflict, Thackeray glossed over the violence of war, washing clean the blood spilled by the colonial uprising.

Moreover, Thackeray portrayed the Indian conflict as a just and noble cause that transcended the shortcomings of government or the bureaucracy of making war. In this regard, his poem was quite unlike Tennyson's, whose 'Light Brigade' 'poignantly memorialized the soldier's martyrdom to arrogant, aristocratic blundering', as Kathryn Ledbetter phrased it.[48] Thackeray's narrative was fixed in time and place, in that its principal action occurs 'on India's troubled shore', but his poem is exceptional as an unapologetic mythological genre mash-up of past heroic battles (the combat between Sparta and Athens in the Peloponnesian War, the fight between David and Goliath in the biblical battle for Canaan, the clash between France and England in the Peninsular War). Seen through Thackeray's imperial lens, these legendary conflicts gave birth to the present colonial war. In short, as Satia observed, Thackeray shaped his present based on his understanding of the past. Consequently, his narrative is redemptive because it appears to legitimize and atone for the destruction of all past wars, in spite of their claims for glory or nationalistic declarations, and its sentiment is deeply nostalgic, even melancholy, because it compensates for the emptiness of the present day and the impossibility of capturing or returning to the lost innocence of youth.[49] Thackeray makes clear that in his view, the insurrection in India was no less significant than those earlier historical examples: an imperial war of conquest; a conflict between East and West; a fight for national glory; a battle for bragging rights in the historical record.

HIDDEN IN PLAIN SIGHT

From the very beginning, Julia Margaret Cameron approached photography as a thoughtful and deliberate artist: she was never idiosyncratic in her choice of subject matter, never haphazard when she titled an image. And yet, the intersection of family, national identity, and imperialism – the three essential pillars that frame the foundation of the present study – remain persistently in the shadows as interpreted by contemporary historians. This was not Cameron's doing, however: rather, she made these relationships explicit in her imagery, sometimes by using allegory, at other times by directly negating visual symbolism altogether. Nowhere is this more apparent than in one of four related photographs that she created in 1872, which

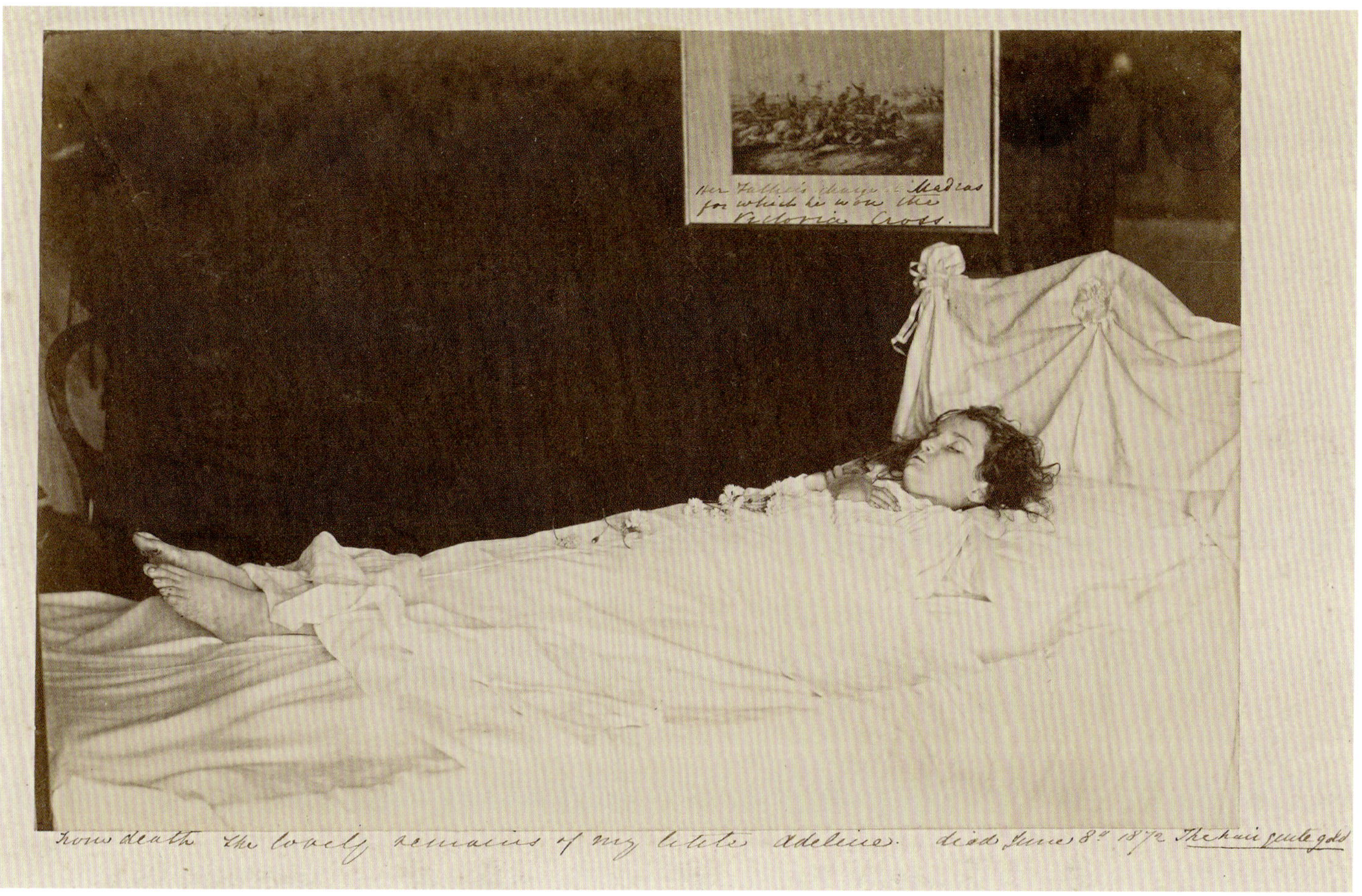

2 Julia Margaret Cameron, *From death / The lovely remains of my little Adeline / died June 8th 1872 / The hair quite gold*, 1872, albumen print, 24.2 × 34.8 cm. Courtesy of Tennyson Research Centre, Lincolnshire County Council. 368a.

portrays the death-bed scene of her great-niece, Adeline Clogstoun, who died unexpectedly from a terrible accident in Cameron's home on the Isle of Wight. Here I argue the Indian Uprising of 1857 lies hidden in plain sight, and the colonial relationship that yokes together family, nation, and empire is left open to viewers without reserve.[50] Titled *The lovely remains of my little Adeline* (Cox/Ford 935), the image uses a methodical array of interlocked visual and textual devices to direct viewers to associations that are personal and familial, symbolic and allegorical, and empirically literal, as Cameron forthrightly embedded the historical legacy of the insurrection in India in the photograph by means of this interconnectedness (fig. 2).

And yet, these signposts have been all but ignored in the historical literature, largely because the photograph has been interpreted as an expression of Cameron's own feminine subjectivity. Such readings privilege a modernistic embrace of artistic self-reflexivity purged of any vestige of political content. Carol Armstrong was among the first to embrace this point of view, arguing that Cameron's approach to photography centred in the maternal home and relied upon 'a visible process rather than a masterfully hidden technique, and her declaration of home-staging' demonstrated 'the personal quality of the truth of her fictions'. As a result, Armstrong held that Cameron's photographs depended upon 'the locus and condition of their making as that of the female domain of the home'.[51] Conceived in this way, Cameron's 'maternal' use of photography is a self-reflexive exercise taking place in a domestic interior, a way for her to allegorize her own artistic practice. As a result, Armstrong wrote that Cameron's photograph depicting the death of *my little Adeline* collapses the photographer's creative identity with maternal grief and despair, a simultaneous expression that merges artistic inspiration with 'the domestic, the incestuously familial and feminine; as something like hysteria – the hysteria of the mother'.[52] In this reading, the photograph becomes a kind of re-enactment of how Cameron used photography to mourn over the untimely death of an innocent and beloved child, one who entered her household with her younger sister after the death of both parents around 1870. In the death-bed photographs of Adeline, Cameron has arranged her body carefully, folded her arms across her breast, surrounded her with white flowers. She has staged this scene in her family's home, experimenting with different background arrangements to insert a tender and loving personal quality. In short, Armstrong contends that Cameron disciplined her pain and anguish and wrestled control over her own 'motherly hysteria' by displacing that grief through the formal and deliberative process of making photographs.

In working through her sadness at the loss of a child, Cameron experimented with the background of the image: while always maintaining her focus on the child's body in the foreground, she included an open window in one image; in a second, she inserted a box camera with its lens open to the light; and in a third, she arranged a framed picture, which appears to hover over the body. Noting these different alterations of the scene, Robin Kelsey extended Armstrong's notion that Cameron used photography self-reflexively but disparaged these background-filling devices as unwanted and untidy distractions. To Kelsey, the three different scenes are nothing more than irrelevant '*self-referential circuits*, whereby the camera was addressed by itself, or its product, or its light' (my emphasis).[53] Kelsey even ignored the fourth image Cameron made of the deceased child, one that lacks any notable background interest whatsoever, deeming it wholly unworthy of his commentary, possibly because it lacks the performative value that this historian prizes. As a result, for Kelsey, Cameron used her camera to look 'past the dead body to a sign of its own vital functions'. After having arrived at these conclusions, he summarily dismissed these 'lifeless' images as 'failures' because, in Cameron's hands, the camera was inert, unable to accomplish any action other than to 'perform for itself'.

In his analysis of the same four photographs, Julian Cox contextualized Cameron's imagery by calling attention to its relationship to the Victorian tradition of eulogizing the untimely death of an innocent child, especially as this sentimental convention was depicted in contemporary novels like Charles Dickens's *The Old Curiosity Shop*. In aligning these two narratives, Cox thereby reframes the subject: in the same way that Little Nell acts as the emotional heart of Dickens's novel, Cox recentres Adeline as the principal subject of the death-bed photograph (and *not* Cameron's self-reflexivity). He emphasizes how both narratives illustrate the purity and sanctity of a harmless child's death and demonstrates how both allegories conspire to present Adeline 'as a virginal child bride of Christ, with flowers strewn on the bed linens and her angelic barefoot form about to ascend and meet her maker'.[54] Cox also recognizes that Cameron does identify with the deceased child through her imagery, noting that in the image with the framed print, she inscribed the words, 'Her father's charge at Madras / for which he won the / Victoria Cross' (fig. 3). Cameron hand-wrote these words in ink on the photograph itself, an unprecedented action that she never repeated. Very likely, she presented the inscribed image to Tennyson, who was deeply affected by the young girl's death.[55] By means of this extraordinary gesture, first by including a framed print depicting Adeline Clogstoun's father and then by inscribing the exact nature of the relationship between that image and dead girl, Cox concluded, 'Cameron linked the daughter to the father and herself to them both'. But his analysis stopped there, leaving unresolved the exact nature of the relationship between the dead girl, the Christian allegory, and Cameron's inscription about the father, a decorated soldier.

Jordan Bear built upon Cox's analysis in his interpretation of this photographic series and, like Cox, focused his analysis on the singular image of the dead girl posed with a framed print depicting her deceased father. He recognized that the framed image Cameron inserted was 'a military scene', and although its resolution is

3 Julia Margaret Cameron, *From death / The lovely remains of my little Adeline* (detail of fig. 2).

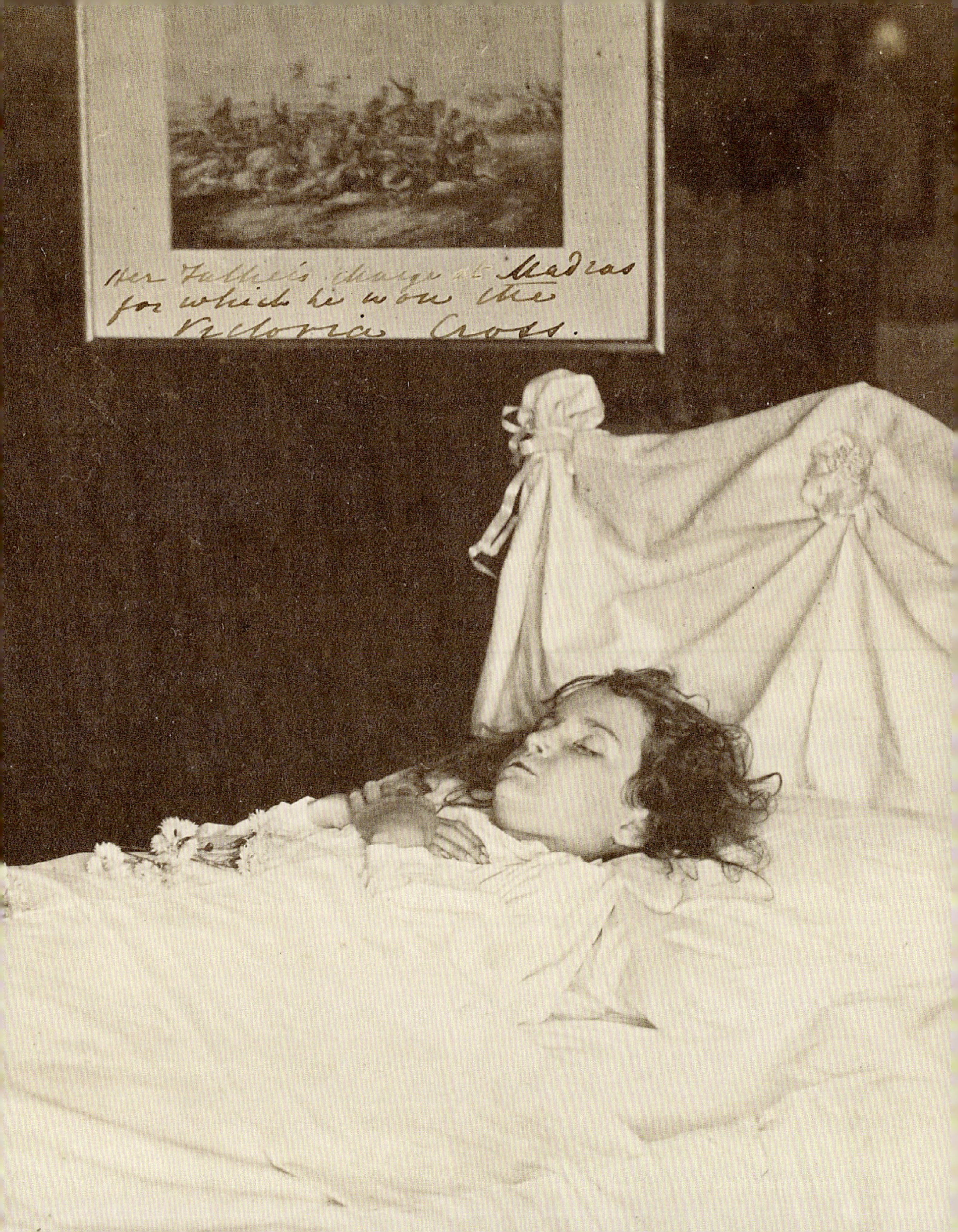
Her Father's charge at Madras
for which he won the
Victoria Cross.

indistinct, he avoided exploring its content because his interpretation was bent on its significance as 'saturated with apparently deferential female agency'.[56] To clarify, Bear referred here to the female photographer who inscribed the scene *and* to the female monarch for whom the child's father served and won the Victoria Cross. But in doing so, Bear once again conjured Cameron's actions as if they were incurably self-reflexive, calling her inscription about Adeline's father a way of 'cloaking her intervention in the description of his gallantry'. Through this act of transference, he argues, the girl's father stands in for the photographer as a foil: by 'transitioning from a darkened cavity in an empty wall to the textual dedication to the father to the visual reflection of the maternal photographer', Cameron 'marks the space as the laboratory of [her] expression of gendered presence'.[57] But Cameron's inscription on the print is not a mere 'dedication to the father', nor is the relationship between father and daughter an abstract and ahistorical association, as Bear misrepresents it here.

Each of these authors has pursued a serious effort to identify and interrogate the objective elements that Cameron presented in this photograph and has contended thoughtfully with the agency of its maker, but each has also privileged a notion that Cameron's activities were based on self-reflexivity and maternal identification.[58] In so doing, these scholars have ignored visual and textual markers that Cameron constructed at the very centre of the image, explicit pointers that she fashioned to help viewers interpret the meaning of this work. For example, the framed print upon which Cameron wrote in this photograph was not just any 'military scene', but a signal episode from the final moments of the widespread war that followed the initial insurrection in India. On 15 January 1859, Captain Herbert Mackworth Clogstoun of the 19th Madras Native Infantry led eight men of the 2nd Hyderabad Cavalry against an Indian rebel force at Chichumbah. After fierce fighting, Clogstoun lost seven of the eight men who accompanied him and was wounded himself; nevertheless, his actions were deemed instrumental in pushing back the rebel force.[59] Clogstoun won the Victoria Cross for this act of courage.

The Victoria Cross had first been bestowed on veterans of the Crimean War in June 1857.[60] For those who served with valour in the war in India, the Queen conferred the Victoria Cross only *after* she had been named Empress, presenting the award to 'Officers and Private Soldiers of Her Majesty's Indian Military Forces, whose claims to the same have been submitted for Her Majesty's approval, on account of Acts of Bravery performed by them in India'. The framed and matted image depicting this military action lies at the centre of Cameron's photograph. It was likely a reproductive print or photograph of a commemorative painting by Orlando Norie, one of the most prolific military painters of his day, whose more than 5,000 images 'graced the walls of military clubs and regimental museums, while others appear in the pages of regimental histories'.[61] The popularity of this imagery was reinforced by Norie's contemporary, Louis Desanges, who created a Victoria Cross Gallery between 1859 and 1862, which was installed as a regular exhibition in the Crystal Palace.[62] Provenance records conserved by the National Army Museum for Norie's image of Clogstoun in action note that Norie's painting was owned by Herbert Clogstoun's brother, Cuthbert, as late as 1912, when the original painting was copied by Lady Isobel Ryder at Burley. Significantly, the museum also conserves an earlier reproductive photograph of the same painting, likely a duplicate of the framed image that Cameron displayed in her house and inserted in her photograph (fig. 4).[63] During this period, the storied Ackermann family of publishers and print sellers distributed reproductions of Norie's work, chiefly through the family's Eclipse Sporting and Military Gallery established in London by Rudolph Ackermann junior, and it is likely that in the early 1860s Cameron acquired her print of Clogstoun's military charge from this source, either at auction or by retail purchase.[64] But what also seems clear is that Cameron did not have far to go in her own home to locate a copy of this print when she wanted to include it within her own photograph.

By inserting this image of Adeline's father in her death-bed photograph, Cameron inserted a record of the anti-colonial rebellion and its aftermath, one that was specific to Captain Herbert Clogstoun, who received his VC in an investiture held in Madras on 19 January 1860, but also emblematic of the war itself. These facts make Cameron's inscription on this print a kind of *anti-allegorical* badge that all but insists viewers deny the formalist

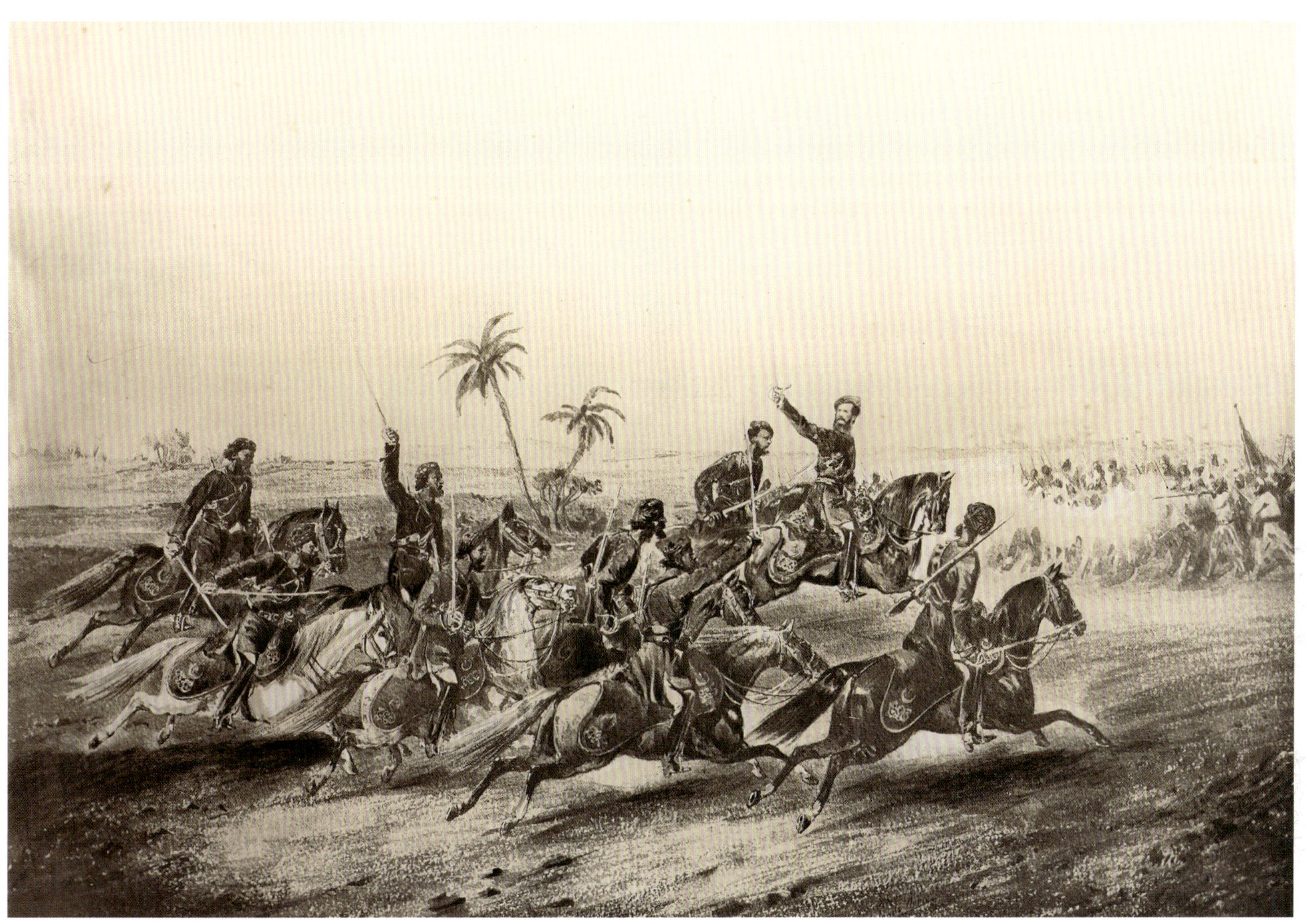

4 Anon., photograph of a watercolour by Orlando Norie, *Capt Herbert M Clogstoun, 19th Madras Native Infantry winning the Victoria Cross when he Charged with Eight Men on the 2nd Hyderabad Cavalry against Rebels at Chichumbah, 15 January 1859*. *c*.1859.
Courtesy of the Council of the National Army Museum, London. 1961–05–8.

and modernist aesthetic of the photograph, reject the allegorical references to *The Old Curiosity Shop*, and discard the notion of self-reflexivity conceived by modern historians. Instead, by implanting a pictorial memento of the war in India, Cameron asks viewers to pay attention to the 'flash of the now' contained within the image, to attend to the unexpected political urgency that she hoped would arrest viewers in this unconventional photograph.[65] Walter Benjamin might have identified the photograph containing the print of Clogstoun in action as a 'dialectical image', a term he coined to describe visual representations that emerge suddenly, as if in a flash. As he wrote in his 'Theses on the Philosophy of History', such imagery is especially potent, and unexpected, because it seizes hold of a historical event 'at a moment of danger'.[66] When she constructed this photograph, Cameron indeed took pains to ensure that the historical record would document Clogstoun's action as a frozen moment of national importance, one electrified by the historical impact of the Uprising: she infused her death-bed photograph with an equivalently charged image, one manifested here by the unexpected inclusion of the white-matted and framed print of the decorated soldier Herbert Clogstoun – which stands apart visually from others in the series for its starkly white presence in the darkened room.

And yet, by means of a clever act of double articulation, Cameron concentrated her viewers' attention precisely here, at the intersection of family, narrative formation, and national identity: visually, she inserted the battlefield scene as a surprising *mise-en-abyme* of the print-within-the-print located at the near-centre of the photograph, an image of war as much as a representation of the deceased father. Positioning the framed print to float above the child's head, she allowed it to disrupt the pictorial conventions of the death-bed archetype and thereby structurally undermine the assumed pathos or literary sentimentality associated with mourning the dead child. Discursively, Cameron's inscribed text on the print-within-the-print also dislodges viewers from pondering the child alone, as if she were isolated as an allegorical stand-in for a virginal child-bride in Christ. And the literal meaning of the inscribed text makes it virtually impossible to take the imaginative leap required to conceive this image as a self-important expression of the photographer's own motherly identity.

In this photograph, Cameron significantly disrupted the conventional death-bed scene in several essential ways that actually *deny* her own maternal identity in relation to the young child. First, she focused her inscription on the dead girl's parentage, which revived the absent father and conjures his presence into the funereal room, even as a relic of patriarchy. Second, she emphasized the patrimonial connection of the association between father and daughter, which is to say, through her inscription, Cameron underscored the child's connection to the child's soldier-father as the *primary* relationship. By contrast, Cameron omits any trace of the girl's mother, Mary Julia Mackenzie, who died in Freshwater in 1870 at the age of 35, as she occupies no symbolic presence in the image whatsoever. Thirdly, Cameron fused together these intertwined legacy-based paternal and national identities with the idea of the *paterfamilias*, a term that consolidates family and nation by referring to the *male* head of the household and its ancestry.[67] As we shall see in chapter 9, this patriarchal term was of vital importance to both Cameron and Herschel. Ironically, then, it is virtually impossible to support the idea that *The lovely remains of my little Adeline* expresses Cameron's 'maternal agency' as claimed by Armstrong, Kelsey, Cox, or Bear, as neither the documentary evidence in the photograph nor the metaphoric logic of symbolism supports this idea.

Instead, I argue that Cameron put this photograph into the service of Britain's imperial project by tapping into the latent 'optical unconscious' of those who would view this print. Walter Benjamin used this term to describe the process by which viewers would discover in photographs an absent, subdued, or repressed memory, one that embedded a historical truth that was absent or disguised in the overt pictorial representation but that was nevertheless present in the viewer's unconscious.[68] By embedding the idea of the *paterfamilias* in this image, Cameron emphasized the primary relationship of the child to her historical ancestors, a legacy that was passed on exclusively through patrimonial descent. Importantly, then, it is essential to note that Herbert Clogstoun, who achieved distinction in the Madras army, was the son-in-law of Lt General Colin Mackenzie, also of the Madras army. During the first Afghan War (1839–42), Mackenzie was imprisoned in Kabul, but at the conclusion of the war emerged as an army hero.[69] After Mackenzie returned to London, the painter James Sant portrayed Mackenzie in his Afghan dress, which he exhibited in 1844 at the Royal Academy (#373) to much acclaim (fig. 5).[70] Recent scholarship has suggested that while Orientalist portraits of this kind often expressed Western ideas of superiority and their right to subjugate Eastern peoples, they also represented for British audiences at home an exotic performance that allowed 'individual Europeans to benefit personally from exotic self-promotion' of their social dominance and power.[71] Most importantly for this story, Mackenzie was Julia Margaret's brother-in-law and an exact contemporary of the Camerons. During their years in Calcutta, the Camerons worked assiduously to try to secure Mackenzie's release from his confinement in Kabul, actions that I describe in greater detail in chapter 1.[72]

By including an image of Herbert Clogstoun in her death-bed photograph of Adeline, Cameron shows us that the young girl is mourned across generations, not only as Cameron's adopted daughter, not only as the girl orphaned by her own parents, but also as *Colin Mackenzie's granddaughter*, the last of her illustrious line.

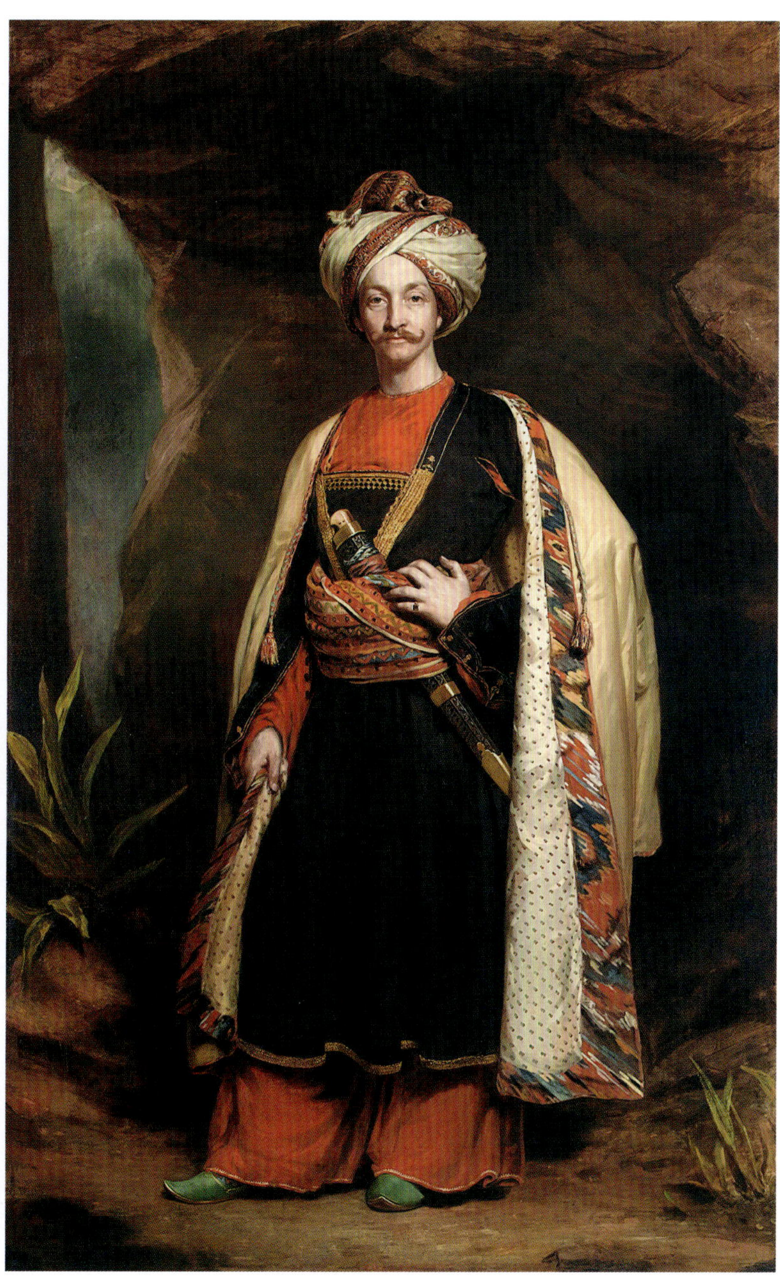

5 James Sant, *Captain Colin Mackenzie, Madras Army, lately a hostage in Cabool, in his Affghan Dress*, c.1842, oil on canvas, 236.8 × 145.5 cm.

Courtesy of the Council of the National Army Museum, London. 1961–10–61–1.

As an extension of this familial interrelationship, Cameron explicitly invoked Herbert Clogstoun's service fighting for Britain against the Indian insurgents, and because she referred to the war obliquely, the Uprising itself is 'present' *but also absent* from the text. So too is Colin Mackenzie, who fought in the North-West Provinces by commanding a Sikh regiment during the rebellion. And yet, by reifying the child's legacy in relation to her father's military honours and as an extension of her ancestry, connecting her directly to her grandfather's illustrious colonial legacy, Cameron triangulated the image, effectively turning the photograph itself into its own kind of war memorial that is as much about the family as it is the nation, as both have endured sacrifices to preserve and advance the imperial cause. In this capacity, this photograph serves as a potent cultural memento that keeps alive the family's imperial heritage, an essential act of patrimonial self-regard.[73] As the Camerons' close friend Thomas Babington Macaulay wrote in his *History of England* (1855), 'A people which takes no pride in the noble achievements of remote ancestors will never achieve anything worthy to be remembered with pride by remote descendants'.[74] Cameron's photograph ensures that her family's pride and its historical role in the imperial enterprise will endure. At the same time, by extolling this patriarchal lineage, Cameron's photograph contributes to the 'great man theory' of history as it was constructed by Macaulay and, as we shall see, by his contemporaries Thomas Carlyle, Charles Hay Cameron, and Henry Thoby Prinsep.[75]

Cameron's handwritten inscription on this photograph also reinforces the role played by Orlando Norie's reproductive print within the photographic image. Framed and reframed in relation to this battleground scene in India, Adeline's body now takes on a new symbolism that allows it to function as a vehicle for Cameron's interest in commemorating a gruesome act from the war, that is, portraying the British children killed during the massacre at Cawnpore. While such an unexpected interpretation might cause a contemporary viewer to lurch away from the physical presence of the young girl, it nevertheless demonstrates how a viewer's subject position must change in relation to its signifier as additional layers of symbolic and historical meaning unfold. As another example, the 1859 date of Clogstoun's act of bravery in India is also significant, as it identifies the scene as an act of British aggression coming *late* in the overall conflict, rather than at a critical point when victory had not yet been won. By 1859, after all, the war in India had been firmly decided, leaving one to ask whether Clogstoun's act of heroism and Cameron's insertion of the image in her own photograph in 1872 marked her satisfied recognition of the outcome of the war or her dispassionate acceptance that Britain's retribution against the Indian insurgents had been justified. Inflected by these overlapping associations, Adeline's death-bed scene then becomes a symbolic referent to the Cawnpore massacre that so outraged the British public, able to invoke yet another source of mourning for innocent British children who were killed in India as much as unresolved shame for the untold acts of retribution committed to avenge those deaths.[76]

In the end, Cameron's photograph continues to startle us today because its narrative is multiplied many times over by these overlapping and intersecting visual and textual elements. They illustrate how even familiar narrative structures, like the Victorian death-bed scene, are constructed on tenuous and unstable foundations, and how, in the hands of a master storyteller like Cameron, a sliver of history can be reclaimed through the 'flash of recognition' that is photography. Photographs become powerful, wrote John Berger,

> when the chosen moment [depicted by the photographer] contains a quantum of truth which is generally applicable, which is as *revealing about what is absent* from the photograph as about what is present in it. [My emphasis][77]

Indeed, Laura Wexler has written, following Berger, 'the photograph depends upon this *linkage with the invisible* for its legibility and for the self-knowledge it confers' (my emphasis).[78]

COLONIAL SHADOWS

Julia Margaret Cameron: The Colonial Shadows of Victorian Photography is organized conceptually in three sections, arranged chronologically, which correspond to Julia Margaret Cameron's complex historical relationship to India and to her close circle of family and friends who were engaged in narrating the imperial project. The first section, 'Outposts of Empire', establishes her colonial roots. Beginning by examining her long friendship with Sir John Herschel, whom Julia Margaret and her husband Charles first met in 1837 in Cape Town, chapter 1, 'Empire's Children', establishes the many ways that Herschel, through his scientific work in Africa, became associated with Britain's colonial expansion across the globe. Critically, this chapter intersects with the contemporaneous activities of the Camerons in India and recognizes Herschel's apprehensions about the East India Company's resolve to release India from colonial bonds. Chapter 2, 'Enchanted Palace', begins after the Camerons quit Calcutta for London, describing the ties that bound the Holland Park circle to one another and to influential political figures, like Lord Lansdowne, who were responsible for approving the charters that licensed the East India Company to operate in India. This chapter also explains Lansdowne's persuasive and revelatory assessment of Herschel as an imperial adventurer and colonial benefactor, attributes that I argue Julia Margaret recognized in her 1859 gift album to Lansdowne, in which she included a contemporary photographic portrait of the astronomer. Chapter 3, 'Letters to Juley', concludes the first section by appraising how Cameron, once situated in the cultural bosom of Little Holland House, absorbed news of the insurrection in India. It examines the letters she exchanged with her adult daughter, Julia Hay Cameron, and her fixation on the massacre of British women and children in the British outpost of Cawnpore, which soon became emblematic of the wide gulf separating India and Britain.

The second section, 'Cross-Cultural Encounters', examines how Julia Margaret contended with new and unexpected sites of imperial transculturation because of the war in India. Like transnationalism, which describes cultural influences that cross national borders, transculturation conveys the intersection of multiple cultural influences and cross-cultural dynamics that arise in the imperial context, examining those diverse elements that collude to produce new, heterogeneous forms of artistic expression.[79] Transcultural spaces are notable because, like the ambiguity that characterizes the colonial relationship, they are unfixed and undefined, subjected to rewriting and revision. Chapter 4, 'Galahad's Homecoming', examines the writing and revision that accompanied the story of Julia Margaret's nephew, Arthur Prinsep, in India. By examining the young soldier's actions and their representation in narratives constructed by the young man and by his contemporaries in India and in London, this chapter compares those accounts with the symbolic portrayals by Thackeray in poetry and by Watts in painting, which fashioned Arthur a national hero. Even Kensington became a transnational zone of cross-cultural conflict when Julia Margaret photographed a native son of India, Iqbal al-Daula, whom she called the 'ex-King of Oude', in the garden behind Little Holland House, and this is the subject of chapter 5, 'An Indian Prince in London'. Chapter 6, 'Blood of the Fathers', closes out this section by examining how Cameron and her circle processed the terrible cost of Britain's imperial wars by elevating the social plight of war orphans, evaluating those works in relation to Julia Margaret's allegorical photographs that illustrate Tennyson's poem 'Enoch Arden', as well as her own Freshwater performance of Tom Taylor's play *Payable on Demand*.

The final section, 'Allegories of Empire', examines Cameron's evolving approach to narrating this history in photographic terms. But this study does not argue for traditional ideas of artistic formation, nor does it make claims for artistic influence. Instead, the book demonstrates how the shared narrative of imperial power that coalesced among Cameron's inner circle of former colonial officials and their literary and artistic company found expressive form in her photographs. When she took up photography, Cameron adopted an allegorical approach to the medium because it allowed her to construct a historical narrative. Allegory communicates through an interrelated, two-part structure: while one part relies upon the precise title an artist assigns to a work, the other part references a well-known literary source or real-world event. These two elements are expressed indirectly in allegory by means of the symbolic language of iconography. Cameron was able to create photographic narratives by drawing upon emblematic forms that her contemporaries would have recognized unambiguously from recent world events and, as we shall see, from the consistent repetition of those narrative accounts in the British press. She relied upon her educated and informed viewers to close the narrative gap left open by this two-part structure, essentially making the task of interpreting her photographic imagery a collaborative act. Chapter 7, 'Triumph and Mourning', provides examples of this approach by examining some of her earliest imagery, photographs that represent these expressions of national sentiment in the wake of the Indian Uprising.

In the final two chapters, I examine two very dissimilar but critically important photographs from the Herschel Album, both created in 1867. These images represent two formal extremes of Cameron's early approach to photography, but both embody the rhetoric of imperial power examined throughout the book. In the Herschel Album itself, Cameron placed her portrait *Sir John Herschel with Cap* (fig. 6) on the first page of the volume and positioned an image she called *At the Well, A Farewell* (fig. 7) on the last page, a fitting pair of bookends for this study. I argue here that the imperial rupture made visible by the 1857 Indian Uprising is present figuratively in both photographs. As we shall see, Cameron approached both types of imagery as vehicles to represent the historical legacy of the rebellion.

In chapter 8, 'Betrayal and Atonement', I analyse an allegorical image that Cameron created by assembling photographic fragments. She first selected imagery containing group arrangements of multiple figures and then cut those photographs apart, retaining key fragments from the compositions and discarding the rest. She then reassembled these selected pieces into a new composition that she titled *At the Well, A Farewell*. This composite image is perhaps one of the least studied and most enigmatic of all of Cameron's allegories. I argue here that Cameron's commemoration of insurrection in India helps to explain this image and that the war becomes visible 'between the lines' as a symbolic presence in the work's iconography, helping to bind its separate parts together into an intelligible whole. In this allegorical photograph, Cameron's narrative hand shaped the iterative glue that unites its parts, providing coherence to the whole as a meaningful work of art.

In chapter 9, 'Paterfamilias', I examine one of Cameron's most celebrated photographs, the portrait she made of her friend, *Sir John Herschel with Cap*. After Cameron showed him his portrait, Herschel recognized that his image embodied the nation's paternal form of imperial authority, effectively representing its patriarchal origins and aristocratic social identity. Acknowledging that his own identity was formed visually and framed

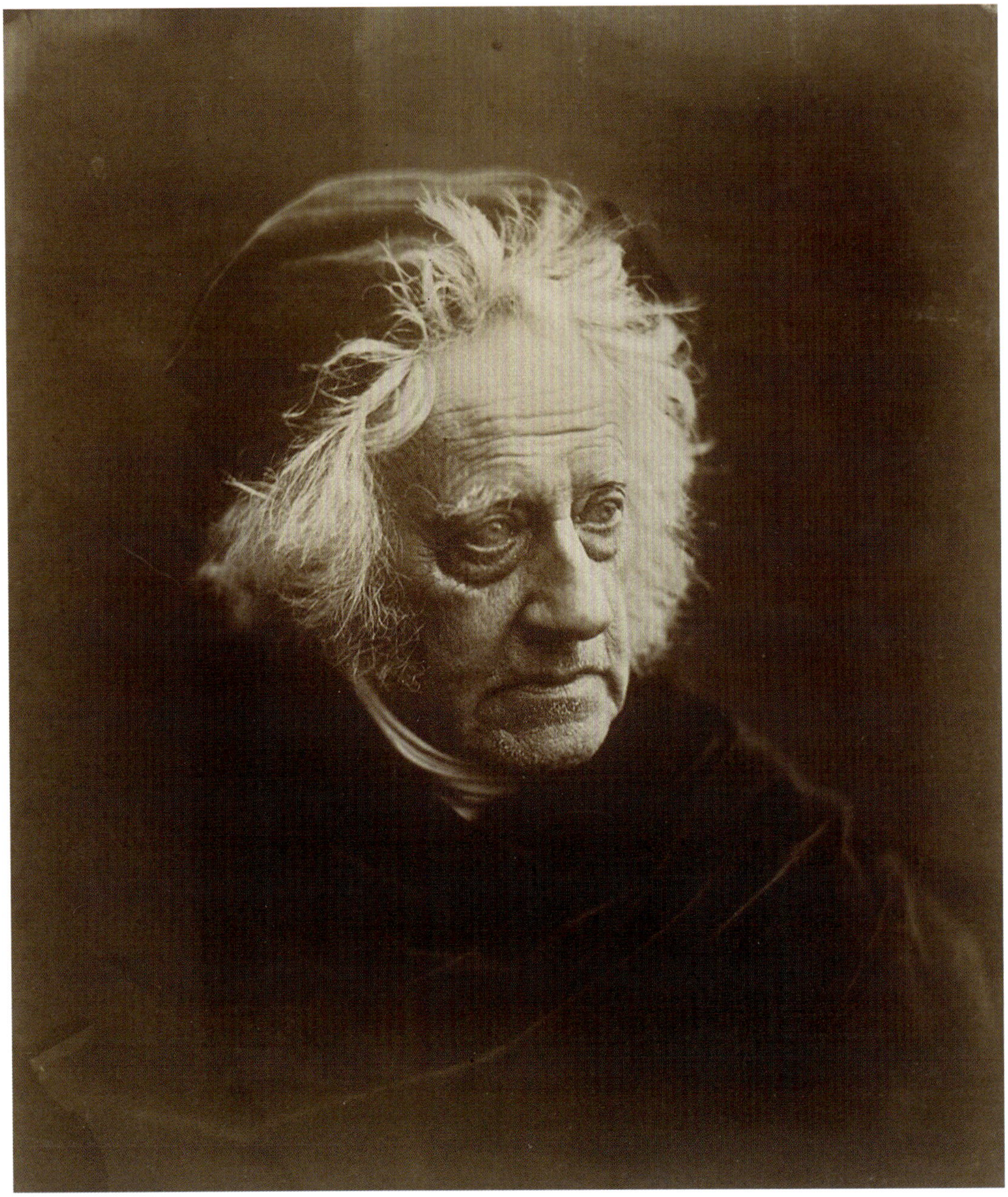

6 Julia Margaret Cameron, *Sir John Herschel with Cap*, April 1867, albumen print, 33.5 × 28 cm.

National Science & Media Museum / Science Museum Group. 1984–5071/1.

7 Julia Margaret Cameron, *At the Well, A Farewell*, 1867, albumen prints; entire album page from the Herschel Album, central image: 10.3 × 11.3 cm.

National Science & Media Museum / Science Museum Group. 1984–5017/92.

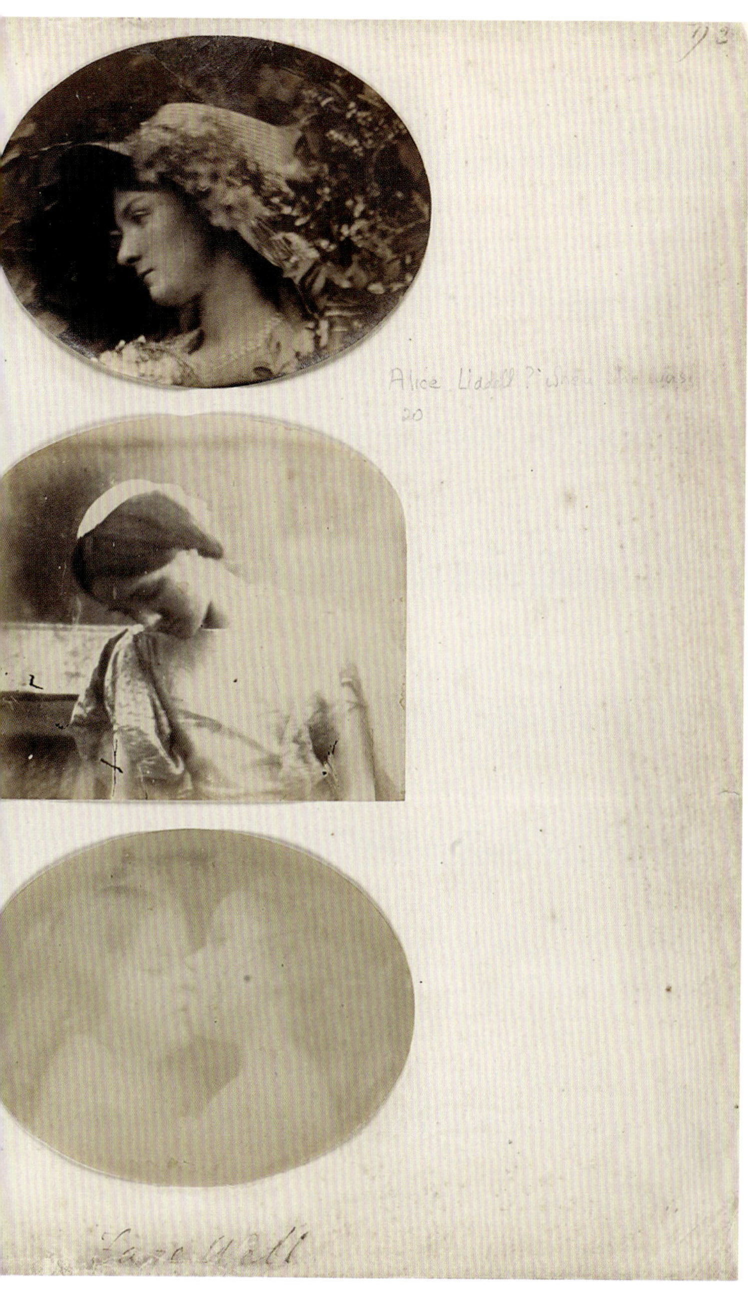

discursively by imperial forces, Herschel informed Cameron that her image captured his own sense of subjecthood. Finally, the Conclusion to this book returns to Herschel's Album itself, to examine the volume's structure and its history-making narrative, by reclaiming for the imperial project her enigmatic photograph *Iago, Study from an Italian* (see fig. 99).

This study demonstrates that Julia Margaret Cameron simultaneously pursued two divergent approaches to photography. On the one hand, she went to elaborate ends to create her own signature style of photographic portraiture, to fill the frame with her subject, to model roundness, as she wrote, in *perfect perfection*. This goal was epitomized by her startling and revealing portrait of Herschel, who recognized in her achievement the embodiment of historical thinking and power that the two friends associated with Britain's imperial project. The same formal elements are present in her photograph of *Iago*. While pursuing this approach to image-making, she 'overlooked photographic realism', as Virginia Woolf recognized, and laid claim to the strategic role of allegory in constructing a historical narrative. By experimenting with photographic fragments, Cameron reimagined how photographs could be arranged on the page and created an image that expressed the nation's triumph and mourning in the wake of the Indian Uprising. Cameron's photographs coalesced in the Herschel Album to help give shape to the visual representation of the nation in the aftermath of this conflict: in her allegorical imagery, she boldly united the fragments of history in a new narrative form, and in her evocative portraiture, she constructed the public face of British imperialism.

Outposts of Empire

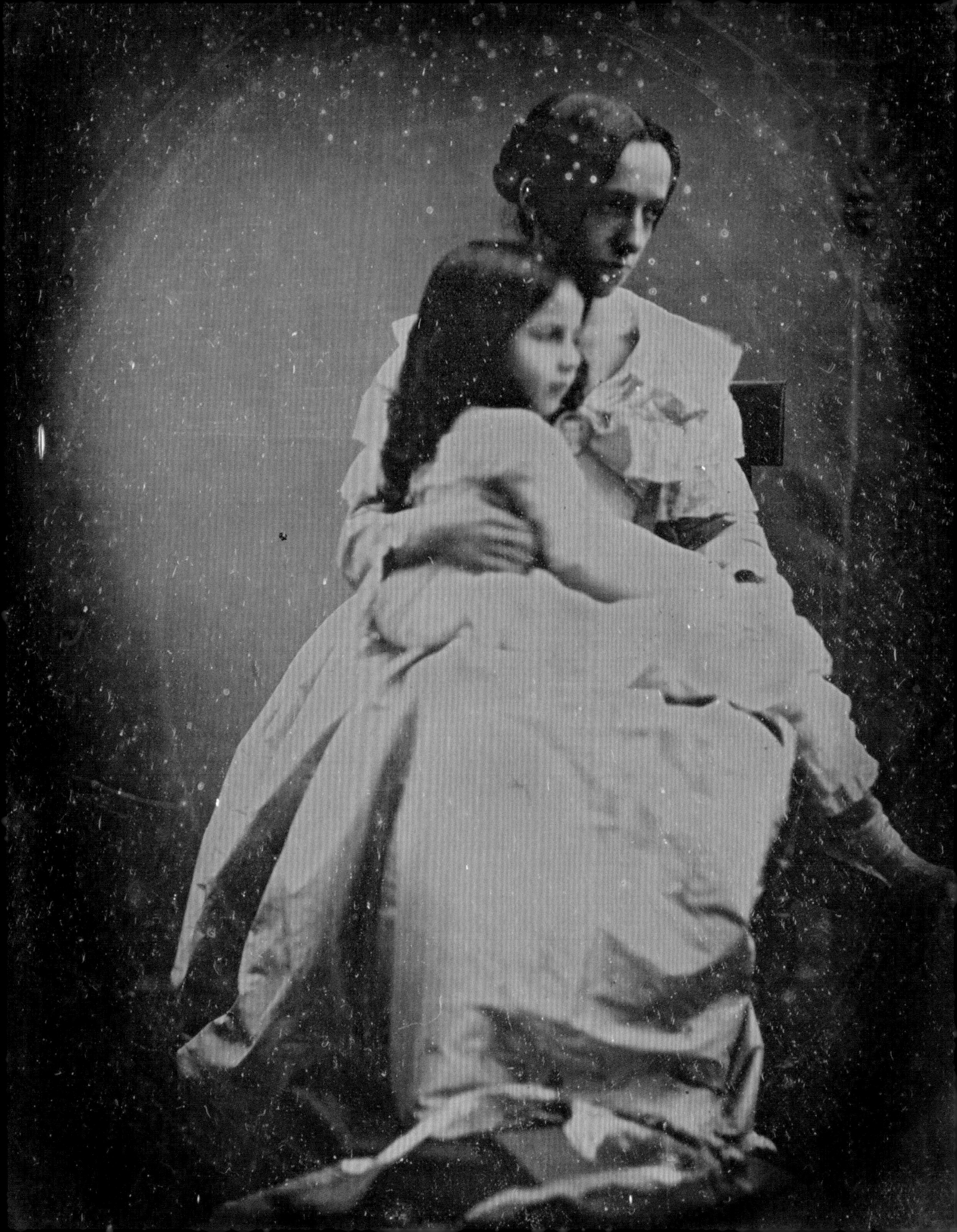

Chapter One
Empire's Children

8 Unknown daguerreotypist, *Julia Hay Cameron with her Mother, Julia Margaret Cameron*, 1845 (detail of fig. 12).

IMPERIAL PARTNERSHIPS

In 1837, Julia Margaret Pattle met Charles Hay Cameron on the Cape Colony. The two had travelled there separately from Calcutta and were each taking a restorative holiday from the oppressive heat. At the Cape, they independently met the esteemed scientist and astronomer Sir John Herschel and his wife Lady Margaret through the small network of British residents in the colony. After a while, the two visitors from India returned to Calcutta, and in 1838, Julia Margaret married Charles Cameron. Their union soon occupied a prominent place among the exclusive society of British residents who ruled India, the men and women who were known collectively as 'Anglo-Indians'. This hyphenated term aptly described their expatriate identity, but also daily life in colonial Calcutta, a city occupied by Britons for three centuries and a destination of choice for young men who wanted to make their mark in the colonies. Meanwhile, in 1838, the Herschels returned to England. Despite the physical distance between the two families, they nonetheless had formed a lifelong friendship from their brief interactions in Cape Town, regularly exchanging letters over the years to mark major holidays, celebrate the births of children, and share notes about daily life in the colonies.[1] Because Herschel introduced Julia Margaret to photography, historians have understandably presumed the new art form was at the centre of the strong bond between them. But their first bonds were of an imperial nature: the two families shared an abiding interest in promoting Britain's colonial interests abroad.

In Calcutta, India's Anglo-Indian governing elite embraced the union of Julia Margaret and Charles Cameron. Their marriage contract created a financial trust, a conventional transaction intended to ensure the financial support of a surviving spouse and children should disaster strike the couple. The Camerons named as trustees Julia Margaret's father, James Pattle, a member of the East India Company's Board of Revenue, and her brother-in-law, Henry Thoby Prinsep, an administrative director of the Company.[2] In addition to Prinsep, who had married Julia Margaret's sister Sara in 1835, three additional Pattle sisters had also wed officials of the East India Company, investing the family deeply in

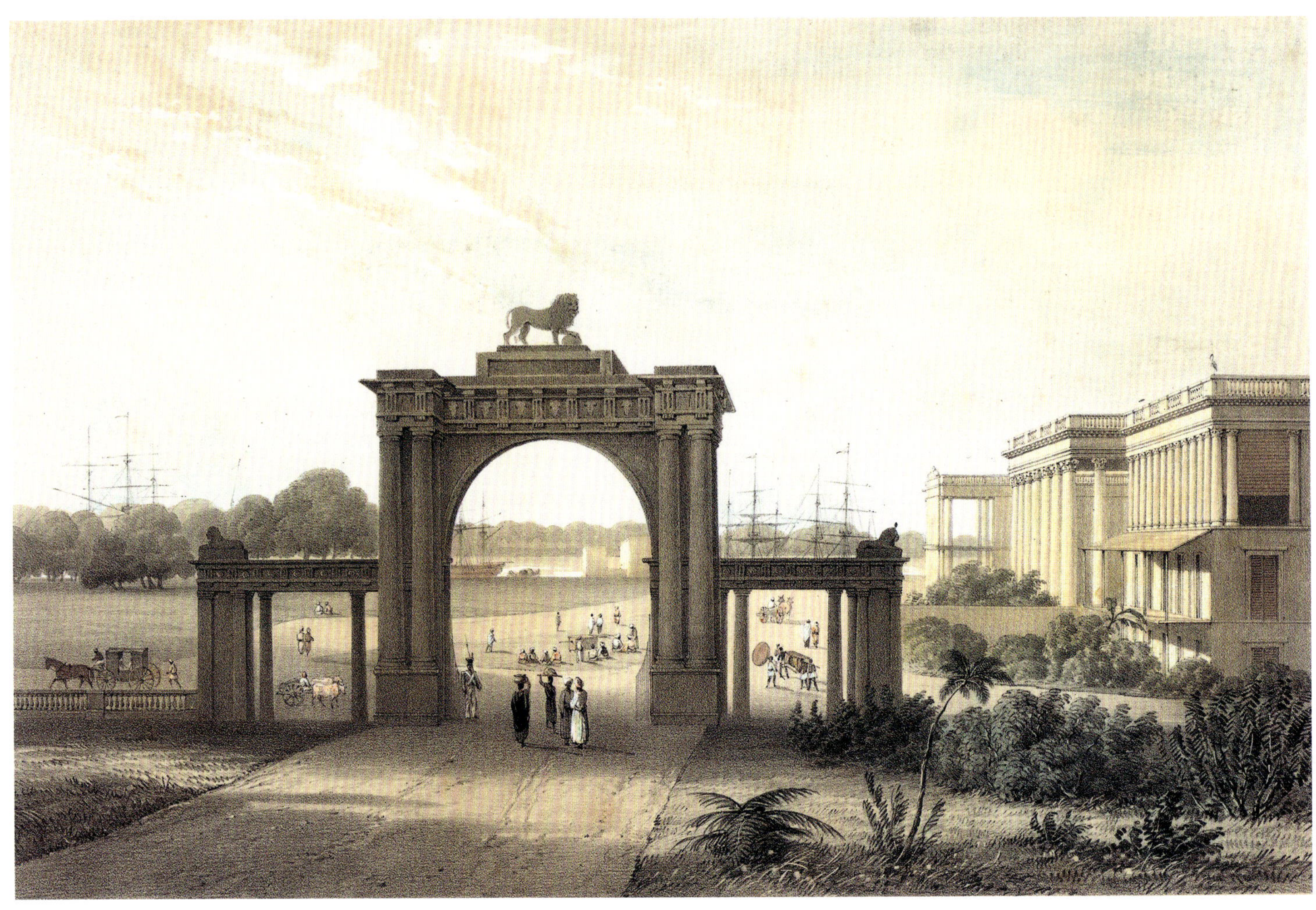

9 Anon., *Esplanade Row, Calcutta, towards Chadpal Ghat, through the west gate of Government House*, 1830, coloured lithograph, 23.8 × 35 cm.

the Company's political future: Adeline married Colin Mackenzie, an officer in the Company's Madras army, in 1832; Maria wed John Jackson, a surgeon in the Indian Medical Service, in 1837; and in 1838, Louisa married Henry Bayley, a writer in the Bengal Civil Service who would later serve as a judge on the Supreme Court.[3] The East India Company was the bedrock upon which Julia Margaret and Charles would build their familial home and establish their cultural future.

Initially set up as a trading company in 1600, the East India Company established itself in Calcutta, in the heart of the city adjoining the banks of the Hooghly River. In 1696, the Company built Fort William on a modest scale to facilitate social interactions with the local population, but by 1781, a new Fort William was built as a commanding edifice that positioned British authority behind high ramparts. The new construction was insulated by a surrounding greensward, a reflection of the territorial expansion of the Company and the growth of its armies.[4] Although the premodern city was built on Romantic notions that so-called 'hybrid spaces' could bridge the social gap between Company officials and indigenous Indians, by the end of the eighteenth century Britain widened the space separating the governing class from those they governed. Early nineteenth-century representations depict how the Company built grand neoclassical structures with sweeping grand facades to house its colonial government.[5] Among the most imposing was Government House, designed by Charles Wyatt and erected in 1802 (fig. 9). Other buildings on Esplanade Row contained the law courts, the town hall, and East

India Company's 'writers' building', that is, the offices that housed its civil administration.[6]

When Parliament passed the Government of India Act on 28 August 1833, Britain's colonial control was formalized by a new charter that transferred and centralized governmental authority under the British Crown and joined together the three provinces of Bengal, Madras, and Bombay under a centralized office ruled by a Governor-General and a four-member advisory Council.[7] Later that year, as the first Governor-General of India, Lord William Bentinck appointed Edward Ryan to the post of Chief Justice of the Supreme Court, and the following year, Thomas Babington Macaulay arrived from England to lead the Supreme Council. One of Macaulay's first actions was to appoint Charles Cameron to the Council as its legal member, a decision he based upon his high regard for Cameron's earlier work in Ceylon as part of a Royal Commission of Eastern Inquiry. In 1833, Cameron's official report on Ceylon, which he authored together with William MacBean George Colebrooke, an Indian army officer and administrator, reimagined Ceylon's legal framework to match Britain's own. While in Ceylon, Cameron purchased large tracts of land that he eventually turned into plantations, first for coffee, then for tea. Cameron's Royal Commission was also concerned with land management. He and Colebrooke proposed replacing traditional forms of labour with 'modern wage labour', recommended introducing English as the official language of the island, and endorsed the creation of a new constitutional government, childhood education as based upon the British model, and a national civil service.[8]

At approximately the same time, from the perch of his private estate, 'Feldhausen', in the Cape Colony, Sir John Herschel blended his mathematical and astronomical studies together with his interest in spreading Britain's civilizing mission in the colonies. Although his scientific expedition was self-funded, the Herschels arrived in Africa in 1834, having sailed from England with the new colonial Governor, Benjamin D'Urban. Upon arrival, D'Urban inherited a fraught and unstable social fabric, one marked by distrust from indigenous Xhosa, Malay, Khoikhoi, Zulu, and !Kung peoples and by restless British plantation owners who were equally anxious about the implementation of new laws that would free thousands of indigenous South African slaves.[9] In February 1834, after settling in, Herschel acquired four coolies to serve as personal household attendants. Avowing that his scientific expedition was his top priority, Herschel resolved to refrain from making overt political or social commentary during his time at the Cape.[10] Nevertheless, the scientist could not isolate himself entirely, as his celebrity in England made him a magnet for numerous visitors, many of whom stopped off on their way to India.[11]

By August, Governor D'Urban had accelerated a conflict with the Xhosa people over land rights that, instead of being resolved, escalated by December into violent hostilities, soon called the Sixth Frontier War.[12] D'Urban was not authorized to annex native territory, however, and the Colonial Office compelled him to return lands to the Xhosa that he had seized during the war. In September 1835, the two sides signed a peace treaty, but these conflicts destabilized Herschel's early impressions of colonial life, and he was appalled by D'Urban's peremptory actions. Deploring the violence and the principle that 'might makes right', Herschel shared with friends in the Cape his view that Britain should educate the Xhosa in the ways of settled agriculture and thereby 'civilize' them socially. Their compliance with British norms would make them fit to live and prosper under colonial rule, he reasoned.[13] Herschel's direct experience with D'Urban's conflict also led to his endorsement of the liberal ideology of self-improvement tied to social progress. He articulated this perspective in public comments on colonial education that he made at an award ceremony for college students after the conclusion of the Sixth Frontier War.[14]

Herschel's views were consistent with the educational policies that Charles Cameron advocated for Ceylon at approximately the same time. To Herschel, the whole population – natives and Europeans alike – should be educated by 'a good practical system of public education', that is, one established with English taught as a core foundation. From this foundation an indigenous administrative class of English-speaking civil servants would emerge, which would then help Britain govern the colony.[15] These were Cameron's views exactly: once in league with Macaulay on the Supreme Council, the two men proceeded to enact measures for India that were like those Cameron had proposed for Ceylon, especially in relation to the teaching of English in public schools and in the administration of governmental affairs. The Camerons' early married life in India therefore took place during a time of fundamental governmental transition that supported Cameron's proposed reforms: the 1833 Charter meant that former East India Company territories were now ceded to the Crown and its commercial monopoly was terminated, replaced by the colonial state. But the Act also empowered and vested the Company's army and centralized the Company's civil service units that had been established earlier in Madras, Bombay, and Bengal, which essentially sustained the Company's influence and its administrative governance.

By acting swiftly to make English the state language of India, Macaulay, Ryan, and Cameron together formed a powerful trio and forged lifelong friendships. They also irrevocably transformed Indian society by imposing a British legal framework, an English-based system of public education, and an Indian Civil Service, soon to be the most formidable administrative corps in the world. These 'Anglicans' reasoned that the English legal system was superior to what they called 'Oriental laws', and that it should be expressed, therefore, in the English language in colonial affairs. Thoby Prinsep and Colin Mackenzie, by contrast, were steadfast Orientalists: each spoke several native Indian languages and advocated for the teaching of Sanskrit, Hindi, and Urdu in public education and in the affairs of state. Both contributed to and supported the activities of the Royal Asiatic Society. John Stuart Mill, then employed as a writer for the East India Company, ultimately helped resolve the policy disagreement over the teaching of English. Although he initially thought that India's languages and traditions should be preserved, Mill came around to Macaulay's viewpoint, articulated in his famous 'Minute on Education' of 2 February 1835. One month later, on 7 March 1835, with Mill's support, India's Governor-General decreed that 'the great object of the British Government ought to be the promotion of European literature and science among the natives of India'.[16]

Despite their differences over the use of English or Indian languages in colonial affairs, family bonds cemented in Calcutta extended throughout the lives of the extended Pattle clan. After Adeline Pattle Mackenzie died at sea in 1836 when she was travelling from India to England, for example, family members in England cared for her young children. Years later, after those children had their own children and the Camerons had relocated to the Isle of Wight, Julia Margaret adopted Adeline's granddaughter Adeline Clogstoun (while George Frederic Watts adopted Adeline's sister Blanche). Cameron also cared for another Anglo-Indian descendant through the Thackeray family, Margie (Daisy) Thackeray, the daughter of Edward 'Tallboots' Thackeray, a cousin of William Makepeace Thackeray, whom the Pattle sisters, Sara and Julia Margaret, came to know during their adolescent years in France.[17] Thackeray's adult daughter Annie adopted young Margie during the 1860s. Herbert Clogstoun and Edward Thackeray later won the Victoria Cross for their bravery as soldiers in the Indian Uprising, but it was not owing to war alone that deep family bonds, established years earlier, secured the family's lineage by caring for its orphans.

FRONTIER DIPLOMACY

From 1838 to 1842, Mackenzie, Prinsep, Bayley, and Charles Cameron played intersecting diplomatic roles in supporting the East India Company's army in its prosecution of a series of battles in Afghanistan and in the Punjab that grew into what became known as the first Anglo-Afghan War. Importantly, their roles were active and strategic, not those of passive administrative functionaries. Early on in Lord Auckland's administration, for example, Colin Mackenzie relied on Thoby Prinsep to disclose the thinking of the Supreme Council; theirs was a coordinated political activity designed to extend British power in the province by sedulously weakening the control of local rajahs.[18] Amid some of the darkest days of this conflict, Julia Margaret and her sister Louisa Bayley joined Charles Cameron and Thoby Prinsep in corresponding with Major George Broadfoot about the progress of the war. Broadfoot was a field officer in the Company's Madras army, and close friend and aide-de-camp to Captain Mackenzie. In 1839, under Auckland's direction, the Army of the Indus, which comprised men of the East India Company's armies from across its three provinces, marched into Afghanistan. The army's ostensible goal was to protect the Company's Indian territories from the possibility of Russian incursions, but its covert objective was to overthrow Afghanistan's ruler and install another more acceptable to the British.[19] But in 1840, in a disastrous turn of events, Afghan soldiers captured the Kabul fort to which Captain Mackenzie and others had fled. Mackenzie was held prisoner until concessions for an orderly retreat could be negotiated among warring tribal leaders.[20] Scores were killed or froze to death in the Khyber Pass as the British retreated to India, marking the Afghan War a major political embarrassment for Lord Auckland and a crushing military defeat for the Company.[21]

Throughout that year, Louisa Bayley maintained regular correspondence with Major Broadfoot about Captain Mackenzie's captivity in Kabul. Broadfoot, who had retreated to Jalalabad, relied upon the understanding that his correspondence would be shared among Bayley's sisters and brothers-in-law and extended his communications to them, too. In a letter dated 20 May 1842, he stated explicitly, 'Give my warmest regards to Bayley, to each of your sisters, and every member of your circle'.[22] Soon thereafter, Broadfoot recounted his tense interactions with those who held Mackenzie captive, and soberly reported the failure of repeated negotiations. Ultimately, he concluded, military force would be necessary to liberate Mackenzie and his fellow soldiers:

> Jellalabad: June 24, 1842.
> My dear Mrs. Bayley, – Some days ago, while in Besood, I had the pleasure of receiving your letter of the 23rd of last month as well as that of the 17th, forwarding letters on to Colin. The day before yesterday I wrote to Mrs. Cameron, telling her all we know of the prisoners, and no fresh intelligence has since been received. Whether Mahomed Shah Khan's offer to negotiate will lead to anything is doubtful. An advance to the capital is our best chance for liberating the captives.[23]

Emily Eden, Lord Auckland's sister, accompanied the Governor throughout his tour of duty and was present for the diverse military preparations and ceremonial formalities that led up to the Afghan conflict.[24] In letters to her sister back in England, Eden recounted the success of early battles in Kandahar and Ghazni but also carefully avoided discussing the numerous military setbacks. These included the insurrection in Kabul, the murder of British envoys, the retreat of Britain's allied forces, headed by Shah Shuja, who had been promised an extended kingdom in exchange for his loyalty and military assistance, and the army's humiliating retreat from Afghanistan in January 1842. Above all was the staggering loss of life. The garrison in Kabul held some 4,500 troops and more than 12,500 retainers, while the British expeditionary force that entered Afghanistan consisted of some 10,000 soldiers, 6,000 Indians under the command of Shah Shuja, more than 38,000 camp followers, and 30,000 camels. Fewer than twenty British soldiers made it back alive, and over the next two years, some 2,000 sepoys and camp followers slowly returned.[25]

By June 1842, Thoby Prinsep was instrumental in recommending Broadfoot for promotion as Resident at the Court of Nepal, what he regarded as 'a post of pure diplomacy'. But Prinsep also wanted to retain Broadfoot in a military role that was a 'frontier post of command'. Broadfoot therefore combined the two roles.[26] In his letter to Louisa Bayley and Cameron's other family members, Broadfoot laid the blame for the disaster in Afghanistan at the feet of Lord Auckland.

> Had Lord Auckland's Government shown any of the energy to have been looked for in the men who undertook so mighty an enterprise as to advance our standards ... into Central Asia, we should long ago have had the prisoners; the murderers would have been in our hands, or in hopeless exile, and the country in quiet subjection.[27]

Emily Eden knew Cameron, Ryan, and Macaulay personally. In 1836, she styled both Charles Cameron and Edward Ryan as youthful schoolboy chums who in their leisure hours established a cricket club in Calcutta. One day she observed their playground competition against British naval officers from two visiting ships. On that same day she also described hosting a dinner party that included Macaulay. The exclusive gathering of forty-six was apparently disrupted by a sudden and violent windstorm.[28] Eden vividly described the colourful parade of British, sepoy, and Sikh troops and the ceremonial flourishes that accompanied their formal departure for war, evidence of her astute eye for pageantry and shrewd awareness of politics. But she was evidently insulated from the violence of colonial warfare: her letters characterized daily life in India as a 'theatre of empire', one attended by numerous servants, sentries, and outriders to provide personal service, special protection, and colourful amusements like cricket matches and other forms of recreation.[29] In retrospect, her letters reveal that an atmosphere of privileged over-confidence made British forces entering Afghanistan inured to the impending danger of the invasion, as the 'sound of teas, cricket, boating, amateur theatricals, and horse racing echoed playfully' in what she called 'the England-away-from-England atmosphere' of the expedition.[30]

Because Broadfoot's correspondence with Louisa Bayley and Julia Margaret Cameron was an instrumental exchange that focused exclusively on military and diplomatic tactics, sensitive negotiations, and political intrigue, their letters avoided supercilious observations. Instead, their correspondence centred on quantifiable political topics such as administrative control, territorial acquisition, army manoeuvres, and the governing policies of Lord Auckland and his successor, Lord Ellenborough, who in 1842 replaced Auckland as Governor. By September of that year, the British had organized a new expeditionary force into Afghanistan. Styled an Army of Retribution, its primary mission was to liberate the hostages in Kabul but also to exact harsh punitive damages upon the country for having earlier routed British forces so mercilessly. As Priya Satia wrote recently, because the concept of vengeance 'did not fit neatly into the liberal narrative of empire', new chronicles of these events had to be written for the British public. These narratives emphasized

> the formidable and terrible nature of the Afghan foe, transmuting Afghani resistance into treachery, thereby glorifying the heroism, however tragic, of both the initial British victory and the bloody retribution.[31]

Meanwhile, Mackenzie ridiculed the welcome prepared to greet the returning British army as an excessive and unseemly spectacle, as Ellenborough lined the procession-way with rows of elephants that led to a gigantic triumphal arch.

> The Governor-General in person superintended the painting of the elephants' trunks and the erection of so ridiculous a triumphal arch, made of bamboos and coloured cotton, and resembling a gigantic gallows, that the soldiers marched under it with peals of laughter.[32]

In contrast to Auckland's humiliation, Mackenzie was heralded a hero upon his release, not simply because he was a hostage survivor, but more importantly as an emissary of the initial force sent to the North-West Frontier to bring 'British order' to the warring tribal peoples of that land. In 1843, John Murray released a portfolio of coloured lithographs under the title *Portraits of the Kabul Prisoners*. Produced after drawings originally made in 1842 by Lieutenant Vincent Eyre, a member of the liberating army, the portfolio featured a portrait of Mackenzie (fig. 10).[33] Eyre portrayed Mackenzie seated on the ground in full Afghan dress, the epitome of calm and assured dignity. As a memento of the Afghan war that featured her brother-in-law Mackenzie, it is likely (but unknown) that Cameron or her sisters acquired a copy of this portfolio. After all, Mackenzie was a unique emblem of what Carlyle had only recently called the destiny of great men. As he framed it in his 1841 book *On Heroes*, Carlyle called these men 'great' because they literally made the history of the world through their brave and illustrious actions: 'universal history, the history of what man has accomplished in this world, is at bottom the history of the great men who have worked here'.[34] Accordingly, Lieutenant Eyre did not represent the 'Army of Retribution' that set out to free the Kabul prisoners. Rather, Mackenzie and his men were celebrated instead as guiding sentinels of British morality.[35]

After his liberation, Mackenzie retreated to England, where the painter James Sant depicted him in the colourful Afghan dress he wore in Kabul. Sant exhibited his portrait at the Royal Academy, depicting Mackenzie as the Orientalist model of patriotic self-sacrifice and duty abroad (see fig. 5).[36] In 1843 in London, Mackenzie remarried, and soon thereafter met and formed a lasting friendship with Thomas Carlyle.[37] By June 1844, Mackenzie had made his way to Scotland, where he spent time

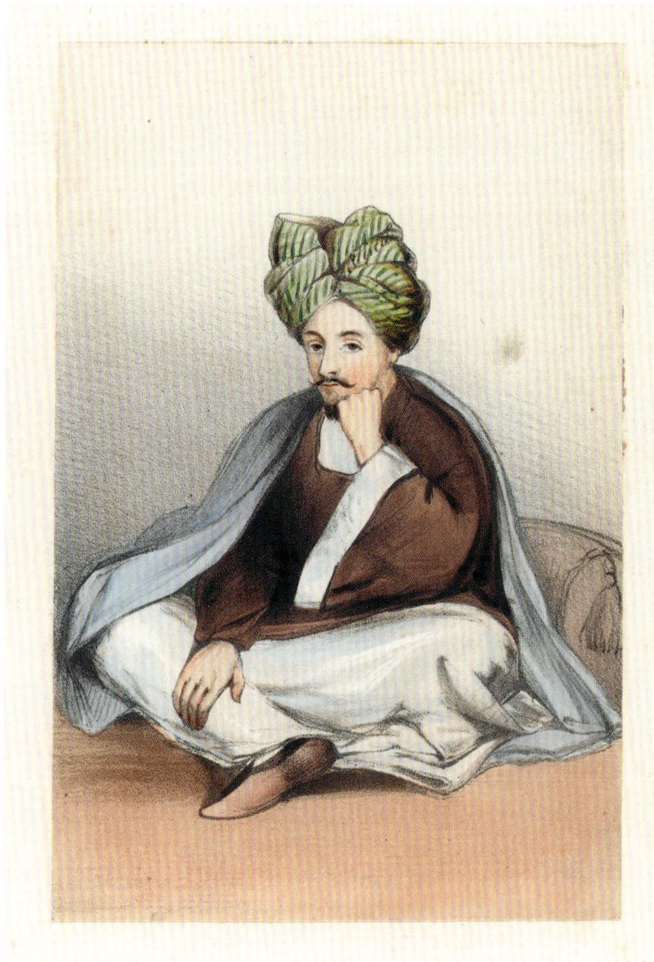

10 *Captain Colin Mackenzie, 48th Madras Native Infantry, attached to the Political Service, 1842*, coloured lithograph after an original drawing by Lt Vincent Eyre, Bengal Artillery, from *Portraits of the Kabul Prisoners* (London: John Murray, 1843).

Courtesy of the Council of the National Army Museum, London. 1950-11-55-8.

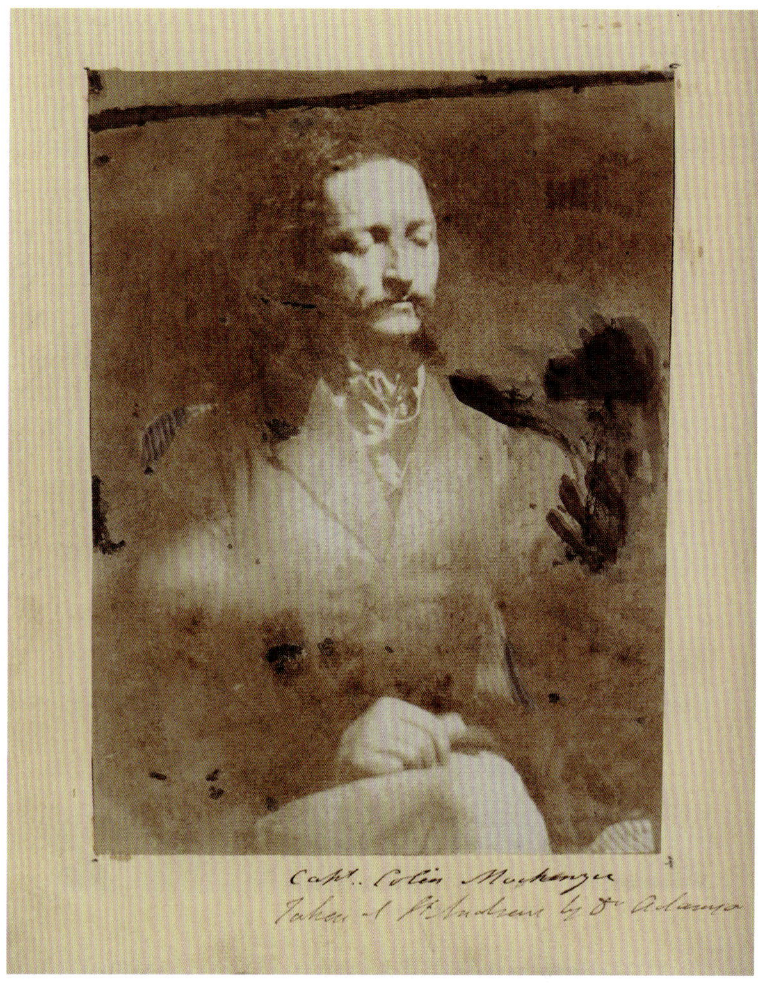

11 Dr John Adamson, *Captain Colin Mackenzie*, *c.*1845, salted paper print from a paper negative, 16.8 × 12.4 cm.

J. Paul Getty Museum, 84.XZ.574.134. Digital image courtesy of Getty's Open Content Program.

with leaders of the breakaway Free Church, where he evidently also met the photographic pioneers Dr John Adamson and his brother, Robert. Mackenzie sat for his portrait by Dr Adamson, and the resulting photograph was acquired at the time by the celebrated scientist Sir David Brewster (fig. 11). A photographic pioneer in Scotland, Brewster shared his earliest experiments with photography's inventor, William Henry Fox Talbot, and compiled one of the earliest albums of salted paper prints.

Back in India, Julia Margaret shared her personal views about Ellenborough in her correspondence with Broadfoot. Although she disparaged Ellenborough, much like her brother-in-law Mackenzie, she reassured Broadfoot that she worked to advance his interests in her discussions with the Governor. She confirmed her position in a letter of 11 September 1843:

> Lord Ellenborough, a very short time ago, spoke of you to me in the highest possible terms; and I assure you I listened and answered in enthusiasm. ... I remarked (what I have often heard my husband remark of you) how rare it was to see a man who could distinguish himself equally in council and in action, in the cabinet and in the field.[38]

In 1844, Ellenborough recognized Broadfoot's earlier contributions in the Afghan war by naming him the Governor-General's political agent for the North-West Frontier. Soon thereafter, however, Ellenborough was recalled to England, leaving a legacy of military aggression throughout northern India that disrupted peaceful coexistence between the British and the native Hindus, Muslims, and Sikhs who inhabited the area for some time.[39]

In the summer of 1844, Sir Henry Hardinge took over from Ellenborough, just as new tensions were developing at the Sutlej River, the acknowledged boundary line separating British India in the south from the kingdom of the Sikhs in the Punjab to the north. Hardinge called upon Charles Cameron to offer legal advice on how to settle longstanding disputes between two warring rajas over property and treasure.[40] But even Cameron's intervention could not help Hardinge avoid stumbling into yet another military conflict. The region had been destabilized since at least 1839, when the Sikh leader Maharajah Ranjit Singh died after decades of peaceful rule and the kingdom fell into disorder, with diverse factions competing for control. During the same period, just south of the Sutlej, the East India Company gradually lost governing authority, as its residents failed to collect taxes, resolve land disputes, fill political vacuums, or quash struggles for supremacy among antipathetic tribal groups.[41] And rather than helping to defuse tensions, Broadfoot's appointment as Britain's political agent for the Sikh states actually escalated the insecurity and conflict because the Sikhs regarded him with mistrust, a legacy of his prominent role in the earlier Afghan war.[42] Nevertheless, Broadfoot intruded even further in Sikh affairs by attempting to manage border crossings at the river, which Sikh chiefs and soldiers perceived as further examples of British interference.[43] And although Broadfoot attempted to mediate between opposing tribal leaders, his efforts were flatly unsuccessful. Anticipating a total breakdown of negotiations and eventual combat, Lord Hardinge increased British forces at the nearby fort of Ambala from 13,600 troops in January 1844 to 32,500 in December 1845.[44] Yet the Sikhs anticipated conflict in the region as well, and assembled more than 15,000 soldiers, 'two-thirds of whom were horsemen', on the northern side of the river.[45]

In December 1845, the Sikh army assembled pontoons to cross the river and struck first against British forces. Fierce fighting ensued, as the Sikh army possessed military discipline and modern weapons of equal strength to those of the British.[46] News of the Sikh 'invasion' reached England some four to six weeks after the conflicts began, as the fastest means to convey the news from India was by steamship. In London, Sir John Herschel avidly consumed news of the war, as he later informed Charles and Julia Margaret. But the British pushed back over the Sutlej and were able to limit this regional conflict to only five military battles. The first two, located near the villages of Moodkee and Ferozeshah, captured the British imagination because the conflict extended into the night and took place in almost total darkness, as the 'fog of war' mixed with the terror of night-time warfare.[47] Broadfoot himself was wounded mortally in the nearby village of Ferozepore. On 1 March 1846, *The Times* of London filled eight pages with news of the conflict, and the *Illustrated London News* published detailed first-hand accounts from British soldiers, one referring to the intensity of the combat as 'the Waterloo of India'.[48]

Although the British won each of these major clashes, it was by narrow margins, and final victory was not claimed until February 1846. After marching into Lahore, the Army of the Sutlej paraded the Sikh cannons it had captured through the city's streets in triumph. Rather than annex the Punjab outright, Governor-General Hardinge determined to weaken the kingdom severely to prevent future uprisings. First, he installed Sir Henry Lawrence as the new Resident in the territory and seeded numerous political agents in Punjabi towns along with British garrisons, and then he fortified India's border with Afghanistan, stripped away the province of Kashmir from Sikh control, seized fertile land on the northern banks of the Sutlej, and assessed the Sikhs a substantial indemnity of £1.5 million.[49] Hardinge's actions thereby planted deep-seated resentments that would later erupt in the 1857 Uprising.

The important point here is that these military activities took place during the Camerons' early married life. They were engaged in formal and informal ways with a clear stake in the outcome, interacting regularly with the Governor-General even as the person who occupied that position

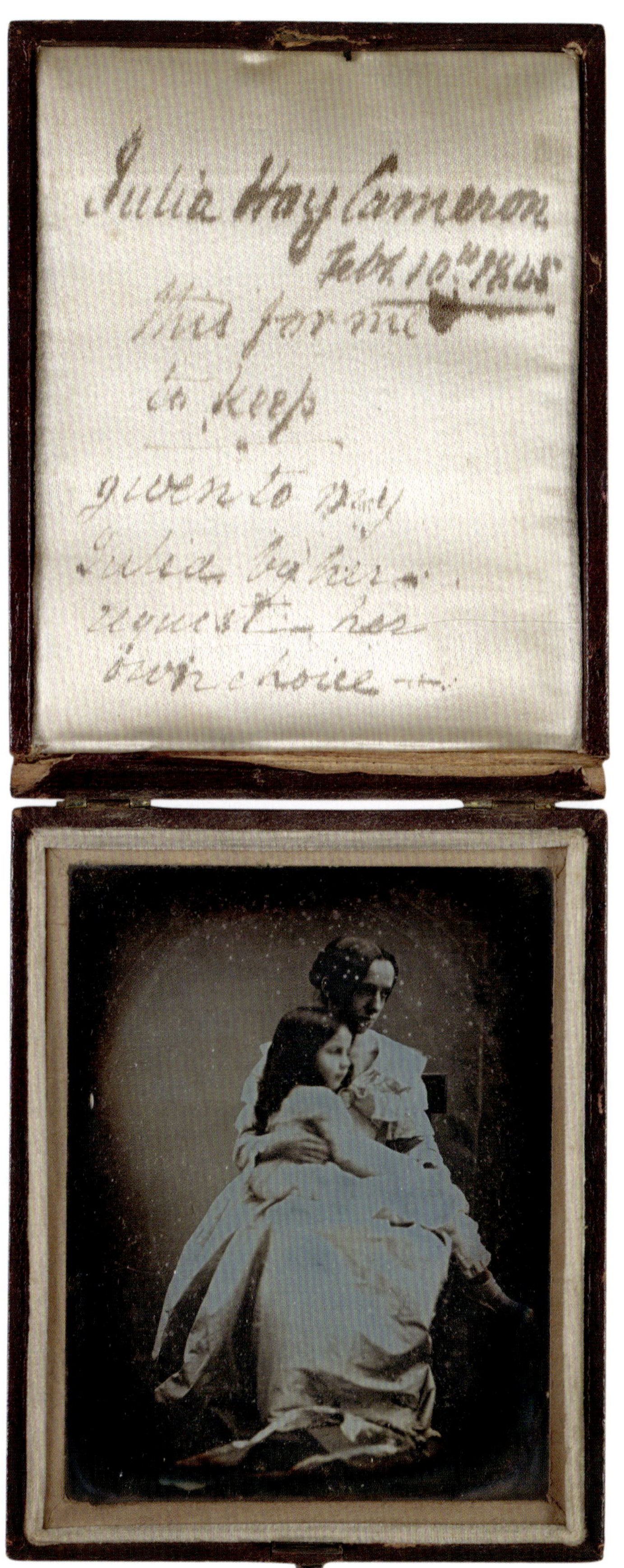

changed several times during the period they resided in Calcutta. Diplomatically they corresponded with Broadfoot on the frontier, and militarily with British forces that fought to maintain colonial control. Yet Julia Margaret's many biographers downplay these years, imagining her role as confined to elaborate party-planning for the Governor-General or preoccupied entirely with child-rearing.[50] In December 1838, Julia Margaret bore her first child, Julia Hay Cameron, and in early 1840 she gave birth to a son, Eugene. Like Lady Herschel, who was pregnant 'more than half the time' she spent with her husband in the Cape Colony, Julia Margaret also gave birth to several children during her early married years in Calcutta. But seen through a different lens, the Camerons' early family life in Calcutta was marked less by the domestic arts than by the chaos of colonial warfare and political influence trading.[51]

EMPIRE'S CHILDREN

By common and longstanding tradition, Anglo-Indian families like the Pattles sent their young children to Europe be raised by family members there. William Makepeace Thackeray, himself a child of empire, deplored such practices because they separated families.[52] Just as Julia Margaret and her sisters had been sent to Versailles as young children to be raised by their maternal grandmother, in 1845 the Camerons dispatched their two older children to England to live with Charles Cameron's unmarried sisters (in 1843, Julia Margaret gave birth to another son, Ewen, who remained as an infant with his mother).[53] Before she left India, five-year-old Juley took along a daguerreotype portrait of herself, shown here sitting on her mother's lap (fig. 12). Julia Margaret holds on to her daughter tightly. The keepsake records their close bonds of affection and is a tangible record of Julia Margaret's early interest in the medium. Julia Margaret found their separation virtually unbearable, noting 'how few who part in India meet again'.[54] The daguerreotype case interior is dated 10 February. By the end of

12 Unknown daguerreotypist, *Julia Hay Cameron with her Mother, Julia Margaret Cameron*, 1845, daguerreotype, approx. 12 × 9.4 cm.
National Science & Media Museum / Science Museum Group. 2007–5000.

the year, Julia Margaret was pregnant once again, carrying her fourth child. On 5 August 1846, she named her new son Hardinge, after India's triumphant Governor-General.

Back in England, Herschel wrote to congratulate the Camerons on the birth of their new son – but also to share his thoughts about colonial affairs in India. Brimming with elation after reading the sensational news in the London press about the army's victory over the Sikhs in the Punjab, Herschel expressed joy and relief the war's outcome had gone Britain's way. Herschel was careful, however, to measure his unchecked enthusiasm for the success of the Company's military expedition by qualifying that he understood its actions were all but altruistic, not a vulgar grab for territory, but rather an extension of Britain's selfless 'civilizing mission'. Herschel's understanding of empire was shaped, at least in part, by his personal experience in the Cape Colony. He cast the East India Company's actions as beneficent and liberating, even as it expanded British territorial control in the region. Regarding Britain's presence in the colony as morally honourable, Herschel agreed with the Company's opposition to traditional Indian religious practices and customs that the British thought corrupt or backward. Herschel made these sentiments clear in his letter.

> What an excited state of feeling of alarm and hope these marvellous events in Northern India must have held you in. Not [in] all the trepidating [*sic*] interest that preceded Waterloo was there a more gasping anxiety prevailing here than in the intervals of the successive announcements of their operations, but it is only now that the alarm of the triumph are [*sic*] over that the real importance of those events is beginning to impress us, and the enormous moral interests at stake begin to be appreciated. They have made India a more integrated part, not of British Empire but of English feeling, than it ever was before, and in the long period of tranquillity that seems now awaiting it, the effects of this will be profoundly felt.[55]

Significantly, Herschel was keen to downplay the violence of British imperial expansion into Afghanistan or the material exploitation of other lands ('*not British Empire*') and instead endorse the self-regarding political position that Britain was an earnest and benevolent custodian of the world's moral development, that its civilizing efforts in colonial lands were selfless, noble, even kind-hearted ('*but of English feeling*'). For Cameron as for Herschel, 'English feeling' was revealed by tangible improvements to colonial life that were made possible by English technology, reflected in virtuous principles of equal treatment under the law that the penal code sought to guarantee, and assured by the administrative rationality and efficiency of the Civil Service.[56] Herschel's expression of his 'excited state of feeling of alarm and hope' also discloses his unmistakable sense of validation that Britain's positive outcome would prevent, in Satia's words, 'the potential menace of an India set loose from the imperial order – such a backward society would certainly collapse into anarchy and wreak havoc in the world'.[57]

Herschel's positive reaction to the conclusion of the war in the Punjab also echoes his own earlier censure of the Frontier War in Africa, which he regarded as a senseless military action that did more harm than good to British interests, in that it neither facilitated harmony among peoples, nor furthered the economic interests of colonial governance. In deploring the war against the Xhosa, he came close to calling such military intervention a criminal act.[58] Cameron and Herschel therefore shared a rhetoric that acclaimed the unquestioned excellence of British civilization, upheld views that discerned between 'advanced' and 'backward' societies, and put their faith in the importance of moral virtue as a guiding principle, in education as in colonial governance. Herschel also perceived the East India Company as a worthy vehicle for helping to shape young men into responsible adults who would advance the goals of the empire, believing that, following the Sikh War, Britain could count on 'the long period of tranquillity that seems now awaiting it' to build even more secure foundations in the colony.

To that end, Herschel confided in Julia Margaret his personal hope that his eldest son, William, would one day enter the administrative corps of the Company and follow in the illustrious careers of so many others who also had started their professional life in the service. An 'entry-level position' in the Indian Civil Service was known as a 'writer', which is to say, working for the Company's administrative corps by inscribing the policies and practices of colonial governance: collecting taxes, administering legal and economic affairs, overseeing social programmes. Eventually, as his son William matured, Herschel enlisted the help of both Charles Cameron and Thoby Prinsep to obtain letters of introduction for the boy to secure his place in the East India Company.[59] William Herschel headed off for Bengal when he turned twenty years old. After attending Haileybury, the Company's training academy, the young man received his first appointment as Assistant Collector and Magistrate at Maldah.[60] In this role, William Herschel essentially served as a revenue collector, the same post that Thackeray parodied in *Vanity Fair* in the character of Jos Sedley, the 'collector of Boggley Wollah, an honourable and lucrative post, as everybody knows'.[61]

Sir John clearly valued the Indian Civil Service, both as a tool of empire and as proving ground for a young man's future livelihood. As he wrote to Julia Margaret,

> there is something in the nature of the [Civil] Service itself which falls in with all y[our] ideas of what is most desireable [*sic*] and most calculated to call into action all the powers of the individual.

This comment suggests that the two had discussed the topic in earlier correspondence, and importantly, that Cameron had expressed her enthusiastic support for the Company's administrative corps.[62] The two friends apparently agreed that, in Herschel's words,

> there is no government on earth which not only so well rewards its servants, but also knows how to apply their abilities, each in the most available manner and according to what they are best fitted for.[63]

Like Herschel, Cameron admired diplomacy over military aggression, and preferred acts of 'civilizing valour' over hostility and oppression. As she wrote three years earlier to Broadfoot, for example,

> Courage, however admirable in the field, however worthy of our respect, admiration, and gratitude, cannot alone entitle a man to promotion and distinction in offices of trust and honour, if he has not, besides courage, the mental and moral qualities required to do justice to that office.[64]

To prevail in its imperial project, Britain could not rely upon courage and moral propriety alone. Those who served the empire had to demonstrate their resilience and commitment to the cause, especially in the face of adversity, imprisonment, or rebellion. An indomitable spirit was required for emigration to the colonies, as was resilience, good health, and good fortune. Julia Margaret Cameron captured these intersecting ideas in the Herschel Album by including a photograph of a child of empire, an otherwise unremarkable photograph of a baby that she titled simply *Baby 'Pictet'* (Cox/Ford 1012; HA-10; fig. 13). She did not identify the infant but wrote below the image, 'One year old infant shipwrecked once in the Madras Surf & again in the wreck of the Colombo Steamer'. Cameron copyrighted the photograph on 30 June 1864. The photograph is unlike any other in her *oeuvre*: it does not represent an allegory or personification, like *Young Astyanax* (HA-60); it does not represent a carefully posed figure study, like *Alice du Cane* (HA-16); nor is this image created as an artistic abstraction, like her close-up portfolio of twelve 'life-size heads' (compare HA-81).

But *Baby 'Pictet'* does portray a child of the empire. She was apparently hearty and resilient, having survived a disaster at sea, the wreck of the P&O Company's *SS Colombo*, on 18 and 19 November 1862 in the Indian Ocean, off the coast of the island of Minicoy, as well as an even earlier mishap that took place 'in the Madras surf'.[65] Baby 'Pictet' was also a family relation: Georgina Anna Mary Pictet, born on 12 September 1862 to Rose Prinsep Mackenzie, the third child of the much-decorated soldier Colin Mackenzie, and Julia Margaret's oldest sister, Adeline Maria (Pattle) Mackenzie, who died in 1836. Young Georgina was therefore Julia Margaret's great-niece. She was the first-born child of Rose Mackenzie's marriage to Francis Frédéric Pictet, who Rose married on 10 December 1861 in Secunderabad, Madras. But Pictet was Rose's *second* husband. Her first husband, David Arnot, died on 18 July 1860 in the aftermath of the Indian Uprising, a Lieutenant in the Madras army's 34th Light Infantry. Their first issue was Colin Mackenzie Arnot, born on 17 December 1857 in Pallavaram, Madras, the child named after his renowned grandfather.[66]

Cameron's inscription and specific reference to Madras is unique in the Herschel Album, as this identification ties young Georgina directly to the British colony. In 1861, after Britain consolidated the Bengal, Madras, and Bombay armed forces

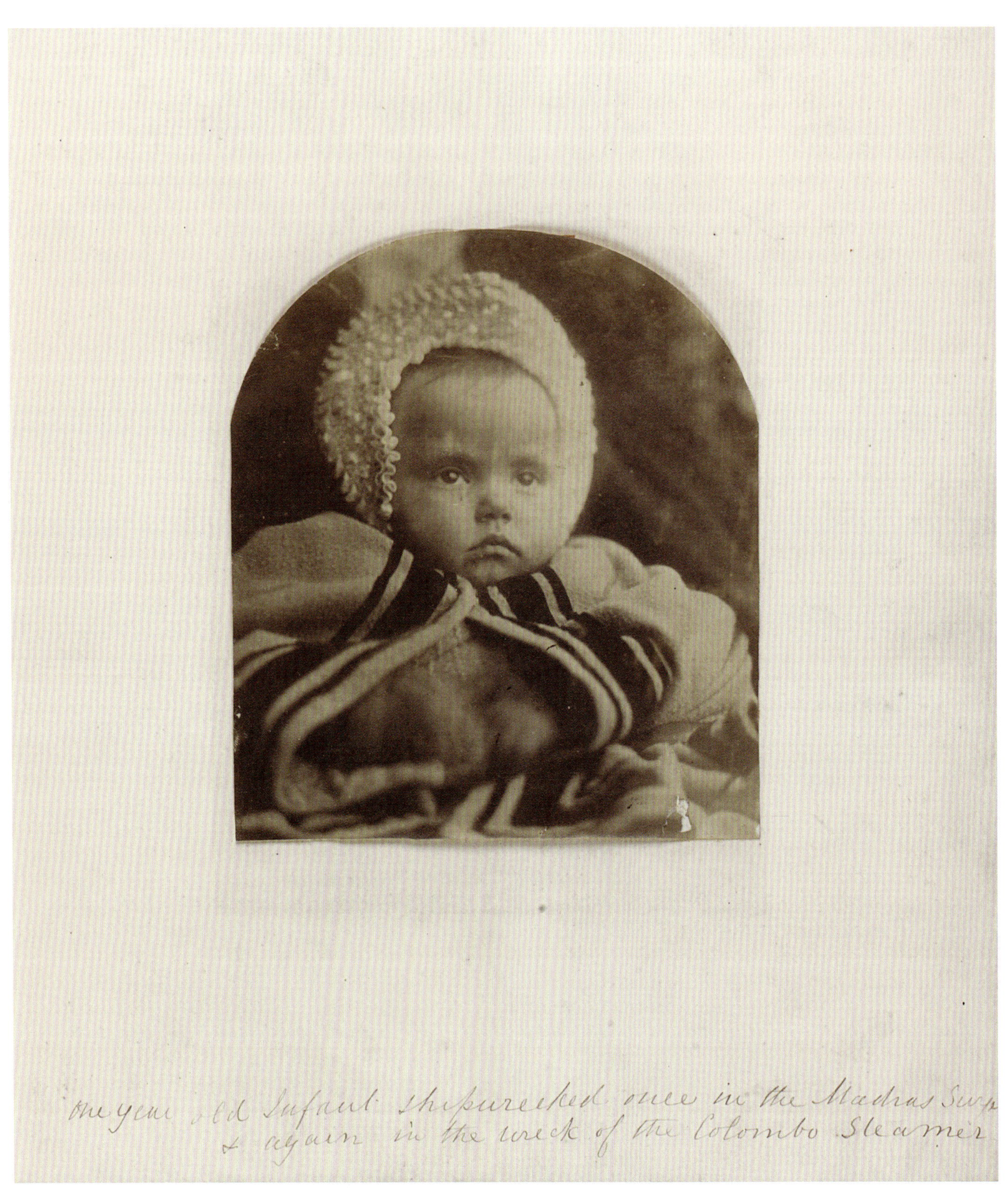

13 Julia Margaret Cameron, *Baby 'Pictet'*, 1864, albumen print, 17.2 × 14.8 cm. Cameron's handwritten inscription reads, 'One year old infant shipwrecked once in the Madras Surf & again in the wreck of the Colombo Steamer'.

National Science & Media Museum / Science Museum Group. 1984–5017/19.

through a formal process called Amalgamation, Captain Pictet petitioned the Secretary of State for India for promotion, an outspoken appeal to the government to elevate the interests of career soldiers over those of newer recruits.[67] But these details about Pictet or the extended Pattle and Mackenzie family history were likely of much less personal importance to Herschel than the young girl's legacy as a child of Madras. After all, when Julia Margaret presented her album to Herschel in 1867, Georgina would have been five years old, a resident of Bath who lived comfortably with her two parents, a younger sister, born in 1864, and younger brother, born in 1866. This family apparently lacked any meaningful connection to Herschel personally. And yet, this photograph is unique in the Herschel Album, as it is inscribed in Cameron's hand specifically as a memento of Madras, suggesting the photograph contained evident symbolic value to Herschel.

Madras signified multiple possible associations, reminders for Herschel as for Cameron how family, nation, and empire intersected once again in this region of India. First, as a child of empire and granddaughter of Colin Mackenzie, Georgina Pictet would have been known to Herschel as a descendant of that celebrated family. Equally likely, he would know from Cameron herself that Francis Frédéric Pictet served in the same regiment as his father-in-law, Colin Mackenzie. Captain Pictet commanded the 49th Madras Native Infantry, the celebrated regiment that performed heroically during the wars in Afghanistan and the Punjab. As we have seen from his correspondence with Julia Margaret, Herschel avidly read news of the Company's wars in the North-West Frontier and would have known of Cameron's personal connection to soldiers in the war, especially Mackenzie and his friend George Broadfoot. After Broadfoot's death, that soldier's heroism was eulogized as a national loss by both Houses of Parliament. To honour his fallen comrade, Sir Henry Havelock, who first won renown in Afghanistan before leading a regiment against insurgents in the 1857 Uprising, christened his youngest son George Broadfoot in 1847, and Governor-General Hardinge remembered Broadfoot with the highest honours. Colin Mackenzie himself placed a tombstone over Broadfoot's grave in Ferozepore, then raised a public subscription to fund an elaborate monument to his name (fig. 14).[68]

The monument to Broadfoot was later erected in St George's Cathedral in Madras, and is discussed in chapter 8. The theatrical nature of such memorials, wrote Priya Satia, contributed to establishing the 'historical template' for commemorating Britain's colonial wars, as these elaborately sculpted tombs were destined for Anglican churches in India. They contributed to creating a narrative that reimagined the army's failures as triumphs, with Broadfoot an archetype of heroism in the mould of Carlyle's heroic model. Cameron's photograph of *Baby 'Pictet'*, as a survivor of not one but two shipwrecks, embeds a similar narrative of triumph over adversity and steadfast commitment to the colonial mission.[69] One additional military association might also be pertinent to Cameron's decision to include this photograph in Herschel's album: during the 1857 Uprising, sepoys in the Madras native regiments apparently 'remained loyal' to their British officers, a fact that led Mackenzie and others in the Madras army to claim their firm hand and benevolent leadership was responsible for suppressing a sepoy revolt within their ranks.[70]

Sir John's particular interest in Madras, however, was more likely familial, related to the scientific activities of his younger son, also named John. In 1864, if Baby 'Pictet' was on her way to England, young John Herschel had just re-enlisted for additional military service in Madras. These movements again make visible the interwoven concerns of family, nation, and empire, for Cameron as for Herschel. That year, Sir John's namesake was commissioned a lieutenant in the Royal Engineers and joined the Great Trigonometric Survey of India, which was based in Madras and located at the Observatory first built in 1786, a longstanding imperial project. Headquartered at the Observatory, the Survey was staffed by military officers who gathered data about the earth and heavens in relation to Britain's overseas territories. Joining together this data with other astronomical observatories across the globe, this scientific work consolidated British colonial, economic, and military interests.[71] The Madras Survey dated to 1802, in fact, when the East India Company established it to create territorial maps based upon precise measurements of land masses,

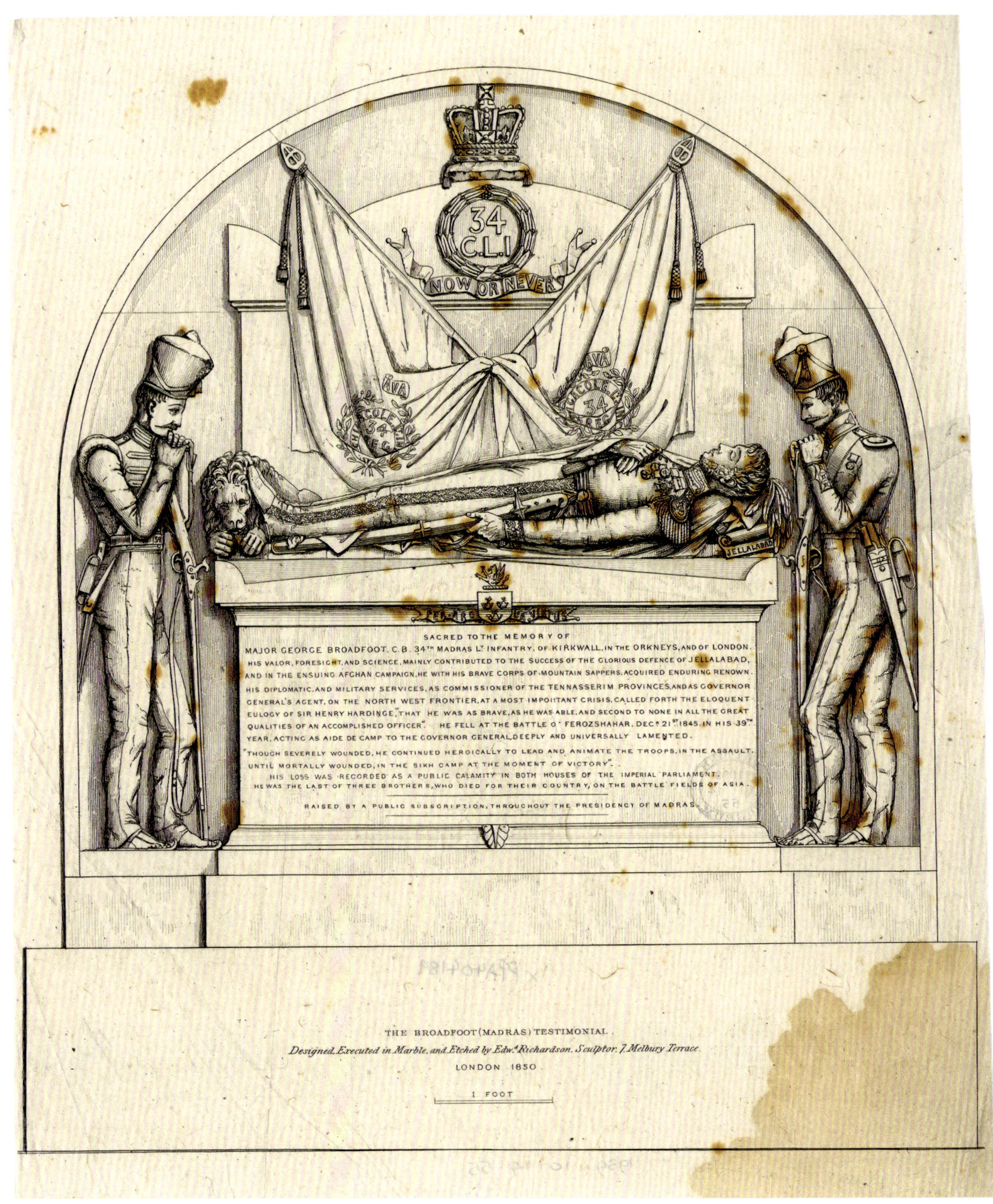

14 Edward Richardson, *The Broadfoot (Madras) Testimonial*, 1850, etching on paper, 28.1 × 22.4 cm. In the letter of the print: 'The Broadfoot (Madras) Testimonial'. 'Designed, Executed in Marble, and Etched by Edw.d Richardson, Sculptor, 7. Melbury Terrace'.

thereby providing reliable estimates of distance between population centres and tactical points of military interest. As a project that represented the extent of Britain's territorial control, the Survey was supported as a strategic initiative by Thoby Prinsep's older brother, Charles, who contributed a sketch of the Calcutta base line in 1832.[72] Even though this work was nominally described as a purely 'scientific' project, the Madras Survey also contributed to the historical narration of the empire's expansion, as it portrayed Britain's military defeats as brimming with future promise, for example, by reframing the 1842 catastrophe in Afghanistan and 1843 annexation of the Punjab as fresh 'opportunit[ies] for a wide extension of geographical knowledge of countries beyond the north-west frontier'.[73] Like his esteemed father, young John Herschel carried out astronomical observations of a similar nature as Sir John did before him, and the young man remained stationed in Madras until 1872.[74] Because of their shared interest in astronomical observations, Sir John could understand the importance of his son's work in Madras and his work for the Great Trigonometric Survey of India as these commitments were tied directly to Herschel's earlier activities on the Cape of Good Hope.

PERFORMANCES OF EMPIRE

For Charles and Julia Margaret Cameron, encouragement for Britain's colonial battles went hand-in-hand with support for its civil service. In December 1846, at the conclusion of the Anglo-Sikh War, the Company's army took over the Esplanade in Calcutta to display the Sikh artillery that it had captured during its war in the Punjab. Like Auckland before him, who assembled triumphal arches south of the Sutlej in 1842 to welcome back the army of retribution that had just invaded Afghanistan, and Lord Ellenborough, who erected a triumphal arch in 1844 in front of the town hall in Calcutta to welcome attendees to his own farewell dinner, Lord Hardinge deployed the ancient iconography once more: Hardinge directed the army to parade the spoils of war through a freshly erected triumphal arch in Calcutta as if it were the return to Rome of an ancient imperial army.[75] The army's parade was commemorated by the *Illustrated London News* in a woodcut depicting the procession taking place on the extensive fairgrounds facing Government House (see fig. 9). Representing the event as a 'Grand Field-Day at Calcutta' (fig. 15), the journal underscored its importance with the following caption:

> In the Sketch, the spectator is supposed to be looking northward; the large building to the right be the Government House, at Calcutta. The captured Sikh guns occupy the left or west side of the open space extending the whole way from the arch to the margin of the view ... In the rear of the guns, the crowd of spectators reach nearly to the river. Beneath the large flag are assembled the Deputy-Governor of Bengal, and his Staff; with ... the Members of the Supreme Council, the Government Secretaries, &c.[76]

Given that Charles Cameron was the sole legal member of the Supreme Council, it is all but certain he was present to witness this ceremonial display of British power and was accompanied by his wife, Julia Margaret.

Colin and Helen Mackenzie returned to India in 1847. They were received initially by the Camerons and stayed with Charles and Julia Margaret in Calcutta before moving on to the North-West Provinces, where Mackenzie assumed command of the 4th Regiment Frontier Brigade. Before departing, Helen Mackenzie noted then how

> Society in Calcutta was still of the old Indian type: there was an amount of show and lavish expenditure which ceased after the Mutiny. The dress of the ladies was gorgeous; sixty servants were to be found in one house; and to a new-comer the strict etiquette and even the wearisome 'bara khánás,' or great dinner-parties, were amusing.[77]

Helen Mackenzie's observations echo those made earlier by Emily Eden, who joined her brother, Lord Auckland, in 1839 for a picnic in the cool mountain air of Simla, where the British had established their summer headquarters to escape the oppressive heat of Calcutta. She, too, reflected on their affluence and advantage, noting her party was eating salmon from Scotland and sardines from the Mediterranean while being entertained by a full band that played ballads from Italian opera for their amusement. She then reflected,

> all this in the face of those high hills, some of which have remained untrodden since the creation and we, 105 Europeans, being surrounded by at least

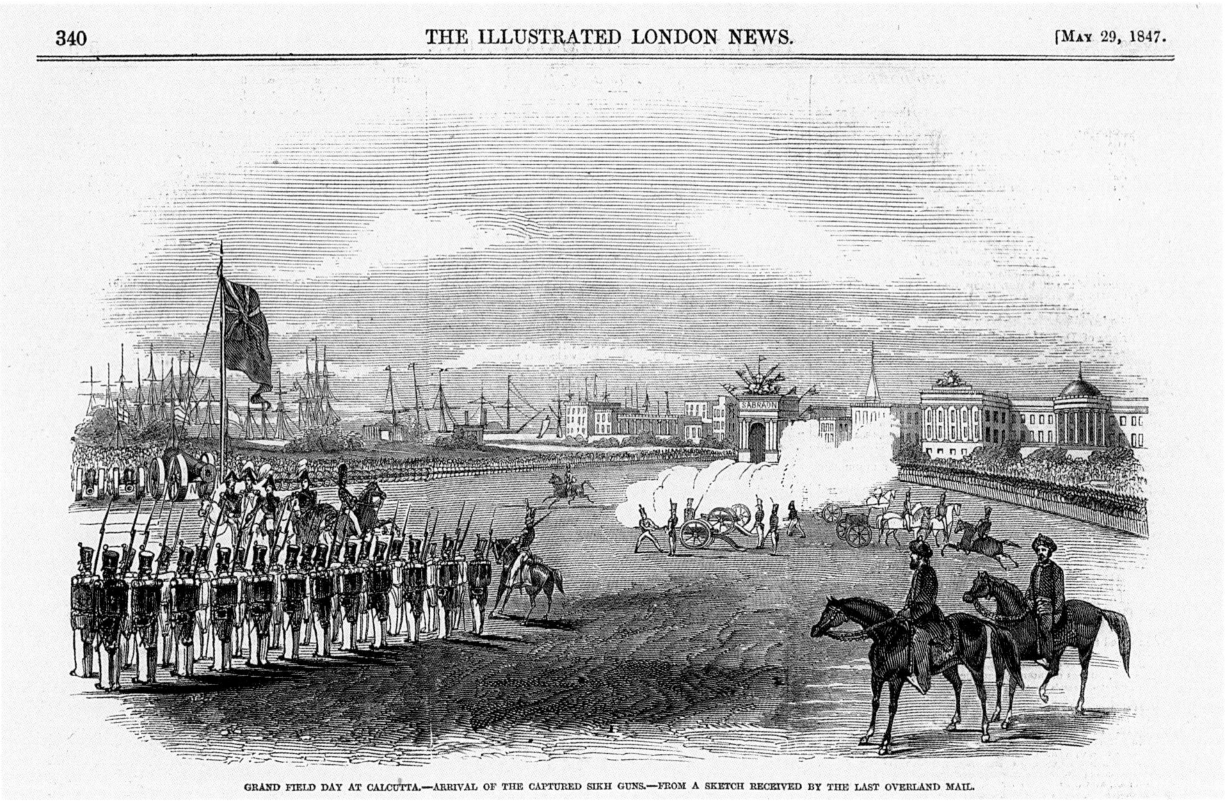

340 THE ILLUSTRATED LONDON NEWS. [MAY 29, 1847.

GRAND FIELD DAY AT CALCUTTA.—ARRIVAL OF THE CAPTURED SIKH GUNS.—FROM A SKETCH RECEIVED BY THE LAST OVERLAND MAIL.

15 *Grand Field Day at Calcutta – Arrival of the Captured Sikh Guns – From a Sketch Received by the last Overland Mail, Illustrated London News*, 29 May 1847, 340.

> 3,000 mountaineers, who, wrapped up on their hill blankets, looked on at what we call our polite amusements, and bowed to the ground if a European came near them. I sometimes wonder they do not cut all our heads off, and say nothing more about it.[78]

Eden's awareness of her privileged status or the risk she took in sitting on a hillside in the open air listening to music should not be mistaken for embarrassment or humility, or even a reflection of her real vulnerability. Rather, her delight in cataloguing the day's pleasures, in meticulously counting off the precise number of individuals present and in articulating Britain's seemingly implausible hold on power, suggests instead a kind of arrogant self-importance, one that must have played well to readers of her letters back home. Today, however, in grasping for wit at the expense of the unnamed servants who attended to her every need, Eden's sense of exposure comes off as false and insincere. Nevertheless, Eden's letters home were emblematic of Britain's preference for understating its authority and how its colonial power was broadly recognized. Equally prejudicial, her letters appear to believe the myths that Britons told themselves about their racial superiority, military power, and cultural dominance.

So too for Sir John Herschel at the Cape of Good Hope. In 1838, just prior to selling the Feldhausen estate, Herschel arranged to retain a circular patch of South African land into perpetuity. Like an explorer planting a stake in 'unknown territory' on behalf of the empire, Herschel marked the spot on which he had erected his telescope as if it were a symbol of civilization carved out of barbarian lands, erecting 'a small cylindrical column of granite engraved "I. H. 1838" representing his initials in Latin'.[79] But this stone marker was soon to be replaced with something much more grand. During his residency at the Cape, Herschel had served as president of the South African Literary and Scientific Institution, and when its members learned of his imminent departure for England, they collected funds to erect a sizable monument to commemorate 'their admiration of one whose talents place him so far above ordinary men, and whose private life was a pattern of every domestic virtue', in the words of Thomas Maclear, who also studied astronomy alongside Herschel.[80] The colony's new governor, Sir George Napier, who replaced D'Urban in January 1838, supervised proceedings that determined the new monument would take the shape of an obelisk and would be made of Craigleith stone from a quarry near Edinburgh.[81] Its hollow base was to contain a time capsule of imperial mementoes, including a map of the colony, engravings of the nebulae and comets observed by Herschel, a six-inch standard scale, data about the Cape settlement, and coins from the British Mint.[82] Above the six-foot-tall base, which was to be aligned to the cardinal points, seven square tapering courses of granite were to be assembled and then topped by a pyramidal cap. The whole would stand 12 feet above the base. After the final stone was laid in February 1842, a bronze plaque was added with a Latin inscription to mark Herschel's achievements.[83] Several years later, this event was memorialized in the published account of the astronomer's observations made during his stay at the Cape Colony, which depicted for readers a picturesque view of the memorial, now called Herschel's Obelisk (fig. 16).

As ancient stone markers, imposing in scale and impressive in precious and polished materials, obelisks had been venerated since biblical times. Native to Phoenicia, Egypt, and Greece, these

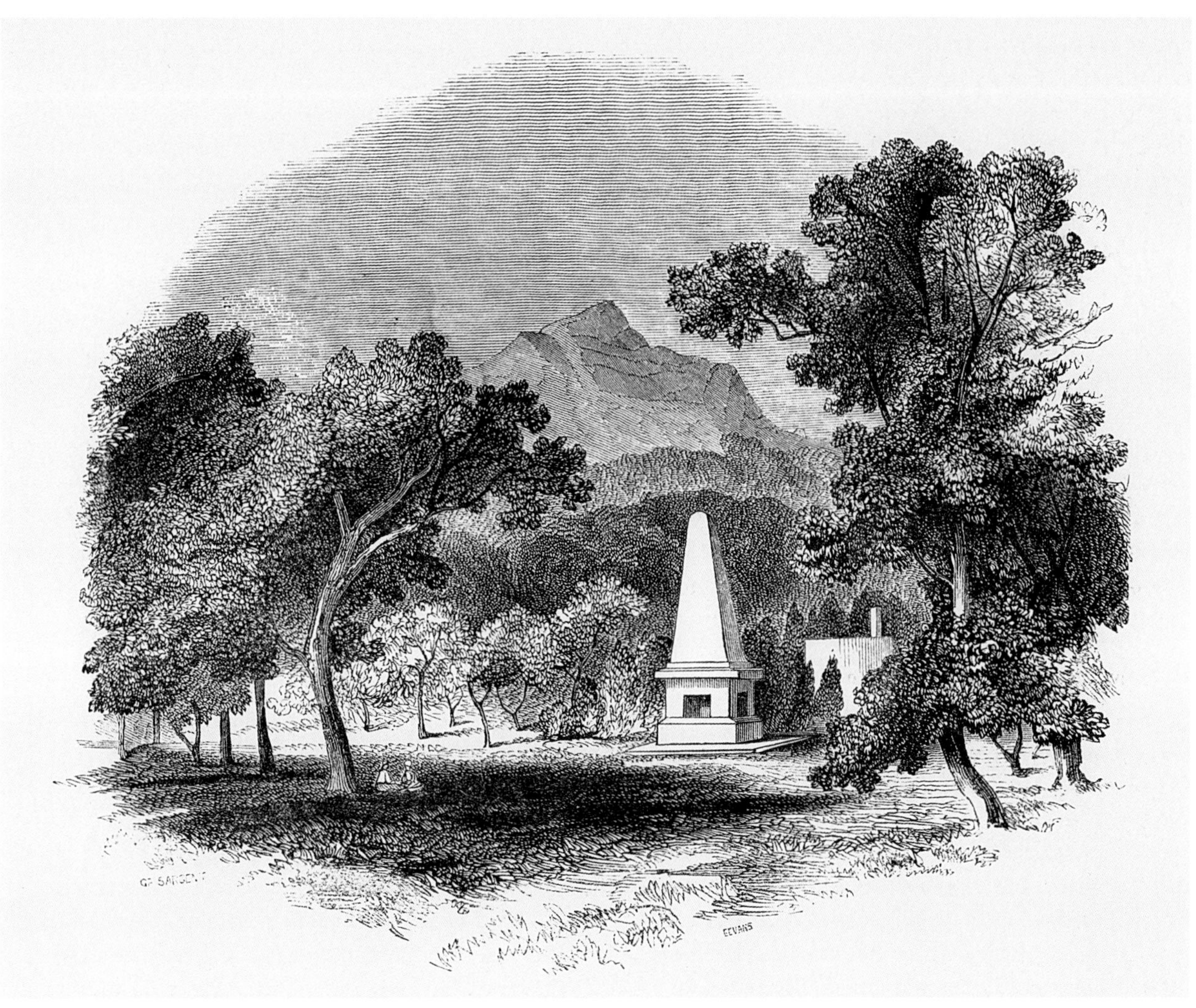

16 Anon., [The Herschel Obelisk] *Results of Astronomical Observations made during the Years 1834, 5, 6, 7, 8, at the Cape of Good Hope, by Sir John F. W. Herschel* (London: Smith, Elder and Co., 1847), 452.

grand visual signposts became known widely for marking significant historical events. Their monumental role in depicting history profoundly influenced the Victorians. In 1859, for example, the sculptor John Bell addressed the Society of the Arts on the historical significance of ancient obelisks to the modern era. Bell noted that their pointed shape represented a narrow ray of light that was associated with 'early profane worship', but importantly, he gave priority to its social function in marking historical time. Obelisks were almost always inscribed by their makers, wrote Bell, emphasizing that the ancient Greek philosopher Strabo called them 'Books of History'.[84] When the ancient Romans conquered Egypt and transported their obelisks to Rome, it was not only to appropriate the power and dominance that these massive symbols represented, but also to confiscate Egyptian history and rewrite cultural memory. As a result, Rome's seizure effectively reinscribed those monuments with a new narrative of power and dominance.[85] For these same reasons, in 1851, Bell wanted to construct an obelisk made of British granite to commemorate the Great Exhibition at the Crystal Palace, an effort to claim the ancient iconography for the modern empire, a uniquely British understanding of imperial power.[86]

The South African Literary and Scientific Institution's decision to erect an obelisk to mark Herschel's achievements was no less politically inspired or conditioned by the shifting meanings associated with this monumental symbol. As a result, Herschel's Obelisk entered different discursive contexts as it met the needs of Cape Town's distinctive communities. For the Literary and Scientific Institution that commissioned the monolith, the obelisk memorialized Herschel's scientific achievements and staked a claim for advancing the society's educational goals in the colony. The obelisk thereby validated the Institution's interests in ancient Egyptian study, particularly its ancient system of weights and measures.[87] For the creators of the buried time capsule, the stone monument marked a triumphant moment in time – a literal recording for the ages, symbolically preserved forever in the earth – that validated Britain's takeover of land held earlier by the Dutch. And despite repeated imperial repossessions of land and the historical transport of obelisks from Egypt to Europe, the erection of Herschel's Obelisk on territory designated 'in perpetuity' as Herschel's own, ironically preserved the same pretensions for the monument's everlasting permanence. Finally, for Governor Napier, who administered the occupation of the Cape settlement itself, the material origins of the obelisk – built as it was from stone transported from a quarry in Scotland – demonstrated the enormous reach and power of the British empire. All these elements conspired together to help brand Herschel's Obelisk – and the small parcel of land in Africa upon which it stood – with a new British identity.

THE 'WOMAN QUESTION'

When the Camerons were still residing in Calcutta, Lady Herschel saw an opportunity to engage Julia Margaret in a venture of her own that might occupy her friend while at the same time helping to promote the imperial project. She wrote to Julia Margaret around 1840, the year after Sarah Stickney Ellis's book *The Women of England, Their Social Duties, and Domestic Habits* was published. In her correspondence, Lady Herschel emphasized the importance of this book to the imperial mission, although it is also possible that Julia Margaret knew of Ellis's work independently. Lady Herschel urged her friend to apply her influence to teach Indian women how to draw upon the British model of domestic life, to use their influence as wives and mothers, and to elevate the moral life of Indian families. By drawing upon Ellis's example, she wrote, Julia Margaret could contribute to advancing England's civilizing mission in India. In *The Women of England*, Ellis claimed the 'respectable, influential, and patriotic women' of Britain as her readers. She urged them to 'carry out the views of an enlightened legislature through those minor channels which form the connection between public and private life', because cultural work that promoted English values at home and abroad was 'of the utmost importance to the welfare of the country in general'.[88] Lady Herschel built upon these same ideas in making her appeal to her friend, Julia Margaret:

> Oh I wish I could animate you to do what you could so well – write a book for the benefit of *Indian ladies*, such as Mrs. Ellis has done for English women, begging them to resist some at least of the customs

> which leave so many sad traces on their children and their own minds afterwards. Must an Indian mother give up her precious ones entirely to the care and guidance of Indian servants? [Original emphasis][89]

Lady Herschel's proposal was undoubtedly sincere, offering Cameron a serious undertaking that she was sure her friend would find fulfilling, while honouring her sympathies and talents. By undertaking such work, she wrote, Julia Margaret could extend the imperial mission while exercising her own authoritative subjectivity, arguing that such a project could help her break free from some of the Victorian era's social constraints on women.[90]

The correspondence between these two imperial women is intriguing, especially in relation to the work of their two husbands, and the dominance of men in legal and governmental positions of authority and power, especially in the colonies. Years ago, Jenny Sharpe observed, 'English women [were] excluded from participating in [the] noble work' of building the empire abroad, in spite of their efforts to promote 'domestic virtues to the civilizing mission'.[91] More recently, Éadaoin Agnew has argued that British women in India did indeed reinforce the prevailing power structures in the colony by means of their cultural and moral authority.[92] Setting aside Lady Herschel's motives in recommending that Cameron undertake the instruction of Indian women in European ways, it is apparent from their correspondence that the two shared a similar understanding that the social role of Indian women intersected with their place in the traditional domestic sphere *and* in relation to British imperial dominance. Which is to say, for Lady Margaret Brodie Stewart Herschel and for Julia Margaret Cameron, the 'woman question' was not about how to transgress the constraints Victorian society imposed upon women or how to promote some sort of maternal self-expression. Rather, as framed by these two friends, the 'woman question', at least in the colonial context, centred on how women could use the levers of power available to them to extend maternal and social influence, and to promote a cohesive imperial identity. In this regard, the 'woman question' was framed as an extension of Britain's civilizing mission.

As Sarah Stickney Ellis argued at the time, the domestic activities and home life of imperial women did not have to disengage them from participating in the social formation of the nation's identity, nor did it absolve them of their duty to contribute to the imperial cause. Indeed, many social observers of the time considered 'the home' to be the principal anchor that maintained the integrity of a nation's moral character. The most popular and well-read of those who advocated this position in England was Ellis. In 1839, for example, she described women's roles as essential to help give shape to the moral authority of the nation's identity.

> The national characteristics of England are the perpetual boast of her patriotic sons; and there is one especially which it behooves [*sic*] all British subjects not only to exult in, but to cherish and maintain. Leaving the justice of her laws, the extent of her commerce, and the amount of her resources, to the orator, the statesman, and the political economist, there yet remains one of the noblest features in her national character, which may not improperly be regarded as within the compass of a woman's understanding, and the province of a woman's pen. It is the domestic character of England – the home comforts, and fireside virtues for which she is so justly celebrated.[93]

From the enthusiastic character of her recommendations of Ellis's writings to Julia Margaret, Lady Herschel undoubtedly idealized such sentiments. And from the character of Julia Margaret's correspondence with Broadfoot during this same time, they no doubt resonated with her as well. For Ellis, domestic life was not confined to household management, nor did her so-called 'conduct books' elevate elegance or refined manners as frivolous distractions.[94] Rather, she advised British women they were the moral centre of family life and therefore represented the very heart of the nation. She urged women to embrace this mission and take a worldly approach by acting in service to others. She also segregated women by class, wanting to elevate the role of middle-class women and downplay both the aristocracy and the poor as unqualified to advance this mission. According to Ellis, 'the middle class must include so vast a portion of the intelligence and moral power of the country at large, that it may not improperly be designated the pillar of our nation's strength'.[95] As a result, she assured bourgeois women that by serving others and devoting themselves to family and community, they would help ensure domestic activity was maintained as a high calling and preserve the national character of the state.

But it is also important to recognize that the correspondence between Lady Herschel and Julia Margaret regarding the status of Indian women rests upon a thinly disguised contempt for indigenous women. This disdain was founded on Britain's religious convictions, which led to its formal opposition to traditional Hindu customs. These included *suttee*, the self-immolation of widows; prohibitions that restricted a woman's ability to remarry; social customs guiding the age when girls could wed; and the practice of polygamy. Policies banning or restricting these customs were central to Britain's civilizing mission and regarded as key ideological justifications for colonial rule, but they were also perceived by indigenous women as unwanted interference. Nevertheless, British missionaries found these and many other Muslim, Jain, and Sikh attitudes towards women anathema to Western norms and regarded indigenous customs long sanctioned by tradition and religious belief as backward, degenerate, and immoral. Attitudes like these were consistent with the anthropological views of Ellis's husband, William Ellis, who studied indigenous peoples in Polynesia and Madagascar during the 1830s and 1840s, and who wrote that the practices of polygamy and infanticide in Polynesia were 'accursed', not only immoral and depraved. With particular attention on the social role of women, in fact, Ellis wrote that these practices embodied 'the essential *anti-type of domesticity*' (my emphasis).[96] William Ellis's idealized norms, of course, were built upon patriarchal social conventions, the Victorian status quo that Sarah Stickney Ellis celebrated in her books.

Partha Chaterjee has pointed out how social and religious practices of Indian women were a major focus of the earliest British reformers in the colony, but also how the same issues persisted throughout the nineteenth century as the intersection of custom, religion, and patriarchy continued to define the 'woman question', even despite global modernism and emergent Indian nationalism. Ironically, in reaction to external pressures, Indian nationalists agreed with Ellis that the family homestead was 'the principal site for expressing the spiritual quality of the national culture', but they firmly opposed Ellis's Western prescriptions to assimilate to British norms: 'No matter what the changes in the external conditions of life for [Indian] women, ... they must not ... become essentially Westernized'.[97] Chaterjee concluded that patriarchy did not disappear during this time but rather circled back to the family home as a way to maintain its central place in shaping society. If it could be employed as a strategic tool *against* colonial rule, he argued, the structure and management of the Indian home could acquire even greater importance because in this gendered space, women could prevent both the rulers and the ruled from entering its privileged domain. As a result, he wrote, these conflicts conferred upon 'the [Indian] home' a special kind of social power as a potential site of resistance.[98] What is apparent, though, is that women's social subordination in India could not be separated from indigenous traditions or from foreign domination alike. For these reasons, liberation movements of Indian women struggled against these same forces well into the twentieth century.[99]

It is evident that the intertwining concerns expressing Britain's 'civilizing mission' to India preoccupied the Camerons and the Herschels and helped bind the two families together in relation to Britain's imperial mission. Their collective understanding was reinforced by their direct experience and ability to influence the social, educational, and legal power structures of their respective colonies, the Camerons in India, the Herschels in Cape Town. The two couples shared commonly held religious and social values that upheld Britain's pre-eminence in such areas as education, language, technology, administrative governance, and gendered social roles. As we have seen, Sir John and Charles Cameron argued on behalf of establishing English as the standard language in formal systems of education in their respective colonies. Both relied too upon their own classical upbringing as the foundation for their beliefs in the superiority of British reasoning and education. While Herschel advocated for the adoption of a standard system of weights and measures in Cape Town, Charles Cameron advocated for a rigorous penal code in India. Both families agreed that the Indian Civil Service provided an ideal model for the world in how to govern indigenous people in colonial territories. And the two imperial women fell into line with respect to their own gendered social roles and how best to evangelize those Western norms to colonial women.

In 1848, the Camerons left India for England. They first moved to Belgravia, in the very heart of London, close to Julia Margaret's sister Sara and brother-in-law Thoby Prinsep, who had preceded them by five years and settled in Holland Park. By 1850, the Camerons entered a peripatetic period that would extend over the next decade spent in London and in cottages in Putney Heath and other small villages in Kent, close to where the Herschels had settled a decade earlier. During this period, the families maintained their intimate social connection, while Charles travelled to Ceylon periodically to manage the family's coffee plantations.[100] Once the Camerons and the Herschels resided in the same English county, they occasionally sent their eldest daughters on summertime exchange visits. This practice became a regular occurrence by 1858, so that when the Camerons moved into a new house in London, at 7 Park Street, Westminster, Julia Margaret reserved 'a spare bed room' at the rear of the house 'to have one of the little Herschel's in it now and then'.[101] In Charles's absence, Julia Margaret embraced new friendships with the eminent Victorians she met in her sister Sara's literary and cultural salon, located at her home, Little Holland House. The following chapter centres on this location, where, on the cusp of the rebellion in India, Julia Margaret was embraced by an expanded family circle of Anglo-Indian expatriates and a new network of prominent artists, writers, and cultural figures.

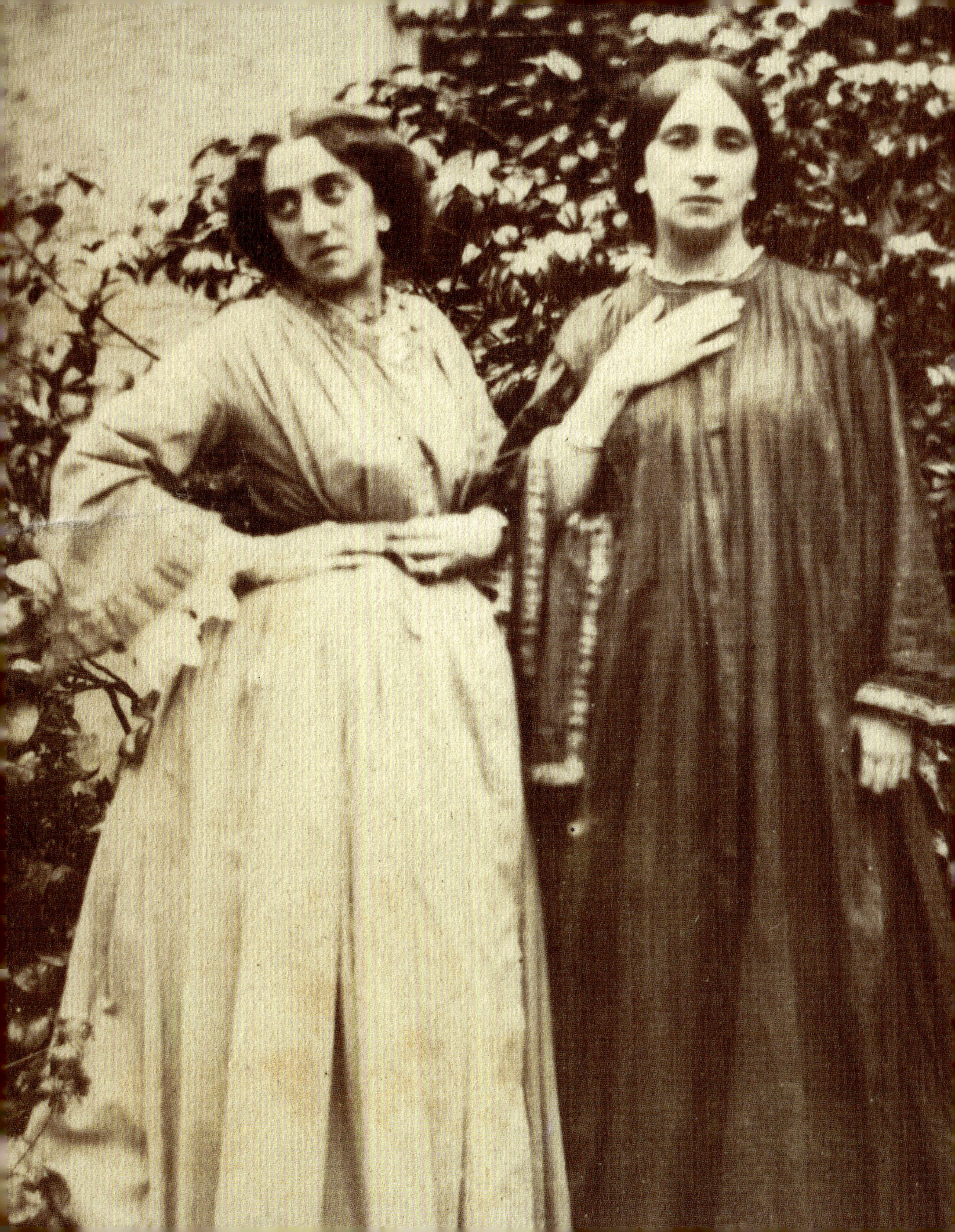

Chapter Two
Enchanted Palace

17 Earl Somers and / or Julia Margaret Cameron, *Mrs Dalrymple and Lady Somers, From Life*, *c.*1858 (detail of fig. 25).

QUITTING INDIA

Before Charles Cameron and Thoby Prinsep retired from governmental service, the two men figured conspicuously among Calcutta's Anglo-Indian elite. In 1850, the artist Colesworthey Grant produced a portfolio of portraits of this influential and exclusive set, which he titled *Lithographic Sketches of the Public Characters of Calcutta ... From 1833 to 1850*.[1] In these seemingly informal portraits, Grant depicted the British governing class in their prime. Grant's illustrations were made on commission for the *India Review* and other English language periodicals published in Calcutta, and Grant assembled these prints afterwards for publication in *Lithographic Sketches*, a volume that contained a total of 167 unique portraits. The volume contained representatives from the East India Company's established institutions of the government and military, the legal and medical societies, and the Church.

Using an informal drawing technique that resembled pen-and-ink sketches, Grant represented his subjects enveloped by the physical comforts and tranquillity of their surroundings. He represented Thoby Prinsep, for example, standing at leisure in front of an immense column (fig. 18). Posed at ease, with his thumb in his pocket and hat in his hand, Prinsep appears to have stepped onto the porch of Government House to take in the afternoon air and look upon the serene view of the Esplanade (compare fig. 9). By depicting Prinsep within a classical Palladian frame, one that had been adopted by architects throughout the British empire to convey its order, strength, and democratic principles, Grant associated Prinsep with the authority of the British empire. Consequently, as depicted in the sketch, the design of Britain's colonial architecture rested upon ideas associated with the ancient Greek and Roman tradition of civilization that informed its principles of governance.[2] By contrast, Grant portrayed Charles Cameron indoors, but he applied the same design principle that depicted an individual's character through his surroundings. Situating Cameron ensconced in an aristocratic clublike parlour or library, Grant portrayed the legal scholar reclining in a padded armchair (fig. 19). Pictured at ease with his foot resting upon an elevated pillow, Cameron's concentration is focused on the open book before him. The impression is one that

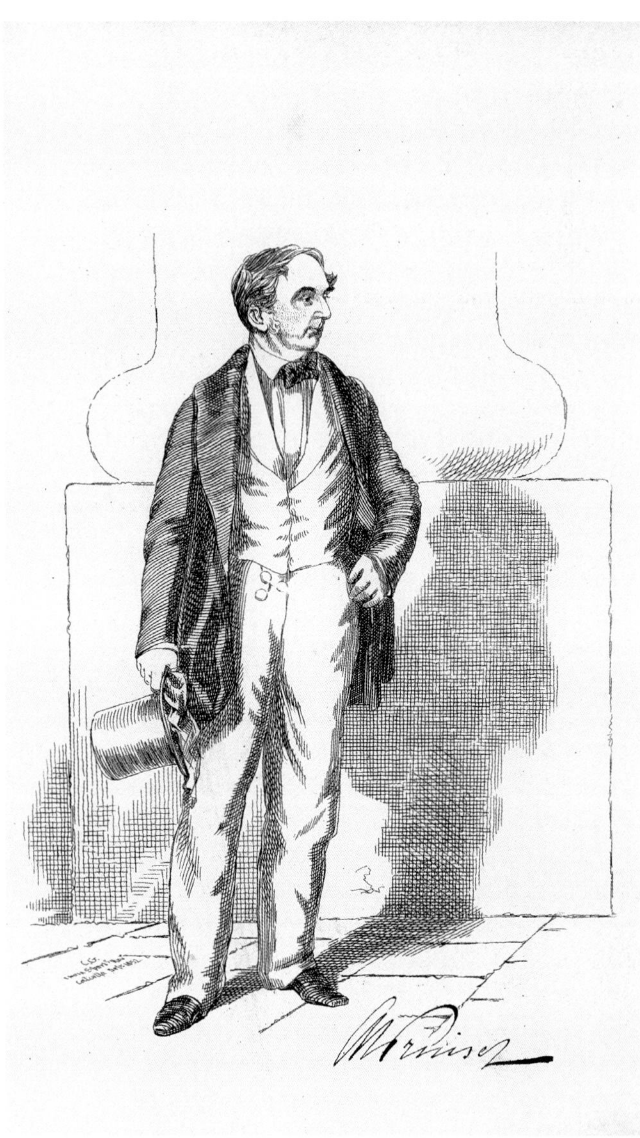

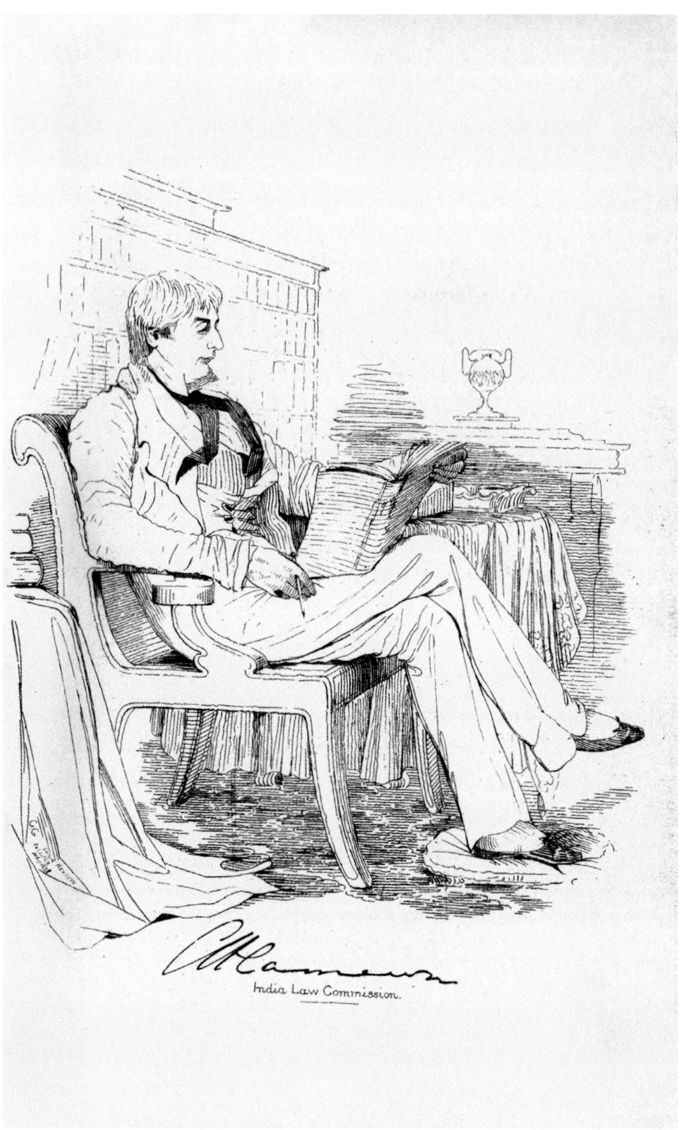

18 Coleswortheу Grant, *Henry Thoby Prinsep*, *c.*1835, lithograph, from *Lithographic Sketches of the Public Characters of Calcutta, 1833 to 1850*.
University of Minnesota Libraries.

19 Colesworthey Grant, *Charles Hay Cameron*, *c.*1835, lithograph, from *Lithographic Sketches of the Public Characters of Calcutta, 1833 to 1850*.
University of Minnesota Libraries.

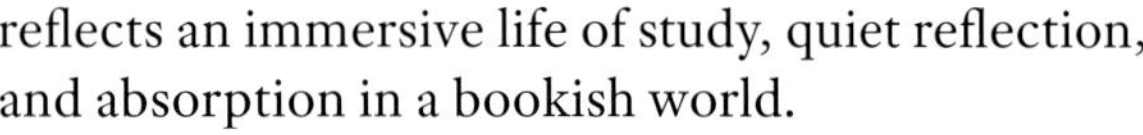

reflects an immersive life of study, quiet reflection, and absorption in a bookish world.

Grant portrayed Prinsep and Cameron as if they were 'at home' in an exported British environment that contained the same patriarchal and theatrical trappings of a London club: elite, protected, exclusively male, dominated by English language and customs.[3] As Ranajit Guha characterized it, drawing upon the memoir of an English soldier in India at the time, the clublike atmosphere that had been transported to India became a 'surrogate for home' in the eyes of the isolated men in colonial service:

> Nearly as small as a cage or caste, it is still a circle of illumination where he can recognize fellow exiles by their heads bent over English newspapers and their thoughts, like his, turned to a place far away from this outpost of empire – a place called home, 'a world,' as he put it, 'whose limits were known.'[4]

More than sharing the signs of a common language and culture, the model of the English club was also a mutually reinforcing environment from which a collective discourse emerged, in part as a consequence of its deliberate isolation from the fabric of daily life, and in part as a bulwark against what John Kaye called the 'differences in race, differences in language, differences in religion, differences of customs, all indeed that could make a great antagonism of sympathies and of interests' that divided all of India into two opposing domains, 'the rulers and the ruled as with a veil of ignorance and obscurity'.[5]

Colesworthey Grant's depiction of tranquillity and self-possession in colonial Calcutta would have been undermined were he to have depicted life out on the frontier, where deep tensions escalated between rival indigenous religious groups and tribal networks in the Punjab. These conflicts, which were accompanied by the simultaneous breakdown of British control in the region, led to additional Sikh rebellions against British rule that culminated in a series of battles between Sikh and British forces in 1848 and 1849. This hostility escalated formally into a second Anglo-Sikh War, which was prosecuted under the direction of Lord Hardinge's successor, Lord Dalhousie. After re-establishing control of the region in the aftermath of war, Dalhousie imperiously annexed the Punjab, pushing British authority all the way to the Indus River.[6] Commenting in 1856 on this earlier period of regional instability and martial activity, the Governor-General reflected on the near-constant presence of rebellious forces that lined up against British colonial rule, a condition that led him to conclude that Britain's hold on power would always be tenuous:

> Experience, frequent hard and recent experience, has taught us, that war from without, or rebellion from within, may at any time be raised against us, in quarters where they were the least to be expected, and by the most feeble and unlikely instruments. No man, therefore, can ever prudently hold forth assurance of continued peace in India.[7]

Responding to this deep sense of vulnerability, uncertainty, and foreboding, the East India Company's armies under Dalhousie tightened their internal practices of discipline as well as their external forces of coercive control, but the serenity of the Calcutta club inhabited by Prinsep and Cameron was not disturbed.

If Emily Eden relied upon a conceit according to which, as she expressed it, Britain's racial and cultural superiority all but guaranteed its dominance over India, under the new Governor-General's command, the raw elements of what the Company acknowledged as its own authoritarian means would increasingly become necessary to maintain governing control. Dalhousie characterized this use of repressive but non-lethal force as the necessary, civilizing recourse of a 'despotic government', a term that Charles Cameron later used following the insurrection in 1857 and, as I analyse in chapter 5, a persistent marker of his approach to colonial policy.[8] But in 1856, under the pretext that the historic Muslim state of Awadh was 'mismanaged', Dalhousie annexed the territory (which the British called the Province of Oude or Oudh). In Lucknow, the ancient seat of Awadh kings, and in Delhi, seat of the Mughal empire, astonishment and resentment formed a seething hostility against the British.[9] However, in London, news of the annexation was greeted with applause for the strategic military and political appropriation, as *The Times* wrote, 'Its greatest victory has been the strengthening and consolidation of the empire. ... The undisputed rule of law and justice has replaced the wild rule of the sword'.[10]

When they were young men, both Charles Cameron and Thoby Prinsep found their fortune abroad and rose to prominence governing the Indian colony. As we have seen, they helped to manage its frontier wars and superintended its territorial expansion. Years later, in 1865, one year after having first presented Sir John Herschel with an album of her photographs, Julia Margaret posed the same two men before her camera. Although she chose not to include them in her album of 1867, Cameron's portraits of her husband and brother-in-law captured the likenesses of the two grizzled men who now were no longer young. At the same time, she personified in the two men the 'old order' of liberal reformers, as these one-time colonial policymakers had now been replaced by governing officials who implemented the new policies following the 1857 insurrection. But when Charles Cameron and Thoby Prinsep retired from their official duties, they were the established *éminences grises* of the Anglo-Indian society they left behind. The two served the empire under the terms of the

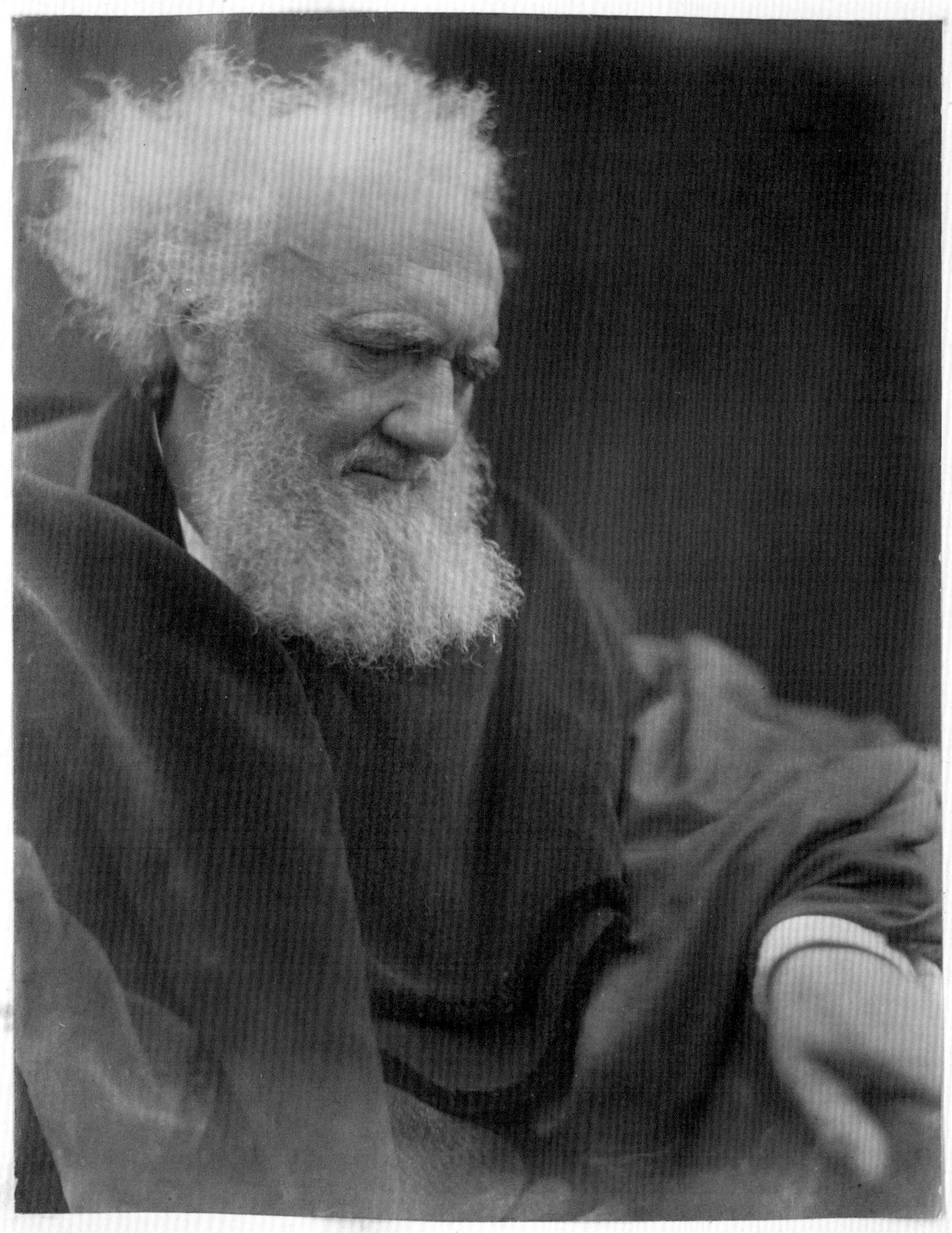

ھنری ٹھوبی پرنسپ

1833 Charter that gave the East India Company the legal right to govern the colony. The terms of this charter extended for renewable twenty-year periods, after which Parliament would evaluate the Company's performance, occasionally renegotiate specific provisions, and determine if it would extend the contract for another twenty years.[11] By 1852, after the Prinseps and the Camerons had quit India and settled in England, Parliament began the process of assessing the performance of the Company's policies before renewing its charter in 1853. For this reason, both Prinsep and Cameron were consulted during this time to offer their perspectives, drawing upon their years of experience and first-hand knowledge in the colony.

Both men published impassioned commentaries that year on the government of India to persuade Members of Parliament towards their way of thinking about events currently affecting the colony and how best to manage its future affairs. These booklets not only revealed their continued interest in steering the course of Indian affairs despite their official retirement, but also reflected their keen desire to affect the outcome of the new charter. For example, Prinsep's pamphlet *The India Question in 1853* argued that since the eighteenth century, the East India Company had successfully managed the economic interests of India and that administration of the colony should be retained under the control of administrators in India. To Prinsep, it was essential to keep the political authority, financial management, and social remapping of the colony out of the hands of Members of Parliament in London.[12] He believed that effective colonial governance could not be consigned to remote supervision and considered Parliament's desire to assume direct control a wrong turn, regarding London politicians as inflected by homegrown ambition and wholly ignorant of colonial governance.

Similarly, Charles Cameron's booklet *An Address to Parliament on the Duties of Great Britain to India, in Respect of the Education of the Natives, and their Official Employment* also affirmed his belief in the importance of relying upon British authority that was managed by knowledgeable leaders from within the colony. Cameron argued that Britain's administration of India should emulate the historical example of Alexander the Great. By uniting the ancient Greeks and Persians under his command, he wrote, Alexander provided a relevant historical example that argued, by extension, in favour of continuing the liberal reforms begun decades earlier by the East India Company to establish English as India's official language. By using Alexander's empire as a historical precedent, Cameron argued that Parliament should approve the Company's plan to employ Indians who were fluent in English as in-country partners to help administer the colonial government. To Charles Cameron, these actions would provide tangible examples of the 'generous philanthropic spirit, the imperial equity' that the East India Company wanted to create in India. As he phrased it, almost echoing Herschel's words of 1846, by learning from the historical example of Alexander and by enacting similar measures to assimilate the empire's subjugated peoples, Britain would extend a positive 'imperial feeling' across the colony.[13] In Cameron's idealized world, an imperial integration of this kind would engender a positive and sentimental emotional response in the indigenous population towards their benevolent rulers, warm feelings that would be comparable to those he imagined were once expressed by the formerly independent countries conquered by Alexander.

In her portraits of Charles Cameron and Thoby Prinsep, Julia Margaret embedded visual and literary signposts that assimilated the personal commitments of each man, using the symbols of visual art to represent their governing principles.[14] Cameron's photograph of Prinsep, which bears his striking signature below the image, provides an example of such an external marker. Signed portraits were not unique to Cameron, of course, but were thought by many to 'add value' to photographs by revealing individual character traits that could not be depicted visually.[15] When she presented her portrait to Prinsep to be autographed, he signed his name in Urdu alongside his name in English (Cox/Ford 737; fig. 20).[16] We might be inclined to take this inscription as a romantic expression of his sentimental attachment to the colony or even an index of his respect for

20 Julia Margaret Cameron, *Henry Thoby Prinsep*, *c.*1865, albumen print, Anne Thackeray Album, image 25.4 × 19.5 cm, on sheet 35.3 × 26.2 cm.
Harry Ransom Humanities Research Center, University of Texas, Austin. 964:0312:0007.

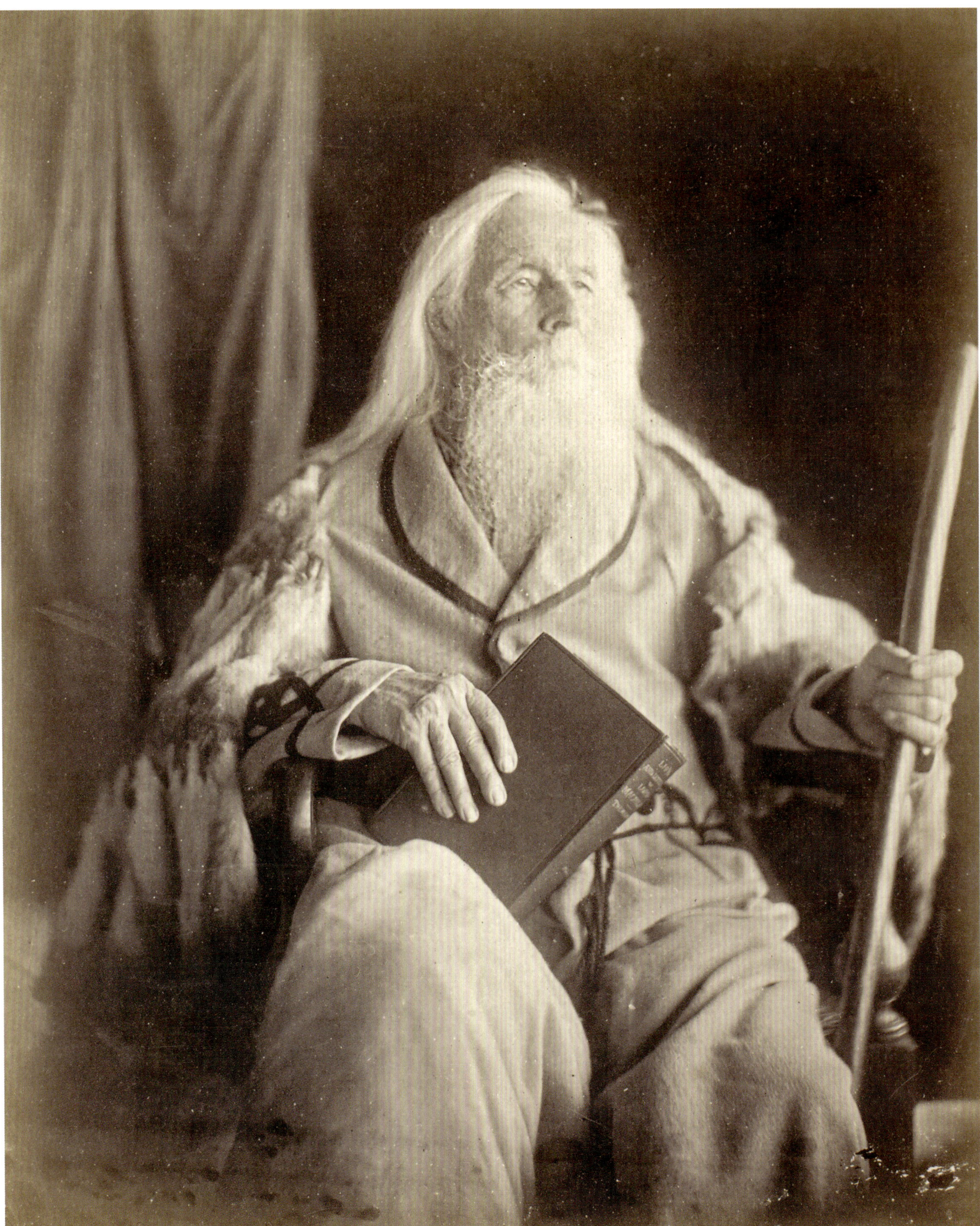

Indian culture, but Prinsep penned his signature in Urdu to mark his fluency in the language. This knowledge identified him as an Orientalist, which is to say, an advocate for practising indigenous languages as an instrument of colonial control.[17] As an East India Company official, knowledge of Urdu was a strategic diplomatic asset for Prinsep and of economic importance to the colony; the language, closely related to Hindi and Persian, was used traditionally in commercial transactions, and importantly was the most widely spoken dialect in West Bengal, a key asset to Prinsep in his role as governmental agent.[18] After his retirement to England, Prinsep's continued use of Urdu marked his ongoing relevance to the Company as an economic and political adviser.

Julia Margaret implanted similar markers in portraits of her husband. In one image, for example, she posed Charles to face a bust of Milton and adorn the sculpture with an oversized laurel crown (Cox/Ford 594).[19] She borrowed the composition from Rembrandt, who posed a man, now thought to be Aristotle, with his hand resting on a bust of Homer, a representation that meditates on the passage of time and on the enduring nature of great art.[20] As in the Rembrandt, Cameron's gesture collapses time between the present and the ancient past, a recognition of Milton's elevated status in the British literary pantheon.[21] But in Cameron's portrait of her husband, Milton's bust also functions as an iconographic signpost that expresses Charles Cameron's investment in establishing Milton as 'required reading' in the Indian educational system. The photograph commemorates the ultimate victory of Macaulay's and Cameron's English policies in India. Yet the teaching of Milton's works in India proved to be deeply controversial, as 'Milton' was taken for a hidden proselytizer because his 'scriptural allusions regularly sent students scurrying to the Bible for their elucidation'.[22] The Company's English language curriculum was therefore politicized as a result and was opposed by Hindus and Muslims alike in their resistance to Christianity, as they were suspicious of the indirect ways that religious ideas could be spread covertly when disguised under the cloak of philology or linguistics.

21 Julia Margaret Cameron, *Charles Hay Cameron*, [1876], albumen print, 28.6 × 22.7 cm.
Art Institute of Chicago, Mary and Leigh Block Endowment Fund, 1998.286, Creative Commons Zero, Public Domain.

Several years later, after the publication of George Otto Trevelyan's book *The Life and Letters of Lord Macaulay* (1876), Julia Margaret photographed her husband Charles once more, posing him seated in quiet contemplation (Cox/Ford 595; fig. 21). Cameron holds on his lap a large book, on the spine of which Trevelyan's title is clearly legible. Macaulay was not only Charles Cameron's employer on the Supreme Council, but he also was instrumental in remaking Indian society as close friend. Macaulay confided in his sisters back home,

> There is a little circle of people whose friendship I value, and in whose conversation I take pleasure: the Chief Justice, Sir Edward Ryan; my old friend, Malkin; Cameron and Macleod, the Law Commissioners ... These, in my opinion, are the flower of Calcutta society, and I often ask some of them to a quiet dinner.[23]

Trevelyan observed that 'on the Friday of every week' these men met 'round Macaulay's breakfast table to discuss the progress which the Law Commission had made in its labours'.[24] Having succeeded in making English the chief language of instruction in the Indian educational system, Macaulay and Cameron then extended British legal principles to the writing of India's penal code.[25]

Compared to the lithographed portraits made three decades earlier by Colesworthey Grant, Julia Margaret's photographs of Cameron and Prinsep depict an insular and cossetted ruling class that had now departed the stage, men whose liberal ideas and administrative decisions were increasingly questioned and even reversed by newer administrators in Calcutta and by the political opposition in Parliament. By coding her portraits of the two men with unmistakable references to the key debates over language and religion and their relation to the ongoing policy debates in the colony, Julia Margaret's photographs embodied the ongoing struggle fought over the policies and practices that would govern India into the future.

ANGLO-INDIANS IN LONDON

These visual and inscribed signposts were also part of a shared discourse that was commonly understood by the Anglo-Indian community of which Julia Margaret Cameron was a part. As we shall see, Cameron cemented these relationships through the presentation of photographic albums. If, as Edward Said insisted, 'the nineteenth-century European novel is a cultural form consolidating but also refining and articulating the authority of the *status quo*', the advent of photographic representation that Cameron practised during this period in the creation and presentation of albums fitted seamlessly into that same structure. These ideas were manifested by the subjects chosen for representation, in relation to the type or genre of forms that were recognized and valued, and in relation to the communities for whom those representations were created.[26] The 'consolidation of authority' for both literary and visual art therefore was knitted into the social fabric, a structure that was bonded ever tighter when families consolidated their wealth through marriage or contractual alliances. As Said wrote,

> [The] consolidation of authority is not simply connected to the functioning of social power and governance, but made to appear both normative and sovereign, that is, self-validating in the course of the narrative. This is paradoxical only if one forgets that the constitution of a narrative subject, however abnormal or unusual, is still a social act *par excellence*, and as such has behind or inside it the authority of history and society.[27]

For Said, creative authors and artists, scientists, narrators of historical and literary works, and their audiences operated together as part of an integrated system, one that was grounded historically and relied upon social norms and historical conventions to locate those narratives in time and space, employing a shared discourse that established their political understanding. At the same time, those conventions provided a valuable discursive context to explain the allegorical references that authors or artists might also embed in their representations.

Cameron's worldview was created in part by marriage, reinforced through her extended family, and enlarged by the social company of her friendship circle centred around Little Holland House, the cultural salon started by her sister Sara Prinsep to which she gravitated after moving to England. It was in Little Holland House that Cameron laced together her intertwined commitments to family, nation, and empire. And it was also the influence of two aristocrats, Sir Henry Holland and Lord Lansdowne (Henry Petty-Fitzmaurice, the 3rd Marquess), who provided a model for this activity, as these men helped unite the cultural figures that intersected their salons and helped establish this discursive authority.[28] Holland and Lansdowne were cousins, and their personal relationship went back decades. Their interwoven cultural influence was extended at dinner parties at both Holland and Lansdowne Houses in London, where Thackeray was also present, as well as prominent governmental figures like Thomas Babington Macaulay, clerics like Henry Hart Milman the Dean of St Paul's, and museum figures like Charles Eastlake.[29] The remainder of this chapter considers the depth of those connections and Cameron's attachment to this group as the essential foundation for a canon of thinking and shared discourse about British imperialism, and India in particular, that helped shape Julia Margaret's worldview.

Importantly, these relationships crossed over from the personal into the political. In practical terms, they collaborated to influence an imperial role for art. As an example, in 1841, Parliament formed a Fine Arts Commission to decorate the new Palace of Westminster. As a top priority, Sir Robert Peel, the Prime Minister, chose well-positioned and influential members to serve on the committee. These included Eastlake, Lansdowne, Macaulay, and Charles Canning, who would later govern India. Among this select group, Macaulay represented India's past, while Lansdowne, a future minister in the 1850 government, and Canning, the future Governor-General who Queen Victoria appointed the first Viceroy of India, represented the colony's future. Commissions comprised of such men were tangible examples of Carlyle's maxim that the ruling society should use the present to possess the past: in *On Heroes*, he wrote, such knowledge

> brings us into closer and clearer relation with the past – with our own possessions in the past. For the whole past, as I keep repeating, is the possession of the present; the past had always something *true* and is a precious possession. [Original emphasis][30]

These ideas informed the painter George Frederic Watts, who entered the 1843 competition and used his prize money to live in Florence with Lord and Lady Holland for the next three years. In 1846, he won top prize in the Commission's third competition and produced a historical panel called *Alfred Inciting the Saxons to Prevent the Landing of the Danes*.[31] Watts's painting was assigned to adorn the Royal Gallery along with other 'subjects related to "the military history and glory of the country"'.[32]

Lansdowne and Macaulay had been friends since their Cambridge days, both Whigs by party affiliation and imperialists by political ambition. Macaulay accorded Lansdowne credit for guiding his ascension into Parliament, and in 1833, the two corresponded about Macaulay's appointment to India to lead the Supreme Council.[33] When Herschel returned from the Cape Colony in 1838, Lansdowne was called upon to represent the British government as well as the Chancellor of Cambridge University at an elaborate dinner held to honour the returning scientist. In his speech to a gathering of more than 400 noblemen, Lansdowne expertly intertwined the exalted cause of scientific exploration to the unbounded project of empire. He started off by observing that the twenty-year peace established since Waterloo had done much to encourage the advancement of science, and that science had likewise kept pace with the expansion of Britain's empire:

> I can recollect when it was a matter of congratulation, that, by establishing [on the southern extremity of Africa] the dominion and authority of Great Britain, we had obtained a stepping-stone and a key to those vast possessions, which it had been the fortune of British arms to acquire, and which since, let me add, it has been the policy of British councillors to improve, south of the line, and in the southern hemisphere. It is no less a matter of congratulation, that having made this acquisition for military and political purposes, we are now called upon to contemplate it in a no less interesting point of view, for the excellent person who sits on the right hand of his Royal Highness has made it, as it were, the outpost of science, for communicating and receiving knowledge.[34]

From Lansdowne's perspective, Herschel had advanced scientific knowledge commensurate to what Britain's military had accomplished in expanding its physical control over foreign territory. Consistent with Said's observation that imperial rhetoric must align with and consolidate a rhetoric of power and governance, Lansdowne constructed a coherent narrative that justified Britain's military expeditions in relation to the spread of science and technology throughout the world:

> Let us recollect, that we are to contemplate that situation not as guarding and commanding extensive territories, but as having opened a new hemisphere to the eye of the scientific observer; as having made accessible to the highest pursuits and aspirations of philosophy, that hemisphere, the riches of which our talented and excellent guest has described to us, and which he has been the means of annexing to the empire of knowledge, making it available for its own purposes, and as it were, conquering itself, for the benefit, not of this country alone, but of all countries and of all after-times.[35]

The same rationale expressed here informed Parliament's ongoing financial support for the Great Trigonometric Survey in Madras. Herschel himself later echoed Lansdowne's very words in his correspondence with Julia Margaret and Charles Cameron. One cannot fail to notice in this short excerpt how Lansdowne deployed an imperial rhetoric of geographic annexation; how words like 'new hemisphere', 'empire of knowledge', and 'conquering', describe his understanding of Britain's imperial purpose and outsized place in dominating world history; how Britain's expansion across the globe made the dissemination and influence of Western thought and ideas possible; in short, how science facilitated the empire's growth and authority.

In London, both Lansdowne House and Holland House, two grand city estates, also offered sometimes-competing cultural attractions, both of which stood independent of the third, Little Holland House, which attracted the poets and writers, government officials, and visual artists that nourished Julia Margaret's ambitions. By the 1850s, a reading by Thackeray at Holland House, for example, could be followed in coming weeks by a performance of Italian singers at Lansdowne House that included Thackeray in attendance. In June 1851, both Lansdowne and Macaulay found themselves at one of Thackeray's lectures.[36] Separately, each attended, and commented on, the

Great Exhibition that opened that year. As both Holland and Lansdowne commissioned Watts to paint interiors for Holland's residence as well as Lansdowne's Bowood House in Wiltshire, their associations with the painter also connected the two aristocrats. The activities of the three London salons apparently overlapped as well. Prominent participants in Sara Prinsep's salon included Pre-Raphaelite painters like William Holman Hunt and John Everett Millais; sculptors like Thomas Woolner and Baron Carlo Marochetti; art critics like John Ruskin, William Michael Rossetti, and Francis Turner Palgrave; members of the royal court, like the Duke of Argyll, who served as Lord Privy Seal, and Henry Taylor, an administrator in the Colonial Office; prominent administrators in the museum world, like Henry Cole, who directed the South Kensington Museum, and Austen Henry Layard, the archaeologist and art dealer, Under-Secretary for Foreign Affairs, and supporter of the nascent National Gallery; as well as popular authors like Thackeray and Alfred Tennyson, the nation's poet laureate. Herschel would have found that Cameron included portraits of many of these denizens of Little Holland House in his 1867 album, including six of Tennyson (HA-6, -72, -73, -74, -76, -84) as well as Tennyson's son Lionel (HA-26), and his friends James Spedding (HA-10) and William Brookfield (HA-17); three of Henry Taylor (HA-7, -21, -71); three of George Frederic Watts (HA-8, -9, -21); and two of Holman Hunt (HA-11 and -23). Later in 1867, Cameron would exhibit these and other portraits of Rossetti, Palgrave, and Layard in her one-woman exhibition in the German Gallery.[37]

Historians have represented these social gatherings at Little Holland House as principally artistic in nature, but during this time Sara Prinsep's salon was also known as a centre for collective political discourse on Anglo-Indian affairs. Experience in India formed much of the intellectual work and cultural activities of the artists and writers, governmental administrators and historians, Anglo-Indian expatriates, and local politicians who gathered there. According to Holman Hunt's memoir of those years, Little Holland House became a focal point for all things Indian and provided a common forum for dialogue, one that enabled participants to articulate a coherent discussion of influential thought and writing about contemporary affairs, especially in relation to colonial India. According to the artist,

> Kensington often then rejoiced in a throng on their way to Little Holland House, who were happy in the certainty of there meeting the most interesting leaders of English society. The days of the old [East] India Company were not yet numbered, and naturally the house represented all matters of East Indian concern to an unlimited degree. The national interests in India alone would have impelled senators of all grades to throng a home where the last questions of Indian affairs were discussed, but Watts's numerous friends added to the charm of the company. Aristocrats there were of ministerial dignity, and generals fresh from flood and field, appearing in unpretending habit, talking with the modesty of real genius, and adding an interest to life such as nothing else could give.[38]

Around this time, Tennyson's wife Emily called Little Holland House 'the Enchanted Palace' and referred explicitly to the imperious Sara Prinsep as 'the *Principessa*'.[39] Perhaps these remarks were made in good-natured fun, although it is difficult to know precisely where the couple came down on the thin line separating gentle mockery from genuine admiration.

In 1850, the Tennysons were newly acquainted with the Camerons. They had already met in the company of Alfred's friends from his student days at Cambridge, Henry Taylor and William Brookfield, and although Thackeray and Tennyson crossed paths at Cambridge, the two were not on friendly terms until the 1830s.[40] Julia Margaret had known Thackeray for nearly as long, since they had both been young adults in Paris, where her grandmother, Thérèse de l'Étang, had supervised the young Miss Pattle's social relations.[41] After the two Anglo-Indian friends had settled in England, Thackeray maintained close family connections to India, in part through letters exchanged with his half-sister, Sarah, whose mother was Indian. Thackeray belonged to one of those colonial families who 'grew up in the compact world that Anglo-Indians made for themselves at home', wrote Thackeray's biographer, Gordon N. Ray, 'a world in which the Indian [civil] service was regarded as a "sacred college of sons and nephews" and there existed "small sympathy for talent without relations".'[42] The Pattle family, too, likely had 'Indian blood in [their] veins', according to a contemporary family relation of Julia Margaret: William Dalrymple observed how his

> beautiful, dark-eyed Calcutta-born great-great-grandmother Sophia Pattle … was descended from a Hindu Bengali woman from Chandernagore who converted to Catholicism and married a French officer in Pondicherry in the 1780s.[43]

Like Harriet Tytler, who was also born in India, the surviving Pattle sisters (Sara, Julia Margaret, Maria, Virginia, and Sophia) exemplified 'that Anglo-Indian woman who does not travel eastward into the estrangement of colonization but who is born into it', in the memorable phrase of Sara Suleri.[44]

In Thackeray's landmark novel *Vanity Fair* (1848), the author lampooned the narrow horizons of the Anglo-Indian community once they had quit Calcutta and reassembled in London, writing that the families sheltered in a 'comfortable Anglo-Indian district' and kept largely to themselves. When he represented 'the respectable abodes of the retired Indian aristocracy' in his novel, Thackeray satirized the grandiosity of the military and civilian heroes of the East India Company whose illustrious names populated this imagined neighbourhood by downgrading their historical pre-eminence to mere place names on a map, like 'Minto Square', 'Great Clive Street', and 'Hastings Street'.[45] For the author, *vanitas* was revealed by the transparent insularity of such a community, especially when it over-estimated its own importance and place in history, and depicted its small cares as conspicuous and grand.

Thackeray also satirized those agents of the East India Company who departed the colony after serving on behalf of the empire only to write the so-called 'great narratives' of their self-proclaimed achievements. In *Vanity Fair*, for example, Thackeray's anti-hero, Major William Dobbin, slides gracelessly into semi-retirement at the end of the novel to write his great *History of the Punjaub*. Here Thackeray offered a gentle caricature of men like Thoby Prinsep, who, in 1834, actually published a historical volume titled *Origin of the Sikh Power in the Punjab*, an account that Prinsep compiled from previous reports of governmental agents, including those of his own father.[46] Thackeray's sly turn in the novel recognized that men like Prinsep spun the violence of Britain's colonial expansion into a tame narrative that made imperial history palatable for easy consumption and mass production. As Prinsep wrote, Britain's influence on the Punjab was salutary because its policies were just:

> The British Government has since 1808 been the protector of the Sikh territory lying between the Sutlej and Jumna: Its officers have been appealed to for the adjustment of all disputes between the chiefs and their neighbours or dependants, and the references to the Supreme Council of Government at the Presidency are frequent, and involve questions of great intricacy.[47]

But Prinsep's narrative of peaceful and benevolent government also washed clean the reality that the indigenous population fiercely resisted British rule. George Broadfoot's account of this same period, by contrast, mentioned that longstanding resentments had seeded numerous 'small mutinies' in the Sikh forces after 1840, directly contradicting Prinsep's self-aggrandizing claims.[48] As a result, Prinsep's historical volume advanced an essentially false but crucial expiatory function in writing the colonial narrative, as Priya Satia asserts: by reasserting that Britain kept the peace in a dangerous world full of chaos and disorder, narratives like Prinsep's reinforced the British public's esteem in its overseas empire.[49]

Personal lives intersected with public personae at Little Holland House, reinforcing these intersecting relationships. Among the artists of the Pre-Raphaelite group, for example, an amicable rivalry emerged pitting Woolner against Baron Marochetti, but it is often hard to tell if the opposition to Marochetti was based upon aesthetic, nationalistic, or generational grounds. Marochetti was courtly and distant, while Woolner was avuncular, on good terms with Palgrave, the Tennysons, and many of the Pre-Raphaelite painters, and some twenty years younger than Marochetti.[50] While Woolner struggled to make his mark, Marochetti had already achieved international renown for his celebrated 1837 sculpture above the High Altar of the Madeleine in Paris, *The Assumption of Mary Magdalene*. And much like the painter Watts, Baron Marochetti was in constant demand. A rendering of his studio around 1860 shows numerous framed prints, portrait busts of contemporaries, plaster casts of

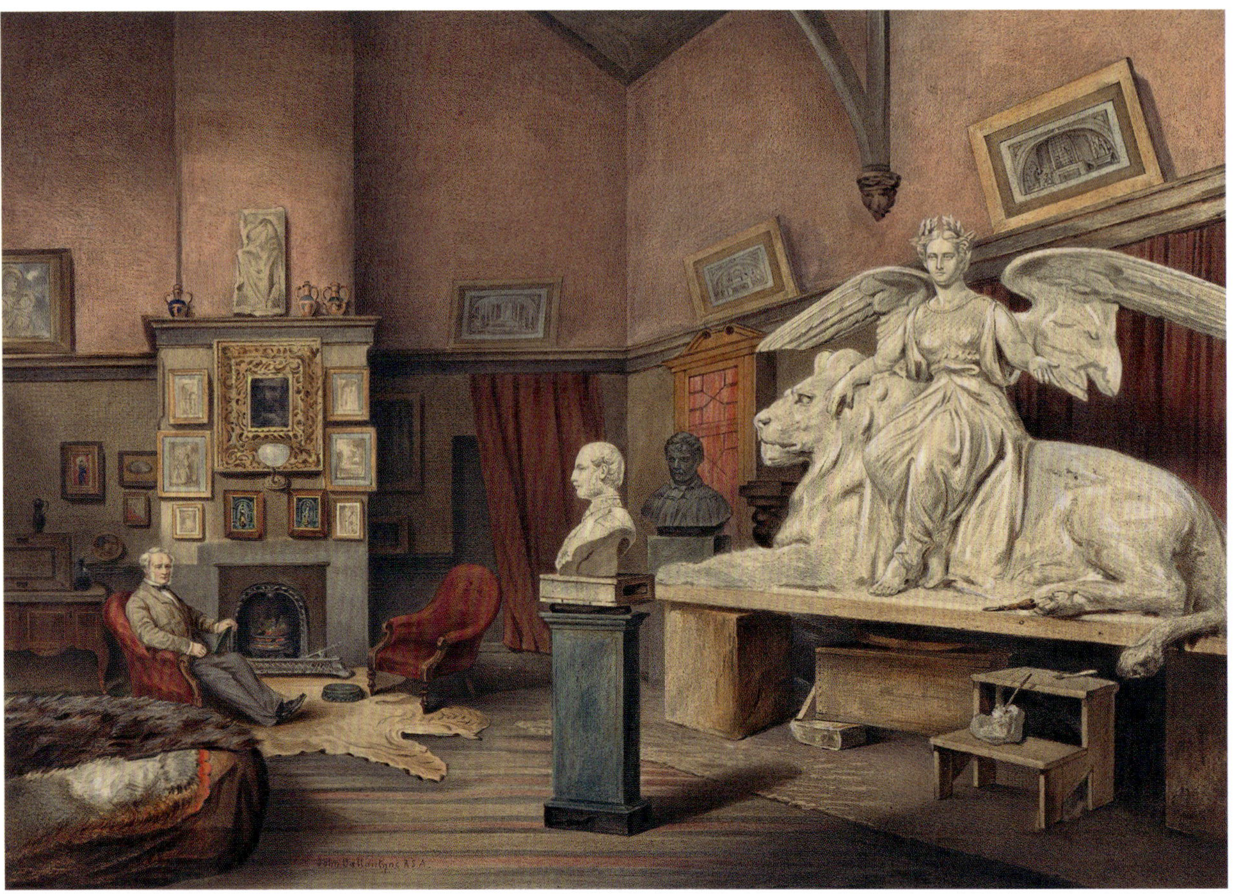

22 Vincent Brooks, *Carlo Marochetti in His Studio*, *c.*1860, chromolithograph after painting by John Ballantyne, 53 × 72.9 cm.

ancient Greek sculpture, and colossal monuments of winged angels and other allegorical figures, depicted in the midst of their design, fabrication, and assembly (fig. 22).[51]

Connections formed at these gatherings often extended beyond one generation and involved intermarriages among families, cementing bonds of affection with political practicality. Sir Frederick Pollock, for example, a Tory politician and Fellow of the Royal Society, succeeded Charles Eastlake in 1855 as president of the Photographic Society of London. But it was Pollock's eldest son, the 2nd Bt, who was on intimate terms with members of Cameron's circle. Rather than distinguishing himself in legal and governmental affairs like his father, the younger Pollock achieved recognition for his published translation of Dante's *La Divina Commedia*, which included engravings by Dalziel after illustrations by George Scharf. Pollock's wife, Juliet, was known among this circle for her enthusiasm for home theatricals, a favourite avocation of Julia Margaret, who sponsored numerous performances in Freshwater after moving there in the 1860s.[52] And Pollock and Lord Lansdowne jointly led a committee at Trinity College to underwrite the creation of a bust of Thomas Babington Macaulay after Lansdowne's friend died in 1859.[53] While at Cambridge in 1834, the younger Pollock was elected to the Apostles' club, where he befriended Tennyson and Brookfield. His acceptance as an Apostle had been facilitated by Stephen Spring Rice, the brother of Theodosia Spring Rice, who in 1839 married Henry Taylor.[54] Consequently, throughout the 1850s and 1860s, these prominent men and women formed a warm and tightly knit group. The Pollocks dined frequently with the Taylors and the Brookfields and were welcomed as intimates by the Holland Park circle, which included the Prinseps, the Camerons, Thackeray, Lord and Lady Goderich, James Spedding, Edward Ryan, and occasionally the Spring Rices as well.[55] Through such connections public careers were often made. It was Lord Lansdowne who helped to appoint Brookfield to his position as inspector of schools, for example, and it was Baron Holland who facilitated Taylor's placement as an administrator in the Colonial Office.

ALBUMS OF AFFILIATION

Julia Margaret Cameron helped consolidate and affirm these mutual connections whenever she could, seeking out Brookfield's congregations when he preached, attending art exhibitions with Mrs Brookfield and Thackeray when notable events occurred.[56] Around this time, in fact, she began to create albums of photographs, assembling them for her sisters and close friends, all of whom circled through Little Holland House. Portraits of Cameron's sisters, Virginia Somers and Sophia Dalrymple, and her young niece, Julia Jackson, also circled through these albums just as they did through the salons themselves, their presence recorded in photographs by Earl Somers, and in paintings and drawings by Watts, Hunt, and Edward Burne-Jones, another member of the Pre-Raphaelite Brotherhood who, in 1858, actually took up residence in the house.[57] That year, Lord Lansdowne bought one of Burne-Jones's drawings that represented Sophia and several other young women in an idealized enclosed garden that the artist called *The Kings' Daughters*.[58] If Burne-Jones was enthralled by Sophia, both Henry Taylor and Thackeray wrote gushing odes to Virginia's beauty in which they famously embarrassed themselves: Taylor in private, at a notable dinner party; Thackeray in public, in the pages of *Punch*.[59] During this period, when Cole, Thackeray, and Marochetti attended events at Little Holland House, their families also developed close personal ties to each other, as all three families lived in close proximity to each other on Onslow Square in Kensington. Marochetti's studio was located just behind his house, while Cole's museum was only a short walk away.[60] Thackeray recorded his first sitting with Marochetti on 1 March 1861 for the writer's own portrait bust, a sculpture that would ultimately end up in Westminster after Thackeray's untimely death in 1863. 'The worlds of *Punch* and Little Holland House might seem an unlikely combination', wrote Carolyn Dakers, but their participants and their mutual influence overlapped with Arthur Lewis's neighbouring salons in Moray Lodge in nearby Campden Hill. Prinsep and Watts hosted evenings that brought together musicians like Lewis together with authors like Thackeray, Dickens, Trollope, and the playwright Tom Taylor. As Dakers wrote, their social gatherings facilitated '"jovial meetings" of the "merry clan"' that encouraged 'male "bonding"' in which many of the participating artists competed to provide illustrations in *Punch*.[61]

When Lansdowne wrote to Virginia Somers in 1855 to invite her to attend a concert at Lansdowne House, he also noted that he had unexpectedly come across a small, sculpted bust of the young Julia Jackson when visiting Marochetti's studio. This chance occurrence might have instigated Julia Margaret's thoughts about creating an album for Lansdowne. Julia Margaret's niece was a striking beauty, even as an adolescent, and owing to her distinctive features and from having undoubtedly made her acquaintance at Little Holland House, Lansdowne immediately recognized Jackson's profile.[62] At the time, Marochetti was working on a tomb sculpture commissioned by Queen Victoria to represent an effigy of her historical relation, Princess Elizabeth, who had died in 1650 at the age of fourteen. Because the young Julia Jackson apparently resembled the princess's likeness, Marochetti had posed her as a model for this work.[63] Because of its exceptional royal patronage, the commission was likely well known among the Pattle sisters. Intriguingly, Marochetti produced his sculpture in the tradition of the shoulder-length portrait busts produced during the Italian Renaissance by artists like Desiderio da Settignano, Andrea del Verrochio, Francesco Laurana, and Andrea della Robbia. As a classically trained sculptor, these important predecessors would have been well known to Marochetti, but they were also valued highly by Henry Cole, who later collected plaster casts of children produced by these same artists for the South Kensington Museum. The Jackson family acquired Marochetti's sculpture of the young Julia and passed it down in the family. Eventually, the bust came into the possession of Vanessa Bell, Jackson's daughter by Leslie Stephen. Years later, Bell posed her own daughter, Angelica, next to Marochetti's sculpture to show off the undeniable family resemblance (fig. 23).

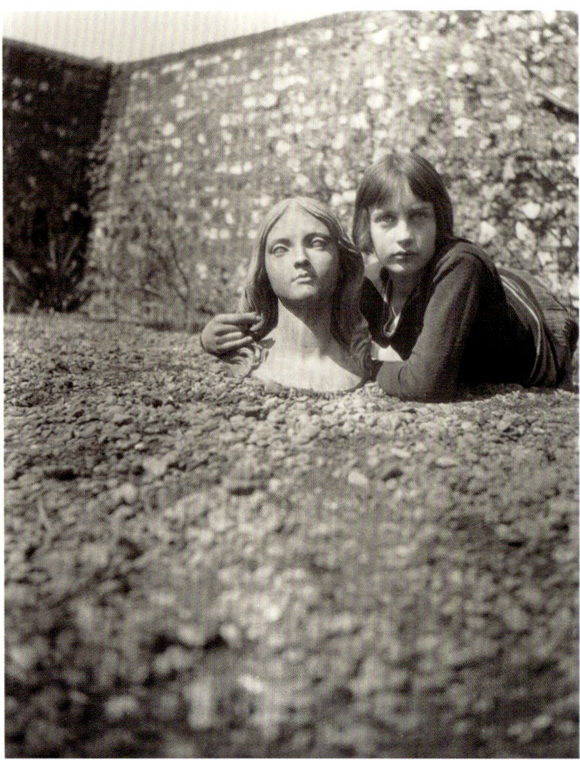

23 Vanessa Bell, *Photograph of Angelica with a Bust of Julia Jackson by Marochetti at Charleston House,* Spring 1930, 11.5 × 85 cm.

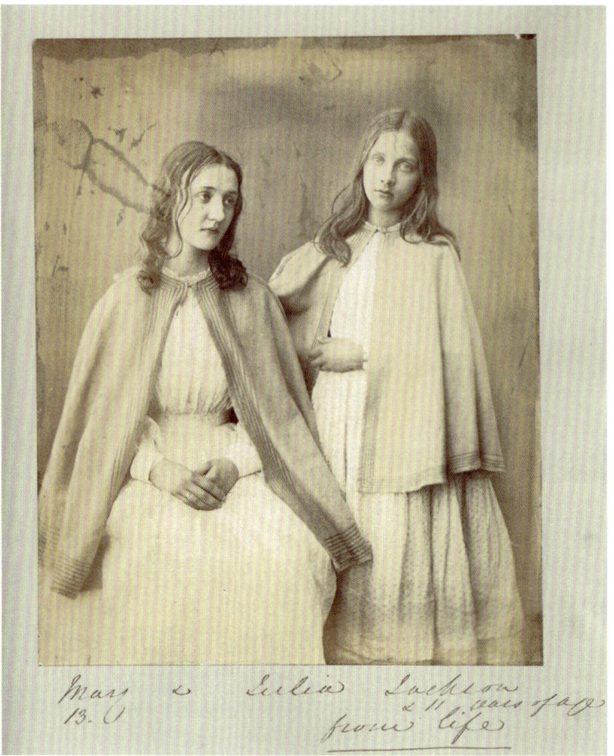

24 Attributed to Earl Somers, *May and Julia Jackson,* *c.*1857–58, albumen print, 19.5 × 15.5 cm. Lansdowne Album, plate 15.

Collection of Charles, Marquis of Lansdowne.

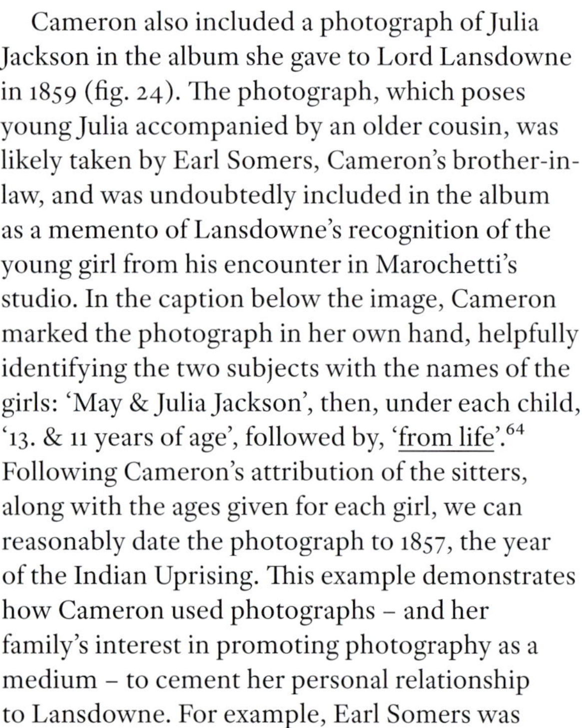

Cameron also included a photograph of Julia Jackson in the album she gave to Lord Lansdowne in 1859 (fig. 24). The photograph, which poses young Julia accompanied by an older cousin, was likely taken by Earl Somers, Cameron's brother-in-law, and was undoubtedly included in the album as a memento of Lansdowne's recognition of the young girl from his encounter in Marochetti's studio. In the caption below the image, Cameron marked the photograph in her own hand, helpfully identifying the two subjects with the names of the girls: 'May & Julia Jackson', then, under each child, '13. & 11 years of age', followed by, 'from life'.[64] Following Cameron's attribution of the sitters, along with the ages given for each girl, we can reasonably date the photograph to 1857, the year of the Indian Uprising. This example demonstrates how Cameron used photographs – and her family's interest in promoting photography as a medium – to cement her personal relationship to Lansdowne. For example, Earl Somers was also Lansdowne's nephew, and the two men occasionally met together with photography's great inventor William Henry Fox Talbot. Lansdowne was also related to Talbot through his wife, Lady Louisa Fox-Strangways, as Lady Louisa was the sister of Talbot's mother, making Talbot another nephew to Lansdowne.[65] Interest in photography and its changing technology, applications, and use also preoccupied their shared activities. In a letter of 1855 to Lansdowne, for example, Talbot referred to a portfolio of Somers's photography as 'distinguished'.[66] And Earl Somers, accompanied by his wife (and Julia Margaret's sister) Virginia, evidently travelled in the same circle as Lansdowne and his son, Lord Shelburne (the 4th Marquess), as this assembled group visited Lacock Abbey, Talbot's home, also in 1855.[67] As a maker of photographic albums, then, Julia Margaret inserted Somers's photographs, especially those depicting life in and around Little Holland House, throughout the many volumes she created during these years. In considering the numerous influences that coalesced to generate the Herschel Album, the photographic album Cameron created for Lord Lansdowne serves as a credible prototype.

Social life at the 'enchanted palace' figures prominently throughout Lansdowne's photographic album, which is now conserved at Bowood, the Fitzmaurice ancestral home. In addition to the photograph depicting younger cousins of the Pattle clan, the album contains two photographs representing the older generation as well. One, an albumen print, also marked 'from life', depicts *Mrs. Dalrymple and Lady Somers*, portraying the two women on a tiled floor with outdoor foliage behind them (fig. 25). Another

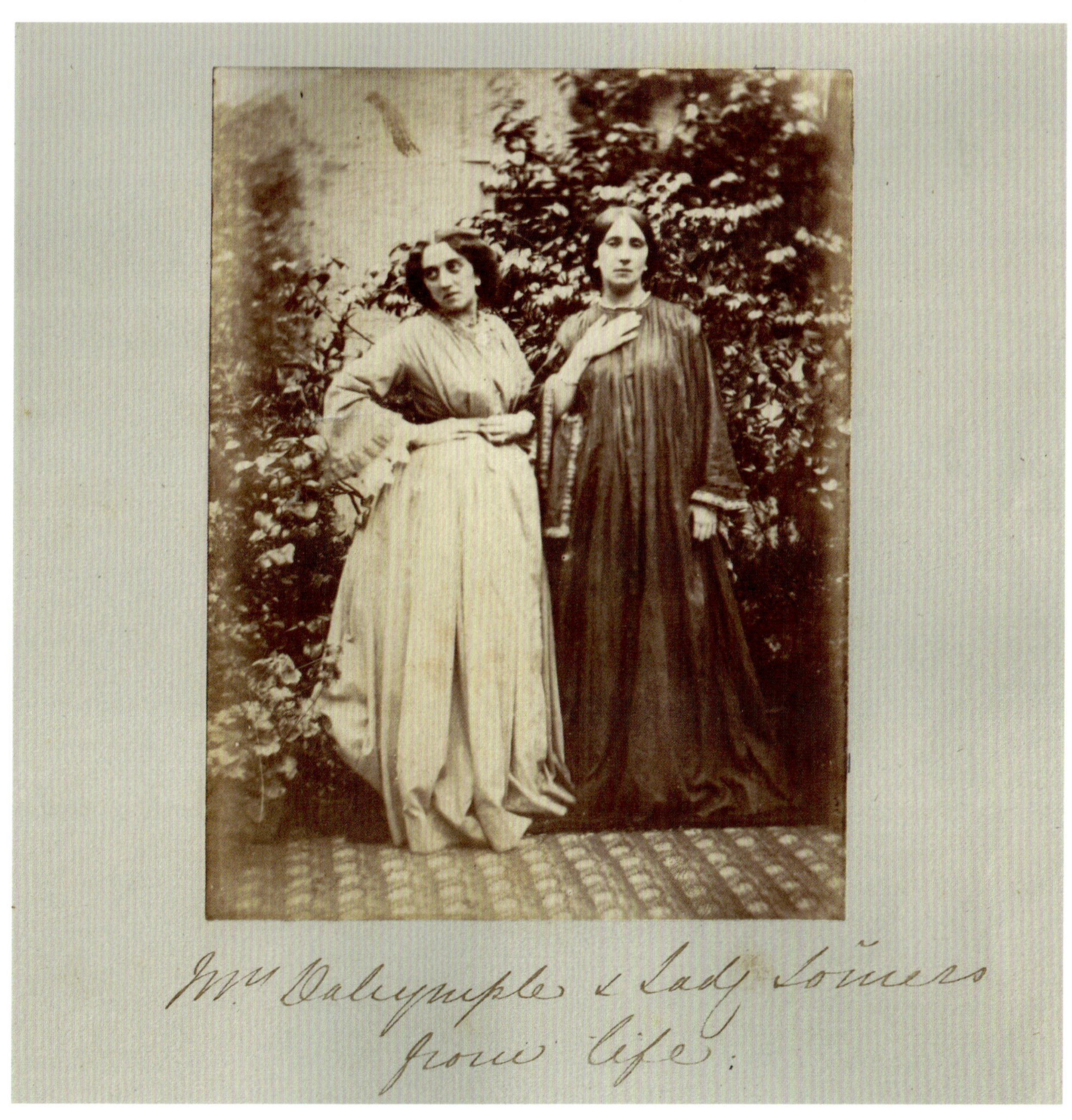

25 Earl Somers and / or Julia Margaret Cameron, *Mrs Dalrymple and Lady Somers, From Life* (portraying Sophia Dalrymple and Virginia Somers), *c.*1858, albumen print, 13.9 × 10 cm, Lansdowne Album, plate 13. Collection of Charles, Marquis of Lansdowne.

photograph reproduces a painting by Watts from 1856 that he titled *The Sisters*, which represents Sophia Dalrymple and Sara Prinsep in brightly coloured and flowing robes, posed on an outdoor porch with an ornamental stone balustrade behind them.[68] The same photograph is also in the collection of the Dalrymple family, likely also part of an album originally created for Sophia and her family, disassembled long ago. A similar photograph depicting the two sisters, also posed against a wall of indistinct outdoor foliage, shows the two women crouched together on a carpet or floormat; while one faces the camera directly, the other twists away. Marked 'Study for a painting' in pencil below the image in an unknown hand, this photograph could have been posed by Watts or a member of the Pre-Raphaelites, as the Dalrymple collection also contains a sketch by Dante Gabriel Rossetti as well as at least three differently sized photographs depicting Virginia Somers's child, Isabel, in various poses and costumes.[69] Interestingly, Julia Margaret did not include a drawing or a photograph representing herself.

Because of the many family subjects in the Lansdowne Album, art historians have reasoned that Cameron assembled the volume in 1859 to recognize some unknown but special connection between the Cameron household and Lord Lansdowne, possibly to recognize financial contributions made by Lansdowne to help support the family.[70] But no evidence is offered to back up this claim. In addition, the Lansdowne Album includes multiple portraits depicting Alfred Tennyson, Thomas Carlyle, James Spedding, and Thomas Wright, which suggests the family-based explanation alone is inadequate to account for these works. In addition, the album includes two photographs of Tennyson by James Mudd that must have been added later, as these portraits date to 1861. Nevertheless, Cameron's presentation album to Lansdowne has persistently been interpreted in a domestic context and as if it were received by the statesman as a finished work of art, the product of thoughtful assembly and archive-minded preservation. The word 'album' almost insists on such an interpretation, with the connotation of interrelated parts and the implication of a coherent narrative, as if the volume constituted a miniaturized and portable exhibition space.

But Cameron's purposeful inclusion of reproductive photographs and works by multiple artists argues that the opposite is more likely true: rather than considering photographic albums like Lansdowne's as evidence of a fixed and immutable archive, it is important to recognize that album spaces shifted over time and were often the product of multiple authors or contributors.[71] Recent research on Victorian women's photographic albums suggest their unfinished quality was an intentional semantic marker of their methodical and tactile assembly, where collage techniques, visual fragmentation, and relational ambiguity characterized their organization, and where their 'cuts and wounds are never fully resolved, never fully "healed", into a smooth continuous surface, neither physically nor conceptually'.[72] In this context, it is useful to ask if Cameron perceived her role as a mere compiler of photographs, one who manipulated photographs that were already well encoded with specific meanings, or whether she conceived her role as a creative author, someone able to engender new interpretations by means of sequencing or arranging different kinds of imagery on the page. Or did Cameron attempt to deny her role as the album's creator entirely, placing herself in the margins, so to speak, to foreground the interests of the recipient of the album, the person for whom she undertook the project?[73]

Lord Lansdowne's album provides no clues in this regard. The volume contains visual material drawn from diffuse sources, including a reproductive photograph of a crayon drawing of Henry Taylor by Watts; another depicting a sculpted medallion of Thomas Carlyle by Woolner; and a photograph of Cameron's two sons, Hardinge and Ewen, playing chess, with no claims made to link or associate the different imagery. Roland Barthes argued that the reader of such albums inhabited a 'multi-dimensional space'

26 Plate 11 from the Lansdowne Album.
Top: Unknown photographer but possibly John Stewart, *Sir J. F. W. Herschel, from life*, *c.*1855, albumen print, 11.4 × 9 cm.
Bottom: Reproductive photograph of a drawing by unknown photographer, *Wright (the great philanthropist) from a drawing by G. F. Watts*, *c.*1855, albumen print, 12 × 10.3 cm.
Collection of Charles, Marquis of Lansdowne.

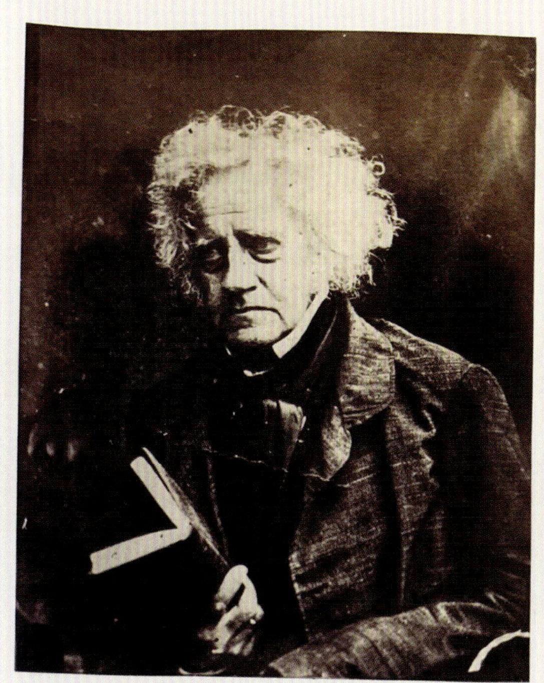

Sir J. F. W. Herschel from life

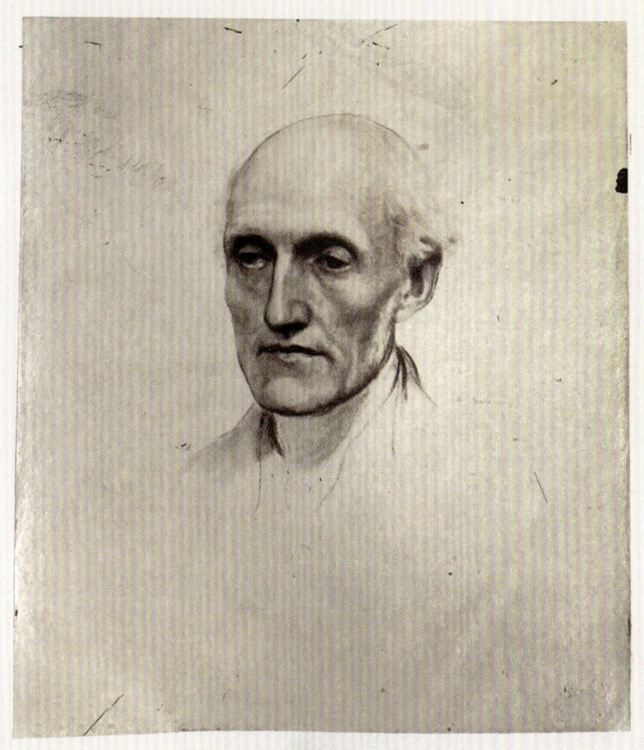

Wright (the great philanthropist) from a drawing by G. F. Watts.

THE

Photographic Album

FOR THE YEAR 1855

BEING CONTRIBUTIONS FROM THE MEMBERS OF

THE PHOTOGRAPHIC CLUB

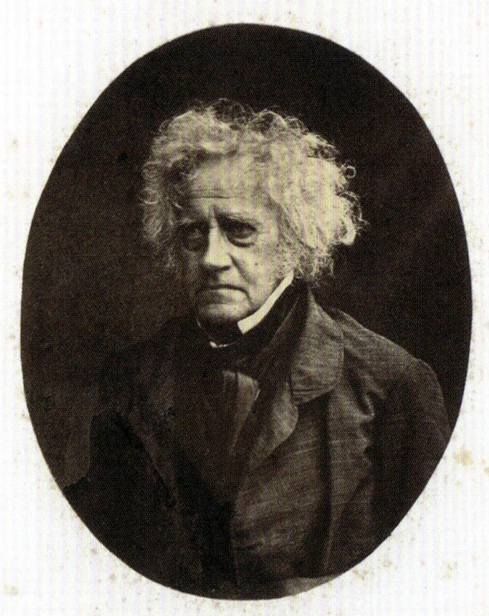

Quis Solem dicere falsum
Audeat? VIRG.

Printed for the Members of the Photographic Club

BY CHARLES WHITTINGHAM

and, by extension, that it was Lansdowne, and *not* Cameron, 'who holds together in a single field all the traces by which the written text [or in this case, the photographic album] is constituted'.[74] This shift in perspective suggests that Lansdowne would not have questioned the multiple sources from which Cameron obtained her imagery and that his possible interpretation of each image in the album was of necessity structured by the discursive and cultural spaces that defined his own experience.

Significantly, the Lansdowne Album contains a unique portrait of Sir John Herschel that puts these questions of authorship and influence in high relief, especially in relation to the historical context in which the photographs in the album were presented, which, following Barthes, affected their interpretation and meaning. Taken around 1855 this photograph of Herschel was likely created by John Stewart (fig. 26, top). Stewart was the brother of Herschel's wife, Lady Margaret Brodie Herschel, which helps to explain his access to his famous subject.[75] From the nature of Victorian collecting and album-making, it is unknown if Cameron originally presented Stewart's portrait in the album when she first gave it to Lansdowne or if she acquired it later and affixed it in place. Equally possible, the image could have been obtained separately by Lansdowne. Regardless of its source, however, the photograph's presence in this album only reinforces the imperial connection established between Lansdowne and Herschel, a relationship that dates from the 1838 ceremonial dinner welcoming Herschel back home when Lansdowne spoke in glowing terms about the scientist.

Stewart's portrait of Herschel depicts the scientist holding an open book before him. This image closely resembles a similar photograph taken in a nearly like pose, but without the open book, also by Stewart (fig. 27). From the visual evidence provided in both photographs, including features such as pose, lighting, and costume, it is likely the two portraits were taken during the same session when Herschel sat before Stewart's camera. Both photographs also date from 1855, but while the first appears uniquely in Lansdowne's album, the second was published in multiple copies as a limited-edition portfolio of works by the Photographic Club. The portfolio was titled *The Photographic Album for the Year 1855*. It is worth comparing the two volumes – one, a hand-made album dedicated to an individual, the other a formally constructed portfolio produced in multiple copies – in relation to their different physical attributes, material organization, and subject matter.

In Lansdowne's album, Cameron pasted Stewart's photograph of Herschel on an album page (Plate 11 of the album) alongside a reproductive photograph of a charcoal drawing depicting Thomas Wright by George Frederic Watts (fig. 26, bottom).[76] Wright was a notable contemporary who devoted his life to the recuperation of wayward children and the rehabilitation of prisoners into society. In admiration for Wright, Watts dedicated his canvas *The Good Samaritan* (1852) to the Manchester Art Gallery. In the context of the album, Herschel and Wright appear with little context to guide the viewer, either in terms of this page alone or in relation to its sequence in the album as a whole. For example, Plate 11 with Herschel and Wright is preceded by a page depicting two children. On Plate 10, Cameron pasted a photograph portraying her seven-year-old son Henry and an unidentified 'Lance Child', aged two years and nine months. No apparent significance is attached to these children. Following the page with the portraits of Herschel and Wright, Plate 12 depicts a clean-shaven Thoby Prinsep, which reproduces a drawing by Watts. Once again, beyond the identification of the sitters, no context or narrative is offered to help readers make sense of the sequence, arrangement, or subject matter of the album pages alone or as a group.

By contrast, in the *Photographic Album for the Year 1855*, Stewart's photograph of Herschel is the sole portrait among the portfolio of forty prints. Intended as an impressive display of artistic and technical virtuosity among club members, the collection reproduces flawless photographs. These prints are all carefully cropped and elegantly presented, materially unlike the Lansdowne

27 John Stewart, *Portrait of Sir John Herschel, Bart., F.R.S., Foreign Associate of the Institute of France*, centre medallion photograph, from *The Photographic Album for the Year, 1855, Being Contributions from the Members of the Photographic Club*. Salted paper print from glass negative, 11.6 × 9 cm.

J. Paul Getty Museum, 84.XA.871.6.1. Digital image courtesy of Getty's Open Content Program.

album's imprecise hand-trimmed angles and awkwardly pasted pages. While Lansdowne's album contains a mixture of portraits of adults and children, public figures and private family members, original and reproductive photographs, and multiple artists, all organized informally, the Photographic Club's portfolio is a model of organizational coherence: Herschel's is the lone portrait, an oval trimmed precisely for display on the frontispiece, framed specifically to honour the subject's distinction. The club's portfolio depicts a wide range of subjects, by design, offering landscapes, architecture, and genre scenes, to demonstrate the wide abilities and interests of club members. In addition, the audience was select, as only fifty-two copies were produced. By carefully controlling the material uniformity of this limited-edition portfolio, club members took pains to impress the public with the look of fine art prints. In 1856, the *Illustrated London News* noted that the producers of this portfolio each received one copy, with the fifty-first presented to Queen Victoria and the fifty-second to the British Museum.[77] The portfolio's royal patronage and its inclusion in a national museum confirmed the positive impression made by this work.

Recent scholarship on photographic albums produced by Victorian women have suggested that volumes like the Lansdowne Album revealed their creators' subject positions, expressing, in Patrizia Di Bello's words, 'cultural norms and social meanings associated with the feminine and the family'.[78] For Marta Weiss, Victorian album-makers like Cameron considered their album-making as material forms of performance, drawing from amateur theatricals and popular entertainment as much as the daily performance of social roles. Consequently, these women constructed each page in a way that was analogous to the theatrical stage: 'With the help of scissors, paste, and watercolour', writes Weiss, women album-makers restaged photographs that they intentionally fragmented, freely reimagining their settings according to their performative role in society.[79] And Elizabeth Edwards explains how the photograph's material status as a three-dimensional object encouraged women to regard them as material and tactile objects of memory, available for album-making precisely because of the modern sensibility that allowed them to be 'handled, framed, cut, crumpled, caressed, pinned on the wall'.[80] Di Bello extended this idea further, arguing that 'women's hands changed the meaning of objects, from commodities valued by price, into fetishes endowed with affective powers'.[81] But it does not seem likely Cameron wanted to imbue her photographic album with enigmatic or magical forces, nor that Lansdowne was prepared to receive the album in such an inscrutable way.

Rather than negotiating Cameron's femininity or mediating constructions of Victorian social performance, it is more likely instead that Cameron regarded her gift album to Lansdowne in the service of the Anglo-Indian and imperial discourse they both shared, one sustained from their regular gatherings at Little Holland House, and, equally important, that the album was received by Lansdowne in this spirit. In the context of Lansdowne's album, the meaning of any single photograph or group of images must rely upon a viewer's amalgamation of multiple possible interpretations, especially as these were understood in relation to other objects in the volume. Such a perspective gives privilege to the recipient of the album rather than the person who assembled the volume. It allows for the viewer to make unexpected discoveries, encounters, relationships, and associations between images; it creates opportunities for introspection and shifting subject positions; and it enables the viewer to prioritize layers of connective meaning, which is to say that it creates the opportunity to examine both what is present and what else might be absent from the album itself.

Some of these associations emerge if we return to Cameron's inclusion of Stewart's portrait of Herschel in the Lansdowne Album. Intriguingly, this photograph predates her own portrait of the scientist by more than a decade (the subject of chapter 9). In fact, in 1855, Stewart's portrait of Herschel was among the earliest of the formal photographs made to honour the scientist. But because of its limited availability as an albumen print, Stewart's photograph was not mass-produced and could not be collected widely, and therefore did not displace the popularity of William Ward's widely collected engraving of 1835, which reproduced Henry William Pickering's painting made that same year. Even ten years later, for example, the *Illustrated London News*

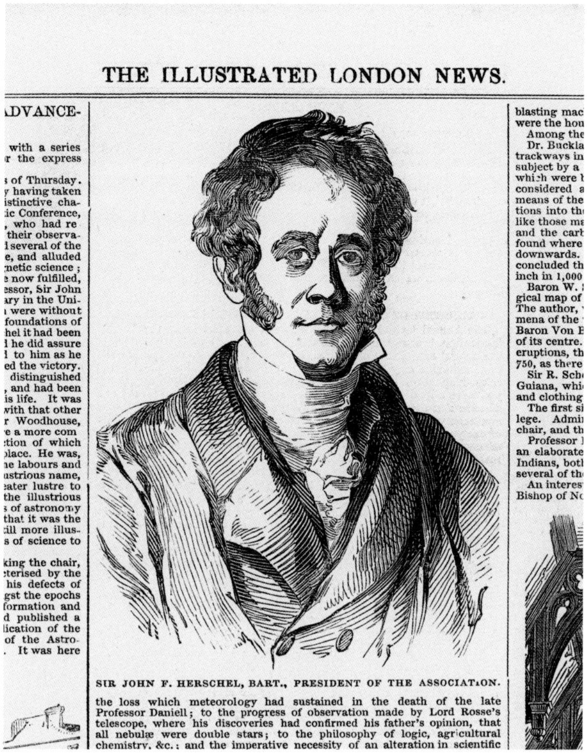

28 Anon., woodcut of Sir John Herschel, *Illustrated London News*, 28 June 1845, 404.

still relied upon Ward's engraving of Herschel to portray the scientist, as the journal included a woodcut version of this image in its article on the 1845 convening of the British Association for the Advancement of Science (fig. 28).[82] But between 1835 and 1850, Herschel's physical appearance changed considerably: his hair whitened and the lines in his face deepened as he aged. The success of his 1847 book *Results of Astronomical Observations made … at the Cape of Good Hope* assured his public renown. But it was not until many years later, in 1860, that Herschel's photographic portrait acquired its own celebrity status and widespread distribution. This came in the form of a mass-produced *carte-de-visite* photograph taken by Maull and Company, an image that is not present in Lansdowne's album.[83] If, in 1860, Lansdowne chose to add the two portraits of Tennyson at that time, he did not choose to expand Cameron's album in a similar way by including the new *carte-de-visite* image of Herschel.

Cameron's influential community was sustained by her personal relationships to Sir John and Lady Herschel, Lord Lansdowne, and the Anglo-Indian circle of those who gathered at Little Holland House. Her early photographic albums must be evaluated in this context. She never did write the book Lady Herschel suggested she author for Indian women, and unfortunately her reply to Lady Herschel about this matter does not survive. Nevertheless, Sarah Stickney Ellis's instructions to English women to fulfil their social roles in the home as an extension of their national and imperial duty must have left a powerful mark on Cameron. Ellis had insisted that useful work, which is to say, the product of making things 'by hand', was distinct from manual labour and therefore must be regarded an honourable activity. Cameron's pursuit of handmade albums fulfils that promise. And while Ellis wrote that modern British women should avoid physical labours, she also encouraged them to pursue hand-crafted work because it empowered women with the opportunity to engage meaningfully in the world, to undertake 'useful purposes' by joining together the material world with 'the moral world'.[84]

In Victorian England, where social connections were determined by class, and family life was constrained by gender norms, Julia Margaret initially prioritized her role as wife and mother before pushing against limits imposed by those social conventions.[85] Her first encounters with photography were through the making of albums, and in a few short years, she created for herself an independent artistic identity, a rare occurrence and real triumph. By 1850, at age thirty-five, she was sufficiently well resourced to vanquish virtually any domestic trouble that came her way.[86] It was unquestionably Julia Margaret who determined where to establish the family home during these years, and it was she who was the engine behind relocating her household to different cottages around Kent in the 1850s, to London towards the end of the decade, and to the Isle of Wight in the 1860s.[87] Only in 1863 did she settle at last in Freshwater, principally to simplify her connection to the Tennysons, who established their home on the island in 1856. And yet, throughout these various adventures and commonplace cares, she was coping with her own disquiet over her husband's persistent longing to travel to Ceylon to visit his plantations.[88] Like her companions in Little Holland House, Julia Margaret Cameron was always looking East.

Tuesday 29 Sep.
1857

My beloved Juley-

I wish I could let my hand write for today as large a letter as I have in my ~~heart~~ heart ready written - but Time is sho as the carriage is ordered early to take us all to the Crystal Palace Y^r Brothers never having seen it I am thank … them - other … ave prefer … & a lette … to … e often … than it can … She said "dear girl a good dear girl!"

Oct 1 -

Miss Julia Hay Cameron
Mr. J. Jackson's
Brent Lodge
Hendon Middlesex.

POSTAGE ONE PENNY
POSTAGE ONE PENNY
LONDON OC 9

Chapter Three
Letters to Juley

29 Detail of a letter from Julia Margaret Cameron to Julia Hay Cameron, 29 September 1857.
Kent County Archives, U310_C75_57.

CRISIS IN INDIA

In May 1850, Herschel wrote to Charles Cameron to continue an earlier conversation the two had shared about the moral question of governing India and whether the colony could one day achieve self-governance and political independence. After considering different arguments, Herschel confided his doubts and worries about what he considered the precarious state of Indian affairs. He directly challenged Cameron, asking his friend how long the East India Company imagined it could continue ruling India:

> I am much obliged by your allowing me a perusal of the arguments of Sir E. Ryan and your self for making a step in the direction of erecting India into a self-governing nation or assemblage of nations a consummation which will not take place in our time or that of our immediate descendants ... That some step of the kind must be taken under pain of rebellion, as some time or other, if we persist in enlightening and educating the natives up to the point of enabling and encouraging them to compare their position as the governed disadvantageous with ours as the governors is clear ... remembering always that the object of a government is not to make its subjects independent of its power but to render them progressively wiser and happier under it.[1]

Although Herschel might have accepted the East India Company's longstanding definition of its benevolent mission to 'enlighten and educate' the indigenous Indian population, his fears about a possible revolt against British rule disclosed his true apprehensions. Or perhaps this letter revealed his disbelief that the Company was genuinely able to deliver on its promises.

Herschel's disquiet apparently lay in the vagueness and uncertainty of what we might call imperialism's 'end game': after years of being on the receiving end of British enlightenment without any input into the terms of their own governance, Herschel asked, why would the Indian populace continue to accept British control, and for how much longer could Britain expect to maintain the status quo? Although he never defined what that watershed moment might look like, Herschel emphasized the ambiguity and precarity of this tenuous position in the phrase 'up to the point'. Herschel's letter ultimately disclosed his recognition that the British government had no intention to release the colony from its control, to allow it to establish a fully autonomous and independent form of self-government. He understood flatly that Indian sovereignty 'will not take place in our time or that of our immediate descendants'. Merely seven years later, to the shock of much of the British public – but perhaps of no genuine surprise to Herschel – India rebelled against the yoke of Britain's colonial rule.

Julia Margaret Cameron first learned of the Indian Uprising by means of the telegraph, and she would dread its periodic reports for many months to come. The revolt – first termed a sepoy rebellion in the press, and then a mutiny – began with a military dispute in Meerut in May 1857. The *Illustrated London News* did not report until June on the spread of the insurrection beyond the initial conflict, but the journal's economy of facts seemed to disclose an accompanied sense of anxiety and alarm. The report stated succinctly, 'A telegraphic despatch received at Bombay from Meerut states that the 3rd Bengal Cavalry were in open mutiny, and that several officers and men had been killed and wounded'.[2]

Mention of 'the Mutiny' itself does not turn up in Cameron's correspondence until July, and her words echo the earlier news reports. On that day, 31 July 1857, when she wrote to her daughter Juley, she was already preoccupied with photography, although she had little experience with the medium. Julia Margaret would surely not have thought of herself as an independent creative artist, although in several short years she would claim for herself a new identity as a photographer.[3] Even by 1857, however, photography was important to Cameron. She avidly consumed photographs to keep in albums and to display in her home, with most of these portrait subjects depicting immediate and past family members. On that day in July, for example, she travelled from her cottage in Putney Heath to the Photographic Institution on New Bond Street in London to have a portrait made of her eldest son Eugene, who was about to report for duty in the Royal Artillery. While she waited in the shop, she hastily posted the letter to her eldest child and only daughter, who was away from the family, spending the summer in Staunton Park.[4] Cameron's letter emphasizes her distress at what she termed the massacre of European women and children reported at the outset of the insurrection, and she projects her outraged sense of betrayal at learning of the duplicity of sepoys who at one moment pledged their allegiance to British officers and then murdered them the next:

> The extra telegraph of today brings shocking acc[oun]ts of the massacre of European Women & Children – & of course this is shocking eno' – but of course also our Soldiers must have been enveloped in defending them – & then other Reg[imen]ts have revolted the 3d R[egiment] I think this was the Reg.t. after swearing fidelity and receiving arms issued & murdered all their officers.[5]

Much is embedded here in the exchange between mother and daughter, as Cameron and her children had once been residents in India themselves and she could easily imagine the vulnerability of being in the same place as those who were killed. Amid her anxiety, however, it also seems apparent that Julia Margaret was working with a paucity of details and jumped to conclusions as a result. As Dan Randall has noted, the telegraph contributed greatly to the 'modern notion of informational immediacy' because it presented seemingly vital news as if it were 'urgent and unignorable', yet the technology obscured the reality of the six-week delay in which telegraphed news was conveyed from India to England. Although it was far quicker than the typical delay caused by a three-month sea voyage, the telegraph nevertheless grossly misrepresented the imminence of events.[6] Early days of the rebellion's coverage in London reflected this sense of crisis and alarm, as news from India was accompanied by numerous exaggerations, outright false accounts, and contradictory reports about the battles. These conflicted with first-hand soldiers' accounts of so-called Indian atrocities as well as inflated tales of British military heroism.

Also embedded in Cameron's words is her implicit contrast between native Indians conscripted into the Bengali forces of the East Indian Company's army – the sepoys – and those murdered at the sepoys' hands, which she identified as 'European Women & Children'. 'European' is the coded word here, one that she used in her correspondence throughout the period of the conflict. Significantly, Cameron did not write 'English' or 'British' to describe the dead women and children, nor did she refer to them as aligned with the 'Company', which would have recognized their attachment to the East India Company. The rhetorical choice reveals something important about how she thought about the British presence in India and the terms she used to report to her daughter about the nature of the revolt. It is useful to address this question here to comprehend Cameron's political state of mind. For Julia Margaret Cameron, it seems apparent, the Indian Uprising was not confined to the treachery of Indian troops who rebelled against their British officers and was more alarming than a conflict contained within the nation's borders: early on in this crisis, Cameron recognized that the revolt in India revealed the gulf separating East and West.

As early as October 1857, Thomas de Quincey, best known for his *Confessions of an English Opium-Eater* (1821), decried the rhetorical shift that called the Indian Uprising a revolt against 'European' control as opposed to 'British' dominance. Elevating this distinction as revealing and important, he claimed the issue was not one of mere semantic preference. Nor did he recognize the preference for 'European' as opposed to 'British' to be the result of the lingering presence of French traders or Dutch agents that still plied their commercial exchange in the colony. According to de Quincey,

> What fiend of foolishness has suggested to our absurd kinsmen in the East, through the last sixty years, to generalise themselves under the name of *Europeans*? As if they were ashamed of their British connections, and precisely at that moment when they are leaving England, they begin to assume continental airs; when bidding farewell to Europe, they begin to style themselves *Europeans*, as if it were a greater thing to take up a visionary connection with the Continent, than to found a true and indestructible nobility upon their relationship to the one immortal island of this planet. [Original emphasis][7]

For de Quincey, preference of 'European' disclosed a naive ideological positioning strategy, an unwise attempt to obscure apparent differences among European citizens through a rhetorical sleight of hand. In denunciating use of the term 'European' for what was indisputably a British colonial conflict, de Quincey criticized those who would denigrate what he regarded as the indisputable and even noble accomplishments of Britain for bringing 'Western civilization' to India through its language, laws, and social institutions.

An unabashed defender of empire, de Quincey censured those who presumed to 'regulate the usage of great nations' by diminishing what he considered Britain's positive influence over Asian lands and peoples. But his censure was more than a preposterous boast. De Quincey understood that Englishmen who obscured their Britishness in favour of calling themselves 'Europeans' used 'the Mutiny' as a coded and racialized term to frame the assumed modernity of Europe against the backward feudalism of the Mughal empire: 'Europeans' was shorthand for the white foreigners against whose rule the dark-skinned insurgents fought, and the 'sepoy mutiny' was not merely confined to a dispute within the army, but symbolized overt hostility to Britain's occupation of India as an unwanted intrusion by a foreign power. In other words, de Quincey recognized that the fighting broke out as an anti-colonial insurrection.

At the same time, ironically, Indian nationalists also employed 'Europeans' as a useful tag to represent the British overseers they hoped to expel. By focusing on the imposition of 'Europeans' in India, leaders of the revolt expressed an urgent need to banish them and their Western thinking, customs, religion, and institutions, at any cost: 'It is no coincidence', wrote Rajat Kanta Ray, 'that on the eve of the outbreak, proclamations appeared in Lucknow in Hindu, Urdu, and Persian, calling upon Hindus and Musalmans to exterminate all Europeans'.[8] Rebels destroyed objects associated with European technology and authority: 'the first targets of destruction were the government buildings, the telegraph wires, the post office, the court, the jail and the record rooms'.[9] John Stuart Mill and others employed by the East India Company regarded technologies like these as evidence of the 'material improvements' the Company had provided, viewing them as contributions to the common good that were intended to improve conditions in the colony. But for Indian nationalists, these institutions and technologies represented Western incursions into the normal social fabric and were associated with a universal threat to Indian traditions and religious customs.[10]

These opposing tensions – British national identity vs Indian autonomy, European rationality and technology vs Asiatic customs and religious traditions, a localized military revolt brought on by sepoy discontent vs a broad social rebellion brought on by widespread cultural opposition – conspired to inform both Charles and Julia Margaret Cameron's bilateral understanding of events as they unfolded in India. This characterization of the Indian rebellion as a British or a European conflict therefore condenses complex understandings about the causes of the Uprising *and* defines the scope of remedies proposed by Britain to regain control of the colony. The two words were not interchangeable, especially as used by Anglo-Indians in Calcutta or in London, and they set up a philosophical and political opposition into which the Camerons would soon be drawn, especially in the public arena. The point here is that their alliances after the 1857 Indian Uprising were inseparable from their earlier public roles as colonialists in India.

As a governing official in Calcutta working alongside Macaulay, Charles Cameron developed laws and policies for India based upon Utilitarian principles. As Mill described it, *Europe's* 'remarkable diversity of character and culture' was responsible for its prosperity and superior culture. To Mill, the Utilitarian principles upon which Britain had based its governing policies formed the best model for future development in India because those policies offered a 'plurality of paths for its progressive and many-sided development', with the European diversity of languages and cultures Mill's shining example.[11] Consequently, attempts to 'reform' India by the East India Company's civil government were based upon these principles.[12] After the 1857 revolt, by contrast, Disraeli led the Tories in London *against* those same principles, claiming the Company's efforts to 'improve' India had been misguided for decades. In the aftermath of revolt, for example, Disraeli rejected the Company's tolerance of India's ancient religions, its respect for native princely rights, and its preservation of the caste system. He rebuked the indigenous traditions of India, not only as 'feudal artefacts', but as regressive symbols that eroded the authority and evident superiority of the Western social institutions Britain had introduced to the colony.[13]

As the Uprising in India continued to unfold and was reported in the British press, Cameron's private reactions to these events were informed by her awareness of this broader political opposition. Her responses to the rebellion abroad therefore emerged alongside her own personal embrace of British nationalism and European superiority, a complex position that even today characterizes multiple conflicting influences and histories that were instigated by an imperial worldview.[14] As a member of an expatriate community of Anglo-Indian families who once held responsible positions in Calcutta's colonial government, the Camerons, the Prinseps, and the extended families around which their relations had built an intimate community also closed ranks as an exclusive society, one that shared news of the Indian insurrection as both a personal misfortune *and* a national calamity.[15]

CRISIS IN THE HOUSE

The crisis in India was all-consuming for Cameron and her circle, as it intermingled expressions of private fear for their family members' well-being abroad together with public statements pronouncing their commitment to Britain's colonial mission. As an example of the former, Cameron's detailed knowledge about the 3rd Regiment of the East India Company's Bengali army discloses her keen awareness about the British men stationed at Meerut who commanded the sepoy regiment there. As she wrote in July 1857, 'the 3d R[egiment] I think this was the Reg.t. after swearing fidelity and receiving arms issued & murdered all their officers'.

Lieutenant Colonel George Carmichael-Smyth had been in command of the sepoy division in Meerut. Carmichael-Smyth was the youngest brother of William Makepeace Thackeray's stepfather, Major Henry Carmichael-Smyth.[16] Julia Margaret surely knew of this close personal relationship and of Carmichael-Smyth's command of the 3rd Regiment: she was Thackeray's close friend and exact contemporary; both were born in Calcutta and each lived under the care of their respective grandmothers in Paris and Versailles during the early 1830s, where Thackeray was on familiar terms with Julia Margaret and her sisters as family friends. Towards the end of that decade, when the two Pattle sisters returned to Calcutta,

Thackeray remained in Europe. Not too long thereafter, however, in 1843 and 1848, when Sara and Julia Margaret returned to London as married women, Thackeray re-established his earlier friendships with the two sisters and their extended families, which deepened in the coming decade.[17] Cameron undoubtedly expressed fear for Carmichael-Smyth's life when she wrote to her daughter Juley. But it is also possible that she was conflicted towards Carmichael-Smyth personally given her own feelings about proper military behaviours as these were expressed earlier in her letters to Broadfoot. After all, Lieutenant Colonel Carmichael-Smyth had a reputation for arrogance and for issuing peremptory and summary directives. For several years preceding the revolt, he had apparently experienced numerous disciplinary problems that negatively affected his command.[18]

During the summer of 1857, Julia Margaret exchanged several more urgent and anxious letters with her daughter Juley. In this correspondence, she repeated her worries and fears about the Indian insurrection and her uncertainty about its aftermath. During this time, the conflict in India was the indisputable focus of the extended Pattle family: they gathered in Little Holland House to discuss the East India Company's prosecution of battles in and around Cawnpore, Lucknow, and Delhi; the British suppression of the revolt; and the terms under which Britain should re-establish its governing authority. Immediate family members were directly involved in India. They were stationed in the East India Company's army, in its administrative operations, and in its medical units. Just prior to the revolt, Julia Margaret's nephew, Arthur Prinsep, her sister Sara's son, enlisted and was assigned to the 4th European Light Cavalry and then, in January 1857, was promoted to lieutenant and called into action from his base in Lucknow.[19] Other family members were also drawn into the conflict. John Jackson, the husband of Julia Margaret's sister Mia, was a doctor in the East India Company's medical corps. At the time of the rebellion, Jackson had already been separated from his wife and children, as he had remained in residence when they moved to London with the expectation that he would soon follow, but Jackson was called upon to remain at his post.[20] By August, John Warrender Dalrymple, the husband of her sister Sophia, was officially recalled to his administrative position as Civil and Sessions Judge for the Bengal Civil Service, serving in Hooghly, north of Calcutta. Although the family expected that he would be reinstated to the post, this news caused much anguish owing to Dalrymple's questionable health.[21] Herbert Clogstoun was also in India, commissioned a major in the Madras army. Clogstoun was married to Mary Julia Mackenzie, the second daughter of Julia Margaret's oldest sister, Adeline, who had died at sea in 1836. First appointed to his post in 1838, Major Clogstoun was transferred in 1856 as second-in-command of the 2nd Cavalry Hyderabad Contingent, just prior to the rebellion, and he participated in several key battles during the war. Also in Madras was Rose Prinsep Mackenzie, Mary Julia's elder sister. At the height of the war, on 16 March 1857, Rose married David Arnot, who served in the 34th Light Infantry.[22]

Although the Pattle sisters no longer called Calcutta home, the renewed stressors of the insurrection in India strengthened their bond to each other, as evidenced in Cameron's many letters to her daughter. Consequently, the Camerons, Prinseps, Dalrymples, and Jacksons, as well as the Mackenzies and their descendants, internalized a personal stake in following the course of the East India Company's army in its prosecution of the war, in supporting the political actions of the Company to re-establish social order, and in preserving Britain's colonial enterprise abroad. Julia Margaret wrote to her daughter about the oppressive weight of these interconnected fears as the extended family faced the risk and uncertainty of service abroad:

> We have all been under some concern & little Soph under great distress by Dal[']s having to go out to India on Friday or Saturday next -- The orders being for all civilians to return to their posts who are not so ill as to be in their beds. Accord[ing]ly Dalrymple is at L. H. H. [Little Holland House] & all possible hurry of preparation going on ... Little Soph is under distress & alarm as well she may be – altho' it is to be hoped that going in a sailing vessel as he is for his doctors think the heat of the Red Sea w[oul]d knock him up that the worst part of the revolt will be over before he arrives.[23]

Two days later, Cameron referred once more to 'Europe' in a follow-up letter to her daughter Juley, using the term as shorthand for the safety of the English 'home base' that it was Dalrymple's misfortune to leave – and to which she presumed he would long to return – as she equated Europe with the loving shelter of his own family while facing unknown peril and uncertainty in India:

> I do pity him for it is a great trial to leave Wife & Children and home and Europe at a moment's notice in this way. I have asked him very particularly and he tells me he must go on Friday night so that it is quite impossible for you to get up in time therefore my darling you must remain quietly.[24]

From the summer of 1857 and throughout the entire next year, during which time British forces re-established military and administrative control of India, Julia Margaret Cameron fervently consumed news of the conflict.

Julia Margaret's personal worries are evident in her correspondence and were certainly justified: 'We have all been under some concern'; 'Soph is under distress & alarm'; 'it is a great trial'. In vain, she declares her fervent hope that 'the worst part of the revolt will be over' before her brother-in-law arrives in the colony, expressing a natural focus on the family's welfare. But beyond discussing their worries for the safety of family members, what has been overlooked in the various accounts of these activities is the concerted effort by which she and her circle gathered to express their own nationalist sentiments in the aftermath of the revolt and to participate in honouring and commemorating British heroes of the Uprising, both military and civilian. The alarm expressed in Cameron's letters attests to the urgency with which she and other family members felt the need to respond to the revolt, but these cannot be dismissed as inward-looking personal cares or as if they were peripheral to her well-being. Rather, they provide insight to a closed society's deep-set anxieties as they blended with patriotic sentiments, especially in the context of the colonial world from which they had recently departed.

That mixture of family and nation was captured admirably by William Holman Hunt, who was present in Little Holland House when a letter arrived from India bearing news about Sara Prinsep's son Arthur. Hunt observed that the fear and grief that spread throughout Little Holland House concerned not only Arthur's unknown fate, but also the very future of India:

> Mrs. Prinsep, the mother, still clung to the hope that her son's regiment would be loyal. But word arrived that its sepoys also had killed nearly all their officers on the parade-ground; and this was followed by news that Arthur had galloped off, followed by numerous shots, and losing his shako, had to ride for three days through the burning sun, being refused succour and even a covering for his head by the villagers he passed on his way. These tidings came from a friend [of Arthur's] who was then on the station nursing him from a sunstroke, from which his glory of hair had not saved him. Every one grieved for the family.[25]

Hunt's narrative of the arrival of the Indian insurrection on the doorstep of Little Holland House only confirmed news accounts the family had read. It exemplifies the 'cloud of fear', the shock and grief in the national mood that reacted in unison to the calamitous events of 1857 and influenced the historical narratives that emerged almost simultaneously from Little Holland House.

An example of this narration can be found in Christina Rossetti's poem of June 1857, called 'In the Round House at Jhansi'. 'Gentle Christina Rossetti', as Hunt called her, did not join her more extroverted brothers in the Pre-Raphaelite circle at Little Holland House very frequently, but she nevertheless wrote her poem in response to one of the many news reports of the war in India. The poem stems from a story that British soldiers and their wives had been confined to the fort at Jhansi and surrounded by rebel forces. Rossetti's narrative imagines an imprisoned couple's last words uttered immediately before a mob of Indian rebels, described as 'swarming howling wretches', breach their fort's defences, the moment just before they resolve to commit suicide rather than fall into the hands of the insurgents. 'In the Round House at Jhansi' illustrates the heightened emotional fear brought on by the rebellion, an alarm that was magnified by a larger symbolic affront to Britain's cultural domesticity and, as Jenny Sharpe has shown, to the threat of Indian men violating the purity of British women.[26] Although Rossetti undoubtedly shared her poem with her brothers, it is unknown if she shared it with others in the house as well, and she did not publish the poem until

August 1859, when it appeared in Charles Dickens's publication *Once a Week*.[27] In later editions of 'In the Round House at Jhansi', she disavowed the historical accuracy of the story that inspired the poem.[28]

Because Cameron's extended family served in prominent public and administrative roles, their historical response to the rebellion is doubly revelatory. Their narration expressed personal knowledge, as in Cameron's awareness of the command of Lieutenant Colonel George Carmichael-Smyth. But they were also nourished by a Romantic sensibility that melded together their veneration of British heroism and grief for the deaths of British women and children with a righteous sense that the East India Company's combat was prosecuted against an insurgency they regarded as illegitimate. As we shall see, the virtuous terms they used to justify the violent suppression of the revolt reinforced their beliefs in duty and sacrifice for the future of India as a British colony. Their unstated presumption that British control would ultimately be restored infused these beliefs, and consequently they regarded the rebellion as only a temporary setback to the permanence of their rule.

CAMERON'S FRIGHT

While the British public was astonished by the Indian revolt and expressed disbelief at the disloyalty of sepoys towards their military commanders, the great shock that electrified Cameron and so many others was the murder of women and children in the garrison town of Cawnpore during the early days of the war. The London presses quickly branded these murders a 'massacre' and inscribed the date, 15 July 1857, as indelible. The city's name consumed the British imagination when it was learned from multiple sources that mutinous sepoys had not only killed their officers but also took some 200 British women and children captive. News reports drew upon the accounts of soldiers who had escaped that the hostages were confined to a building near the Ganges called the '*Bibighar*', a name given to a small house that a British man had once used to keep his Indian mistress. After the initial revolt that had spread to Cawnpore from Meerut, a small number of British soldiers had survived the initial combat and were taken hostage. These soldiers were promised safe passage in boats down the Ganges on the following day, while the insurgents were to keep the women and children behind as prisoners. But once the men had boarded in the morning, miscommunications and the chaos of war led to a bloodbath on the river and only a few British men escaped with their lives. The river massacre took place in the open and was sanctioned brazenly as an overt act of war, later written about as a 'spectacle' that displayed the rebels' power and their public resistance to British authority.[29]

At some point during or after these events (depending upon various accounts), a rebel leader by the name of Nana Sahib emerged to give new focus, direction, and accountability to their earlier confusion and disarray. For the British public, Nana Sahib came to personalize the Uprising itself as the rebels' diabolical leader. After first pledging to release the British hostages as an act of mercy, Nana Sahib turned about instead and ordered the mass killing of the women and children held in the *Bibighar*.[30] The order and execution of this mass murder took place in a closed space, unlike the river battle, later interpreted as an 'act of retreat' that took place in response to fresh reports that British garrisons would soon be bearing down on the city.[31] The British soldiers who ultimately relieved Cawnpore wrote about the *Bibighar* as if they had encountered a 'slaughter-house'. Several soldiers' accounts, all later refuted, described how they waded through a blood-soaked floor and saw blood-stained walls. One of those first soldiers, Lieutenant Charles Wade Crump, wrote about the fate of the women and children:

> It was told me, as an actual and literal fact, that the floor of the inner room [of the *Bibighar*] was two inches deep in blood. It came over men's shoes as they stepped. Tresses of women's hair, and children's shoes, and articles of female wear, broad hats and bonnets, books, and such like things, lay scattered all about the rooms ... The bodies of the victims had been thrown down a well, just behind the house, and were there to be seen, a mangled heap, with an arm or leg protruding here and there. If the Black Hole of Calcutta brought down much retribution on its perpetrator, what vengeance can be meted out for this?[32]

When variations of this account were reprinted in news publications in London, the *Bibighar* was re-christened the 'Slaughter House', and, consistent with all myths of origin, the massacre at Cawnpore established Nana Sahib's incomparable violent reputation, effectively turning him into an iconic enemy of singular wickedness. In the British press, Nana Sahib was portrayed as villainous, evil, heartless, and barbaric.[33] By September 1857, the *Illustrated London News* solidified this perception in an engraved portrait of the man, representing him as a conniving Oriental despot (fig. 30). The journal's portrait was accompanied by the following description: 'This demon has, with his own hand, given the signal for the slaughter of six or seven hundred of our own kith and kin'.[34] Lieutenant Crump's eyewitness accounts were substantiated by sketches he made while 'on the spot' of the massacre itself. In February 1858, three of these sketches were turned into lithographs and published by the firm of Henry Graves. The three were entitled *A Pictorial Record of the Cawnpore Massacre*. One depicted the desolate scene of the British encampment. Another depicted the *Bibighar*, which was titled, *The Chamber of Blood*. The third depicted the notorious well located outside the *Bibighar*, site of the mass burial of women and children after the massacre (fig. 31).

The final indignity of Cawnpore was the callous disposal of the victim's lifeless and dying bodies into the community's water well. Apparently, when the well could no longer contain additional bodies, rebels cast the remainder in the Ganges. The well came to hold particularly gruesome associations once this news reached Britain and consequently acquired incomparable representational significance over time as an enduring symbol, one that embodied the substantial loss of life, the sepoys' 'mutinous betrayal', the mass burial of innocent victims, and the apparent effort to conceal those murders. Worse, as George Trevelyan described it in 1865 in

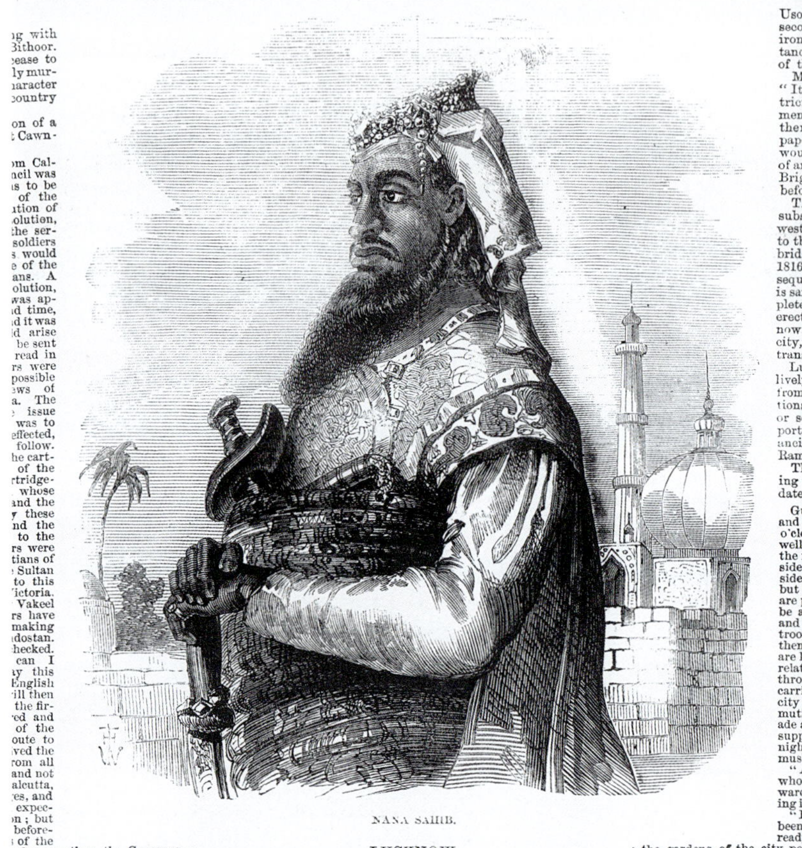

THE ILLUSTRATED LONDON NEWS

M U T I N Y I N I N

NANA SAHIB.

LUCKNOW.

Of this capital of the territory of Oude we this week engrave two Views, from sketches by Mr. W. Carpenter, jun. These are the Illustration upon the front page of the present Number, which shows a

30 *Nana Sahib*, woodcut engraving from *Illustrated London News*, 26 September 1857, 328.

31 Vincent Brooks after Charles Wade Crump, *The Exterior of the House and Well*, 1858, tinted lithograph, 41 × 56 cm, published in Henry Graves, *A Pictorial Record of the Cawnpore Massacre by Charles Wade Crump* (London: H. Graves, 1858).

Anne S. K. Brown Military Collection, Brown University Library, Providence, RI.

his book *Cawnpore*, were the 'base motives' of the mutineers, whose actions had no apparent strategic aim or military objective:

> The great crime of Cawnpore blackens the page of history with a far deeper stain than Sicilian Vespers, or September massacres: for this atrocious act was prompted, not by diseased and mistaken patriotism, nor by the madness of superstition, nor yet by incontrollable fear that knew not pity. The motives of the deed were as mean as the execution was cowardly and treacherous. Among the subordinate villains there might be some who were possessed by bigotry and class-hatred: but the chief of the gang was actuated by no higher impulses than ruffled pride and disappointed greed.[35]

As if ticking off possible ways that could explain how the initial revolt could lead to the killing of civilians, Trevelyan first listed those passions that he attributed to nationalism, religion, and fear of the unknown, before naming what he considered self-evidently dishonourable motivations, like spinelessness, deceit, and intolerance. Finally, he came to what he considered blatantly corrupt and immoral drives, base humiliations that he thought were not only unjustifiable and undignified, but depraved and unethical, motivations that were just short of human. In short, Trevelyan censured the mass execution as an act that was based upon nothing more than what he called the 'trivial impulses' of a defective culture that essentially proved its inferiority by the fact of the massacre itself. To Trevelyan, the episode created its own unique historical narrative by virtue of its crime against humanity; as he wrote, it 'blackens the page of history'.

In British news accounts, the burial well was described repeatedly as an unfathomable 'scene of horror', a term worth exploring for its rhetorical and historical associations and emotional resonance. For one, the well was indisputably a mass burial; consequently, it was impossible to identify any individual who had perished or to sanctify that person's remains. The well was also an anonymous tomb that contained an unknown number of bodies, and the buried were innocent women and children, not soldiers, unknown to the risks of military conflict. As a burial site on colonial ground, the well remained an unmarked grave, at least until a suitable marker could be fashioned. Therefore, the well became a unique site that was unlike any other, a physical space with its own distinctive character. Michel Foucault called such spaces 'heterotopias' because they stood apart in spatial terms, 'outside of all places, even though it may be possible to indicate their location in reality'.[36] The well at Cawnpore was neither a traditional cemetery nor a formal battlefield. It simultaneously occupied both sacred and profane ground. It condensed a discrete moment in time but also marked 'an absolute break' with traditional time. And although the well was physically accessible in the public square, it was also remote and spatially distant, inaccessible on foreign land many thousands of miles from London. These contradictory characteristics led Trevelyan to call this singular site 'unrepresentable'.

Nevertheless, the well became a complex symbol in the British press. When represented as a tomb containing the bodies of British women and children and in opposition to Nana Sahib, the despot who ordered their destruction, the well became an emblem of innocence and purity. The well also symbolized history repeating itself, as it was a tangible reminder of the so-called 'Patna Massacre' of 1763, in which British officers were killed in a local revolt and whose bodies had also been disposed of in a water well.[37] Consequently, the well contained an enduring narrative of British conflict in India, a story of the colonists' ever-present vulnerability in a hostile land. The curse of historical repetition also defined this narrative because the British experience in Patna seemed to confirm the enduring myth of the 'Black Hole of Calcutta', which dated to 1756, when Fort William was under siege. In that episode, Indian insurgents took British soldiers captive overnight and held them in a small enclosure that left only a few survivors.[38] In 1857, these historical episodes confirmed for the British that the vengeful acts of 'Indian savagery' that once took place in Patna and Calcutta required their continued presence in the colony.

In London, the Cawnpore well acquired additional mournful associations. As a common burial ground, the well dishonoured the dead in Christian terms. First, the location was profane, an ordinary source for obtaining well-water. As a public gathering site, it was unsanctified ground. But worse, the mass grave prevented sacrifices made by individuals from being recognized and honoured; there was no way to identify the dead. To the British, the wreckage of the well and the dilapidated roughness of the site was considered undignified for these 'martyrs'. And finally, because the well contained innocent women and children, this 'unholy tomb' needed to be consecrated in Christian terms to redefine the burial ground as a 'sacred well'. Left unattended and unmarked, the well represented an open wound; left in a desecrated state, the well became a site of blasphemy.[39] Indeed, when he first visited the site after his appointment as the new Governor-General replacing Lord Dalhousie, Charles Canning recognized the profane character of the site and resolved to consecrate the grounds and build a suitable monument to recognize the British lives lost. At Cawnpore 'the world splits apart', wrote Patrick Brantlinger, 'the well becomes a widening chasm dividing the forces of absolute righteousness from the demonic armies of the night'.[40] At no point did those 'forces of absolute righteousness' acknowledge the insurgents had branded them a common enemy and had good reason to expel them, 'root and branch, from the face of all India', as these sentiments were articulated by Nana Sahib's vizier, Azimullah Khan.[41]

Turning against their military superiors was one thing but killing innocent English women and children was quite another, and the British press vilified the insurgents not only as disloyal, but as barbaric and cruel. These bitter sentiments led the earliest accounts of the 'massacre' to publish inaccurate reports – amplified by racial animus – about how unclean and disreputable sepoys defiled and tortured pure white women, accounts that were later dismissed as fabricated.[42] Nevertheless, calls to 'avenge the honour' of British women animated the military's hostile suppression that followed, just as George Trevelyan's 1865 history of the event referred repeatedly to the restoration of order as an act of British 'chivalry', a term coded to convey Victorian admiration for virtuous women and the veneration of their purity.[43] While the revolt itself jolted London out of its general indifference towards Britain's relationship to its colonies, this murderous episode caused disbelief and outrage as much as horror. Consequently, the 'massacre at Cawnpore' was referred to repeatedly for years: '*Remember Cawnpore!*' became a rallying cry for the military, just as 'the Slaughter House' and 'the Well at Cawnpore' were used repeatedly in the British press as shorthand for the atrocity.

That summer, the news from India saturated the London press, and by August, Julia Margaret Cameron's anxiety and fear about receiving distressing news from India seemed to haunt her state of mind. Her letters to Juley in the coming months expressed a mixture of worries and fears, for the safety not only of the extended family but also for the nation. After directing the Photographic Institution to make prints of her son Eugene in July to commemorate his military commission, she returned two weeks later in mid-August to order additional portraits of her sister Sophia's children for her husband to take with him to India as family keepsakes. As she wrote to her daughter, 'Little Soph and Dal being so exceedingly anxious to get good photos of themselves for each other and of the children for poor Dal before he leaves'.[44] As Victoria Olsen has astutely observed, Cameron 'used photographs to mediate absence and separations'.[45] In this correspondence, she blended family worries together with national concerns, often displaying a stream-of-consciousness style of writing in which the flowing together of the private life was intertwined with the public. A typical example of the combination of these concerns infused the postscript to her letter of 10 August 1857:

> Write me by return of post
> Y[our] loving Mother
> August 10th 5PM
> No further news fr[om] Eugene
> The Indian telegraph
> is expected tomorrow. I dread the coming in of those mails.
> Soph leaves Brighton & talks of spending the Winter with her children at Versailles.[46]

During this time, the extended circle that gathered at Little Holland House was consumed by news of the Indian Uprising. Significantly, the freshness of the violence itself made an immediate impact on Julia Margaret. By her own account, by late September, the combat in India was affecting her peace of mind. She complained to her daughter often of bouts of dizziness, fatigue, and occasionally, shortness of breath. As she wrote to her daughter from the quiet village commons of Bromley,

> I am well nigh weary of pen ink and paper and envy the sheep nibbling on this pasturage in a little Paradise where peace seems shut in & all such images as the scenes in India shut out – & seemingly impossible – But yet they force themselves before me & that massacre of those women & children in Nana Sahib's Slaughter House seems as vivid a picture to me in all its solemn reality.[47]

By this time, Cameron had clearly absorbed many of the written and visual representations of 'the massacre of the innocents' and the disturbing horror of what she termed 'Nana Sahib's Slaughter House' from accounts in *The Times* and *Illustrated London News*. Her letter expresses dread at the idea of consuming even worse news, exhaustion from the relentless pace of the reporting, restlessness, and exhaustion from the stress of absorbing the tragedy and dealing with the haunting imagery of massacred innocents. She also experienced fright from the disturbing imagery these scenes caused in her fertile imagination: '*But yet they force themselves before me*', Cameron insisted. Cumulatively, the telegraphs and letters, published news reports, family worries, and shared conversation in Little Holland House about the war in India created an indelible visual impression, in Cameron's words, '*a vivid picture*' of the '*massacre of those women & children*'.

CAMERON'S PANIC

The young soldier Arthur Prinsep himself accounted for his combat wound in an undated letter to his mother Sara, who apparently shared the news immediately with her sisters. The letter survives because Julia Margaret borrowed Arthur's letter and enclosed it with her own correspondence to her daughter Juley, dated 1 October 1857, to inform her of the news. She implored Juley to share the letter widely:

> Shew it to Auntie Soo [Sophia Dalrymple] & tell Auntie Mia [Maria Jackson] have it to shew to Adeline [Cameron's niece, Mia's daughter] & [her husband, Henry] Halford [Vaughan] & then bring it with you [presumably, to Little Holland House, where the family had gathered] on Saturday.[48]

The Pattle clan was circling its wagons.

In his letter home, Arthur wrote that he had initially tried to inform his family immediately about his injury, but was unable to write himself because of the physical damage to his arm. 'I got Grey of the Artillery to write you a long acct of my escape whilst at Goojeranawalla which I hope you have received', he wrote.[49] As described above, Holman Hunt witnessed how this earlier letter had been received and spread alarm throughout the house. Arthur's letter brought the extended family a first-hand account of the insurrection as it was experienced in real time. Prior to getting shot, he wrote, he had been to Cawnpore with a soldier name Shepherd, possibly in July, to relieve the garrison following the mass killing of women and children. In August, he saw action against the rebel forces in Sealkote (*Sialkot*), site of another important battle that took place in the Punjab. The day after the fight against sepoys in Sealkote, Arthur was aided by a fellow British soldier (Blane of the 52nd) and one of the Sikhs who fought alongside the British ('one of our Seikhs' ... recognized 'my watch hanging out of the pocket'). In Fort Lahore, while recovering from his injury, he received assistance from a soldier named White, who 'has written all my letters [and] cut up my food at dinner', a Mr Willock of the 6th Cavalry, and a Colonel McPherson, who restocked the young man's wardrobe. Arthur expressed gratitude for their help and reassured his family, 'My health & spirits have never been better than since I was wounded, and my arm having ceased to be painful after the first weeks I have altogether had a very jolly time of it'.[50]

In closing his letter, he sent love to his older brother Val, asked Watts to write to him in India, and enclosed a special note to his father.[51] Even as he recuperated in his hospital bed, Arthur wrote to his family back home describing how he narrowly escaped death on the frontline.

> Certainly I had a nearer look at Death than most men have and if the ball had touched any of the muscles, or any part of the bone[,] I should have been rendered helpless immed[iate]l[y] & the trooper w[oul]d. have potted me directly. I shall never forget the sensation of feeling the ball strike me – I gave myself up for lost thinking that the bone must have been touched / and knowing that the trooper in pursuit was better

> nourished than I, but directly I found that I could draw my sword I was as jolly as could be –.[52]

By October 1857, having now re-joined his countrymen and recovered from his fright, the young soldier also apparently regained his enthusiasm for the fight, even expressing some eagerness to return to combat:

> My arm will I hope be quite well & unloosed from the bandages which it now has in a week's time & at furthest & I shall then apply for some appointments with the Irregular Calvary [*sic*] – I only hope I shall be able to get down Delhi wards in time to see a little of the fun & pay off some of the mutineers – Don't get into a fright because I say this dearest Mama as Delhi is as safe a place as any as these. With European troops we are sure of having no mutiny in the night. I cannot tell what will be done with me, but I shall certainly volunteer to go to Delhi.

By the date of this letter, the battle north of Lahore, like the suppression of the revolt at Cawnpore, were now historical facts. With each defeat of rebel strongholds, the tide had turned to the advantage of British forces. However, given the time delay in reporting such facts to London, the British public was still digesting the news and uncertain of the outcome.

As summer turned to autumn, rebels fleeing Cawnpore and other sites travelled to Delhi, despite that city's being under siege since June. Their aim was to rally around the last Mughal king, Bahadur Shah Zafar, to unite the rebellion as a national cause and spread the insurgency beyond the province where it had begun. Delhi therefore became the next vital site for British forces in its suppression of the rebellion. As the former capital of the Mughal empire, the city was important militarily and symbolically for both sides. For the insurgents, Delhi's ancient Kashmiri Gate represented the city's endurance, especially against foreign invaders. The Gate was an emblem of strength and independence since it was first built during the seventeenth century, and its survival made the king a central figure. While under the East India Company's control, the British had acknowledged this symbolic power, allowing Bahadur Shah to retain his title as King of Delhi as an honorific, a way to maintain goodwill. The stakes were therefore high. As William Dalrymple phrased it, 'it was clear from the outset that the British had to recapture Delhi or lose their Indian empire for ever', and from the rebels' point of view, the sepoys 'realised that if they lost Delhi they lost everything'.[53]

From the Company's perspective, Delhi held a place of strategic importance. Were it to remain in Indian control, the city and the king could become a rallying point for the rebellion to spread, whereas by recapturing Delhi, an important symbolic victory would be denied the rebels. British commanders also reasoned that once the city was taken, the rebellion could be stopped in its tracks and prevented from spreading to other cities.[54] After the British and Indian armies built up their respective forces between June and September, British soldiers broke through the defences at Delhi at the end of September 1857 and occupied the city. Their destruction of the Kashmiri Gate was decisive.[55] The news must have soon reached Fort Lahore, as Arthur Prinsep's confident boast to his mother that 'Delhi is as safe a place as any' was only made possible because, as he wrote, 'European troops' had already retaken the city.

After recovering from his injury, Arthur shared with the extended Pattle clan that his very next thoughts turned to retribution. His reference was as clear as it was casual, as if responding to a spontaneous and naive adolescent urge to 'see a little of the fun & pay off some of the mutineers'. In this passage, Arthur downplayed the British destruction of Delhi and normalized his participation in the subsequent acts of vengeance that took place against the Indian population. Perhaps his use of the term 'European' for the invading British army also discloses the racial animosity he expressed in craving to join what he referred to as 'the Irregular Calvary', a term that emerged for the ad hoc bands of renegade soldiers who formed spontaneously to exact reprisals. On reading these lines, Julia Margaret could very well have wondered how the cruelty and ruthlessness of war had turned her gentle nephew into a seemingly callous soldier, how a fair English boy could have suspended the moral compass of his upbringing and considered the indiscriminate killing of a defeated population as if it were 'a little fun'; how he could join marauding British forces to 'pay off some of the mutineers' under the guise of dispensing justice.[56] Christopher Herbert analysed these base impulses in uncompromising terms:

> The unmistakable note of something like exhilaration that mingles with fury in much of the most extreme Mutiny rhetoric is the note of a severely repressed cultural force suddenly able to cast off its inhibitions, to display itself in undisguised form, and to assert itself, under the militant banner of 'Retribution,' as the salvation not only of British India but also of the national soul.[57]

Arthur's letter home does not disclose his motives in joining the army of vengeance. Nevertheless, his intentions became common knowledge throughout Little Holland House.

Thoby and Sara Prinsep could also have received word of their son's well-being in India from another family relation who was stationed in the colony. Young Arthur figures by name in the diaries of Augusta Becher, who was the daughter of Augustus Prinsep and therefore a generational cousin of Thoby Prinsep's sons Val and Arthur.[58] Augusta had married an East India army officer named Septimus Becher and accompanied her husband to India in 1849. She and her children were repatriated to England in 1857 following the insurrection. In her diaries, which were later published in 1930, Becher recorded her presence at the siege of Delhi and her awareness of the British destruction of the city. In one entry, she indicated that Arthur Prinsep managed to telegraph the Bechers in advance of his arrival in Delhi, suggesting he knew of their movements in-country:

> Arthur [Prinsep] telegraphed 'come down', and next day a storming note from Fan at Kussowlee, saying she had a pony dak waiting all day for him. …
>
> Of that terrible siege I shall say no word, 'tis historical; but our suspense and anxiety were what none can understand but those who *know*. …
>
> At last on the 7th September Delhi was carried by assault – at what cost! Arthur had been wounded shortly before in a skirmish, but he had no notion of leaving camp before the fall of the town. …
>
> Arthur soon after arranged to come up the hill, Sir Colin Campbell having been sent out from England as Commander-in-Chief. The staff had to await the first opportunity of joining him, then impossible, and Arthur's wound being in the right arm he was unfit for service. The day he came up we went along the road towards the Entrance to meet him and Fan, and as he was well known to everyone, much liked, and moreover the first returned from Delhi, there was quite a little crowd following our party.[59]

Unfortunately, no surviving letters exist from this episode, but Becher does confirm Arthur's presence in Delhi. If Arthur Prinsep did enlist with one of the 'flying brigades' that were formed under the command of Colonel Edward Greathed to pillage Delhi or if, when he marched along the Grand Trunk road between Delhi and Cawnpore, he killed insurgents and destroyed villages for sport, as he claimed he wanted to do, no records survive confirming his participation in such acts of retribution. Nevertheless, it was from the ranks of soldiers like those in Fort Lahore that Greathed drew his willing conscripts, even though those soldiers, already traumatized by the insurrection, paid a heavy price.[60] Becher confided to her diary, for example, that her husband's participation in the column assembled to 'dispense justice' to the native population ultimately destroyed his kind personality and peace of mind, turning him into 'a grave, and even at times *almost*, a soured man'.[61]

Concerns in Britain during this time expanded from thinking the initial sepoy rebellion in India could be confined to the Company's military into a much greater fear that the insurrection would sweep over the entire colony, and this anxiety informed Julia Margaret's correspondence with her daughter. It reflected the awareness shared by Colonel John Becher, Augusta Prinsep Becher's brother-in-law, which had been communicated in another letter from this time:

> The whole native army without a single exception has either mutinied or been disarmed and disbanded, and it is little less than a miracle that the massacres have not been general from one end of India to the other. From Allahabad to Meerut, and thence to Neemuch and Mhow, is an enemy's country. The barbarous atrocities committed are beyond belief.[62]

In closing her note to Juley that accompanied Arthur Prinsep's letter home, Julia Margaret confided her sense that 'the public news seems worse than ever'. She then told her daughter about receiving yet another letter, from a soldier named Gerard, who reported the insurrection had begun to spread widely across India. This letter was sent 'on his way to Ahmedabad' and posted from Bombay, spreading news of the wide dispersion of the rebellion. Basing her knowledge upon this correspondence, Julia Margaret expressed her gravest fears: 'all the Bombay troops are disposed to mutiny & are sure to mutiny if the fall of Delhi or the arrival of European Troops do not arrest the spread of mutiny by creating Panic'.[63]

From these surviving communications we cannot conclude that Julia Margaret and her family had learned that the British had recaptured Delhi by October, when she wrote her letter to Juley. Nevertheless, Cameron's letters took on a sense of renewed urgency that accompanied her deepest anxiety. In sharing this news, she was also spreading certain alarm about the spread of the insurgency (the Bombay sepoys 'are sure to mutiny'). In her own words, the experience of receiving (and in distributing) this news was responsible for 'creating Panic'. Cameron's letter communicates the gravity of the situation by describing her own anxieties and worry, perhaps with the intention of binding her daughter closer to her mother. But panic also politicizes the discourse by injecting fear and distress into the public sphere. Discursively and psychologically, panic displaces certainty with contingency, but more importantly, it binds together people who may be widely dispersed across space and time.[64] In narratives of the colonial encounter, therefore, anxiety is the antithesis of enthusiasm, which typically dominates discourses of conquest and expansion, the rhetoric of lawful governance, and the civilizing mission that affirmed to colonizers the impression they were improving the societies they had conquered. Anxiety intrudes upon this triumphant language and disrupts its inevitability because of its sudden, indefinite, and uncanny qualities.[65]

PICTURING TIME

How did Julia Margaret confront her sense of dread and overcome her feelings of panic, and how did she process the disturbing visual imagery from the conflict in India that 'forced itself' upon her in Britain? During the 1840s, while still in Calcutta, she became acquainted with the power of photography to represent frozen moments in time. She learned the medium could preserve the present forever and came to understand that its subjects always remained a part of the past. While in India, she received examples of Talbot's early calotype process from Sir John Herschel, and as we have seen, she sent her daughter Juley to England with a daguerreotype in her hand (see fig. 12). Herschel's letters encouraged Cameron to expand her horizons, to take a historical perspective by thinking about how she might want to use the medium and what subjects she valued. His are perhaps the first words of encouragement she received to imagine herself as a photographer:

> The enclosed are a few specimens of what is doing in England in that and all but miraculous art of Photography of which I dare say you have seen plenty of the French or Daguerrotype [*sic*] specimens. Your Indian Architecture would afford superb subjects and I never look on these things without longing to be at work on those venerable monuments in which India abounds.[66]

To Herschel, photographs made excellent historical documents: because of their independent, material form, because they can be scrutinized as objects, photographs provided a heightened understanding of all that lies before us. Whether these things are imperceptible to the naked eye or lie on the surface of the ordinary world, Herschel intimated, photographs make visible that which may lie latent to our awareness or even hidden from our everyday perception.

Cameron was enamoured with the medium. As we have seen, she actively collected imagery produced by others and arranged them in albums. Yet a significant interval of time exists between Herschel's letter of the early 1840s, when he shared his prescient observations about the new medium and sent her examples of the craft, and 1864, when Julia Margaret first shared with him photographs that she had made by her own hand. This interval also defines an important time-lag in political terms, as it represents another temporal gap in relation to colonialism. During the 1840s, at the conclusion of the first Afghan War, Herschel and Cameron first confided to each other their shared belief that Britain's colonial government was a benevolent gift to India; recall that in 1846, Herschel claimed that 'there is no government on earth which is so thoroughly well served, and in whose maintenance and well working the civilization of mankind has so deep a stake'.[67] But by 1857, that belief was shaken by the shocking moment of the Indian Uprising against Britain's colonial rule. As Herschel had phrased it only several years before, Britain's role in

> enlightening and educating the natives up to the point of enabling and encouraging them to compare their position as the governed [had become] disadvantageous with ours as the governors.[68]

This time-lag in historical awareness and representation corresponds to what Homi Bhabha has called the '*signifying lag* between event and enunciation', a way of characterizing the spatial and temporal distance that separates historical episodes themselves from their creation as narratives, thereby dividing 'the Great Event and its circulation as a historical sign'.[69] Two stories may be said to describe Britain's control of India during this time, which helps to illustrate this apparent contradiction. Both narratives are incompatible and effectively cancel each other out, as historical accounts and in relation to their symbolic representation. While Britain argued that its 'civilizing mission' expressed genuine benevolence towards those it governed, for example, the East India Company actually imposed a repressive regime under the legal and governing principle it called 'despotic governance'. Bhabha theorized that it was not possible to represent a discontinuity such as this in real time. Rather, he theorized that new forms of representation would be created only after a temporal break had occurred, as they were able to take shape only after a suitable duration had transpired. At that point, new narratives could then emerge to incorporate personal memory (expressed in myth, in history, and in reminiscence). Counter-narratives could then arise to respond to forms of 'social and psychic identification', because the time-lag between the event and its representation would create new opportunities to overcome and reconcile social dissonance. For Julia Margaret Cameron, photography became the expressive vehicle by which she could come to terms with the gap between the colonial mission and the repressive regime in India, thereby filling an empty space wherein she could reconcile the 'panicked feelings' she experienced from the news reports of the insurrection, a means of controlling the anxiety and dread provoked by her correspondence, and a palpable way to try to reconcile the disjunctive fissure in colonial governance that the Uprising made visible. Cameron therefore approached the medium as a new kind of representational space; she took up Herschel's challenge as a *modern* means of representation. As Bhabha wrote, 'Modernity as a *sign* of the present emerges in that process of splitting, that *lag*, that gives the practice of everyday life its consistency as *being contemporary*'.[70]

Where might we find evidence of Cameron's effort to resolve this dislocation in her photography? In the Herschel Album, she included a new portrait of William Holman Hunt where she made this symbolic representation visible and communicated a new kind of historical narrative in contemporary terms. She photographed the Pre-Raphaelite painter in the Eastern costume he wore in Jerusalem, where he lived and worked in 1854 in search of inspiration for his religious subjects. Cameron photographed Hunt in 1864 but also included her portrait of him in the 1867 Herschel Album. This photograph, *W. Holman Hunt in his Eastern dress* (Cox/Ford 686; HA-11; fig. 32), is not simply an expression of the painter's infatuation with the exoticism of the East or his self-flattering identification with the native inhabitants of Jerusalem. After returning to London, Hunt commented that his Eastern costume had allowed him to depict 'accurate representations' of the people who still occupied the legendary Mount of Olives. Ironically, he claimed this masquerade gave him access to the unvarnished truth, writing,

> Since the days when Godfrey de Bouillon, with his crusaders, were chased from Jerusalem, no Christian, except in disguise or by stratagem, at a risk of very probable death, had ever entered its precincts.[71]

By his own admission, then, the Eastern dress that he wore while abroad was a sign of his infiltration into that closed society, a penetration for which only a disguise could provide cover and protection, a shield against possible discovery and exposure as a Western intruder.

Hunt therefore collaborated with Cameron, one might say, by engineering the making of his portrait as if it were a performative record some ten years after the fact. Several layers of fabrication are present. For one, Hunt's description discloses the physical dislocation of Jerusalem and London, makes plain the lines separating East and West.

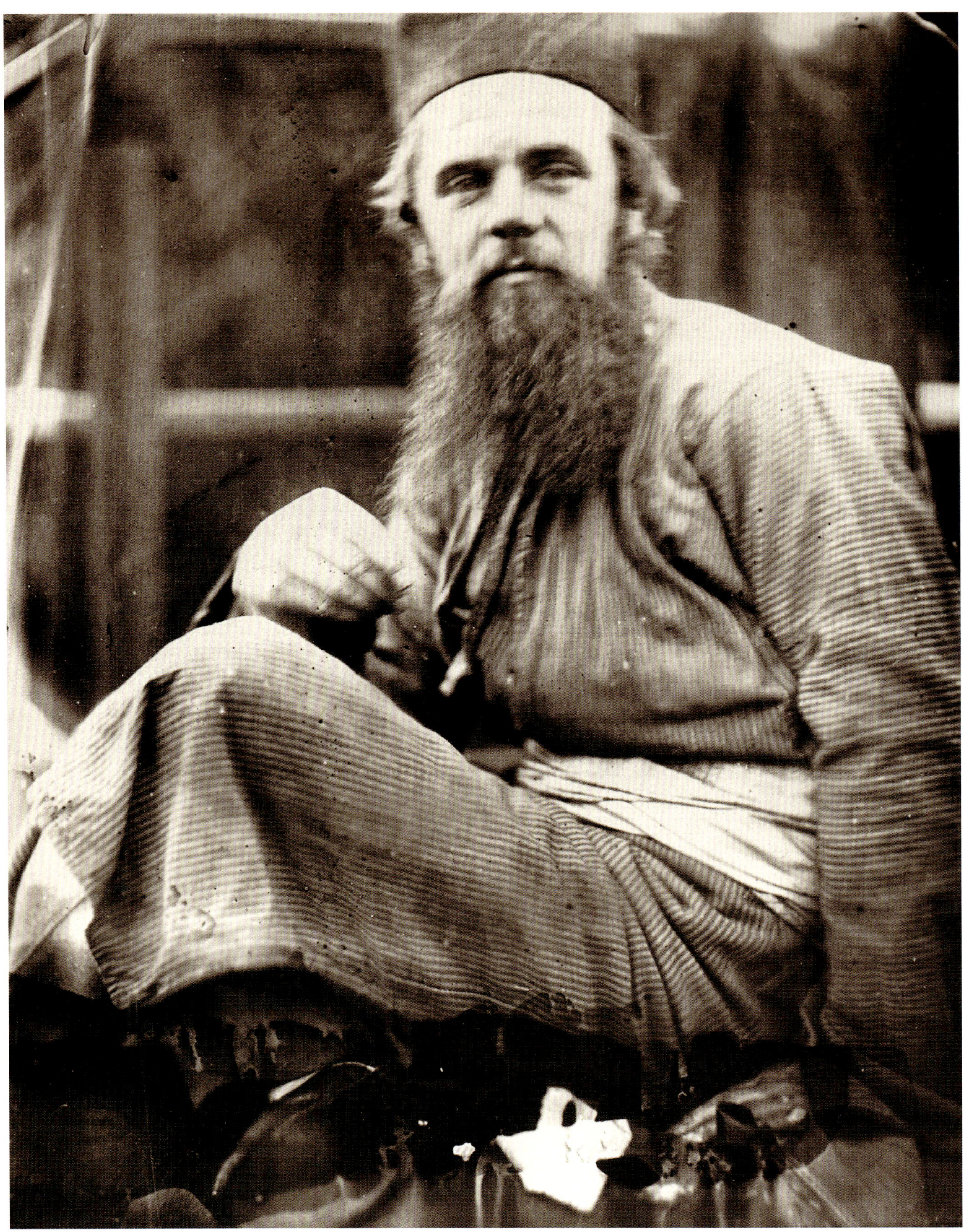

His self-flattery relies upon embellishing historical markers that define and elevate the refinement of his subterfuge as he compares them favourably to the coarseness of earlier Crusaders. Hunt also regards his attire as a means to emphasize his theatrical re-enactment. As a result, the costume itself becomes a tangible emblem of his colonial agency and a marker of his identity as a Western subject, a relic that also 'bears witness' to the time-lag between the first Western ruler of the Holy Land (Godfrey de Bouillon) and that of the nineteenth-century ruler, the Ottoman empire. Cameron therefore used Hunt to construct a coherent historical narrative that captures the 'memory and moral of the event' in terms that would be honoured by British imperialists. She portrayed those markers here as references for Hunt's double identity, a condition which effectively splits contemporary life in the Victorian age and therefore exposes a compelling sign of the modern condition.[72]

Cameron's photograph of Hunt was among her first portraits of the double articulation made visible by colonialism, a simple portrait that nevertheless discloses the 'time-lag' between a historical event like the Indian insurrection and its representation as a historical narrative. As we have seen, her 1865 portrait of her brother-in-law Thoby Prinsep that bears his signature inscribed in Urdu (see fig. 20) and her photograph depicting her husband Charles crowning a bust of Milton with laurel also contain an analogous temporal break that splits time, making visible the gap that separates a historical episode from its symbolic representation. Disguise and costume made it possible for Hunt to assume a double (modern) identity. For Cameron, performing such a makeover before the camera was not unique to her representation of Hunt. In 1867 and 1868, for example, she created photographs of several others in her circle who camouflaged their British identity in similar ways, notably William Gifford Palgrave (Cox/Ford 733), Richard Francis Burton (Cox/Ford 845), and Austen Henry Layard (Cox/Ford 700). Although she chose not to include these portraits in the Herschel Album, she displayed them together the following year in London in her German Gallery exhibition. Discursively, Palgrave, Burton, and Layard almost always defined their identity in neutral terms, as 'adventurers' or 'explorers'. But these men also served as political agents abroad, interlopers and intelligence-gatherers. Like the men who brought the scientific and military surveying work of the Great Trigonometric Survey to a human scale and helped the West understand whether the seeds of insurrection in India had spread beyond its origins in the colony, these English travellers reported back to European governments about the state of colonial governance in the Holy Land and Arabia.[73]

32 Julia Margaret Cameron, *W. Holman Hunt in his Eastern dress*, May 1864, albumen print, 25.9 × 20.8 cm. National Science & Media Museum / Science Museum Group. 1984–5017/11.

RETRIBUTION / ATONEMENT

By autumn, Julia Margaret was still processing her reactions to the war in India. On 1 October 1857, she sent Juley another letter that discussed her plans to take a day trip to visit the Crystal Palace in Sydenham, informing her eldest that she planned to take along Juley's two youngest brothers (see fig. 29):

> I wish I could let my hand write you today as large a letter as I have in my heart [al]ready written – but Time is short – as the Carriage is ordered early to take us all to the Crystal Palace [.] Your Brothers never having seen it – I am thankful to take them – otherwise I should have preferred myself this lovely dawn and a letter to you – [74]

The precise destination for this family outing is intriguing and its timing could not have been more portentous. Although no extant follow-up correspondence spells out their actual purpose for visiting the Crystal Palace, the most likely plausible explanation is that it was in anticipation of the 'Day of National Humiliation, Fasting, and Prayer' that had just been announced to mark the British response to the Indian Uprising. Queen Victoria had declared this national holiday only the week before, on 25 September 1857, proclaiming Wednesday 7 October a 'public day of solemn fast, humiliation, and prayer' in consideration of 'the grievous mutiny and disturbances which have broken out in India'.[75]

To mark the occasion, the journal *Punch* reproduced a solemn cartoon a few days later depicting the Queen in mourning with her eyes raised to heaven, kneeling on the ground to provide comfort to a collapsed group of British women and children, now widowed and orphaned by the war in India (fig. 33). The women portrayed in this image are clothed in black mourning attire; their heads are bowed earnestly, or they pray fervently to heaven with clasped hands and grief-stricken expressions. *Punch* gave its illustration a caption taken from Shakespeare's history play *Henry V* (Act IV): 'O God of Battles! Steel My Soldiers' Hearts!'[76] Henry's lament, of course, was as much a battle cry as an outpouring of existential grief. By invoking an epic battle of historic and national importance, *Punch* consolidated the literary, nationalistic, and religious sentiments of Shakespeare's time and applied those lessons to the modern crisis.

The physical spot designated to host this event of conciliation and hope appropriated a national and commercial space – the Crystal Palace – and turned it into a religious venue. As Thomas Richards and Don Randall described the planning for this event, the vast stage created 'a new kind of political theatre' in which the building's physical lightness and transparency was equated with a 'moral mission of imperial enterprise, suggesting a world-embracing clarity' over religious doubt.[77] In Sydenham, preparations for the actual ceremony included the erection of a portable pulpit in the northeast corner of the Centre Transept in anticipation of large crowds that would be drawn from London. On the day of the event, some 24,000 people gathered at the Crystal Palace, while across England and Ireland, more than 190 churches offered multiple services during the day, and numerous collections were taken from churchgoers to support the families of those lost in India.[78] Six days prior to the event, then, Julia Margaret and her children could very well have paid a visit to the Palace to familiarize themselves with its building and grounds. And if she did not actually attend the religious service held in Sydenham that day, it is unlikely that Cameron and her family, much less the entire Holland Park circle, would have avoided or missed one of the many public church services devoted to express grief and sorrow for the loss of British lives and to process Britain's moral response to the crisis.

Reverend Charles Spurgeon addressed the crowd at the Crystal Palace. He recited the ninth chapter of the Book of Daniel, offered prayers and a sermon, sang hymns, collected donations.[79]

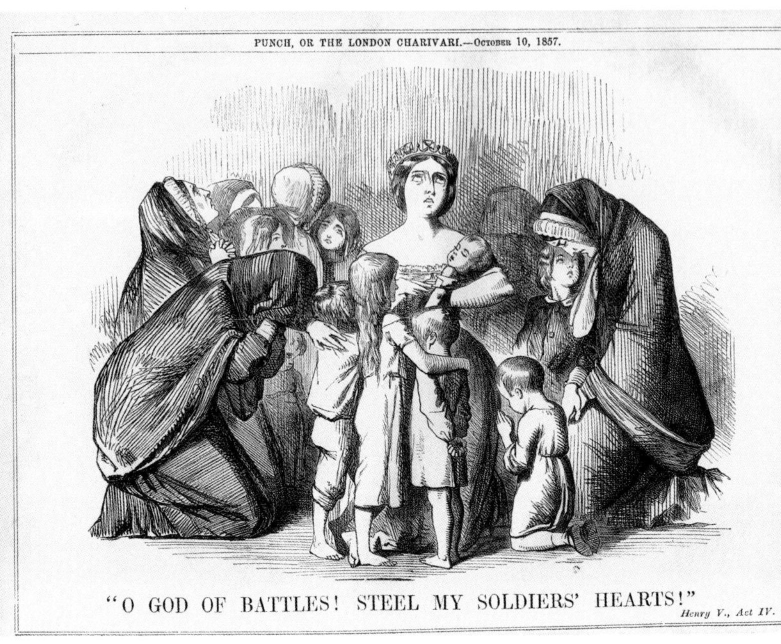

33 *'O God of Battles! Steel My Soldiers' Hearts'*, woodcut engraving from *Punch*, 10 October 1857.

After first calling upon the assembled crowd to feel humility before God and to rejoice in his mercy, he then pivoted to petition God to punish the rebellious sepoys and exact revenge against all those who rebelled against Britain's 'benevolent' rule: 'Give strength to our soldiers to execute upon the criminals the sentence which justice dictates', he preached; 'Lead them on to battle, cheer their hearts; bid them remember that they are not warriors merely, but executioners'.[80] It would seem the language of extermination was neither Christian nor moral, but to Spurgeon, Britain's 'failure' in its recent governance of the colony, as he put it, was owed to its failure to properly civilize the subject races under its charge, for not having the courage to impose Christianity across the whole of the Indian populace, and for undervaluing the importance religion plays in creating moral lessons, in reinforcing obedience, and in providing society with a principled structure and purpose. The *Illustrated London News* depicted the pious speaker and took stock of the enormous crowd (fig. 34).

Cameron and her sons would have heard from Spurgeon that the rebellion was, in fact, a 'Mutiny' against Britain and could not be considered the 'legitimate' rebellion of a subjugated people fighting for their freedom. The preacher reasoned that because 'the rebellious sepoys' had 'voluntarily given themselves up to our dominion and had taken the oath of fealty to her Majesty', they had forfeited their independence in favour of the British sovereign. According to Spurgeon's logic, this meant that the sepoy revolt 'was not that of a nation, as when patriots strove to free their country from the yoke of an oppressor'. In reporting on this event, the *Illustrated London News* repeated what Spurgeon regarded as Britain's failure 'to have suppressed the vile religion of the Hindoos by the strong hand'.[81] According to Rasiah Sugirtharajah, of the many different sermons offered that day, those that were published in press accounts like this one revealed a striking political unity that delegitimized Indian grievances, including

> the active and direct providence of God in the affairs of the British, the British as victims, a chance once again to make Britain worthy of her call, and an opportunity to preach repentance and prayer as a way of avoiding God's chastisement.[82]

34 'The Reverend C. H. Spurgeon', *Illustrated London News*, 17 October 1857, 400.

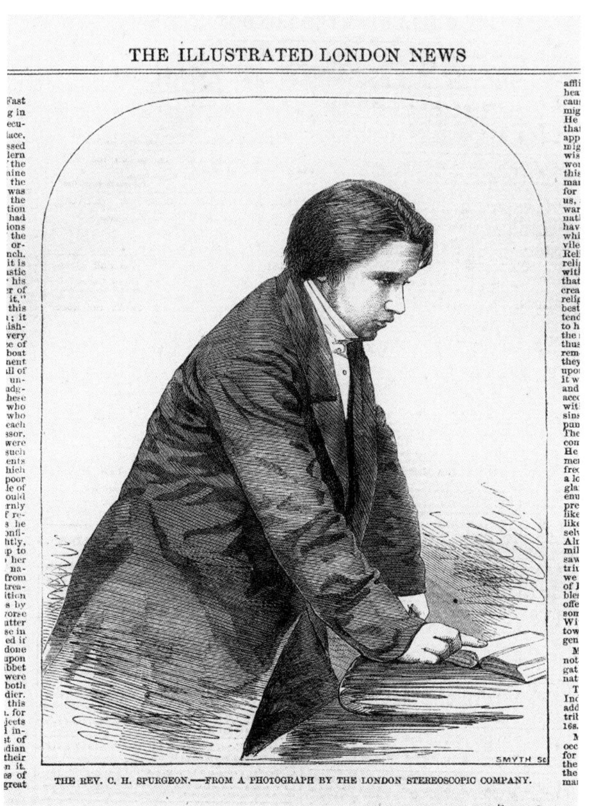

Spurgeon's notion of 'national self-examination', of course, did not consider colonialism oppressive, nor economic development exploitative, nor territorial occupation problematic. Rather, the military underlayment that made imperial control possible was taken as an extension of Britain's evident superiority, its ability to extract wealth from the subcontinent a natural consequence.

Spurgeon's sermon took aim at expunging what he called 'public sins' of the East India Company for its role in creating this national crisis ('the sins of the Government of India are black and deep!') as well as the Company's official position to avoid interference in India's indigenous religions, again laying blame on the Company for refusing to impose Christianity on the colony. Yet Spurgeon's explicitly Christian sermon did not please everyone, especially those in the former government like Thomas Babington Macaulay, Charles Cameron, and Sir Charles Wood, all of whom had advised earlier Parliaments against imposing Christianity on Hindus and Muslims. Following Utilitarian principles, these men established policies to ensure compatibility and compromise among all religious groups.

Writing in his diary of the events of that day, Macaulay despaired of Britain's turn to the vindictive and unforgiving, and reviled Spurgeon's explicitly righteous tone. In response to the Day of National Humiliation and Prayer, Macaulay complained,

> The sermon was detestable; ignorance, stupidity, bigotry. He [Rev. Spurgeon] would have the Government plant missionaries everywhere, invite the sepoy to listen to Christian instruction, and turn the Government schools into Christian seminaries.[83]

Macaulay, like Charles Cameron with whom he served, was not opposed to Christian instruction on principled grounds. Rather, they both had long been convinced that religious indoctrination would backfire against the British and destabilize the social order, thereby undermining the authority of the colonial government. For this self-serving reason, rather than to win doctrinarian disputes over moral grounds, earlier colonial governments in India had pursued a strict policy of religious neutrality. These issues would soon be raised once more in the public forum, especially once Queen Victoria proclaimed herself Empress of India and reconfigured the colonial government.

Cross-Cultural Encounters

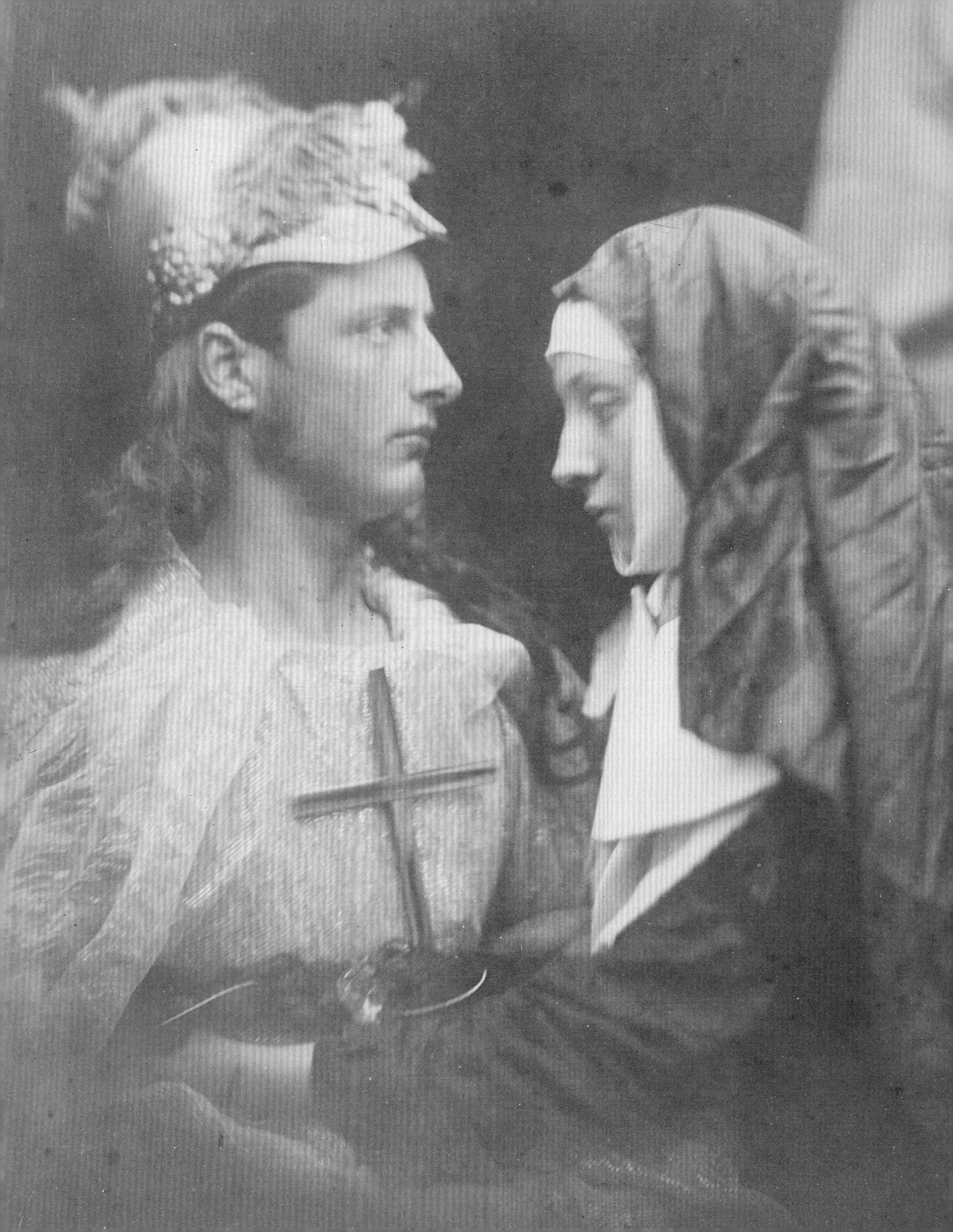

Chapter Four
Galahad's Homecoming

35 Julia Margaret Cameron, *Sir Galahad and the Pale Nun*, 1874 (detail of fig. 42).

EMPIRE'S DESCENDANTS

Julia Margaret's preoccupation with and anxiety about the course of the Indian Uprising was happily side-tracked when she relocated the family dwelling to London at the close of 1858. In leaving the quiet of rural Kent for the bustle of the city, she very much welcomed the change of scenery. At the very least, her new townhouse in Westminster meant that it would be easier to visit her sister Sara and the community of Little Holland House in Kensington. Writing to her daughter Juley, she shared her thoughts about the family's new home and its suitability for their changing needs:

> last ev[ening] we all dined in the new home & slept there & entered upon our new life to day cheerfully & thankfully – Your Papa entirely approves of the house & all the arrangements which is a great blessing to me[.] The children also are very well pleased & I must endeavour also that you should be well pleased & against your return I hope to have your room quite quite ready. I have robbed you of the huge space front room & given you the long back room as little Henry being perpetually in his nursery is amused by the omnibuses passing & all that goes on in the high road – You will not mind a sacrifice to your Henry & Mother[']s is a back room too & a very small one – [1]

The Camerons' move to London in December also allowed Julia Margaret the liberty to imagine how she could deepen the family's connection to the Herschels. She recalled with fondness how Juley had enjoyed her summertime visit to Collingwood, Herschel's estate, and Julia Margaret wanted to reciprocate. In their new London house, she wrote to her daughter about having 'one of the little Herschels' visit occasionally, even planning ahead to the following summer:

> I will write to Lady Herschel when I have breathing time – or breathing power ... I am very glad you repeated Lycidas to dear Sir John Herschel[.] I have so strong a love for him that I felt grateful & happy & proud when I saw you seated with him starting under his face to go to his home & Lady Herschel has written to me most lovingly ab[ou]t you.

Like the Camerons, during the past two years Sir John and Lady Margaret were equally focused on Britain's conflict in India, as their two eldest sons were serving in the East India Company's administration.

Both of Herschel's sons managed to avoid physical danger and did not engage in military conflict. As Sir John had shared with Julia Margaret in 1846, he hoped his older son, William James, would join the Company as a writer. Even aristocrats like the Herschels regarded employment in the Indian Civil Service an honourable occupation for their offspring. To help facilitate William's acceptance, Charles Cameron sent letters of introduction for the young man to advance his position with the Company and smooth his social interaction.[2] Because he was initially stationed in Jangipur, far from the major battlegrounds of the rebellion, William Herschel did not participate as a soldier in the war. In 1857, the young tax collector even complained to his relatives in England that he was 'missing the excitement' of war, although he apparently took some credit for disarming several Indian deserters in the aftermath of a nearby conflict.[3] Sir John's younger son, named John after his father, also entered the East India Company's service. After attending Addiscombe, the Company's military academy, in 1856, he entered the Bengal Engineers. Though prepared for army service, he was not sent to India until after the fighting had concluded and Britain had restored control of the colony (it was not until 1864 that John would join the Great Trigonometric Survey in Madras). Towards the end of 1857, when he grew convinced that his sons had escaped serious danger, Sir John expressed great relief at the prospect of their safe return. In October and November 1857, he received assurances from friends based upon news reports and fresh correspondence contained in the Indian mail.[4] And by 1859, his two sons returned to England on leave bearing photographs that depicted scenes in India for their parents.[5] Arthur Prinsep, too, had re-joined his parents in Little Holland House around this time.

The young man had apparently recovered from the wound to his arm sufficiently well to allow him to sit for a family photograph along with his older brother, Val. In the group portrait, the Prinsep boys sit with their cousins, Julia Margaret's two younger sons, Henry and Charles. They have been posed on a large fallen tree trunk in the back garden lawn of Little Holland House, the site of their usual family gatherings, especially in 1859, when the Camerons also lived in London.[6] The Cameron brothers were several years younger than the Prinsep boys. While the older two slump into their postures, affecting adolescent insouciance, the two younger boys appear awkward and stiff. A fifth boy also appears in the photograph and stares curiously out at the viewer from his spot in the exact centre of the image, though to this day he remains unidentified (fig. 36).

In the photograph, the Cameron brothers face the camera with their legs in front of the tree, with Henry on the far left and Charles on the right. Sitting with his legs to the rear of the fallen tree is Val Prinsep, wearing a cap, on the far right. Arthur Prinsep is on the left, the only one of the boys depicted in profile. Likely composed and taken by Earl Somers, Julia Margaret's brother-in-law, the photograph represents an idyllic scene of leisure and privilege, young cousins gathered together for a family event, or more likely corralled to sit still for a family photograph. Although Arthur Prinsep must have returned from his military service abroad shortly before the photograph was taken, he does not stand out as exceptional from the others represented. Little is known about how easily he fitted back into the extended family in London after his wartime service, how well he reintegrated with family life in Kensington, or when he re-joined his unit. Any documents that might shed light on how the Little Holland House circle absorbed the news about Arthur's purported acts of wartime retribution, or whether they found his actions moral or just, do not survive. And while Somers's photograph did not extol the soldier's virtues, heroism, or personal trials, the young man soon came to represent the national drama of the Indian Uprising on a much larger stage. Julia Margaret made sure that Earl Somers's photograph portraying the Cameron and Prinsep boys was shared widely. She pasted copies in the Lansdowne Album, the Signor Album (dedicated to Watts), and the album she gave to her sister, Maria Jackson. By portraying the extended Pattle cousins, the photograph of the Cameron and Prinsep boys plays a role in these albums that is similar to Cameron's photographs of her two nieces, *Isabel and Adeline Somers*, which she included in the Herschel Album and the Overstone Album (Cox/Ford 1015; HA-34; fig. 37), and the photograph of Julia Jackson and her cousin from the Lansdowne Album (see fig. 24).

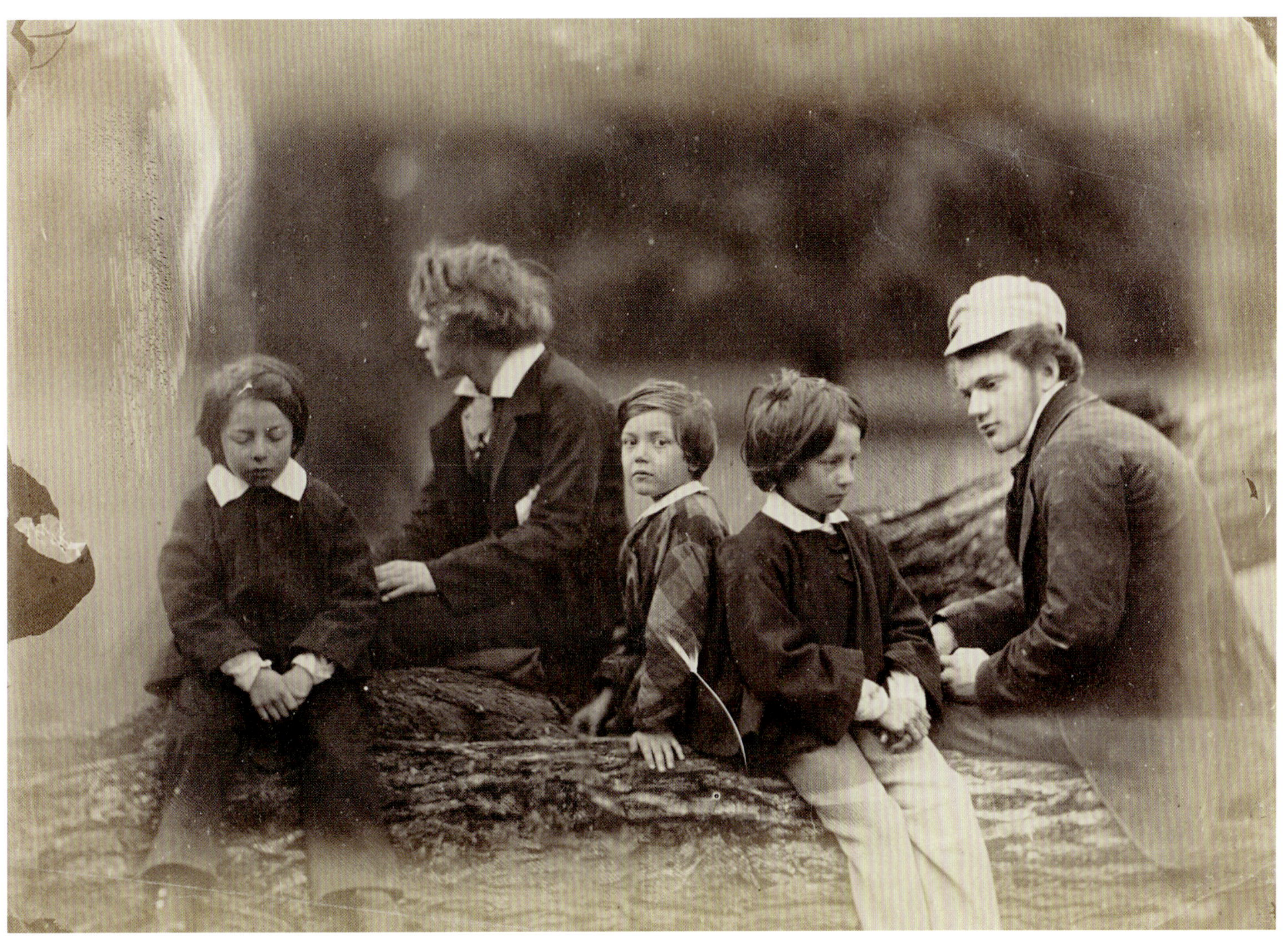

36 Unknown photographer, possibly Lord Somers, untitled family group with (l. to r.) Henry Herschel Hay Cameron, Arthur Prinsep, unknown sitter, Charlie Hay Cameron, Val Prinsep, *c.*1860, albumen print. 15.7 × 20.7 cm.
National Science & Media Museum / Science Museum Group. 2003–5054.

Yet in none of these albums did Cameron include photographs of veterans of the Indian Uprising who were close to the extended family and with whom they likely shared regular correspondence, like Herbert Clogstoun, Septimus Becher, or David Arnot. Many stories of the family's experience in India did not survive.[7] Among the Cameron sisters, for example, the experiences of Cameron's brothers-in-law, John Jackson, Colin Mackenzie, and John Dalrymple, are lost to time, although Mackenzie's activities were remembered in diary form by his second wife, Helen, in her 1857 publication *Six Years in India*, and later, in 1884, in an extensive account of Mackenzie's military exploits written after his death, *Storms and Sunshine of a Soldier's Life*.[8] And although Julia Margaret apparently displayed a framed print in her home that depicted Herbert Clogstoun in action, it is unknown precisely when she acquired it.

The Pattle clan even absorbed Thackeray's cousin, Edward, who had served in India in the company of the Bengal Sappers and Miners and was apparently among the first regiments to respond to the insurgency's outbreak in Meerut. After the war, he too returned to England and, as Ferdinand Mount has written, 'drifted into the family circle of his cousin William Makepeace Thackeray who greeted him with great affection'.[9]

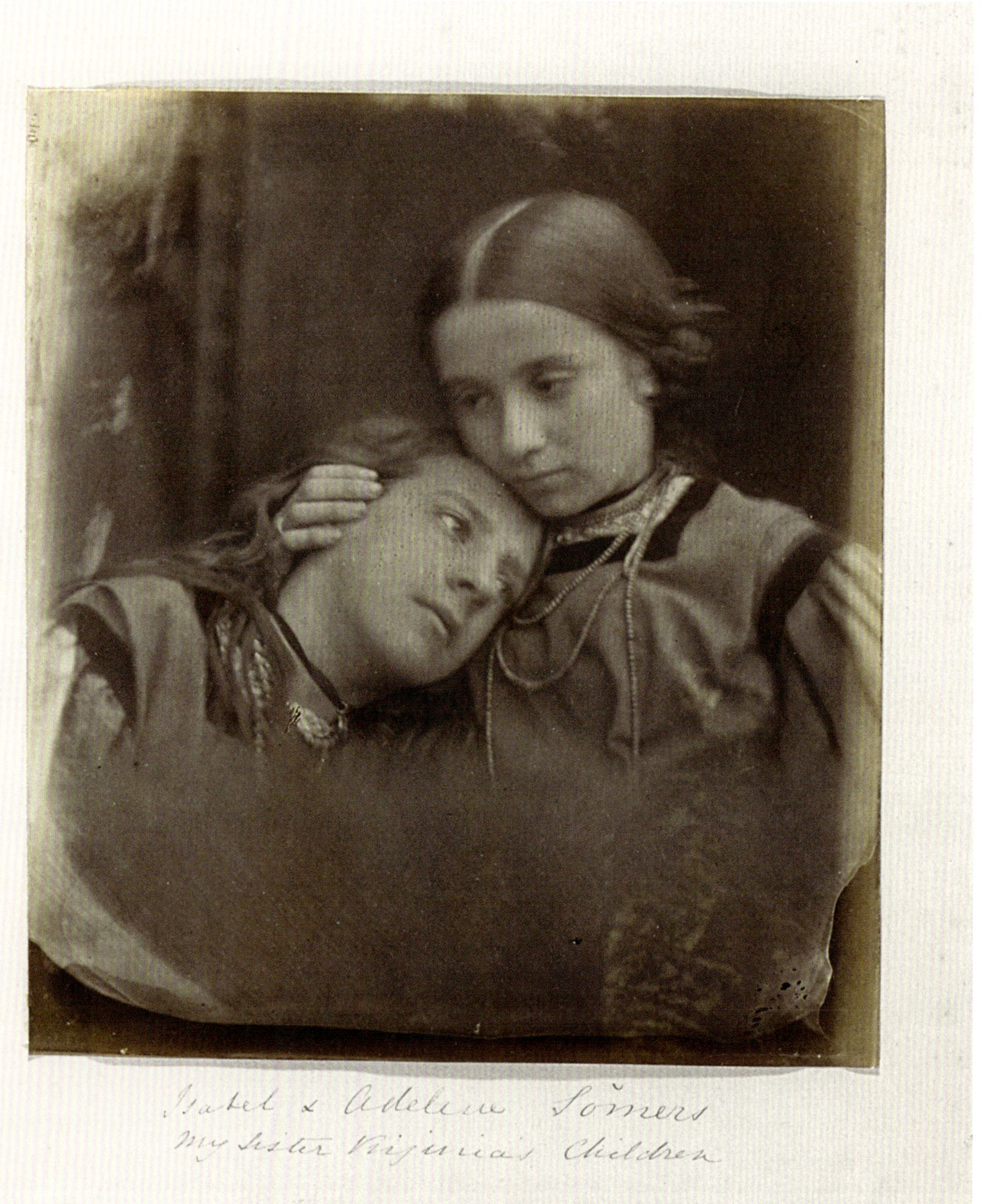

37 Julia Margaret Cameron, *Isabel and Adeline Somers, my Sister Virginia's Children*, 1864, albumen print, 25.2 × 22 cm.

National Science & Media Museum / Science Museum Group. 1984–5017/34.

The author of *Vanity Fair* apparently boasted to his daughters, Annie and Minnie, that their soldier cousin would soon be awarded the Victoria Cross for his bravery in the war, even though Edward Thackeray did not receive the medal until 1862. Nevertheless, in anticipation of his arrival, young Annie reflected that their older cousin's army experience in India would bring honour to the family:

> Papa says, bravery is the best thing in the world & makes everyone more friendly & enthusiastic than cleverness or wisdom, or learning or rank or whatnot, & so it is no wonder that we all feel proud to have a VC come into the family.[10]

After settling in London, Edward Thackeray married Amy Crowe, a member of Thackeray's extended household. The couple later travelled to India, where his wife had two daughters before dying in childbirth with a third. Thackeray's daughters Annie and Minnie took in their two baby cousins, Margie and 'little Annie', whom they raised in London and on the Isle of Wight among the extended Cameron family.[11]

For Julia Margaret Cameron, these young children were both casualties of war and constant reminders of the rebellion. Cameron welcomed them into her home on the Isle of Wight and the children became extensions of her own family and intimate circle. She celebrated their legacy, recognizing the young Clogstouns and young Thackerays as extensions of their soldier-fathers who had won the Victoria Cross. And she photographed them in sympathetic poses, grouping Blanche, Mary, and Adeline Clogstoun, for example, in tender arrangements (Cox/Ford 930–931; fig. 38), or portraying young Margie Thackeray repeatedly surrounded by flowers and bouncing curls (Cox/Ford 1042–1047; fig. 39) or conferring upon her the title *Our Island Daisy* (Cox/Ford 1045). But the common story told today defines these charming photographs of young children in relation to Cameron's altruism and maternal self-identification or to the children's

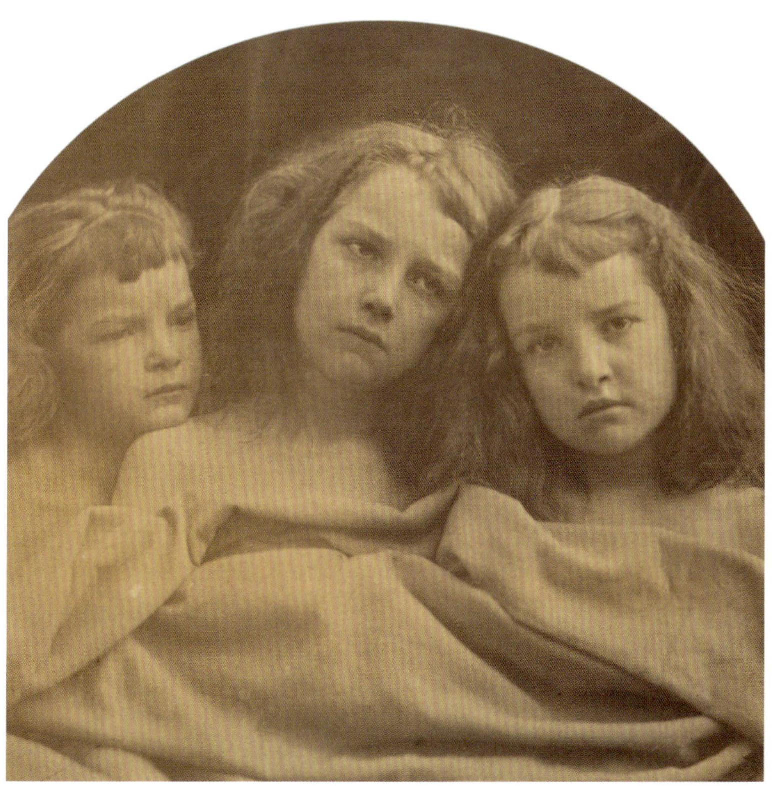

38 Julia Margaret Cameron, *Untitled* (portraying Blanche, Mary, and Adeline Clogstoun), *c.*1868, albumen print, 28.6 × 28.9 cm.
Image courtesy of Heritage Auctions.

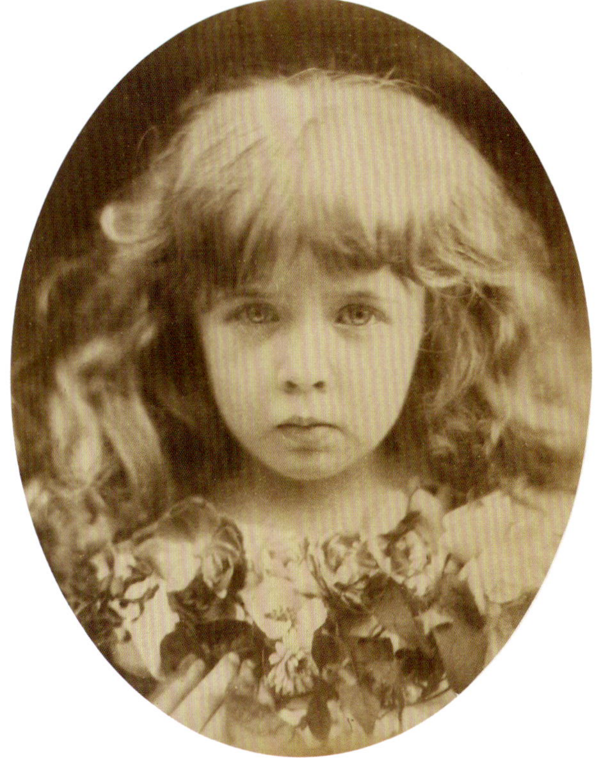

39 Julia Margaret Cameron, *Untitled* (portrait of Margie Thackeray), *c.*1868, albumen print, 30 × 26.6 cm.
 RPS.1243:1–2017.

individual characters and behaviours in the domestic scene. Their colonial context has been effectively stripped away in favour of a historical revision borne of a modernist conceit about artistic self-reflexivity, a position that centres attention on the photographer and ignores the subject's historical context, erasing the sad estrangement of these fathers and daughters, concealing the tragic dissolution of their families of origin, and occluding the imperial story that gave rise to this imagery. For example, Herbert Clogstoun died in 1862 on the battlefield in Madras, and when his children were orphaned in 1870 they were separated: Blanche went to live in Little Holland House as Watts's adoptive daughter and her two sisters moved into the Cameron household in Freshwater. After young Adeline's untimely death in 1872, Mary remained with the Camerons and eventually, in 1875, travelled with them to Ceylon.[12] And yet in Cameron's photograph the three girls huddle close together, almost squeezed into the frame, as if to forestall their later physical separation. Edward Thackeray complained to his cousin Annie that, as a father, he was miserable because his two young daughters 'never utter in his presence', and although he married again and produced four more children, he remained aloof from the children of his first marriage and spent the final thirty years of his life in virtual seclusion in the Mediterranean coastal village of Bordighera.[13]

And yet it is also true that Cameron devoted her life to nurture and rear these children, to make them a part of her vibrant household. But their status as *imagery*, as photographic representations that she produced, collected, and assembled in albums, and then disseminated to family members and friends, is not the same thing as their domestic status as young children in a Victorian household, where their individual personalities for acting in ways that were silly, bashful, daring, retiring, or outgoing, for example, would have defined their relations within the family. The colonial context (as opposed to the familial background) provides a different perspective to the way we might understand how these photographs functioned as representations. Cameron's approach to making photographs and collecting them in albums was also inflected by the after-effects and consequences of colonialism on the British public. These two perspectives come together by means of the trope of inclusion, which emerges as the chief organizing principle that Cameron used to picture the Clogstouns and the Thackerays as part of the extended Pattle clan. No longer war orphans, they have been reclaimed – through the act of photography – and are represented as *belonging* to a loving family. No longer alone or estranged, they are presented as full participants in the collective aesthetic of bourgeois respectability in Victorian England, where they share the same mode of performing an idealized childhood as the one Lord Somers represented in his photograph of the Prinsep and Cameron boys (see fig. 36) or in Julia Margaret's photograph of the two Somers sisters (see fig. 37). More critically, Margie Thackeray, like all three Clogstoun sisters, and even Arthur Prinsep, has been repossessed for the nation by the agency of photography. Recovered at a moment of danger and crisis, these children have been reclaimed by the family precisely when they were most vulnerable. They have been welcomed into the bower of home, and these photographs stand as a testament to, or evidence of, that inclusion. As Laura Peters has affirmed,

> the blood relations and shared language give this home – in the sense of the wider community – an unmistakable difference. It is the myth of an essentialised origin to which the memory will return and which will command 'affection' and, crucially, loyalty. However, implicit in this are a number of disturbing assumptions: the reference to blood relations especially in conjunction with notions of native community constructs a racial grouping; the emphasis on indigeneity distinguishes between the 'natives' and the immigrants; the emphasis on rootedness differentiates this community from travelling and diasporic peoples.[14]

Cameron has recuperated these children – through their photographic portraits – *for the family*, but she has also reintegrated them as subjects *of the nation*. As photographs, they serve as visual emblems that symbolize inclusion, national identity, and the unbreakable continuity of family descendants, while at the same time, their presence in albums assures their future social integration as productive citizens. By rehabilitating their iterative value as signs, these photographs replace 'war orphan' with a distinguished ancestral legacy, which thereby reinscribes their place in the cultural memory of the family and the modern nation.

ARTHUR'S FIRST WOUND

The Day of National Humiliation brought together private lives and community grieving but also fused together civic theatre and religious performance, turning the Crystal Palace into the largest-ever enclosure of the Anglican public square. The event also framed the Indian Uprising as a national symbol for Victoria's reign, as the revolt created an urgent need to represent British power as unwavering and sure. In this unstable and turbulent climate, nationalistic passion was the lens through which families of the East India Company experienced even the smallest of personal dramas. As a result, Arthur Prinsep's story did not end with the private letters the young man sent home to his family. Rather, Arthur's injury, in the context of the 'Indian Mutiny', became a vivid topic of conversation in and beyond Little Holland House. The story inspired William Makepeace Thackeray, Cameron's longstanding friend and a regular guest at the house, to write a poetic tribute to Arthur.

Arthur's personal sacrifice – his war injury – became for Thackeray an indelible emblem and embodiment of national honour. Composed after learning of the event from Arthur's correspondence, Thackeray titled his poem 'Arthur's First Wound'. The entire poem is reprinted as this book's Prologue. In this poem, Thackeray revoked two crucial judgements that made his novel *Vanity Fair* (1848) such an insightful social critique. For one, he transformed Arthur, Thoby Prinsep's younger son, into a heaven-sent warrior-hero, all but reversing his earlier cynical appraisal of heroism in *Vanity Fair*. In the novel, Thackeray regarded heroism with suspicion, so much so that he appended the subtitle 'a novel without a hero'. Thackeray's panegyric to Arthur is therefore an ironic about-face from his treatment of the fictional characters in the novel. Unlike Dobbin, for example, whom Thackeray portrayed as a passive 'non-hero' because he casually slides from one colonial war to another without passion or commitment, he now portrayed the young Arthur as if he possessed fire in the belly. Thackeray also distanced himself in the poem from the shrewd observation made in *Vanity Fair* that favourably reimagined the blurring of national identities in Europe, where a new cosmopolitan unity was then being forged by the steady march of international capitalism. By contrast, in the wake of the rebellion in India, Thackeray now embraced the exact opposite point of view, asserting that Europe should erect formidable boundaries to distance itself from the infernal character of Asia.

In the autumn of 1857, Thackeray read this poem to a small gathering of friends and family at Little Holland House. Hunt recorded that his audience included himself, Tom Hughes and his wife, and Sir Henry Taylor, as well as regular members of this closed circle like Sara and Thoby Prinsep and their extended families. As the close confidant of the Prinseps and a personal friend of the young Arthur, Watts was most certainly present as well. According to Hunt's recollection of the event, many of the men assembled for the reading could barely conceal their tears as they listened to Thackeray, suggesting that even world-toughened and mature men were completely undone by the family's grief and wept openly as they identified with the young boy's personal hardship or in sympathy with the rousing national sentiments that Thackeray stirred.[15] Thackeray's poem was also known to others in Cameron's circle, notably Tennyson and the Oxford theologian Benjamin Jowett, who exchanged letters about its message and the role of poetry during this time of national crisis.

After Cameron took up photography in 1864, some six years after this recital took place, she made photographic portraits of each of the men who witnessed the event, other than Thackeray himself, who died unexpectedly in December 1863. But Cameron's photographs of those in attendance – Hunt, Prinsep, Hughes, Watts, Taylor, Tennyson, and Jowett – became among the most celebrated portraits of this era, emblematic representations of a Victorian high culture and sensibility that was cerebral, philosophical, austere, nationalistic, and male. Cameron included portraits of Hunt (HA-11, -23), Watts (HA-8, -9, -38), Taylor (HA-7, -21, -71), and Tennyson (HA-3, -6, -72, -73, -74, -76, -84) in the Herschel Album, and later displayed photographs of the other men in this select group at her solo exhibitions at the French and German Galleries. And yet, because each of Cameron's portraits represented these men in isolation from the group, we naturally consider their individual personalities and the unique accomplishments of each man apart from the others. But the group also defines a mutually reinforcing collective who shared a common discourse and experience as Thackeray's sounding board and, as gathered in Little Holland House, who shared his understanding about Britain's historical war in India in relation to the nation's imperial ambitions.

On 11 February 1858, Thackeray published 'Arthur's First Wound' in *The Times* (p. 10), thereby engaging a large public audience that far eclipsed the small numbers of the Holland Park circle. But Arthur Prinsep was never identified personally, consistent with the anonymous character of myth-making: for *The Times*, Arthur's identity was irrelevant because the young man represented 'every soldier' who fought in harm's way for Queen and country. Consequently, 'Arthur' became the ideal example of a Victorian hero, where youth and innocence are tested by a merciless adversary; where fearlessness and bravery are rewarded because personal virtue overpowers all hardships, especially those inflicted by opponents deemed morally unworthy; and where moral behaviour is honoured, especially in the face of peril, because the cause is just. But Thackeray did not conceive these heroic qualities in the abstract. The Indian adversary was well known, the moral repute of the British cause beyond reproach, the imperial mission a moral imperative. As the nation required soldiers who exhibited selfless disregard for their own personal safety, a battlefield wound becomes a badge of honour. As a result, the heroic outcome of young Arthur's triumph was all but foreordained.

By analysing several key stanzas from the whole, we might identify the author's sentiments about what he called the justness of the struggle for control of India. The poem is at once a historical narrative and a heroic mythology: intermixed here is the young man's personal misfortune that is accompanied by a magnified sense of alarm resulting from the larger struggle between East and West. Importantly, Thackeray's story is told as if in urgency but is moderated by the need to recite the triumphant legacy of earlier historic battles. Taking on the historian's point of view, he asked his readers to consider the relationship between grand historical events and the small and seemingly insignificant moments of daily life. As he wrote in *Vanity Fair*, 'Are there not little chapters in everybody's life that seem to be nothing, and yet affect all the rest of history?'[16] At stake in this overseas conflict, it should be stressed, was the still-unresolved outcome of Britain's stake in India, but Thackeray did not articulate this concern explicitly, because he did not have to, given the weight of the historical narrative he wrapped around Arthur's story:

> A fragile child no more
> On far India's troubled shore, –
> 'Gainst wild revolt and massacre our English Arthur strives.
> Charge! is the given word,
> And he fearless draws his sword,
> While around him fall a hecatomb of lives.
>
> Now, God be with the right!
> Teach the slender hands to smite,
> As when Israel's champion shepherd foiled the huge Goliath's thrust;
> Where our young sons make their stand –
> The Davids of our land –
> Let the Giant of Revolt bite the dust!

Capitalizing on the popularity of his contemporaneous book *The Newcomes* (1855), Thackeray signed the poem '*Thomas Newcome*' when he published it in *The Times*. One possible reason that Thackeray used his known pseudonym was to adopt a literary contrivance, a strategy that constructed a fictitious framing device to convey the realism of his own Anglo-Indian experience. This approach was like his authorship of *The Newcomes*, which, he wrote, was edited by another alter-ego, 'Arthur Pendennis, Esq'. In the novel, Thackeray portrayed Colonel Newcome as a veteran of several unnamed Indian conflicts. Another motive would be to deflect his own sentimental feelings, borne of his personal connection to the extended Pattle family, onto an alias to divert attention and maintain emotional distance from the domestic story. A third rationale could be Thackeray's interest in emphasizing the power of narrative myth-making, as if to say to his audience: although 'Arthur' suffered his 'first wound' only recently in the battle for India, the experience of colonial warfare and national cry to unite behind all the Arthurs who now fight on behalf of the nation and empire is particular to this very moment, but also timeless and true. As a result, it is to 'Colonel Newcome' that we owe the memory, and the allegory, of Arthur's first wound.

To Thackeray, Britain's war to suppress the rebellion and re-establish control in India was waged legitimately; he saw it as a strike against treason and massacre. Consequently, he considered Indian lives killed in the war utterly dehumanized, even meaningless, as he likened their existence, and their deaths, to a 'hecatomb', an ancient term used to describe a Greek ritual in which priests killed a hundred oxen as a sacrifice to the gods. After comparing youthful Arthur to the biblical David of ancient Judah who bravely saved his nation in battling the giant, Goliath of Philistine, Thackeray brought the comparison home to contemporary London. At the end of the poem, he nostalgically likened young Arthur Prinsep to the nation's modern-day hero, Arthur Wellesley. As Duke of Wellington, Arthur Wellesley defeated Napoleon at Waterloo, a victory that brought him unparalleled military distinction and national fame. But unlike in *Vanity Fair*, where the author famously avoided narrating the ferocious battlefield mêlée that took place that day, Thackeray elevated the Battle of Waterloo in 'Arthur's First Wound' as the decisive turning point that both saved and defined the modern British nation:

> Arthur! thou bear'st the name
> Of that warrior dear to Fame,
> Who, after all his battles, so calmly sank to sleep, –
> With the dint of faded scars
> From the old triumphant wars, –
> In the hush of love and Walmer's castled keep.

In this stanza, the poet emphasized Waterloo as the singular, crucial event that turned the Duke into a national hero. Thackeray linked the famous battle to the nation's contemporary fight to suppress the revolt in India, but also to the earlier historical period of the sixteenth century, when Henry VIII built the armoury at Walmer Castle to create a national system of artillery fortifications to defend the homeland. Collapsing together those two distinct moments of historical time, which metaphorically responded to the nation's shared fear for its existential survival, Thackeray reminded his readers that just five years earlier, on 14 September 1852, the Duke of Wellington had died while in residence at Walmer. Such a reminder would hardly seem necessary, as the Duke's death and funeral in November that year was one of the most significant public events in the nation's history. When the funeral cortege processed through central London, the spectacle was witnessed by more than one million people.[17]

Finally, Thackeray concluded his elegy by paying homage to the contributions of numerous anonymous soldiers who fought to restore the country's honour in the wake of the Indian Uprising, with young Arthur Prinsep now elevated as one among their heroic number:

> May thy name – which now is known
> To loving friends alone –
> Be one thy country yet shall link with many a famous fight;
> And old men give this praise –
> 'His first wound was in those days
> 'When rebel India crouched to Britain's might!'

As William Holman Hunt observed, when the poem was recited at Little Holland House those in attendance 'shared in sympathy in both personal and national tribulation'.[18]

But Thackeray also turned the Prinsep family's (and Pattle clan's) personal worries and hardship into an allegory of national triumph, a victory that makes sense only in opposition to the purported viciousness of the dehumanized Indian rebels against whose 'wild revolt and massacre' Arthur fought, as represented in the poem. Thackeray has all but identified Arthur's Indian adversaries as 'racialized bogeys', as Christopher Herbert called them, 'the projections, scapegoats, surrogates of some dread ultimately not external but internal'.[19] Consequently, the Indian insurgents are represented as dispensable villains, barely human, sacrifices that must be forfeited to the greater cause of colonial expansion. In portraying their deaths as martyrs to a false god, as in a collective hecatomb, Thackeray drew a metaphorical contrast to the notorious site of the massacre at Cawnpore, where a tomb of Christian women and children lay. By referencing this imagery, Thackeray again called to mind an affront so grievous that it alone could legitimize Britain's retributive violence against the colony.

It is also striking that Thackeray embraced the ancient historical account of Thucydides ('Historians have told / How the Spartan boys, of old') to convey to his audience that he was following an established form of historical narration. Priya Satia called this rhetorical device an example of using a historical template that represents 'national glory and redemption pivoting around a central trial of temporary defeat'.[20] At the same time, by invoking and updating Thucydides for his account of the bloody conflict in India, Thackeray aligned his story to the Romanticism of heroic warfare that his readers would have associated with the ancient epic battle between Sparta and Athens. The civil war analogy is not far off, in fact, as Britain's continual use of the term 'Mutiny' for the Indian Uprising suggests that it recognized the mutual interdependence of the two opposing sides, a latent understanding of the conflict embedded in Thackeray's narration. Christopher Herbert identified these same passions and the intensity of Britain's attachment to its 'loyal sepoys' as the chief rationale that informed its outrage at their disloyalty, calling this human bond 'the profound strain of emotion that runs throughout this myth of betrayed interracial homosocial love'.[21] Thackeray built upon this unacknowledged interdependence, and union, by drawing upon the ancient Greek story to ratchet up the historical stakes of his poetic tale. After all, by this time, Thucydides's *History of the Peloponnesian War* had been translated into English numerous times and came to define the idealized sensibilities of *Western* civilization.[22] Therefore, Thackeray's opening lines reminded his audience how a small skirmish involving an anonymous soldier was emblematic of the lightning bolt dividing East and West that was made freshly visible by the Indian Uprising.

And yet, perhaps because Thackeray could not acknowledge what Herbert calls the 'interracial homosocial love' between the British colonizers and Indian insurgents, his poem also reads like an unresolved holdover from his own formative schoolboy days at Charterhouse. Adopting the musical cadence of sing-song Romantic poems that he might have consumed as a child, 'Arthur's First Wound' also reads like a formulaic tribute to the elite, authoritarian, single-sex world that shaped Thackeray's own sense of history and that made him respectable as a Victorian gentleman. In this regard, Thackeray turned Arthur's battlefield wound into another kind of allegory altogether, a rite of passage or gauntlet through which English youths must pass in order to become men. The public-school upbringing referred to here was famously described in Thomas Hughes's novel *Tom Brown's School Days*, first published in 1857, perhaps the era's most famous allegory of such austere upbringing. In Hughes's novel, the book's protagonist first overcomes brutal bullying by classmates and then becomes protector to another boy whom he helps develop into a proper, honest, and upstanding young gentleman. Another version of the childhood bullying story was told by Thackeray himself in *Vanity Fair*, as when Cuff squares off against Dobbin in Dr Swishtail's school early in the novel.[23] It is striking in this regard that Hughes was present for Thackeray's initial reading of the poem, although no formal reaction from Hughes apparently survives.

Chivalry and patriarchy also infuse these verses, undoubtedly informed by the social world of which Thackeray was a part, but also by his own knowledge of news reports about the British women and children who were entangled in the Indian conflict and who perished in Cawnpore. By invoking the divine forces of providence to intervene, shelter, and defend them, however, he avoided the inescapable conclusion that British forces were ineffective, or too late, to secure their safety:

> Protect them, holy Heaven!
> By the bitter war-cry given
> Of our women and our children in their pain!

As Julia Margaret wrote just a few months earlier to her daughter Juley while sitting in the pastoral comfort of Bromley Common, the image of defenceless women and children portrayed in news accounts of the massacre at Cawnpore would not leave her thoughts:

> they force themselves before me & that massacre of those women & children in Nana Sahib's Slaughter House seems as vivid a picture to me in all its solemn reality as is this lovely lawn with its stately cedars.[24]

By connecting the 'bitter war-cry' directly to the pain of '*our* women' and '*our* children', Thackeray's poem emphasizes British losses as a way of keeping these mournful feelings alive.

Thackeray's lines referencing British women and children were also connected to his working

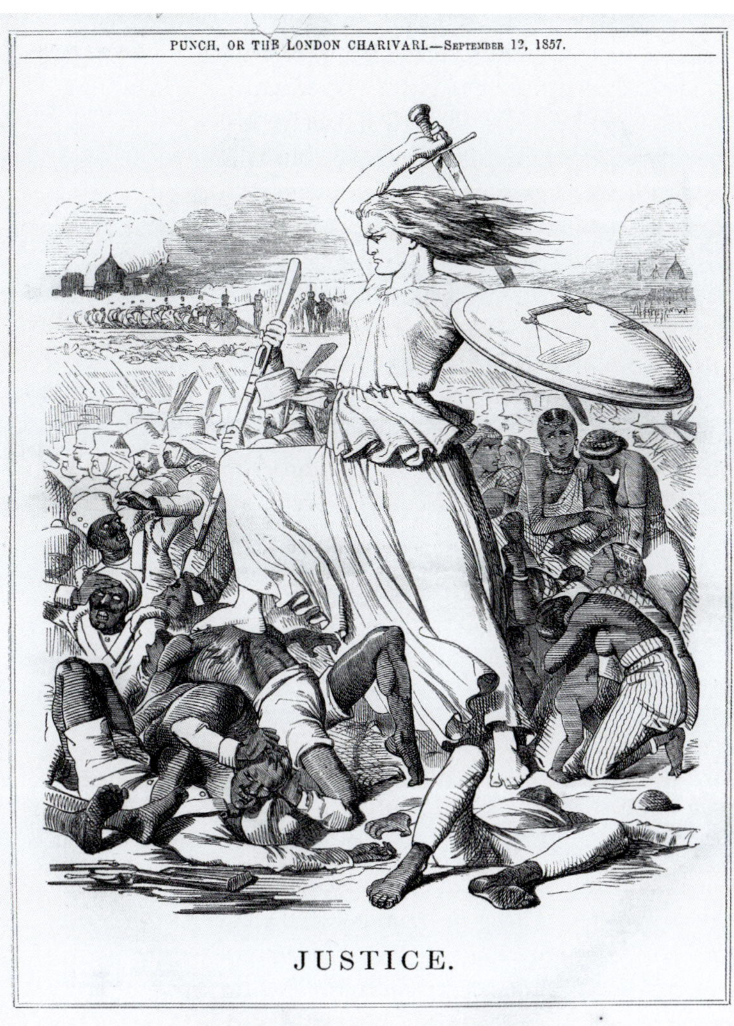

40 Anon., *Justice*, woodcut engraving from *Punch, or the London Charivari*, 12 September 1857, 109.

relationship to the journal *Punch*, as he had been closely associated with its editors since the 1840s.[25] It therefore does not seem coincidental that, precisely around the same time Arthur Prinsep's news describing his battlefield wound first reached Little Holland House in September 1857, *Punch* published a provocative line drawing depicting an allegory of British fury performing 'justice' against Indian rebels, who are represented in the cartoon as sepoys.[26] The journal simply titled the drawing *Justice* (fig. 40), but it could equally have been called '*Rebel India crouch[ing] to Britain's might*', as Thackeray had written. Thackeray's connection to *Punch* cannot be overlooked, as the author regularly gathered around what the *Punch* editors called 'the Mahogany Tree' to select the primary political cartoon of each issue.[27] This cartoon certainly qualified as timely and significant, as it portrayed a gargantuan, stern-faced, and noticeably white figure of Britannia wielding an enormous sword of retribution upon diminutive, frenzied, and dark-skinned Indian men.

In the cartoon, the sepoys are portrayed half-clothed, dazed, trembling and dying, while off to the side, a small group of Indian women plead in vain for mercy, like the huddled, scared women off to the corner in Jacques-Louis David's *Oath of the Horatii*, helpless against the British giant warrior and unable to affect the outcome of the battle. Following Britannia's lead, the formidable British army is depicted as an endless mass of uniformed soldiers who march in sync behind the colossal sword-bearer. These soldiers are represented as exemplars of order and discipline, facelessly alike in their unvarying regularity. Marching in solemn formation, they sweep up the middle ground in a blur of bayonets. Behind them, artillery forces assemble cannons in preparation to deliver Britain's particular form of 'justice' known as 'blowing away' the enemy from the mouths of cannons.[28] And to reinforce the 'justness' of its solemn cause, the artist has represented on Britannia's shield an imprint of the scales of justice. Just as the army is portrayed as faceless, the subjugated Indians are likewise invisible, as if they were unworthy of compassion or kindness, their humanity and hardships imperceptible to the strident Britannia, and presumably too, to the journal's many readers.

MODERNISING 'BOADICEA'

Tennyson was not to be outperformed by Thackeray in creating a poetic commemoration of the Indian Uprising or in commanding national attention. Since 1850, he had been the nation's poet laureate, and had earlier spoken out patriotically at times of national crisis, as with 'The Charge of the Light Brigade', which commemorated British heroism and lives lost during the Crimean War. In poems like 'Britons, Guard Your Own', 'The Third of February, 1852', and 'Hands All Round', he embraced an unabashedly nationalist, commercial, and democratic point of view, as anti-elite as it was anti-French. By publishing these works in the national press, the poet 'was enjoying the publicity game', as Kathryn Ledbetter has demonstrated, anchoring himself in the process 'to middle-class readers who have a grammar or public school education', invoking 'a heroic past with a call to heroic attitudes'.[29]

But in the aftermath of the Indian Uprising, Tennyson was at an immediate loss for how to respond to the outbreak of the fierce war in India. In January 1858, after learning from news reports of the death of General Henry Havelock, who commanded British forces in Cawnpore and Lucknow, Tennyson composed a brief, four-stanza poem and dedicated it to the fallen soldier's memory, even backdating it to Havelock's death, 25 November 1857.[30] After the Cawnpore disaster, Havelock had recaptured the city and then marched north to Lucknow with a British garrison in an initial, unsuccessful attempt to free its besieged stronghold. He then fought alongside reinforcements led by General James Outram in a second assault, one that was ultimately successful. But then Havelock died of dysentery, and not in the heat of battle, making Tennyson's intended elegy an invented story of battlefield heroism, another contribution to the heroic myth-making associated with celebrating Havelock.[31]

Tennyson never published his 1858 poem to honour Havelock. But he did not leave the nationalistic subject matter alone. As the London press gave increasingly greater attention to the insurrection in India, Tennyson was in the middle of composing 'Guinevere', his treasonous foil to King Arthur's ideal example of purity and virtue. Contemporary politics informed Tennyson's imperial storyline that structures *Idylls of the King*, and in 'Guinevere', King Arthur dispenses forgiveness as an act of religious piety, but meets treasonous behaviour with lethal force. Matthew Bevis regarded these oppositional moral principles in the poem as embedded analogies for Britain's response to the anti-colonial revolt as the harsh reaction to a personal betrayal. As Bevis asserted, Tennyson's poem 'Guinevere' points

> to a realm beyond secular politics, but it also acknowledges that imperialist politics demand intervention, and it was this dispute between a Christian religious imperative and the call for military force which had been at the forefront of the public debate over the Indian Mutiny.[32]

Years later, in 1879, Tennyson published 'The Defence of Lucknow', which Victor Kiernan pointedly observed was 'about the dogged British defence of the Residency, not the savage British assault on the city'.[33] Tennyson's nationalism celebrated how the besieged British army overcame sickness and starvation, and he represented the English banner that flew over the Lucknow garrison as a symbolic marker of English endurance and pride. Triumph consumed Tennyson; he was not interested in acts of retribution or revenge. The poet also expressed his patriotic support from a safe distance: as Kiernan commented, 'from the vantage-point of empire he could admire and applaud his England, and reassure himself that beneath all appearances it was still inwardly sound'.[34] Because of this strong conviction, Tennyson praised the British army's valour and its military sacrifice in India in 'The Defence of Lucknow'. Consistent with the elevation of ordinary men into national heroes, he singled out Havelock's name in the final three lines of the poem, thereby combining the great man theory of history with a personal eulogy. In this way, Tennyson reimagined 'Lucknow' as an epic battle worthy of King Arthur: 'Saved by the valour of Havelock, saved by the blessing of heaven! / "Hold it for fifteen days!" we have held it for eighty-seven! / And ever aloft on the palace roof the old banner of England blew' (ll. 104–6).

As numerous families with ties to the colony were absorbing news of the rebellion, Tennyson's closest friends, like Benjamin Jowett, urged him to write a new poem to commemorate the British lives lost in India. Jowett's idea was to persuade Tennyson to expand upon the mournful sentiments that the poet had expressed earlier, as in his widely popular poem 'In Memoriam', thinking that a similar kind of elegy could provide solace to those whose loved ones had perished abroad. Perhaps Jowett was moved by the recent loss of his own brother, Alfred, a surgeon who served in the Indian Medical Service and who was killed in Banta on 4 October 1858.[35] Just two months later, in a letter of December 1858, Jowett even appealed to Tennyson's wife Emily to intercede on his behalf as he urged his friend to consider writing a new poem about the war. 'The subject I mean is "In Memoriam" for the dead in India', he wrote. To clarify, he suggested Tennyson might consider including

> some scenes of Cawnpore and Lucknow; or quite simply and slightly, 'Relatives in India,' the schemings and hopings and imaginings about them, and the fatal missive suddenly announcing their death.[36]

In making this suggestion, Jowett was motivated to use Tennyson's celebrity to provide a means of comforting and consoling readers who were also affected personally by the war. His focus was on mourning, death, and loss. Although he realized that a poetic commemoration set in Cawnpore or Lucknow would inescapably evoke the massacre or the siege that took place in those cities, Jowett believed nevertheless that a poem of this kind could honour the British lives that perished in India in a meaningful way. Of course, his letters are mute about the Indian lives lost during the rebellion or how he thought Tennyson should represent their fates, if at all.

In his correspondence with the Tennysons, Jowett also suggested a range of possible related subjects that were inspired by his own interest in classical Greek history and mythology. But Tennyson overlooked these ideas, which Thackeray used to such advantage in 'Arthur's First Wound'. Instead, Tennyson marked the 1857 rebellion by reaching back to the colonial Roman era of British history and resurrected the name of a legendary tribal queen to allegorize British heroism and rally around the national defence. This figure was Boudicca, Queen of the Iceni tribe, a leader venerated for her military prowess as a defender of her people against the occupying Romans. Styled as 'Boadicea' by Tennyson and others, the warrior queen had already been conjured in contemporary London as a subject on the dramatic stage. In the visual arts, Boadicea was considered an apt subject for the painted designs of the rebuilt Palace at Westminster, where she would represent a pivotal moment in the formation of English identity.[37] Boadicea also enjoyed royal patronage as an ancestral historical figure. Following Britain's mixed success in the Crimean War (even though Britain 'won' the war, the numerous soldiers who were killed in action disrupted the sure moral authority of its leaders), Prince Albert sought to lay claim to the nation's victory in military terms. He did so by associating the ancient warrior queen to Queen Victoria directly: in 1856, Albert commissioned Thomas Thornycroft to design a grand public statue to Boadicea, associating her leadership with Victoria's, an enduring symbol of British strength and national identity.[38]

These representations updated Boadicea as a model for British society, providing a unifying type of Britannia who emblematically could blend the fierce independence of Victorian England with the resurgent nationalism of Boadicea's Iceni tribe. Although Thornycroft's design and the plans for the painting cycle at Westminster both downplayed overt references to Boadicea's historical violence, in 1858, Tennyson seized upon the figure of 'Britain's might' as a potent literary trope for a new poem dedicated to the warrior queen. This meant, of course, that Jowett's well-meaning suggestions for expressing comfort and sorrow never found their compassionate champion. Like the graphic representation of *Justice* in *Punch*, Tennyson conceived his poem 'Boadicea' that year – exactly during the height of Britain's efforts to suppress widespread rebellion and re-establish order in India – and he completed it in 1859.[39] Emily Tennyson recalled that Alfred recited the poem to a group of friends and admirers on 14 February 1859, and then again on 27 April 1860. Of these readings, Tennyson expressed some grudging unhappiness with the poem's ungainly metre, which he claimed made it impossible for anyone else to read the poem as it was truly meant to be heard (and even less possible for Emily to set it to music, as she had with other poems of the 1850s, helping to spread their popular appeal). The poet delayed publishing 'Boadicea' until 1864, when it appeared in the volume *Enoch Arden and Other Poems*.[40]

Despite the poet's misgivings, Tennyson depicted the wild violence in 'Boadicea' without restraint and, it should be noted, as sanctioned by providential approval. The poem is filled with images of fierce battle: anger, thunder, fire. The war's terrible cost is tolled in terms of human pain and loss: moans, wails, agonies. The language is intense and forceful, the images bloody, the sentiments extreme, the victory hard-won yet, above all, necessary and justified:

> [The Gods] have told us all their anger in
> miraculous utterances,
> Thunder, a flying fire in heaven, a murmur
> heard aërially,

Phantom sound of blows descending, moan of an enemy massacred,
Phantom wail of women and children, multitudinous agonies.

Bloodily flow'd the Tamesa rolling phantom bodies of horses and men;
Then a phantom colony smoulder'd on the refluent estuary;
Lastly yonder yester-even, suddenly giddily tottering –
There was one who watch'd and told me – down their statue of Victory fell. (ll. 23–30)

This poem is less a solemn and reflective memorial to those lost in battle than it is a robust call for bloody revenge and violent retaliation.

In the poem, when the warrior queen shrieks 'Trample them under us!' (l. 69) to rally Britons against the occupying Romans, she closely resembles Thackeray's own 'Let the Giant of Revolt bite the dust!'. Both poems give animated voice to the strident figure of a gargantuan Britannia leading her forces in formation across India as depicted visually in *Punch*'s cartoon *Justice*. For Thackeray, the 'barbarians' were the rebellious Indians who must be subdued. For Tennyson, India's rebellion was equivalent to Britain's betrayal, which metaphorically breathed new life into its ancient taste for vengeance and reanimated the national heroics of a mythic queen. Tennyson's graphic imagery was as vivid as Thackeray's: blood flows on the Thames as 'phantom bodies' of horses and men float by, while the cries of massacred women and children echo in the air. The allusions to Cawnpore are unmistakable. Historians have suggested that Tennyson's poem used the so-called savagery of Boadicea's 'primitivism' to stoke anxieties against Victorian women who threatened to rebel against their subjugated place in society, and this parallel might lie latent in the poem.[41] But it is the anti-colonial rebellion in India that links 'Boadicea' to 'Arthur's First Wound', as well as the fact that both poems found their first public audience in Little Holland House. Several years later, Tennyson famously justified Britain's violent reprisals in India when he was confronted again by the nation's suppression of a different insurrection, this time in 1865 in Jamaica, when British soldiers once more crushed a colonial rebellion: in response to being reminded of Britain's merciless suppression of the 1857 revolt in India, Tennyson replied, 'That's not like Oriental cruelty'.[42]

Amid the multiple crises of 1857 and 1858, Jowett shared with Tennyson his thoughts that the day's political challenges called for a new kind of empathetic poetic response, a healing gesture. In a world seemingly coming apart at the seams, he wrote, Tennyson should respond to the great need for what he called the unifying power of poetry. He sympathized that it was difficult for anyone to know how best to respond to pain and grief in the world, acknowledging that easy and uncomplicated answers were difficult to find, and that Thackeray was a hard act to follow. Despairing of his own meagre advice in this regard, Jowett unburdened his sentiments to Tennyson in an undated letter:

> the whole world is morbid with dissecting and analysing itself and wants to be comforted and put together again. Might not this be the poet's office, to utter the 'better voice' while Thackeray is uttering the worse one? I don't mean to blame Thackeray, for I desire to take the world as it is in this present age, crammed with self-consciousness, and no doubt Thackeray's views are of some value in the direction of anti-humbug.
>
> But there is another note needed afterwards to show the good side of human nature and to condone its frailties which Thackeray will never strike. That note would be most thankfully received by the better part of the world.[43]

Tennyson's son Hallam, who preserved Jowett's words, did not speculate what worldly sorrows Jowett had in mind when he penned his letter to Tennyson, allowing for multiple interpretations. One historian asserted that Jowett's allusion here to 'the two voices' corresponds well to Tennyson's poem of the same title, published in 1842, which reflects the narrator's indecision and internal psychological distress. Another scholar, drawing equally viable conclusions, suggested that political, ideological, and social factions of the day made it impossible to discern how one should recognize 'the good side of human nature' from its opposite, citing the fact that Thackeray, for example, had censured French colonialism in Algeria while at the very same time applauded Britain's suppression of the Sikhs in the Punjab.[44]

It is also possible that Jowett's desire to balance 'the good side of human nature' with its opposite could not ultimately be achieved, because the world seems unable to balance the grand illusions of nationalistic identity together with the accidental, but intensely meaningful 'little chapters in everybody's life' that 'affect all the rest of history', as Thackeray wrote in *Vanity Fair*. It would seem yet another mark of hubris, ripe for Thackeray's ridicule, to give priority to either the grand narrative or the 'little chapter'. In *Vanity Fair*, Thackeray notably avoided using a regal example to define English identity, suggesting instead that a more commonplace sense of nationalistic pride could never be represented adequately. For example, immediately following the scene in which the cannonballs flew over Waterloo, he wrote,

> All of us have read of what occurred during that interval. *The tale is in every Englishman's mouth*; and you and I, who were children when the great battle was won and lost, are never tired of hearing and recounting the history of that famous action. Its remembrance rankles still in the bosoms of millions of the countrymen of those brave men who lost the day. They pant for an opportunity of revenging that humiliation; and if a contest, ending in a victory on their part, should ensue, elating them in their turn, and leaving its cursed legacy of hatred and rage behind to us, there is no end to the so-called glory and shame, and to the alternations of successful and unsuccessful murder, in which two high-spirited nations might engage.[45]

It is striking to recognize that Thackeray imagined that bloodlust for revenge lay dormant in the aftermath of every political war, from Waterloo to the Indian Uprising.

GALAHAD'S HOMECOMING

George Frederic Watts, the painter who resided at Little Holland House, could not have avoided the full-throated display of national pride that erupted when Sara Prinsep talked about her son's military service. During this time, Watts was engaged in his own patriotic endeavour, depicting portraits of national heroes for a British 'Hall of Fame'. Julia Margaret Cameron was certainly aware of this ambitious project, as she petitioned Watts in 1860 to include her friend Sir Henry Taylor as part of Watts's project, all but demanding of the painter that he 'fulfil your reiterated intention & paint for your gallery of great men this great head'.[46] In turn, Watts specifically asked for her help in 1861 to secure sittings for him from Michael Faraday, the scientist who discovered electromagnetism, and Richard Owen, the renowned biologist.[47] Although Watts never painted those two portraits, Julia Margaret understood Watts's 'Hall of Fame' in nationalistic terms and was eager to capitalize on a nascent celebrity culture that encouraged the public to collect *carte-de-visite* portrait photographs of eminent Victorians.[48]

More than likely, Watts was also directly involved in conversations with the Prinseps about their son in India, as Watts was very fond of Arthur, who reciprocated the painter's affection. In his letter home, Arthur asked his mother specifically to give his personal regards to 'the Signor', the family's pet name for Watts.[49] Writing a letter to Arthur in India was unlikely to have come easily from Watts, as he complained to Julia Margaret that it was often difficult for him to find the right words: 'I have not like you a pocket full of word money,' he claimed; 'mine has to be dug with labour out of the mine in the rough metal & shaped with disheartening toil before it can be made to represent the current coin'.[50] Were he to have received news of the Indian Uprising directly from Arthur's letter or had he been present for Thackeray's reading, Watts would have understood the young soldier's first-hand account of his thirst for revenge.

After Arthur Prinsep returned to England, perhaps while on leave from his unit in India, Watts posed the young soldier as a chivalric warrior for a painting that he titled *Sir Galahad* (fig. 41). In 1862, Watts completed the painting and exhibited it at the Royal Academy. The painting depicted Galahad as the fair knight from King Arthur's circle who was 'just and faithful', much as Tennyson had first conjured in 1842 in his poem of the same name, the same knight who later assumed a prominent role in the *Idylls of the King*. Unlike Rossetti's woodcut image of *Galahad* in the 1857 *Moxon Tennyson*, where that artist portrayed the knight indoors, at night and in the 'Ruined Chapel', Watts depicted Sir Galahad after he has dismounted from his white horse in a dense forest. The young knight strikes an attitude of devotion, his helmet off, hands clasped before him, quiet and serene, seemingly innocent of the unworldly vision of the Holy Grail that soon awaits him.

Watts's painting became immediately popular after its exhibition, resonating with at least three overlapping audiences. One responded to the growing public admiration for the legend of King Arthur. The poem's associations of manly strength tempered by innocence could not be dissociated from the painting, especially in the wake of the recent wars in Crimea and in India that took so many of the nation's young sons. Britain portrayed its war in India, as Evangelical leaders like Reverend Spurgeon insisted, as a moral and just conflict, making Tennyson's knight a warrior for modern times: Galahad says in the poem, 'My strength is as the strength of ten, / Because my heart is pure.' These sentiments enhanced the popularity of the poem, especially after 1859, when Tennyson published the poem as part of *Idylls of the King*. According to Hallam Tennyson, 'ten thousand copies [of the *Idylls*] had been sold in the first week', and hundreds more were selling monthly, especially after positive critical reviews were published in the *Spectator*, the *Edinburgh Review*, and the *Quarterly Review*.[51]

A second set of associations emerged from Watts's painting that connected Galahad's slender physical appearance to Tennyson's depiction of youthful virtue. The poem described Galahad as a 'maiden knight'. But the poet tethered this feminine quality to the youth's emerging masculinity, helping crystalize an idealized type of virile young manhood who is virtuous precisely because he is fearless in his innocence. This legend of Galahad could not be separated from the 'manly Christianity' and Victorian chivalry idealized by writers like Thomas Hughes, Charles Kingsley, and Charlotte Yonge.[52] For this reason, inexpensive reproductions of Watts's painting were soon 'hung in nurseries and schoolrooms throughout England and the British Empire'.[53] Watts apparently demurred that Tennyson's verses had anything to do with his painting, citing earlier drawings he had made of Arthur Prinsep dating from 1855, prior to the young man's commission in the Indian army. And although Watts's drawings of Arthur do bear a certain resemblance to his painting of Sir Galahad, they also resemble an androgynous likeness to the actress Ellen Terry, whom Watts later married in 1864.[54]

Watts's painting was also claimed by a public who wanted to commemorate the tragic loss of

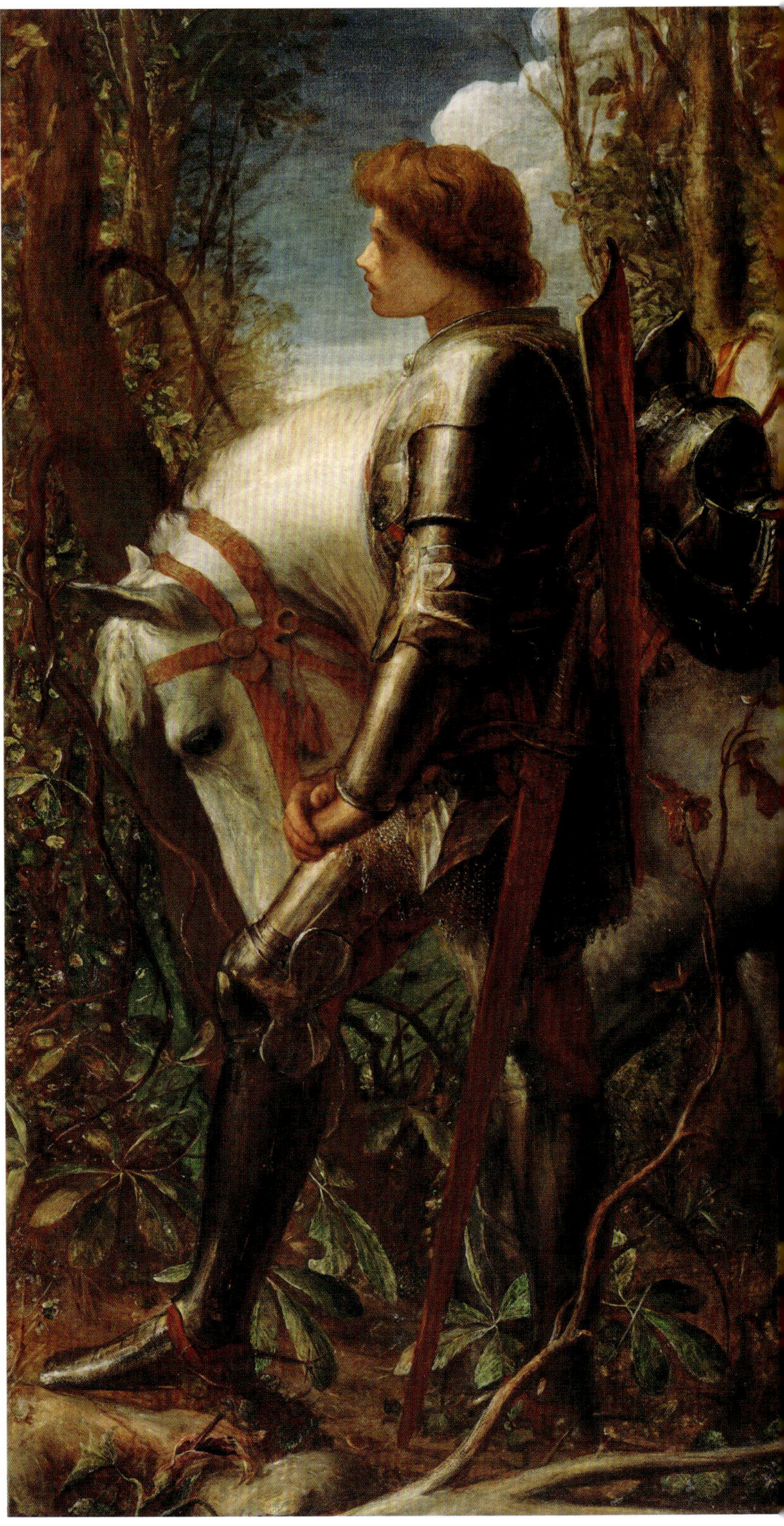

41 George Frederic Watts, *Sir Galahad*, 1860–2, oil on canvas, 191.8 × 107 cm.

Harvard Art Museums / Fogg Museum, Bequest of Grenville L. Winthrop, © President and Fellows of Harvard College. 1943.209.

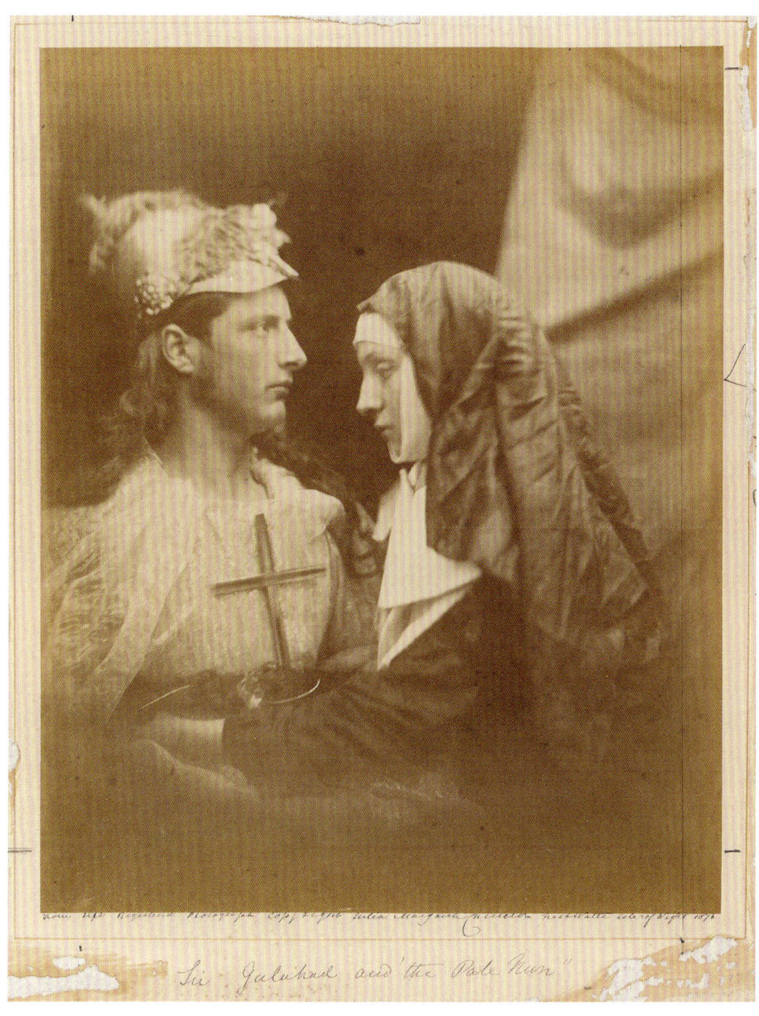

42 Julia Margaret Cameron, *Sir Galahad and the Pale Nun*, 1874, albumen print, 34.3 × 26.5 cm.

© Royal Photographic Society / Victoria and Albert Museum, London. RPS.896–2017.

a son or brother who died overseas, in which case *Sir Galahad* became an emblem of national sacrifice. It is striking, however, that critics of the time chose not to associate *Sir Galahad* directly with any contemporary wars, and equally fascinating that they did not know Watts's model, Arthur Prinsep, served the nation as a soldier in India. For his part, Watts never drew an explicit connection to either point. As Watts was never taken for a modern allegorist, it makes sense that contemporary critical responses ignored overseas conflicts and interpreted *Sir Galahad* strictly in relation to the moral codes of medieval chivalry. And yet, Arthur Prinsep's actions in India provide a powerful counter-narrative that complicates the association of Watts's model for the pure and innocent *Sir Galahad*. After all, the young soldier's actions to suppress the Indian Uprising were entirely *anti*-chivalric. Crusading knights were supposed to be virtuous, moral defenders of the faith. Vengeance and retaliation, by contrast, are wholly antithetical to, one might even say an entire repudiation of, the morally high principles of honour, mercy, and justice that defined the ancient chivalric code.

While this example demonstrates the disjunction (and apparent irrelevance) between the life of an artist's model and his represented form in allegorical or mythological painting, it also sheds light on ways in which historical events that inform those allegories, like the insurrection in India, can be expunged from the historical record by means of aesthetic transformation, even one that ironically makes the legend of King Arthur's court accessible through inexpensive and popular reproductions. In *Sir Galahad*, Watts metaphorically restaged the colonial battleground upon which Arthur Prinsep 'lost his shako' and suffered a flesh wound to his arm as a soldier in the East India Company's army. Watts then metaphorically healed and resurrected the young, wounded Arthur Prinsep in symbolic form and, like Thackeray, portrayed the soldier as the timeless medieval knight of legend whose life is blessed by providence.

GALAHAD IN FRESHWATER

Years later, in 1874, long after Watts's painting had gained celebrity, and fifteen years after Tennyson first published *Idylls of the King*, Cameron issued her own photographic interpretation of selections from the poem. In her portfolio, she matched her photographs with specific excerpts from the poem that she wrote out in her own hand. That year, she portrayed *Sir Galahad and the Pale Nun* (Cox/Ford 1169; fig. 42). Rather than drawing her inspiration from the 1842 poem 'Sir Galahad', Cameron chose her scene from 'The Holy Grail' in the 1859 *Idylls of the King*. Here, Tennyson describes the exchange that takes place between the fair knight and a fervently inspired nun who believes her visions of the Grail's return to earth could heal the broken world. Accordingly, Cameron's photograph depicts the moment when the nun bestows upon Galahad magical powers. She encircles him in 'a strong sword-belt, and wove with silver thread / And crimson in the belt a strange device, / A crimson grail with a silver beam' (ll. 153–5). In this version of Galahad's story, the knight represents evangelizing faith triumphing over militarism, hope and anticipation prevailing over hopelessness and despair, unity succeeding over discord. Cameron embarked upon her project with zeal and intensity, her aim to elevate photography to the moral example of Tennyson's poetry, her stated goal to surpass earlier interpretations of the poem by artists like Dante Gabriel Rossetti and Gustave Doré.[55] In her earnestness, Cameron staged each image in the portfolio carefully and chose just the right models to embody her characters' emotional state and portray the dramatic action of the scene.

But in 1923, Virginia Woolf, Cameron's great-niece, was having none of it. In the play she wrote that year, *Freshwater*, Woolf lampooned Cameron and her circle as hopelessly dated and archaic. She interpreted the photographic portfolios that Cameron made depicting Tennyson's *Idylls* as prime examples of an outmoded Victorian mindset, overworked and overly sentimental. For Woolf, *Sir Galahad and the Pale Nun* was emblematic: she found Cameron's staged narratives unconvincing, her search for ideal models pompous, and her attempt to re-create the mythical and idyllic past an anti-modern exercise in futility. As a result, Woolf seized on Cameron's representation of Sir Galahad for noteworthy ridicule in *Freshwater*. In setting up the action of the first scene, Woolf cues Cameron's character (here styled as 'Mrs. C.') by having a maid inform her that the family's bags have been packed in preparation for their travel abroad. They are off to India:

> MRS. C. Packed – why packed? Ah – I remember. We start for India at two thirty sharp. ... Did you ever hear anything so provoking? I've only just time to finish my study of Sir Galahad watching the Holy Grail by moonlight. Cook was posed. The light superb. At the last moment up comes word that Galahad has to take the sheep to Yarmouth. It's market day. Sheep! Market day! [*With great scorn*] Where I'm to find another Galahad heaven only knows![56]

In *Freshwater*, Woolf poked fun at Cameron's obsessions as the misdirected ambitions of pursuing 'high art' and derided her feverish intensity as exasperating narcissism. My purpose in raising Woolf's objections here is not to defend or support Cameron's interpretation of Tennyson's poem or Woolf's appraisal of Julia Margaret's photograph. In the philosophical and aesthetic debates that separate the acolytes of modernism from its Victorian, Romantic opposite, Woolf and Cameron square off in well-known opposing corners.

But by specifically invoking *India*, Woolf has inserted something important and essential, reclaiming a historical truth: she has re-situated the representation of Sir Galahad in relation to the story's imperial context by reframing the Kingdom of King Arthur in relation to Britain's global empire. *Why India*? In this scene from the play, Woolf encourages us to imagine Cameron composing her representation of Galahad as inflected by latent images of Britain's multiple historical conflicts in India, where colonial wars of the 1840s and 1850s and the ghostly scars of the Indian Uprising were still visible in the present. For Woolf, modernism makes it possible to reinscribe this cultural narrative, even by allowing everyday life to intercede, as she did in her novels, because that intercession enabled readers to capture and reckon with the interwoven texture of the present and the past, especially the bloody and violent past from which the modern world could not escape.

And by summoning *India* to her imagined scene of art-making on the Isle of Wight, Woolf even manages to 'get it wrong', but very likely by design. In 1875, as Virginia Woolf knew quite well, the Camerons were preparing to travel to *Ceylon*, not India. And yet, for Woolf, it was the 1857 Indian Uprising that cast the long shadow of history onto Cameron and her creative activities in Freshwater, which explains its presence here, like a talisman that symbolizes something so terrible it cannot be named. The very memory of India cannot be erased. In a diary entry of January 1918, for example, Woolf returned to a conversation she had had recently with Lady Jane Grant Strachey (the mother of her friend Lytton Strachey of the Bloomsbury Group). Lady Strachey's father served in the Indian Civil Service after the 1857 Uprising and later went on to serve as Lieutenant-Governor of Bengal. Woolf reflected upon their exchange:

> I suppose [Lady Strachey] ruminates over her past. According to her it was a splendid time to live in. For one thing, *she remembers India before the Mutiny*.

> 'Splendid men they were, the [East India] Company servants. Your Prinsep relations among the finest. Fancy my horror when I went to see the Delhi pictures the other day, & found they'd called the Prinsep Pier the Princes Pier!' [My emphasis][57]

For Woolf's brand of modernism, the past never completely disappeared, and the present was always populated by revenants. Consequently, her play, *Freshwater*, collapses Cameron's preparation for travel to India together with the making of a mythological subject in art, effectively capturing the intertwined texture in which staging a representation of Sir Galahad could not be separated from the past life and daily experience that informed the present.

Perhaps the most absurd moment in this imagined dialogue from *Freshwater* is Woolf's insistence that a fixed timetable literally coerces Julia Margaret Cameron's activities. Time is imminent and running short in this scene: Cameron appears to be 'on the clock' and must hurry up as she prepares to depart for India, *precisely* at 'two thirty sharp', no earlier, no later.[58] But the force of Virginia Woolf's critique – that is, her insistent focus on *time* – makes it clear that Woolf believed Julia Margaret's cultural moment had actually *passed her by*: in 1874, in other words, it was no longer possible to depict Sir Galahad outside of history, as if his essence could be captured as a mythical hero or crusading saviour who could liberate the Holy Land by bringing Christianity to the heathen. At least Woolf could not take such a proposition seriously. But Cameron had not yet received this message, as she was still trying to mythologize the past, much like Thackeray, Tennyson, and Watts did before her. To Woolf, Cameron was still quite stuck in that antiquated mindset. But Woolf imagined the inescapable force of time rushing by and inserted the mystical presence of India as a magical colonial destination to which Cameron was returning. In so doing, Woolf swept irony aside and injected instead an understated but nonetheless powerful historical sensibility, one that effectively disrupts the ahistorical and apolitical farce she had been writing about her Great-Aunt Julia. If the era of timeless mythology was now a thing of the past, Woolf suggests, so too was the plausible fiction that made Cameron's photographed *tableaux vivants* possible, as these too were self-evidently mired in the ageless and Romantic world of Victoriana.

But more insightfully, Woolf also intimates in this scene that the historical moment had *not yet come* for Cameron to be able to reclaim Galahad's antiquarian roots – that is, in relation to the colonial struggle for India – because only Woolf's later brand of detached modernism could make that relationship visible. In *Freshwater*, Julia Margaret's character is insensible to these nuances of time and place, unconcerned to disentangle myth from history, unable to reconcile the present and the past. But by collapsing Julia Margaret's 'return to India' with the photographer's attempt to portray *Sir Galahad watching the Holy Grail by moonlight*, Woolf implies that the past *can* be reinterpreted successfully and understood anew, but only from a much later vantage point. From the full distance of time, India and Galahad can now be reinscribed in a fresh historical narrative, one that recaptures that which has been, but is now forgotten: the ardent nationalism that inspired Tennyson; the committed colonialism that shaped Cameron; in addition, the threat to the imperial regime posed by the Indian Uprising; the threat to the moral order laid visible by Britain's acts of retribution. But these complex and intertwined political identities are unavailable to the oblivious photographer, at least as Woolf represents her in the play. As Woolf explains, Cameron's moments are *interfered with* by the pressure of the infernal clock ('two thirty sharp'), and *interrupted by* the ordinary and routine facts of daily life, the rude and unwelcome need for her model to step out of the frame and take the sheep to market.

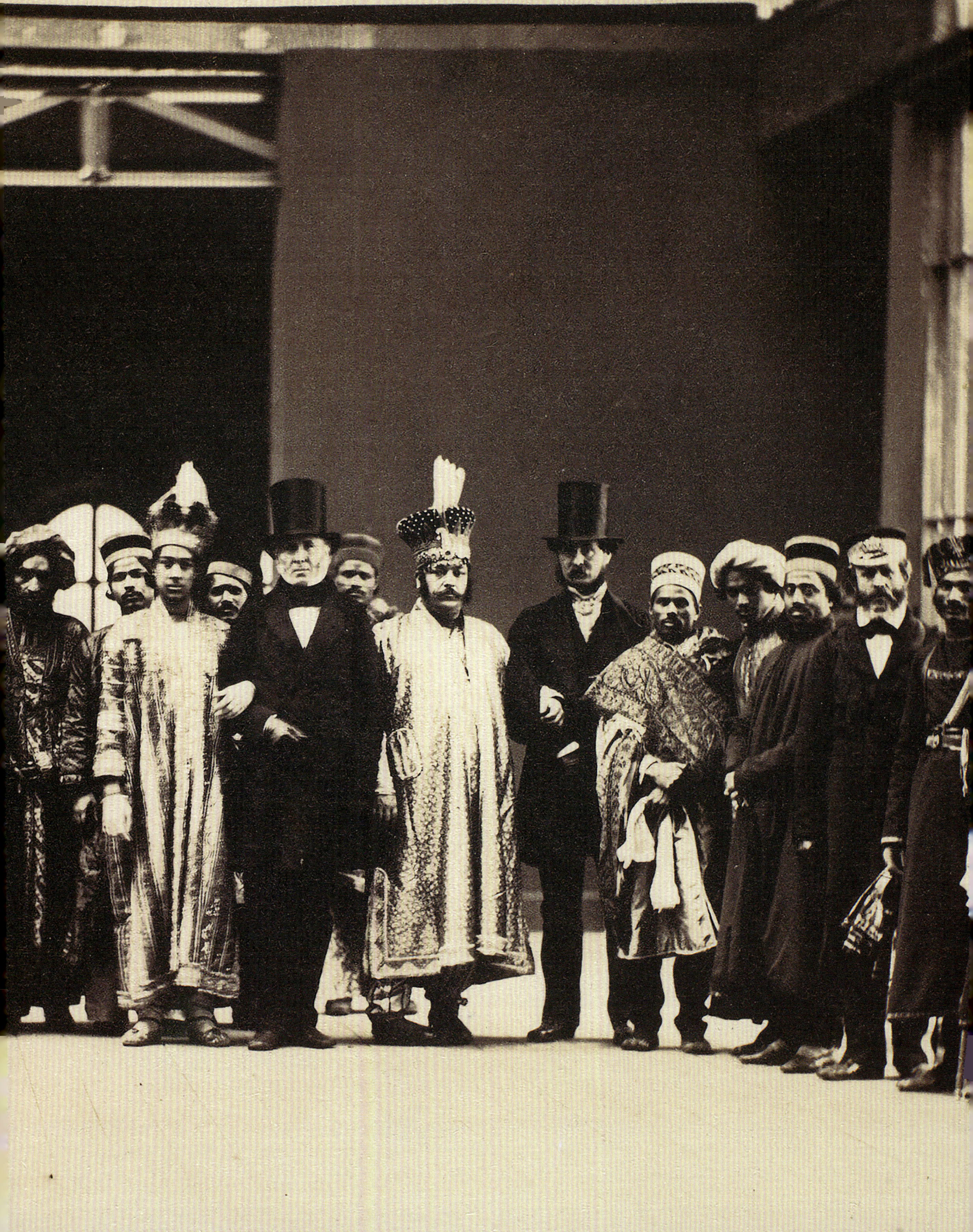

Chapter Five
An Indian Prince in London

43 Leonida Caldisi, *The Princes of Oude, India, at Manchester Art Treasures, April 1857* (detail of fig. 51).

A QUESTION OF SOVEREIGNTY

In 1850, when Sir John Herschel engaged Charles Cameron to ask about the East India Company's policies 'for making a step in the direction of erecting India into a self-governing nation or assemblage of nations', he was opening for discussion the question of Indian sovereignty. Sovereignty refers specifically to self-government, which is to say, the authority of the people living in a state to govern themselves. But in the *colonial* context, sovereignty also refers to the extension of state rule *beyond the nation's borders*, that is, to the governance of others in foreign lands. This concept presumes that some sort of national cohesion exists, a defined common sense of statehood to which those living in the nation's territory identify or belong. The concept relies for its authority upon the 'rule of law'.[1]

Statehood, in turn, creates the necessary precondition for the idea of a person's subjecthood, which is the foundation for the legal status that defines an individual's public identity as a citizen. These terms are not only political, but they also define legal and cultural identity. Because the East India Company first established its rule in India as a private company and not as a state, yet established its legal claims based upon charters granted by the English Crown and approved by Parliament, questions of sovereignty were kept deliberately ambiguous by the East India Company for centuries, leaving the status of the subjecthood of indigenous Indians equally unclear into the nineteenth century.[2] In seeking greater clarity about the nature of this relationship from Cameron in his letter, Herschel addressed these very questions head-on, as Charles Cameron, the legal member of the Supreme Council, was an acknowledged expert on this topic.

The Indian Uprising magnified the ambiguous status of native Indian subjecthood, as colonial governance of the vast territories held by the Company had really been accomplished for some time by its Residents' coordination with local officials in the name of kings, princes, rajahs, lords, and other indigenous leaders. The eighteenth-century Residency system, by which the Company installed political agents to control regional territories, effectively extended the empire's influence without incurring economic costs or military risks. This system, called *indirect rule*, relied upon the Company's nominal acceptance of Mughal sovereignty and a series of unequal treaties made with native princes.[3] Because the system permitted the Mughal emperor to retain honorifics and conduct rituals, but exercise no real power, indirect rule was referred to as a 'masked system'.[4] Thoby Prinsep was among the earliest to implement this system as one of the Company's valued political agents, where he played a significant role in governing the colony. For example, Prinsep was involved in the disputes surrounding the replacement of Charles Metcalfe in 1827 as Resident of Delhi, the dismissal of Sir Edward Colebrooke in 1829, and the subsequent installation of Charles Trevelyan as an advisor to the Raja of Bharatpur.[5]

Indirect rule was also responsible for establishing the elaborate series of diplomatic conventions and ceremonial practices in which the Company's agents were expected to perform.[6] One such political attaché was Major George Broadfoot, with whom Julia Margaret Cameron corresponded in 1844 and 1845. Broadfoot had been appointed the Company's Resident in the Punjab by Governor-General Hardinge. As Company agent, he held a double identity as a civil servant and military officer. In the regional areas, territorial and political authority was shared with traditional leaders like native princes and tribal heads, although their lands were fragmented, and their control decentralized. In the North-West Provinces and in Awadh, aristocratic *zamindars* and *taluqdars*, the indigenous tax collectors of those regions, also exerted control over the indigenous population. And political influence affecting taxation and land rights was exerted at times by special envoys connected to the Mughal emperor in Delhi, even though successive Company charters had largely delegitimized his sovereign status.

Decentralized power relationships of this kind in India meant the Company's definition of imperial subjecthood was not unified in policy or in practice, and therefore this issue became an inescapable problem for managing colonial governance. Because the question was one of legal authority, Charles Cameron, who served as Law Commissioner alongside Thomas Babington Macaulay, was tasked with resolving the matter in policy. In their 1838 draft of the Indian Penal Code, the two legal minds addressed the question of British sovereignty and Indian subjecthood directly. Macaulay and Cameron expressed the issue in historical terms for Parliament by drawing upon the example of shifting allegiances of English, French, and German peoples across the long arc of European history. According to their joint testimony,

> The East India Company was, during a long course of years, in theory at least, under two masters. It was subject to the King of England; it was subject also to the Great Mogul. It derived its corporate existence from the British Parliament. It held its territorial possessions by a grant from the Durbar of Delhi. The situation of the native subjects of the Company bore some analogy to that of the inhabitants of Mindelheim, while that fief of the empire was held by the Duke of Marlborough. The inhabitants of Mindelheim were subjects of the Duke of Marlborough, but they owed no allegiance to the English Crown, though their sovereign was subject to that Crown. It was in this way that the British Empire in India originated.[7]

Although Macaulay and Cameron confronted the question directly, they could offer only an obsolete historical analogy to explain the present circumstances. Worse, perhaps, was their argument that 'the situation of native subjects' was not a *function* of their independent agency, but rather a *consequence* of the vicissitudes of empire, an equivocal legitimation that only reinforced the status quo. As Sudipta Sen has written, it was apparent that the British used shifting definitions of sovereignty under the law 'as a tool of political legitimacy', but also 'as a measure *and* limit of imperial power' (original emphasis).[8] Were Britain's treaties with Oriental rulers really to be regarded as valid because they were made with sovereign states? Partha Chaterjee observed that to admit as much would tacitly mean that Indian rulers possessed an equal status to European royalty or governmental leaders of other nations, while to deny their sovereign authority would effectively nullify the legal standing of those treaties.[9]

Nevertheless, Macaulay and Cameron's Law Commission left the following questions unanswered. Were native Indians considered 'British subjects', and if so, should their allegiance be to the Crown or to the Company? Given the Mughal emperor's marginalized status and honorific as a nominal sovereign, under what conditions should Britain tolerate residual expressions of feudal loyalty shown the emperor? If indigenous Indians were to act against the Company's interests in some way, could such individuals be tried for treason? Such questions were unnerving to the Law Commissioners because they appeared to undermine the very legitimacy of the Residency system upon which the Company relied to govern the colony. That is, because the penal code would differentiate between modern and traditional laws and customs, distinguish between civil and feudal societies, and establish one set of rights for British citizens and another for indigenous Indians, the unsettling question remained: to which citizens was the Company's Resident accountable, and why?[10] Of equal importance: to which side would indigenous Indians give their allegiance? In 1865, Julia Margaret Cameron would confront these very questions directly, when a visiting prince of India, Iqbal al-Daula, joined her company in the garden behind Little Holland House for her to make his photographic portrait.[11]

The Law Commission's efforts to create a viable penal code for British India remained in draft form for many years, and the law languished unfinished, meaning that Indians never had a definitive code of imperial citizenship to which they could refer. As Sukanya Banerjee has written,

> emphasizing the various articulations of citizenship that ensued in the absence of such a code draws attention to the extra-legal life of citizenship, the modes of self-representation it generates even before it is codified, the political claims it triggers because it is deferred.[12]

Cameron's penal code was not authorized by Parliament until 1860. By that time, in the *aftermath* of the 1857 Uprising, questions of Indian sovereignty had been definitively resolved, at least in practice. In 1858, the British Crown claimed full control of the colony by means of an Act of Parliament passed on 2 August, and by the end of the year the Mughal emperor was captured, tried, and exiled, as was the King of Awadh (or Oude, as the British called the province). The Queen's Proclamation of 1 November ended the Company's rule and transferred its sovereignty to the Crown, renamed Governor-General Canning her first Viceroy, and created a Secretary of State for India to replace the Company's Board of Control and Court of Directors. The Queen herself even pledged amnesty towards all those who had rebelled against British rule but desired to return to their peaceful lives as British subjects. After the Proclamation, Company 'Residents' were replaced by 'political agents' of the Crown, retaining the same job function but under a different name. And once the penal code was enacted, political agents' powers were extended, allowing them to investigate crimes committed by British subjects in regions outside the jurisdiction of the law.[13] The year 1858 therefore marked a clear and substantive turning point in Britain's legal relationship with India. Moreover, because the new order preserved the earlier governing policy of indirect rule, the Crown solidified British power in India well into the twentieth century.[14]

As a result, from the end of 1857 through the passage of the new law establishing Queen Victoria as Empress of India, the question about the formal constitution of Britain's government in India again took centre stage. In many ways, the chief issues that had been left unsettled in 1838, when Macaulay and Cameron had reported to Parliament, remained unresolved even in 1853, when Parliament scheduled debates on the renewal of the Company's charter. These latter activities took place under Lord Aberdeen's government, a coalition of ministers representing the nation's opposing parties whose political views often clashed.[15] Several of these men were well-known personally to Charles and Julia Margaret Cameron, including Lord Lansdowne, the Duke of Argyll, Earl Grey, Lord Granville, and Sir Charles Wood, most of whom had attended social events at Little Holland House. A popular engraving of 1857 represented their portraits as governmental leaders.[16]

ANGELS IN THE PUBLIC SQUARE

In 1853, both Charles Cameron and Thoby Prinsep gave testimony as a part of those Parliamentary debates, as did Macaulay. These were three representatives of the old order, which is to say, men of the East India Company who served in Calcutta under the previous Charter of 1833 and who now had retired to England. Although

Cameron and Prinsep disagreed about the importance of teaching English in the education system, the two found solidarity on the principle that India's legal system should be based upon British principles and that the dual form of government in Calcutta and London should be retained.[17] In 1854, many of these matters appeared to have been resolved, as Parliament passed the new Charter Act and appointed an English Law Commission to codify Indian law. Members also established a higher education system and installed English as the principal language of instruction to create an Indian middle class. Plans for reforming the Civil Service were even approved to permit educated Indians to be employed in governmental service. But no sooner were these policies resolved in principle for determining India's governance after 1853 than they were suspended abruptly when Parliament pivoted to address the brewing crisis in Crimea.[18]

In the years leading up to 1858, as we have seen, Lord Lansdowne played an increasingly significant role in the Camerons' personal and public lives. Lansdowne, for example, assumed a prominent role in creating governmental commissions to erect public national monuments, especially those designed to commemorate Britain's triumph in the colonial wars. While still in Aberdeen's government, he was involved in commissioning Baron Marochetti to create a memorial to Britain's soldiers who died during the Crimean War, a monument called 'the Scutari' after the location of the British Army Hospital at Üsküdar. In 1855, even as the conflict in Crimea still raged, Lansdowne visited Marochetti's studio in the company of Lord Panmure, who had advanced this commission in Parliament. During that occasion, when Lansdowne inadvertently came across Marochetti's *maquette* of Julia Jackson (see fig. 23), the actual reason for his studio visit was to check on the artist's progress with the Scutari commission. In May 1856, after war in Crimea had finally ceased, Marochetti unveiled a scaled-down model of his monument in a public event at the Crystal Palace in Sydenham, an event that was celebrated with a prominent illustration in the *Illustrated London News* (fig. 44).[19] John Tenniel vividly represented this ceremony in a watercolour made expressly for the Queen that same year (fig. 45).[20] Two months later, on 8 July 1856, Lord Panmure argued

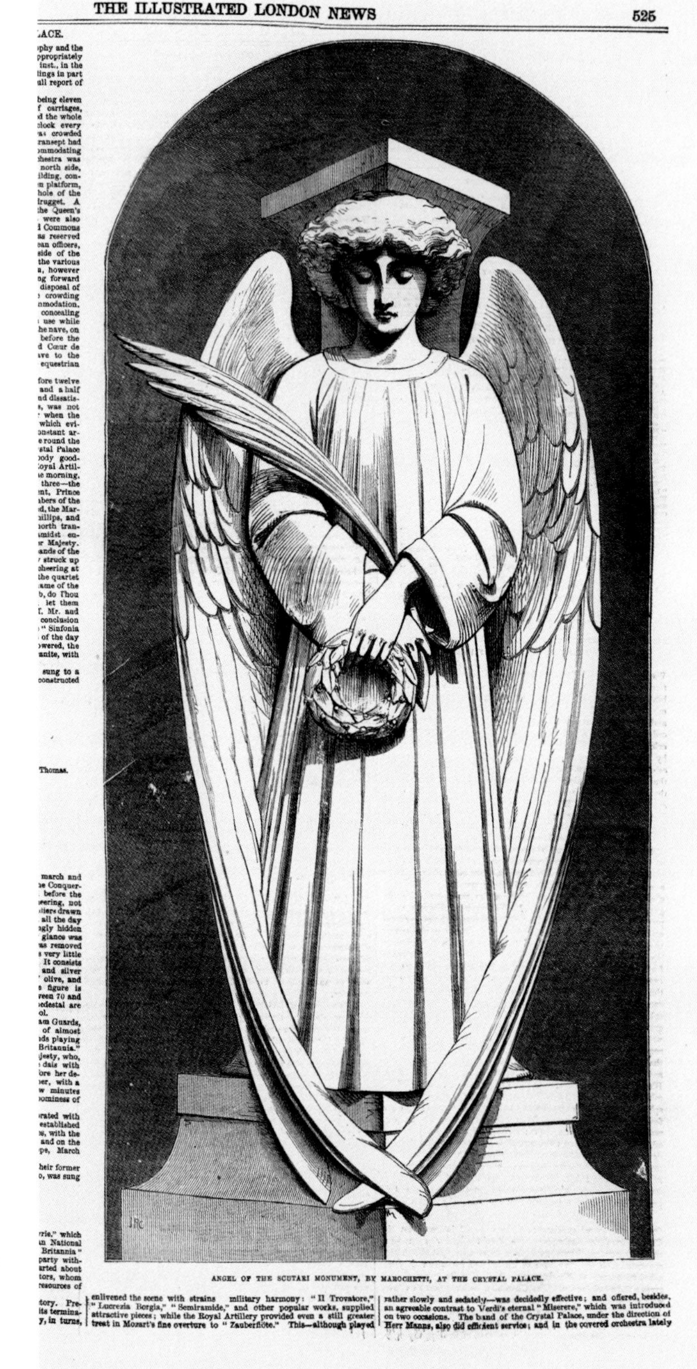
THE ILLUSTRATED LONDON NEWS 525

ANGEL OF THE SCUTARI MONUMENT, BY MAROCHETTI, AT THE CRYSTAL PALACE.

enlivened the scene with strains military harmony: "Il Trovatore," "Lucrezia Borgia," "Semiramide," and other popular works, supplied attractive pieces; while the Royal Artillery provided even a still greater treat in Mozart's fine overture to "Zauberflöte." This—although played rather slowly and sedately—was decidedly effective; and offered, besides, an agreeable contrast to Verdi's eternal "Miserere," which was introduced on two occasions. The band of the Crystal Palace, under the direction of Herr Manns, also did efficient service; and in the covered orchestra lately

44 Anon., *Angel of the Scutari Monument, by Marochetti, at the Crystal Palace*, woodcut from *Illustrated London News*, 17 May 1856, 525.

45 Sir John Tenniel, *The Inauguration of the Scutari Monument and the Peace Trophy at the Crystal Palace, Sydenham*, 9 May *1856*, 1856, pencil, watercolour and bodycolour, 47.7 × 33.6 cm.

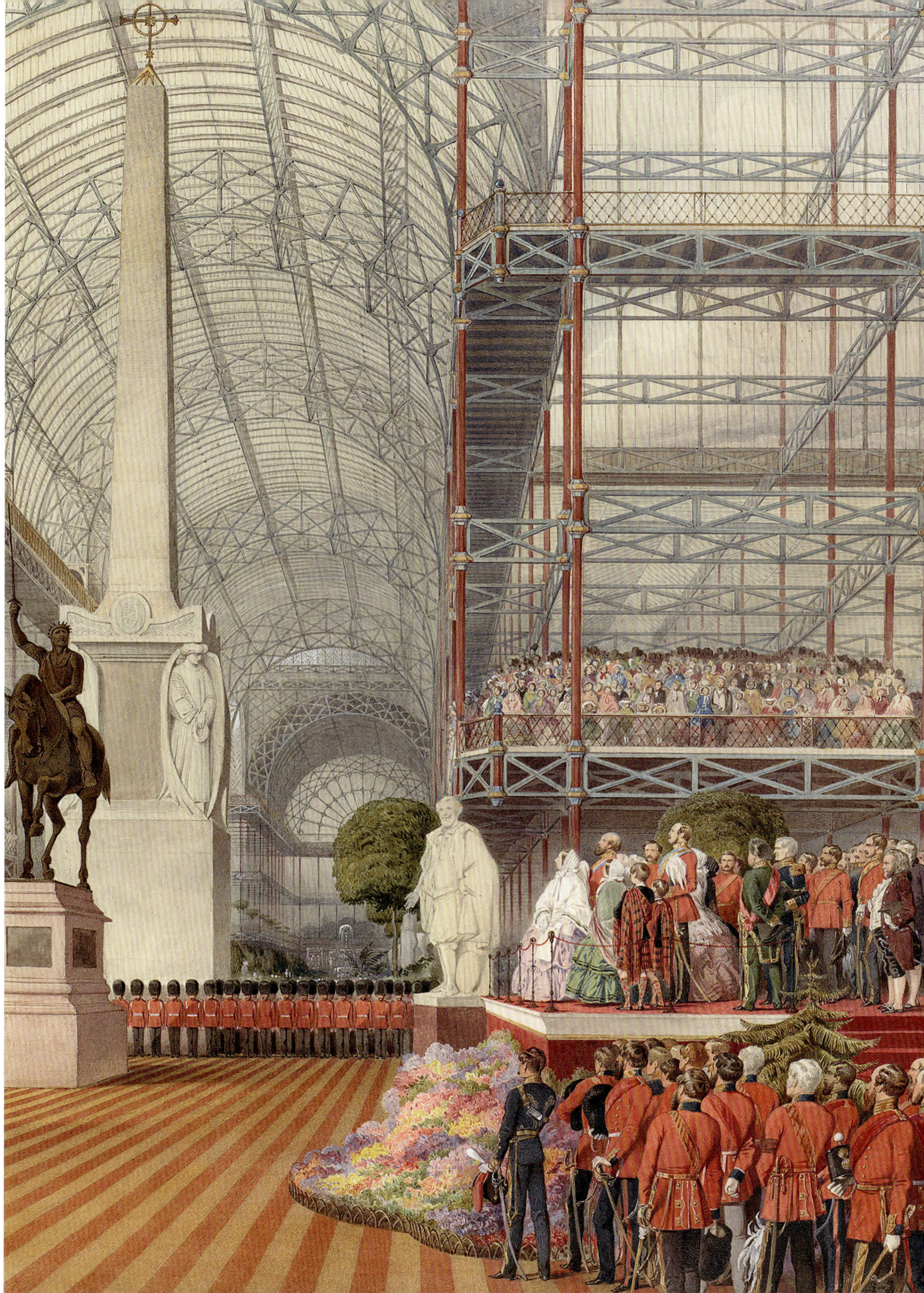

successfully that Parliament should approve the artist's final design. Once Marochetti's work was completed, it was sent by ship to Istanbul, arriving on 10 April 1858, and was erected in the British military cemetery.[21] Francis Frith, or a photographer in his employ, photographed the monument as part of his 'Universal Series' archive of topographical sites (fig. 46).

Although he had emigrated to Britain years earlier, Marochetti repeatedly had to defend his patriotism and assert his right to represent British subjects. Although his English competitors labelled him a foreigner for his Italian birth and Parisian education, he nevertheless became one of Queen Victoria's favourite sculptors. He was also a favourite of the Holland Park set, an intimate friend of Thackeray's if not of the Pre-Raphaelites. His public works, like the equestrian statue of *Richard Coeur de Lion*, first exhibited in plaster in 1851 for the Great Exhibition at the Crystal Palace, gained him wide notoriety and esteem. During the mid-1850s, Lord Lansdowne lent his support for casting Marochetti's *Richard* statue in bronze and moving it to a location near the Palace of Westminster. This project required a combination of private funding, public support, and royal patronage, and created a predictable dispute about where the statue should ultimately be installed in the city.[22] When the Crystal Palace relocated to Sydenham in 1854, so too did the statue. Julia Margaret Cameron undoubtedly saw it herself when she visited the Palace in 1857 in the week prior to the Day of National Humiliation, Fasting, and Prayer.[23] Lansdowne supported monumental sculpture of this kind, particularly public works that celebrated individuals who had sacrificed their lives in defence of their country, whether historical figures or contemporary heroes.

In March 1858, when the dust had not yet settled on where Marochetti's *Richard* sculpture would end up, Lansdowne initiated yet another new commission, this one to erect a statue to honour General Henry Havelock, now styled the hero of Cawnpore, in recognition of his final military campaigns in India. On 19 March 1858, Lansdowne joined Prince George, the Duke of Cambridge, to announce the creation of the 'Havelock Memorial Fund'. The following day, *The Times* quoted the Duke's speech at the event, noting his high appraisal of General Havelock:

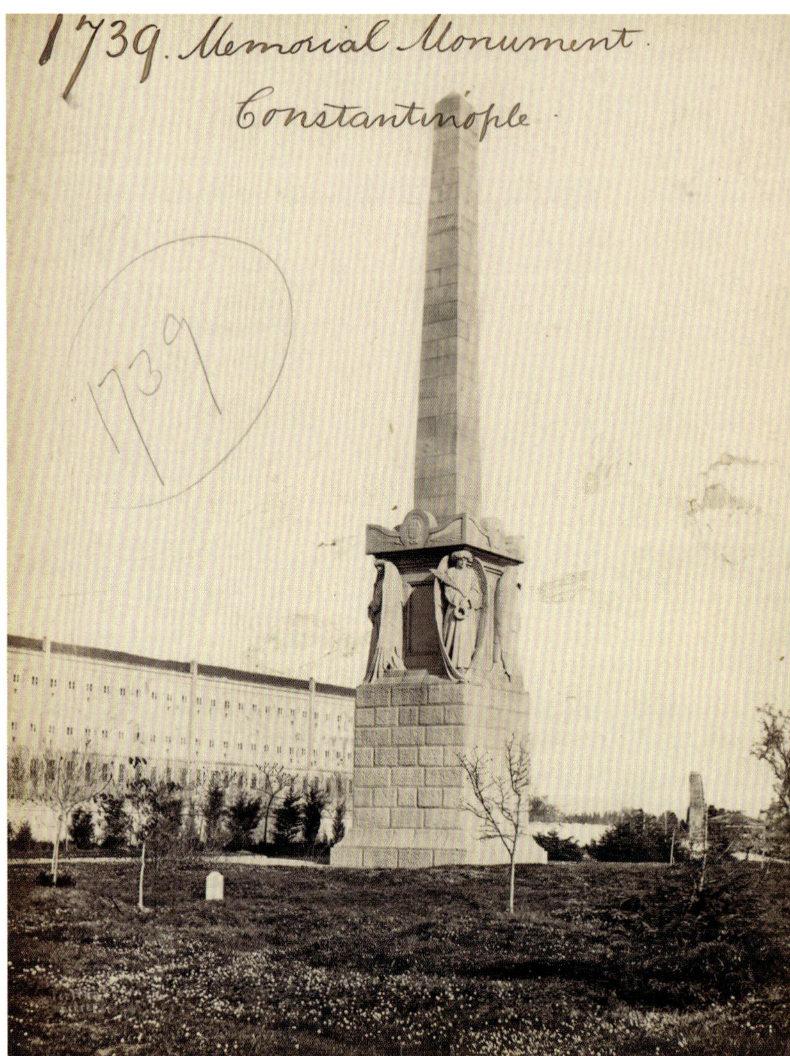

46 Francis Frith, *Memorial Monument Constantinople*, *c.*1856–7, albumen photograph, 15.2 × 21 cm.
Acquired from F. Frith and Company, 1954. © Victoria and Albert Museum, London. E.208:1097–1994.

> He at a moment of the greatest anxiety, the greatest uncertainty, the greatest difficulty and danger, was the man who was selected by the Indian Government to lead the column of troops which first made a successful advance on Cawnpore, and then moved on to Lucknow.[24]

At nearly the same time, John Kaye was memorializing the avenging acts of Brigadier-General Neill, whose personal command oversaw the murder of many thousands of native Indians in Cawnpore and Lucknow.[25] The assembled dignitaries of the Havelock Memorial Fund went on to announce that the Queen had granted a prominent site in Trafalgar Square for the erection of the monument.[26]

March 1858 also marked the date when the East India Company's armies had finally removed the two most prominent indigenous rulers who had controlled the earlier kingdoms that Havelock had vanquished, and that General Neill had subdued. These prominent symbols of Indian authority were represented visually for readers of the *Illustrated London News* in October and November 1857 (figs 47 and 48), long before there was reason for the British to celebrate the actual restitution of order or to erect memorials to the fallen, like Havelock. Wajid Ali Shah, now called the 'ex-King of Oude', had been deposed earlier, in 1856, when the East India Company had annexed the kingdom of Awadh. But it was only after the rebellion, when the Company forcibly relocated Wajid Ali Shah and his court to Calcutta, that he was effectively exiled from the province, ensuring his supplication to British power. Similarly, Emperor Bahadur Shah Zafar, whose capture was announced in *The Times* on 1 December 1857, was put on trial in January 1858 after the fall of Delhi. Found guilty in March and stripped of his royal title, the Company exiled him to Rangoon, in Burma, styling him now the 'ex-King of Delhi'.[27]

News accounts in the *Illustrated London News* reminded readers about the 'Oriental effeminacy' of the two ex-kings and itemized their many deprivations using familiar stereotypes about their lavish lifestyles and excessive appetites.[28] Long forgotten were Lord Clive's treaties with the Mughal emperor or the Company's commercial treaties of the 1830s with the Awadh king. Metaphorically, in relation to the story the British press was telling its readers, it was necessary to expunge the two ex-kings from the chronology – and from the historical archive – to remove any memory of the historical sovereignty of the two rulers and their former legitimacy. 'The rebel has no place in this history as the subject of rebellion', as Ranajit Guha commented about 'official histories' of 'the Mutiny'.[29] The two kings' unceremonious removal therefore constituted an erasure of powerful symbols. By removing

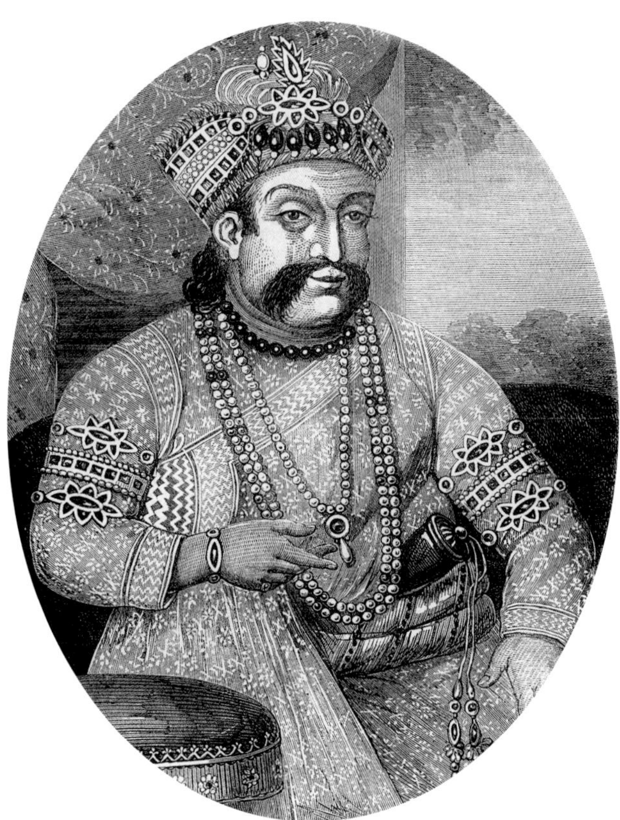

47 *Ex-King of Oude, Illustrated London News*, 28 November 1857, 549.

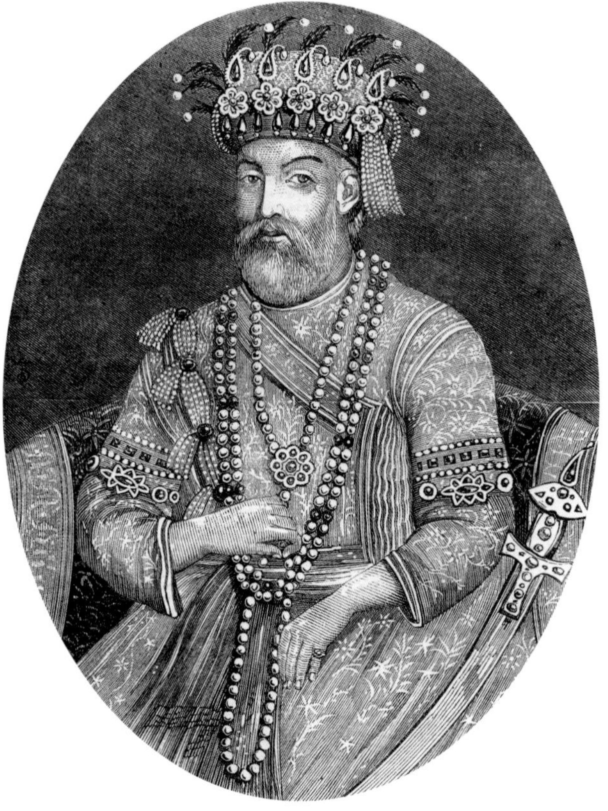

48 *Ex-King of Delhi, Illustrated London News*, 10 October 1857, 353.

them, Britain also excised visible emblems of the insurgency and removed the possibility that former rulers could be restored to power, especially because 'love of the country in those days meant love of one's own homeland ruled by one's traditional ruler'.[30] As a result, the elimination of the two kings helped to ensure the narrative of British power was written as continuous and unbroken.

In the aftermath of the insurrection in India, the symbolic erasure of the rebels continued in the London art world, as English painters joined sculptors in representing the justice of the British cause. At the opening banquet of the annual exhibition of the Royal Academy of Arts that year, Lord Lansdowne once again addressed the noble company about matters of shared civic importance and national concern. On Saturday 1 May 1858, the ceremony was presided over by Charles Eastlake, the Academy's president. Among the many guests were the Duke of Cambridge; the Earls Grey, Derby, and Granville; Baron Pollock; the Bishops of London and Oxford; Sir Charles Wood; Thackeray and Dickens. Virtually all had attended Sara Prinsep's salon at Little Holland House. Given the prominence of this event at the very heart of the art world, their activities were certainly known to Watts, Cameron, and the Holland Park set.

While the obligatory first toast of the evening was offered to the health of the Prince Consort, the second was to the valour and lasting memory of the departed Havelock, whose distinction in classical studies, ironically enough, was extolled as a kind of humanistic balance to the abject violence of his Indian campaigns.[31] As the year's most cataclysmic and disruptive political event, the Indian Uprising was therefore brought directly into the opening ceremony designed to honour the year's most important contributions in the visual arts. At the banquet, Havelock's cultural pedigree and scholarly accomplishments were emphasized, burnishing his credentials with the art set while avoiding mention of military combat. In this genteel setting, Joseph Noël Paton alone represented the war in India on the Academy's walls with his painting *In Memoriam*. In the painting, Paton portrayed a huddled group of women and children praying for deliverance in a confined interior while, beyond their sight, menacing armed sepoys appear ready to breach their doorway and threaten their lives. Although Paton's work was a wholly imagined re-enactment of the *Bibighar* massacre, many critics were repelled by the subject, finding its depiction too realistic or gruesome. Reacting harshly to the subject, they rejected Paton's painting as 'horrific' because it vividly represented innocents stoically awaiting their demise.[32] John Ruskin joined these critics, commenting that 'art may face horror, but should not dwell with it'.[33]

In response, Paton reclaimed his canvas and painted out the threatening sepoys, replacing them with Scottish Highlanders, which emphasized deliverance of the women and children and the valour of British rescuers. Still, critics were not assuaged by this revision. One French writer accused Paton of undoing his painting's original historical realism by reducing 'his noble tragedy to a melodrama'.[34] And of course, the Highlanders were too late to prevent the *Bibighar* massacre, too late to save the day, as depicted in the painting. This controversy was still fresh in 1862 when William Simmons reproduced the painting as a popular engraving. Intriguingly, Simmons added an unambiguous dedication in the letter of the print that explicitly refocused the subject, shifting the painting's reading from the rebellion of Indian sepoys against British commanders to a scene of explicit pathos focusing on defenceless women. The inscription reads, 'Designed to Commemorate the Christian Heroism of the British Ladies in India during the Mutiny of 1857, and their Ultimate Deliverance by British Prowess' (fig. 49). Simmons's print therefore served double duty, as it now memorialized the British women killed in Cawnpore *and* proclaimed British military superiority. In this way, visual art also helped shift the public's attention away from acts of retribution perpetrated by the Company's armies against indigenous Indians, as paintings like Paton's and prints like Simmons's kept the focus on the helpless British women.

49 William Henry Simmons, engraving after Joseph Noël Paton, *In Memoriam* (1858), 1862, oil on canvas, 86.4 × 68.5 cm.

Printed below the image: 'Designed to Commemorate the Christian Heroism of the British Ladies in India during the Mutiny of 1857, and their Ultimate Deliverance by British Prowess' and 'Yea though I walk through the shadow of the Valley of Death, I will fear no evil, for thou art with me'.

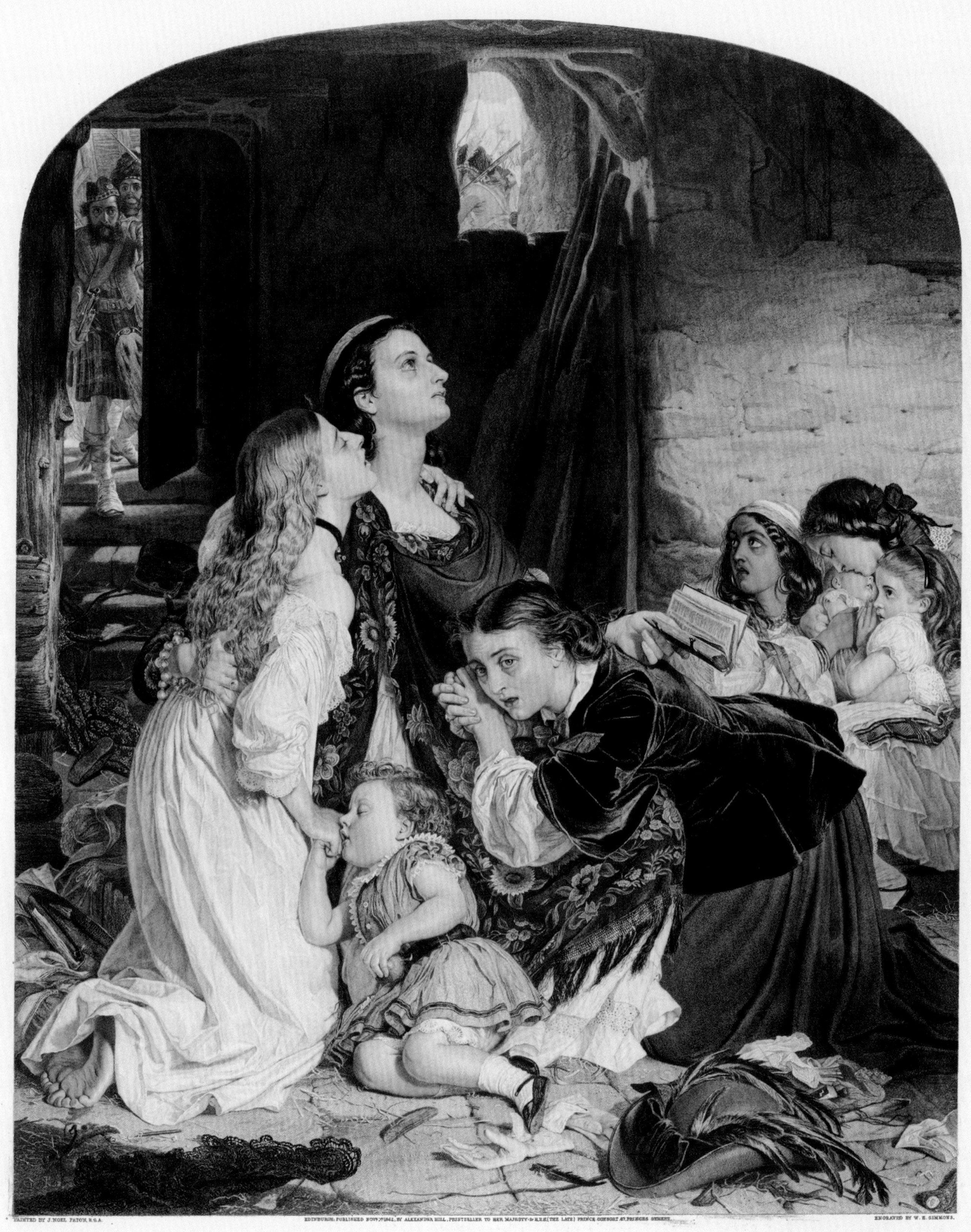

PAINTED BY J. NOEL PATON, R.S.A. — EDINBURGH: PUBLISHED NOV. 1862, BY ALEXANDER HILL, PRINTSELLER TO HER MAJESTY & H.R.H. (THE LATE) PRINCE CONSORT, 67 PRINCES STREET. — ENGRAVED BY W. H. SIMMONS.

In Memoriam

Designed to Commemorate
The Christian Heroism of the British Ladies in India during the Mutiny of 1857,
and their Ultimate Deliverance by British Prowess

"Yea though I walk through the Valley of the Shadow of Death, I will fear no evil for Thou art with me."

Printed by McQueen

DESPOTIC GOVERNANCE REVIVED

In 1852 and 1853, Charles Cameron had offered his ideas about India's governance and legal system before Parliament and to members of Lord Aberdeen's Cabinet, only to have his recommendations postponed – or rejected outright – as unwanted and outmoded reforms.[35] But in 1858, Cameron was emboldened to see his proposals given new life amid the contemporary crisis and public uncertainty about how to re-establish governmental control in the colony, now that the immediate danger of revolt had passed. This unexpected political revival came in January 1858, when the *National Review* published an extensive analysis on the 'Principles of Indian Government'. In this essay, the author elevated Charles Cameron's tract of 1853 and accorded it a new status as a valuable strategic planning document.[36] Likely written by Walter Bagehot, the journal's chief writer and editor, this essay held the East India Company virtually blameless for the insurrection in India by claiming that the Company's 'sins' were 'those of omission and of oversight alone'.[37] In this regard, Bagehot flatly contradicted the earlier Evangelical condemnation of Reverend Spurgeon, effectively throwing out Spurgeon's religious denunciation of the Utilitarians' moral failures and reviving the civilizing argument upholding Britain's practical duties and its responsibilities related to colonial governance. In making his argument, Bagehot drew directly from Cameron's testimony before Parliament, arguing the Company had set the 'right course' all along, that Dalhousie's 1856 annexation of the province of Oude was legitimate and justified, and that the Company's financial inducements to local princes were reasonable. Bagehot, who established his economic *bona fides* as head of his family's banking firm, reframed these administrative and governmental decisions as unquestionably appropriate – a legitimate cost of doing business. To Bagehot, for example, the Company's refusal to allow native Indians to be employed in the Civil Service was a rational and practical necessity. He essentially agreed with Company administrators that Indians were 'not yet ready' to assume responsibility for their own governance because they lacked the essential discipline necessary for self-determination.

Bagehot quoted Charles Cameron at length in defending these positions, which is something of a revelation today in relation to how scholars have earlier interpreted Julia Margaret's relationship to her husband, a connection that has been presumed to be one of aesthetic, and not political, compatibility. But as one of the prominent architects of India's colonial government prior to 1857, Charles Cameron held a unique public role in helping determine the political aftermath of the rebellion, a position from which he exerted an exceptional influence upon his family's attitudes towards Britain's colonial policies, and therefore one that was undoubtedly compatible with his wife's political worldview as well. Of particular importance in this regard is Bagehot's vigorous endorsement of Charles Cameron's earlier Parliamentary testimony of 1853 in which he argued that 'the best government for India … is a despotic government',

> and that the inhabitants of that country, European as well as Asiatic, should derive the assurance which they ought to possess against the abuse of power, not from any political privileges exercised by themselves, but first from the fact that none are admitted to the highest offices in the country but those who (whatever may be their origin) have received the moral and intellectual training of British functionaries: secondly, for the fact that all the proceedings of the Indian governments are submitted in detail to the criticism and correction of authorities in England: and lastly, from the fact that those authorities are responsible to the British Parliament.[38]

Framed in this way, argued Bagehot in his endorsement of Cameron's views, a despotic attitude towards the colony would express true benevolence towards India's indigenous population because it would put a fledgling and inexperienced colonial administration under the superior and proven authority of British administrative control. The formal policies that emerged from this approach to colonial governance became known collectively as expressions of 'paternal despotism'.[39]

What were the goals of this new policy? Drawing upon Cameron's authority, Bagehot reasoned that the influence of rational British governance would further reinforce its hold on the colony, even draw it closer to England, perhaps, as a permanent dependency. He concluded, 'there is no reason, moral or material, why we should not retain our Indian empire for all time. We believe that we are under a solemn obligation to retain it'.[40] By contrast, John Stuart Mill wrote that permanent dependency should *not* be the goal of Britain's colonial government, but that it should work instead to enable the colony to assume future autonomy, a position articulated earlier by Herschel. Mill also argued that paternal protection and guidance, such as that established by Britain's rational government, should mark the limits of its distinctive control over India. Consequently, for Mill and others, the administrative Civil Service rose in importance and became essential to Britain's philosophical and practical success. Likewise, Bagehot also fundamentally agreed with Cameron that Britain's administrative Civil Service represented bureaucracy as the highest form of state-sponsored altruism, because the men of the service were trained, impersonal, apolitical, rational, and disciplined. Effective colonial governance, to these Victorian policymakers, became redefined in dispassionate, logical, and bureaucratic terms: 'Good governance', they reasoned, 'did not belong to the inhabitants' of the colony and 'did not belong to the British people'. Rather, as Bagehot argued, supported by Cameron's reasoning, 'good government' resulted from 'a body of trained experts'.[41]

Defined in this way, despotic government was essential to Cameron and to Bagehot because its policies made the indigenous population less prone to resist Britain's rule, much less to rebel against it outright in the future. 'Despotism', wrote Mill, 'is a legitimate mode of government in dealing with barbarians, provided the end be their improvement, and the means justified by actually effecting that end'.[42] Under this logic, Britain's role was to provide educational and moral guidance; Indian progress could then be measured soberly and recorded through public demonstrations of social discipline. Charles Cameron argued for the underlying paternalistic notions of trusteeship that are built into this framework because such policies reinforced the Utilitarians' founding philosophical principles: accountability would be derived from morally faultless, British-bred bureaucrats; administrative oversight would be provided by transparent practices associated with 'the criticism and correction of authorities in England'; superintendence, oversight, and ultimate responsibility would rest with the British Parliament. Only now, under Crown rule, where an approved system of paternalistic despotism was made possible by *direct* British control, Indian 'improvement' would no longer be the expressed ambition. Rather, in the new regime fashioned after 1858, governance of India would be guaranteed by the laws written *for* it, especially the penal code written earlier by Macaulay and Cameron. 'English virtue – virtue as such – was embodied in English law, now bestowed on India', wrote Priya Satia; 'it was "the gospel of the English," made none the worse for the fact that it was a "compulsory gospel which admits of no dissent and no disobedience".'[43]

Bagehot's sense of enduring British governance also mirrored the sentiments articulated earlier by Macaulay. Additional symbols of continuity with this approach took shape in government in London. In 1859, when Sir Charles Wood was appointed Secretary of State for India, he encountered a tangle of unfinished administrative business left unresolved from the work of the earlier Board of Control. Now installed in his new role, Wood proposed reviving policies that relied upon governing principles articulated earlier by Charles Cameron. Bagehot endorsed these policies enthusiastically, taking a megaphone to Cameron's ideas in the *National Review*. Even if his audience did not equal the size of Spurgeon's captive crowd at the Crystal Palace, Bagehot's influence was unparalleled among the political economists, members of government, bankers and diplomats, and former Company officials, as well as the elite members of society that made up Cameron's circle.

One of those core principles was the perceived continuing usefulness of the caste system as an instrument of British control, a principle long advocated by Charles Cameron. Previously considered an outmoded relic of India's pre-modern and 'barbaric' social order, caste was now redefined explicitly as a useful tool of colonial governance. According to Cameron,

> the system of caste must have prevented the growth of that predilection which elsewhere commonly arises in men's minds in favour of a national government. That singular system [caste] was calculated to engender a complete indifference in the subject multitude as

> to who might be exercising over them the powers of government; provided only that the persons placed in that position confined themselves within those limits which are recognised in the system itself. ... A true imperial government, though foreign in blood, cannot be considered so foreign in feeling and interest to the races over whom its sway may extend as the ruling caste of Hindoos was to the castes excluded from participation in the government.[44]

Because caste inhibited nation-building from within, it helped avert social disorder. Cameron's defence of the persistence of caste therefore aligns perfectly with Michel Foucault's contemporary understanding of 'governmentality', in which an individual citizen's agency is restricted, and where conduct and liberty are regulated severely by the state.[45] Britain's manipulation of caste took this ancient form of social organization and hierarchy, and rationally integrated those policy goals in practice, regulating the social conduct of native Indians, limiting their access to self-governance, and restricting their political participation. If in 1850, Sir John Herschel expressed concern that Indian self-government appeared a far distant goal, by 1858, Herschel could only imagine that the goalposts had been moved further still. Charles Cameron's policy recommendations regarding the usefulness of caste to British governance were therefore instrumental to its resumption of political control over the colony. Significantly, the British maintained the caste system into the twentieth century.

In 1855, after Lord Aberdeen's ministry was disbanded and with it Lansdowne's service in the Cabinet, Wood remained in his post at the board under Lord Palmerston and was retained in the position through Palmerston's first and second governments to oversee large segments of India's reconstruction based upon these same principles.[46] With Britain's military, political, and structural power in India now fully restored and its governmental integrity assured in Parliament, it was left to the India Office to supervise administrative affairs in India. Yet the 'structure and split of the Home government of the East India Company in the shape of the Council of India, coupled with the failure of parliament to cultivate and of the Crown to sustain a continued, active interest in Indian affairs' led only to the mildest of reforms under Wood's helm, which continued into the 1860s.[47] Open wounds remained, however. The most persistent, destabilizing, and longstanding were multiple claims made against the Company by descendants of the kings of Awadh, the largest and most coherent of the North-West Provinces with an established capital in Lucknow and major commercial centres in Cawnpore and Benares. The British had long called the presidency by the name of Oudh or Oude and were mindful of its historical independence. Since the eighteenth century, Awadh's kings resisted what they considered British interference in its affairs by the Company's Resident. But over time, after a series of poor treaty agreements and outright usurpations, the Awadh dynasty lost large amounts of territory and treasure to the East India Company.

Before considering Julia Margaret Cameron's unique photograph of one of Awadh's rulers, it is useful to provide a brief overview comparing the differing perspectives of governance that were experienced by the Company and by Awadh's kings. John Stuart Mill's experience illustrates the Company's perspective of governing the province over the course of many years. His legacy is instructive, not only for his commentary about Awadh's governance but also in relation to British sovereignty. In 1823, Mill joined the Company as a writer, where he served until 1858, the year it was dissolved by the Queen's Proclamation, and he played a major role in determining the internal affairs of Awadh and its relationship to Britain.[48] From Mill's perspective, disagreements between the Company's Resident and Awadh's leaders resulted from complaints made by two persistent sources: British merchants, on the one hand, who resisted the Company's restraints on trade, and *taluqdars*, the local tax collectors, who disliked the erratic collection of revenues. The deteriorating relationship took years to develop. In 1834, for example, Lord Bentinck threatened the Awadh king that the British would annex and govern the province unless he took steps to improve these economic conditions, and Mill observed greater compliance following this intervention. But in 1837, the kingdom experienced a financial crisis, and Lord Auckland recommended the king be deposed. Mill argued against this action, citing the political cost of removing what he recognized was the last major Muslim state in northern India. Instead,

Mill urged the Company to take what he called an 'intermediate course' by exerting greater control over Awadh's internal affairs. Conditions between the Company and Awadh's rulers deteriorated once again after 1840, but even after 1842, when a new king was installed, Mill was still not impressed, writing in 1845 that while the kingdom appeared to be 'on the brink of anarchy', it had not yet 'suffered permanent deterioration from this perpetually recurring misrule'.[49] This litany of complaints increased under Lord Hardinge, who once again threatened annexation after receiving reports about declining revenues, neglected agriculture, and chaos in the Awadh royal court. Finally, in 1856, Mill ultimately supported Lord Dalhousie's proposal to annex the province, thereby shifting it from indirect to direct rule to bring 'order and regulation' to the system of collecting revenue.

REPRESENTING IQBAL AL-DAULA

The indigenous rulers of Awadh experienced this period quite differently from Mill. Most offensive and distressing to the Awadh royal court was the Company's effort to manipulate and rewrite the kingdom's established history of royal succession by interfering with its ancestral lines. In 1837, for example, the Company's Resident deposed the established ruler, who was the presumed son of the recently deceased king, Nasir al-Din Haydar, and installed in his place a much older and previously exiled uncle. This decision outraged Nasir al-Din's immediate heirs, but perhaps none more so than his cousin, Iqbal al-Daula, who protested vigorously that the British had interfered with his rightful claim to assume the throne, following Awadh's traditional lines of royal succession.[50] After complaining directly to the Company in Calcutta, without success, Iqbal al-Daula took the surprising – although not unprecedented – step of bringing his appeal to London to make his case directly to the British Crown.[51]

Iqbal al-Daula arrived in 1838 and remained in Britain for almost two years. He lived in luxury, toured England and Ireland, visited France, and commissioned former British officers to plead his case.[52] While the Company's directors refused to acknowledge him, he found a sympathetic ear from the political opposition, notably Disraeli. Correspondence between the president of the East India Company's Board of Control and Lord Auckland reveals the fraught political dynamic caused by his presence in London:

> [I] wish that you had not permitted [Iqbal al-Daula Bahadur] to leave Benares – If these *Bahaudoors* are to come to England, they will give infinite trouble, and throw no small suspicion on the wisdom or justice of our Indian government. This man has managed to interest several persons in his favour, and intends to prosecute his claims in Parliament after they shall have been rejected by the Court ... In the meantime I have refused to present the Oude Prince [to the British king], or to take any notice of him; and the same course has been followed by all of us [in Cabinet], except Lord Holland, who returned his card *mistaking him for the Turkish Ambassador!!!* [Original emphasis][53]

Lord Holland's 'mistake' may reveal his evident confusion over diplomatic protocols among foreign governments, but his misunderstanding in this case also discloses that, at the highest level of state authority, diplomats were bewildered by Iqbal al-Daula's complaint and did not possess the capacity to understand its legitimacy. At the same time, it is hard to fathom how Lord Holland could have overlooked the fact that Iqbal al-Daula occupied luxurious apartments close to his own home in nearby Regents Park.[54] Claims made by Iqbal al-Daula's 'Oude delegation' in London were not perceived as a simple private dispute, therefore, but rather took on the character of a state grievance.[55] Yet the petitioner was essentially stateless, a condition that compounded the evident confusion of his official status in relation to Parliament.

The deposed prince then commissioned a Captain W. White to present his grievance to the British public, making Iqbal al-Daula a public figure in London. White's book advocated for Iqbal's restitution to the Awadh throne by arguing against the validity of the East India Company's treaties with the province, which further embarrassed the Company.[56] Predictably, Iqbal's delegation turned into a public spectacle, one that was captured visually in hand-tinted coloured lithographs printed by Ackermann around 1840 (fig. 50).[57] Around the same time, Iqbal al-Daula also sat for a formal portrait by the painter John Smart in which Smart imagined his subject standing on a terrace overlooking Lucknow, a city to which he would

50 'King of Oude', hand-tinted lithograph, *c.*1840, from *The King of Oude, his Brother, and Attendants: Sketched while on their Visit to England, by a Lady* (London: Ackermann, *c.*1840).

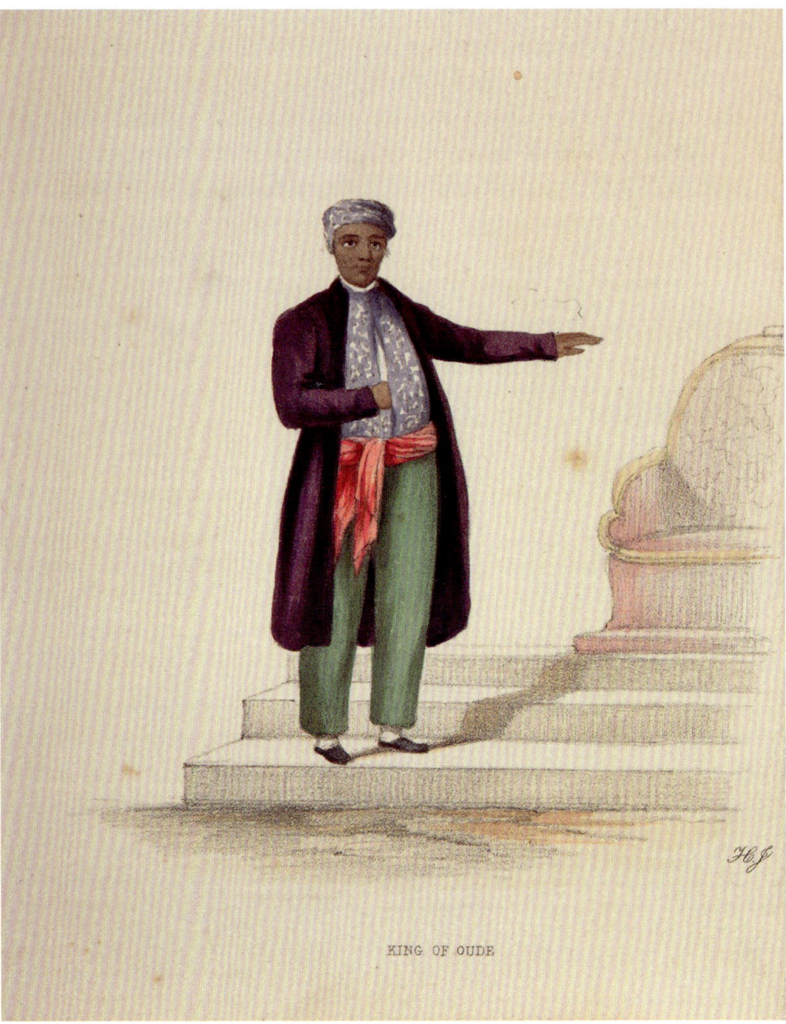

never return.[58] Despite his considerable efforts, Iqbal al-Daula did not prevail in his ambition to be restored to the Awadh throne and he remained in exile. After abandoning his efforts, he retired to Baghdad, where he received British protection.[59] He would appear once again in London, but only *after* the 1857 Uprising.

The Company's interference in Awadh's kingdom continued until 1856, when Lord Dalhousie determined it was necessary to annex the province. As we have seen, the Company deposed Wajid Ali Shah (who had assumed the throne in Iqbal al-Daula's place) and exiled him to Calcutta just prior to the revolt of sepoys in Meerut, which historians have called another of the many incidents that likely precipitated the 1857 Uprising. In response to his ouster from Lucknow, Wajid Ali Shah was determined to plead his case in London, as did Iqbal al-Daula before him. But the Company flatly refused his petition to travel. In response, the deposed king sent a delegation that included his mother, brother, and son. Their mission was to reverse Dalhousie's imposed annexation and reinstall Wajid Ali Shah, an ambition they were forced to abandon once the anti-colonial insurrection broke out in 1857.

Nevertheless, the 'Oude Delegation', as the group came to be known, proved to be quite savvy in creating their own public relations in England. In March 1857, they attended a performance at the Drury Lane Theatre, where they were captured occupying a loge box which the *Illustrated London News* represented graphically the following week.[60] In April, the Oude delegation accompanied several unnamed dignitaries to Manchester to attend the Art Treasures exhibition, where the group was photographed by Leonida Caldisi. Prince Albert collected a print of the ensemble on its way to view the exhibition for one of his photographic albums (fig. 51). And in August 1857, this group was represented once again in the *Illustrated London News* in a full-page woodcut made after a photograph by Mayall (fig. 52).[61] In an awkward understatement, the article accompanying the illustration noted that recent news from India about a sepoy uprising raised some discomfort in London regarding the delegation's public appearances:

> The news just received from India of the implication of the ex-King of Oude in the conspiracy which has led to the Indian mutinies, his lodgment [*sic*] in Fort William, and the disarming of his followers, invests the history of the Royal Family with additional interest.[62]

51 Leonida Caldisi, *The Princes of Oude, India, at Manchester Art Treasures, April 1857*, salted paper print, 13.6 × 20.7 cm.

52 Anon., *The Princes of Oude and Suite – From a Photograph by Mayall*, woodcut from *Illustrated London News Supplement*, 1 August 1857, 121.

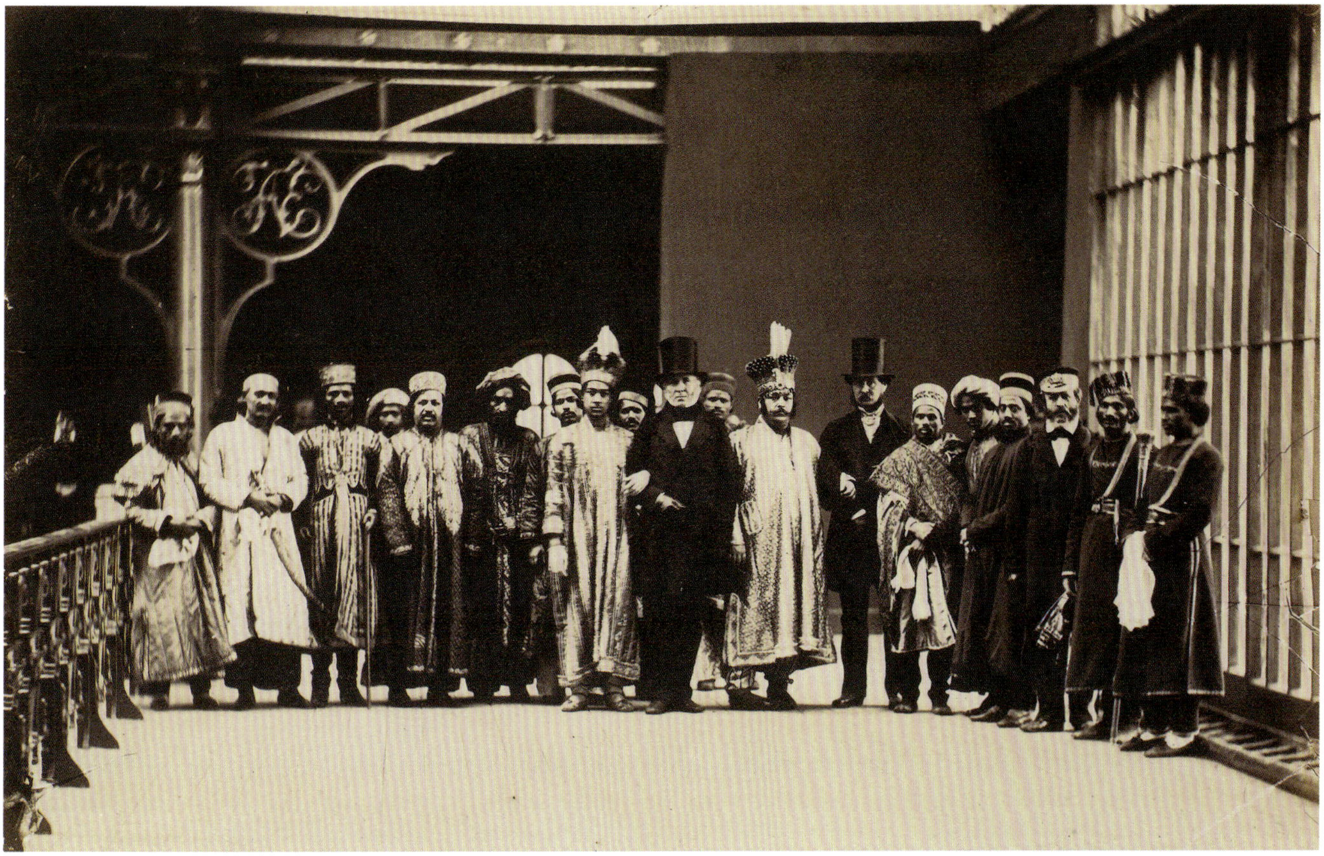

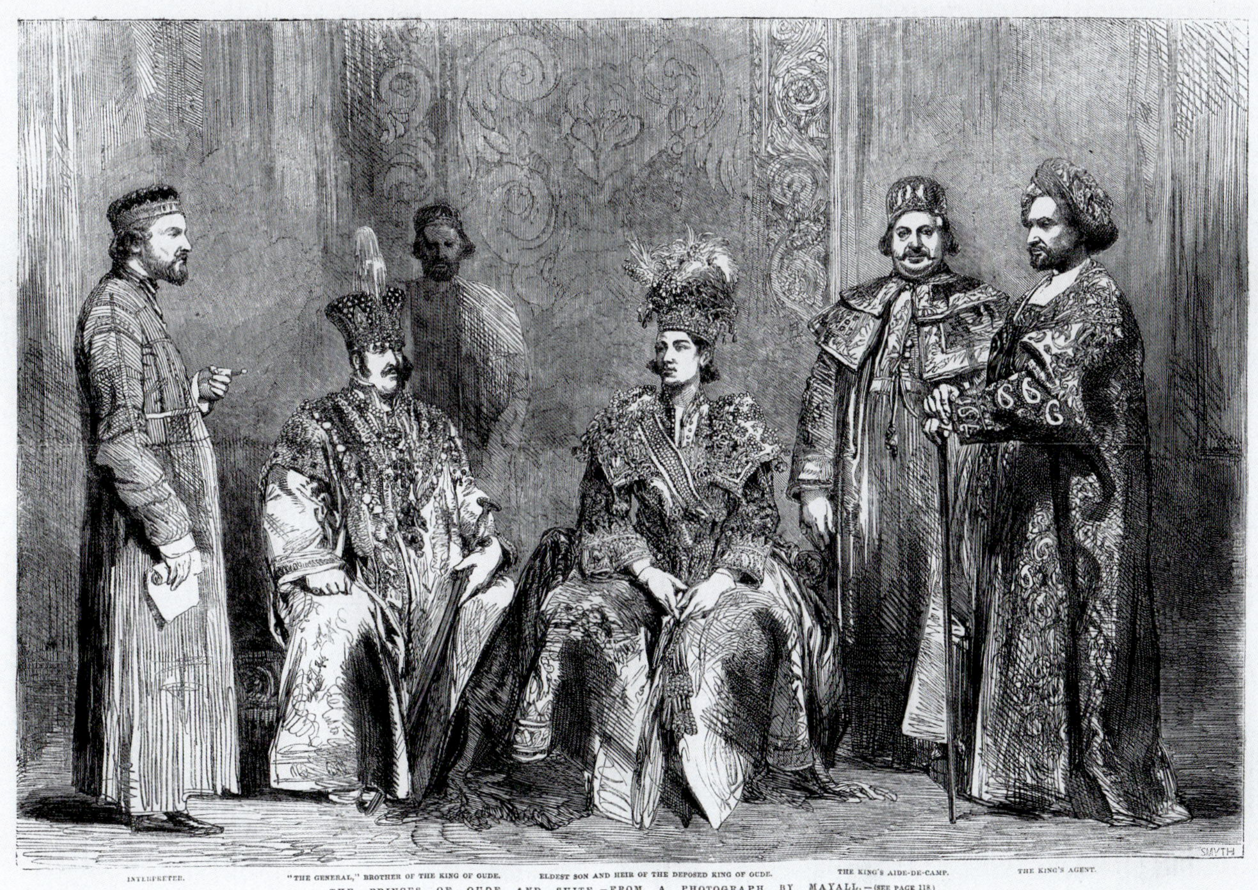

INTERPRETER. "THE GENERAL," BROTHER OF THE KING OF OUDE. ELDEST SON AND HEIR OF THE DEPOSED KING OF OUDE. THE KING'S AIDE-DE-CAMP. THE KING'S AGENT.

THE PRINCES OF OUDE AND SUITE—FROM A PHOTOGRAPH BY MAYALL.—(SEE PAGE 118.)

Nevertheless, the Oude delegation was successful in manipulating Parliamentary legislators in London, as well as members of the East India Company Board of Control and the court of public opinion, much like Iqbal al-Daula's first delegation of 1838.[63] These two examples demonstrate that the deposed kings of Awadh undertook their travels to London because they tacitly accepted British sovereignty.[64] That is, in making their appeals to Parliament and the Crown directly, both Iqbal al-Daula and Wajid Ali Shah apparently understood themselves to be 'British subjects'.

Ironically, their two distinct claims to the throne depended upon their confidence that eighteenth-century European nationality laws applied to them, too. Under these provisions, the chief criterion for determining an individual's claim to legal inheritance was defined by his place of birth under the sovereignty of a monarch (*jus soli*) and his claim of parental descent (*jus sanguinis*); in short, a subject's nationality was determined by 'blood and descent'.[65] But as we have seen, the deposed kings of Oude and Delhi also came to appreciate these esteemed principles held no water. Even more bitter was the reality that earlier treaties their royal ancestors had signed with the Company had since become invalid, largely owing to the deceitful practices of Governor-General Warren Hastings, who in 1819 effectively *created* the royal lineage of Awadh. At that time, the East India Company elevated the status of Awadh's rulers from 'Nawab', a title indicating support for the sovereign Mughal emperor, to that of 'king'. By elevating the nominal status of the Awadh 'king', the Company simultaneously diminished the real power of emperor's throne in Delhi. At the same time, the Company installed a Resident as a political intermediary to manage internal affairs of the kingdom. Therefore, in exchange for conceding their real authority into perpetuity, the new king received only superficial symbols of his elevated status. These included empty symbolic and ceremonial promises, including a lavish formal coronation, a performance of *God Save the King*, and a twenty-one-gun salute.[66]

Amid these distractions in the years leading up to the Indian Uprising, the East India Company created several new laws designed to pre-empt both Islamic and Hindu legal customs. The new policies affected both legal practice and administrative governance, on two accounts. For one, the Company created a policy it called the 'Doctrine of Lapse', which allowed its Governors-General to annex the territory of India's princely states.[67] The doctrine was a legal and political strategy that deliberately interfered with traditional lines of succession. For example, although Hindu law permitted adoption when there was no direct heir, the Company insisted that adoptions by native rulers required its prior approval. Should the Company deny its consent, it could invoke the Doctrine of Lapse to assume territorial control. Dalhousie applied this new legal act broadly, even in the case of Awadh, whose rulers were Muslim and not Hindu.[68] Like the earlier feudal law of escheat, if an individual died without legal heirs, property of the deceased reverted to state control. Mill incidentally considered the annexation of Awadh by this policy a criminal 'discharge of an imperative duty', but he stood by it, nonetheless.[69]

In addition, the Company implemented a second legal prerogative to accompany the Doctrine of Lapse. This legal claim also rested on questions of sovereignty because it rejected the legal traditions and precedent of Mughal emperors who had for generations claimed Islamic law as the *de facto* 'territorial law' of British India. Charles Cameron's Indian Law Commission of 1840 countered instead that the Company was forced to reject Islamic law outright, explicitly on the ground that it was 'intolerant of other religions'. English law was superior, the Law Commissioners argued, because it was subjected to the 'deliberative laws of men'. In this way, the Company paved the way for new forms of social control: 'English law, as it does not profess to be a revelation from God, may be changed by Parliament in the way of legislation, and by the Courts of law'.[70] Although in 1840, the Commission was not able to implement these recommendations when they were first conceived, these guiding principles nevertheless established the unambiguous legal precedent that prevented any future possibility that religious law of any kind would be imposed to govern India.

Although the Queen's Proclamation ousted the authority of the native Indian princes and replaced their rule with a British empress, the royal court of Awadh did not disappear entirely. While Wajid Ali Shah remained in exile in Calcutta, his cousin,

Iqbal al-Daula, became a notable philanthropist as a member of the British India Society, an anti-slavery group.[71] From his residence in Baghdad, he also managed a controlling financial interest in the so-called 'Oudh Bequest', which promoted humanitarian relief and educational opportunities. During these years, the Oudh Bequest moved more than 6 million rupees from Awadh to cities then controlled by the Ottoman empire, including Najaf and Karbala, and Kazimayn, a sector in Baghdad.[72] In 1865, Iqbal al-Daula travelled to London once again, but this time to petition the British government to accord him greater control of the bequest, as he wanted to restrict the legacy to members of the former ruling family of Awadh, and to Indian and Kashmiri paupers.[73] He travelled with Austen Henry Layard, the archaeologist of Nineveh, whose projects to excavate archaeological sites in the region had also taken him through Baghdad.

In London, Layard introduced Iqbal al-Daula to the cultured, politically connected, and aristocratic society of Julia Margaret Cameron's Holland Park circle. On 19 January 1865, Lady Enid Guest, who was Layard's cousin and future wife, welcomed Iqbal al-Daula to her home for a salon-like winter evening of cultivated amusements, including *tableaux vivants*. Lady Guest wrote the following entry in her diary that day to commemorate the event:

> At 7:30 the old Ex King of Oude Ak bal od owlah – & Ld & Lady Carmarthen came ... After dinner we had tableaux vivants – the 4 seasons. *Spring*, Mr and Mrs C. Forbes – in Paul and Virginia. *Summer*, Mr C. Gurney & Mr Layard as Rebecca at the Wall [*sic*]. *Autumn*. Mrs Hambro & Mr C. Gurney as Italian peasants. – *Winter* Lady Felmer & Ivor in a russian [*sic*] skating scene. Mrs Hambro was the beauty looking lovely with a sheaf on her head. We then went on dancing & danced till 2.[74]

Who joined 'the old Ex King of Oude' in these parlour games that evening? The Marquess of Carmarthen was a British peer, the 8th Duke of Leeds, and Charles Gurney was another member of the Holland Park set, as he was Thoby and Sara Prinsep's son-in-law, the husband of their daughter Alice. The Gurney family virtually resided with the Prinseps in Little Holland House, and Julia Margaret later photographed the Gurneys' two children, Rachel and Laura, dressed up in angel wings. Ivor was Lady Enid's brother, and Mrs Hambro another family member.[75] Together with Lady Enid, this exclusive group mixed with the Prince of Wales as members of the 'Marlborough House Set', the self-designated club-house name they gave to their own privileged company.[76] Their theatrical re-enactments that day combined classical drama (*The Four Seasons*), with biblical stories (*Rebecca at the Well*), and imagined genre scenes portraying the unknown hardships of Italian peasants. Contemporary literature was represented by *Paul and Virginia*, the popular romance novel by Jacques-Henri Bernardin de Saint Pierre that sentimentally idealized the lives of impoverished, exiled children who lived with their mothers in a slave colony on an isolated island in the middle of the Indian Ocean.[77] When Layard wed Lady Enid in 1869, Cameron composed portrait studies of the two members of this elite society (for Layard, see Cox/Ford 700; for Lady Enid, see Cox/Ford 343) as well as Lady Enid's youngest sister, Blanche (Cox/Ford 230). And Julia Margaret included a portrait of Alice Prinsep Gurney in the album she made for her daughter Juley, although that photograph was probably taken by Oscar Gustave Rejlander.[78]

Several months later, during the summer, Julia Margaret Cameron welcomed Iqbal al-Daula to Little Holland House to photograph him outside in the gardens (fig. 53). Cameron did not record how he arrived on her doorstep in London, nor did any members of the Marlborough House set or Pre-Raphaelite Brotherhood record this encounter. After composing her Indian visitor before her lens and printing his image, she omitted the sitter's name when she titled her print and relied instead on his social status: *ex-King of Oude by Right of Birth* (Cox/Ford 729). The photograph captures a curious amalgam of the sitter's deposed royal standing: *ex-King*, as Lady Guest referred to her Indian visitor, but with the added significant qualifying legalistic phrase, *by Right of Birth*, which emphasizes, or rather calls into question, his nationality and subjecthood. By labelling her photograph in this way, Cameron conceded her awareness that Iqbal al-Daula believed himself to be the rightful sovereign of Awadh as well as his claim that the East India Company's annexation of his kingdom was unlawful.

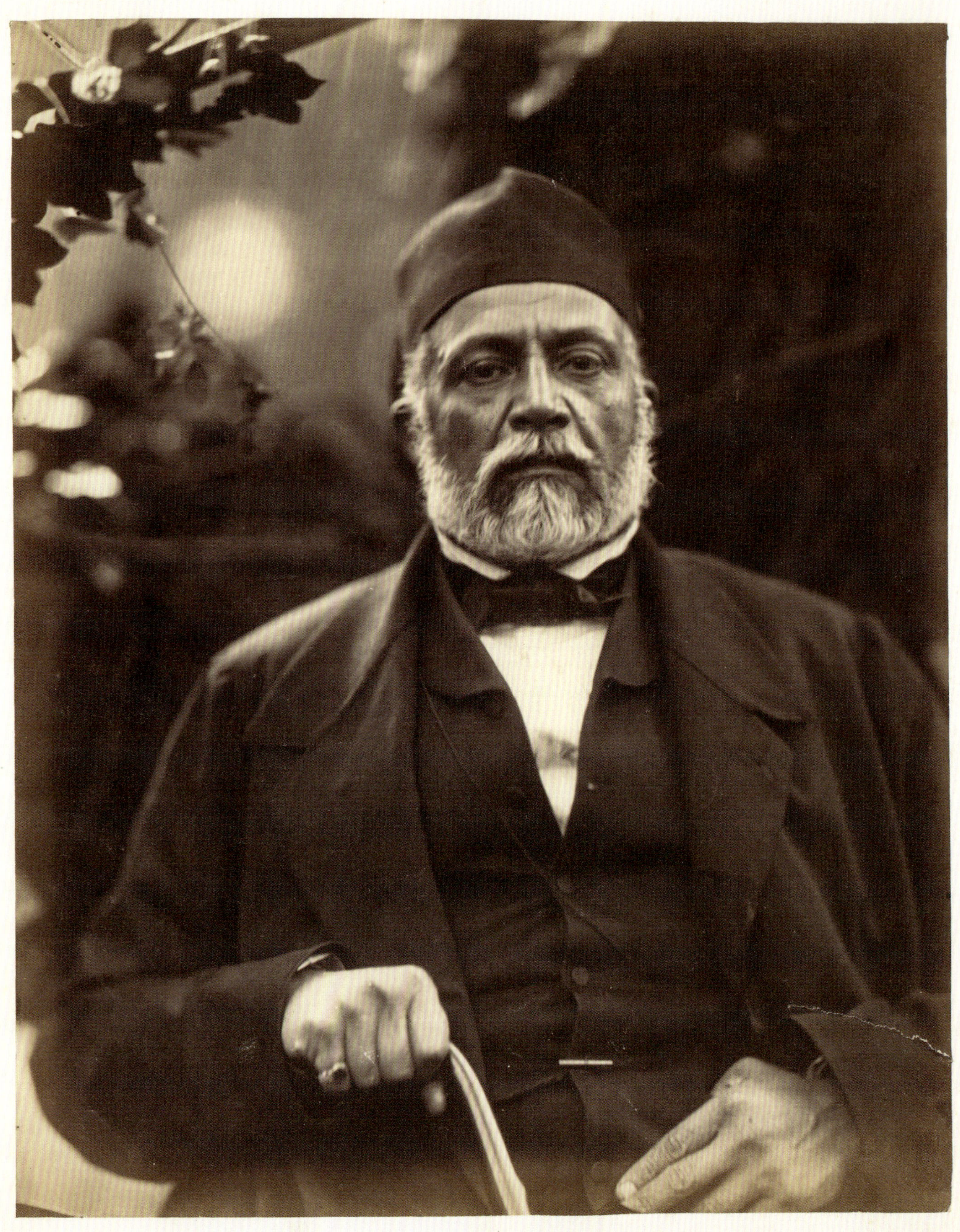

King of Oude by right of birth

Iqbal al-Daula was displaced in space and time: out-of-place as a foreign visitor to London, he was also dispossessed of his royal position and native land, an evident curiosity in English society. In her portrait, Cameron represented Iqbal al-Daula in a double role, but never referred to him by name. She depicted him as an Indian visitor presenting himself in the contemporary Western dress he wore while in London: he wears a fashionable vested suit, starched white shirt, black cravat, and displays what appears to be a modest piece of jewellery, perhaps a fob attached to a watch chain. His expression is serious, and his gestures are deliberate. His right hand grasps the head of a walking cane, his left thumb tucked into his vest pocket. Formal bourgeois attire of this kind was designed to convey dignity and status, intelligence and self-awareness, and a thoroughly modern bearing. These common attributes are also assigned to Cameron's established Victorian sitters – especially the cultivated men who witnessed Thackeray's recital of 'Arthur's First Wound' – Hunt, Prinsep, Hughes, Watts, Taylor, Tennyson, and Jowett – men in whose company she was familiar and whose portraits she took repeatedly over the years. Unlike Iqbal al-Daula, however, these men exude quiet self-confidence as they display symbols expressing their high status in British society or project the serenity of their esteemed social position. At Little Holland House, and later, in Freshwater, they were literally in dialogue with one another. By contrast, Iqbal al-Daula was isolated. He stares intently and directly at the white British woman positioned behind the camera, an evident outsider to the regular proceedings of the House.

Cameron's portrait of Iqbal al-Daula cannot escape the historical fact of the Indian Uprising: by emphasizing her sitter's regal position in her title, she situated Iqbal al-Daula in relation to the province of Oude, the Indian territory where the insurrection broke out, and in relation to the ex-king ousted by the British, Wajid Ali Shah, who was exiled in Calcutta. But Cameron also inscribed an additional marker of her sitter's subjecthood in relation to colonialism when she emphasized his birth-right, thereby calling attention to Iqbal al-Daula's simultaneous identity as both deposed sovereign *and* British subject. In her photograph, she has depicted him as a 'civilized Nawab', an Indian aristocrat who was loyal to British rule and therefore revered by the empire as a so-called 'faithful subject'. And yet, even though he abided by British authority, he also was marked a reviled imposter. Despite the Western clothing he wears to help blend into London society as a contemporary European, Iqbal al-Daula also wears a *kufi* cap, a sign of his Muslim faith and marker of his outsider status. As a result, Cameron captured the key discursive signifiers that defined how her sitter's subjecthood was constructed – and mediated by – external historical forces that constructed his national identity and determined his subjecthood. As we have seen, Iqbal al-Daula's claims to the Awadh throne depended upon Britain's legal recognition of his native birth-right.

53 Julia Margaret Cameron, *Ex-King of Oude by Right of Birth*, *c.*1865, albumen print, 25.5 × 19.8 cm.
Henry Taylor Album, fol. 47r. Bodleian Libraries, University of Oxford.

In Cameron's photograph, her subject expresses an element of suppressed or latent hostility, perhaps a response to the camera's mechanical status as a covert weapon of war. In 1863, from his vantage point in Simla, the summer home of Britain's Indian government, Samuel Bourne noted how the practice of photography interfered with daily life in the colony:

> the curious tripod with its mysterious chamber and mouth of brass taught the natives of this country that their conquerors were the inventors of other instruments beside the formidable guns of their artillery, which, though as suspicious perhaps in appearance, attained their object with less noise and smoke.[79]

Following Bourne, Ariella Azoulay more recently called the camera an instrument of violence and photography a technology of division, one that isolates the person represented in time and space while separating the sitter from the body politic.[80] In recognizing the camera's use as a surreptitious instrument of violence, Bourne's remarks actually presage by several years Britain's rigorous efforts to use photography to document and classify India's distinct indigenous tribes and religious castes as a formal approach to social mapping and control. That massive project, *The People of India*, reproduced more than 400 portraits of the Indian population. Although it was not published until 1868, its origins lay in the private collection of Governor-General Canning before he was named Viceroy, making ethnographic photography a longstanding proxy for the expansion of imperial control.[81] Although Cameron's photograph was never intended to make a similar contribution to an imperial archive like Canning's, as an isolated cultural document it functions in much the same capacity, chiefly because its genesis depended upon the legacy of Britain's colonial war in India.

Around this time, although the exact timing is uncertain, Iqbal al-Daula sought to exert control over his own photographic representation by having his portrait made and reproduced as a *carte-de-visite* photograph. Portraits of this kind were mass produced in the reduced size of visiting cards. They were fashionable items, either responding to, or helping to foster, the vogue for collecting celebrity portraits that was popular in Victorian Britain at the time.[82] It is not exactly clear how or why Iqbal al-Daula participated in this fad, but he established a formal tie to the London studio of Hellis and Son, had his image taken and visiting cards produced. Although Hellis's *carte-de-visite* portrait of Iqbal al-Daula has not been located, the firm advertised its connection to the Awadh king's celebrity status. On the reverse side of the cardboard stock that the firm used for all kinds of portraits, Hellis printed the legend, 'Photographers to His Highness Akbaloddowla, Ex-King of Oude', over a stylized script in Urdu.[83]

In the absence of Hellis's portrait of Iqbal al-Daula, it is tempting to posit that he might have wished to test his own identity as British subject through this act of photographic self-representation, perhaps by conforming to the typical conventions associated with the *carte-de-visite* format. In one major respect, for example, all *cartes-de-visite* looked alike, chiefly because sitters were presented frontally before a common studio-produced painted backdrop, a stage-set used repeatedly by the photographer for everyone, irrespective of their occupation or social position. The format almost always represented individuals in a sitting or standing posture and showed the entire body. Possessing such a portrait meant attachment to a social group.[84] Consequently, the *carte* format signalled to the world that the individual represented belonged to polite or bourgeois society, that is, the photograph helped to convey a 'textualization of citizenship' in visual terms. Sukanya Banerjee described this kind of photography as a social tool,

> a mode of inquiry that is sensitive to the narrative constituents of its claims as well as its statutory prescriptions, both of which speak to the imaginative framings through which the category of citizenship consolidates itself.[85]

But the *carte-de-visite* format also carried negative attributes as well. Owing to the format's uniform size and appearance, *cartes* emphasized their sameness to each other. As Christopher Pinney has argued, consumers of the medium in India disapproved of its apparent 'levelling and uniformity' because they found its visual sameness banal and commonplace as well as a threat to caste distinctions and social hierarchies.[86] But that sameness could also influence their choice of self-representation: as Julie Codell has observed, colonial subjects 'were aware of the reception of their look and of the reality that tailorized and dandified identities were becoming as ready-made as modern clothes'; consequently, they were particularly conscious to *avoid* any type of imagery that might stereotype them as 'exotic' outsiders.[87]

Iqbal al-Daula undoubtedly was aware of earlier group photographs of Wajid Ali Shah's Indian delegation (see figs 51 and 52). It is also possible that Austen Henry Layard or perhaps Alice Prinsep Gurney introduced him to the comparatively novel photographic style then being practised by Julia Margaret Cameron. They could have shared examples of her portraits in photographic albums or even accompanied him to her print sellers, which included P. & D. Colnaghi & Company in Pall Mall, Spooner's on the Strand, and John Mitchell on Old Bond Street.[88] In comparison to the banal sameness and diminutive size of the *carte-de-visite*, Cameron's signature style and impressively sized format must have seemed highly desirable as a distinguished alternative. Because Iqbal al-Daula was almost certainly conscious of the power of photography to fashion his own self-representation, he could have exploited his connection to Layard and Gurney to meet Alice's father, Henry Thoby

Prinsep, secure an invitation to Little Holland House, and facilitate a portrait session with Julia Margaret Cameron. And because Prinsep and Iqbal al-Daula were both prominent members of the Royal Asiatic Society, it is also possible the two men had been acquainted earlier, making Thoby Prinsep, as a speaker of Urdu (see fig. 20), the likely intermediary to have enabled the introduction between Iqbal al-Daula and Cameron that gave rise to this portrait.[89]

And yet, even though Cameron's photograph of Iqbal al-Daula was not destined for mass production, and she did not use the typical props or backdrops of those who operated *cartes-de-visite* studios, her portrait of the Indian man objectified its subject. Cameron's photograph was unlike the typical formula common to *cartes-de-visite*, which framed their subject in a distant middle ground. By contrast, Cameron and her subject were much closer in physical proximity. And yet, this relative closeness makes visible an evident power imbalance that emanates from the portrait, which is to say, Iqbal al-Daula's image captures inescapable differences in gender, class, and race that separated the photographer from her sitter, factors that would be far less apparent in a reduced-size *carte-de-visite*. Even by 1865, Iqbal al-Daula was unlikely to have ever directly confronted a British woman in such a domestic setting, much less one who met him eye-to-eye – albeit mediated by a camera – in a European city far from his home, in a formal garden behind an elite city residence, and in a controlled environment that was defined exclusively by her and her society, and not by him.

Very likely the two were not alone in the garden, and certainly not in the house. Iqbal travelled with attendants, and Cameron relied upon assistants to help with her apparatus. Nevertheless, it was necessary for the two to interact directly, even if Prinsep acted as a verbal mediator, to instruct Iqbal to hold still, for example, or for Cameron to indicate precisely when she intended to expose the sensitized plate to light. Owing to his religious and social upbringing, Iqbal was sensitive to gender differences. In 1838, for example, when he first travelled to Britain with his mother and small delegation, Iqbal al-Daula took elaborate pains to guard the modesty of the women in his company as an observant Muslim. We do not know if, as a native ruler, he believed his social place was divinely sanctioned to exert control over others, especially women, or if he held notions of essential differences that separated the sexes under Shia law. While similar kinds of social convention, although largely devoid of religious associations, determined unequal power relations between men and women in Victorian England, we might ask of this portrait session: was Iqbal al-Daula risking an affront to his regal standing or contravening religious doctrine by virtue of his proximity to Cameron?

As a native prince of India, Iqbal al-Daula was also likely to have considered his own paternalistic and aristocratic station in life as elevated above that of the female photographer who was taking his portrait, perhaps even considering her operation of a camera as menial labour and therefore further beneath his station. It would not be possible, in other words, for the Indian prince to ignore or deny Cameron's racial and gender differences. He might even have had to overcome possible offence from Cameron's atypical and curt social mannerisms, which even her English peers called peremptory, eccentric, and brusque. But perhaps Iqbal al-Daula's intense expression was not one of overt hostility towards Cameron but rather the mien of pain and grief, the result of what bell hooks called 'a process of fetishization', an approach 'that takes the black masculine "menace" and renders it feminine through a process of patriarchal objectification'.[90] Visible anguish of this kind could also have resulted from trauma inflicted by racial conflict, as a result of the legacy of suffering inflicted by the colonial war, or even owing to the violence of what hooks called 'the dispossessed, colonised black body politic'. As the critic explained,

> The blackness/darkness of the colonised body that marks it as other to the white coloniser is always framed within a gendered context wherein the metaphors of emasculation and castration symbolically articulate the psychic wounds of the colonised. That pain is then inscribed always as the pain of men inflicted upon them by other men. ...
>
> To establish fraternal order ... critical dialogue among men is necessary, as is the recognition of shared subjectivity. The presence of the female disrupts the possibility of this unmediated bonding.[91]

Crucially, then, as a female photographer, Cameron could not have established a common bond, what hooks called 'the recognition of shared subjectivity' that would otherwise result from the fraternal order of the status quo. Nor could Cameron, as a British subject, have presumed the two shared a neutral common ground upon which some sort of 'unmediated bonding' could take place. By contrast, evident racial differences marked the foreign subjecthood of colonized subjects who visited London.[92] And yet, it also appears that Iqbal al-Daula occupied an *in-between status* as both 'British subject' and 'not-British subject', returning us to the question of his legal sovereignty in post-'Mutiny' Britain, where it is apparent that his subjectivity was, by definition, ambiguous.

But in his portrait session with Cameron, the male/female and black/white dynamic that Iqbal al-Daula experienced could *not* have been interpreted as indefinite, like the question of his legal subjectivity before the lens. As bell hooks framed the social and historical context of their likely physical interaction that day, Julia Margaret's female presence disrupted their encounter, which made any recognition of shared subjectivity or unmediated bonding impossible. We might also add that the camera's material presence, which occupied an in-between space separating the female colonizer and the colonized man, also represented an additional physical barrier between them, yet one additional impediment to mutual recognition and understanding, yet one more obstacle to shared subjectivity. Combined, these apparent barriers could only impede what hooks called the 'psychic healing of wounds inflicted not only by the dysfunctions created by racism but by the myriad dysfunctions rooted in traumas'.[93] In the aftermath of the 1857 Uprising, as we have seen, those psychological traumas were experienced on both sides of the camera. For Iqbal al-Daula, it was the trauma of dispossession from his ancestral lineage, the exile from his homeland, the violence of colonial war. For her part, Cameron experienced trauma through the 'panic' she described from reading newspaper accounts of the war in India and letters from her nephew, as well as the 'vivid picture' of bloodshed and the death of British women and children in Cawnpore that 'haunted her thoughts'.[94]

Embedded in this portrait, then, is Cameron's portrayal of Iqbal al-Daula not only as a survivor of the anti-colonial rebellion, but as one who occupies two positions at once. On the one hand, she has appropriated his image as a compliant British subject, a model of decorum and practised civility. On the other hand, she has represented him as an incongruous alien in London, an Indian prince still clinging to his former status and title despite the assumption of Queen Victoria as empress, a misplaced revenant who can never recover his former archaic position.[95] As Judith Butler writes, this dynamic interaction describes an exchange relationship that is, at its root, antipathetic and unresolvable:

> Making the demand to become a citizen is no easy task, but debating the terms by which that citizenship is conferred is surely even more difficult. In this perspective, the citizen *is itself* a coalitional exchange; in other words, there is no singly or multiply determined subject, but a dynamic social process, a subject who is not only under way, but constituted and reconstituted in the course of social exchange. One is not only entitled to a certain status as a citizen, but this status is itself determined and revised in the course of social interaction. [Original emphasis][96]

As a result, Iqbal al-Daula's session before the camera produced an unstable portrait because the photographer captured his social status as ambivalent: vacillating between two discursive positions, his very citizenship 'constituted and reconstituted in the course of social exchange', Cameron could only embed her own ambivalence after experiencing the 'panic' she once felt in the wake of the Indian Uprising. Consequently, her portrait of Iqbal al-Daula also embodies unstable symbolic associations.[97]

But because the photograph's instability replicates the Indian man's undefined legal *and* cultural status in Britain, Cameron's representation of deposed Indian royalty cannot fix or inscribe the 'lessons of the past' in the present.[98] Having been denied 'the rights of succession' in legal terms and yet fruitlessly seeking restitution to the Awadh throne, Cameron represented Iqbal al-Daula's cause as one of vanity but also futility. The photograph survives as a complicated and unresolved archival document of the British empire in relation to its Indian colony: sitting before her, Iqbal al-Daula became *her* subject, a reminder to those who viewed this portrait that the 1857 Uprising put an end to what Charles Cameron and his colleagues in the East India Company considered the Oriental tyranny and unjust rule of successive Mughal rulers. After the rebellion, and certainly by 1865, which captures the brief interval when Charles Cameron's brand of paternal despotism was first disrupted, and then reinstated, the kings of Awadh and their royal descendants were irrevocably displaced by what the Camerons considered the wise and benevolent government of the British Crown. That transfer of power did not resolve the colony's conflicted notions of British subjecthood, although it did put an end to the promise of Indian self-governance, at least until the next century. Consequently, Cameron's portrait of Iqbal al-Daula contains the same unresolved power dynamic and contradictions of colonialism.

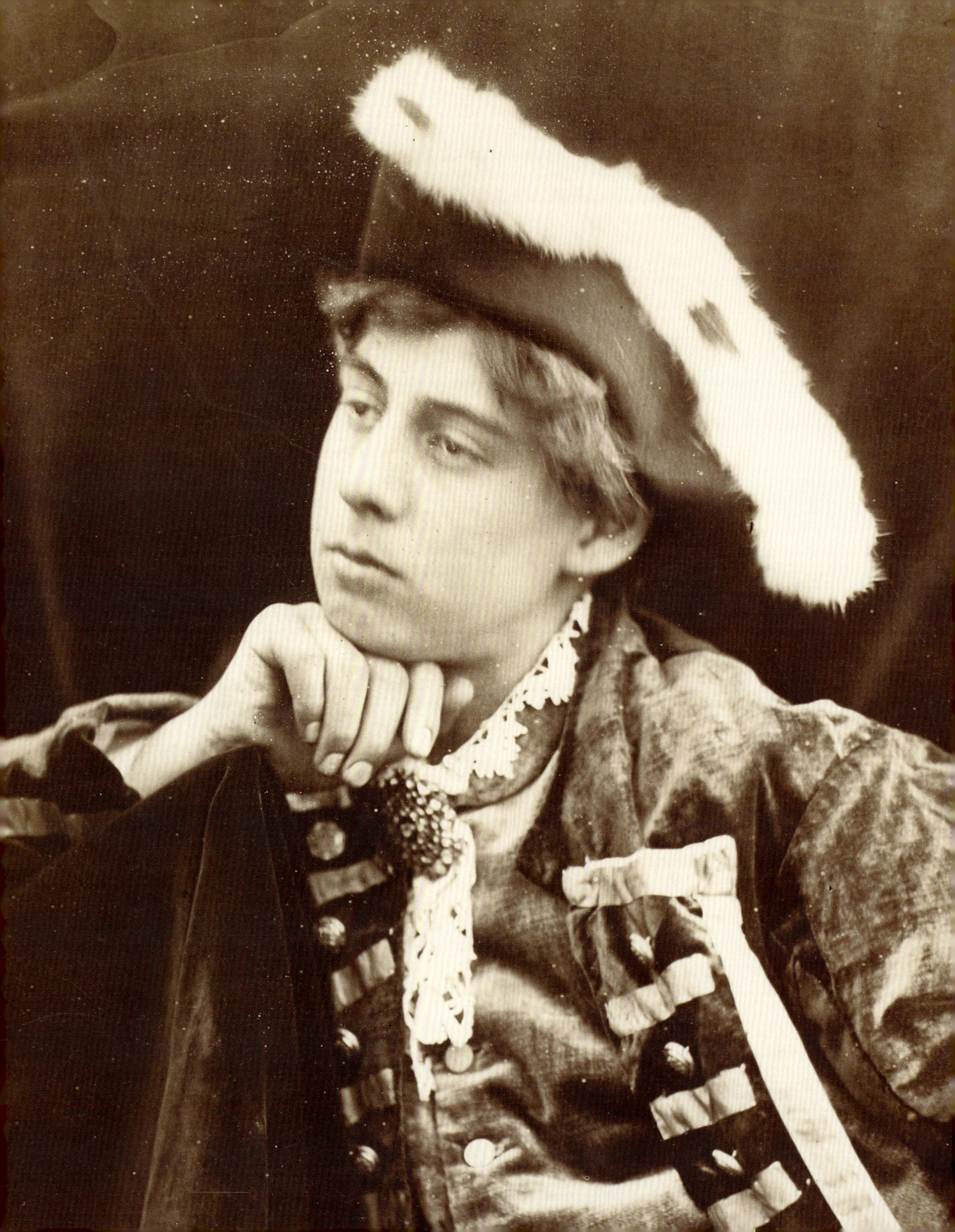

Chapter Six
Blood of the Fathers

54 Julia Margaret Cameron, *Lionel Tennyson in the Character of the Marquis de St. Cast*, 1869 (detail of fig. 63).

A WORLD WITHOUT MEN

As many of Cameron's biographers have affirmed, Julia Margaret was no 'angel in the house'. She was unconventional in dress and habits, assertively spoke her mind, was peremptory with others, and often demanding. She needed none of the warnings against slipping into the 'melancholy spectacle' of the 'languid, listless, and inert young ladies' that Sarah Stickney Ellis disdained.[1] Nor was she content to 'know her place' as willingly subservient, at least as that social position was counselled for women by the Tractarian cleric Edward Pusey, who so inspired the novelist Charlotte Yonge.[2] Yonge devoutly followed Pusey, but there is no evidence to support the idea that Julia Margaret was similarly smitten by that same brand of Evangelical Christianity.[3] Nor was Emily Eden Julia Margaret's role model. Cameron was no more interested in feasting on European delicacies, as did Eden on the hills of Simla, than in reclining languidly on couches or ordering *punkhawallahs* to cool her brow. Always industrious and busy, even a decade after returning to England, Julia Margaret Cameron enlarged her social activities as an 'imperial wife' by taking on new philanthropic causes. In 1859, she focused her energies to attend to the needs of the nation's war orphans.[4]

In February of that year, one month after her daughter Juley married Charles Norman, Julia Margaret embraced this role by hosting a formal event for children orphaned by the Crimean War, what might be called a kind of pleasure outing or amusement intended to provide fun and distraction, to take place on her own estate. As the Uprising in India had followed quickly on the heels of the Crimean War, many in Britain had still not fully processed the human cost of the earlier war. Dispatches from India had displaced reports of Russian incursions in Ukraine, and news stories about the conflict in Crimea had eventually receded from the daily press. Far greater emotional weight was now expressed in the press for vigorously defending Britain's presence in the empire's largest colony. In the court of public opinion, the earlier war seemed remote and, worse, was little understood. Yet two years after the traumatic colonial rebellion in India, the spectacle of war orphans emerged as the most visible everyday reminder of both wars, and even as she faced down her own anxiety over the mounting losses in India, Julia Margaret did not forget the most vulnerable orphans of the Crimean War. By underwriting an amusement designed to benefit orphans of that conflict, she was again 'doing her part' for the imperial cause, as Sarah Stickney Ellis would have it, by carving out for herself 'a new, powerful, discursive identity that was still rooted in Victorian femininity'.[5]

At this occasion, even though Cameron was joined by Sibella Norman, her friend and son-in-law's mother, as co-hostess of the event, she found the event disquieting, causing her thoughts to be filled once more with feelings of sorrow, mourning, and loss. Most of the war orphans were barely toddlers, she observed, and therefore sadly unaware of their precarious circumstances. Cameron described the scene to her daughter Juley using these terms:

> Some fifty of them were little tots of 2 & 3 & 4 years of age and I ranged them all in rows on the floor and we gave them all a bun and an orange apiece and feasted them besides on the fragments that remained and they were vastly happy and busy – They filled the floor of each room and then we let them escape and they all stood under the awning and sang 'God save the Queen.' Every one was more or less interested in them – dearest Mrs. Norman looked upon them with the tenderest deepest interest and when one thought that the Blood of all those Fathers (for we had 128 orphans with us) had been spilt in the Crimea in our service one felt a sore pity and compassion but they were all chubby – rosy creatures quite unconscious of sorrow and of the nature of their loss. For in this charitable country orphans are generally better provided for as to the real wants of life, than the poor who depend upon the efforts of their parents can be – [6]

Julia Margaret's charity event was certainly an act of kindness and benevolence, but also one that connected her once again to sorrow brought on by the sacrifices demanded of the imperial cause.

Cameron's verbal description of this event recalls John Everett Millais's two Crimean war paintings, *Peace Concluded, 1856* (fig. 55) and *L'enfant du regiment*. Both paintings received much critical praise in 1856 at the exhibition of the Royal Academy.[7] In the paintings, children take centre-stage as they are depicted as unmistakably but quietly traumatized by their separation from family and from the violence of war. In *Peace Concluded, 1856*, two children, accompanied by their weary mother, welcome home their shattered father, who sits exhausted, and is possibly wounded. In *L'enfant du regiment*, Millais depicted a wounded orphan, covered by her absent father's military coat, fast asleep on the effigy of a medieval knight. Millais's paintings were well known to the Holland Park circle, of course, and his success at the exhibition seems to have galled others among the competitive group of Pre-Raphaelites. In exasperation, for example, Rossetti called *Peace Concluded*, 'a very stupid affair to suit the day – but very big, and fetching him £900!, without copyright, for which he expects £1,000 more!', presumably thinking Millais would be able to collect this additional amount from engraved reproductions of the painting.[8] Julia Margaret almost certainly would have connected the plight of the war orphans she entertained to their representation in Millais's painting. Some critics found Millais's use of symbolism in *Peace Concluded* heavy-handed, as one child plays with the dove of peace in the foreground while the other plays with little figurines representing emblems of the warring countries. But the artist balanced his use of symbolism with realistic depictions of everyday contemporary objects, including a rumpled copy of the London *Times* announcing the news, and a well-read instalment of Thackeray's novel *The Newcomes*. Both are associated with the returning soldier: the novel is tucked behind his pillow, while he holds on to the journal in his left hand. Consequently, Millais connected the war abroad to contemporary depictions of these events in popular culture, which helped to convey the scene's immediate social impact. Millais also made the imperial cause explicit in this painting, as Thackeray described his novel's protagonist, Colonel Newcome, as a veteran of several earlier wars in India. After the 1857 Uprising, Millais's two paintings reminded viewers that Britain's imperial might was being severely tested once more. And in 1858, Thackeray helped to cement Crimea and India together as the source of so much despair, while

55 John Everett Millais, *Peace Concluded, 1856*, oil on canvas, 116.8 × 91.4 cm.
The Putnam Dana McMillan Fund, Minneapolis Institute of Art. 69.48.

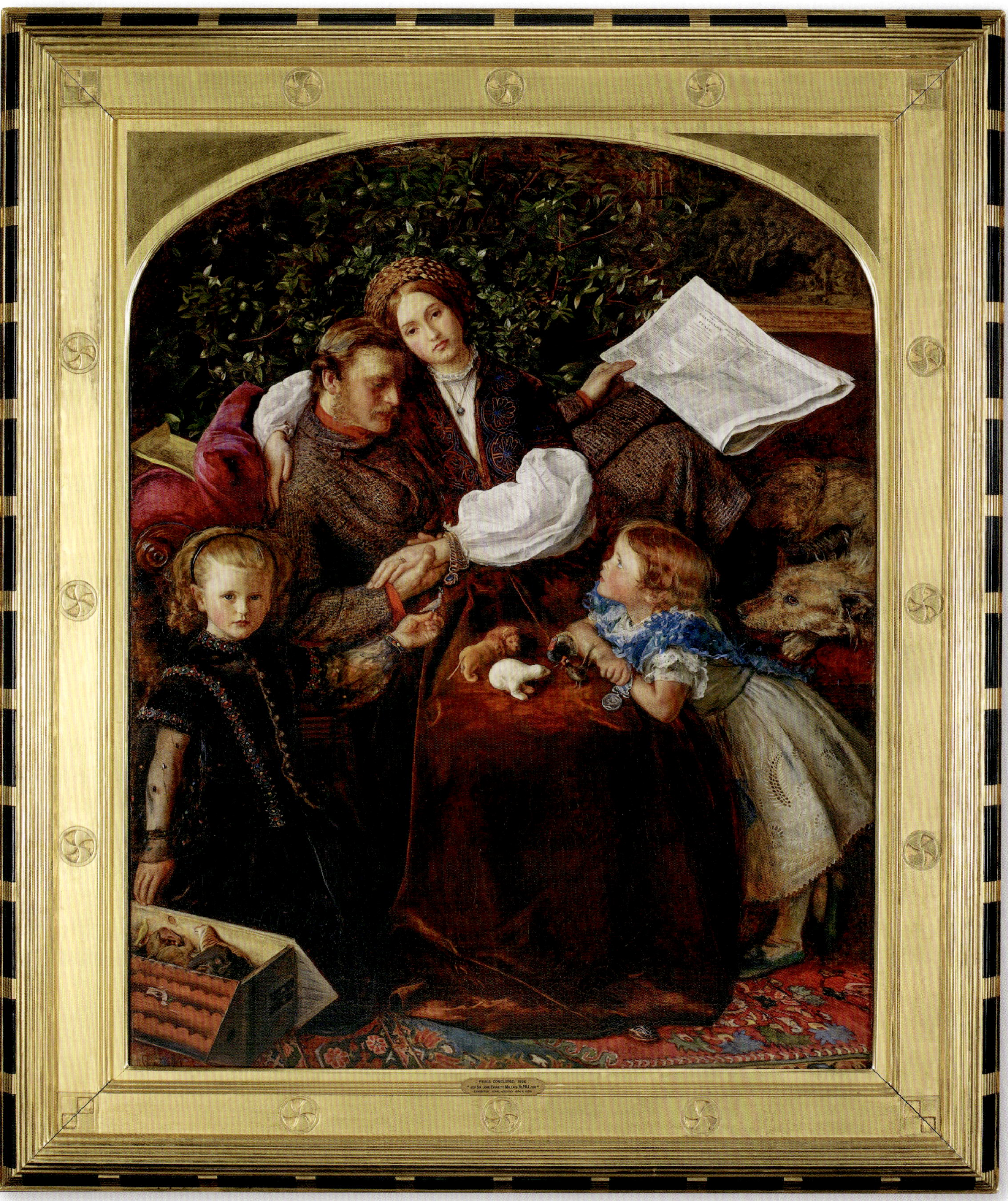
PEACE CONCLUDED. 1856

also alluding to national honour and military glory, when he signed his poem in *The Times*, 'Arthur's First Wound', with 'Colonel Newcome'.

Cameron's remark that England showed greater compassion to the offspring of the soldiers who died serving their country over the treatment of its poorest citizens who needed their help is a curious observation. Both were deprived populations, but the burden fell disproportionately on women and children. In remarking on these parallel conditions, Cameron implicitly criticized the Poor Laws that did not recognize the wives of soldiers who married without permission and were thereby prevented from receiving welfare benefits. When a 'Royal Patriotic Fund' was established in 1854 to aid war widows and their orphaned children, that fund depended upon the support of volunteers, to which Cameron clearly contributed.[9] Accurate numbers of war dead for both overseas conflicts are also impossible to determine. Historians estimate some 750,000 soldiers died in the Crimean War, approximately one-third of them on the British side of the conflict.[10] But for the war in India, Britain documented a mere 2,400 records of its own soldiers' casualties, although estimates of Indian losses ranged between 100,000 and several millions of lives, and both appraisals seem woefully inadequate.[11] As Ferdinand Mount has accurately observed, 'no serious historian of the Mutiny has attempted to offer a figure for the numbers who died over the whole period from May 1857 to April 1859'.[12] Recent studies examining how the East India Company addressed the financial needs of widows and children of men who had been in its service have found that the Company dispensed widely unequal responses to widows making formal requests for compensation – from the total denial of pecuniary assistance to the granting of full pensions – depending upon the status of the deceased soldier or administrative employee.[13] Julia Margaret might have also been responding to reports of unequal treatment of war widows and orphans stemming from the differential between those receiving East Indian Company benefits following the Indian Uprising and those dispensed by the Crown following the Crimean War, which were themselves widely perceived to be more generous for widows of officers and administrators than for ordinary regimental soldiers.[14]

Relief organizers who gathered in London to support the fund for widows and orphans in India inevitably associated their activities with efforts to ameliorate the suffering of the earlier war, with one key difference.[15] Drawing upon news reports about the loss of British lives, especially widows and orphans, the inaugural meeting of the Indian Mutiny Relief Fund drew more women than men, and organizers soon estimated there would be four times the number of sufferers from the rebellion in comparison with the earlier war owing to the increased number of troops and the presence of those 'civil sufferers'.[16] Finally, funds were collected to benefit British widows and orphans from a global community of sympathizers. For example, in September 1857, the *Economist* reported on a donation received from Napoleon III; the *Port of Spain Gazette* reported on contributions received from Trinidad; and the *Albion* reported on relief efforts and contributions taken in America to benefit British survivors.[17]

Orphans were therefore everyday reminders of the two imperial wars. As defenceless children, they embodied fraught social anxieties connected to their future upbringing, class affiliation, and workforce productivity. Their very presence visualized these concerns. They also represented for Victorian society unknown social consequences connected to being raised in a world without men. After 1857, these intertwined fears were magnified by the possibility that a first husband who went off to war – and who was wounded, missing, or lost – might later return home only to find he had been usurped by a second husband. The 1857 Matrimonial Causes Act made divorce possible for women whose husbands were presumed dead, ushering in the possibility that war widows could claim better economic and social futures, at the risk, or perhaps at the cost, of their earlier religiously sanctified marriages.[18] Coincidentally, also in 1857, in Wandsworth, south of London and not far from the location where Cameron held her outing for the group of war orphans, Queen Victoria laid the foundation stone for the Royal Victoria Patriotic Asylum. This facility was under construction in 1858 and began housing girls orphaned by the Crimean War in the summer of 1859, only several months after Cameron held her own social outing for fatherless children orphaned by the war.[19]

These interconnected activities undoubtedly informed the personal concern Julia Margaret expressed in 1861 concerning her eldest son's pending marriage to Caroline Browne. Eugene Cameron intended to marry before leaving England that year to accept a new appointment in Barbados as Secretary and Aide-de-Camp to Governor James Walker.[20] Barbados was important to the empire as a sugar-producing colony and had survived a bloody slave revolt in 1816. This conflict ultimately contributed to Britain's legal prohibition of slavery in 1834, but the new law upended the economic calculus of British plantation owners, many of whom brought slave labourers to the island from Africa and Asia. Simmering conflicts between owners and labourers persisted into the 1860s, only to erupt again in 1865 in nearby Jamaica. Although both Charles and Julia Margaret supported Eugene's military appointment as advantageous to their son's career aspirations, they were not confident about the proposed marriage union. Julia Margaret was adamant that Eugene and Caroline wed before her son embark for the West Indies so that the economic security of any of their progeny would be assured. She ultimately succeeded in pressing her husband Charles to iron out the family's differences with Caroline's father to facilitate a successful union within the family.[21] As these episodes demonstrate, Julia Margaret's family activities were intertwined with her self-appointed obligations to serve the nation by honouring the ancestry, and future legacy, of the empire. Moreover, her family's concern for their future offspring during this period of heightened awareness about colonial conflict, like her charity work on behalf of children orphaned by colonial wars, was informed by the social and political consequences of recent legislation, particularly those laws affecting the fate of women and children.

Cameron brought the Crimean War directly into her own photography. As a kind of pendant to her group photograph of the family's orphaned children, Blanche, Mary, and Adeline Grace Clogstoun, discussed earlier (see fig. 38), Cameron posed the three girls once again for a very different composition (Cox/Ford 930). Both photographs depict the Clogstoun sisters frontally, as a group, but if the former depicts the three girls as angelic in their pose or beatific in their costume of folded dark drapery, the latter portrays the three sisters as if they were industrious children hard at work on behalf of the empire. On a small round table before them, the sisters handle bundles of an unidentified white substance, the child at the centre looking up in consternation. One copy of this image, handed down within the Somers-Cocks family (Julia Margaret's sister), bears the following inscription on the reverse to explain the activity of the children and identify the material in the foreground: *3 Clogstouns / Picking Hemp for / Crimean War*. Yet the actual circumstances of this unusual message are indeed unclear. Why would Julia Margaret have portrayed the three Clogstoun children cultivating hemp, and why do so in a photograph, which Cameron apparently created after 1867? What possible significance could this activity have held – more than a decade *after* the war in Crimea had ended?

The range of possible associations could only be symbolic: hemp was an indispensable commodity throughout Europe as it was essential to the fabrication of cordage and sails used by sailing ships worldwide. Hemp therefore propelled international commerce and made it possible to equip naval warships. The crop was vital to sailing vessels and was cultivated and traded globally. Until the full takeover of naval fleets by steamships, hemp was in constant demand by virtually every nation's navy.[22] But surely Cameron did not portray her adopted girls undertaking actual menial labour. Rather, in this photograph she recreated or simulated this activity for a specific purpose. Perhaps the image commemorates the family's sense of national commitment to British veterans of overseas wars or expresses Cameron's own sense of shared obligations for the best interests of the nation. Perhaps she wanted to portray the Clogstoun sisters – actual orphans of the Indian Uprising – as an expression of solidarity with orphans of the Crimean War, an allegorical recognition of their shared privation and sacrifices. Or perhaps this photograph commemorates an actual recent memory on the Isle of Wight. On 23 April 1856, sailing ships of war, bound for Crimea, paraded formally on the Solent. Called the 'Grand Review of the Fleet', the naval display also was designed to honour Queen Victoria, who was present for the spectacle.[23] In advance of this marine procession, *The Times* promoted the event for weeks. On the appointed day, Alfred and Emily Tennyson left Freshwater for the piers at Yarmouth to witness the parade, very likely joined by Julia Margaret Cameron and her family. Emily Tennyson described the day's outing as inspirational for herself and her husband:

> We both of us went to the Grand Review in the little Solent and saw things very comfortably and well. … I am glad I went. The firing along the whole line when the Queen was saluted, the clearing of the smoke when ships and distant hills began to be seen again, the long line of ships standing up still and grand like an avenue of sphinxes, the cheering, the manning the yards, the great ships turning in slow majesty one after the other. We are glad to have seen so grand a sight.[24]

Memories of such grand spectacles of military might lingered long after those events took place. But it is equally likely that Cameron's photograph of the Clogstoun girls 'at work' helping stock ships destined for Crimea might also symbolize a celebration of the *aftermath* of war. In fact, peace was declared in Crimea just *after* the magnificent parade of warships took place in the Solent in April 1856, meaning that Britain's navy would not have to send its fleet into Asia after all, and the nation could rest easy in knowing its sailors would not come into harm's way. As a result, the *Illustrated London News* recorded a palpable sense of relief in its issue of 26 April 1856:

> The people who met in 1854 and 1855 to cheer our gallant sailors to their duty again assemble to cheer them for its performance. Peace has come, and with it – at least for the present – the naval and military labours of the country end.[25]

In this regard, Cameron's photograph of the children 'picking hemp' for war in Crimea could function in the same commemorative way as Millais's painting *Peace Concluded*, that is, not in relation to actual preparations for war, but as a marker of a return to peacetime reconciliation.

Before the war in India captured the Victorian imagination, then, Britain's military heroes were the soldiers it sent to fight in Crimea. These too were the model for Thackeray, who embraced the military motto of that time, 'Do or die', in 'Arthur's First Wound'. And yet, before the newer war could also produce fatherless children, publications like *Punch* represented deep concern for the women left behind when the nation sent its soldiers abroad. In April 1854, for example, just as soldiers left for Crimea, *Punch* published the poem 'A Soldier's Dream', a meditation on modern warfare. The soldier's dream is really a nightmare, an ominous foretelling that his absence will bring starvation upon his children and suffering to his wife. To the family's rescue comes 'an angel of grace', however, who offers material relief and moral succour that 'comes from the country your husband defends, / Which to you pays a debt that to him it feels owed'.[26] As Julia Margaret Cameron's photograph of the Clogstoun children demonstrates, the fears connected to Crimea prepared the nation for, and merged seamlessly with, the panic unleashed by the anti-colonial rebellion in India.

THE ORPHAN'S UNHAPPY RETURN

In 1861 and 1862, after hearing his friend Thomas Woolner recite the tale of a fisherman who was apparently lost at sea, Tennyson wrote his poem 'Enoch Arden'. The story describes an ambitious sailor who becomes marooned after a shipwreck. After a long absence from his family, the fisherman returns home only to find he has been forgotten, presumed dead. His wife has remarried, his children are unknown to him. Tennyson only slightly modified the tale for his poem, a story with ancient roots in Homer's *Odyssey* and Shakespeare's *The Winter's Tale*. But Tennyson made it new for Victorian audiences. As numerous commentators have remarked, during a period of foreign warfare, overseas commercial trade, and colonial emigration, stories like 'Enoch Arden' were avidly consumed and well-received by the British public as they responded to anxieties brought on by the nation's global expansion, commercial aspirations, and population growth.[27] The poignant theme corresponded to these social anxieties and formed the principal storyline for numerous short stories, novels, and poems. Male protagonists in these stories separate themselves – some reluctantly, others enthusiastically – from the warm bower of family, all hoping their absence from home will be temporary, but instead spend years adrift in heart-breaking wandering and isolation. Upon returning home, they learn their abandoned families have indeed suffered severely because of their desertion. They face the agonies of their wives, who were forced to resist the overtures of unwanted suitors in the husband's absence. Yet one day, the lonely, suffering wife remarries, hoping for a better life, and the moral quandary results when the first husband unexpectedly returns.

In 1862, when Tennyson read 'Enoch Arden' to a small audience of close friends in Freshwater, Henry Taylor observed that Julia Margaret's sister, Maria Jackson, 'went into hysterics' as Tennyson reached the poem's conclusion, and Emily Tennyson logged similar observations in her diary that day. She was particularly unsettled by what she called the strange behaviour of Maria's two daughters, who were also in attendance. (These were likely Mary and Julia Jackson, as their older sister Adeline was then married to Henry Halford Vaughan and living in Hampstead.) To Emily Tennyson, the reaction of the Jackson family was notable. Speaking of the Jackson sisters, she wrote, 'Her two dream girls *haunt* one. They seem to come out of some Nibelungenlied' (my emphasis).[28] In referencing the German medieval epic poem *Nibelungenlied*, Emily Tennyson did not spell out whether she regarded the sisters as tragic, histrionic, or simply theatrical, but melodrama effectively describes the intended effect of 'Enoch Arden', which links this medieval story to Tennyson's modern poem. Perhaps the sisters amplified the 'hysterics' of their mother. Emily Tennyson could have also used the term 'haunting' in a different sense, to convey something more romantic than unhinged, perhaps perceiving Cameron's two nieces as absorbed in a fantasy-like space, one shaped by desire, longing, and dreaminess, and for that reason might have concluded they were overtaken by some kind of melancholia. But the term 'poetry of sensation', which often is used to describe such work, describes only one aspect of this poem, as 'Enoch Arden' was conspicuously moralistic, even didactic. In the poem's most famous scene, after Enoch has returned home and then observes the happiness of his wife's second family, he selflessly determines not to destroy it by announcing his presence. P. G. Scott memorably called Enoch's observation of Annie's second family a 'voyeurism of the hearth'.[29] Here, Tennyson was explicit in outlining for the reader Enoch's proper moral choice, and critics considered the poem's overt moralism a kind of corrective to the sensation novel popular during this time in England.[30]

And yet, it is also no exaggeration to say that a *haunting* pervades the poem's narrative, as a persistent ghostly presence troubles both Enoch and his wife Annie and provokes uncanny feelings of dislocation and dissociation in them both. Having waited ten years after her husband's disappearance, Annie has remarried their onetime childhood friend, Philip Ray, who has now grown up to become a successful mill-owner. She then almost immediately experiences her absent husband in the form of an ominous presence, a supernatural haunting:

> … never merrily beat Annie's heart.
> A footstep seemed to fall beside her path,
> She knew not whence; a whisper on her ear,
> She knew not what; nor loved she to be left
> Alone at home, nor ventured out alone.
> What ail'd her then that, ere she enter'd, often
> Her hand dwelt lingeringly on the latch,
> Fearing to enter? (ll. 509–16)

Annie's nervous experience of haunting and melancholy parallels Enoch's physical isolation on the island where he is stranded along with two other shipwrecked men. The island provides all they require for daily sustenance, but they ache to be restored to their homeland. After Enoch's two companions die, his separation from the world is all but complete. He bears his solitude and outcast status stoically by constantly looking out for 'a sail', which represents for him human company, a return to civilization, and moral salvation:

> There often as he watch'd or seem'd to watch,
> So still the golden lizard on him paused,
> A phantom made of many phantoms moved
> Before him haunting him, or he himself
> Moved haunting people, things, and places, known
> Far in a darker isle beyond the line; (ll. 596–601)

On his lonely island, Enoch's sensory experiences are intensified: haunted by phantoms, he sees brilliant 'scarlet shafts of sunrise' before his eyes by day, which then are filled by 'the great stars' in heaven at night; he feels 'the hollower-bellowing ocean' in his bones; he reconstructs the parish bells of home 'in the ringing of his ears'.

The phantoms that plague Enoch are much like those that disquiet Annie in the sense that they remind him of what remains unresolved in his life and unacknowledged from the past, making the present anxious and tense. Enoch's wish-fulfilling phantoms also resemble Annie's expectant dream that takes place in Enoch's absence and immediately prior to her decision to remarry. On that fateful day, she selects a biblical verse at random but misinterprets the scriptural meaning of the text. Then she passes an unsettled night of disturbing dreams. In the morning, she misapprehends both experiences as providential signs that confirm her belief that Enoch has died, which then frees her to marry Philip. Yet Annie's state of mourning results from her uncertainty, which is complicated by ill-fated chance, confusion, and doubt as she seeks to answer the question: is Enoch still alive? Meanwhile, in his forced isolation, Enoch's phantoms hasten his own decline, as he increasingly becomes dissociated from his own identity and his nation. He becomes 'long-hair'd, long-bearded solitary, / Brown, looking hardly human, strangely clad, / Muttering and mumbling, idiot-like' (ll. 633–5); Enoch asks himself in vain, 'But homeward – home – what home? Had he a home? – ' (l. 663).

Tennyson's poem is important because it is linked to what I earlier called Cameron's intersecting obligations to family, nation, and empire and because the poem engages symbolic representations of anxiety, mourning, and loss, tying together interconnected symbolic forms to express contested histories and imperfect recollections. The poem also captures the anxieties of growing up in a world without men. Early in the story, for example, Tennyson establishes that Enoch is an orphan, although he does not explain how Enoch's father died. The theme was a compelling one for Tennyson, as the narrator of his earlier poem 'Locksley Hall' (1842) was also orphaned and a child of empire, his father having been killed in 'Mahratta-battle', a reference to the three successive wars prosecuted by the East India Company against the Maratha confederacy before 1818. In 'Enoch Arden', the three children grow up virtually on their own; together, they play a version of 'house' and take on the social roles of the Victorian patriarchal family. But with a twist: to keep the two boys from quarrelling, Annie plays 'little wife to both' (l. 36). 'Enoch Arden' became a potent cultural artefact during this period. Its intersecting emotions and ideas circulated among Cameron's family and friends, filled the halls of Little Holland House, and preoccupied the British reading public, which devoured *Enoch Arden and Other Poems* when it was published in the summer of 1864. This volume of poems was among Tennyson's most popular, selling 17,000 copies on its first day and, by the end of the year, its entire first run of 60,000 copies.[31]

We know these powerful and interconnected themes held great importance for Julia Margaret, as she chose 'Enoch Arden' as a source for several of her earliest allegorical photographs. One depicted Philip, Annie, and Enoch grouped together (Cox/Ford 905–906; fig. 56).[32] Another depicted the young *Annie Lee* alone (Cox/Ford 907; fig. 57). As Cameron emphatically wrote in her autobiography, she delved into photography with passion and zeal after receiving her first camera in December 1863. But in the immediate months that followed, she did not record the actual sequence in which she chose new subjects, and historians have no way to reconstruct this order. Although she dated her childhood portrait of Annie Philpot (her 'first success') to January 1864, for example, she did not register this photograph for copyright immediately, but waited instead until June 1864 to record her entry – along with thirty-five other photographs representing a diverse array of subjects, making it impossible to tease out a semblance of her order or priority. And in the preceding month of May, she recorded ten prints in the registers, also a mixture of portraits and allegories, which she later called 'fancy subjects'.

Among Cameron's earliest photographs are images of children. Through them, she portrayed anxiety, mourning, and loss through the vehicle of the popular literary characters they represented. By means of these narrative choices, she represented the larger concerns of the family, the nation, and the empire, particularly in images that represent orphaned children. Critically, these diverse stories represented an unstable and dangerous world in transition, where children bear the burden of a society they have inherited but did not make. Julia Margaret embraced these themes in her earliest photographs, representing the

56 Julia Margaret Cameron, *Philip Ray, Annie Lee, and Enoch Arden*, *c*.1864, albumen print, 24.3 × 21.1 cm.
Henry Taylor Album, Arch. K b.12, fol. 28v.
Bodleian Libraries, University of Oxford.

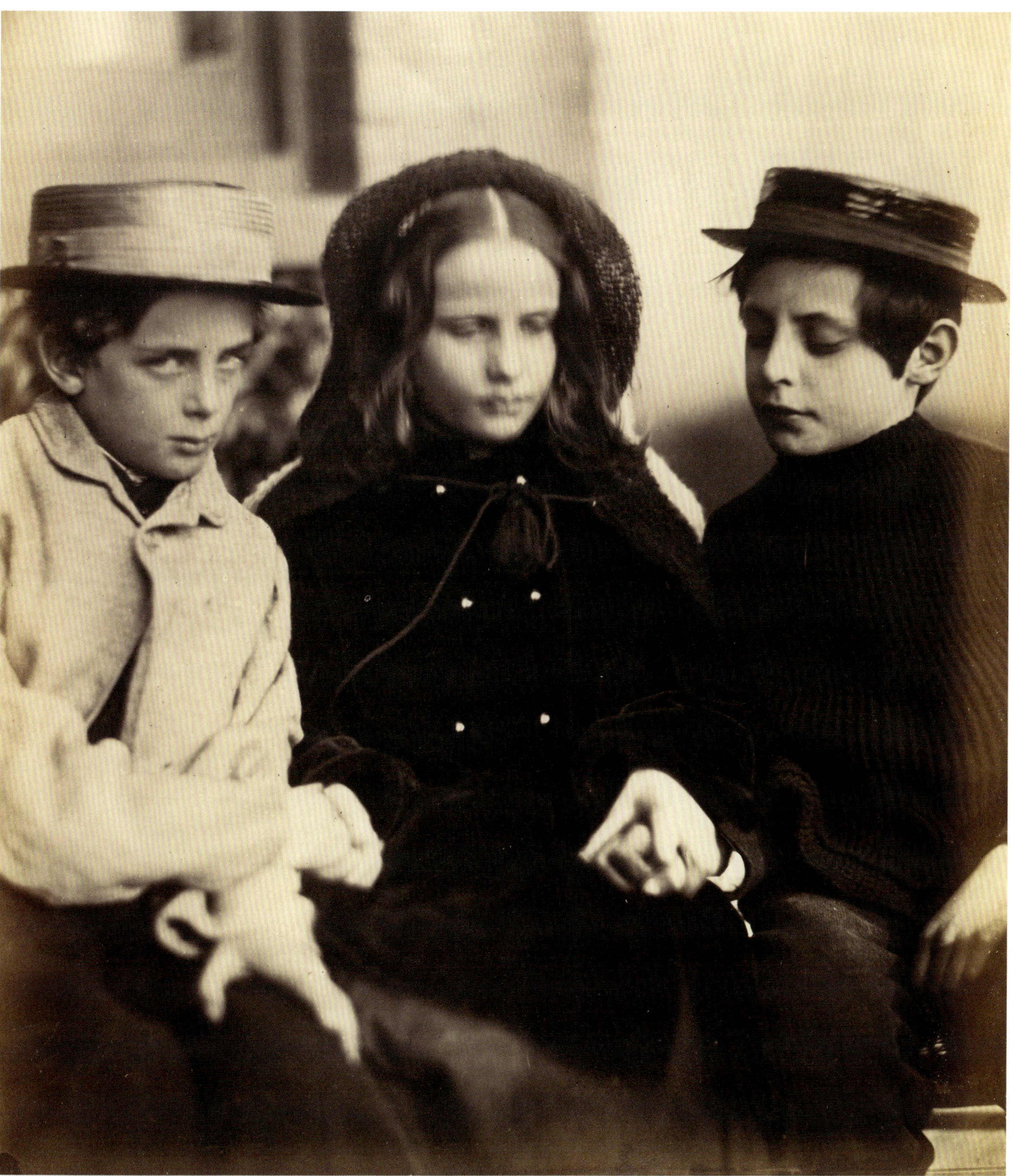

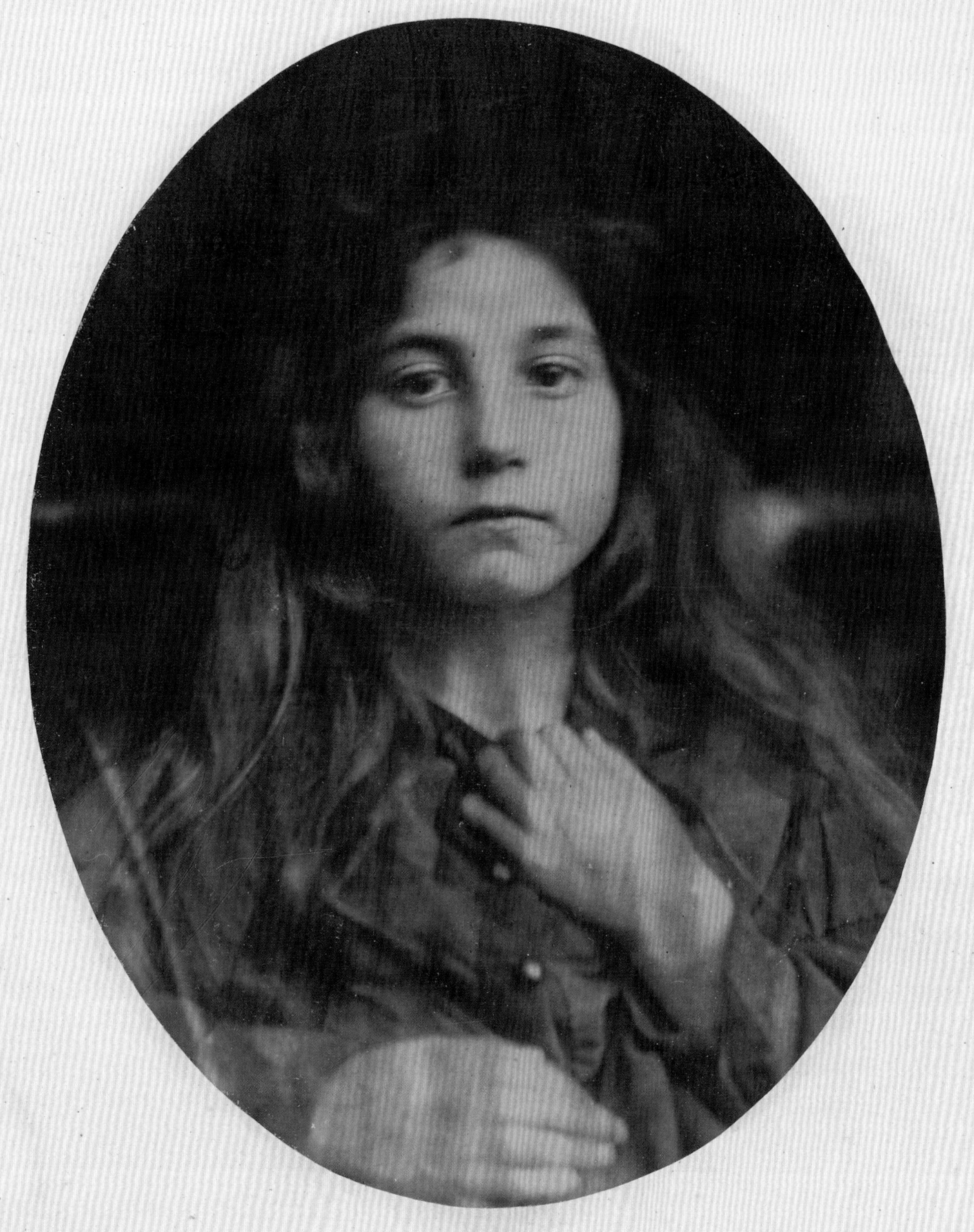

Annie Lee.
From life

Julia Margaret Cameron

principal childhood characters in 'Enoch Arden' in at least three separate compositions. Around this time, Cameron also represented the two young protagonists of Jacques-Henri Bernardin de Saint-Pierre's novel *Paul and Virginia*, even though she did not register that photograph until 1865 (Cox/Ford 20–23). Popular in Britain and an international success, Saint-Pierre's novel tells the story of two fatherless outcasts who live with their mothers on a primordial island paradise in the middle of the Indian Ocean. Like 'Enoch Arden', Saint-Pierre's novel was one of the period's most widely read books.[33] These connected storylines depict the act of mourning *avant la lettre*, as the children are unaware of their life's trajectory and too young to comprehend their precarity in the world. Both photographs depict children in mournful poses, quiet, internally focused, solemn, and contemplative.

As stories that start off in an orphaned childhood, these characters also foreshadow the protagonist's absence from the patriarchal hearth and therefore anticipate the nation's mourning of that absence. In 'Enoch Arden', the protagonist's repressed memories symbolize his longing to regain that position. For Marion Shaw, they also represent Enoch's commitment to the imperial cause:

> As an inadvertent colonialist, Enoch ... strives to become a true son of Britain and of Empire by imposing English values on his 'orient' island through the scenes, scents, and people of English memory. But it is a phantasmal enterprise, a ghostly and grotesque paradigm of imperial acculturalization.[34]

Consequently, the phantoms and hauntings that circle through 'Enoch Arden' reveal two additional elements of the world disrupted by Enoch's disappearance. On the one hand, Enoch's island ghosts take shape as remnants of the violent trespasses practised by mercantile tradesmen and colonial explorers, whose history of abuses and exploitations demand a reckoning in the present. On the other, Annie's phantoms signify the interior disquiet that reflects her unsettled state of mind, which turns the act of mourning into a symbolic act of remembering the past. Perhaps these unsettling images were of the kind that disturbed the Jackson sisters when they listened to Tennyson's reading and attracted Julia Margaret to attempt their representation in photography. In the end, the phantoms haunting both Enoch and Annie are emblematic of the partial and contested experiences brought on by this disquiet and are amplified because history and memory, as Tennyson's poem demonstrates, are prone to gaps and misinterpretations.

Tennyson tackled similar themes of love and loss earlier, as in his elegy to Arthur Hallam, 'In Memoriam' (1850), where he expressed yearning for the physical return of his dead friend: 'Ah dear, but come thou back to me! / Whatever change the years have wrought, / I find not yet one lonely thought / That cries against my wish for thee' (XC, ll. 21–4). As the reader of 'Enoch Arden' pieces together the narrative of intertwined forces that conspire to haunt both Annie and Enoch, perhaps even recalling these lines from 'In Memoriam', the 'repressed and buried reality' of their tragic circumstances become vividly apparent as the poem reaches its heart-rending conclusion.[35] Tension builds when Enoch returns to his village as a revenant because his very presence threatens to disrupt the harmony built between Annie and Philip, a moralizing threat that would undo the secure union the two had established, and destabilize the relationship between past and present. Enoch never truly confronts the real betrayal, writes Anne Humpherys, which would entail recognizing Annie's return for Philip's love.[36] Instead, because Enoch assumed a kind of 'cloak of invisibility' when he returned to the village and then spied from afar on the happy family scene of Annie with her new husband, Enoch had become a ghostly revenant who possesses a scopic power, the uncanny ability 'to see without being seen'.[37] Tennyson's poem cautions his readers that only through the revenant's eyes can the awful reality of the imperfect and unresolved past be truly revealed.

57 Julia Margaret Cameron, *Annie Lee*, 1864, albumen print, 21 × 16.2 cm.

J. Paul Getty Museum, 84.XM.443.53. Digital image courtesy of Getty's Open Content Program.

ANGELS ON HEAVEN AND EARTH

During this same period, Cameron also composed images of very young children in numerous other allegorical representations. She portrayed them as holy angels accompanying the Madonna in the manner of Raphael's *Sistine Madonna*, as mythological figures (cupids and putti), and as the subject of contemporary fables like the 'water babies' of Charles Kingsley's 1862–3 story of the same name. 'The peasantry of our island is very handsome', she noted in her autobiography,[38] but in using her island neighbours as models she erased their Victorian identities by turning them into literary subjects. As Virginia Woolf claimed, by inverting photography's 'hold on the real' and introducing the metaphorical language of symbols, she broke apart the camera's lock on realism. In Cameron's hands, cherubic infants play numerous possible roles, mythological or religious, their meanings based upon the narrative context represented in the image or signified by the title. But Cameron assigned titles inconsistently and many of her photographs do not correspond well to the plainly factual descriptions she wrote in the copyright registers when she recorded these works.[39] Early in 1864, for example, in seeking guidance on composition but also appropriate titles for her imagery, Cameron shared numerous prints with George Frederic Watts, asking for his critical feedback and advice.[40]

A review of the copyright registers for this period reveals that she could have assigned many possible titles to describe multiple photographs in which she arranged infants or very young children in nearly identical poses:

7. Child's head from life, like a cherub, full face inclined [30 May 1864]

41. Child, Hair flowing down, light on top of head ¾ face, coat with large buttons [30 June 1864]

56. Annie Lee, hat on, hair flowing, full face, left hand raised to throat [10 October 1864]

84. Lizzie Koewen, Child full length, shift falling off from each arm otherwise undressed [4 November 1864]

93. The Water Babies. Two Children seated as if floating, both nearly full face, nearly naked [12 December 1864]

107. Child (Alice Ducane), nearly naked, full face, long hair, hand on leg near ankle [12 December 1864]

114. Two girls in white drapery, kissing each other, one profile, the other face ¾ turned away [11 January 1865]

115. Girl in long cape kissing forehead of other girl who bends downwards [11 January 1865][41]

Except for #93, *The Water Babies*, a title that corresponds directly to Kingsley's invented fable, or #56, *Annie Lee* (see fig. 57), which viewers would recognize as the name of the female protagonist in Tennyson's poem 'Enoch Arden', the incomplete and imprecise descriptions of these copyright registers is simply inadequate to match up to titles she assigned later. Complicating the matter is the fact that at this early stage in her career, Cameron created many similar compositions of the same subjects during a very brief window of time, and when she produced new versions of these works, she did not always record those efforts in the copyright office. Cameron's other title choices for her infant models only confound matters further. She titled other photographs of young children using enigmatic or obscure references, including *The Infant Bridal*, *The Double Star*, and *A Story of the Heavens*.[42] In short, by using titles like these interchangeably or by not assigning titles at all, Cameron complicated not only the symbolic associations of her imagery but also their intended use and meaning. After all, the religious or secular associations of angels, cupids, and putti depend entirely upon the iconographic context in which they appear.[43]

Once transformed into heavenly beings or mythological figures or even fantasy creatures, Cameron's child models acquired the graphic language of iconography.[44] For example, Cameron's photograph of *Cherub and Seraph* which she included in the Herschel Album, (Cox/Ford 872; HA-41; fig. 58), portrays particular kinds of angels in the history of art that, since the Italian Renaissance, were associated with the top level in the 'hierarchy of angels' as described in the Bible (Genesis 3:24; Ezekiel 10). Often, these angels were depicted as human heads surrounded only by pairs of wings. This visual type signifies their unique place in Raphael's *Sistine Madonna*, for example, which portrays the Virgin and Child adored by two of these heavenly angels at the base of the painting. Prince Albert was a notable admirer of Raphael's works and helped to popularize these subjects through his collecting. At the time, Raphael's painted canvas was installed in Dresden, but the image was

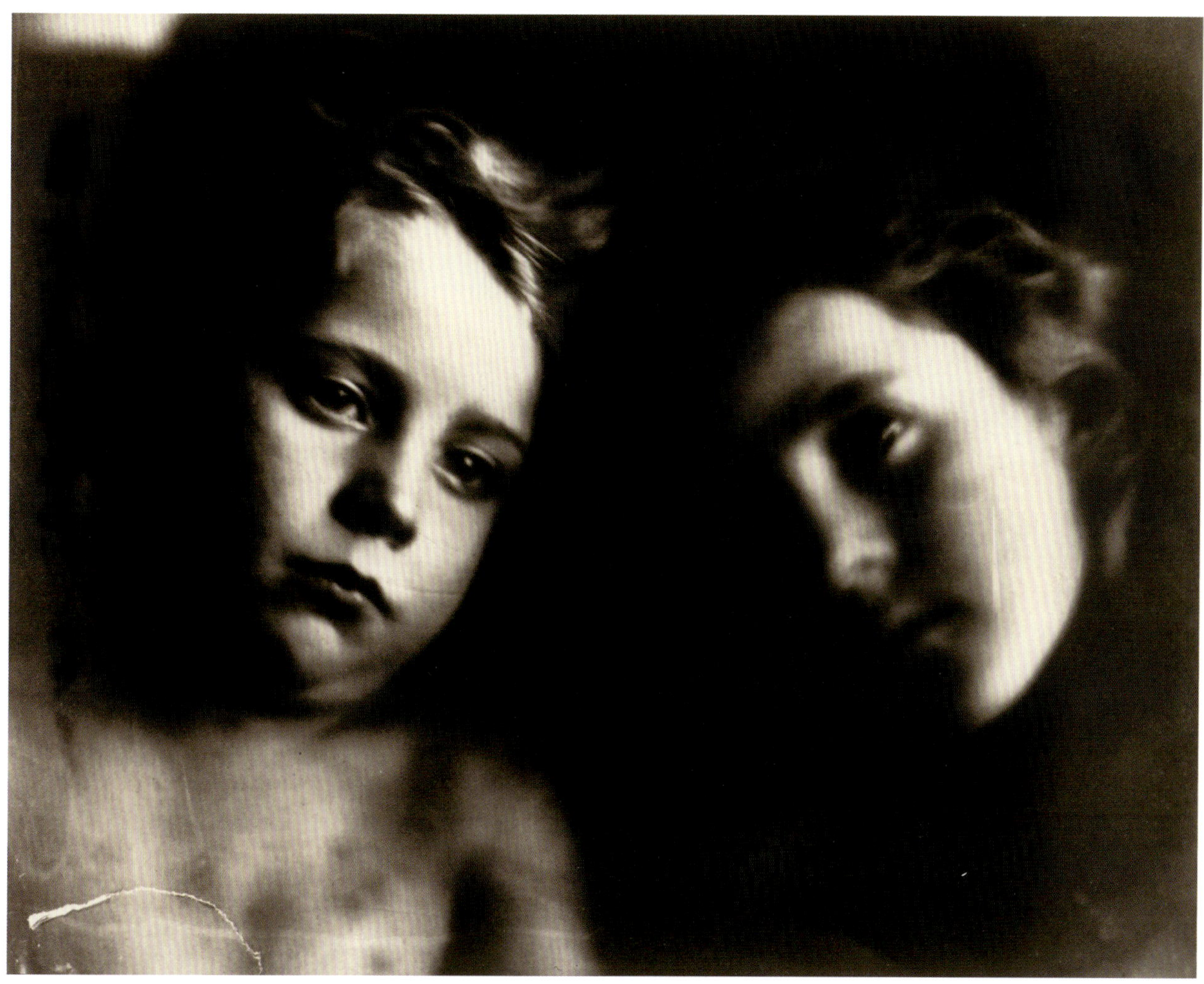

58 Julia Margaret Cameron, *Cherub and Seraph*, *c.*1866, albumen print, 23.3 × 28.8 cm.
National Science & Media Museum / Science Museum Group. 1990–5036/11505.

known throughout the world as a reproductive engraving.[45] In 1853, Albert embarked upon a grand project to create an album containing prints of all of Raphael's paintings. Towards that end, he collected numerous prints of the *Sistine Madonna*, even commissioning photographers to document Raphael's paintings and drawings in British collections.[46] So enthralled was Albert with the *Sistine Madonna*, he commissioned Leonida Caldesi to photograph his young son, Arthur, posed in the manner of one of Raphael's angels. Cameron herself understood the wide popularity of Raphael's angels at the same time and posed two children in precisely the same manner in at least one of her photographs of the Madonna and Child.[47]

Cameron was exposed to numerous other representations of young children in similar poses by artists, ancient and modern, and came to understand how artists depicted angelic figures like putti to announce a divine presence on earth, to mediate between heaven and earth, or simply to provide some light-hearted amusement or visual distraction. In her photography, Cameron posed the two children in *The Turtle Doves* (Cox/Ford 858–859; fig. 59), for example, as if they were putti embracing in the model of numerous examples she might have known in sacred art from the Renaissance, which historians have most frequently cited as her source material.[48] But putti are also present in examples of secular art where they are used to convey heavenly approval for some sort of earthly activity. For example, in

Thomas Stothard's print *The Voyage of the Sable Venus from Angola to the West Indies* (*c.*1800; fig. 60), the artist deployed putti to portray slavery as if it were a heaven-sent gift. Their presence glorifies the transport of slaves across the ocean. They frolic in the air surrounding the captive woman as if welcoming the birth of a goddess. In this way, the artist signified the divine endorsement of human bondage. By equating the delivery of female slaves to work the plantations of Jamaica to the mystical Birth of Venus, Stothard used putti to distract viewers from the violence of the capture or the cruelty and oppression of holding men and women in captivity. Drawing upon the much-admired example of embracing angels who celebrate the mystical birth of Venus in Sandro Botticelli's painting of the 1480s, Stothard effectively turned the allegory upside-down, using putti to sanction the mortal actions of men and convey the blessings of providence.

Cameron herself encountered similar representations of putti in a painting explicitly intended to express nationalistic and imperial themes. In November 1859 in London, she paid a visit to her brother-in-law, Thoby Prinsep, where he worked in the financial offices of India House, the administrative centre of the government's control of India, which had replaced the East India Company only the year before.[49] At India House, Cameron would certainly have encountered Spiridione Roma's celebrated painting *The East Offering its Riches to Britannia* (1778), an oil on canvas designed for the ceiling (fig. 61). Roma depicted putti conspicuously in the upper left-hand section of the painting to represent divine support for the colonial relationship: Britannia shelters these dancing babes and protects them

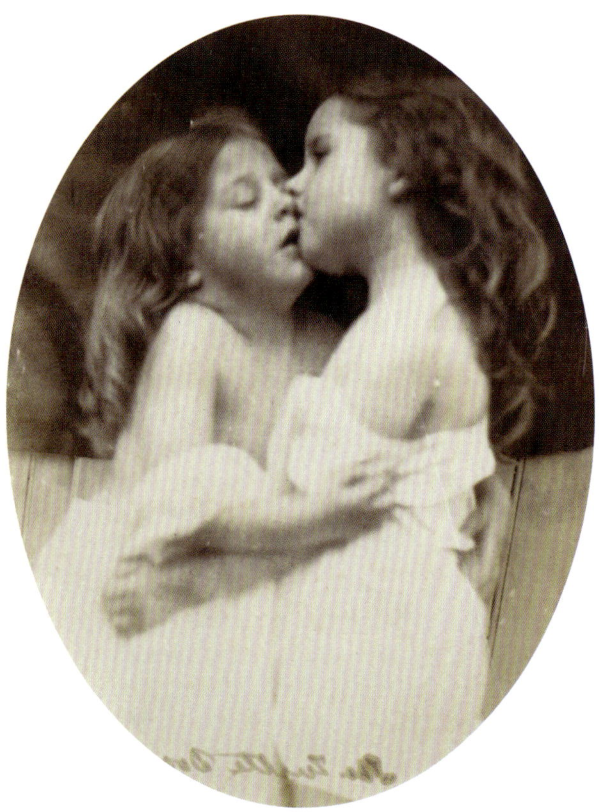

59 Julia Margaret Cameron, *The Turtle Doves*, 1864, albumen print, 18.8 × 14.4 cm.

© Victoria and Albert Museum, London. PH.241–1982.

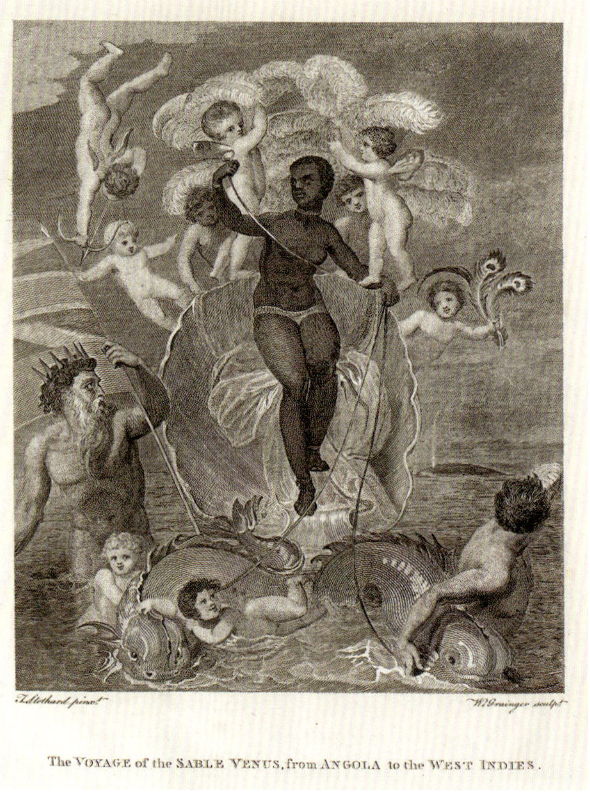

60 Thomas Stothard, *The Voyage of the Sable Venus from Angola to the West Indies*, *c.*1800, etching and engraving, 20.3 × 16.4 cm.

National Maritime Museum, Greenwich, London, Michael Graham-Stewart Slavery Collection. Acquired with the assistance of the Heritage Lottery Fund. ZBA2520.

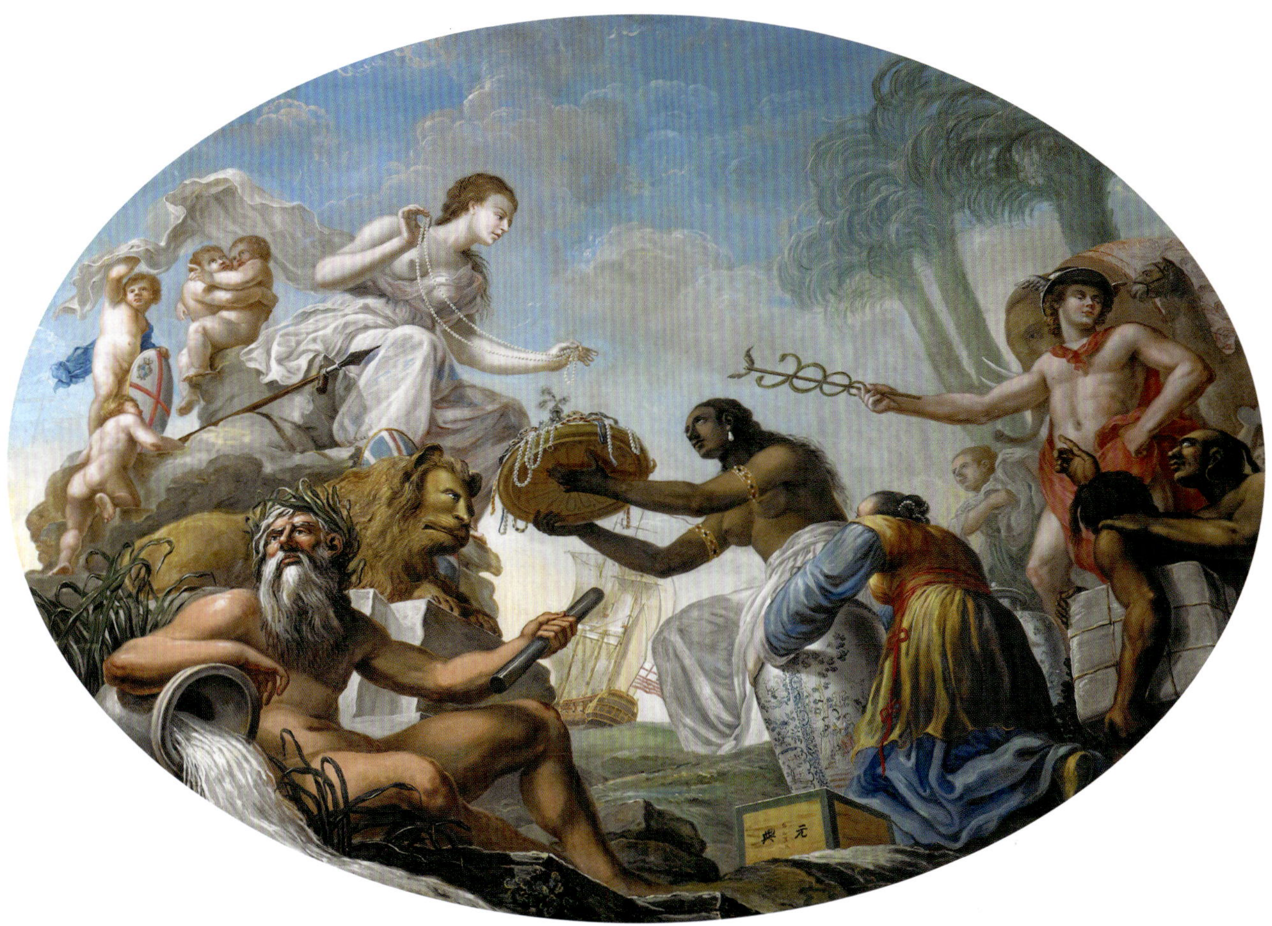

61 Spiridione Roma, *The East Offering its Riches to Britannia*, 1778, ceiling painting originally for the Revenue Committee Room of the East India House, London, now in the Foreign and Commonwealth Office, London.

© The British Library Board. Foster 245. Shelfmark: IOSM F245.

from harm. Standing behind the East India Company's ceremonial shield, the naked children represent its worldly actions as justified. Their presence oversees the transfer of wealth from Asia to Britain as if it were providential and peaceful. Surmounting the rock upon which Britannia sits, the putti communicate divine approval of the Company's rule over the nations of 'the East' to appropriate the world's material prosperity as its own. Intriguingly, in Cameron's photograph of *The Turtle Doves*, she replicated the same pose of the putti's embrace as in Roma's painting, although this visual resemblance is more likely a function of parallel modelling from the archetype established in Renaissance Italy than a deliberate appropriation from Roma.[50] The point here is that the iconographic trope was a shared discourse and could be found in numerous examples of sacred and secular art.

Because of George Frederic Watts's standing at Little Holland House and because Cameron replicated his subjects in many of her earliest photographs, scholars have represented Watts's artistic impression on Cameron as highly influential. But Cameron did not restrict her inspiration to Watts's example exclusively and did not confine her early allegorical imagery to children alone. After 1862, she enlisted the help of Oscar Gustave Rejlander, a Swedish emigrant to England who had made a significant impression upon the world of photography from his display of an allegorical image, *The Two Ways of Life*, at the 1857 Manchester Art Treasures Exhibition. Several years later, Rejlander's fame grew owing to the photographs he displayed at the International Exhibition of 1862. As we shall see, Cameron drew upon his experience with genre imagery to further her understanding of how to embed narrative storytelling in photographic representations of children.

The official *Record* of the International Exhibition singled out Rejlander's photograph *A Night in the Streets of London* for special acclaim (fig. 62).[51] As a prototypical genre picture, the photograph embodied the sentimental expressions of Romanticism. Depicting a shoeless, poor boy in dirty rags, posed alone on a doorway stoop where 'every line in the figure suggests destitution and wretchedness', the *Record* called the photograph 'a true portrait of the youthful pariah of a great civilized city'.[52] Yet nothing in Rejlander's photograph was 'true' in the sense of factual or documentary veracity, as the child portrayed in the photograph was selected as a studio model, dressed in a ragged costume, and positioned in a fabricated setting. And yet, while Rejlander constructed the image as a form of theatrical fiction, he nevertheless also embedded a kernel of realism that revealed something authentic about London's class structure: as the official guidebook acknowledged, while the youthful subject embodied associations of 'childhood innocence' common to genre studies, it also personified the discarded outcasts living at the margins of society.[53] These two spheres merged in much of Rejlander's photography, which Cameron would have seen at the London exhibition, especially as they were singled out for commendation. That same year, perhaps during the summer, Cameron welcomed Rejlander to the Isle of Wight as her guest. Scholars agree the two collaborated or made several photographs together, with Rejlander presumably in the teaching role and Cameron learning to compose and print.[54]

At some point, *A Night in the Streets of London* acquired the title *Poor Jo*, which transformed Rejlander's photograph from an artful representation of a street pauper into a fictional character straight out of Dickens's novel *Bleak House* (1852–3). The photograph soon became ubiquitous, reproduced in numerous forms and media.[55] Dickens's character, Poor Jo, is an urban street urchin of distinctly English origins; 'he is not a genuine foreign-grown savage', Dickens's narrator tells us, but rather, 'he is the ordinary home-made article':

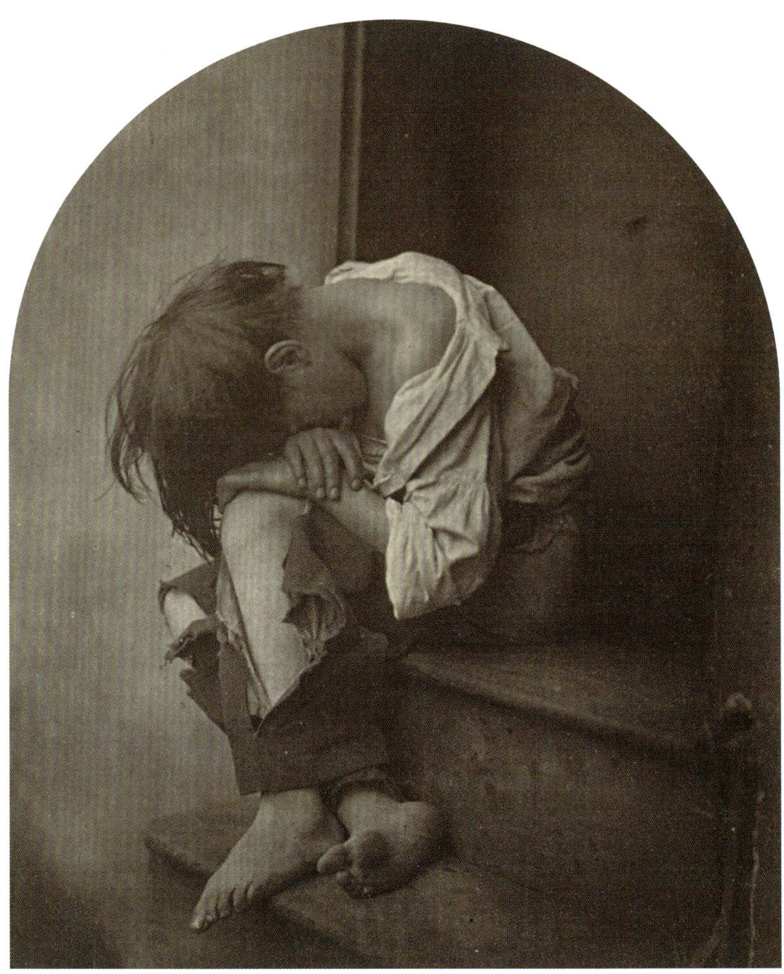

62 Oscar Gustave Rejlander, *A Night in the Streets of London*, *c.*1857, photograph, 26 × 32 cm.
National Science & Media Museum / Science Museum Group. 1987–0211.

> Dirty, ugly, disagreeable to all the senses, in a body a common creature of the common streets, only in soul a heathen. Homely filth begrimes him, homely parasites devour him, homely sores are in him, homely rags are on him: native ignorance, the growth of English soil and climate, sinks his immortal nature lower than the beasts that perish.[56]

As represented visually by Rejlander, Jo embodies the flip side of Cameron's rehabilitated orphans. For Dickens, Jo's misery is exacerbated by his extreme poverty, a consequence of his homelessness amid the urban squalor, but also his abject separation from society. Likewise, Rejlander portrayed him alone, separated from society. In *Bleak House*, Dickens established Jo as a kind of home-grown exile, a character who is *of* the nation but simultaneously *apart* from it, a native insider but also a disruptive outsider. By contrast, Cameron's orphans have been saved from this fate. Reclaimed by their extended families, reintegrated into domestic life, reconnected with the nation's sense of duty and obligation, they have been reimagined as productive descendants of the family line.

AN ORPHAN'S REDEMPTION

In 1859, London's Olympic Theatre produced Tom Taylor's play *Payable on Demand*. Ten years later, Julia Margaret Cameron performed the same play in Freshwater as part of her ongoing series of 'amateur theatricals'. Apparently, Tennyson's younger son, Lionel, and Cameron's son Henry both shared a love of acting. In the Cameron's home, the family put on such popular performances, spent weeks in rehearsal, printed announcements, and occasionally posed for Julia Margaret to stage a photograph or two depicting scenes from the play to which the entire Freshwater community was invited.[57] On the reverse of one such photograph depicting Lionel Tennyson (Cox/Ford 1033; fig. 63), she wrote the following lines:

> *Lionel Tennyson*
> *In the character of the Marquis de St. Cast*
> *in the play of Payable on Demand*
> *As acted in the Cameron's Private Theatricals*
> *in aid of our Freshwater [Village Hospital] for orphans*

As we shall see, in dedicating her performances to benefit children orphaned by the nation's recent wars, Julia Margaret used Taylor's play *Payable on Demand*, a story of a rehabilitated orphan in the role of the Marquis de St Cast, to consolidate the sympathies of her audience and lend support to the imperial cause, anticipating that their approval of the staged production would loosen their pocketbooks to help support the care of orphans at Freshwater's local hospital.

Unlike commercial performances such as the ones produced for the Olympic, which used professional actors, amateur theatricals were a form of domestic entertainment that relied heavily on children and young adults. The charm of these productions was enhanced by the spectators who recognized the performers personally and were eager to participate in suspending awareness of their true identities while they acted on stage, a pleasure unique to a knowing audience, as Jane Austen described it in *Mansfield Park* (1814). As home-based theatricals, the audiences were typically drawn from the same social group as the performers, true then for Austen as much as for Cameron fifty years later. Victorian amateur theatricals were not exclusively home entertainments, however. These productions are also associated with popular entertainments that went beyond small audiences, like Charles Dickens's productions of the 1840s and 1850s, which brought his performances to America, or as Thackeray represented the pastime in his novel *Vanity Fair*, when Becky Sharp took on the role of Clytemnestra as a calculated way to ensnare another suitor. In addition, recent scholarship has also documented that amateur theatricals were exported to the British colonies, where they enjoyed wide participation among expatriate and military audiences, not only for popular entertainment but to express national solidarity and British identity for those who were far from home.[58] Whether these performances were acted in playhouses or in makeshift quarters, amateur presentations of this kind provided audiences new spaces for socialization and, like letters or newspapers, 'served as a lifeline to the home country': 'Watching or performing in a play allowed them to strip away their colonial identity and feel part of "civilization" – if only for the duration of the performance'.[59] Moreover, staging an amateur performance was an established way to raise money to underwrite a worthy cause. In the summer of 1867, for example, Tom Taylor joined his friends from the *Punch* crowd to perform *A Sheep in Wolf's Clothing* to benefit the widow and children of Charles Bennett, a recently deceased *Punch* artist.[60]

Payable on Demand is a two-act play with few characters.[61] In Taylor's historical narrative, the action follows the French Revolution and the subsequent Wars of Liberation, when Britain formed alliances with several European states to fight against Napoleon's incursions on the Continent, but Taylor billed the play as a 'domestic drama'.[62] The first act takes place in Frankfort, during the Terror, and the second in London, just before news of Napoleon's abdication reached England. Throughout this interval, and despite the change in setting, the same actors can perform in their role throughout the play, as the story told involves the same characters or their offspring. The effect of this limited approach to casting creates a striking doubling effect. By making use of the trope of the double, Taylor's play enables the actor who portrays a father in the first act to perform in the role of his son in the second and enables the actor who plays a mother in the first act to perform in the role of her daughter in the second. Remaining unchanged throughout the play, although ageing suitably to convey the passage of time from Act I to Act II, is the Jewish moneylender, Reuben Goldsched, who plays a pivotal role in the drama. Taylor secured the famous actor Frederick Robson to act the principal role of Goldsched.[63]

The following lines summarize the narrative. The Marquis de St Cast, a French aristocrat, is introduced in the first act. He is on the run, desperately trying to safeguard a large sum of money and avoid the troops of the French Republic, who occupy the town. The Marquis deposits his wealth with Goldsched with instructions to benefit his wife and child in the case of his death. Goldsched at first forgets to write the Marquis a receipt, but then the nobleman returns and Goldsched writes a receipt, but in invisible ink. Goldsched's pregnant wife Lina, who is not of Jewish descent, guarantees the receipt by witnessing it with her signature. To avoid detection from the French soldiers, they hide the receipt in a portable desk carried by the Marquis. But as the first act ends, the Marquis is killed and the moneylender invests the deposit, soon to become a wealthy broker. When the second act opens, some twenty years have passed. Goldsched is now rich, but he seeks to leverage even greater wealth by gambling a large sum on Napoleon's defeat in the war. He will either lose everything or win substantial gains depending on the outcome. Although his wife has died, he is raising their daughter, also named Lina, who takes music lessons from a teacher who visits the house regularly. Unknown to all, the teacher is really the disguised son of the late Marquis. After buying an antique French desk for Lina as a gift, Goldsched discovers that it is the very same portable desk once owned by the Marquis. Rifling through its drawers, they find the hidden receipt and Goldsched acknowledges his moral commitment to the Marquis's son, just as the music teacher reveals his identity and declares his love for Lina. With these revelations, Taylor has set the conditions for

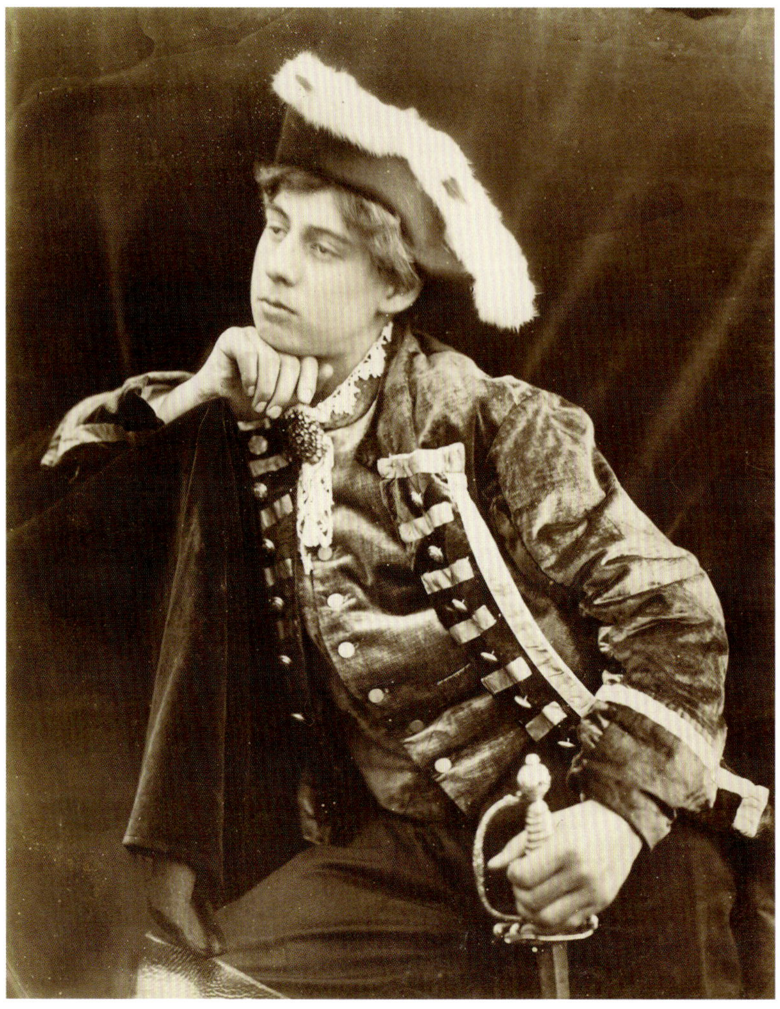

63 Julia Margaret Cameron, *Lionel Tennyson in the Character of the Marquis de St. Cast*, 1869, albumen print, 33.5 × 27.8 cm.

Courtesy Tennyson Research Centre, Lincolnshire County Council. 5466a.

intersecting moral dilemmas. These are accentuated by the fact that news of the war's outcome has been delayed and that Goldsched has not yet learned whether his gamble has paid off. Will Goldsched honour his pledge to the Marquis before God and his deceased wife; will Goldsched's love for his daughter outweigh his craving for wealth; will the music teacher, now a penniless Marquis in name only, be true to the young Lina, even if Goldsched's bet fails and his fortune disappears?

The London critics were favourably impressed with the play, especially the performance by Robson acting the part of Reuben Goldsched. The *Spectator*'s critic was emblematic, portraying the chief dilemma of the drama as a struggle within Goldsched for his own conscience, whether to 'destroy a receipt of which no one but himself has ever heard, and thus save himself from' ruin, or 'pursue the path of honour', and divulge his debt to the Marquis's son. 'Virtue in the end is triumphant', wrote the critic,

> chiefly because Reuben, if always perplexed by a fiend in his heart, is perpetually guarded by an angel in his domicile. In the first act this angel is his wife, who insists on his giving a proper receipt ...; in the second, it is his daughter, so completely the image of her mother ... who on hearing the case of conscience prompts her father to do right without regard to expediency.[64]

The Jew's conscience is thus saved by 'the angel in the house', an allusion not only to Lina's female, domestic presence, but also to her Christian identity. The critic for the *Athenaeum* was equally effusive about Robson in the role of the Jew, but first linked the play to the legend of the Rothschild's family's wealth, 'that in some such circumstance the greatness of this house originated'. For this critic, the drama owed its sharp cultural resonance to the Rothschild's Jewish identity and its familial wealth, especially as this was contrasted to the nation's current economic worries. Aside from the obvious negative aspersions cast against the Rothschild house, this critic's economic focus implied that the drama gained currency from playing 'on the fears of a society newly alert to the anxieties and embarrassments of a capitalist system', which is to say that financial speculation of the kind that Goldsched engaged in was analogous to the same commercial gambles that ruined traders in railroad stock or other risky investments, thereby adding to the tension in the play.[65]

In the *Illustrated London News*, the journal's critic joined together these observations about cultural identity and economic precarity, writing how 'an Oriental colouring is thrown over the action, and the character of the Jew is brought into relief'. As the *Spectator*'s critic noted, Robson played his part 'in that Jewish dialect, which he has not used since the days when he first made an impression on the London public by his burlesque Shylock'.[66] Taylor's character therefore reinforced the cultural differences that made 'uncivilized' Jews – those who resisted assimilation in language and in dress – outliers in British society. Yet Taylor represented Goldsched as redeemable, able still to observe the values and mores of respectable society because his avaricious character has been tempered by his wife's Christian efforts. To reinforce this relationship, the *Illustrated London News* commissioned an artist to portray the scene (fig. 64)

> when the conscientious wife of Reuben swears him on the Old Testament, that book of the law which was once his father's, to act honestly in relation to the deposit, the head of their daughter's cradle serving as the altar for the solemn rite.[67]

Taylor's drama left critics with the unmistakable impression that Goldsched's honourable actions towards the Marquis could only be assured because of the explicitly female and Christian intervention of his wife, Lina.

Like all dramatic performances, Taylor's play was presented to Victorian audiences and interpreted by critics in relation to the social imperatives and political priorities of the day, even as these were inflected by different audiences and theatre locales in London.[68] For his part, Taylor continued his interest in exploring these themes the following year, when he adapted for the stage Charles Dickens's *A Tale of Two Cities* (1860).[69] But while that drama also focused on questions of national identity as it was constructed in the wake of broad social upheaval – in this case once again, the French Revolution – an analysis of Taylor's adaptation is beyond the scope of this analysis, as *A Tale of Two Cities* was destined only for the professional playhouses.[70] As an amateur production, however, *Payable on Demand* retained textual references to the Jewish money-lender's Orientalism and the moral dilemma over the money's return, especially as these were represented in critical reviews of the play.

But the moral centre of the drama shifted when the audience did as well. When the production venue shifted from the Olympic Theatre in London to Cameron's 'Thatched House' theatre in Freshwater, the play could be performed to strike a different emphasis.[71] Because Cameron's performance was acted by and for members of her own intimate society, which comprised the same social group of family and friends who were also performing on stage, Cameron could ensure that

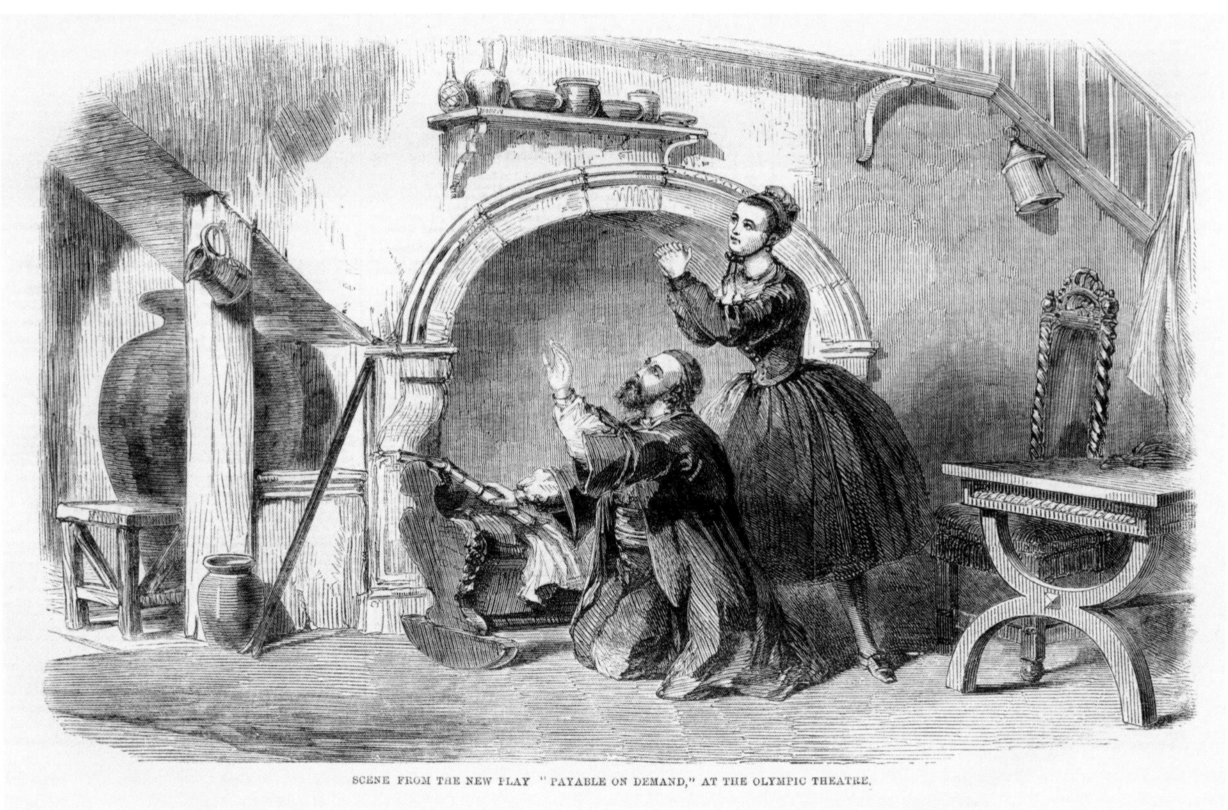

64 Anon., *Payable on Demand*, woodcut from *Illustrated London News*, 6 August 1859, 13.

the interests of that society took pre-eminence over secondary or less resonant themes within the text. And by 1869, some ten years after offering a pleasurable diversion for Crimean War orphans in her own home, and ten years after the play was first performed in London, Julia Margaret was able to commission an amateur performance to reinforce the idea that, as she had written to her daughter Juley in 1859, 'in this charitable country orphans are generally better provided for as to the real wants of life, than the poor' (see p. 136).

Why would Cameron have chosen to perform *Payable on Demand* in Freshwater, ten years after its run at the Olympic had concluded? One possible reason would be to capitalize on the evident success of the play and thereby secure an entranced audience. Another would be the opportunity to emphasize and reinforce obvious cultural divisions manifested in the original production (for example: Orientalized Jew vs European Christian; English vs French; affluent aristocracy vs impoverished masses). A third could be tied to the play's easily staged qualities in relation to the demands of the actors' performance, as the roles of the Marquis de St Cast and that of Lina, for example, were doubled from one act to the other, which is to say, these two roles could be performed by the same actors throughout the play with minimal costume changes made between the acts. Moreover, Cameron was never shy about making sure her own needs were met, and this play was performed for a specific purpose, to benefit the orphans in Freshwater's hospital. Therefore, it is reasonable too that the emphasis of the performance was shifted accordingly to accentuate the plight of the orphan at the centre of the play. Unlike at the Olympic, where the focus was on the professional actor Robsen in the role of Goldsched, at Cameron's Thatched House theatre, the moral centre was likely shifted to that character whose fortunes turn on the conscience of the moneylender, that is, the young man who acted in the role of the Marquis de St Cast, Lionel Tennyson.

Reuben Goldsched utters the key lines, however, that would have crystalized the audience's attention in Freshwater. Still in the throes of indecision about whether to burn the found receipt or not ('who'd be wiser – who'd be worse?', he wonders aloud), Goldsched examines the fateful document carefully, one last time. He brings it closer to the fire to better read the invisible ink, where he recognizes his own signature, plainly enough. But then, he peers even closer at the aged paper, where he is finally able to confront his conscience through the image of his departed wife, and makes an important discovery.

> ... and what's this? 'Witnessed – Lina Goldsched.' My Lina's own trembling characters. (*kisses them*) No, I can't burn these, I can't – I can't! Oh, how glad you would have been, my blessed one, to see this day! She spoke of it on her death bed – *of that widow and orphan, and bade me never rest till I found them out.* I swore again to her then, as I swore that 22nd of October. *I have found the orphan.* [My emphasis][72]

Critically, it is here, in Act II, when the young Marquis de St Cast – who earlier had been disguised as Lina's music teacher – is revealed as the child who had been orphaned when his father was killed by Republican soldiers. The orphan, after all, had been hiding in plain sight.

The Marquis's restoration is an uncanny kind of return. As an actor who is 'doubled' in the play, the Marquis de St Cast uncannily resembles the likeness of his father, the fleeing aristocrat of the first act. In Act II, the young Marquis's discovery is therefore portrayed as a kind of return. As a result, this figurative doubling helps to reinforce the impact of Goldsched's ability to re-establish the young man's familial wealth and with that restoration, allow him to reclaim his aristocratic ancestry. For the young Marquis of Act II, Goldsched's unexpected financial windfall reverses his personal financial ruin, but more importantly, it reinstates his family's honourable name. As a result of Reuben's reckoning with his original promise, the Marquis can now be restored to full citizenship in a post-Revolutionary world. Moreover, such restitution cannot be measured simply by financial recovery alone, Taylor's play insists. Rather, it is achieved through reintegration with the family and animated by a broad social acceptance. To reinforce this point, Goldsched's reception of the Marquis as his daughter's future husband embraces the orphaned young man within a widening bower of an extended family. Finally, because Reuben's pledge to 'find that widow and orphan' was sealed at his wife's death-bed, the Christian goodness of Lina is credited with helping assure such an outcome: her final, sacred act was one of Christian kindness, duty, obligation, and domestic sentiment. When Goldsched exclaims '*I have found the orphan*', it is the crucial turning point of the whole drama, and this revelation must have resonated accordingly in Cameron's Thatched House theatre. With the Marquis now reintegrated into the family, the blood of the fathers can be redeemed at last. If Taylor's professional critics were limited to seeing only stereotypes in Taylor's characterization of the Orientalized Jewish moneylender or the Christian goodness of a dedicated wife who acts the 'angel in the house', it is likely that Cameron's amateur performance was able to repurpose that narrative yet again.

For Cameron, then, the central character in *Payable on Demand* was not Goldsched, but rather the restored Marquis de St Cast, no longer a social outcast, now reintegrated as a cherished family member. Reframed in this way, the central moral quandary of the play was not one of potentially defrauding an absent investor, but rather a noble search for the restoration of a family's broken national heritage. As a result, the key redemptive act was not in returning money to its rightful owner, but in having the Marquis honour his forebears by reclaiming the family title. Once redeemed, the Marquis, previously exiled from France and then displaced in England, can claim a new, imperial identity in the modern world as a social equal. For Cameron, as we have seen, it was essential to restore orphans to their families of origin as an expression of their relationship to the nation, chiefly because she considered an individual's identity and his or her subjecthood as inseparable. Sukanya Banerjee reinforces this point when she maintains, 'it was the empire, rather than a pre-existing prototype of nation, that generated a consciousness of the formal equality of citizenship'.[73] In her backyard theatre, Julia Margaret Cameron's staging of *Payable on Demand* offered her most intimate community a dramatic model for reintegrating the orphan into a civil society that the British empire had remade as a modern, imperial world. As a record of the performance itself, Cameron's photograph of *Lionel Tennyson in the role of the Marquis de St. Cast* accomplishes the same act of social redemption.[74]

Allegories of Empire

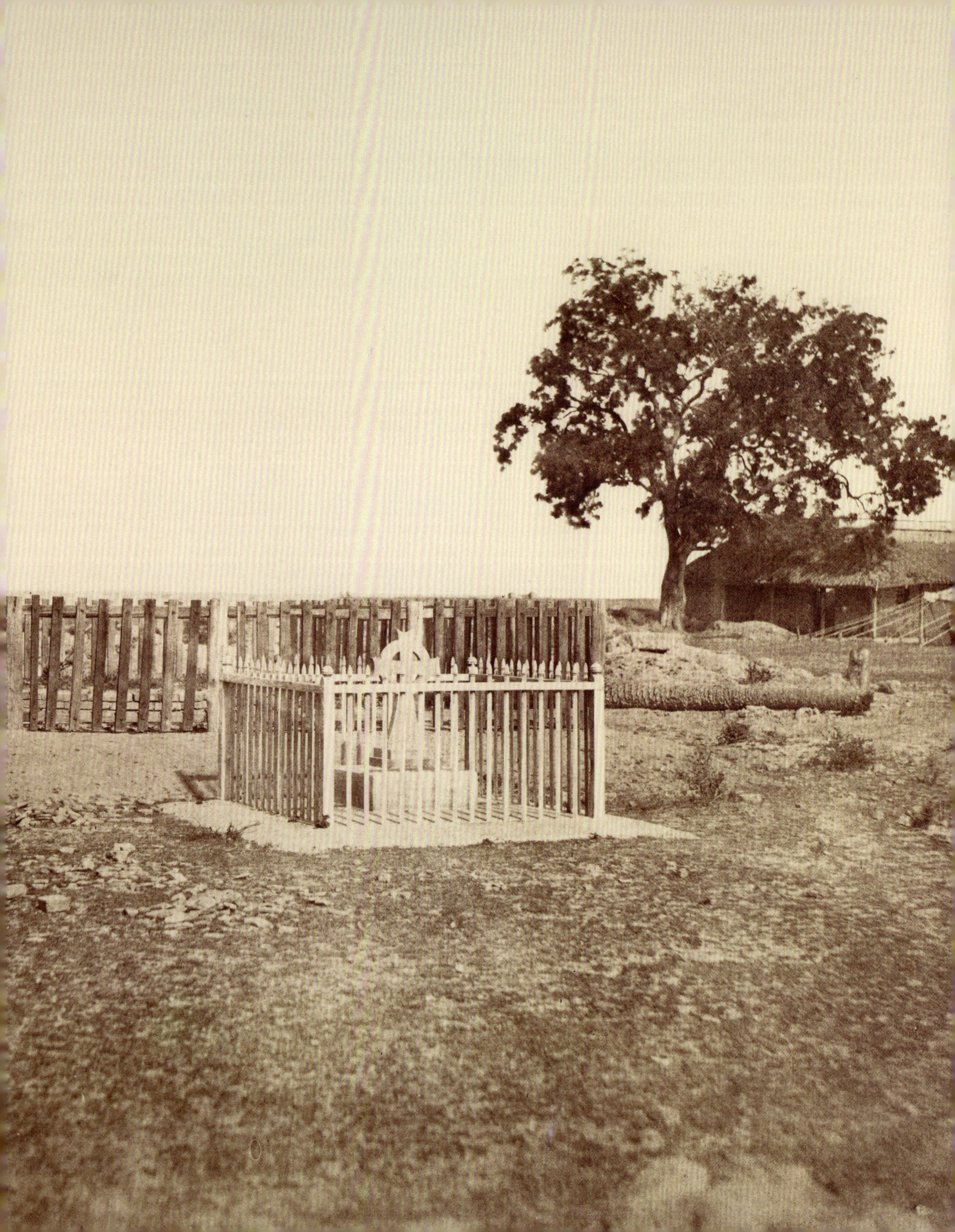

Chapter Seven
Triumph and Mourning

65 Harriet Tytler and Major Robert Christopher Tytler, *The [Bibighar] Well, Cawnpore*, 1858 (detail of fig. 67).

PICTURING CAWNPORE

In the London press, the well at Cawnpore was without peer in the ongoing project of writing the nation's history of the Indian Uprising. From the first reports of its outbreak in 1857, through to 1865, when Baron Carlo Marochetti's winged angel statue was installed to mark the site in Cawnpore, the overarching narrative of the massacre of British women and children was associated with numerous intersecting and conflicting accounts, each with their own hero and villain, each telling only part of the story: Nana Sahib's treachery, Havelock's heroism, the bravery of stranded British women, the sacrifices made on behalf of Britain's civilizing mission. Even by 1858, British publishers were churning out numerous first-hand accounts: soldiers' letters, widows' diaries and memoirs, journalistic reports.[1] Taken together, each author and virtually every episode hinted at the much larger storyline, one that told of mourning for the lives lost in India accompanied by fulsome expressions of pride in Britain's commitment to achieving the imperial mission.

In *The Times* and in other journals, these years were defined by a persistently articulated need to establish the site in Cawnpore as sacred ground, which led to numerous public demands to consecrate the burial well. But as a powerful *visual* emblem, one able to embody intersecting associations of national grief and pride, the transformation of the well into a cultural symbol is a fascinating study that combines remembrance and historiography, and as a result, tells a powerful story of the construction of imperial iconography.[2] Between 1857 and 1865, in fact, the well became appropriated in several significant ways, but crucially remained the centrepiece of narratives about the war in India. Rechristened by the London press as a 'Memorial Well', its location in Cawnpore became reified as a site of memory, a solemn marker of deep and abiding loss, and a Christian emblem of resurrection. In visual representations reproduced during this time in graphic art, sculpture, and photography, the Memorial Well also became a national symbol of mourning, a unique site that was soon called the nation's first 'mutiny memorial'.[3] Commemorative memorials of this kind, especially those built on foreign soil, helped to create an essential narrative that defined British national identity because the site embodied the 'deep national past that differentiated a given culture both from its European and its non-European others'.[4] This chapter examines the making of the new iconography, how it acquired narrative authority in cultural terms, how key players in Cameron's circle participated in this creating and distributing its imagery, and how Julia Margaret herself explored ways to represent the impact of Cawnpore in her own emerging approach to photography.

We have seen how for Cameron concern for orphans of the Crimean War blended into actions taken to benefit orphans of the Indian Uprising. In the public arena, too, monuments created to mark the earlier war merged with public memorials fashioned to honour those who had fallen in India. For Cameron's contemporaries, the Scutari monument erected in Istanbul stood as an archetype, with Marochetti's winged angels standing guard to mark the continuing British presence in the soldiers' graveyard on the Bosporus (see figs 44, 45, 46). Likewise, from 1858, public sentiment, at least as expressed in letters to *The Times*, called repeatedly for a new memorial to be built in Cawnpore that would literally carve out a section of earth and mark it as British land. Because Baron Carlo Marochetti was selected to erect the monuments for both sites, his work acquired an unusual public visibility.

And yet, there were fundamental differences between the two locations. For one, the Scutari marked a defined military burial ground: gendered male, the cemetery organized conventional soldiers' gravesites whose overall impression expressed the consolidation of imperial power and victory, even in death. For the marker, Marochetti created four identical winged angels, also called 'weeping victories', which he positioned on the four sides of a base upon which rose a giant obelisk. The angels hold palm fronds, ancient symbols of military victory, and wreaths, representing suffering and sacrifice. In Christian terms, the two emblems represented the soldiers' sacrifice, but also the victory of eternal life. Yet because the four sculptures also functioned structurally like caryatids, the angels appeared to be constrained, hemmed in from the overhanging canopy above. On 8 July 1856, Lord Harrington even complained in the House of Lords about the sculpture's proportions, comparing it unfavourably to Cleopatra's Needle. Nevertheless, because of its graveyard site as much as the historical form it took from Egyptian obelisks, the Scutari monument was regarded positively for conveying patriotic duty, selfless bravery, and national honour.[5] Because its angels look outward across the four cardinal directions, they take on the look of sentries and convey the stern demeanour of guardians, especially in a military graveyard.

By contrast, Cawnpore's Memorial Well was a different kind of cultural and national touchstone, equally conceived in patriotism but not in military terms: gendered female, even before Marochetti's angel was installed over the well, the site symbolized innocence, helplessness, and sacrifice.[6] Associated with the women who accompanied Britain's sons and who worked to improve India in Western terms, the deceased were not soldiers or missionaries but nevertheless helped to spread English culture throughout the colony.[7] Their sense of duty was reinforced by missionary tracts but also by the secular writings of Sarah Stickney Ellis. Because Victorian women embodied the core of the nation's moral identity, as Ellis had written, their presence in India helped to define Britain's civilizing mission. Marochetti chose a single winged angel to represent the dead as a cultural statement. Gone is the obelisk and the grave-like marker. Approached from a single viewpoint behind a protective screen, a single Cawnpore angel hovers uncannily over the well-head itself. Once conceived, the memorial took years to execute and even longer before it was installed in India.

From the ancient Egyptian Pyramids to the modern-day churchyard, monuments erected in memory of the dead brought together a wide array of visual artists, including architects, sculptors, and landscape designers. Because the Cawnpore memorial represented not only those who died but the nation's cultural identity as well, a wide range of British artists wanted to design and erect the Memorial Well. Paradoxically, though, the site itself was wholly unknown to the British public. The earliest published visual representations of Cawnpore in England did not even picture the overall location or the well itself, perhaps to avoid appearing mawkish or indelicate. On 23 January 1858, the *Illustrated London News* published one of the first attempts, a simple line drawing representing the '*Bibighar*', the house in which the women and children were murdered, and which Julia Margaret referred to in her letters as the 'Slaughter House'. The accompanying article reminded readers that the British army completely levelled the structure in order to obliterate any chance that the building would be preserved. Therefore, the journal's drawing could only represent an approximation of the *Bibighar*'s former physical presence. Historical erasures of this kind often preceded the erection of new monuments in their place to provide a historical correction or rededication. In this way, victors asserted their control over interpreting a site's future narrative. Paradoxically, as Fredric Jameson has demonstrated, while the narrative of national triumph acquired a singular authority, it also remained locked together with its opposite, that is, grief and mourning, as well as the equally suppressed story of the Indian experience at Cawnpore.[8]

As it was in Awadh that the 1857 revolt first erupted, so it was in Awadh that Viscount Canning began the task of restoring British rule to India. His so-called 'Oudh Proclamation' of 3 March 1858, issued in anticipation of the fall of Lucknow, proposed to act on 'the principle that, before pronouncing sentence on the guilty, it was just and proper to reward the innocent', and therefore he pledged to protect those who had 'remained faithful' to Britain's rule by issuing an amnesty.[9] In practice this meant restoring the province's traditional power structure, particularly the *taluqdari* system of land tenure. But it also meant that Canning reaffirmed the legality of Dalhousie's annexation of Awadh's territory, thereby extending the land mass of Britain's colony. By taking the question of land rights off the table, Canning forced the *taluqdars* to accept a 'free and incontestable grant from [Britain as] the paramount power' to resume their earlier positions.[10] As a result, Canning expunged their earlier entitlements with a heavy hand that compelled them to recognize British authority.

Contesting voices in Britain objected to Canning's offer of clemency and protested the reinstatement of *taluqdars*, seeking even greater retribution against them. Others in London objected to the continued annexation of Awadh, and hoped to restore the exiled king and exit fully from India.[11] These contradictory demands reflected the initial opposing views in Parliament regarding Britain's control of the colony. But in 1858, Parliament ratified a new brand of liberal economic policies that acted on two fronts. The first was Canning's determination to reinstall elements of the earlier feudal order. This action dismantled the Utilitarians' earlier social reform policies by removing financial control from large landowners. The second went together with the first: in order to enhance the independence of landlords, Canning instituted new policies of *laissez faire* economics to remove governmental restrictions on agriculture.[12] These directives were intended to address immediate practical and social insecurities, soon to be followed by deeper structural and transformative policies that would rewrite India's financial future.

In 1859, James Wilson, the apostle of free trade, publisher of the *Economist*, and president of the Board of Trade, assumed the financial seat on the Supreme Council of India. Once in Calcutta, with Canning's blessing, he proposed instituting a brand-new income tax, a licence tax on trade, a tobacco tax, and a new paper currency, substantive economic reforms that were designed to erase Britain's enormous war deficit and help restore the colony's financial health. When Wilson died unexpectedly of dysentery in 1860, Walter Bagehot, his son-in-law, took over the reins of the *Economist* and used the magazine to advance his support for these reforms.[13] As we have seen, Bagehot relied upon Charles Cameron's moral and legal arguments, including his support for maintaining the caste system as well as a British-dominated civil service. As a result,

> with Bagehot the English in India sought a stable balanced society, in which government was entrusted to 'a select few' and the poorer classes rendered due respect and deference to their social superiors.[14]

As Partha Chaterjee observed, paternal despotism soon became institutionalized throughout the colony, as subsequent British governments upheld the 'normative superiority of modern Western institutional practices' in India by promoting 'a gradual and balanced process of change in which the imperial power had to hold the balance and make the decisions, because otherwise native society would collapse'.[15]

Once these policies were implemented through the legal channels and institutions formerly administered by the East India Company, Viscount Canning and his wife, Lady Charlotte, turned their attention to commemorate British lives lost during the Uprising. In tackling the matter of representation head-on, the Cannings exerted their privilege to narrate the recent history of Britain in India in monumental terms, no different in principle from Herschel's desire years earlier to erect a stone obelisk to mark his territory in Cape Town. In 1859, the Cannings took control over how the historical narrative of Cawnpore would be framed by defining the symbolism used to commemorate the recently concluded war. Their patronage shaped the very narrative of remembering. In London's daily press, Canning captured headlines as he moved to establish both narrative and symbolic control of the notorious well-head at Cawnpore. After first consecrating the land by the Anglican Bishop of Calcutta, he then established a memorial fund to mark the tomb. The Cannings' patronage also shaped the symbolism of the memorial statue itself: working through trusted intermediaries in London – notably, Lady Waterford, Charlotte's sister, and Earl Granville, Charles Canning's friend and peer – they influenced the choice of sculptor and the iconographic form the work would ultimately take. Importantly for this story, the Cannings were related to influential members of Julia Margaret Cameron's intimate circle – in particular, her brother-in-law, Earl Somers, who was Lady Waterford's cousin, the sculptor Baron Carlo Marochetti, and her friend and neighbour on the Isle of Wight, Alfred Tennyson. As a result, the rhetoric of an imperial and commemorative language, particularly as it concerned debates surrounding the representation of the Memorial Well, coincided with Julia Margaret's emergence as a creator of photographic imagery.

After the Queen's Proclamation, the British press intensified its coverage of the Cawnpore well, largely in response to numerous letters calling for establishing a permanent memorial for the British women and children killed there. Lady Canning wrote to Queen Victoria personally about the devastation she encountered as an eyewitness in India.[16] She also corresponded with her sister, Louisa Anne Beresford, the Marchioness of

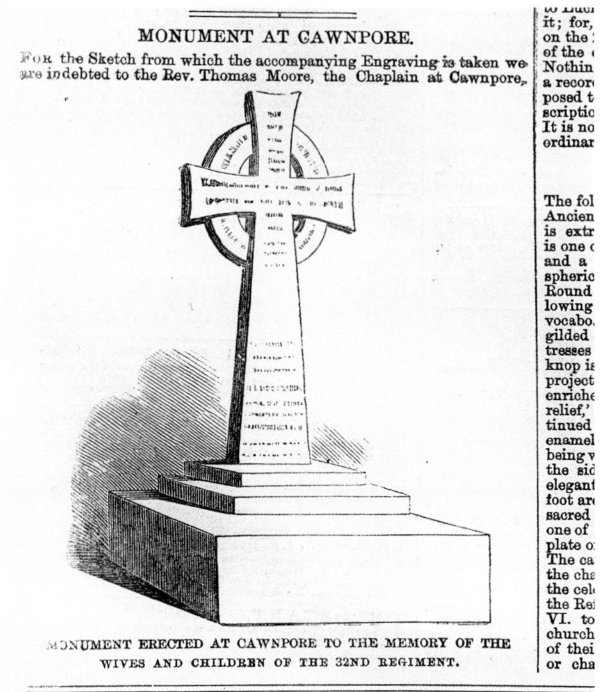
MONUMENT AT CAWNPORE.

FOR the Sketch from which the accompanying Engraving is taken we are indebted to the Rev. Thomas Moore, the Chaplain at Cawnpore.

MONUMENT ERECTED AT CAWNPORE TO THE MEMORY OF THE WIVES AND CHILDREN OF THE 32ND REGIMENT.

London: Printed and Published at the Office, 198, Strand, in the Paris

66 *Monument Erected at Cawnpore to the Memory of the Wives and Children of the 32nd Regiment*, line drawing, *Illustrated London News*, 27 March 1858.

Waterford, about her impressions of Cawnpore, and solicited her sister's input on a design that might fittingly commemorate the sacrifice of British lives. The two sisters were accomplished artists. During the 1850s, Lady Waterford studied drawing and painting in earnest, visited Holman Hunt at his studio and met others in the Pre-Raphaelite Brotherhood, and began an extensive correspondence with the art critic John Ruskin, who likely was introduced to Lady Waterford by Cameron's brother-in-law, Earl Somers.[17] After the Cannings arrived in India in 1856, Lady Charlotte sent her sister numerous drawings and photographs from India. When they discussed a possible sculptor for creating a monument to mark the well in Cawnpore, Louisa recommended Baron Marochetti, not only for his recently completed sculpture for the Scutari cemetery, but more personally because of the high regard she had for the portrait bust of her late husband that she had commissioned from the artist.[18]

After the *Illustrated London News* published its line drawing in January depicting the *Bibighar*, other representations soon followed. On 27 March

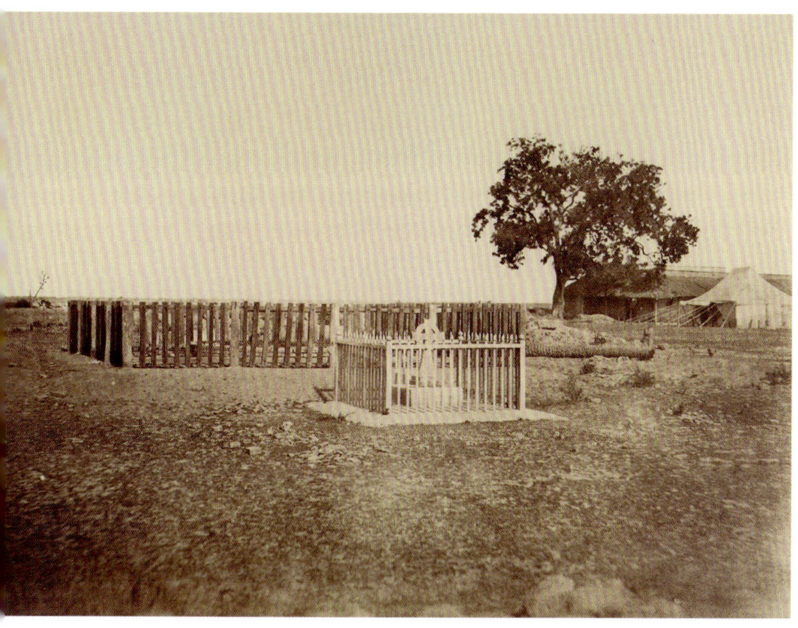

67 Harriet Tytler and Major Robert Christopher Tytler, *The [Bibighar] Well, Cawnpore*, 1858, photograph.

68 John Murray, *The Well and Monument, Slaughter House, Cawnpore*, 1858, photograph.

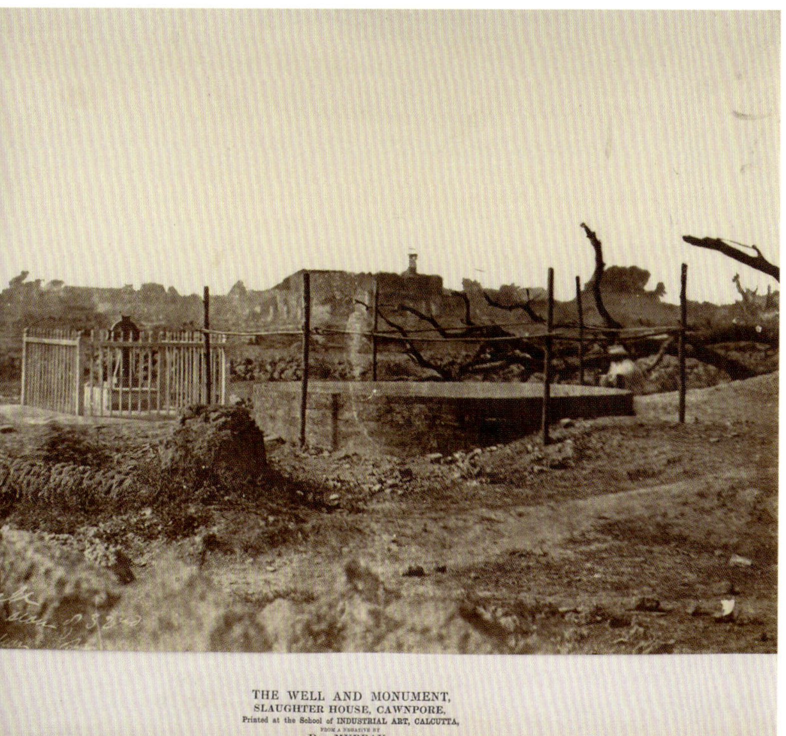

1858, while the British public was still absorbing news of the rebellion, the same journal published a drawing of a Celtic cross erected specifically on the site of the well-head. And yet, the drawing presented the site as an abstract rendering, an isolated cross lacking any visual clues regarding its perspective, scale, or context in relation to the landscape (fig. 66).[19] The image did not indicate its actual size or even the material used for its construction. The drawing was titled simply 'Monument Erected at Cawnpore to the Memory of the Wives and Children of the 32nd Regiment', but it is even unclear if this was the journal's caption or if it represented an actual inscription at the site. The size of the well was left to the imagination as was the condition of the overall site. And although the journal tried to authenticate the image as having originated from a sketch made by the British chaplain at Cawnpore, the journal's engraver could easily have embellished or removed details from the image. Astute readers or print collectors would have had difficulty aligning this representation to the depiction of the scene in lithographs made after Lieutenant Charles Wade Crump's drawings of the well and *Bibighar* (compare fig. 31).

By contrast, the earliest photographic representations of Cawnpore situated the well and the cross more explicitly in the landscape and in relation to each other, even though the scale was still indistinct owing to the scarcity of physical landmarks, like trees, buildings, people, or other environmental details. At some point in early 1858, several British photographers made their way to Cawnpore. One was Major Robert Christopher Tytler, a soldier in the East India Company's army. Tytler was accompanied by his wife, Harriet Tytler, an accomplished photographer who published her memoirs of this period after the couple returned to England. Like other photographs of empty spaces in India taken by the photographers, Christopher Pinney called this image 'a vacant space waiting for its historical inscription' (fig. 67).[20] Another photographer who visited the site was Dr John Murray, a physician employed in the service of the Company.[21] Governor-General Canning specifically commissioned Murray to produce photographs of the site, suggesting a keen interest in securing reliable images of the location (fig. 68).[22] And in February 1859, the Tytlers' photographs were exhibited in Calcutta at a meeting of the Photographic Society of Bengal.[23]

These photographs depicting Cawnpore are remarkable for their common focus on the well itself. In the centre-ground of each photograph, both depict a prominent Celtic cross on a raised plinth, enclosed by a short, stockade-style fence, signs that the enclosure marked a sacred or protected site. Yet, in both photographs, the cross appears to stand barely taller than the surrounding fence and is not immediately legible as a Christian emblem. The landscape appears desolate and sterile, the materials marking the site flimsy and impermanent, the location undistinguished and bleak. Both photographs portray an unmarked circular structure that is slightly raised off the dusty ground to denote the notorious well-head. This round structure is visible behind the fenced enclosure in the Tytlers' photograph and in the near foreground of Murray's photograph, appearing almost as a kind of afterthought, as if the main attraction was the small cross protected behind the rickety fence and not the burial tomb itself. Both photographs depict the unmistakable barrenness of the site, a location so forlorn it required no need for signposts or markers to guide visitors, so abandoned and apparently forgotten there appears no reason for people to visit at all.[24]

It was not until February 1859 that the Photographic Society of London presented the first exhibition of photographs of India following the Indian Uprising, but according to the checklist from the exhibition, neither Murray's nor the Tytlers' photographs were exhibited.[25] Rather, the Photographic Society displayed

> portraits of a phalanx of Indian heroes, Lord Clyde, Napier, Birch, Greathed, and many others known to fame, the views of public buildings and localities in the city connected for ever with the chivalry of Havelock, and the successes of Outram and Clyde, [which] are the most striking and memorable.[26]

Demand for visual imagery of India gave currency to Murray's earlier work, even though these were picturesque views of India taken prior to the revolt.[27] Picturesque landscape conventions also dominated Murray's photographs of Indian scenes exhibited by the Photographic Society in 1858 and by the Architectural Photographic Association, which in 1861 exhibited additional photographs from India taken by Murray.[28] As a result, interested London viewers could not immediately examine photographic documentation of the Memorial Well, as both Murray's and Tytlers' works were not exhibited publicly, but rather were insulated in portfolios of limited production. For some readers of *The Times*, however, these photographs provided visual documentation that ran counter to press reports.

In an extraordinary series of 'Letters to the Editor' that the paper published about the dilapidated state of the Memorial Well, *Times* readers learned from first-hand accounts that they had been misled from earlier reports about the cross erected to honour the British dead. Often it appears the publication strategy of *The Times* was one of embarrassing the government into action by providing evidence of the site's neglect and thereby scolding Members of Parliament for their inaction. For example, an emotionally charged letter published on 14 January 1860 effectively accused the government of blatant negligence:

> We pray the patience of our readers while we describe a painful scene. It has taken us hours to learn the situation of the melancholy spot – and many people visiting or passing through Cawnpore are altogether unable to find it – so insignificant are deemed the associations connected with it. ... Near at hand one observes at last another enclosure – a cattle-pen looking sort of place, a rough rude paling encircling a patch of dilapidated brickwork; and the visitor starts with horror on learning that this is the monument marking the tomb of our sisters and our children, whose butchery close by drove all England half mad with horror and awe ... The palings [around the cross] bid fair to tumble down speedily from injury by white ants. The brickwork [around the well] is all crumbling to pieces already. Originally the work so called consisted of three or four layers of bricks in a circle covering the earth with which the well was filled in. That earth sank in the middle, owing, we suppose, to the rains, and of course broke up the brickwork above. And so it remains now ... Already the accumulation of dust and dirt has half hidden the still sinking mound, and in a few months, when the palings have rotted away and tumbled down, little there will remain to mark the spot.[29]

The author was plainly underwhelmed by the small size of the cross and equally upset by the derelict condition of the well-head. Both criticisms seem valid from the visual evidence presented in Murray's and the Tytlers' photographs. But the writer essentially called the site a forgotten remnant of war and condemned the lack of a suitable memorial to the dead. The letter was a strident call for action: 'We remember two years ago seeing in the *Illustrated London News* a picture supposed to represent a monumental cross erected at the slaughter hole', he wrote (referring to the image reproduced in fig. 66), 'for it purported to be worthy of the spot. It was a barbarous falsehood'.[30]

Three days later, on 17 January, another letter in *The Times* answered these accusations by reprinting yet another letter of October 1858 that Viceroy Canning sent to Sir John Inglis affirming Canning's intention to honour the memory of the dead with a suitable memorial. Canning wrote,

> The Government has undertaken to raise a monument over the well into which the bodies of the women and children murdered on the 15th of July 1857, were thrown. The ground round the well will be made a garden and carefully tended.[31]

Canning also supported the idea of erecting a new structure in the form of a church nearby 'for the use of native Christians' to be used as a sanctuary to pray for those who were lost. Above all, he wanted to assure the public that 'The designs for the monument are in progress'. Two days later, on 19 January, *The Times* responded once again to the provocative letter printed only the week before by reprinting a letter from Lieutenant-Colonel Carmichael of the 32nd Light Infantry, who was stationed in Suffolk. The Colonel wanted to defend the small wooden cross erected by his battalion when they were in India. He insisted that the cross was erected by soldiers – a mere twenty men, all fatigued and battle-scarred, none of whom were trained engineers and all of whom were motivated by good intentions. They were on their way from Cawnpore to Lucknow, he wrote, the cross was erected only as a temporary offering.[32]

To fulfil Canning's promise, the Public Works Department of Bengal issued new plans to make good on creating a permanent marker. On 29 March 1861, *The Times* published the specific plans for the two wells extant at the site. One of these wells was associated with the defence of Cawnpore, ordered by its commander, Major General Hugh Wheeler. It was part of the entrenchment dug by the British, a small but deep water well that was used to sustain the British troops confined there during the siege. As Trevelyan's book explained, Indian forces had destroyed the machinery for drawing up water from the depth of 60 feet, and so volunteers had to risk their lives to pull up buckets hand over hand. The second well was dry and much larger in diameter and depth; it was located outside the entrenchment and was used as the notorious burial site. Accordingly, Canning's administrative unit proposed building two monuments. For the first, the plans called for building 'a massive Iona cross on an appropriate basement', and

> for that other well, west of the canal, will consist of an octagonal Gothic screen and platform enclosing the closed well. Both the screen and the platform will be executed in stone. Over or by the side of the well will be placed a marble statue.[33]

Both Murray and the Tytlers had earlier photographed the larger second well, for which Canning created the artistic competition that would come to be known as the Memorial Well.

Around this same time, an extraordinary photographic album was then being assembled by John Nicholas Tressider, a surgeon employed by the East India Company who was stationed in Cawnpore. In one of his album's pages, Tressider represented the chief difference between the two memorials.[34] Pictured on the top half of the page is a photograph of a barren site that depicts the two wooden fences the soldiers had erected for the larger of the two wells stationed outside the *Bibighar*, or 'Slaughter House'. The smaller fence depicted in the image encloses a small marker for the site, while the larger structure surrounds the well itself. On the bottom half of the album page is a photograph depicting the Iona cross designed for the smaller well outside Wheeler's compound, showing a man and woman visiting the site. Both are marked *c.*1858 in the Tressider Album. However, since Governor-General Canning's plans were not released until 25 January 1861 and were published in *The Times* only in March of that year, the dates written in this album were likely made in error.

The Bengal Public Works Department erected the Iona cross. The marker was massive in size and stood at least 18 feet off the ground. The face of the cross itself was inscribed:

> In a well under this cross were laid, by the hands of their fellows in suffering, the bodies of men, women, and children, who died hard by during the heroic defence of Wheeler's Intrenchment when beleaguered by the rebel Nana, June 6th to 27th, AD, MDCCCLVII.

On the pedestal of the cross the following lines were inscribed:

> Our bones are scattered at the grave's mouth as when one cutteth and cleaveth wood upon the earth. But our eyes are unto Thee, O God the Lord. – Psal. CXLI.[35]

And yet, while this marker appeared to address an immediate religious imperative, its symbolic representation was still absent.

AN ALLEGORY FOR CAWNPORE

Around the same time that *The Times* described this monument, Canning had already taken steps to commission an artist in London to design an appropriate statue for the site, writing in March 1861 to his friend, Lord Granville, that he wanted to create an allegorical representation.

> I have a commission for you about a monument over the well at Cawnpore into which the massacred women and children were thrown. It will not be very troublesome after you have once read the papers which I shall send you, but it will require the descreetest [*sic*] taste and judgment in deciding whom to employ. The plans &c. are not ready yet.[36]

While in India, Canning discussed this matter with his wife, Lady Charlotte, who in turn wrote to her sister, Louisa, about their plans to commemorate the large well outside the site where the *Bibighar* once stood:

> The hope of the Resurrection is the only thought which can calm sorrow or bring comfort in connection with the awful catastrophe which is connected to the place; therefore let a statue of the Angel of the Resurrection be placed over the well.[37]

In his historical account of the events at Cawnpore, published in 1865, George Trevelyan would declare that the horrors of Cawnpore were ultimately unrepresentable:

> the dire agony of Cawnpore needs not to be figured in marble, or cut into granite, or cast of bronze. There is no fear lest we should forget the story of our people. The whole place is their tomb, and the name thereof is their epitaph.[38]

The Cannings, however, clearly thought otherwise, and set upon choosing an appropriate allegory to mark the tomb. It is striking how they engaged the Victorian artistic community – including Julia Margaret Cameron's family and their closest associates – to guide them in how to deploy symbolism and iconography to mark this momentous historical event.

As an example, Lady Waterford created a notable drawing of an angel in response to Lady Charlotte's correspondence, thinking that such a design could serve as a model for the sculpture (fig. 69).[39] This angelic figure bears a striking similarity to Marochetti's sculpted angels for the Scutari monument. Both depict solitary, standing angels with enormous wings. These are adult-sized figures, not small and childlike, like cupids or putti. In addition, both Lady Waterford's drawing and Marochetti's Scutari angels are robed dramatically in long gowns that touch the floor. In both cases, the angels hold palm fronds, symbols of eternal life. Marochetti's sculptures cross their arms at the wrists, with one hand holding a laurel wreath, a symbol of victory over death, while the arms of the angel in Lady Waterford's drawing are folded at the breast, displaying a similar kind of wreath or circlet that hangs from the angel's draped arm. And while Marochetti sculpted a male angel to mark the dead soldiers of the Scutari cemetery, Lady Waterford's angel appears to be gendered female, perhaps reflecting a feminized response that recognizes the women and children killed at Cawnpore.

Around this time, Julia Margaret Cameron, her brother-in-law Lord Somers, and two of her sisters – Virginia Somers and Sophia Dalrymple – visited Louisa's residence, known as Highcliffe Castle, where Lady Waterford dwelled during the summer months. Earl Somers was Lady Waterford's first cousin, making it plausible that the four visitors to Highcliffe that day were also invited guests.[40] The site is located on the Dorset coast bordering Hampshire and faces the Solent to the south. The castle is also relatively close in proximity to the Isle of Wight, where in 1861, the Camerons

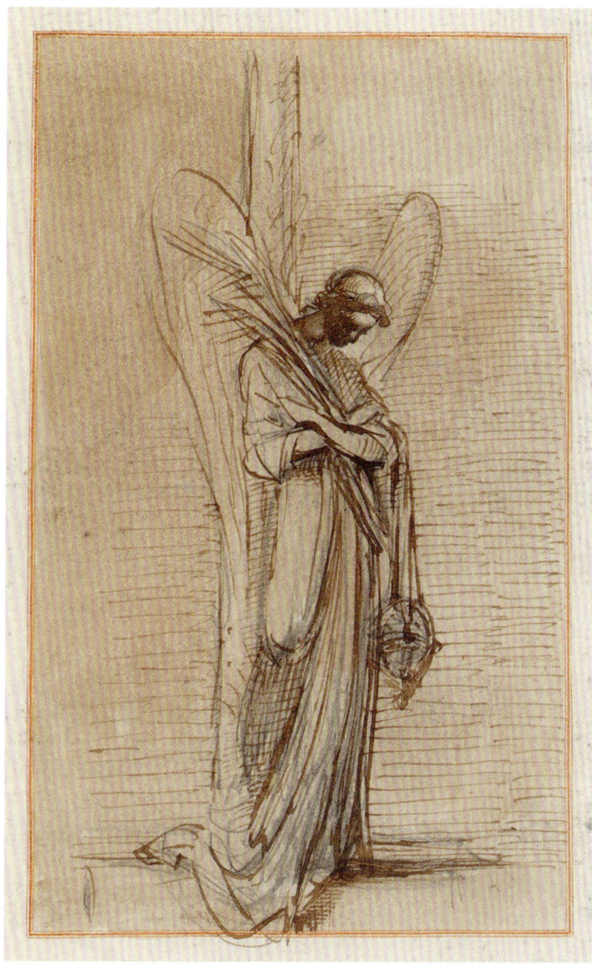

69 Louisa Anne Beresford, Marchioness of Waterford, *Sketch for the Statue of the Cawnpore Angel*, *c.*1860, drawing.

were residing in Colwell Bay, which looks north to the Solent with a view towards the Hampshire coastline.[41] From their cottage facing the small bay, Cameron even reported that she could easily see Hurst Castle close by on the island's promontory.[42] Given this particular view, looking north and west from her cottage's location, Cameron also could likely see in the near distance, only some ten miles down the coast, the outlines of Highcliffe Castle, which is perched high on a bluff.

Lord Somers and two of the Pattle sisters collaborated that day in posing for and creating photographs. While these photographs document their physical presence at Highcliffe, we do not know many specific elements of the visit, such as when the party visited the castle, whether Lady Waterford and her visitors discussed the Canning's proposals for designing the Cawnpore sculpture, or even if she shared her evocative drawing with them. All were interested in the new art of photography, however. Lord Somers served as vice president of the Photographic Society of London; as described above, his imagery was known to Talbot and Lord Lansdowne. Lady Waterford, who received photographs from her sister in India during this period, also discussed photography with the art critic John Ruskin. A member of the Holland Park circle and friend of the Pre-Raphaelite Brotherhood, Ruskin had encouraged Louisa's development in drawing and painting during this time.[43]

While at Highcliffe, Julia Margaret and Lord Somers posed Cameron's sister, Virginia Somers, in an architectural setting in the grounds. In the photograph, the model stands against an exterior stone wall with an empty urn at her side and an ornamented wall niche – perhaps a piscina – just above her head. While the authorship of the image might have been shared between Julia Margaret and Lord Somers, Cameron apparently marked the resulting photograph in her hand alone with the inscription 'From Life. Taken at High Cliffe' (fig. 70). Because of the formal similarities of this image to Lady Waterford's drawing described above, it is intriguing to speculate that Lady Waterford's image was known to Ruskin and, through Ruskin, the artistic circle of the Little Holland House. But the point of the comparison here is not to ascribe 'artistic influence' of the one to the other, but rather to demonstrate that a common set of visual and allegorical conventions was in play among the extended members of Cameron's circle. One might even say, following Pinney, that this network of artistic friends embodied a shared 'imperial habitus', one shaped by the shared discourse of mourning and triumph that accompanied memorial art after the Uprising. In this context, a 'tacit system of codes' defined their shared understanding of imperial discourses of power.[44] Significantly, the photograph taken by Somers and Cameron appears to insist on the camera's authority to situate a real subject in a specific setting, that is, Highcliffe Castle, and yet, the image also denies the realism of the camera by obscuring the identity of the subject. The symbolism suggested by the model's pose is indistinct. In this photograph, Virginia Somers becomes an allegorical figure because her attitude, gestures, and location have been portrayed ambiguously.

When Cameron marked this photograph 'From life. Taken at High Cliffe', it was perhaps among the earliest instances of her inscribing of photographs in this way.[45] As others have suggested, she might have written 'From Life' to indicate that the photograph depicted a living subject and was not a rendering of sculpture or graphic art reproduction. Other examples in the Watts and Lansdowne Albums did, in fact, reproduce line drawings and paintings. But the photograph of Lady Somers is also very different in quality and subject matter from other photographs depicting family subjects, like the more documentary photographs that depict the Prinsep and Cameron cousins or the children of the Somers, discussed earlier (see figs 36 and 37). And although the model in this image might indeed portray Cameron's sister Virginia, obviously a close family member, the enigmatic quality of the image is unlike that group family portrait of related children. As an allegorical composition, the arrangement of the subject is even somewhat mysterious, as the dark cloak worn by Cameron's model disguises her identity and the soft blur around her hands obscures their gesture or purpose. The model's head is bent forward slightly; her eyes closed. And while this figure appears to be standing in an exterior niche of an ornamented chapel-like structure in the grounds of Highcliffe, her relationship to these architectural details is unclear.

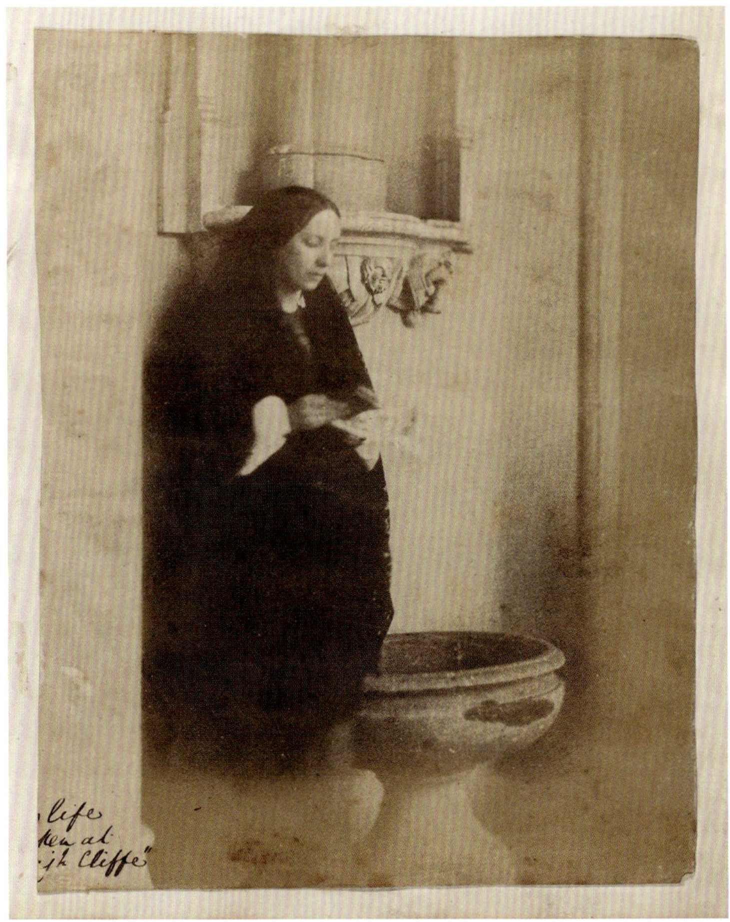

70 3rd Earl Somers and Julia Margaret Cameron (?), *Untitled*, photograph portraying Lady Somers at Highcliffe Castle, *c.*1857–60, 22.3 × 17 cm, inscribed by Julia Margaret Cameron, 'From life. Taken at High Cliffe', Watts Album.
Courtesy of Sotheby's.

Lord Granville had taken his friend Canning's ideas to heart and, significantly, he approached several members of Cameron's circle, notably Marochetti and Woolner, about creating an allegorical statue for the monument, and he drew the Lansdowne family into the discussion as well. Writing to her sister and brother-in-law in India, Lady Waterford set aside her earlier drawing of an angel and proposed a new representation that was not symbolic at all, a representation that portrayed a 'woman clinging to a cross with the bodies of murdered children near her', a sketch that does not survive, if it was made at all. In response to this idea, Canning objected strenuously, calling this idea precisely the kind of literal and didactic, not to say gruesome, design that gave him 'alarm': 'This is the sort of design I wish to avoid', he wrote emphatically to Granville. 'It would be a very painful record to some English families, and a very exasperating one to our fellow-countrymen – soldiers for instance'. Canning was explicitly searching for an *allegorical solution*, an iconography of symbolism, a design that contained narrative complexity, a form that evoked moral and political truths as they were then being defined by Victorian Britain. The winning design, he wrote, 'should not represent flesh and blood, but angels and guardian spirits':

> I am afraid that I said something about a Rachel weeping for her children which may have misled you on this point; but even that subject (if it were to be

> chosen) should be treated quietly and *allegorically*. The crisis of murder and terror is not the moment to be perpetuated, nor is the first great agony of grief; but rather the after-condition of sober mournfulness sustained and cheered by hopefulness. [My emphasis][46]

Woolner apparently misunderstood Canning's preference and might have even been misdirected by Lady Waterford. Woolner designed a plaster maquette that depicted a grief-stricken woman leaning wearily against a large Celtic cross, her eyes closed, body drooping, expression agonized. Even more disconcerting, she seems to have just let go of a dead or dying infant from her outstretched arms. The child lies at her feet, motionless (fig. 71). Although Woolner's composition was metaphorical, in that he did not represent a single individual, the metaphor did not cross over into allegory and certainly did not represent optimism. Even the sculptor's friend James Anthony Froude questioned Woolner's thinking in proposing such a maudlin design: 'the figure appeared to me intensely expressive but expressive of unthinkable agony. The child appeared as if it had just dropped from the hands. Did you mean that?'.[47]

In his next letter to Canning, Granville reported on his subsequent efforts to obtain designs for the memorial competition by soliciting the views of the Lansdowne family, notably, appraisals by Lady Waterford and Lady Shelburne, Lord Lansdowne's daughter-in-law. Granville added that he would 'decide chiefly according to the advice given me by the Lansdowne family, Lady Waterford, and [Henry Labouchere, Baron] Taunton'.[48] In the same letter, Granville favourably described one of the new designs as 'a new sort of Britannia', but then wrote how Marochetti preferred a 'St. George in Armour', which Lady Waterford thought 'beautiful' but which Lady Shelburne called 'hideous'. Responding two weeks later, Canning voiced his dislike for the idea of 'a Britannia as a monument over a grave' but expressed relief at being able to steer 'clear of the horrible', by which he meant Woolner's proposal, which he flatly rejected earlier.[49] Despite this seemingly forward progress, Canning's competition for the monument languished until early 1862, when Granville happily conveyed the following news to India:

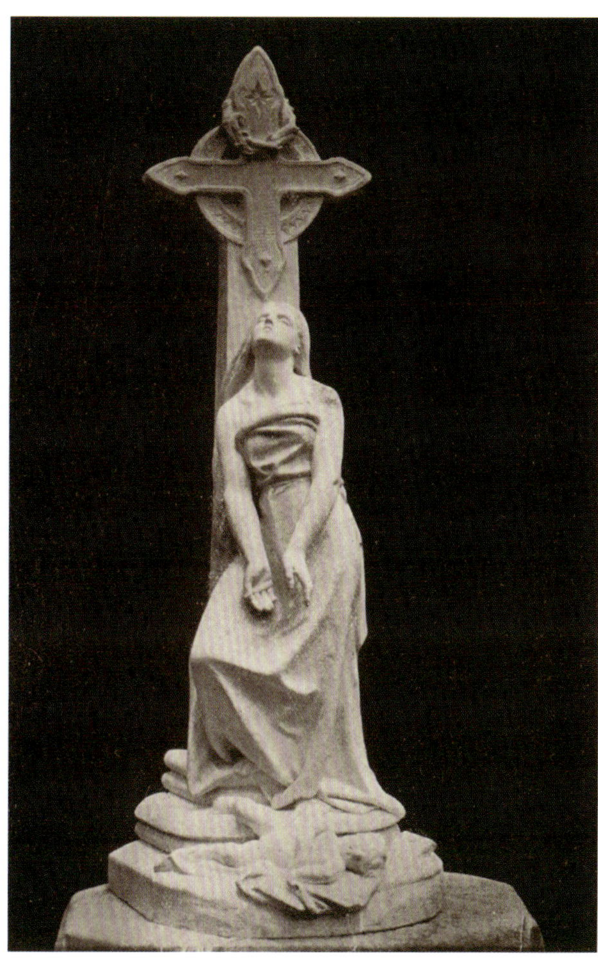

71 Thomas Woolner, *Cawnpore Memorial*, 1861, maquette; photograph in Amy Woolner, *Thomas Woolner, R.A., Sculptor and Poet. His Life in Letters* (New York: E. P. Dutton, 1917), facing p. 85.

> Marochetti has been very dilatory about your commission, but most amiable at the same time. He is now going to have ready before your return, a figure suggested by Lady Waterford, as the embodiment of what she has reason to believe was the intention of her sister, which she has gathered from several letters.[50]

The source of that figure was undoubtedly Lady Waterford's figure drawing, discussed above (see fig. 69).

By April, Canning was back in England, but unexpectedly fell ill and died in June. His wife had predeceased him the year before, having died of malaria in Calcutta. A few days before the Viceroy's death, however, Canning sent the plans and a scaled-down model for the Memorial Well at Cawnpore to the International Exhibition, where the exhibition's organizers granted it a special space in the English architectural gallery. On 1 May 1862, Earl Granville, the exhibition's Chief Commissioner, opened the event to the public, and so this addition in July represented a 'late entry'. Nevertheless, *The Times* reported that Prince Alfred and Princess Mary of Cambridge visited Marochetti's new model almost immediately, expressing royal approval. The maquette was constructed on the scale of half-an-inch to the foot. It displayed a gothic screen, as described in earlier designs of the Bengal Public Works Department, to be 'made by native stonecutters at Allahabad' from Agra soapstone. At its centre, raised above the well itself, a place was reserved for Marochetti's monumental sculpture of a single angel, which still had not yet been completed. *The Times* reported that the site would bear the following inscription:

> Sacred to the perpetual memory of a great company of Christian people, chiefly women and children, who near this spot were cruelly massacred by the followers of the rebel Nana Dhoondopunt of Bithoor, and cast, the dying with the dead, into the well below, on the 15th day of July, 1857.[51]

Almost five years to the day after the event, then, plans for erecting a national monument over the Memorial Well preserved the prevailing narrative about the massacre 'of a great company' of Christian women and children by 'the rebel Nana'. The persistent reporting kept the site fresh in the public's mind. The Christian symbolism was emphasized. A marble angel holding palm fronds would be installed as if hovering over the well, bearing emblems of resurrection and martyrdom. The gothic screen would define the memorial and its surroundings as a sacred space and hallowed ground, an out-of-doors churchyard. A sanctuary would thereby be encircled, providing dignity and privacy, and the elevated structure would provide a physical buffer from the profane world. Finally, garden-like surroundings, with fountains sourced by the Ganges, would be maintained to provide an idyllic Eden-like setting, 'a smiling garden – almost a pleasure ground – in the midst of surrounding sterility', as *The Times* maintained. Thus would horror be turned into harmony and mourning into triumph.

The relentless pace of public events organized to memorialize the women and children buried in Cawnpore persisted for the next several years. Reports in *The Times* kept the subject alive for months on end as it appeared self-conscious of its role in narrating the history of the insurrection and its aftermath. Consequently, reports focused readers' attention on the symbolic commemoration of those events. In 1863, for example, Lord Elgin, who replaced Canning as Viceroy, travelled to Cawnpore with the Bishop of Calcutta on a mission to sanctify the Memorial Well and surrounding gardens. *The Times* commented on this event extensively, noting that the Bishop's address on 13 February,

> befitted the occasion and suggests many a reflection on the present prosperous state of our empire five years after an occurrence intended to sweep us from Asia ... But the most solemn service at which the Viceroy was present was two days before at the Slaughterhouse Well, where from 120 to 130 of our women and children were mercilessly butchered. On Saturday, the 27th of June 1857, the doomed garrison, under promise of protection, made over their guns and treasure to the Nana, and at sunrise began their march to the Suttee Chowra Ghat on the Ganges, about a mile off, where the previous day three of their number had seen and approved 24 boats prepared for their reception. The Ghat was surrounded by guns concealed, and parties of Sepoys with loaded muskets. You know the story.[52]

You know the story. Thackeray expressed the same thoughts when he wrote in *Vanity Fair* about the battle of Waterloo: *The tale is in every Englishman's mouth*. Not only had the story of Cawnpore been repeated endlessly in news accounts, as we have seen, but the parable of mourning and triumph had been told in multiple other forms as well: in Thackeray's poem 'Arthur's First Wound'; in Paton's painting *In Memoriam* (see fig. 49); and in Marochetti's allegorical sculpture, which was then nearing completion. The maquette's display at the International Exhibition kept the historical narrative current, its symbolic content in front of everyone's eyes, the tale in every Englishman's mouth. As *The Times* reminded its readers, 'The well itself within is vaulted over and covered with a pedestal which awaits the statue Lord Canning promised to order from Baron Marochetti'.[53]

Narrative repetition of this kind served many interconnected purposes. Facts, like dates

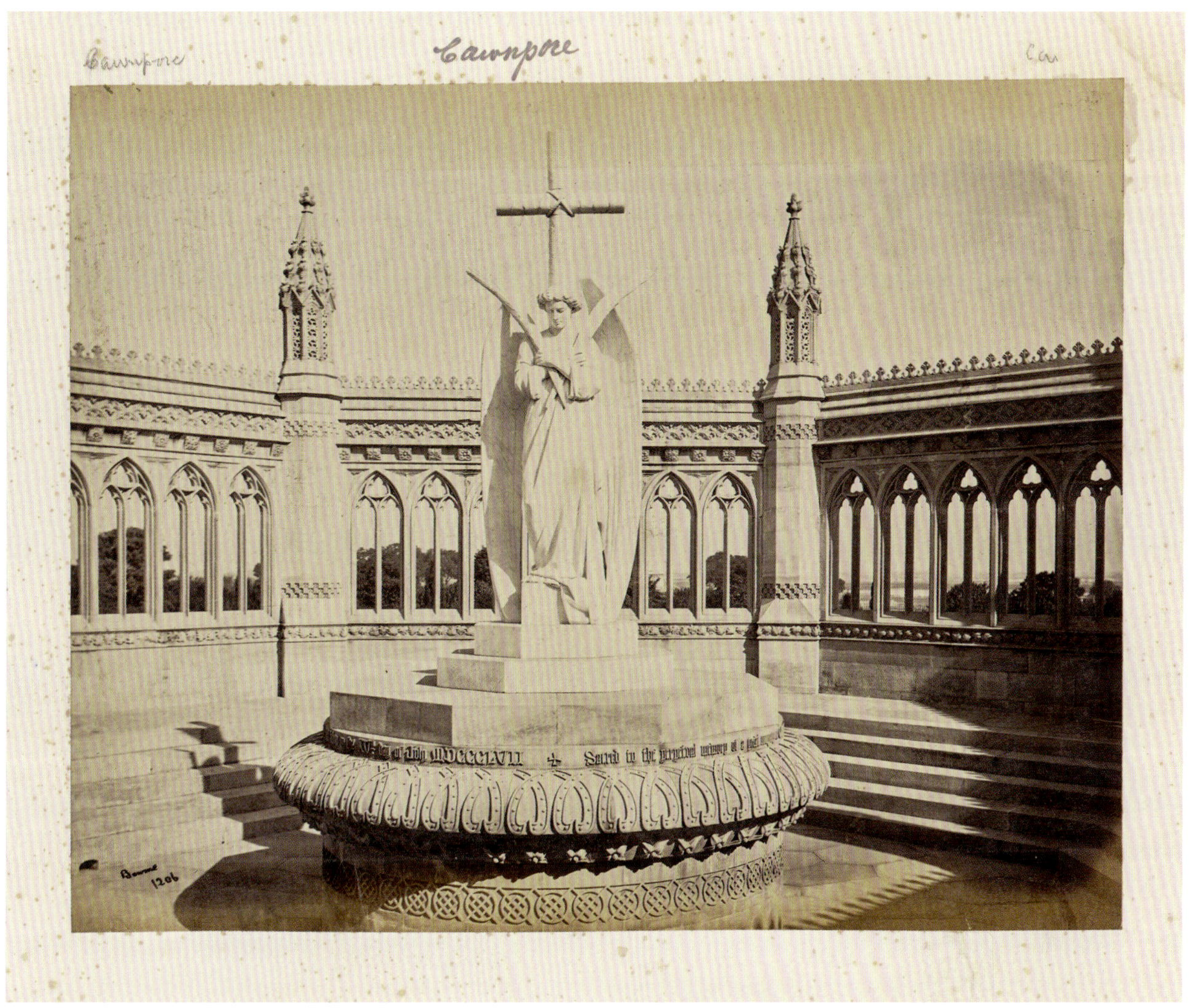

72 Samuel Bourne, *Cawnpore; The Memorial Well, the Marble Statue by Marochetti, from the Entrance,* 1865, albumen silver print, 23.6 × 29.2 cm.

J. Paul Getty Museum, 84.XO.1358.13. Digital image courtesy of Getty's Open Content Program.

and locations, or the numbers of dead women and children buried in the well, helped to sear these details in readers' memories. Historical interpretations, like the article's notable observation that the empire stood 'prosperous' even five years after the insurrection initially took place, vindicated the victor's dedication to its cause and justified the defence of the colony, even despite the material losses it suffered. Repetition of this kind occurred even after 1865, when Marochetti finally completed his sculpture for the Cawnpore memorial. That year, after being installed above the Memorial Well, the monument was photographed by Samuel Bourne and received widespread acclaim (fig. 72).[54] By standing firm against the revolt, Britain's commitment to India ultimately demonstrated the resilience of its imperial designs, and writers used the monument to confirm these actions, to reassert the legitimacy of the British cause. At the same time, metaphorical symbolism, like the term 'Slaughterhouse Well' that served as a shorthand expression for the burial ground itself, consolidated the overarching narrative in a mere economy of words. But this metonymic compound also created a neologism, one that replaced 'Slaughter House' for *Bibighar* and 'Well' for the burial tomb, thereby forming a new amalgamation that effectively communicated the intertwined associations of mourning and triumph discussed here. Narrative repetition of this kind therefore performed the idealizing work of empire, as it infused nostalgia and romanticism in symbolic form.[55] Narrative repetition also produced the illusion of decisiveness, the sense that 'the truth' had been captured and contained, that knowledge about the event had been affirmed, structured, reviewed, even finalized by authoritative means.[56] In short, narrative repetition as it was expressed here made it possible to create and refine a 'canon of historical thinking and power', which is to say, to project a given reality outward into culture through the language of symbols and iconography.[57]

As a result, narrative repetition makes allegory possible, chiefly because the symbolic representation at the heart of allegory relies upon the unity of a shared discourse. Moreover, wrote Gilles Deleuze, repetition helps to define a historical moment in time, first by displacing that event metonymically in relation to itself (e.g. 'Slaughterhouse Well'), and then by disguising its representation in relation to the 'real event' it purports to narrate historically.[58] For example, *The Times*'s almost compulsive retelling of the historical account ('where from 120 to 130 of our women and children were mercilessly butchered') and its repeated references to the designs, plans, models, and exhibition of the Memorial Well in different contexts ('the well itself within is vaulted over and covered with a pedestal') confirms Deleuze's contention that such representations of the event disclose the intermixed and repressed emotional responses to the nation's expressions of mourning and triumph over its conflict with India. But repetition also represses counter-narratives, for example, by erasing the story of British retribution from these accounts.[59] Consequently, the symbolic representation of British women and children as innocent victims helped the British empire comprehend the reprisals committed in its name as necessary to restore order in the colony, making the 'Slaughter House Well' a potent allegorical emblem of cause and effect. 'Allegorical empire', wrote Don Randall,

> like the historical empire upon which it is predicated, is sustained by a violence that never achieves its final act. One cannot put an end to the Mutiny story, one can only return to it – again and again.[60]

Moreover, fear of the *next* anti-colonial revolt also animated these repeated narratives, making allegory an essential tool of empire because it effectively reinscribed key narratives and reinforced the imperial mission. Over time, the repeated narrative of massacred British women in India shifted the 'colonial system of meaning from self-interest and moral superiority to self-sacrifice and racial superiority', as Jenny Sharpe has argued.[61] Framed in this way, the cause of empire accorded new importance to racial difference, redefining Europe's unholy 'Other' by embracing inflammatory cultural terms.[62]

But because allegories also contain inherent ambiguities, representations of victory over India were accompanied by their symbolic opposite, which is to say, the allegorical process inevitably contained the rebellion's opposition to Britain's occupation, uncannily reviving an absent counter-narrative buried deep in the anti-colonial struggle. Said another way, if the Memorial Well symbolically marked a British triumph over Indian treachery, it was also necessary to disavow the legitimacy of the opposing forces. And because the mythical forces and symbolic forms that epitomized these fears could never definitively be erased, they soon emerged in theatrical form, as we shall see, as spectres of the past that remain invisible in the present.[63] They are present in tales of loss and grief told by members of the Holland Park set, reminders of what remained unresolved and unacknowledged from imperial conflicts of the past. Representations of Cawnpore therefore provided a continual reminder of the precarity of British imperialism in India, a nagging memory, and a suppressed fear.

THE WELL IN FRESHWATER

The International Exhibition of 1862 reinforced this prevailing narrative. There is no chance that Julia Margaret could have missed attending the exhibition. Throughout the summer of 1861, at the height of the building's construction in South Kensington, Cameron's daughter Juley was residing at 1 Cromwell Place, just a block or so from the building site.[64] More importantly, many of the exhibition's artistic exhibitors and honoured guests provided a 'who's who' of those in her inner circle. The exhibition itself was the brainchild of Cameron's friend Sir Henry Cole, a regular visitor to Little Holland House. Earl Granville, the exhibition's Chief Commissioner, was on familiar terms with Lord Lansdowne, Lady Waterford, and the Cannings. Her friend Tennyson was present on Opening Day to hear a performance of his *Ode* to the exhibition sung for the assembled guests. Two months later, in late July, Tennyson returned to the site once more to take a private tour with his wife, Emily, where they were sure to pass by the English architectural gallery.[65] Tennyson's friend Francis Turner Palgrave, another regular at Little Holland House, had been commissioned to write the official guide to the works of fine art on display at the International Exhibition. Palgrave wrote an opinionated text that praised the work of the Pre-Raphaelite painters, Hunt and Millais, as 'the Future of English Art', while his comments disparaging the 'empty extravagance' of Marochetti's sculptures provoked a vigorous backlash.[66] Nevertheless, because of the wide range of historical and contemporary English works that were selected for display, the cultural networks of Little Holland House and Lansdowne House were deeply engaged. Holman Hunt declared, for example, that the International Exhibition 'captured all of London's attention', despite the cloud of sadness cast by the recent death of Prince Albert.

The historical chain of interconnected narrative elements described above provides a useful critical foundation from which to examine Julia Margaret Cameron's early work in photography. The earliest of her photographic allegories, produced in Freshwater even before she began copyrighting her work or making pictures of children as angels, depicts imagery of women posed around a water well. Cameron's formal interest in and narrative investigation of this iconography is the central focus of these early photographic explorations. In pursuing this theme, she was not working naively: *You know the story*, *The Times* reminded its readers. Likewise, Cameron expected that the photographic stories she wanted to tell were also known broadly. Like the narrative of the Memorial Well at Cawnpore, these stories were part of the cultural firmament. Writing about Cameron's allegorical subject matter, Mike Weaver asserted, 'Her stories were already known to everyone'.[67] From the evidence of Julia Margaret Cameron's earliest photographic explorations, she believed there was yet one more story to tell.

The 1862 International Exhibition appears to have been an important catalyst, as the same event displayed Marochetti's reduced-scale monument (see fig. 72) and exhibited Rejlander's photograph *A Night in the Streets of London* (see fig. 62). That same year, perhaps during the summer, Cameron welcomed Rejlander to the Isle of Wight as her guest. Scholars agree the two collaborated or made several photographs together, with Rejlander presumably in the teaching role and Cameron learning to compose and print.[68] The two apparently also collaborated in determining subject matter, as Rejlander made several photographs depicting young women in Cameron's household as well as her young granddaughter, Charlotte Norman. During the summer of 1864, Cameron shared some of these earliest photographs with Lewis Carroll, who visited her on the Isle of Wight. Carroll remarked that one evening they

> had a mutual exhibition of photographs. Hers are all taken purposely out of focus – some are very picturesque – some merely hideous. However she talks of them as if they were triumphs of art.[69]

The question for us is not whether she achieved those 'triumphs of art', as Carroll phrased it, but rather how she engaged members of her circle to discover how she could use the medium to represent narrative subject matter.

Rejlander's prints of *Irish and Isle of Wight Peasants* (also called *The Three Graces*) appears to have been made inside Cameron's Freshwater house (fig. 73), for example, and a photograph of Cameron and her maids receiving letters from a postman, perhaps taken with Lord Somers, is posed just outside her cottage's secondary doorway. Rejlander himself also came in front of the camera to take on a dramatic role, pretending to be an organ-grinder for a photograph he called *The Hurdy-Gurdy Man*. To Rejlander and Cameron alike, the photographic identity of the models emphasized their performance as actors, as if their purpose was to narrate a story on a theatrical set. As with all genre pictures, an easily perceived and prominent visual narrative provided structure to the image and accorded primary meaning to its subject. Like *A Night in the Streets of London*, photographs like those described here drew upon the aesthetic tradition in visual art that idealized rural and itinerant labour, just as they recorded social and class divisions, as if these scenes were composed 'naturally'. Cameron sent prints *Irish and*

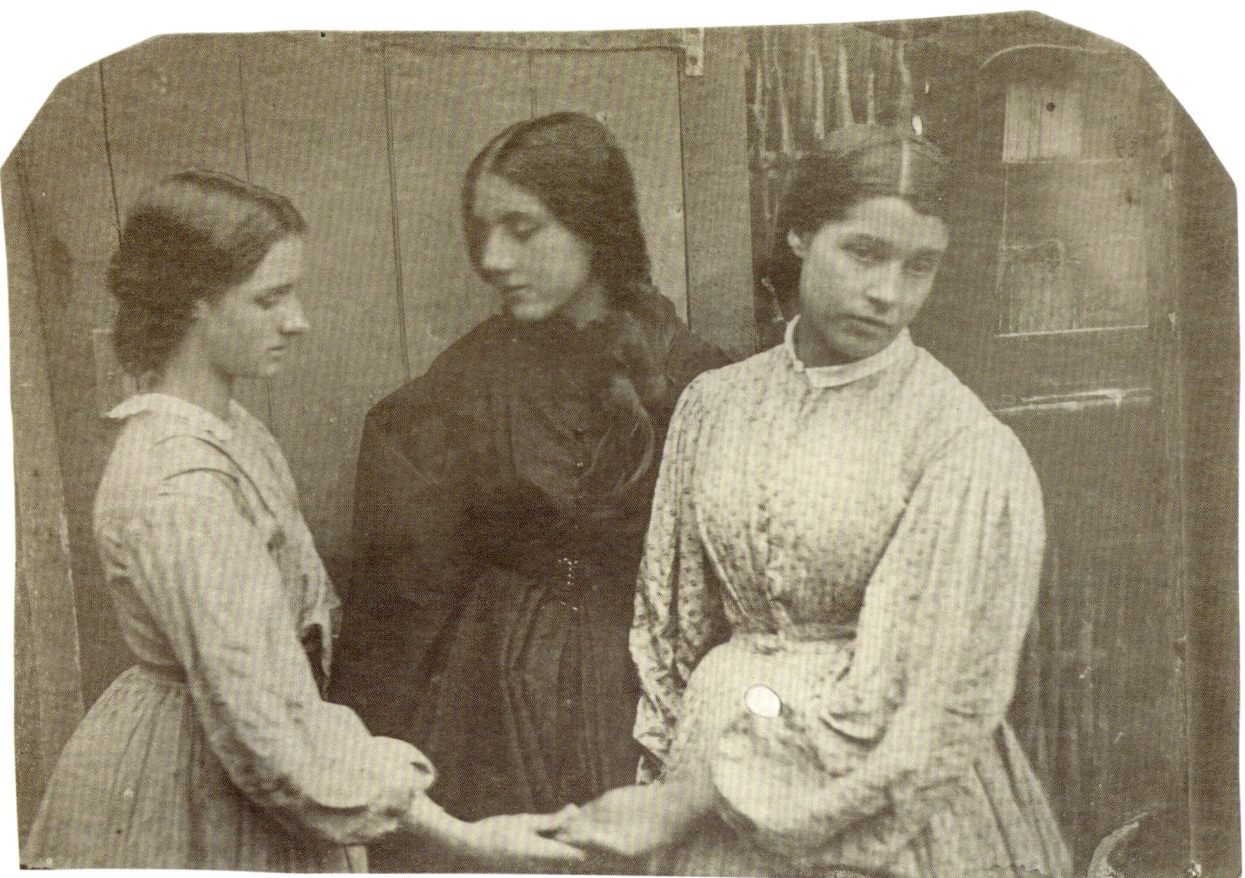

73 Oscar Gustave Rejlander (with Lord Somers, possibly), *Irish and Isle of Wight Peasants* (also called *The Three Graces*), *c.*1860, albumen print (Mia Album 97), 11 × 16 cm.
Collection of Michael Mattis and Judy Hochberg, New York.

Isle of Wight Peasants and *The Hurdy-Gurdy Man* to her sister Maria in 1863 for inclusion in her album of photographs.[70]

Cameron and Rejlander also collaborated in the making of two additional photographs that depict household maids drawing water from a well-head (figs 74 and 75), although she copyrighted these images in her own name – that is, claiming these images as products of her own hand – and registered one on 30 June and the other on 10 October 1864.[71] At first, these two untitled photographs appear to be part of a series of genre subjects that represent household maids at work, like those described above. As photographs related by subject matter, they share common models and rely upon the same domestic setting. Posed in arrested action like actors on a stage, these two photographs possess no more 'documentary value' than does Rejlander's *A Night in the Streets of London*. In one of the two photographs, for example, a young man is posed to lean against a nearby ladder that has been propped up close to the well, and in both images Cameron's actual housemaids may have been recruited to serve as models, or, as some have suggested, visitors to the house may also have been asked to pose, but just as with *A Night in the Streets of London*, their identities as individuals are not essential to unlocking the possible meanings of the imagery.[72]

In both photographs, a female model holds a pitcher as a kind of studio prop. And although physical labour is depicted here – as the maids appear to have just pulled up a tub full of water – their poses suggest something like weariness or even dreaminess, as if the photographer was uncertain if the actual subject of the photograph was the exertion of drawing water from the well, the aftermath of that labour, the iconography associated with water, or the symbolic importance of the well-head itself. Alternatively, it is possible that the models themselves were unsure of their stage directions, uncertain if they should portray rest or work, or perhaps some biblical personification, like 'Rachel at the Well', particularly owing to the well-known iconography of this Old Testament story, which typically represents the interaction of Leah, Rachel, and Jacob in the same composition. In the absence of clear instructions, however, Cameron's models appear unnatural before the lens and act self-consciously, expressing embarrassment. In their awkwardness and in reflecting their apparent awareness of the camera, the models break the illusion expected of genre subjects.

This example may reveal Cameron's inexperience with the new medium or expose her naïveté in setting up a credible photographic illusion. The two images do not correspond to a well-known narrative and do not tell a new or persuasive story of their own. These two photographs, however, are useful as early examples of what Roland Barthes called the 'deictic language' of photographs. Barthes appropriated this term from linguistics to illustrate why photographs must rely upon contextual information to make their meanings clear, much in the same way that words and phrases also require context to situate meaning. He wrote, 'the photograph is never anything but an antiphon of "Look," "See," "Here it is;" it points a finger at certain *vis-à-vis*, and cannot escape this pure deictic language'.[73] Without any situational, literary, or historical context, in other words, Cameron's photographs are wholly enigmatic. In the absence of an explicit narrative, photographs can only 'point a finger' at something depicted by the camera, but like a signpost that points to no

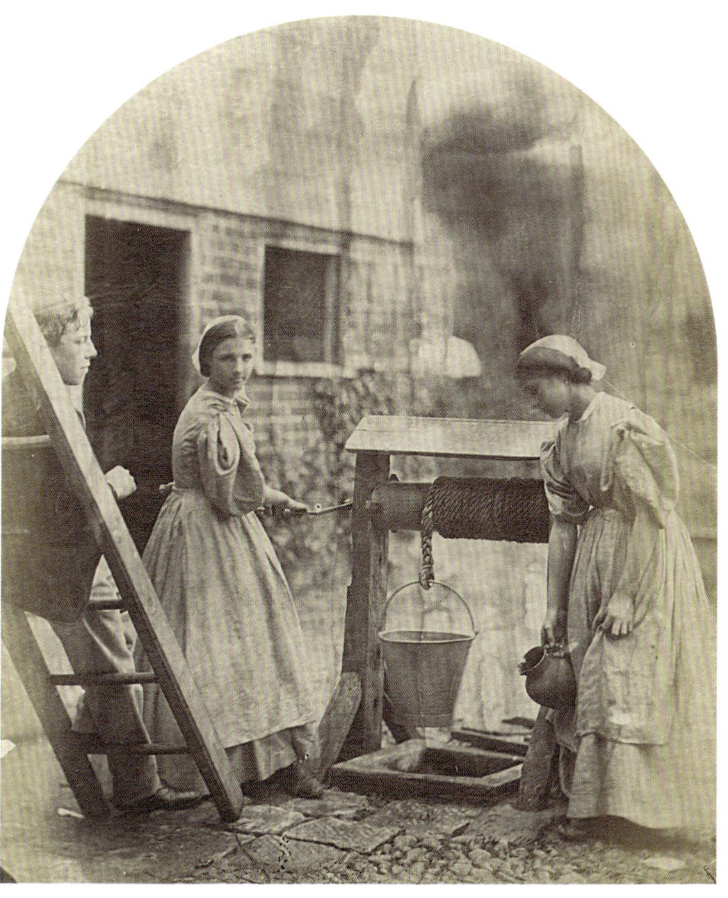

74 Oscar Gustave Rejlander and Julia Margaret Cameron, *At the Well*, *c.*1863, albumen print (Mia Album 73), 17.5 × 14.5 cm.

Collection of Michael Mattis and Judy Hochberg, New York.

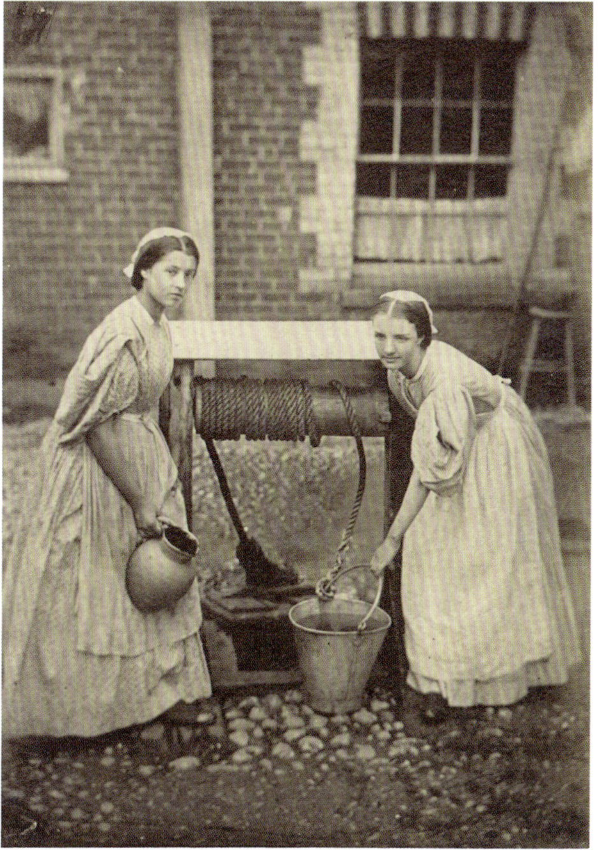

75 Oscar Gustave Rejlander and Julia Margaret Cameron, *Untitled*, *c.*1863, albumen print (Mia Album 80), 15.3 × 10.6 cm.

Collection of Michael Mattis and Judy Hochberg, New York.

obvious destination, the meaning behind such imagery can only remain mysterious if context is lacking. To avoid this conundrum, wrote Barthes, photographs 'require a secondary action of knowledge or of reflection' to enable their viewers to apprehend the photograph's intended signifier.[74] Because Cameron understood the value of evocative titles, for example, we can place *Annie Lee* in her English fishing village and visualize *Paul and Virginia* on their secluded island.

Yet the two photographs of women at the well described here both lack titles and context. As viewers, we can only 'point a finger' at the action depicted and, like Barthes, identify what we see using descriptive terms. Rejlander and Cameron chose an ordinary setting of a well near a house and they costumed models using theatrical props, but these factors alone are hardly adequate to convey the various possible meanings of the imagery beyond what we see with our eyes alone. Following Rejlander's lead, however, Cameron began to append signifying titles to her photographs. That summer, either in Rejlander's presence while the two were at work, or perhaps at some later point after he had departed from her company, Cameron produced her own photograph of a woman at the well. The outdoor setting was the same and the model posed similarly, but this image is not identical to the photographs made by the two. In 1864, Cameron included the new picture in the first Herschel Album, very likely in the same position as the one in which it was placed in 1867, on the last page of the album. At the bottom of the page, she appended the word *Farewell* (Cox/Ford 169; fig. 76).[75] Cameron's notation below the print might have been inscribed as a personal signoff to Herschel or, in the absence of a Table of Contents to the 1864 album, it could equally serve as the title to this work, which, for our purposes following Barthes, usefully identifies the image.

Significantly, Cameron registered this new photograph for copyright protection on 10 October 1864 but did not assign it a formal title. Unlike her photographs of young children described above, *Farewell* does not represent religious, mythological, or literary iconography, nor does it presume to document a typical Victorian household activity. And although the photograph may resemble the scene of the two

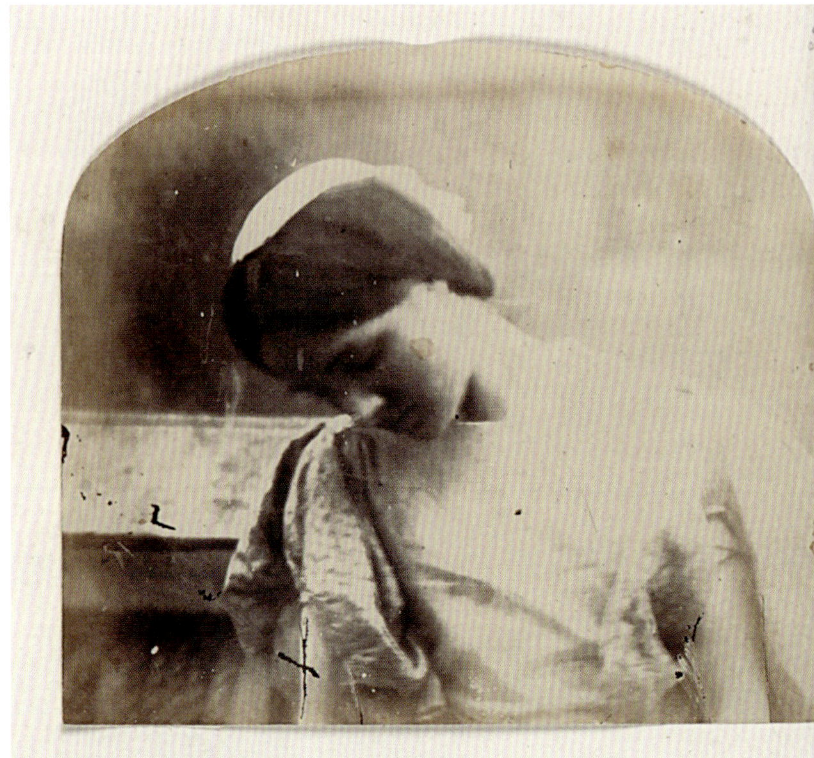

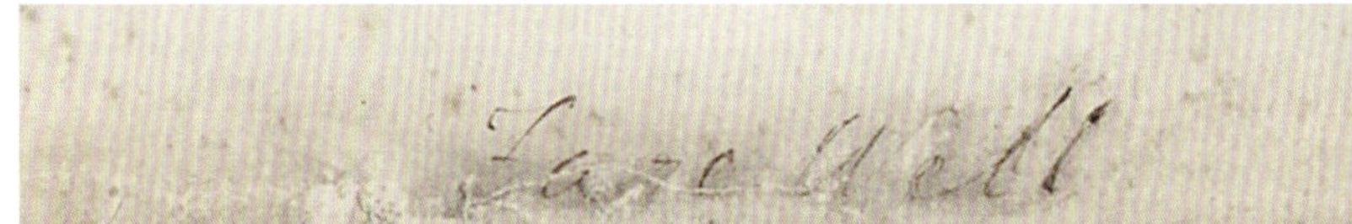

76a and b Julia Margaret Cameron, details of a page from the Herschel Album (see fig. 7).

women at the well that she produced alongside Rejlander, *Farewell* is also not composed as a conventional genre picture, because the solitary figure is cast in shadow, depicted only from the waist up, and framed alone in a scene that provides even less context than the others. And even though this photograph may depict one of the same models as in the earlier photographs taken with Rejlander, the costume is entirely different, there are no props, and the model's attitude has changed. Cameron claimed this new photograph as her own, and three years later, she reconceived the image once more.

But before examining that material and conceptual transformation, it is useful to ask several questions to help determine how Cameron might have assigned meaning to this photograph in 1864. We might ask first if page sequencing was an important factor. The associations with such placement could prove useful since Cameron affixed the photograph to the last page in the album where the reader prepares to take his or her leave of the volume. In this regard, Cameron's inscription on the bottom of the album page does differ from the titles she gave to other works. From this perspective, the image could have functioned metaphorically as if a way to bid the reader 'farewell'. But Victorian photographic albums were not read exclusively in one direction, from front to back, as if they possessed a single narrative through-line. For example, of Maria Jackson's album, Colin Ford wrote, 'Start from one end and you see only Cameron prints. Start at the other, and there are pictures by a number of mainly unknown and unidentifiable photographers'.[76] As described above, the earlier Lansdowne Album also lacks defined sequencing and narrative coherence, and the same is true of the Watts and Norman Albums. In addition, Cameron produced albums that she simply left incomplete, as she intended to add additional prints later, as with the volume she created for her sister Maria. In Lansdowne's album, which Cameron gave to the Marquis in 1859, either she or the Marquis himself added new photographs of Tennyson around 1861, as we have seen. Even more complicated, Julia Margaret constructed the so-called 'Mia Album' with two beginnings and two endings, as the reader was supposed to flip the book over and begin again from the other side. Readers of the Mia Album could therefore open the volume from either direction, beginning anywhere.

What about the Romantic affect expressed in this photograph? With the model's sad demeanour, her head bent forward, eyes downcast, *Farewell* might seem to conform to visual conventions associated with sentimental genre painting. Much like Rejlander's *A Night in the Streets of London*, where the child's head is bent forward and the body slumped over to convey dejection and despair, Cameron's photograph also elicits an emotional response. Titles were important to Cameron. Were sentimental references important to her representation, it is reasonable to conclude, she would have selected an appropriately evocative title from the familiar stock house of genre subjects, like 'Sadness at Parting', 'A Melancholy Good-bye', or 'Grieving a Loss', in order to make the sad emotions explicit. Or she might have borrowed a sentimental line or two from Byron or Tennyson that expressed similar kinds of sombre feeling. She clearly knew this tradition in visual art well, as she would later append such mournful titles to evoke feelings of melancholy and dejection, as in examples like *The Disappointment*, *Sadness*, *The Fisherman's Farewell*, or *The Passion Flower at the Gate*. Explicit titles like these and precise references to poems like 'Enoch Arden' or novels like *Paul and Virginia* situate such imagery unambiguously as genre pictures and thereby help viewers channel their primary emotional associations.

Finally, we might ask if the iconographic history of costume helps to convey a particular interpretation, how the model's attire, and the physical objects she holds or is pictured with, help us understand the domestic context of *Farewell* in relation to Victorian social mores. For example, the pitcher held by the model in the two photographs made earlier with Rejlander could refer to earlier works of visual art in which an idealized female (typically a nude) holds a pitcher as an emblem for a water source or eternal spring, a visual metaphor for female fertility, the muse of artistic inspiration, or the wellspring of creativity. Painters like Watts and Ingres drew upon this iconographic language and history. But in these two examples, Rejlander's and Cameron's models resemble ordinary maids in contemporary dress rather than timeless goddesses or water nymphs. They are situated in contemporary time rather than an ageless arcadia. Their props are commonplace and familiar; and, of course, water does not magically flow from the pitcher. We might compare these maid's lace caps to a similar type of headdress worn by a domestic servant as portrayed in George Dunlop Leslie's painting *Afternoon Tea* (1865). Viewed from the rear, the maid's lace cap covers the back of her head, its frill providing a frame-like surround to her face when seen from the front (fig. 77).

While it may be possible to connect the two photographs of Cameron's housemaids at the well taken by Rejlander and Cameron to earlier conventions in painting, these observations do not explain the importance of the well or the models' relationship to the title *Farewell*. And yet, Cameron ensured that an essential marker was present in the head-covering worn by the model in this image. Unlike the maid's caps worn by the two women represented in the earlier imagery, this model's headdress is a white mourning cap and signifies that she is *not* in domestic service. Rather, the head-covering depicted in *Farewell* – sometimes called a 'chapel cap' – would have been worn by upper-class women to demonstrate their faith, humility, piety, or devotion, especially in a religious setting. Unlike a maid's cap used as a hair-covering for a servant girl, as represented in Leslie's painting, mourning or chapel caps were carefully positioned to cover only the top of the woman's head. Over time, these pious coverings were refined stylistically to come to a point towards the forehead. Therefore, in this photograph, Julia Margaret Cameron has depicted a widow, not a housemaid.

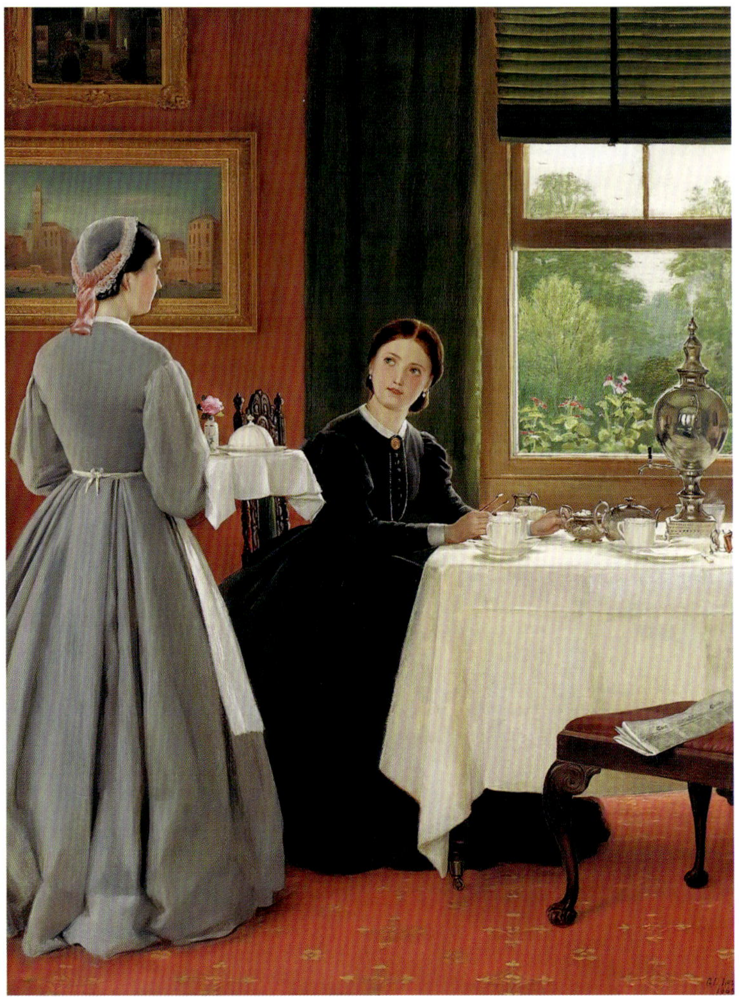

77 George Dunlop Leslie, *Afternoon Tea*, 1865, oil on canvas, 62.3 × 46.7 cm.
Private collection, public domain.

THE WAR WIDOWS' FUTURE

Widow's caps were worn commonly during the 1850s and 1860s in England, but the tradition of widows wearing mourning apparel to signify their personal grief dated from practices in the eighteenth century.[77] And in the Victorian era, mourning dress was associated with social isolation, because generally speaking, widows were expected to avoid social functions.[78] The practice of signifying loss by wearing mourning attire was especially important during times of war, when a mourning dress accompanied by a widow's cap took on even greater significance. As we saw earlier, the journal *Punch* portrayed Queen Victoria in mourning attire as she grieved for the nation. Gathering war widows and orphans into her orbit, she leans down to offer comfort and security. Paradoxically, however, this image also depicts consolation and grief coupled with a national call for revenge, its double meaning articulated by the caption 'O God of Battles! Steel My Soldiers' Hearts' (see fig. 33).

Following the 1857 war in India, the young British widow of a clergyman who had been posted to Lucknow published her *Lady's Diary* of the war, a text that attracted a wide audience.[79] In her account, Mrs James Harris wrote of the importance of mourning garments to signify her personal loss to the world. In an entry marked December 1857, for example, she described the scene in Allahabad Fort following the siege of that city:

> Mrs. Polehampton and I went round the barracks and took down the names of all the widows belonging to the Artillery and the 32nd, for Mrs. Spry, who is going to give them each a black dress from the relief fund. Some of the poor things are in great distress, having come out of Lucknow with only the clothes they wore.[80]

The practice of using such attire to signify widowhood was of exceptional importance in the aftermath of the 1857 Uprising because it re-established 'conventional mourning patterns that unified Britons' in the field. In fact,

> one of the very first priorities for relief workers ... was to distribute proper mourning attire to women

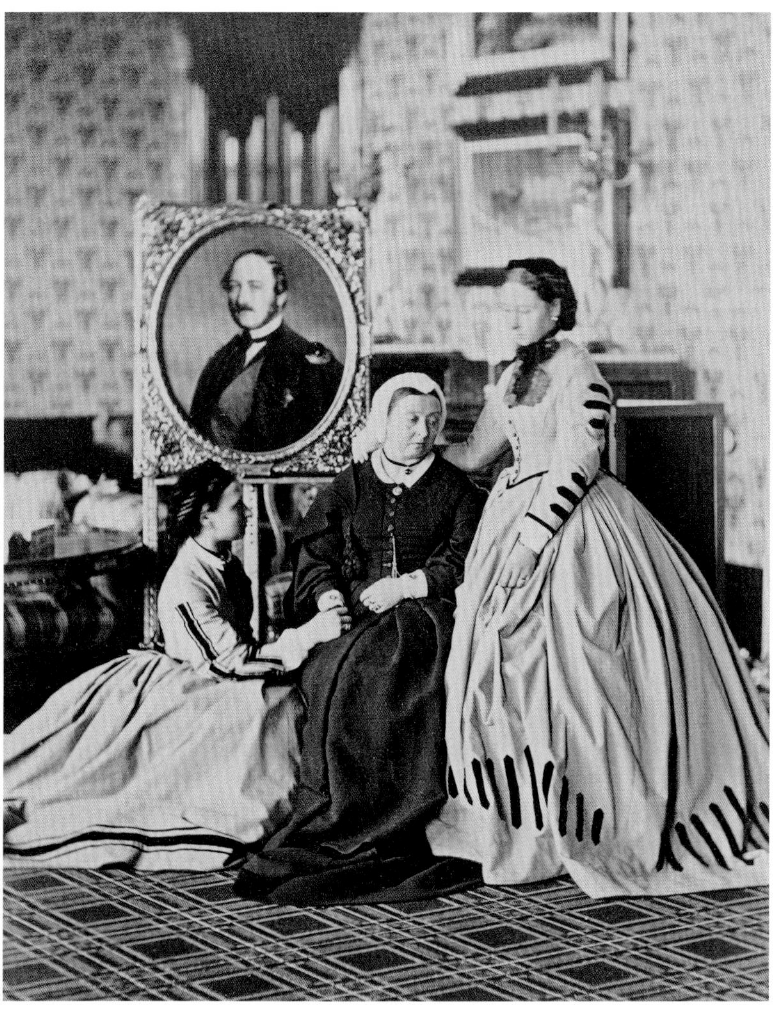

78 George Washington Wilson, *The Queen, Princess Louis of Hesse [Princess Alice] and Princess Louise, Balmoral, Oct. 1863*, albumen print, 10.7 × 7.7 cm. Royal Collection Trust / © His Majesty King Charles III 2023. RCIN 2900814.

> survivors as they travelled from Lucknow to Calcutta. The widow's black dress or mourning cap instantly identified her as someone who had sacrificed for Britain, while provoking established outlets for expressing grief.[81]

In this way, mourning attire cemented public duty with extreme personal sacrifice and expressed nationalistic commitment together with a commonly shared British identity.

The popularity of these practices among women grew even more resolute after Prince Albert's death in 1861, when Queen Victoria made *white* widow's caps identifiable with public displays of grief and mourning (fig. 78).[82] For example, in this photograph dated October 1863, the Queen wears a white widow's cap as she sits between two of her daughters in front of a painting of the late Prince Consort. Moreover, during this era, *young* widowhood was associated directly with widows who lost husbands from the two wars in Crimea and India.[83] As Susan Casteras has observed, mourning attire worn by 'the widow who was young, attractive, and vulnerable' created 'a potent formula to excite pathos' in Victorian England.[84] In Cameron's photograph *Farewell*, the figure's young womanhood is accentuated by her bare arms, which pointedly do not conform to stereotypical black and dreary 'widow's weeds', and therefore the image emphasizes her youthfulness as appealing. A similar unconventional approach to young widowhood was expressed in contemporary literature. In Anthony Trollope's *Barchester Towers* (1857), for example, when the author introduces his readers to Eleanor Bold, he describes her as being still young and attractive, despite the widow's cap she wears to grieve the loss of her late husband. Designed to be worn in a solemn indoor setting (as opposed to a veil, which would be worn outdoors), these articles of clothing conveyed feminine modesty, humility, and sexual restraint, while bringing an unmistakable devout or sacred context to a particular setting.

In Cameron's photograph, the model's bare arms and white chapel cap suggests still another possible interpretation, one that implies Cameron was interested in depicting a transgressive statement about this subject, one that censured depictions of 'traditional' mourning. Why might Cameron have broken from the familiar template of dreary black mourning weeds? Rebecca Mitchell offers a compelling reason, writing that Victorian

> women with the means and the desire could use mourning dress in surprising ways, appropriating its ambivalence, controlling the emotional messages it communicated, and actively negotiating the marketplace for mourning goods to assert erotic, social, and economic agency. Widows' fashion could be read as a symbol of bereavement, but it could also signal a woman's new availability or sexual experience.[85]

Evidence for this transgressive attitude appears once again in Trollope. For example, in his novel *Can You Forgive Her?* (1864), his character Arabella Greenow self-consciously enjoys her youth and independence while entertaining two potential suitors at once. As a young widow, she flaunts her desirability and attractiveness. Unexpectedly, she revels in her extensive mourning wardrobe as if it were 'a trousseau' and changes her widow's caps regularly, consciously making different fashion statements according to the particular social occasion she pursues.[86] Given this example of a contemporary though fictional portrayal, Cameron's representation of a widow at the well could be interpreted as a portrait of a demure, inward-looking, and self-aware widow, but also as a representation of a widow much like Arabella Greenow, who is coy and alluring, who uses her attire to feign only a pretence to modesty or sadness, while actually emphasizing her availability and feminine attractiveness. Conceived in this way, Cameron's widow before the well may function as does Trollope's, that is, 'as the junction point at which compulsory mourning and compulsory heterosexuality wrestle for control of narrative ends'. In this regard, the widow must, on the one hand, mourn her first husband as a loss and, on the other, 'forget him in order to facilitate the marriage that will signify the closure of her loose narrative ends; the alternative is a kind of narrative oblivion'.[87]

Cameron's photograph *Farewell* has been among the most overlooked of her early allegorical works, and yet this image remains powerful today because it embodies Cameron's highly personal interpretation of national mourning in the aftermath of the 1857 Indian Uprising. The melancholy pose and demeanour conveys sadness and grief, while her bowed head and white widow's cap express religious devotion and sorrow. Moreover, the figure's depiction in an outdoor setting conveys public attention and awareness, and the model's choice of attire suggests an expression of self-consciousness and self-aware sexuality. The water well appears present though indistinct behind her, where its relevance to her social status is ambiguous. Nevertheless, Cameron's female figure is also defined in relation to the well behind her, and the well's symbolic associations with the burial site at Cawnpore in relation to the photograph's title reinforces the overall effect.

Although such a reading provides narrative coherence, it is also important to recognize that this photograph is also complicated by what is *not pictured* in the image: Cameron's photograph of a white woman dressed in white mourning attire in front of a water well represents a British (or European) subject – and not an Indian woman. This distinction makes evident the stark religious and cultural differences that projected opposing values on the social role and performance of widowhood in British and Indian societies after the war. For British Anglicans, mourning apparel signified the accepted performance ritual associated with marking death in a family, and its public recognition conveyed broad public sympathy for widows' personal and social sacrifices. By contrast, traditional Hindu customs were entirely at odds with the British example. As seen through imperial eyes, the social practice of Hindu widows was a marker of that religion's uncivilized cruelty, since widows were supposed to sacrifice their lives to honour their dead husbands in the ritual practice of *suttee*, or self-immolation. In 1829, the East India Company outlawed *suttee* under the Governorship of William Bentinck, calling it 'barbarous and inhuman'. Nevertheless, the matter came up again two years later in Parliament, when Lord Lansdowne presented the question as a matter for the Privy Council to decide in a petition before the House of Lords, where Bentinck's prohibition was ultimately upheld.[88]

Bentinck's ban on *suttee* was especially provocative, as it was used specifically to justify Britain's intervention in India on so-called humanitarian grounds and to justify the Company's continued presence in India thereafter as a civilizing influence. But as the practice continued despite having been outlawed, the Company introduced additional measures to constrain the practice. In 1856, for example, Lord Dalhousie passed the Hindu Widows' Remarriage Act, but that new law was once again considered yet another affront to Brahmin religious practices because it required widows to give up their wealth and property before remarrying. As a result, the British law actually reinforced class and caste biases in India, making it even more difficult and unlikely for a widow to remarry.[89] Consequently, the fate of Indian women once again was 'caught between patriarchy and imperialism', as Gayatri Chakravorty Spivak notably described it.[90] Regarded in this light, by promoting British conceptions of 'appropriate behaviour' for widows in her photograph, Cameron's image of a British woman mourning in front of a water well provided both a discursive and didactic response to the Indian practice of *suttee*, a proper Western example, and corrective, to the 'barbaric' Indian practice. Interpreted in this way, the photograph's message accords well with Sarah Stickney Ellis's advice to 'imperial women' to use their considerable influence to transmit the moral superiority of British society.

In creating a series of photographs in 1863 and 1864 built around the domestic setting of a water well, it hardly seems possible that Cameron could have detached her composition from the narrative repetition of the 'Memorial Well' that kept this symbol alive in the public's mind as an emblem of grief and mourning. As we have seen, before its installation in 1865 in India, Marochetti's sculpture was accorded a place of honour as a scaled-down model at the 1862 International Exhibition, a public reminder of Canning's national promise, making the Memorial Well an inescapable reminder of the war. The *Illustrated London News* directed those who attended the exhibition to view the model in the English architectural gallery.[91] Every step of the monument's progress in design and construction was chronicled almost daily in *The Times* and other papers. Its financial underwriting, first discussed as a national priority, was then assumed by Lord Canning and his wife as a personal commitment. Their sponsorship liberated Parliament from bankrolling the cost of the monument, but the associations of Marochetti's 'Angel of the Resurrection' statue extended beyond Cawnpore to represent all British lives lost during the war.

Cameron's photograph *Farewell* consolidates these diverse associations. As an allegorical photograph, it relies upon a shared discourse of mourning and triumph. The image represents a focal point of national remembrance for the war, a commemorative memorial that mourns over those who died, a cultural statement honouring British widows and their indomitable spirit, and an emblem of triumph over the forces that would have ousted the British from India. In the photograph, Cameron's model mourns figuratively not only for the loss of the women and children buried in the well at Cawnpore, but also for the lost soldiers who fought on behalf of the empire, and by extension, for their widows and orphaned offspring as well. Moreover, in creating *Farewell*, Cameron feminized the male genre in which warfare was typically commemorated, by incorporating narrative codes of importance to female viewers, like the white chapel cap and the modern apparel that was likely a meaningful symbol to younger widows. And as a work of mourning, this photograph shared common ground with her allegorical photographs depicting 'Enoch Arden' and *Paul and Virginia*, as these subjects also narrate the story of young orphans who were abandoned by the empire and must make their way in a world alone, unaccompanied by men. Cameron's female mourner stands apart from the well but she also haunts the scene, representing the unresolved and unknown losses that defined Cawnpore as a site of unimaginable grief, but imperfect remembering. In this image, Cameron pays homage to Britain's unresolved collective memory of the war in India.

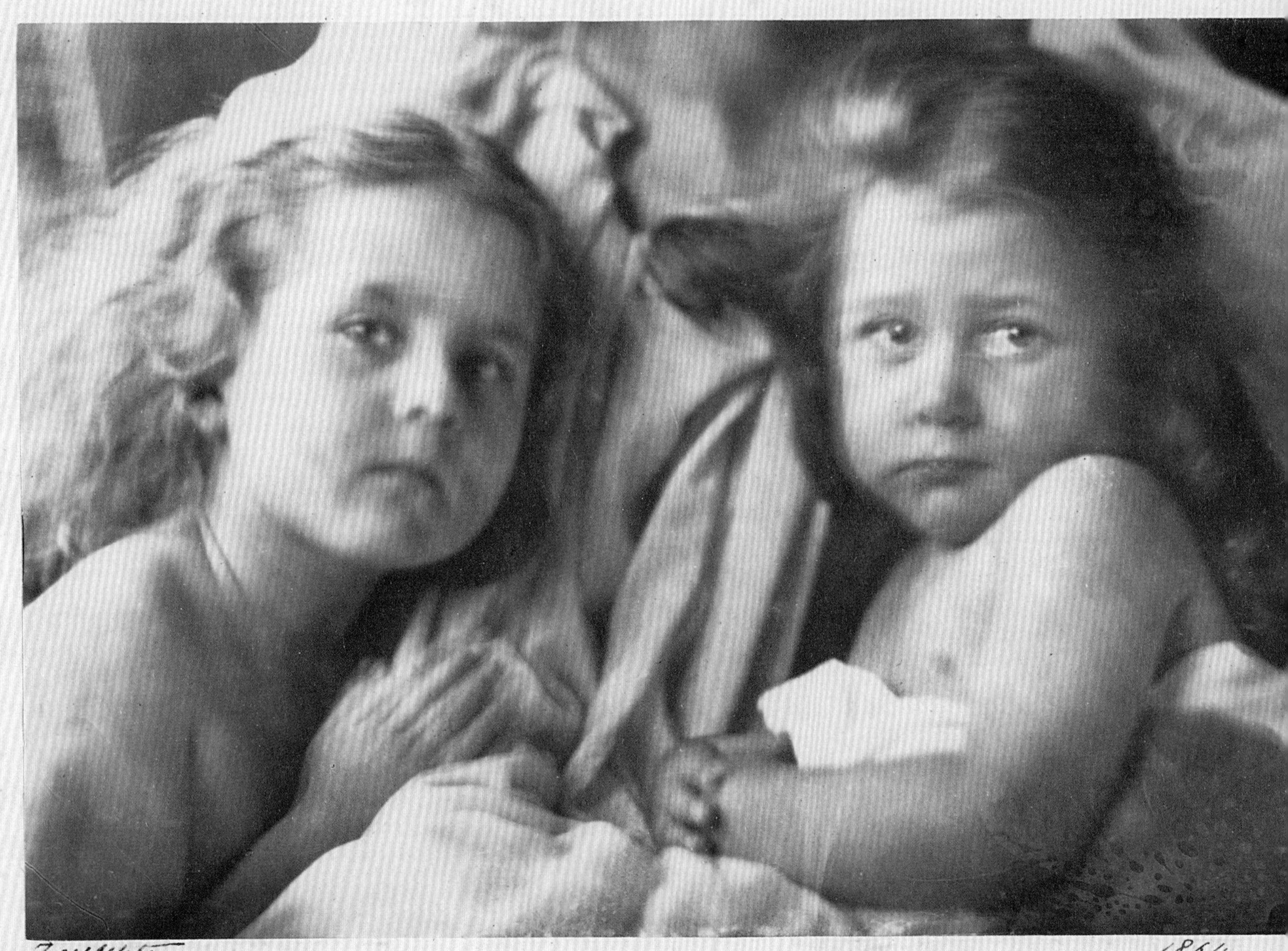

Freshwater 1864

The bereaved Babes

Chapter Eight Betrayal and Atonement

79 Julia Margaret Cameron, *The bereaved Babes*, 1864 (see fig. 83).

NANA SAHIB'S RETURN

During the second half of the nineteenth century, British novels featuring the Indian Uprising formed a distinct category of popular literature, one that enabled authors to represent familiar tropes facing off in moral and mortal opposition. These idioms included British valour and Oriental tyranny; heroes and antiheroes; mercy and vengeance; lightness and darkness; betrayal and loyalty; injustice and righteousness. At least sixty so-called 'Mutiny novels' appeared during this time, according to Christopher Herbert's estimate, most of which contain references to the traumatic break inflicted by the combined effects of the Uprising and Britain's violent suppression of it afterwards.[1] Gautam Chakravarty has observed that so-called 'Mutiny narratives' rested on an equally fictitious historical archive of the conflict, one that

> was hardly self-contained or without wider reference to genres, disciplines and institutions that produced, systematised and disseminated British knowledge and representations of India in all the years since the *diwani* [that is, the year 1765, when Governor-General Robert Clive won rights from the Mughal emperor for the East India Company to collect land taxes].[2]

And Patrick Brantlinger has shown that among the many narratives of the conflict in India – both the 'historical archive' and the fictionalized representations – there is 'an obsessive emphasis on Cawnpore and Nana Sahib', who became 'one of the most familiar villains in novels and melodramas, and by far the most familiar Indian character' of the rebellion.[3]

In 1866, 'Nana Sahib' made his figurative reappearance in Cameron's circle, courtesy of the playwright Tom Taylor. From the mid-1850s, Taylor was a regular presence at Little Holland House, a close friend of Thackeray and a gregarious member of the *Punch* crowd. When he visited his friends, he often brought along the famous acting Terry sisters, Kate and Ellen, as entertaining company. In 1864, when the professional performances of *Payable on Demand* moved from London to Canterbury, Kate Terry played the dual role of Lina, as wife and then as daughter to Reuben Goldsched.[4] And although Ellen Terry had married George Frederic Watts that same year, the two quickly parted ways, while Ellen's acting career, especially in Taylor's productions, continued to flourish. In 1865, Taylor finished writing a new play that he called *A Sister's Penance*, and he assigned the two leading roles to the Terry sisters. When the Camerons and the Prinseps joined the Tennysons in Freshwater, Tom Taylor also shifted his visits from Kensington to the Isle of Wight. To William Allingham, a poet and friend of Rossetti and others in the Pre-Raphaelite Brotherhood, the 'enchanted palace' of Little Holland House in Kensington, as branded earlier by Emily Tennyson, was now reassigned to Tennyson's home, Farringford. In his diary, Allingham described his journey to visit the new gathering place of the cultural literati:

> I crossed by the evening boat, walked over the bridge, and after two or three miles of beautiful greensided roads, spoilt here and there by Forts, reached the enchanted realm of Farringford.[5]

'More than any other eyewitness', wrote Colin Ford, Allingham 'seems to catch the authentic tone of voice of Alfred and Julia'.[6]

Towards the close of 1866, Tom Taylor invited Allingham to spend a few days with him in London. One evening in December, Allingham was whisked off by Taylor to the Adelphi Theatre to see his newest play. Allingham recorded the event in his diary.

> SATURDAY DEC. 22 [1866]: To Tom Taylor's, Lavender Sweep, for Christmas. Clapham Junction, all trains late. Reach the hospitable house about 7, in good time for dinner. Then T. T. hurries me off to the Junction again, and from Waterloo we take a cab to the Adelphi, and see *The Sister's Penance*, [*sic*] with Kate Terry. The Indian Mutiny scene, Ahmedvolah. In a stage-box the Terry family (including Nellie) and their Yorkshire friends. We just catch train at Waterloo and get home about half-past twelve.[7]

With a production run of eighty-three sold-out performances in London, *A Sister's Penance* was considered highly successful, and despite some harsh reviews, the play was well-received by critics and the public alike. In March 1867, after concluding its run at the Adelphi, the play moved

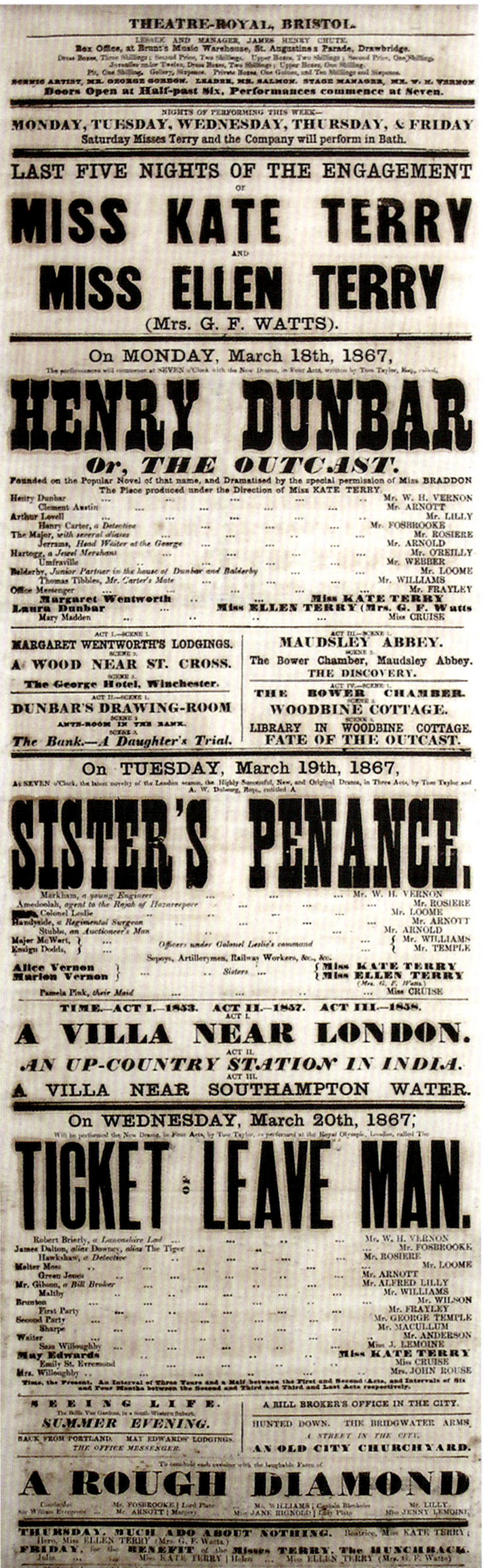

80 'Henry Dunbar at the Theatre-Royal, Bristol, and *A Sister's Penance* and *Ticket of Leave Man*', playbill, 1866.

Collection of Smallhythe Place, Kent, 1117284. © National Trust / Andrew Fetherston.

on to the Theatre-Royal in Bristol, where the Terrys continued in the same roles throughout most of the year (fig. 80).[8]

Tom Taylor timed his play to be performed at the ten-year anniversary of the Indian Uprising, which made his storyline both topical and newsworthy. As a play designed for the London stage, the drama built upon the popularity of numerous so-called 'Mutiny novels' that were published during this period, but *A Sister's Penance* has managed to escape notice in the scholarship surrounding the historical impact of these publications. Brantlinger and Herbert have demonstrated these stories were important for keeping the mutiny narrative alive. Their regular publication since 1857 downplayed residual anxieties about Britain's violent suppression of the Uprising in India, while helping to reinforce the enduring hostilities, racial animus, and moral justification for punishing India's betrayal. Tennyson apparently consumed sensational fiction of this kind, like Trollope's Irish Famine drama *Castle Richmond* (1859) and Mary Elizabeth Braddon's *Lady Audley's Secret* (1862), both set in the aftermath of the 1857 insurrection.[9] Ten years later, these fictional reminders became all but institutionalized. For example, anniversaries of the Uprising were marked in India in government-sponsored commemorative *durbars* for that purpose.[10] This chapter begins by examining Taylor's play in the context of its reception among the Freshwater circle, where Tennyson and Cameron held court, in order to discover how Cameron used her new interest in photography to reimagine the story of the anti-colonial revolt in a new light.

Taylor's drama, *A Sister's Penance*, unfolds on the eve of the 1857 Indian Uprising. Although the play is structured in three acts as a familiar Victorian tale centred around a predictable love triangle, the melodrama acquired its immediacy for Victorian audiences – and an electrified sense of menace – when the setting moves from England to India, and then back again. The return trip is essential to the story. A brief plot summary is useful. Act I begins near London in 1855, where two sisters, Alice and Marion, face an uncertain future as the unmarried daughters of a failed investor, whose unspecified commercial enterprise took place in India. The sisters compete for the attentions of Markham, a British railway engineer, whose company also has business commitments in India, and their home is frequented by their father's business associate, a high-born Indian named Ahmedoolah (whom Allingham misremembered in his diary as 'Ahmedvolah'). Taylor stresses this character's commercial connection to the family, designating him 'an agent to the Rajah of Hazareepore'.

Taylor built the character of Ahmedoolah by combining two sources, one factual, the other fictitious. The imaginary model was supplied by Thackeray, whose character Rummun was also styled an Indian commercial agent as portrayed in his 1854 novel *The Newcomes*. Although Colonel Newcome does not trust the Indian at first, he eventually goes into business with Rummun. But by naming his Indian character Ahmedoolah, Taylor decidedly aligned him with the real story of Azimullah Khan, known colloquially as Azimullah. As a child, Azimullah was rescued from starvation by British missionaries in Cawnpore, taught English, wore British clothing, came to understand British culture and politics. As an adult, he became Nana Sahib's chief advisor. In 1853, Nana Sahib sent Azimullah to London under the protection of Lady Duff-Gordon, cousin of the then Prime Minister. His mission was to petition the Board of Control of the East India Company to restore an annual pension that had been promised to Nana Sahib's father, but which the Company had rescinded. After two years in London, Azimullah failed to win back the pension. Nursing his grief, wrote Andrew Ward, Azimullah 'began to brood on what had seemed too outlandish a notion to consider seriously: the expulsion of the British from India'.[11]

In Taylor's play, Ahmedoolah secretly harbours amorous feelings towards Alice, but the sisters' family refers to him as a racial 'Other', calling him their 'black prince'. Ahmedoolah also repeatedly demonstrates his loyalty, both to the family and to the British cause, while he also harbours repressed animosity of the kind experienced by the real Azimullah. In Act I, for example, Ahmedoolah reveals himself to Alice:

> I am a Mahomedan, dark skinned, an Indian native. How can my masters be expected to know I am a gentleman? Here you receive me as an equal, but in India I must bear myself before you as a servant – a slave servant – and yet my family counts ten generations of learned Moollahs, wise councillors,

> brave soldiers. You admit me to your colleges, I may study your tongue and lay its lessons to heart, I am eligible to be a vakeel – an attorney in your Indian courts, or even a sub-stipendiary magistrate at three hundred rupees a month. This is what your gracious Government does for the gentlemen of India. Can you wonder we are grateful to it?[12]

Lying dormant in this putatively sincere declaration of gratitude, Ahmedoolah harbours his true resentments quietly. Meanwhile, Markham and Marion become engaged to marry, but soon thereafter, Markham accepts a position in India and breaks off the engagement. He then has misgivings and writes a letter to Marion formally proposing marriage. But he unwisely entrusts that letter to Alice, who deceptively withholds it from her sister. Believing Markham no longer a part of her future, Marion marries a different suitor, while Alice pursues Markham to India in the company of her uncle, an army colonel. During this same time, Ahmedoolah returns to India and to the service of his Maharajah.

Act II shifts to India in 1857, just before the outbreak of the rebellion, where Ahmedoolah has become a major antagonist to British rule. He warns Alice, 'I told you not to come to India. The country was meant for us, not for you English'. Yet on the eve of the rebellion itself, Ahmedoolah unexpectedly declares his love for Alice and asks her to 'become a queen among these people – a centre of light and knowledge, loved, trusted, looked up to'. But Alice rejects Ahmedoolah, expressing undisguised racial hatred as she fights him off:

> They were right who warned me against your race. Base, treacherous, insolent! ... *You* rise against *us*! You dare not; you know if there was only one Englishman left alive in India he would be your master![13]

As 'shots and sounds of fierce and rapid conflict' take place outside their residence, Alice's uncle, Colonel Leslie, is killed. Markham is seriously wounded, and Ahmedoolah escapes. In the third and final act, which takes place one year later in Southampton, Ahmedoolah re-emerges in the guise of Habib, a dark-skinned, bearded Indian ship servant, now unrecognizable from his earlier refined appearance. Markham's appearance has also changed noticeably, as he survived the insurrection an invalid. When a servant prepares a restorative tonic for the weakened Markham, Habib covertly poisons the glass as an act of revenge. But Alice carelessly drinks the tonic instead, and Ahmedoolah reappears suddenly – casting off his disguise – to prevent her from being poisoned. In despair, believing he acted too late, Ahmedoolah/Habib jumps from a window to his death on the cliffs outside. Yet Alice does not die, because unknown to all concerned, one of the servants had surreptitiously replaced the poison with harmless water. Alice then reconciles with her sister and expiates her guilt for having concealed Markham's letter.

Critics were divided in their reviews: the *Observer* wrote disparagingly about the drama, calling the action stilted, the dialogue poor, the slow length of the play 'a drag'.[14] But the play had its many enthusiasts, too. *Punch*, for example, wrote excitedly about what it called 'the Indian Mutiny passage' in the second act, which culminated

> in a scene of such physical strain and excitement, that the audience hold their breath, and men who have known the real horrors of Cawnpore and Agra, of Arrah and Jhansi, feel the terrible remembrances of that time revived.[15]

The critic for the *Illustrated London News* appreciated how Ahmedoolah pursued Alice 'with all the fierce heat of an Oriental and a Mohammedan'.[16] And the *Athenaeum*'s critic was equally captivated by the portrayal of the Indian Uprising, once again focusing on the cartoonishly animated character of Ahmedoolah, whose amorous overtures towards Alice are spurned in the third act.[17]

Taylor's account of 'the Mutiny scene' was hardly original. Indeed, as Christopher Herbert and others have demonstrated, 'repetitive, compulsive-seeming, redundant, exorbitant retelling ... is indeed the fundamental trope of narrative' in such literature.[18] Recirculated from earlier accounts, for example, are Ahmedoolah's use of chapattis (flat unleavened bread), which were used by sepoys as covert signals in their plot to oust the British.[19] Alice even articulates the conservative, imperial views of Lady Herschel or Sarah Stickney Ellis when she speaks on behalf of British colonialists, but especially British women, in declaring 'We have made [India] ours, and must do our duty. ... To keep what we have won, and rule it wisely'. Later, Alice even emphasizes the point as a gender-inflected imperative:

> When I first came out here, I dreamt of a life so different! I thought an Englishwoman might teach and guide her native sisters, help to make them worthy of the men our English rule should mould.[20]

As a result, Taylor's drama unabashedly provided yet one more opportunity for British audiences to vilify the ungrateful sepoys (who epitomize Oriental treachery and deceit in their attempt to infiltrate established, polite society) and praise the nation's earnest, everyday heroes: the railway engineer intent upon improving India (symbolized here by bringing new technology – the modern railroad – to the interior of the colony) and the selfless English woman intent on providing guidance, however misguided, to enlighten and Westernize 'her native sisters'.

Above all, Taylor's play made it possible for audiences to sustain and even embolden their feelings of righteous indignation towards India. More recent insurrections, like the Jamaican revolt in 1865 or the 1867 Fenian incursions in Canada, instantly recalled the Uprising in India for British nationalists. These revolts became proxies for anxieties about future colonial rebellions, not only in India but across the empire, while stoking deep-seated hatred against those who spurned Britain's beneficence. In November 1867, for example, Allingham disclosed in his diary that he read Carlyle's tract 'Shooting Niagara', which disparaged the former slaves of Jamaica for their ingratitude towards the empire, and admitted to himself that he was largely persuaded by Carlyle's argument against the black plantation workers who rebelled. Carlyle's essay, and the events in Jamaica and Canada, also became topics of conversation in Freshwater. In November and December 1867, Tennyson let loose his rage against the Fenians, proclaiming 'Kelts are all mad furious fools'.[21] Even by 1872, in a conversation with Matthew Arnold, Allingham affirmed Tennyson's and Carlyle's shared interests in the necessity of 'keeping together the Empire – Canada, Australia, India, etc.'[22]

At the end of Act II of the play, Taylor emphasized the gender and racial animosity held by the British towards indigenous Indians by recirculating the infamous tale of Eliza Wheeler, the daughter of Colonel Hugh Wheeler of the Cawnpore garrison, an episode of war in India that Charles Ball made legendary in his published *History* of 1858.[23] The brave Miss Wheeler, who commits suicide rather than be captured by invading sepoys, was the narrative prototype for Taylor's fictional scene. In *A Sister's Penance*, Alice expresses her fear that Ahmedoolah intends to break into their compound in order to kidnap and possess her as his own. For Alice, an honourable death is preferable to a profane captivity:

> MARK. Hark, the bloodhounds are upon us!
> ALICE. Then do me one more mercy; do not let me fall alive into Ahmedoolah's hands. I should not care for death from you. If they come, promise you will shoot me before you die! (*offers him pistol.*)
> MARK. (*takes pistol and turns away*) I promise.[24]

This scene also recalls the suicidal pact described in Christina Rossetti's poem 'In the Roundhouse at Jhansi', created at the outbreak of the rebellion. But in *A Sister's Penance*, where 'melodrama reduces social and moral complexities to simplistic oppositions between good and evil, victims and villains', the drama's plot emphasizes the racial polarization that grew engrained after the Indian Uprising.[25] In Act II, for example, the racist language is explicit and vile, as the British characters refer repeatedly to Indians as 'niggers', 'black varmints', and 'savages'.[26] And in visual terms, the scene all but reimagines Joseph Noel Paton's painting *In Memoriam*, and the engraving that made this work famous (see fig. 49). The 'terror' inflicted by Ahmedoolah, the stereotyped 'fierce heat' of his sexual pursuit of one of the sisters, and his ultimately seditious act towards the play's two heroines all function dramatically as an analogical substitute for the persistent evil represented by Nana Sahib, a racial and gender-based threat. As Brantlinger reminds us, 'his evil visage peers out of countless texts, the miragelike product of the projective mechanisms by which Victorians displaced their repressed sexual desire and guilt for imperial domination'.[27] Consequently, Taylor's script embedded British fears of miscegenation in Alice's repulsion to Ahmedoolah's romantic intentions, as the drama sets up his inclusion in British society as a threat to its idealized conception of racial purity.

Ironically, Ahmedoolah's storyline also *inverts* the infamous legend of Eliza Wheeler. Kidnapped early in the conflict, she was supposed to have lain in wait until nightfall before abruptly shedding her Victorian feminine inhibitions, rising up to kill her captors in cold blood.[28] In the British retelling, Miss Wheeler's brand of moral heroism stands in opposition to Ahmedoolah's anti-heroic treachery, although both die by their own hand. But in both cases, the vigour motivating their actions is embedded and unknown, disguised and contained. Therefore, its sudden reappearance is even more unexpected and startling. Freud called this phenomenon 'the return of the repressed', a condition in which past traumas that have been forgotten and buried deep in the unconscious reappear suddenly to disrupt the present day. In the guise of Habib, Ahmedoolah resurfaces suddenly as a revenant, seeking to unburden himself from the unresolved ordeal of the insurrection, from British hostility towards his race, and from having been dispossessed of his sovereign royal line.[29] But because such painful memories can be suppressed for only so long, they spring forth in dramatic form when the restraints that have held them in abeyance are relaxed or removed.[30] Although Eliza Wheeler's harrowing tale was written into the many heroic narratives of British resistance to Indian treachery, the rhetoric of empire made stock characters of representations of indigenous Indians who survived the war, even fictional characters like Ahmedoolah.

Taylor's play also demonstrates Christopher Herbert's thesis that the Indian Uprising inflicted upon British society 'the shock of what seemed to be a catastrophic wound to the moral order itself'.[31] In this context, Ahmedoolah is an evident bogeyman, but also a thin disguise for Nana Sahib, who at first evaded capture after the Cawnpore massacre, or even Azimullah, who pleaded his case in London. As a character in Taylor's play, the role made an impression on Allingham and must have resonated with others on the Isle of Wight, yet critical reception in the British press emphasized that Ahmedoolah was not only regarded as 'the Other', but *in his disguise* was perceived a vicious hybrid, because the apparently loyal Indian agent of Act I turns into a venomous brute and revolutionary in Act II. By Act III, the concealed dual character of Ahmedoolah/Habib lies in wait as a clandestine and mysterious subterranean presence. Cloaked as a docile servant, he is invisible to the oblivious British family. Taylor's camouflaged Indian revolutionary therefore represents Britain's psychological tether to the betrayal, deceit, and trauma of the initial sepoy insurrection, as the threat of sedition and revolt remained ever-present but unseen to Taylor and his contemporaries. As a result, Ahmedoolah/Habib is a repressed memory figure, a survivor of the conflict but also one who returned menacingly to threaten the lives of his oppressors. Even in 1866, after almost a decade had passed since the Indian Uprising, it is apparent that the war in India was still alive to 'men who have known the real horrors of Cawnpore', because the violence had not been fully expiated. Through repeated allusions to the death of British women and children at Cawnpore, the 'wound to the moral order' was kept alive, years after the event occurred. Trauma associated with Cawnpore – the site of Eliza Wheeler's heroics, and her tragic end – could become renewed once more as fresh reminders that Britain's moral order had once been upset, but that its guard would not easily be lowered again.

Steps towards atonement, however, were taken by the women who survived the conflict, like the fictional Alice of *A Sister's Penance*, who undertakes her Indian sojourn thinking she could fulfil her duty to the empire by edifying her 'native sisters'. It was also epitomized after the war by those who donned mourning attire to signify their personal grief and represent their loss as a public injury. The social performance of grieving allowed these women to claim a collective role with others who had endured extreme loss for the nation.[32] Mourning attire allowed war widows to emphasize their role in shaping a domestic sphere that reinforced British national identity and its conception of idealized morality, as Sarah Stickney Ellis might have declared, or in Lady Herschel's assessment, as a moral example for the native populations in Britain's colonies. This image was multiplied repeatedly in different forms, as we have seen. In sympathy with these views, Julia Margaret Cameron made mourning attire a centrepiece to *Farewell*, her photograph of a woman before a well. Cameron might also have been marking the ten-year anniversary of the Indian Uprising, when the event would be remembered once again as a symbol of national sacrifice, and an emblem of honour and duty.[33]

In 1867, Julia Margaret modified this image significantly, first by reinterpreting its central iconography and secondly by altering its material presentation as a composite image on the page. At the same time, she changed the photograph's title in relation to its new incarnation, which she destined for the last page of the Herschel Album. What she had called *Farewell* in 1864, she retitled, as her new composition in 1867, *At the Well, A Farewell*. By examining this transformation, I propose that Cameron created her new composite image as a gendered reimagining of the narrative of the Cawnpore massacres. Three dimensions describe this symbolic and physical makeover. The first element centres on Cameron's allegorical image of a woman in mourning attire in front of a water well and offers a nuanced interpretation of *A Sister's Penance* that builds upon the key principle of atonement in Taylor's drama. The second examines Cameron's material and experimental approach to photography and its formal presentation as two-dimensional design, centring on the ways she experimented with her printed photographs in material terms. The third element investigates Cameron's interest in exploring new iconographic sources for the revised composition, especially in relation to her interest in symbols drawn from Italian Renaissance humanism, Christian funerary sculpture, and gendered performances of mourning.

ATONEMENT

Atonement is central to *A Sister's Penance*, as Marion, the wronged sister, forgives her sibling Alice for her transgressions. But the play might equally be called *A Sisters' Penance*, which is to say, by moving the possessive from the singular to the plural, the drama aptly represents the collective atonement of the sisters – and as expressed by the British nation – for the multiple offences it committed against India. In Taylor's play, penance is paid for one sister's misbehaviour and indiscretions, and Alice's expiation to both Markham and Marion rights her frayed relationship within the family. But the play also lays bare the ongoing abuse of Britain's colonial oppression in India, especially as it is represented in the play by economic exploitation, racial acrimony, and the dispossession of royal titles and territories from the indigenous population. Also exposed in *A Sister's Penance* is Britain's colonial duplicity in relation to the question of Indian sovereignty. Because the play denies Ahmedoolah's subjecthood as a 'British subject', he is portrayed as a homeless man in exile, locked into an 'in-between' status, much like the real-life experience of Iqbal al-Daula, the 'ex-King of Oude'. At the beginning of *A Sister's Penance*, Taylor presents Ahmedoolah's double identity to the audience. He is identified as a commercial *vakir* (or legal agent) who navigates between Indian and British society and therefore occupies an established and 'natural' intermediary role, because mercantilism governs their commercial interactions. But by the end of the play, the double identity of Ahmedoolah/Habib is presented as *unnatural*, a contortion of his identity as a man, as a son of royal lineage, and as a proud Indian. When he rejects that status in his bid to wed Alice in Act I, Ahmedoolah forsakes his Rajah but still imagines that Alice can enter his world as 'queen', deluded in this belief just as he is in thinking that she would even wish to do so. Taylor demonstrates that Ahmedoolah is mistaken on both accounts. By Act III, under the cover of disguise, Ahmedoolah/Habib denies his high caste for the low caste status of a lascar, debasing himself once more, while making any possible union with Alice even more unlikely. And yet, throughout the play, Ahmedoolah must disavow his sexual desire to possess Alice in the face of his hatred of the British occupation. One might say his character occupies two identities at once, neither of which can be reconciled.[34]

Ultimately, Ahmedoolah finds his split identity untenable, resulting in his self-inflicted death. But by means of this figurative act of doubling, Ahmedoolah also enables the play's characters to face themselves, to consider what it might mean to invert their roles as colonizer and colonized, to imagine ties that bind the white-skinned Briton to the dark-skinned Indian, and in the end, to express a shared penance for the British presence in India. This is not Spurgeon's idea of 'national humiliation' for Britain's part in the Indian war, which was really only a renewed call for vengeance. Rather, in Taylor's play, doubling exposes the bind that joins the two worlds, and as a result, shines light on the relationship that both unites and separates the imperial centre from the colonial periphery. It also exposes what Jacques Derrida called an 'originary wrong': it is the 'birth wound' of imperialism that afflicts Ahmedoolah, 'a bottomless wound, an irreparable tragedy'; tormented in this way, Ahmedoolah can only 'become an inheritor, redresser of wrongs, that is, only by castigating, punishing, killing'.[35]

Penance, atonement, and compassion stand in opposition to the vengeful actions that prolonged the initial rebellion into protracted and bloody war and that animated the ongoing resentments that explained, in part, the public appeal of *A Sister's Penance*. The antidote to cruelty, violence, and the inhumanity of war depends upon compassion, a sentiment expressed in mourning and that lies as the foundation of atonement. But on the Isle of Wight, these emotions either lay dormant or went unanswered, as Allingham recorded numerous instances in his diary where he expressed overtly racist attitudes that were magnified by the 1857 Uprising. As early as 1864, for example, watching survivors of the war in India disembark from a P&O steamship in Southampton, Allingham expressed undisguised contempt for the appearance of a native Indian woman, writing, 'A single one of these brown slender women with black eyes and undulatory movements (they must have soft bones), in muslin and gold ornaments, makes all Hindustan real'.[36] Allingham's patriarchal admiration for Oriental exoticism, however, was tempered by his evident miscegenation anxieties. He expressed those fears in August 1868 in the presence of the African child-Prince Alamayou, who was visiting the Isle of Wight following the British war in Abyssinia, a war that orphaned the boy and exiled him from the land of his birth. Allingham taunted Thackeray's daughters, Annie and Minnie, by suggesting that their young fair and blonde cousin Margery (Margie) Thackeray (whom Julia Margaret portrayed in fig. 39), should wed the dark-skinned African boy.[37] And on 15 October 1868, Allingham recorded making another visit to the Thackeray sisters at Cameron's home, where the assembled company was joined by two British émigrés from the recent war in India, a Captain Irving and his daughter or sister, a Miss Emma Irving. Once assembled, the group went to dine with Mrs Cameron, and after dinner, Allingham relayed what he recalled 'a true ghost story' of a man's decapitated head, apparently taken by a British soldier as an Indian war trophy. In Allingham's telling, the head fell out of a medical student's bag and rolled down the street, only to stop at the door of slave-dealer, who nearly fainted when he opened his door.[38] Allingham peppered this repugnant story with racial epithets of the same kind Taylor used in his play. And although Allingham's story could certainly have been told as an unbelievable 'tall tale' from the war, such accounts demonstrate the Isle of Wight group's lingering animosity and unconcealed racism towards indigenous Indians who participated in the rebellion. Consequently, Allingham comes off as less a playful and worldly cosmopolitan and more a malicious agitator.

Mourning and atonement, by contrast, are the prevailing sentiments in Cameron's allegorical image of the young woman at the well that she called *Farewell*. When the image was rededicated in 1867 under a new title, *At the Well, A Farewell*, Cameron made its allusions to the Cawnpore well even more explicit. Because this title asks viewers to resolve a formal relationship between the standing figure in white mourning attire and the water well situated behind her, Cameron calls viewers' attention to the iconography of the woman in relation to the metonymy of 'the Well'. Complicating that relationship, Cameron added two photographic fragments in 1867 – one above and one below the image containing the central figure at the well. Since Herschel's day, the critical literature about this photograph has been virtually silent, even though the cultural ideas, symbolic forms, and narrative elements embedded in the imagery were connected to numerous instances of popular and high art that crossed the boundaries of literature and the visual arts for years after the rebellion had taken place. Given the shared discursive spaces they occupied and the interconnected narrative representations of this imagery, I turn next to investigate how Cameron pursued experimental practices with the material nature of photography to widen the interpretive possibilities for this composite image.

MATERIAL CULTURE

From her earliest days as a photographer, Julia Margaret Cameron had to determine how she wanted her photographs to be received and viewed formally, which is to say, she needed to

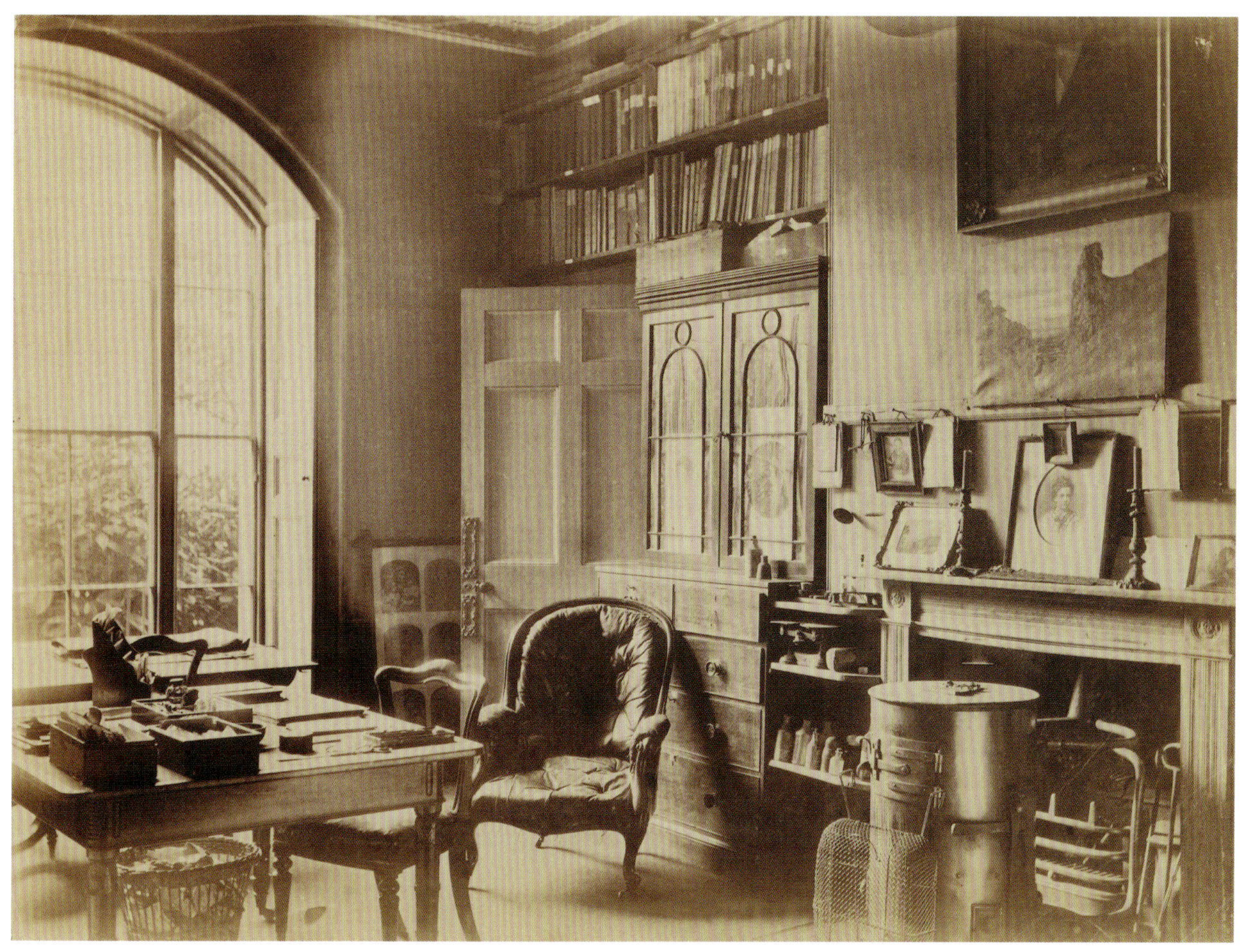

81 Unknown photographer, *Grandpapa's study, laboratory through the door (the house of Sir John Herschel)*, *c.*1860, albumen print, 15.2 × 20 cm. NPG x44700.

determine whether her prints were made for public exhibition or for private viewing. For years she had constructed albums, as we have seen, and experimented with their format and size. But in 1864, she began to think systematically about different kinds of complex subject matter and how those images related to each other – or how they could be assembled in novel ways – to create a compelling integrated ensemble, what she called a *series* of related works. For example, when she sent a large, framed group of nine photographs on 31 December 1864 to her friends Sir John and Lady Margaret Herschel, she explained the *series* was intended to be displayed as arranged in its accompanying frame. She titled this group of photographs *The Fruits of the Spirit*, wrote about the series as a coherent 'theological work of some interest', and explained that the collective title corresponded explicitly to the New Testament Epistle of Paul to the Galatians (5:22–3).[39] For his part, Herschel understood that this photographic series – as Cameron presented it to him – was to be retained in its large frame and regarded as an integral work of art. In a contemporaneous view of Herschel's study, for example, we can see that the scientist propped Cameron's frame against a back wall. There it remained intact, as a single unit, when someone photographed this interior space (fig. 81). On 12 January 1865, she sent the same *Fruits of the Spirit* photographic series to the British Museum, apparently framed in the identical manner. Unbeknown to the photographer, the Museum later disassembled the large frame she provided in order to conserve the nine photographs separately.[40]

In other photographs of this same period, however, Cameron experimented freely with dramatically different framing devices and formal presentation techniques to explore distinctive means of creating and displaying her subject matter. Typically, we think that photographic experimentation chiefly takes place as a function of purely photographic techniques. One common approach is 'through the lens', which is to say that the experimental process originates in the camera or in the darkroom. The approach centres on the making of a unique negative from which countless positive prints can be produced. Another, related process of experimentation can occur in the process of making positive prints. In this approach, a photographer experiments with light transmitted through the negative, or with the use of photographic chemistry to create special effects that modify the look of each positive print.[41] But these two optical and chemical processing-based means are not the only methods by which a photographer can experiment with the outcome of her final prints. Importantly, Cameron pursued a third way of experimentation that manipulated the arrangement of finished prints. In short, she altered the physical properties of otherwise 'completed' final prints by treating these works as if they were 'raw material' for her experimental practice. Critically, this experimentation took shape directly on a cutting-room board in her studio or, more likely, while working in broad daylight in her home with a stack of prints atop her dining-room table.

This kind of photographic experimentation is physical and material rather than immaterial and ephemeral. It is aligned more closely to the creation of photocollages and scrapbooks in which images from *cartes-de-visite* and other photographic formats were snipped and pasted into fanciful albums.[42] This was a site where the so-called 'truthfulness' of a realistic image was not exalted as the only measure of success for a photograph and where the finished print was not always destined for an elaborate frame. By contrast, Cameron's material practice of cutting

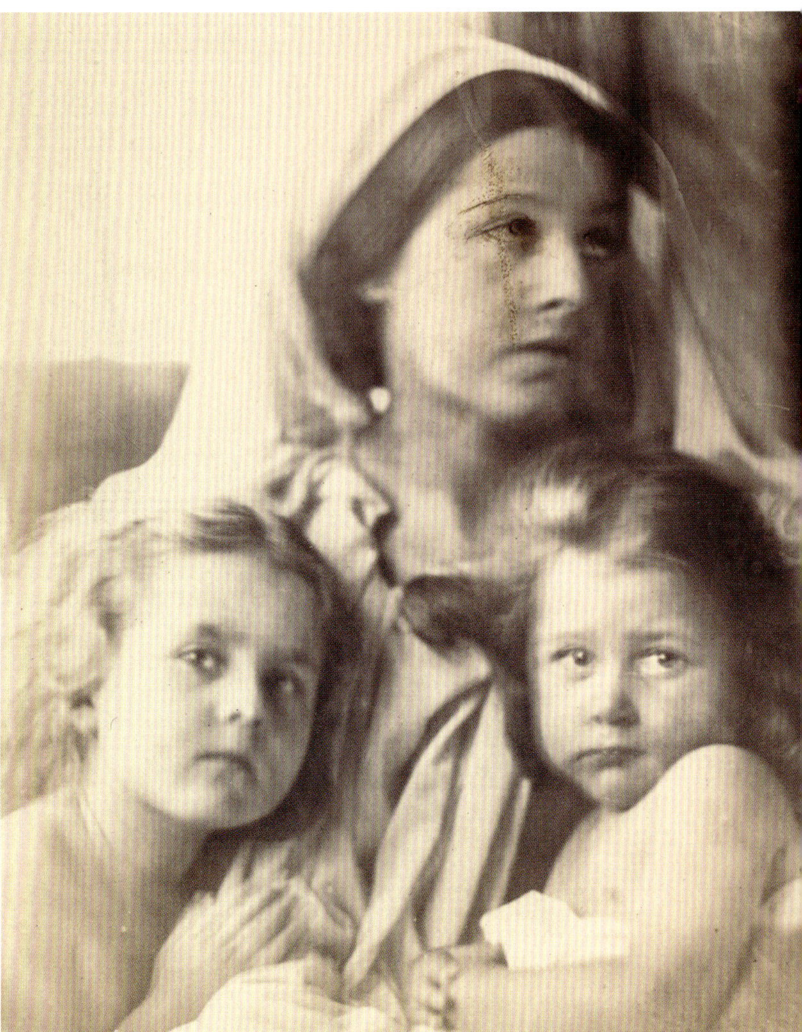

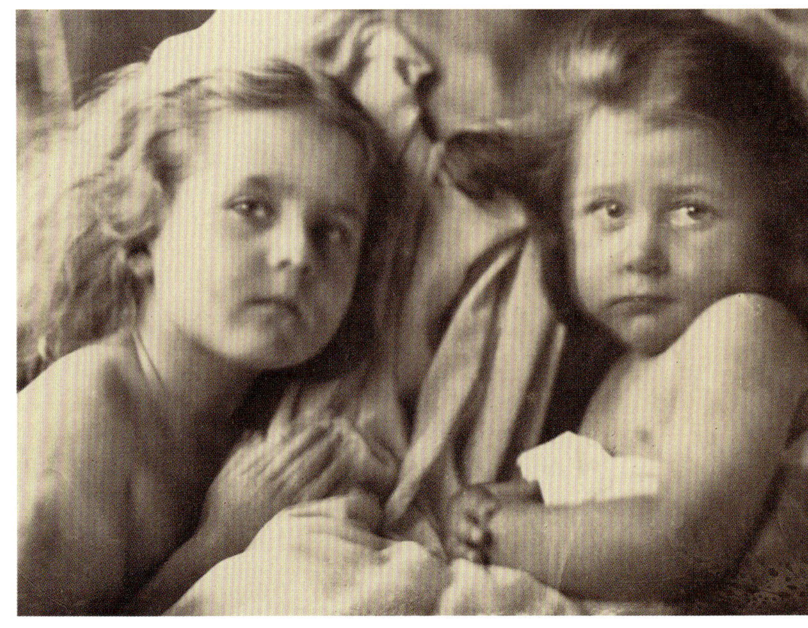

82 Julia Margaret Cameron, *Madonna with Two Children*, 1864, albumen print, 23.7 × 19.8 cm.

83 Julia Margaret Cameron, *The bereaved Babes*, 1864, albumen print, 14.3 × 19.6 cm.

J. Paul Getty Museum, 84.XZ.186.86. Digital image courtesy of Getty's Open Content Program.

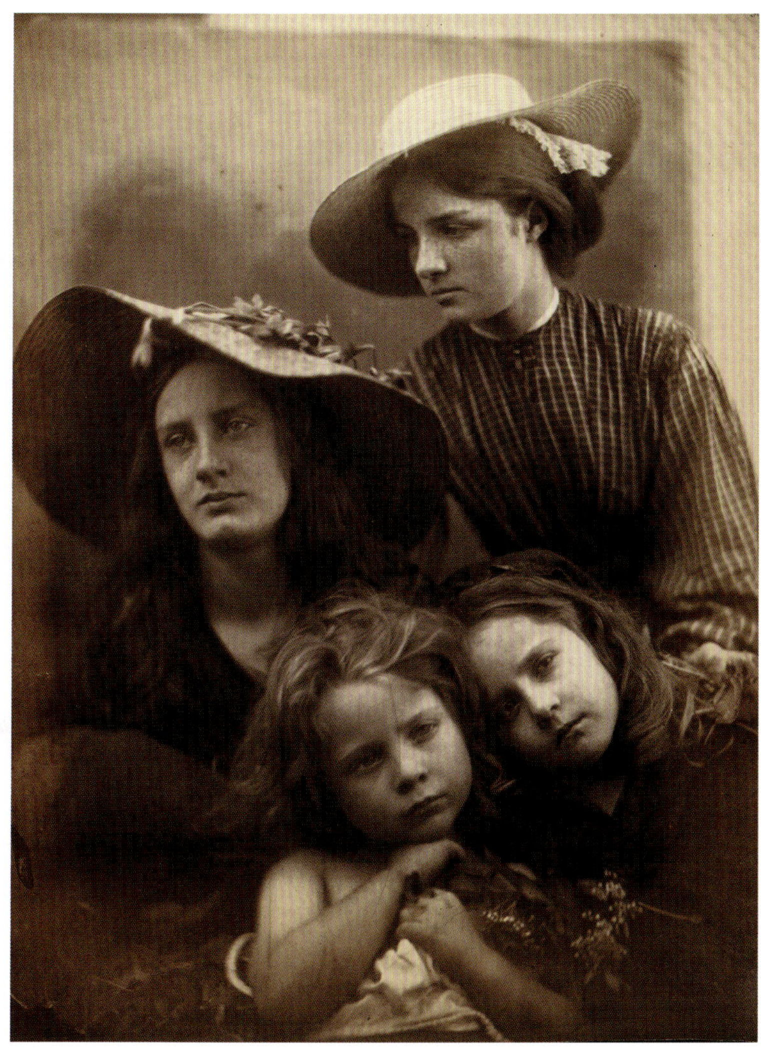

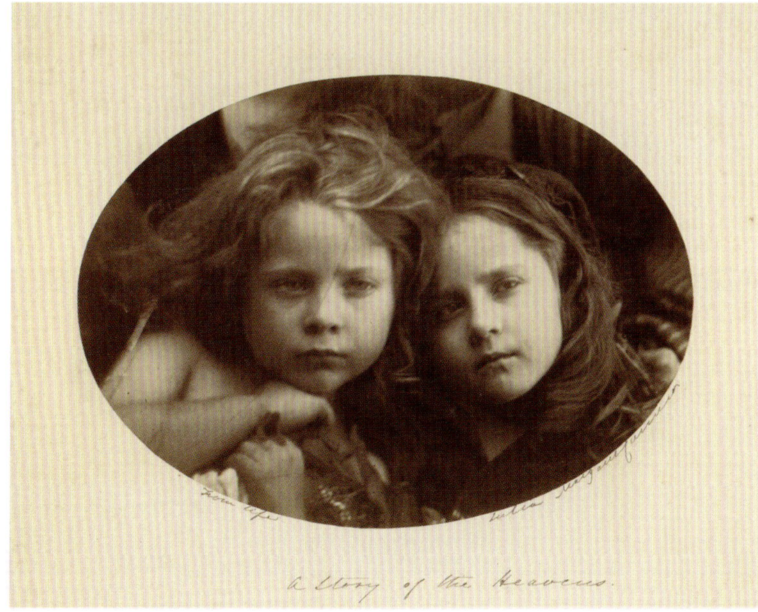

up images and reconceiving their use measured success by reimagining the value of photographic fragments and experimenting with their potential new relationship to one another. Conceived now as material culture to be manipulated and arranged as the artist saw fit, Cameron began to regard photographs as cultural artefacts rather than immutable works of art.

Cameron often explored new subjects when deciding how to manipulate her imagery in this way. Often this meant reconceptualizing larger compositions, and she did not hesitate to crop her photographs severely by cutting them down into smaller pictures, often isolating one or two figures and discarding the rest. In 1864, for example, Cameron truncated a photographic print of the *Madonna with Two Children* (Cox/Ford 72; fig. 82) by *editing out* the Madonna. In the new version, she isolated the two children and made *them* the principal subject of her new photograph. She then titled the new image *The bereaved Babes* (Cox/Ford 869; fig. 83), effectively signifying that the children in the image now represented allegorical characters made famous in Charles Kingsley's fable *The Water Babies*. This example demonstrates that Cameron consciously reimagined the iconography of her 'original' exposure. By excising the female model, she turned the two children who portrayed Christ and St John in the *Madonna* photograph into two of the diminutive water-fairies that populate Kingsley's story. Cameron used the albums she constructed to mix and match up fragmented works like these. In the Overstone Album, for example, she included *The bereaved Babes* to accompany three other photographs that she also titled as *Water Babies*.[43] She also refashioned another one of those prints from a different, larger composition.

Cameron repeated this kind of iconographic and material reimagining once again in 1866 when she

84 Julia Margaret Cameron, *Summer Days*, 1866, albumen print, 35.2 × 27.2 cm.

Henry Taylor Album, Arch. K b.12, fol. 38r. Bodleian Libraries, University of Oxford. Creative Commons License CC-BY-NC 4.0.

85 Julia Margaret Cameron, *A Story of the Heavens*, 1866, albumen print, 13.8 × 18.5 cm.

J. Paul Getty Museum, 84.XM.443.13. Digital image courtesy of Getty's Open Content Program.

cut down another photograph that portrayed two women and two children in a group composition that she originally called *Summer Days* (Cox/Ford 1096; fig. 84). When Cameron isolated the children as a separate image and discarded the portion of the photograph representing the two women, she called the new photograph *A Story of the Heavens* (Cox/Ford 870; fig. 85). Evidence of this practice upends today's modernist bias that prefers a rendering of the entire negative over disassembled pieces. We are not accustomed to thinking of Cameron disposing of the rest of this image, which depicted Mary Ryan and May Prinsep in floppy summer hats. But Cameron even used this apparently 'discarded' portion as new source material for making other experiments. In the Mia Album, for example, Cameron pasted a close-up detail from *Summer Days* that portrayed Mary Ryan apart from the original group, measuring only 12.9 cm in diameter (fig. 86). In this way, a circular detail of this 'remainder portion' became its own isolated fragment. She repeated the process for the same image in a nearly square frame, measuring 13.0 × 13.2 cm (fig. 87). This alteration in form suggests that she was interested in examining ways that different framing formats could affect the meaning of the same image. As another example, in one version of *A Story of the Heavens* she framed the image of the two children in an oval shape, and in another version of the same subject she cleverly twisted the negative image in its frame. The resulting image possesses a new kind of dynamism that has been rendered somewhat mysterious, as she simultaneously darkened the space surrounding the children in this print (Cox/Ford 871). Cameron's awareness of these formal differences in the visual appearance of the final print suggests that she returned to the darkroom to execute an idea that emerged after first cutting down a larger image. As a result, the children portrayed in *A Story of the Heavens* more closely resemble other photographs of angels, like the photograph she called *Cherub and Seraph* (Cox/Ford 872; HA-41; see fig. 58), which she composed during the same year using the same two child models.

These examples of Cameron's interest in experimenting with her imagery demonstrate that although she might have used *May Day* and *The Turtle Doves* (see fig. 59) as fragments from which

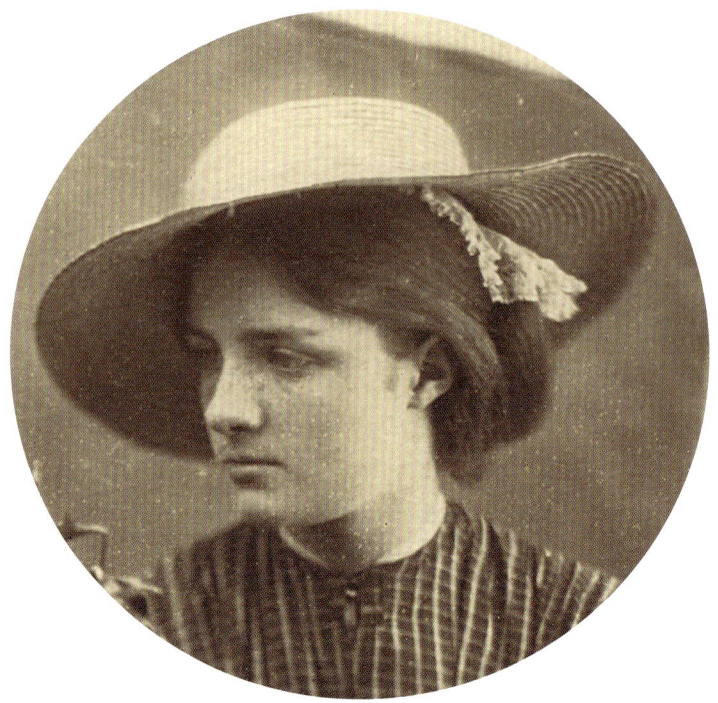

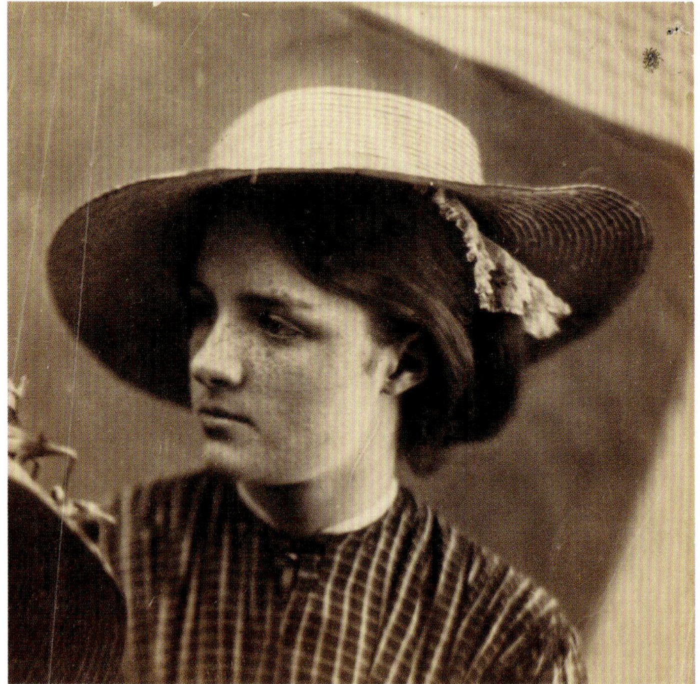

86 Julia Margaret Cameron, circular detail from *Summer Days*, 1866, albumen print, (Mia Album, 41), 12.9 cm diameter.

Collection of Michael Mattis and Judy Hochberg, New York.

87 Julia Margaret Cameron, nearly square detail from *Summer Days*, 1866, albumen print, 13.0 × 13.2 cm.

Courtesy Dominic Winter Auctioneers, Lot 13, 19 May 2021.

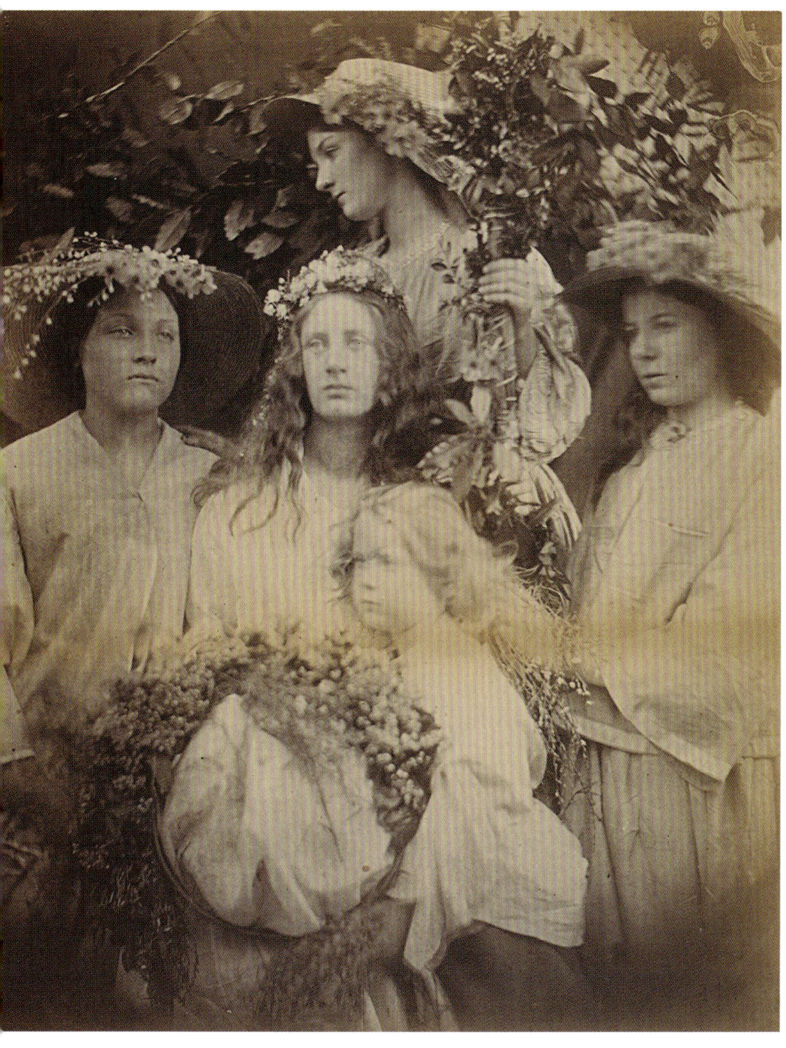

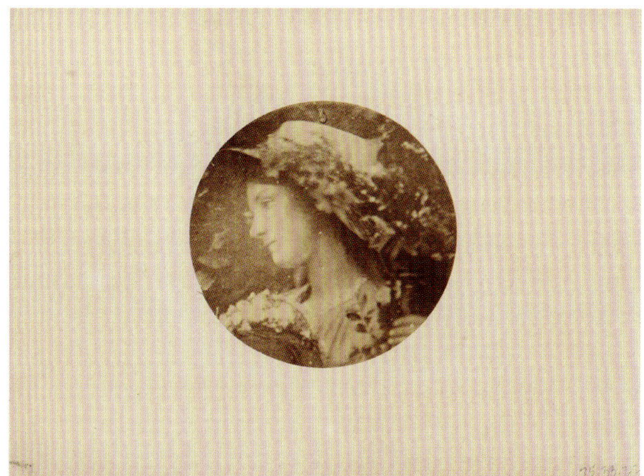

88 Julia Margaret Cameron, *May Day*, 1866, albumen print, 35.2 × 28.9 cm.

© Royal Photographic Society / Victoria and Albert Museum, London. RPS.896–2017.

89 Julia Margaret Cameron, circular detail from *May Day*, albumen print, approx. 9.5 cm diameter.

Eskenazi Museum of Art, Indiana University, 75.38.22 Photo Credit: Eskenazi Museum of Art/Shanti Knight.

she then created *At the Well, A Farewell*, there is no reason to assume she would have retained those titles to identify the same images when she created the new composition. In the Table of Contents to the Herschel Album, each of these 'source' images are not identified separately. Rather, the singular title for the album page suggests that Cameron wanted the viewer to consider the ensemble as an integral work. Indeed, were they to be exhibited or used as separate photographs, like *The bereaved Babes* or *A Story of the Heavens*, Cameron would have assigned these fragments with distinctive titles as well. From her earliest photographs of narrative subjects, then, Cameron's process-based experimentation, which led her to cut down prints in search of creating other subject matter, was aligned with her regular practice of assigning narrative titles to give her photographs a clear identity and allegorical reference. This kind of process-based work was not executed in opposition to the practice of producing traditional finished works like the *Fruits of the Spirit*. Rather, she produced both forms simultaneously, working from a wholly different conception from what we might mean now by photographic originality.

Additional examples reinforce this point. In the same manner as when she cut apart *Summer Days*, she also created a fragment of the larger composition she called *May Day* (fig. 88) by cutting out a circular detail of the topmost figure that portrays Mary Ryan in a hat strewn with flowers. By isolating this figure and discarding the rest, Cameron once again reimagined how different sizes and shapes of the smaller detail, as well as with its placement on the page, could affect the meaning of the image. For example, in an album now at the Eskenazi Museum of Art, she shaped the small headshot of Mary Ryan in a circular format and placed it in the middle of the page (fig. 89). But in another version of the same image, now in the Henry Taylor Album at the Bodleian Library, she shaped the fragment as an oval.[44] At some point, this album page also acquired a portrait of James Spedding, presumably a later addition that was affixed, somewhat clumsily, by either Cameron or

Taylor (fig. 90). Also present in Taylor's album is a cut-out oval detail of *The Turtle Doves*, which is paired on the page, in a more balanced way than in the earlier example, to accompany a circular-shaped detail that once again depicts a headshot of Mary Ryan, but this time taken from the print known as *Summer Days*, rather than *May Day* (fig. 91). While experimenting with these material forms, Cameron left no notes explaining her process or her reasons for creating such different sizes, shapes, arrangements and compositions. As remnants of her wide-ranging experimental practice, these examples suggest a fluid approach to the medium and evince a disinclination to think that any negative was so precious that its prints could not be altered or that a final print must be presented to a viewer in any one way.

Cameron's material experimentation with photography – its size and shape in relation to its iconography – provides a foundation for analysing the composition she called *At the Well, A Farewell*, in the Herschel Album (see fig. 7). As discussed earlier, she reclaimed the album from Herschel in 1867 with the intention to refresh the volume with new imagery. Yet the ensemble of three photographs on the last page of the album remains enigmatic today. Several possible reasons account for this inscrutability. For one, the photograph's formal presentation in the album was wholly unlike her frame containing *The Fruits of the Spirit* series, which presented the series together, in sequence, in a constructed frame. By contrast, uncertainty surrounds the composition, framing, and presentation of *At the Well, A Farewell* in the 1867 Herschel Album. This composition appears incomplete, unlike the comparatively refined presentation of Madonnas in the *Fruits of the Spirit* frame, which scholars

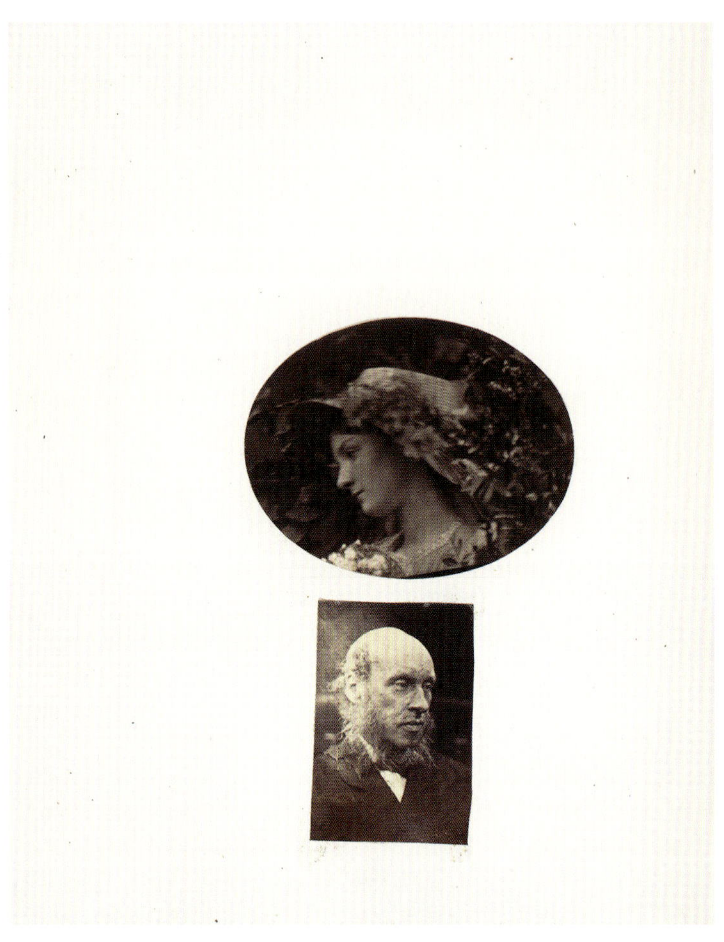

90 Julia Margaret Cameron, untitled detail from *May Day*, and untitled portrait of James Spedding, albumen prints.

Henry Taylor Album, Arch. K b.12, fol. 44v. Bodleian Libraries, University of Oxford.

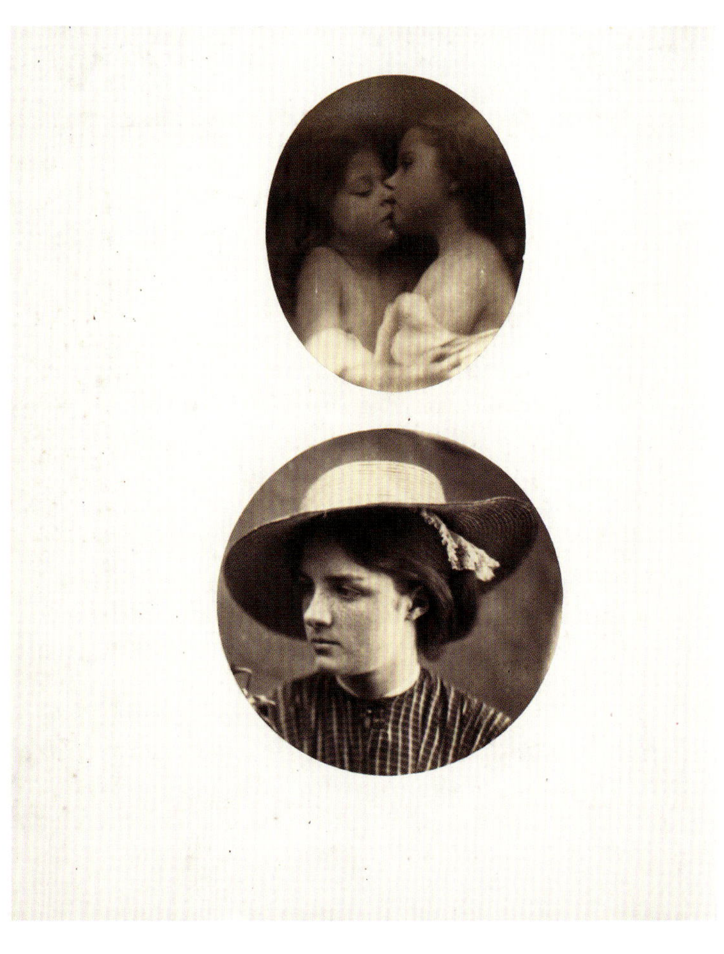

91 Julia Margaret Cameron, cropped version of *Turtle Doves* and circular detail from *Summer Days*, albumen prints.

Henry Taylor Album, Arch. K b.12, fol. 68v. Bodleian Libraries, University of Oxford.

have assumed reflected Cameron's preferred approach to presenting her work. But we might be misguided in this assumption: when she cut down final prints and assigned those fragments different iconographic subjects and titles, or experimented with different formats and sizes, she was exploring the different physical forms and meanings her prints could take. This practice suggests she wanted to visualize different types of presentation or composition that might affect the interpretation of a subject, perhaps because of dissatisfaction with earlier efforts or to explore different formal options and see if new arrangements were able to impart different allegorical meanings. *At the Well, A Farewell* is also unique to the Herschel Album. Cameron did not discuss the subject in her letters, and because she did not display the photograph in public exhibitions alongside other works, this image has evaded critical reception. It also seems that her contemporaries – even Herschel – did not comment on the image.

In 1867, when Cameron reconceived her photograph for Herschel, she retained the placement of *Farewell* in the centre of the page and then added two photographic fragments to create a new composition. She cut these two fragments into oval shapes and affixed them vertically, with one image above and the other below the central figure of the woman at the well. Critically, she did not place them to the left or to the right of the central image, so that all three would appear in a horizontal line, nor did she sort the fragments randomly across the page, as if it were a stitching sampler or scrapbook of arbitrary subjects. She then retitled the album page on which the three photographic fragments appeared and inscribed the new title in the volume's Table of Contents. The earlier inscription, *Farewell*, still appeared at the base of the last page from its 1864 version. Because titles provide essential clues to help viewers comprehend the meaning of an allegorical image, the 1867 title asks viewers to discern the relationship of the woman to the well, leading us to draw the reasonable conclusion that the well is central to the image and its meaning. The larger question, then, is how that central image relates to the other two portions of the composition. For insight into the relationship of the parts to the whole in this composition, I turn now to examine the iconography of the fragments.

ICONOGRAPHY

Today, our familiarity with Cameron's large archive enables us to recognize the image on top as a fragment of the large group portrait that she called *May Day* (1866; Cox/Ford 1098; see fig. 88). We also recognize the section on the bottom from a different photograph, sometimes called *The Turtle Doves* (1864; Cox/Ford 859; see fig. 59 and fig. 91 (top)). In 1867, Herschel likely did not have access to this knowledge unless Cameron provided it to him separately. And although he surely recognized the central image, *Farewell*, from the earlier album, he could not have been aware of the other two photographs that she cut into ovals from more recent photographs in her growing *oeuvre*. Neither *May Day* nor *The Turtle Doves* appears independently in the new album, and importantly they are not listed separately in Cameron's Table of Contents. No other context is provided for interpreting the relationship between the two fragments and the central image. In short, because Cameron did not provide unique titles for the top and bottom images, she left their relationship to the central image ambiguous.

The unique formal arrangement of *At the Well, A Farewell* also invites viewers to consider how the three photographs cohere as a composite image *and* why Cameron might have chosen to unify her ensemble under this new title. How might we make sense of the iconographic ambiguity described above, and what clues suggest she imagined the three images could combine to convey a persuasive allegorical narrative? To be comprehensible, such a complex work must contain an evident relationship between its allegorical title and its visual iconography, ideally one that is aligned to its overall formal structure. And why in 1867? The timing of Cameron's new imagery corresponds exactly with Tom Taylor's play *A Sister's Penance*, a commercial success in the theatre and known to the Freshwater circle from Taylor's multiple visits along with the Terry sisters. Importantly, narratives of the 1857 Uprising in India had not passed quietly into history. Rather, the popularity of Taylor's play made stories of the insurrection new again by reviving cultural memories along with earlier narratives of the war and its aftermath. Additional clues emerge from Cameron's connection to Sir Henry Cole, who directed the South Kensington Museum, and to the Arundel Society, as both institutions promoted the funereal iconography of Italian Renaissance art.

By this time, Cameron had presented photographs to Cole, seeking his approval and encouragement. Writing on 20 May 1865 from Little Holland House, she alerted him to expect a portfolio of photographs sent from her dealer, Colnaghi: 'I should be so proud and pleased if this complete series could go into the South Kensington Museum', she wrote. In a postscript, she sweetened her appeal with a social invitation: 'Mrs. Prinsep says she joins me in the hope that you and Mrs Cole and your daughters will come to our shady garden here tomorrow afternoon. Yes?'[45] Cole ended up buying eighty photographs from Cameron for the Museum, sending one set to the Art Library and another to the Circulation Department. In gratitude, on 27 September 1865, Cameron sent Cole thirty-four additional prints. Mark Haworth-Booth noted that Cole chose four of these photographs specifically for Godfrey Sykes, the Museum's chief designer. He theorized that Cameron knew of Sykes's designs to decorate new rooms in the Museum as well as his preference for ornamental figures of women and children in the style of the Italian Renaissance. In other words, Cameron sought approval from Sykes because she believed her photographs were essentially 'in a similar style, reminiscent of the sculptures of Desiderio da Settignano and other masters'.[46]

A contemporary interior view of the Museum undergoing architectural renovations features Sykes's courtyard designs (fig. 92). As captured in the photograph, Sykes's terracotta columns display segments of figurative sculptures fashioned together with alternating sections of simple plain and abstracted designs. Although Cole had a hand in introducing Sykes and Cameron, we simply do not know the extent of their discussions about art, architecture, two-dimensional design, and formal composition, although it is enticing to contemplate the possibility that the two shared thoughts about Sykes's designs for the Museum. As a result, this image could provide a possible design template for Cameron, one that illustrates how an architectural model could function artistically as a framework for two-dimensional design, one that Cameron could adopt in photography. The approach was not unique to Sykes. Other prominent models in which British architects used decorative or structural fragments to create coherent design pieces existed elsewhere in London, as in the 'pasticcio' column designed by Sir John Soane and displayed in his house museum, for example.[47]

When she created the three-part composition that forms *At the Well, A Farewell*, it is likely that Cameron drew upon the history of Italian Renaissance art to create the unexpected visual relationship between the three elements in her photographic composition. Cole, Sykes, and Cameron shared a common interest in the popular revival of Italian Renaissance art. In addition to Sykes's designs, Cole was interested in collecting funerary sculpture, particularly the church-based wall tombs called *avelli*. This term was used to describe memorials placed against the interior walls of a church apse or nave. Since the Renaissance, this design was characterized by a vertical, tripartite structure and borrowed architectural elements like columns and arches to help define space while suggesting an impressive vertical presence. This sculptural form also emphasized symbols associated with the human condition, notably, the separation of the body from the soul after death, divine acceptance of human frailty, and the pain inflicted by loss, grief, or separation. Drawing upon these iconographic roots, the Italian Renaissance wall tomb was much in vogue in Cameron's circle, especially as its design features were popularized after 1860 by the Arundel Society and the South Kensington Museum.

Renaissance funerary sculpture was promoted in South Kensington chiefly for its association with high art, that is, the Museum considered this art form a positive example for the applied arts and manufacturing of the present day. Secondly, the Museum used the older art form to demonstrate how iconography was used to depict human loss and commemorate the lives of national heroes. Initially reserved for popes and royalty, church-based wall tombs acquired broad acceptance over time when they were applied more widely for nobles, military officers, and important cultural figures. As a result, by the mid-nineteenth century, the style became commonplace throughout Europe.[48] In addition to recognizing the function of the vertical three-part structure, viewers were expected to be familiar, through the common and shared language of funerary iconography, with the interplay of allegorical figures like angels and

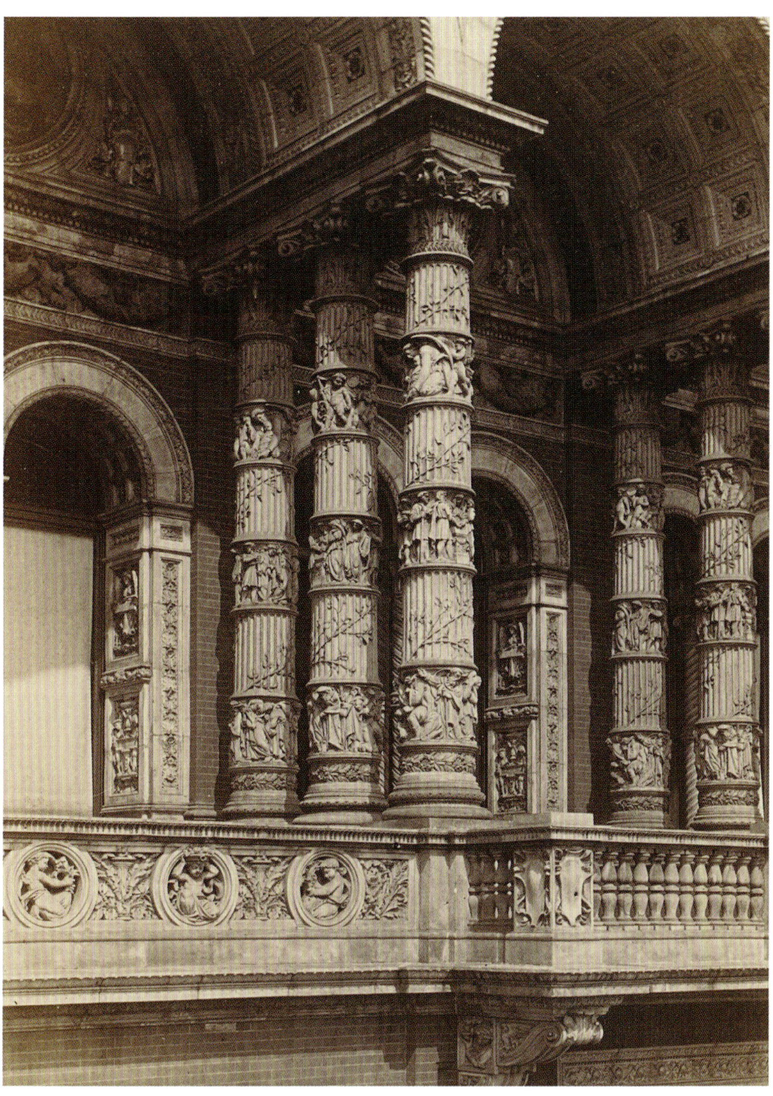

92 Unknown photographer, *South Kensington Museum, Terracotta Decoration and Columns of the Lecture Theatre Facade, Designed by Godfrey Sykes and Made by Blanchard & Co., c.1865*, albumen photograph, *c.*1875, 21.6 × 15.4 cm.
© Victoria and Albert Museum, London. 76531.

putti in communicating meanings traditionally associated with these classical symbols. A kind of visual template gained currency. The top-most register, for example, contained angels who were present to welcome the soul of the deceased person into heaven. Other symbols could also be present, such as emblems representing victory, divine rule, or eternal life, for example. In the centre register, the departed was often represented in human terms, sometimes in effigy, sometimes as if entombed or resting in peace. In this register, the deceased might also be surrounded by grieving family members, sorrowful angels, or others who knew the individual on earth and lament their loss. Finally, on the bottom register, secondary angels or putti might surround an effigy of the dead or may be present to call mourners' attention to an inscribed testimonial that celebrates the earthly accomplishments of the deceased. If present, these heavenly figures express sadness and grief or symbolize the closure of the decedent's worldly concerns as they help convey his soul to heaven. Other common architectural elements may also be present in the structure of Renaissance wall tombs, including tabernacle frames, Roman aediculae, and triumphal arches, all of which provide visual coherence to the overall structure while emphasizing certain symbolic attributes connected to the deceased.

As Barbara Groseclose has established, from the eighteenth century through to the period of the 1857 Indian Uprising, the East India Company exported to India numerous church-based wall tombs to honour the lives of those who served the Company. Over time, as the Company filled churches in Calcutta, Madras, and Bombay, these funerary monuments contributed to building up the presence of Britain in India, a presence that combined religious sacrament with public and national service.[49] Groseclose demonstrated that the Company exported wall tombs to India for installation in church interiors for an explicitly imperial purpose: to appropriate a religious iconography and structural framework to commemorate public lives that had been devoted to the empire. As a result, Britain's impetus to disseminate church-based monuments in India helped to instil and reinforce behaviours in the colony that were deemed useful to the state, an effective way to extend nationalistic sentiments abroad. According to Groseclose,

> Church monuments sanctify memory, public monuments adjure memory, and their appeal to a common interest is strongest and most direct when that interest can be seen as national. With the claim that the common good is the national good, church monuments' former signification of spiritual reward and God's favour is exchanged for the secular memorability and royal approval that public statuary betokens.[50]

When she resided in India, Julia Margaret Cameron would have been familiar with many of the funerary monuments described by Groseclose, as she and Charles Cameron were married in Calcutta in St Paul's Cathedral, the interior design of which consciously reproduced the solemn ambiance of Victorian college chapels.[51] Given her close connection to Major George Broadfoot, perhaps she was also familiar with Edward Richardson's 1850 etching of the design for Broadfoot's tomb (see fig. 14), created in the manner of Renaissance-inspired *avelli*, that was circulated to raise funds to erect his memorial in St George's Cathedral in Madras.[52] In Broadfoot's wall tomb, the deceased soldier is laid out in effigy in the centre register, flanked by two members of his infantry unit who stand erect with reversed guns. In the panel below, Broadfoot's worldly accomplishments and service to the empire are inscribed as lasting tributes. Draped immediately above him in the top register are the colours of the East India Company's army, above which floats the laurel wreath of triumph and eternal life, while uppermost in the composition the British crown is represented as if a floating, mystical presence, where it is suspended in air, symbolic of imperial triumph. Because death monuments like Broadfoot's turned a person's lived experience into a form of historical narration, these artistic forms embodied the storyteller's role, wrote Walter Benjamin: 'Death is the sanction of everything the storyteller can tell', he wrote. 'He has borrowed his authority from death.'[53]

In London, Cameron could also have seen numerous contemporary examples of church-based wall tombs for heroes of the empire that combined symbolic elements of personal duty and national sacrifice. These could be found in the sacred spaces of Westminster Abbey and St Paul's Cathedral and in the secular halls of the Crystal Palace or South Kensington Museum. At South Kensington, Henry Cole had been acquiring and cataloguing examples of *avelli*, both actual period monuments and in plaster casts made from originals. In 1862, for example, under the direction of Sir John Charles Robinson, the South Kensington Museum produced an important catalogue of Italian sculpture called *Italian Sculpture of the Middle Ages and Period of the Revival of Art*.[54] Robinson's catalogue – and the Museum's growing collection – was intended to influence contemporary production of works of applied art. Between 1859 and 1863, under Cole's guidance, Robinson acquired drawings and paintings for the Museum and consolidated the Italian sculpture collection.[55] In lectures given in South Kensington in 1858, John Ruskin extolled the virtues of Italian Renaissance art, calling 'the Florentine school' in particular 'the perfect expression of human emotion – the showing of the effects of passion in the human face and gesture'.[56] In England, one of the most well-known examples of Italian Renaissance wall tombs was exemplified by the sculpture made to honour Cardinal Ascanio Sforza, originally created around 1505 by Andrea Sansovino and then years later, around 1852, cast in plaster for permanent display in the Crystal Palace (fig. 93).[57]

The public competition for the memorial of the Duke of Wellington inside St Paul's Cathedral

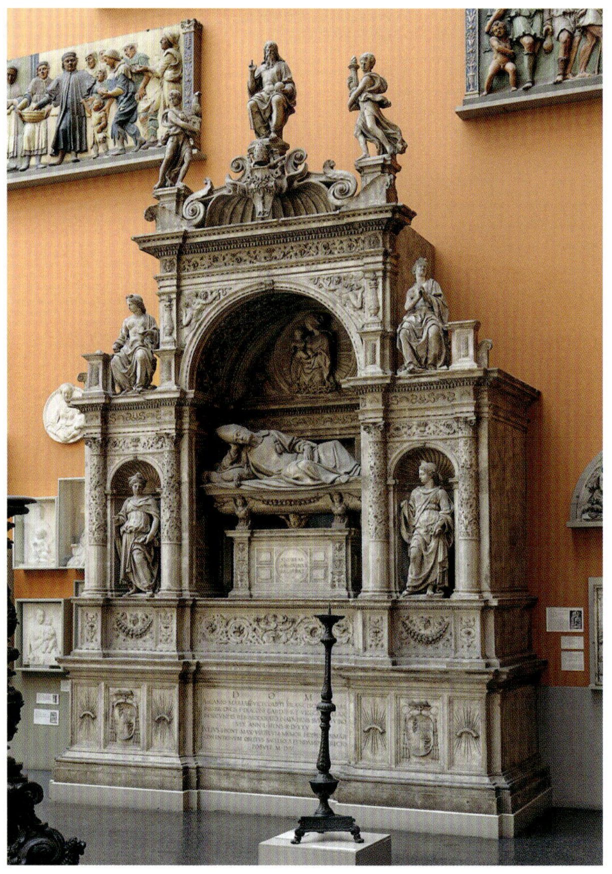

93 Andrea Sansovino, *Tomb of Cardinal Ascanio Sforza*, 1505–9 (sculpted), 1852–4 (cast), plaster cast.
Given by the Trustees of the Crystal Palace, © Victoria and Albert Museum, London. REPRO.A.1938–12.

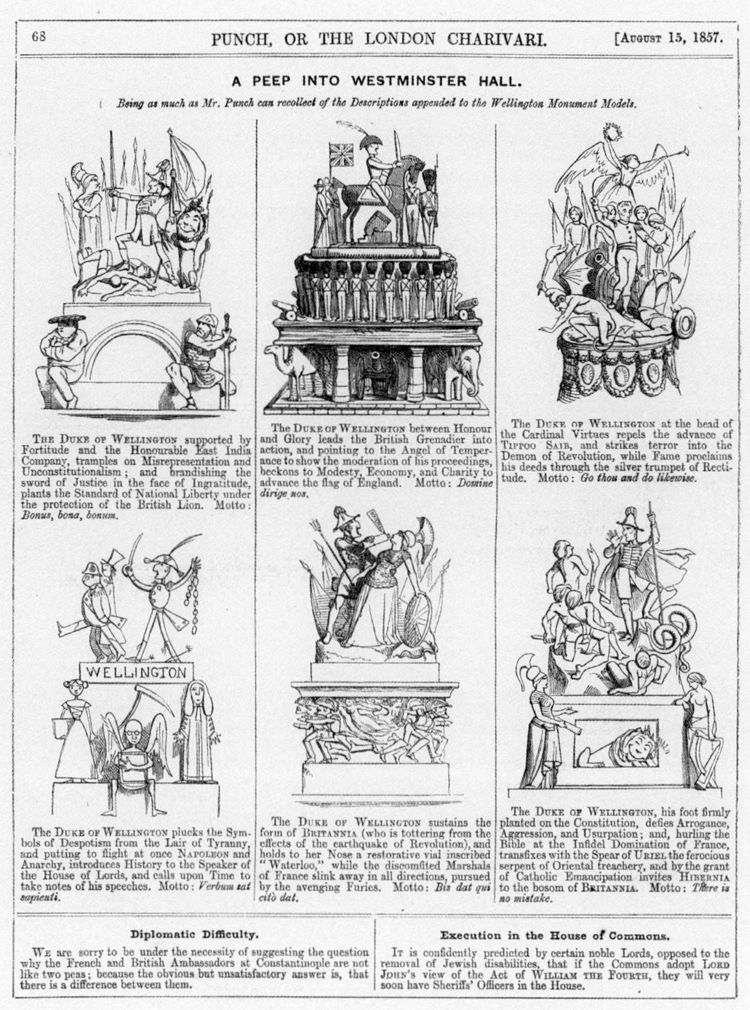

68 PUNCH, OR THE LONDON CHARIVARI. [August 15, 1857.

A PEEP INTO WESTMINSTER HALL.

Being as much as Mr. Punch can recollect of the Descriptions appended to the Wellington Monument Models.

The Duke of Wellington supported by Fortitude and the Honourable East India Company, tramples on Misrepresentation and Unconstitutionalism; and brandishing the sword of Justice in the face of Ingratitude, plants the Standard of National Liberty under the protection of the British Lion. Motto: *Bonus, bona, bonum.*

The Duke of Wellington between Honour and Glory leads the British Grenadier into action, and pointing to the Angel of Temperance to show the moderation of his proceedings, beckons to Modesty, Economy, and Charity to advance the flag of England. Motto: *Domine dirige nos.*

The Duke of Wellington at the head of the Cardinal Virtues repels the advance of Tippoo Saib, and strikes terror into the Demon of Revolution, while Fame proclaims his deeds through the silver trumpet of Rectitude. Motto: *Go thou and do likewise.*

The Duke of Wellington plucks the Symbols of Despotism from the Lair of Tyranny, and putting to flight at once Napoleon and Anarchy, introduces History to the Speaker of the House of Lords, and calls upon Time to take notes of his speeches. Motto: *Verbum sat sapienti.*

The Duke of Wellington sustains the form of Britannia (who is tottering from the effects of the earthquake of Revolution), and holds to her Nose a restorative vial inscribed "Waterloo," while the discomfited Marshals of France slink away in all directions, pursued by the avenging Furies. Motto: *Bis dat qui citò dat.*

The Duke of Wellington, his foot firmly planted on the Constitution, defies Arrogance, Aggression, and Usurpation; and, hurling the Bible at the Infidel Domination of France, transfixes with the Spear of Uriel the ferocious serpent of Oriental treachery, and by the grant of Catholic Emancipation invites Hibernia to the bosom of Britannia. Motto: *There is no mistake.*

Diplomatic Difficulty.

We are sorry to be under the necessity of suggesting the question why the French and British Ambassadors at Constantinople are not like two peas; because the obvious but unsatisfactory answer is, that there is a difference between them.

Execution in the House of Commons.

It is confidently predicted by certain noble Lords, opposed to the removal of Jewish disabilities, that if the Commons adopt Lord John's view of the Act of William the Fourth, they will very soon have Sheriffs' Officers in the House.

94 Anon., *A Peep into Westminster Hall*, woodcut from *Punch*, 15 August 1857, 68.

provided yet another contemporary example of this tripartite design feature for a sculpted tomb. During his long life, numerous public sculptures had already honoured the soldier and statesman, but a new commission was announced in 1852, after the Duke's death, that would be the first monument designed to honour him in a sacred space. Accordingly, the *avelli* wall tomb format was chosen as the preferred structure. Regrettably, however, the competition was marked by controversy for decades.[58] Critics openly called for the commission to go to an 'English artist', not only to honour the patriotic sentiments associated with the departed national hero, but also to spurn Baron Marochetti, despite his long residence in Britain and much-favoured status with England's royal family. In 1856, for example, William Michael Rossetti inflamed British resentments by writing in the *Crayon* that Marochetti's selection was all but a shoo-in.[59] His mischievous commentary stoked fears and anger, as the competition was supposed to be open, and at the time of his writing had not yet been decided.

In 1857, *Punch* disparaged the entire affair by lampooning the entries submitted for display in Westminster Hall, publishing a derisive and cartoonish parody of nine of the scaled-down sculptural models (fig. 94).[60] In each simplified caricature, the journal depicted the Duke of Wellington in the act of fighting for some noble cause or against some sort of grave injustice. He rides a noble horse, brandishes a sword of justice, or stands aloft flanked by lions or in the company of angels. Each of these familiar tropes is represented in a simplified symbolic form with allegorical figures stacked one atop the other in two or three registers, once again following the familiar design structure. As an example,

> The Duke of Wellington supported by Fortitude and the Honourable East India Company, tramples on Misrepresentation and Unconstitutionalism; and brandishing the sword of Justice in the face of Ingratitude, plants the Standard of National Liberty under the protection of the British Lion. Motto: *Bonus, bona, bonum.*[61]

Punch's caricatures ridiculed the wall tomb's tripartite structure as inflexible and mocked its repetitive use of well-worn (some would say tired and restrictive) allegorical figures that the iconography allowed, exposing the devices artists used to express noble sentiments and heroic virtue as worn-out clichés. But it was also apparent that the journal's parody of the Wellington Monument competition exposed the extent to which the discursive model for this structure had become well-established artistic vernacular, no longer an esoteric or highbrow formal language, and therefore, ironically, a fitting and popular tribute to honour the great national hero. Each of the legends beneath the nine drawings pokes similar fun at the repetitive and formulaic use of this now-common funereal symbolic form.

In the end, Alfred Stevens won the Wellington Monument competition, not because his allegories were deemed superior, but because his entry was judged to fit best in the restricted architectural confines of St Paul's, where it would occupy space under an archway in the nave. (In 1878, the South Kensington Museum acquired Stevens's model for its collections.)[62] Meanwhile, broad popular interest in Italian Renaissance sculpture was disseminated even more widely by the Arundel Society. This group was founded in 1848 to promote knowledge of works of art through the publication of reproductive prints, but also to promote application of those high-art principles to applied design and manufacturing. The Arundel Society's mission, therefore, was much like that of the Science and Art Department of the South Kensington Museum, and the two worked collaboratively to achieve the same end. As an example, the society commissioned original watercolour drawings from professional artists to create chromolithographs for mass production, and the Museum in turn acquired many of those original drawings for its collection, while making the society's reproductive prints of those images available for purchase.[63]

In 1859, Julia Margaret Cameron formally joined the Arundel Society as a member. Her friend, Lord Lansdowne, was among the society's founders, and as we have seen, Cameron delivered a photographic album to Lansdowne in February of that year.[64] Other members in Cameron's friendship circle included Lord Lindsay, Lord Elcho, John Ruskin, and Austen Henry Layard. The year before, Layard wrote an extensive essay for the *Quarterly Review* about Italian frescoes produced during the Renaissance, where he centred on ways that artists used allegory to convey meaning and developed complex narratives by individualizing figures and realistic landscapes. Using the Lorenzetti's *Allegory of Good and Bad Government* as a historical example for ways that artists historically commented on contemporary politics, Layard elevated this Italian Renaissance fresco as a model that could be applied to the present day.[65]

Excellence in art, according to Layard, resulted from Renaissance Italy's wholesome moral environment. But when Italy's painters 'no longer painted for the people', he wrote, moral and spiritual decay began to set in: rather than remembering the high purpose of using art to enhance public instruction, artists lost their way, became more interested in glorifying popes and decorating palaces of the nobility, and began employing meaningless ornamentation in churches without any elevated purpose in mind.[66] But the public role of art, Layard insisted in 1859, was found in a nation's most elevated ambitions and moral purpose: great art promoted 'National subjects, worthily exercising its best and highest mission among us'.[67] In this regard, Layard's pronouncements about national art were in accord with those of Ruskin. A nation's successful artistic production, wrote the critic, was connected to its struggle against 'national degradation', an aim that could be achieved only if society prioritized three principles: first, its ability to resist 'indolence and sensuality'; second, its ability to serve high religious purposes without stooping to idolatry, superstition, falsehood, or vice; and third, its ability to defy countercultural forces that might surface unexpectedly that would dignify cruelty and unkindness.

Ruskin delivered this high-minded commentary in January 1858 at the South Kensington Museum.[68] Predictably, his archetype for 'national degradation' was represented by India, as he regarded the recent anti-colonial rebellion as synonymous with 'barbarism', cruelty, and 'the lowest level of possible humanity'. According to his printed lecture,

> Since the race of man began its course of sin on this earth, nothing has ever been done by it so significative of all bestial, and lower than bestial degradation, as the acts of the Indian race in the year that has just passed by.[69]

India's art, he cautioned, uses

> meaningless fragments of colour and flowings of hue; or if it represents any living creature, it represents that creature under some distorted and monstrous form. To all the facts and forms of nature it wilfully and resolutely opposes itself.[70]

'Authentic art', by contrast, was found only in nature, according to Ruskin. Archetypes of true 'national art' could be found by contrasting British and Indian examples, with the recent experience of the Indian Uprising instructive. For Britain, Ruskin chose the traditional arts of Scotland, no doubt because the Highlanders distinguished themselves in military warfare on behalf of the empire. For India, Ruskin's model was the untrustworthy

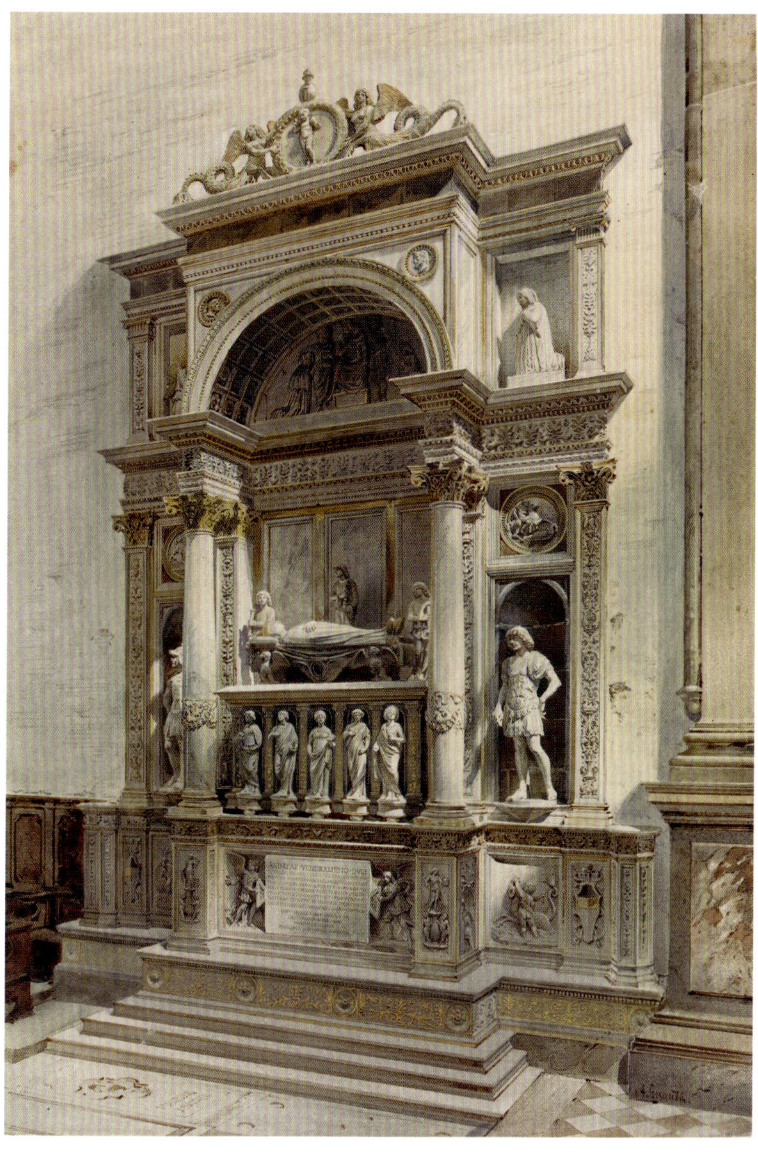

95 Adolf Gnauth, *Monument to the Doge Andrea Vendramin*, 1867, watercolour drawing on paper, 43.9 × 28.7 cm.

sepoy, once a dependable ally under Britain's benevolent tutelage and now used metaphorically to describe a despised colonial inferior: 'Out of the peat cottage come faith, courage, self-sacrifice, purity, and piety', claimed Ruskin, whereas, 'out of the ivory palace come treachery, cruelty, cowardice, idolatry, bestiality'.[71]

Ruskin's derogatory remarks bear witness to the enduring cost of the Indian Uprising on British civil society, as the critic soured on virtually everything Indian. His comments demonstrate that the nation's sense of colonial betrayal and the trauma of warfare had even intruded upon the South Kensington Museum's broad public commitment to teach appreciation for diverse forms of artistic expression as they occurred in different historical periods and from across the world. This is even more surprising because Henry Cole had been acquiring works of Indian art systematically over the course of the previous decade. His efforts began in earnest after the 1851 Great Exhibition at the Crystal Palace, when he purchased at auction several displays that the East India Company had commissioned, and he used these pieces to form the 'Indian Section' of the Museum in 1857.[72] When the Company was dismantled after 1858, so too was its museum, and without a home, the Indian art collections wandered throughout the 1860s 'from place to place as dispute raged over the relative merits of housing them in the British Museum, in South Kensington, or in a new museum to be built at Whitehall near the new India Office'.[73]

As a result, it is fascinating that in 1867, Cole acquired Marochetti's model of the Cawnpore Angel and installed this reduced-scale sculpture in the lower gallery suite that he called the 'Indian Museum'.[74] Marochetti, of course, achieved renown as an English artist, and the sculpture itself represented an angelic figure in the Christian tradition. In no way, then, could this work be misconstrued as a product of Indian artistic sensibilities. There remains the unanswered question of why Cole chose this particular gallery – apparently outside the main exhibition halls – to display Marochetti's sculpture, especially after so much public attention had been given to the commission and the selection of Marochetti to execute it for Cawnpore. It is also curious that this installation in the South Kensington Museum all but escaped notice in the press or elsewhere. And although Ruskin enjoyed an outsized critical influence in the evaluation of contemporary art and with respect to artistic education in general, no record remains of his reaction to Cole's new and expanded 'Indian Section' of the Museum.

Finally, the coordinated efforts of the Arundel Society and the South Kensington Museum are instructive, as Cole valued the Arundel Society's promotion of Italian Renaissance art to demonstrate the alignment of high art forms of the past with modern practices of applied art and manufacturing. Cole's ideas began to take shape in 1862, using works of art on loan from the International Exhibition, which he housed in the South Court of the Museum. He believed that photography could help disseminate these artistic principles, a rationale for his support of Cameron's work in photography. By 1866, the Arundel Society had more than two thousand members, and in concert with the Museum, the society continued to promote Italian Renaissance art and reproduce the imagery of funerary sculpture from this era. In 1867, for example, the society commissioned the professional artist Adolf Gnauth to create watercolour drawings of Renaissance tombs that the society then intended to publish as chromolithographs. A useful example is the *Monument to the Doge Andrea Vendramin* (fig. 95), which became a popular print. The society used this example to illustrate how the historical wall tomb commemorated the life of the Venetian official. The design incorporates a classicizing triumphal arch style, much like Stevens's design, along with the conspicuous use of ornamental putti, which is incorporated into the conventional wall tomb structure. It uses putti in the lowermost register to call attention to an inscribed tribute that celebrates the life of the deceased (*putti reggistema*), while in the topmost register, a putto stands in isolated glory, enclosed by a roundel created by two sirens who join two garlands (the sirens act as *putti reggifestone*).[75]

By this time, John Charles Robinson's special loan exhibition of Renaissance art held in 1863 in the Museum's South Court established the broad popularity of this sculptural legacy to collectors in Britain as well as its importance to the Museum.[76] In order to demonstrate her awareness and support of this trend in Victorian high art and taste, Julia Margaret Cameron included in the photographic portfolio she sent to Cole examples of portraits of life-size heads of young children that date to 1865 and 1866. These photographs consciously adopted the frontal posing of Italian Renaissance portrait busts and the naturalistic style of artists like Desiderio da Settignano, Antonio Rossellino, and Andrea della Robbia (fig. 96), which Cole was then collecting for the Museum. In formal terms, the soft lines of Cameron's life-size heads, but also her direct and formal approach to portraiture, vividly resemble the idealized portrait bust that Marochetti produced years earlier that depicted her niece, Julia Jackson (see fig. 23). Cameron included two of these photographs in the Herschel Album. She titled one *No. 3 of series of 12 Life sized heads* (fig. 97) and the other *Young Astyanax* (HA-60), and sent the entire group of 'Life sized heads' to her print dealer, Colnaghi, for sale.[77]

Cameron's well-grounded familiarity with the three-dimensional design template of Italian Renaissance *avelli* helps to explain the principal source for the formal organization of her photograph *At the Well, A Farewell*, because the formal arrangement of the fragments in the photograph embraces the iconography of funerary sculpture (compare fig. 7). In the photograph, the three separate elements are united in a new formal relationship. In the image on top, the woman's covered head is framed and positioned

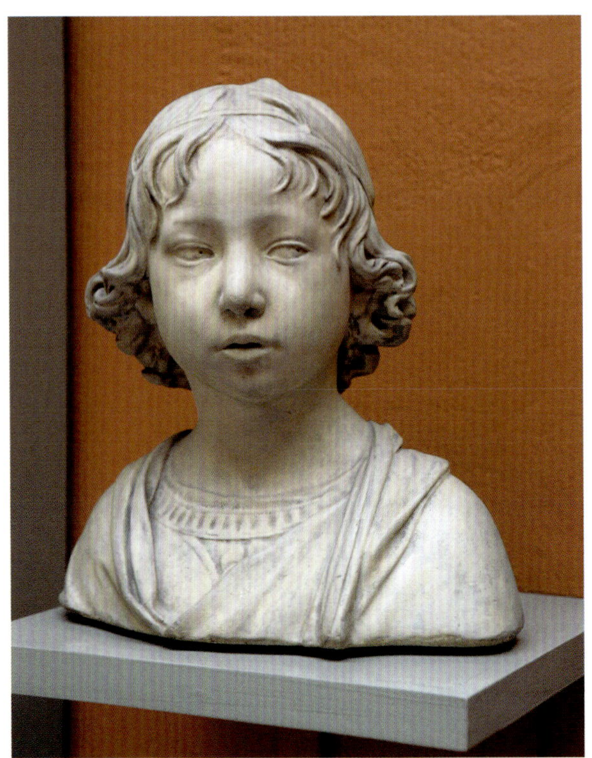

96 Andrea della Robbia, *Bust of a Child*, *c.*1460–90 (sculpted), *c.*1867 (cast), plaster cast.
© Victoria and Albert Museum, London. REPRO.1867–182.

97 Julia Margaret Cameron, *No. 3 of series of 12 Life sized heads*, 1866, albumen print, 35.6 × 28.7 cm.
National Science & Media Museum / Science Museum Group. 1984–5017/81.

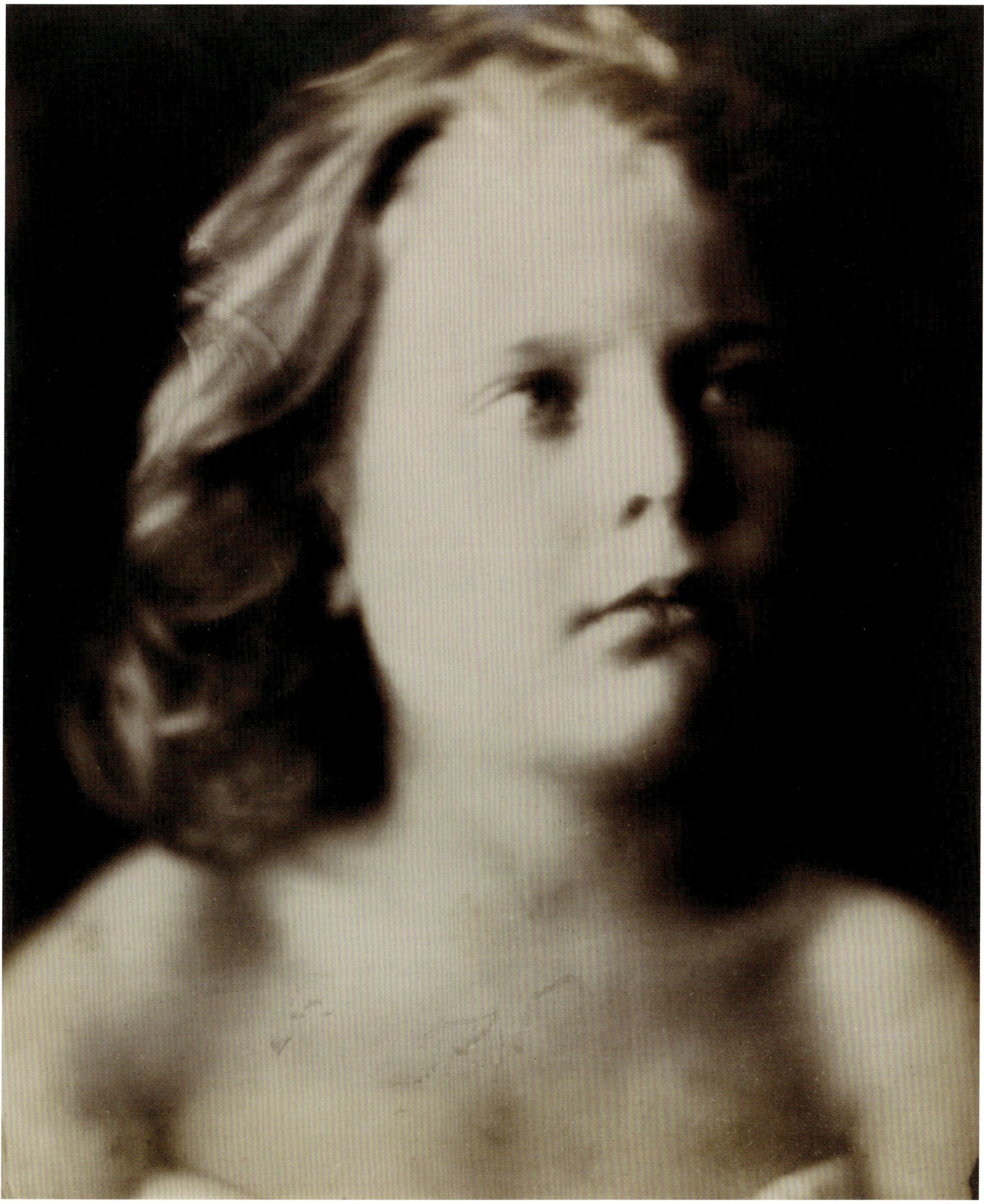

to look down upon the centre image of a woman in mourning, standing before a well in a white chapel cap, while on the bottom of the page, two naked children kiss and embrace while appearing to look upward. Translated into allegorical terms, a seraphim angel looks down upon a woman who mourns for dead women and children lost in Britain's war with India and welcomes their souls to heaven. As the angel's divine light sanctifies the scene, enhancing the whiteness of the woman before the well, putti on the bottom register figuratively lift the souls of the martyred to heaven, there to be received by the attending angel. Conceived compositionally in this way, *At the Well, A Farewell* becomes reanimated as a new kind of devotional object, one that expresses a religious reconciliation that laments the human cost of war while at the same time expressing atonement for the imperial project.

By adopting the structural composition of Italian Renaissance funerary wall sculpture as a model for this photograph, by surrounding her central image vertically with angelic figures above and below, Cameron would have manipulated an older art form and remade it through the new medium of photography. In doing so, she would have surely executed one of the foundational 'high art' principles that the Arundel Society and South Kensington Museum advocated with respect to influencing the arts and manufactures, which is to say that Cameron's composition would have exemplified the application of high art to the mechanical process of photography.[78] Conceived of in this way, Cameron's composite photograph would have united the formal elements of Renaissance sculpture together with symbolic iconography used in funerary design. Moreover, because her experimental practice made her familiar with isolating and moving around different photographic fragments, she was able to adapt an established formal design structure that drew upon iconography of the Italian Renaissance and then combine those fragments into a new allegorical representation. In her new composition, *At the Well, A Farewell,* Cameron could therefore emphasize symbolism over realism and use structural elements borrowed from architecture to call viewers' attention to the constructed nature of the image. And by embracing the familiar three-part design, she could emphasize the religious associations of this composite image and attach its meaning to monumental funerary sculpture. Conceived in this way, it appears that Cameron devised her composition to convey the nobility of 'a sign, which would afford it access to the dignity of language', as Barthes wrote.[79] Photographs seldom achieve this aim.[80]

TOMB OF THE UNKNOWN

In his book *Imagined Communities*, Benedict Anderson analysed how modern societies try to atone for the grievous losses that take place during wartime, a seemingly unattainable task given the impossibility of expiating the trauma and collective guilt of sending children into battle. Because of that irretrievable sense of loss, he argued that 'no more arresting emblems of the modern culture of nationalism exist than cenotaphs and tombs of Unknown Soldiers'. Memorials like these command reverence, he insisted, 'precisely *because* they are deliberately empty or no one knows who lies inside them', claiming that such practice 'has no true precedence in earlier times'.[81] As a result, memorials to anonymous or unknown soldiers also present a representational dilemma because they invert the genuine function of a tomb and deny the act of commemorating a single life. They exist in a physical space that has been overturned, having become a 'placeless place', in the words of Michel Foucault, because they occupy a 'simultaneously mythic and real contestation of the space in which we live'.

Mass tombs like the Cawnpore well are like the tombs of the unknown. For Foucault, they disturb the nature of time itself because they represent an 'an absolute break with their traditional time'; yet simultaneously they also represent a 'perpetual and indefinite accumulation of time in an immobile place'.[82] Consequently, monuments like the 'Memorial Well' are paradoxically locked forever in place. And yet, these sites also become timeless, that is, they existed outside the conventional ways of marking time. For that reason, George Trevelyan believed the well at Cawnpore was ultimately unrepresentable because it was impossible to tell the magnitude of the story in physical form. Because of their enormity, burial sites of this kind, concluded Anderson, become symbols of larger, unmet ambitions: in his words, they become 'saturated with ghostly *national* imaginings' (original emphasis).[83]

In paying homage to the mass burial at Cawnpore, Cameron's photograph, *At the Well, A Farewell*, accomplishes a similar double purpose: it directly honours the human sacrifices made by British women and children during the Indian Uprising and at the same time celebrates the restitution of British power after the war had concluded. By embodying this otherworldly presence of ethereal and contradictory nationalism, we might say that Cameron's composite photograph also occupies two worlds at once. Operating at the intersection of memory and storytelling, mediating between national identity and the iconography of the funerary eternal, this photograph negotiates heroic myths, embodies moral imperatives, and narrates historical triumph. Yet it also expresses compassion for the vanquished, whose lives are expiated through the overtly religious and humanistic iconography. By using allegory to represent the Memorial Well in Cawnpore and then by adopting the model of the Italian Renaissance wall tomb to structure the design of her composite photograph, Cameron reinforced this emblem of the war in India as a symbol of the strength and endurance of the British empire, but also as an atonement for its past sins.

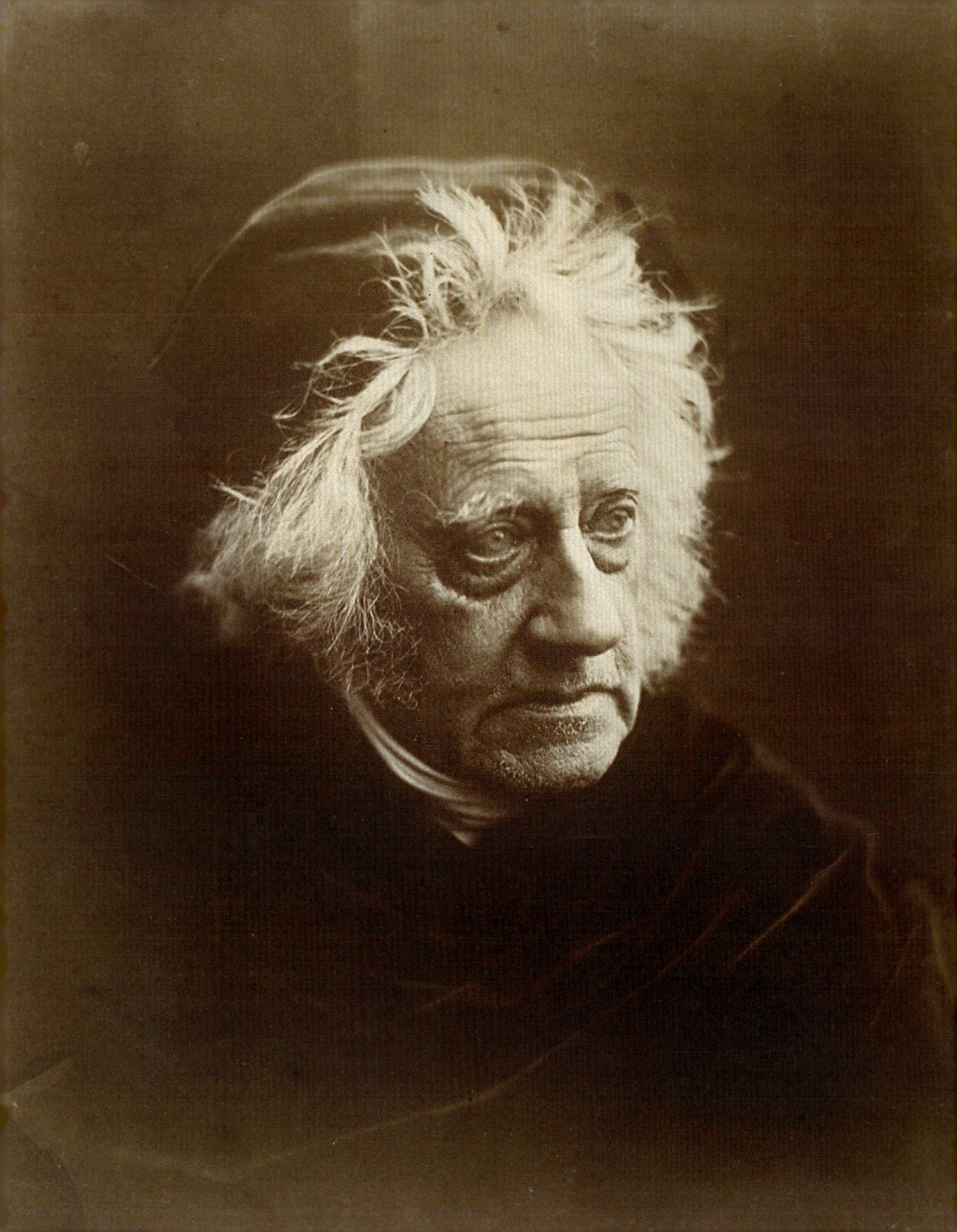

Chapter Nine
Paterfamilias

98 Julia Margaret Cameron, *Sir John Herschel with Cap* (detail of fig. 6).

FILLING THE FRAME

In the spring of 1866, Julia Margaret Cameron acquired a new camera and lens to replace the apparatus her daughter had given her two years earlier. The new technology still used the process of collodion-on-glass, but Cameron's new equipment allowed her to create photographs that were sized 15" × 12" without enlarging the negative plate, a grand size that was comparable to folio-size paper used in book publication and fine art printmaking.[1] This aspect ratio was also far larger than ordinary photographs like the 6" × 4" dimension of cabinet cards or the 4.5" × 2.5" of reduced-size *cartes-de-visite* produced during the same era. Importantly, the new lens also enabled her to work in low-light conditions by using a wide aperture. By using this apparatus, Cameron could create a shallow depth of field, which she realized could be used to enhance the soft-focus approach that she had grown to favour.[2]

And yet, because professional photography was associated with precision, and because sharpness was valued above all for documentary purposes like record-keeping, Cameron's soft-focus look, like her cut-up details and photographic fragments, was considered entirely unconventional. In fact, professionals disregarded her approach to the medium as the practice of amateur work.[3] Nevertheless, Cameron's soft-focus photographs caught the attention of contemporary art critics, who called them blurred and even out of focus. These insights have influenced art historians today who have evaluated her work in these terms, examining, for example, how she cultivated 'accidental glitches' to her creative process in order to enhance ill-defined outcomes, or how she used selective focus and multiple printing to blur distinct lines and emphasize her sense of artistic effect, or how she deliberately employed soft focus to signal the gendered identity of her imagery of women and children.[4] In 1864, after all, Cameron famously complained, 'What is focus – & who has a right to say what focus is the legitimate focus – '.[5]

Cameron's perplexed query – 'what is focus?' – seems to reflect her exasperation with critics as much as her derision for their misplaced superficial emphasis on the surface appearance of her photographs. Yet an alternative reading of her inquiry into the appropriate use of focus emerges from examining the reasons behind her purchase of a new camera and lens, because one might also conclude that the new apparatus was designed to help her shift the conversation *away* from focus and to centre instead on the content or subject matter of her photographs. Focus, in other words, was a distraction, a critical misdirection and wrong-headed emphasis, one that mistakenly concentrated interest on the surface detail of a print, an insignificant element that made critics miss the point of her work entirely. Cameron's new apparatus, by contrast, was designed to enable her to *magnify* the image. By means of the new apparatus, the enlarged size of the negative image would now enable her to produce equally large high-quality prints. As a result, she could intensify the impact of her subject matter, divert attention away from surface and onto questions of substance. In fact, the new 'Rapid Rectilinear' lens of 1866 allowed her to cover nearly the entire surface of her large glass negatives with her subject's image.[6] One might reason that her critics would follow suit, opening up questions of content, iconography, allegory, and subject matter.

As Julian Cox observed, Cameron's acquisition of these new 'symmetrical, flat-field' optics allowed her to produce the 'characteristic [effect] of slightly magnifying the subject and thereby increasing its size in the image'.[7] In other words, by adopting this apparatus, Cameron was able to *fill the frame* with her photographic subject. The closer that she moved her new camera to her sitter, the larger the image size would appear on the camera's ground-glass. At the same time, by physically moving closer to the subject, depth of field in the image would proportionally *decrease* in a corresponding fashion. As a result, Cameron's new camera and lens allowed her to make portraits that were grand and imposing while also appearing soft-focused at the edges. This ability allowed her to refine her artistic objectives once more, because she found a new alignment between her apparatus and formal approach to her subjects, one that united her interest in taking portraits of the 'great men' of her time, like the 'life-size heads' and sculpted torsos inspired by Italian Renaissance prototypes. Cameron was deliberative in her approach to the medium and in her choice of subjects: she enhanced these new-found visual effects by merging the intensified magnification of the apparatus together with theatrical lighting effects, a performative combination that she celebrated because the new materials and the enhanced size of her imagery brought out minute features of her sitters in vivid and dramatic ways.

When she shared photographs with her friend Sir John Herschel, he likened the results of her new approach to carvings found in deeply modelled sculpture. Of one image that Cameron later included in the 1867 album, he wrote that the photograph, titled *The Mountain Nymph Sweet Liberty*, 'is really a most astonishing piece of high relief – [the model is] absolutely alive and thrusting out her head from the paper into the air' (Cox/Ford 335; HA-82).[8] Cameron herself emphasized the sculptural impact of these effects when she called her portrait of Thomas Carlyle 'like a rough block of Michael Angelo's sculpture', and even posed sitters to resemble statues from the Parthenon's pediment.[9] And as we have seen, she portrayed the heads and shoulders of young children in her series of 'Life sized heads', all taken with the new camera and lens, as if they were modern-day equivalents to the Renaissance-era busts then being collected by John Charles Robinson and Henry Cole for the South Kensington Museum.

Herschel emphatically endorsed his friend's new approach as early as February 1866. He enquired after Cameron's process of experimentation, using his awareness of her interest in combining theatrical effects to suggest, astutely, that she mix this with an enhancement of three-dimensional affect:

> Have you ever tried the effect of draping all the figures of a group in pure white – whitening their *faces* & *hands* & *hair* and then photographing your group as a sculpture – the background also and all of the appendages being white or grey? [Original emphasis][10]

By invoking sculpture explicitly, it should be apparent that Herschel understood Cameron was not interested in pursuing accidental artistic effects when she created her new imagery, nor in seeking to record a transitory act or recreate a theatrical performance for the camera.[11]

Rather, Cameron's stated ambition was to achieve impeccable and exact precision, especially as this was expressed by flawlessness in execution, which is to say, she wanted to match the evident perfection of her subjects by achieving excellence in the aesthetic outcome of her final prints. She stated these aims explicitly in a letter to Henry Cole of February 1866.

> I hope it is no vain imagination of mine to say that the like have never been produced and never can be

> surpassed! ... They are quite ready quite ready – a new series of 12 [life-sized heads] – and if you watch my opport[unity] for me and acquaint me I will answer at once by sending you the supply. Mr Thurston Thompson I hope *will* be delighted this time. [Original emphasis]
>
> Won't the South Kensington Museum give me a crown! Not of diamond stones but those better diamonds laurel leaves – or a medal or honorable [*sic*] mention if this series of photographs of mine surpasses all others –
>
> Talk of roundness I have it in *perfect perfection*. [My emphasis][12]

By this date, Cameron had moved beyond any possible worries she might have harboured about imprecise focus, expressing instead an affirmative and optimistic ambition to represent '*roundness*' in a two-dimensional photograph, *human scale* (which is to say, life-size proportions) in the rendering, and '*perfect perfection*' in the execution. Her new determination and approach were made possible by three coinciding factors. First, her new camera and lens enabled her to fill the frame with her subject, providing life-size imagery. Second, she derived new inspiration from the national prototypes of Italian Renaissance portrait busts and wall tombs, in accord with the emphasis on these forms that was promoted by the Arundel Society and South Kensington Museum. And third, she undertook a new commitment to use photography to communicate narrative meaning, both in formal portraits and allegorical images. If the theoretical and aesthetic grounding for this work came from Layard and Ruskin, photographic encouragement came from Cole and Thurston Thompson.

Charles Thurston Thompson was well known to the Holland Park set but his influence on Cameron's artistic formation has not been fully explored. A wood-engraver by trade, he produced woodcuts in 1851 after illustrations made by Richard Doyle for Ruskin's fable *The King of the Golden River*. After that date, Henry Cole employed him to photograph works on display at the Crystal Palace. In 1856, Cole appointed Thompson, who was also his brother-in-law, to the post of 'superintendent of photography' at the South Kensington Museum.[13] The following year, Dante Gabriel Rossetti hired Thompson to make photographs of drawings created by the artist to illustrate Moxon's 1857 edition of Tennyson's poems, and Rossetti later displayed these reproductive photographs at the 1857 Pre-Raphaelite exhibition in Fitzroy Square.[14] Between 1856 and 1859, years associated with East India Company's annexation of Oude and the Uprising itself, and years when Cameron was collecting photographs and assembling albums, Thompson taught eighty-five non-commissioned officers of the Royal Engineers how to photograph in the field. This educational programme was delivered to the army under the auspices of the South Kensington Museum.[15]

It also seems apparent that Thompson achieved artistic results that Cameron admired. An example is Thompson's photograph *A Quiet Moment* (1854), portraying a young girl backed up against an ivy-covered wall expressing a moment of introspection or melancholy common to other genre pictures. The photograph was displayed at the first exhibition of the Photographic Society of London and later collected by Prince Albert and Queen Victoria.[16] Even before acquiring her new camera and lens, Cameron's photographs of children, as in the examples of the *Water Babies* imagery discussed earlier, seem to replicate Thompson's artistic approach to genre photography, especially his use of narrow depth of field, full-frame exposure, dramatic lighting, and enhanced sculptural effect. With her new apparatus in hand, Cameron clearly sought out his artistic approval, intending that her 'Life sized heads' should favourably impress the photographer.

In March 1867, Cameron made arrangements to take Herschel's portrait at his home, Collingwood, a project she had anticipated for some time. Because the collodion process required chemical processing immediately after exposure, she needed to transport her camera and chemical solutions to her subject's location. She would also take along one of her household maids as an assistant, but first required Lady Herschel's assistance in advance to help her prepare a suitable studio environment:

> The room cannot be too humble, if it is capable of having all light excluded except that of the one window or one aperture which I will myself cover with a yellow calico that is all I desire.[17]

After posing Herschel in this neutral, unadorned space, she covered up his everyday clothes under a black cloth, tousled his freshly washed grey hair, and bade him wear a black cap. Directing a beam of raking light from the side, she illuminated his face and hair and filled the frame with her subject's sideways gaze.

The great amount of sharpness and detail on the large plate revealed heavy bags sagging under his eyes, every forehead crease and furrow, and day-old beard stubble present on his upper lip and chin. Cameron made no effort to clean up Herschel's appearance. She made several exposures during this portrait sitting and sent the results to her friend. Herschel wrote to Cameron with thanks, noting that he found one portrait outdid all her other efforts. He wrote his thoughts on the reverse side of the image when he returned the print to Cameron:

> The picture of the old paterfamilias with the black cap on is, I think, the climax of photographic art, and beats hollow anything I ever beheld in photography before.[18]

Cameron placed that image, *Sir John Herschel with Cap*, in the first position in the restored album she dedicated to him later that year (see fig. 6). And yet, although it was received by Cameron and accepted as a badge of honour, the presence of this inscription remained unknown until the album was dismantled in the twentieth century.

Colin Ford noted that Cameron's portrait of Herschel in the black cap, like others taken using the same technology, 'gave her subjects' eyes a particular intensity, an "abstracted look".'[19] Cameron apparently cultivated this new approach to her portraits and applied these lessons to making new photographs of Carlyle and Tennyson that she also included in the Herschel Album. In this way, Herschel became a kind of 'founding father' for her new portrait aesthetic of close-up intensity and her emerging archive of national subjects. Although Cameron never used this term to describe the collective portraits in the album that she gave Herschel, she nevertheless began to think of her portraits as a coherent body of imagery. After taking Herschel's portrait, for example, she extracted from him 'a promise to her not to sit for one to any other artist-photographer'.[20] Cameron obtained this pledge from him not, as has been suggested, because other portraits of Herschel would flood the marketplace and thereby diminish the commercial value of her own portrait, but rather because she had accomplished something unique in formal terms and understandably wanted to take credit for it alone. She intended to capitalize upon this opportunity. The following year, she begged Herschel's forgiveness in sending him blank mounts upon which she would later affix copies of this portrait, 'trusting to your goodness to sign them when you can', having already 'marked the place with pencil for your dear name'.[21]

ALTER EGO

Herschel's observation that he appeared 'the picture of the old paterfamilias' is a striking commentary by the sitter, even if this declaration was discreetly hidden away, like a diary entry or secret letter. Since that time, historians have cited Herschel's comment as evidence of his unqualified praise, a kind of confirmation that in one stroke, Cameron captured the unparalleled likeness of her mentor while achieving her own self-conscious aspirations to create a work of high art. But Herschel's unique statement is also a mark of identification, even a self-described recognition of a truth captured by the photographer, and perhaps one that held personal meaning for Cameron.[22] And so, it is important to ask, what could Herschel have meant by referring to himself as 'the old paterfamilias' and, equally important, what did Cameron hear when he uttered those words? I tease out a range of possible meanings below.

We might begin by first considering Cameron's abiding personal affection for Herschel. In 1864, she confided her sentiments in a letter to her friend using the most endearing and tender tone:

> Your eye can best detect & your imagination conceive all that is to be done & is still left undone for you were my first Teacher & to you I owe all the first experiences & insights which were given to me when you sent me in India a score of years ago – the first specimens of Talbotype of photographs coloured by the juices of plants &c &c.[23]

Cameron's high regard and personal appreciation for her mentor, and deep recognition of Herschel's mutual affection for her, come through in this letter, and certainly one can deduce what we might call a certain fatherly attachment ('you were my first Teacher'). The 'paterfamilias', of course, was the traditional 'head of the family', a male authority figure associated with ancient Rome, though not necessarily the father. In Renaissance Italy, the head of the family was also expected to be the family's guide, civic teacher, and moral centre. According to Leon Battista Alberti, for example, 'in the well-conducted family, elders exercise care and discretion in the training of the young, and the young, in turn, behave as they are obliged and duty-bound to do toward their elders'. In this context, one of the obligations of the paterfamilias was to provide guidance to the young on 'how to rule and preserve your own person'.[24] By this time, Herschel had fathered twelve children, a fact well known to Cameron. Even so, given that Cameron was not Herschel's own child, his use of the term 'paterfamilias' in relation to Cameron makes sense as a kind of reciprocal acknowledgement of their deep and longstanding personal attachment, offered by Herschel perhaps as a mutual 'term of endearment' that cements the warmth and affection felt by both parties. By 1867, the two had been friends for some three decades.

Another possible interpretation for Herschel's use of 'paterfamilias' is connected to his role as one of the scientific fathers of photography, as Herschel's chemical experiments with the medium in its early days led to his discovery of how to stop the chemical reaction of unexposed silver salts. Herschel's scientific breakthrough was to submerge the water-saturated paper-based image into a solution of water mixed with potassium-cyanide. This process, called 'fixing' the image, soon came to be practised widely despite its attendant hazards, as cyanide was a known poison. Again in 1864, Cameron honoured Herschel's scientific impact on the practice of photography by connecting his achievements with the Scottish scientist Sir David Brewster, whose optical experiments had also helped refine the medium. She offered to send him a copy of Brewster's most recent speech before the Photographic Society of Scotland, to which she had just been elected a member: 'When I read it I could not help wishing you had been writing on the subject'.[25] And after watching Cameron develop and fix his own photographic portrait in 1867 at Collingwood, Herschel wrote to implore his friend to exercise greater caution with her handling of the dangerous chemistry:

> Since you left us I have been getting more & more uneasy about your free use of that dreadful poison the Cyanide of Potassium – letting it run over your hands so profusely – Pray! Pray! Be more cautious.[26]

A third point of reference that Cameron shared with Herschel was their common interest in the humanistic art of Renaissance Italy, a fact that also inflects our understanding of how Cameron possibly received Herschel's words. Although she did not artificially whiten Herschel's face in 1867, as he had suggested to her prior to their portrait session, Herschel nevertheless recognized that Cameron's artistic rendering of his likeness was fashioned after the aesthetic model of portrait busts sculpted by the ancient Romans. By using the Latin term 'paterfamilias', Herschel could then possibly have signalled his understanding that Cameron's interest in Renaissance sculpture led her to borrow from this earlier aesthetic form, that he approved of her efforts to depict the noble traits and powerful legacy of aristocratic patricians in Rome and the values they hoped to transmit through their sculpture. For her part, Cameron understood that her recent success with Henry Cole at the South Kensington Museum was directly connected to her adoption of the humanistic iconography of these Renaissance-inspired portrait busts. But it may also be that Herschel understood 'paterfamilias' in these terms, which is to say, that like the sculptural examples discussed earlier, he found that Cameron's photographs embodied the Renaissance ideals of family lineage and national identity.

These intersecting ideas were embraced in Victorian Britain. The paterfamilias prototype reinforced an imperial understanding that emphasized the importance of providing for the *nation's* future, not simply an archaic personal concern for representing an individual family's past ancestors or the patriarchal legacy of the father. In Italian Renaissance thinking, especially as it was expressed in humanistic and civic literature, 'one finds increasing discourse on the idea that the fate of both family and state rests upon the moral integrity of its citizens, with special emphasis on its children'.[27] In his book, *I libri della famiglia*, Alberti made this advice an explicit moral and civic imperative:

> [the father] must attempt to make his children moral and upright. Thus may they serve the advantage of the family – moral character being no less precious in a young man than wealth – and be an ornament and credit to their family, their country, and themselves.[28]

The social role of the Victorian paterfamilias, then, was to draw upon this history as a model to cultivate the future society and strengthen the nation by ensuring the integrity of its moral character. This goal would be accomplished by emphasizing the interconnectedness of familial and social responsibility. By nurturing his children in the family institution, the head of the household was understood to be seeding the future participation of his children in relation to the body politic and helping them take their rightful place as citizens, because the family was a microcosm of the state. Embedded in this practice was the stability and preservation of the social and political status quo, a matter of high value for Renaissance Florence as much as for Victorian England. In this way, the continuity of the ancient patrimony could assure the preservation of the nation's character, at home and abroad. In 'Arthur's First Wound', Thackeray invoked the 'fragility' of childhood, the 'slender hands' of 'our young sons', and the need for the nation to protect 'our women and our children in their pain'. These moral and social imperatives reinforced the Victorian's sense of their honourable national character, which in turn was a cornerstone of the imperial mission. These intersecting ideas resonated in Victorian Britain, where the role of the child was undergoing an important rethinking.[29]

But the alignment of national character, imperialism, and scientific advancement was also embedded in Herschel's own career as a public figure. In 1845, for example, at the celebratory dinner of the British Association for the Advancement of Science held in Cambridge in his honour, Herschel was once again welcomed back from the Cape Colony, his reputation now burnished as a kind of 'scientific paterfamilias'. At the reception following the meal, the Dean of Ely Cathedral invoked Herschel's most recent astronomical achievements as the very embodiment of his own patrimony, his fame a reflection of his personal inheritance, and his example an inspiration for future achievements:

> [Herschel] was, indeed, the inheritor of an immortal name. (Loud cheers.). The labours and pursuits of a long life, devoted to the vindication of his illustrious name, would tend, he did trust, to transmit that name with still greater lustre to his descendants. (Continued cheers.) It was the boast of the illustrious family of the Cassinis that they were eminent in the pursuits of astronomy and science to the third and fourth generations. Need he say that it was the prayer of every member of the British Association that the still more illustrious name of Herschel would also be eminent in the annals of science to the third and fourth generation? (Cheers.)[30]

To members of the British Association, Herschel's Obelisk, then under construction in Cape Town, was the physical manifestation of Herschel's personal name and imperial legacy, rendered as a lasting monument across the globe (see fig. 16). As a marker of this ancestral claim, the obelisk also symbolized the scientist's high professional standards, which established future ambitions for all who might follow in his shoes. And because the empire could not be conceived or promoted without appropriate visual representation, in 1845, the *Illustrated London News* reproduced a new engraving of the association's most illustrious honouree (see fig. 28).

Admittedly, these associations are largely symbolic. But in Victorian England, the term 'paterfamilias' was also used as a political and class-based term to convey unquestionable authority, especially among the aristocracy. Herschel's upbringing and classical background would have made these associations familiar.[31] As a social and political term, Hannah Arendt wrote that the meaning and application of 'paterfamilias' was structured by the formal public responsibilities of the citizen:

> the *paterfamilias*, the *dominus*, ruled over his household of slaves and family. And this was not because the power of the city's ruler was matched and checked by the combined powers of household heads, but because absolute, uncontested rule and a political realm properly speaking were mutually exclusive.[32]

The locus of power of individual families, particularly those of the landed aristocracy, was reinforced in Victorian England by these founding ideas. In philological terms, the idea of the *dominus* derives from the actions of an imperial ruler. In political economy, the *dominus* was also a theoretical foundation that informed the governing policies of 'despotic rule' that Parliament imposed over Britain's colonies, particularly India. As we have seen, these intertwined ideas informed Walter Bagehot's essay of 1858 in the aftermath of the Indian Uprising, where he cited the legal arguments of Charles Cameron, as well as the contemporaneous influential political theories of John Stuart Mill about the limits of representative government.

The unquestioned authority of the Victorian paterfamilias was demonstrated by three interlocking features: first, parental authority was reinforced by the physical remoteness of the father from his children; second, social control was established by virtue of the father's sole discretion in manipulating wealth and privilege in his sovereign management of the household; and third, the father's benevolent character was exhibited by his largesse to both family and society. As David Roberts has argued,

> The paternal authority of such fathers extended beyond the living-room of a nuclear family. It made paternal authority generalized, impersonal, and hierarchical; not intimate, confining or enveloping. It formed a pattern of authority that was repeated in the public schools and universities, in the army and navy, and in the Church and local government.[33]

At the same time, however, the class-based austerity revealed by these examples was mitigated somewhat by idealized portraits of tender fathers then being portrayed in British periodicals of the time. These essays and sketches were directed at a middle-class reading public and provided fresh examples of a new and emerging role model for polite society, that of the affectionate father. Tender fathers of this kind regarded the fragility of their newborn infants 'with a look of pitying love', as Thackeray phrased it in his poem 'Arthur's First Wound'.[34] As used in specific texts of the time, then, 'paterfamilias' was a potent allegory for an evolving, mutable kind of male authority that was directly associated with the family and the nation, a term of great importance to the Victorian age.

IN PLAIN SIGHT

Cameron channelled a beam of sunlight into the temporary studio Lady Margaret helped her construct in Herschel's home to reveal these complex and intertwined traits, a photographic technique that she had used for several years, as it emphasized the internal character of her sitters. As early as December 1864, in fact, photographic critics celebrated how Cameron used raking light for this purpose, calling it 'Rembrandt lighting'.[35] This characterization, of course, associated her lighting effects with the artistic control of light as it was painted by Vermeer and Rembrandt, but also, as Richard Dyer has suggested, with the prevailing brilliant white sources of light that are commonly represented in Northern European painting.[36] In formal terms, Cameron's portraits of Carlyle, Tennyson, and Herschel that she photographed with her new apparatus in 1867 depict each sitter at life size in the very front of the picture plane and use Rembrandt lighting to associate their sitters with an idealized and spiritual light, as if their individual characters emanate light from within rather than reflect it. These lighting techniques appealed to Cameron's Pre-Raphaelite contemporaries and can be found in works like Holman Hunt's painting *The Light of the World* (1854). In iconographic terms, light from a celestial source as it was depicted by Hunt and others was associated with the goodness of heaven, while darkness accompanied representations of evil or hell. Dyer also reminds us that so-called 'Northern light' eventually became associated 'literally and symbolically' with 'superior light' because it emanated from 'the region of North Europeans, the whitest whites in the white racial hierarchy'.[37] In this regard, Herschel's advice to Cameron to whiten the faces, hair, and hands of her portrait subjects might have disclosed his awareness of the relationship between visual representations of this kind and the 'pure, white' idealization of patriarchy, masculinity, and European ancestry that this iconographic archetype embodied.

Cameron photographed Herschel, literally and symbolically, 'at home' at Collingwood. Years earlier, the photographer and her sitter met as expatriates in Britain's South African colony and had now returned home, to England. But in her photograph of Herschel, Cameron obscured all possible referents to 'home': she did not photograph him in his study, but rather concealed her sitter's contemporary clothes and masked his modern dwelling and its interior by darkening the room. As an accomplice in this subtle act of camouflage, we might even say that Herschel participated in his own self-representation. The net effect was to create a portrait in which Herschel expressed the stability and permanence of his world. Every temporal, changing, or historical element has been removed. Herschel is paradoxically planted in space and yet locked into the camera's shallow picture plane; his intellectual eminence is displayed by the luminous raking light as if it were radiating forth from his body.

These formal qualities undoubtedly contributed to Herschel's sense of being securely rooted in time, place, and culture, which also likely contributed to his confident assessment that he appeared 'the old paterfamilias'. And yet, although Herschel's self-identification discloses his critical awareness of how his physical likeness reflected certain familial and social realities, psychoanalytic thought stresses that self-identification of this kind is never completely 'finished' or 'known' as a final product. Rather, identification emerges *over time* and is created *in dialogue* with the sitter's own representation. This is because the photograph itself, and the subject's identification with his own portrait, are both recognized to be artificial, constructed realities. Homi Bhabha described the problem in these terms:

> The image is only an *appurtenance* to authority and identity; it must never be read mimetically as the 'appearance' of a 'reality.' The access to the image of identity is only ever possible in the *negation* of any sense of originality or plenitude, through the principle of displacement and differentiation (absence/presence; representation/repetition) that always renders it a liminal reality. The image is at once a metaphoric substitution, an illusion of presence and by that same token a metonym, a sign of its absence and loss. [Original emphasis][38]

As an extension of these ideas, Herschel's statement (to himself and to Cameron) declaring his identity as 'the old paterfamilias' can be understood in relation to the discursive processes in which identification takes shape as a provisional kind of interpretation, an assessment that is of necessity unstable and fluid. By means of Herschel's multiple and overlapping dialogues – with himself, the sitter, and with Cameron, the image-maker – he applied the term 'old paterfamilias' to construct his identity metaphorically and concretely as a 'sovereign subject'.[39] After all, a sovereign subject is one who resists being objectified, who defies easy categorization, and who cannot be discovered conclusively or represented straightforwardly as a knowable, graspable 'object of knowledge'. Therefore, Herschel's declaration is revealing because the subject position that he assumed, recognized, or took for granted was one of empowerment made possible by virtue of his own self-definition. This confrontation with the self takes on even greater importance because Herschel inscribed his own identity as 'the old paterfamilias'. Framed in this way, as articulated by the sovereign subject who was at the same time the portrait subject, we might now recognize 'the old paterfamilias' as the reified embodiment of patriarchal *and* imperial power.

The relative difference in the subject and object positions I have been describing here is clarified even further by comparing Cameron's representation of Herschel in his black cap to her earlier portrait of Iqbal al-Daula (compare fig. 53). As we have seen, the 'ex-King of Oude' confronted the photographer uncomfortably but directly. If she presented Herschel firmly rooted in space, representative of an aristocratic and patrician culture that was settled, 'at home', mature, and 'known', she portrayed Iqbal al-Daula as if appearing to tip back in his chair, gazing sceptically at Cameron through the camera's lens, as if expressing the opposite experience, a colonized culture that was unsettled, uprooted, and displaced, a reflection of Iqbal's disinherited and nomadic status. 'Exiles look at non-exiles with resentment', remarked Edward Said: '*They* belong in their surroundings, you feel, whereas an exile is always out of place.'[40] By extension, Herschel appears composed, even serene, in his far-away 'abstracted' gaze off to the side, a quality that lends to his portrait a 'timeless' quality associated with a national identity that was self-assured in its own authoritative place and historical legacy. Iqbal al-Daula, by contrast, stares back at the photographer and expresses his self-conscious awareness of being objectified through the lens. Iqbal's portrait could almost stand in for the prototype of 'the picture of a gentleman', the term Christopher Pinney used to describe 'the default setting of nineteenth-century photographic apparatus'.[41]

Moreover, Herschel exercised the gift of speech in his dialogue with Cameron, whereas it appears that she photographed Iqbal al-Daula without any commentary from her sitter, or at least, the record of any verbal exchange that might have taken place between the two does not survive. But the self-conscious voice of the kind Herschel expressed to Cameron is one of the essential ways that individuals humanize themselves to themselves, as bell hooks wrote in her seminal book *Talking Back*.[42] Herschel's declaration was therefore an expression of empowered speech because it was from a position of autonomy and liberation, which allowed him to participate in the process of self-identification, whereas Iqbal al-Daula could not 'talk back' within the context of the photographic exchange, and therefore was unable to move from the camera's objectified presence to become its fully realized subject.[43] As a result, Herschel was able to 'complete' his portrait through a conscious and intentionally performative act of his own making. In *Camera Lucida*, Roland Barthes argued that the real power of photography derived from its ability to structure such a performance as it mediated between the photograph and its subject.[44] For Barthes, therefore, posing was an act of self-representation: 'once I feel myself observed by the lens', he wrote, 'everything changes: I constitute myself in the process of "posing," I instantaneously make another body for myself, I transform myself in advance into an image'.[45]

Cameron portrayed Herschel's face emanating from the dark cloak and cap that surrounds him, and, in this way, she defied the temporal relationship of the subject to a fixed position in time. By contrast, Cameron defined Iqbal al-Daula as a transitory figure in space, time, and history: *here*, in this garden behind Little Holland House, facing a member of the former East India Company's governing elite; *here*, eight years after the unsuccessful anti-colonial rebellion, after which the British Crown emphatically ousted the ancestral line of Awadh kings; *here*, in London, separated physically from his homeland in India. In this domestic but ultimately alien space, Cameron represented Iqbal al-Daula in exile, which is to say: nationalism's opposite.[46] Iqbal al-Daula's portrait therefore contains semiotic markers of his identity as a historically defined 'Indian subject': a foreign traveller represented after Britain had assumed governing of the colony, an ex-king stripped of power and authority. In Hannah Arendt's terms, Cameron portrayed Iqbal al-Daula as 'worldless', the terminology Arendt used to describe the condition where one is left without a world in which to dwell.[47] And yet, as an Indian in London wearing dignified European clothes, Iqbal al-Daula participated in his own self-representation, much as Herschel consented to his black drapery and black cap. Consequently, Cameron's representation of Iqbal al-Daula simultaneously portrayed both his cosmopolitan and his imperial status, a recognition of his double identity that creates – and results in – his evident ambivalent expression before the camera.[48]

Because of this complicated status, Iqbal al-Daula's gaze differs markedly from that of Herschel. Herschel stares off to the side and into oblivion, creating an abstract gaze that could connote wonder, perceptiveness, or delight. By contrast, Iqbal al-Daula's confrontation with Cameron reflects the direct and penetrating gaze of awkward self-consciousness. Edward Said theorized that this response, especially as it was expressed by a colonized person in front of a camera operated by a European hand, was the result of learning to live under colonialism. Although Iqbal al-Daula's self-awareness marked him as a 'colonised subject', according to Said, that awareness also taught him how to see more intensely, equipping him with a deeper and more penetrating perspective than merely relying upon his own singular point of view. For Said, this 'deeper kind of seeing' became an asset for colonized peoples when they became exiled or displaced from their homelands:

> The essential privilege of exile is to have, not just one set of eyes but half a dozen, each of them corresponding to the places you have been. ... There is always a kind of doubleness to that experience, and the more places you have been the more displacements you've gone through, as every exile does.[49]

Cameron's portrait of Iqbal al-Daula embodies this unique sense of doubleness. On the one hand, because she omitted his name from her title, Cameron erased her sitter's individuality, rendering him invisible. And yet, she also identified her subject using terms that only further objectified him in both time and place by using categorizing language to define his royal lineage, to situate his geographical origins, and identify his ethnic history. Presented to her public as the *ex-King of Oude by right of birth*, Cameron's title can only be called classificatory, even taxonomic, the anonymous tools of modern ethnography. Framed in this way, she signified the exact opposite of the timelessness and permanence that she embodied in her portrait of Herschel. The 'old paterfamilias' is unmarked by time and place and therefore universalized in humanistic terms associated with the fine arts tradition. By contrast, in Cameron's portrait of Iqbal al-Daula, her sitter stares right back at her, directly confronting the photographer's imperialist eyes, a living embodiment of the shadow of colonialism.

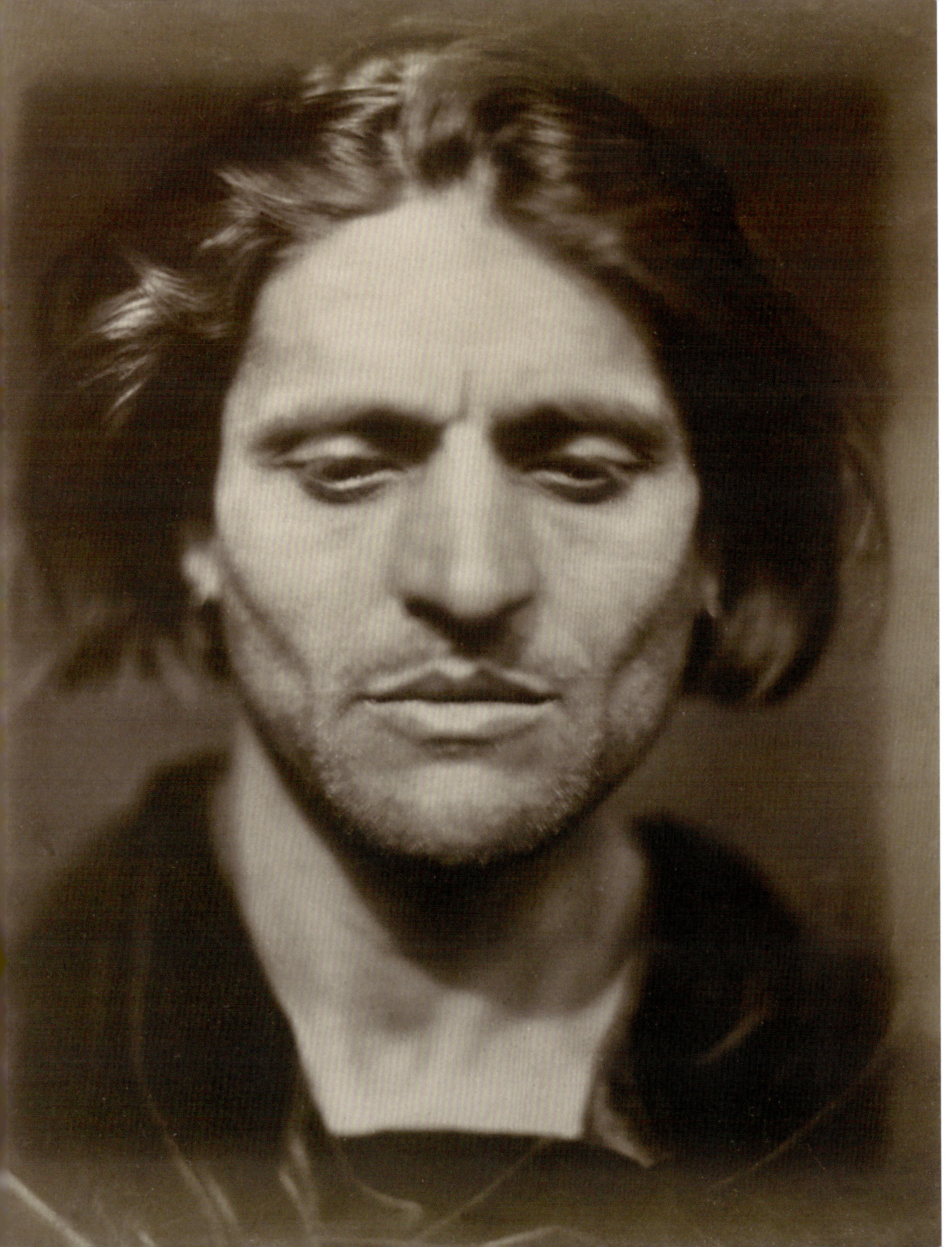

Conclusion
Reclaiming 'Iago'

99 Julia Margaret Cameron, *Iago, Study from an Italian*, 1867, albumen print, 33.4 × 24.8 cm. National Science & Media Museum / Science Museum Group. 1984–5017/69.

THE MEMORIAL WELL AT TEN YEARS

Julia Margaret Cameron dedicated her photographic album to Herschel on 8 September 1867. Two months later, the British Viceroy, Sir John Lawrence, and the colonial government's Resident in Awadh, Sir John Strachey, held an elaborate pageant in Lucknow to cement the new power structure that Britain established in the former kingdom, where the real power of the deposed princes was now only nominal. This ceremonial pageant, called a *durbar*, was held to mark the ten-year anniversary of the Uprising against the government of the East India Company. Held over several days, the event included a state visit to important governmental sites, a formal reception with the Viceroy and Resident hosting the historical royal family of Awadh, now deposed, and a mile-long procession of English and Indian dignitaries that featured thousands of attendees and more than 400 elephants.[1] The ceremony in Lucknow established the prototype for future coronation *durbars* that were to follow in Delhi in 1877, 1903, and 1911.[2]

As an eyewitness to this event, the London-based reporter for *The Times* also wrote about visiting the site of the Cawnpore Well, his first occasion to do so since reporting as a correspondent during the rebellion. Now, ten years later, he was finally able to view Baron Marochetti's sculpted angel in situ. The sculpture itself was finally installed in 1865 and popularized in a photograph by Samuel Bourne (see fig. 72). In the aftermath of the revolt, once the British restored order, this site soon became a pilgrimage spot on what became known as 'mutiny tours'. Shifting from the *durbar* to the Memorial Well, *The Times*'s reporter emphasized this sense of visiting a holy shrine, offering an assessment from one of the faithful:

> The Well is approached by a mound, around which stands an octagonal screen of exquisitely carved stonework. Entering by a door carefully watched, as the whole garden is, we descend to the pit's mouth, around which the bones were literally scattered. From it, on a pedestal, arises Baron Marochetti's figure of Pity, or Mercy, or Hope, or Triumph, or all combined – a female figure, dressed in angel's robes, with angel's wings, and bearing in her hands the 'martyr's holy palms'.[3]

Curiously, the reporter recites a narrow range of possible meanings conveyed by Marochetti's statue – 'Pity, or Mercy, or Hope, or Triumph, or all combined' – making it clear the writer was *not* intending to be complementary about the multiple and overlapping symbolic associations. In his account, he even complained further about the look of the angel itself. Noting it was 'dressed in angel's robes' and even possessed 'angel's wings', it was nevertheless unremarkable as fully 'angelic' in his eyes. As if in exasperation, he declared, 'there is no expression in the face, no grace in attitude, no meaning in the position of the arms and palm branches'. One imagines he was not alone in expressing disappointment for the angel's inscrutable expression and its many possible intersecting symbolic references.

This account raises important considerations about the many ways artists convey meaning in the visual arts and the equally complex nature of interpretation. We have seen that, in Britain, the dominant story of the historical events in Cawnpore was dependent upon narrative repetition, but also that Viceroy Canning himself struggled to define an appropriate symbolic attitude and allegorical reference point for the statue he had commissioned. It is therefore useful to examine the intersecting symbolic references listed here. And it is also important to remember that such associations are not fixed forever as immutable emblems. Rather, a viewer's relationship to works of art invariably alters and is revised over time, as an individual changes and matures, confronts new influences, or acquires new knowledge or historical insights. Equally important, legends, stories, personal accounts, and private memories fade, just as letters, diaries, and newspapers are often discarded. In short, no two moments in time are likely to produce precisely the same impact upon any one viewer or group of viewers, and an English visitor to the Memorial Well might very well experience mourning one day and triumph the next. As *The Times*'s reporter wrote, 'Pity, or Mercy, or Hope, or Triumph, or all combined'. But because 'the story is in every Englishman's mouth', as Thackeray wrote, *The Times*'s correspondent was able to find that emblems of mourning *and* triumph were *both* present in the statue's emblematic form.

Ironically (in relation to the correspondent's complaints), Marochetti's sculpted angel actually *reaffirmed* the narrative authority of the story *and* endorsed the semiotic success of the intertwined iconography. In short, a mere ten years after the Uprising, the legend of the massacre at the Cawnpore Well had apparently 'passed from history to nature', as Roland Barthes phrased it, meaning that the angel sculpture over the Memorial Well had entered the realm of mythology. Paradoxically, wrote Barthes, once symbols become myths, they lose their historical specificity:

> In passing from history to nature, myth acts economically: it abolishes the complexity of human acts, it gives them the simplicity of essences, it does away with all dialectics, with any going back beyond what is immediately visible, it organizes a world which is without contradictions because it is without depth, a world wide open and wallowing in the evident, it establishes a blissful clarity.[4]

Like stereotypes and other examples of endlessly repeated symbolic forms, mythologies similarly require narrative repetition, not because they are wholly without meaning otherwise, but because their world, constructed apparently free of contradictions, is inherently unstable and requires regular reaffirmation and reminder.

These observations about the conflicting interpretations of symbolic form apply equally to Cameron's photography. A prime example is illustrated by the debates of contemporary art historians concerning a unique photograph in the Herschel Album that she titled *Iago, Study from an Italian* (Cox/Ford 634; HA-69; fig. 99). Only a single image is known today, and scholars disagree widely about its interpretation. For some, the 'blissful clarity' about which Barthes wrote is not evident in Cameron's photograph, despite the photograph's explicit title, which references one of the two main characters in Shakespeare's play *Othello, the Moor of Venice*. At first glance, the photograph, a head shot of a man, appears much like one of Cameron's 'series of 12 Life sized heads' (see fig. 97), the full-framed compositions that the photographer captured using her new camera and lens in the shortened depth-of-field she favoured. Moreover, situated as it is in the Herschel Album, *Iago* is accompanied in the volume by another close-up portrait depicting a different character in Shakespeare's plays, that of Henry Taylor in the role of *Prospero* (Cox/Ford 779; HA-75; fig. 100).

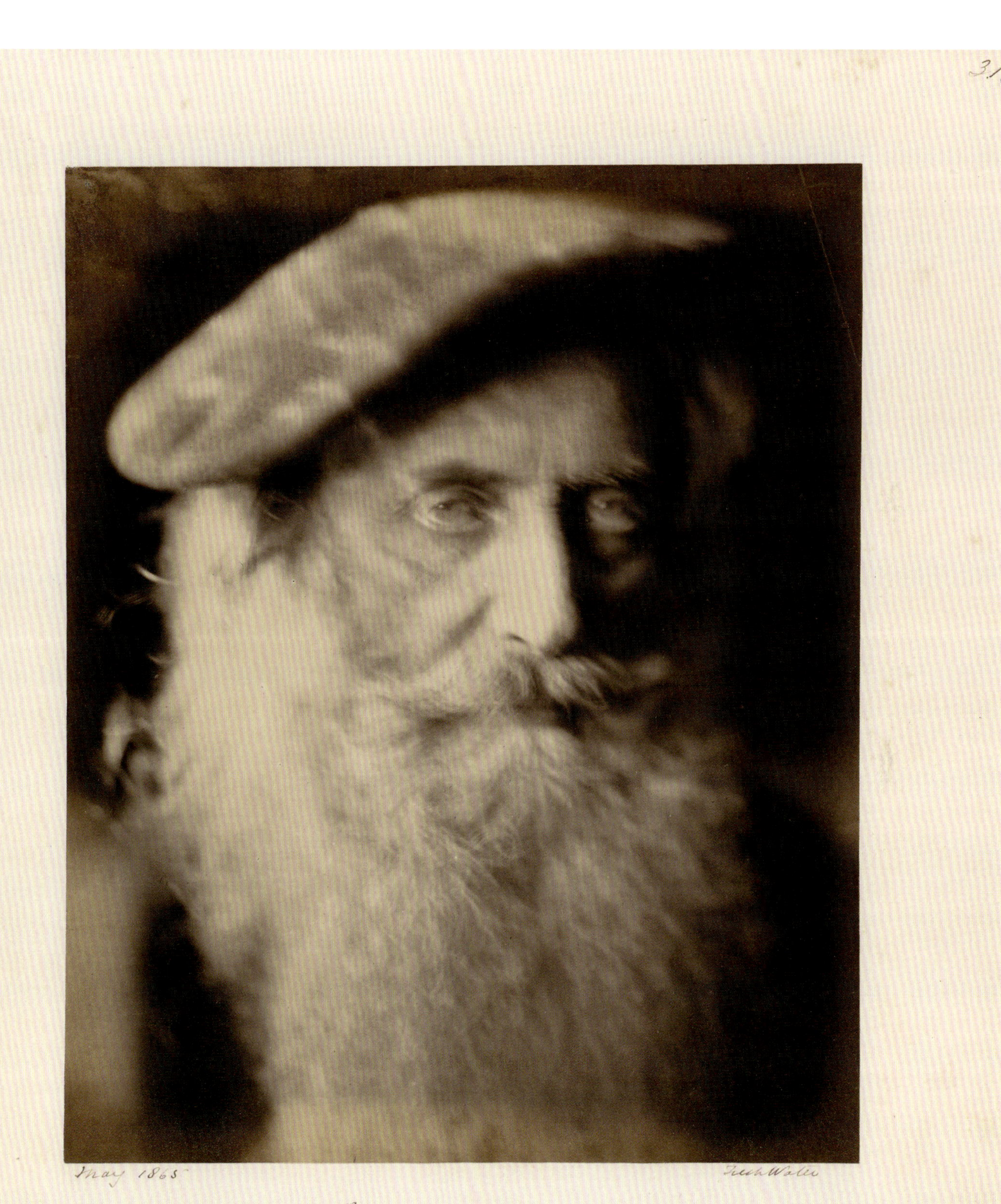

100 Julia Margaret Cameron, *Prospero*, 1865, albumen print, 26.8 × 21.4 cm.

J. Paul Getty Museum, 84.XZ.186.32. Digital image courtesy of Getty's Open Content Program.

Conceptually and compositionally, the two photographs are more alike visually than they are different. Both representations are close-up character studies of a man's face, but beyond physical similarities, interpretation of these two photographs varies drastically. *Prospero*, for example, has been seamlessly woven into the Cameron canon as a stellar example of her portraits of 'great men', where the image and model's physiognomy is interpreted as the embodiment of timeless human values. As an example, Julian Cox writes that Cameron's model and Shakespeare's character are aligned, both sympathetically and artistically. For Shakespeare, Cox argues, Prospero was understood as

> a mercurial scholar who learns the secret powers of nature after many years of laborious study. [In her photograph,] Cameron depicts the character as a sage-like figure with an arresting appearance. Taylor's head entirely fills the frame; Cameron underscores the realism of his portrait in proportion and personality by inscribing the mount of the print with the word 'Life'.[5]

As seen here, Cox implies that Cameron's genius as a photographer was to recognize and then capitalize on joining the unique look and personality of her sitter, Taylor, to the equally 'sage-like' attributes of Shakespeare's character, Prospero. By contrast, *Iago* has confounded modern historians and entered the current period as if this image must be continually renegotiated. Like the multiple associations attached to Marochetti's angel, 'Pity, or Mercy, or Hope, or Triumph, or all combined', as it was expressed in 1867, contemporary historians similarly express dissatisfaction with, and doubt about, Cameron's representation of Iago. They have questioned her choice of model, mistrusted her use of extreme lighting effects, quarrelled over the model's detached and downward gaze, and distrusted the apparent opacity of the image. The net effect has been to undermine the narrative authority of the subject itself.

This renegotiation is quite unlike like the apparent dissatisfaction expressed by *The Times*'s reporter as described above, whose frustration at least did not discredit the very depiction of the angel, but asked instead how to settle on one or another of the symbolic associations the angel represented. Conversely, the contemporary controversy over Cameron's *Iago* has exposed open disagreement and frank denial about her depiction of the character itself and led to an eagerness for disregarding her use of explicit titles altogether, as if her intended subject was open to second-guessing. Several open doors in the historical record have made such an interpretive reassessment possible. Unlike the numerous copies of *Prospero*, for example, only one print exists of *Iago*, as Cameron might have damaged or broken the glass negative. And Herschel, the intended recipient of the image, either never recorded his reaction to the photograph or, if he did, his sentiments are now lost. Complicating this history of the photograph is the fact that Cameron never publicly exhibited the print, which is to say that her representation of Iago has escaped a historical critical assessment from the moment she first produced the image, leaving its interpretation open to later historians.

IAGO'S INSCRUTABILITY

Depending upon one's perspective, viewers tend to find this photographic portrait either sympathetic or harsh; they ascribe the model's demeanour as menacing or tranquil; they find the image dark and frightening or light and serene. Cameron's photograph seems to invite such opposing reactions; rarely do viewers find these inverse qualities are present simultaneously. Ironically, then, the photograph may be said to have achieved at least one measure of Cameron's success in rendering a believable portrait of a split identity. Said another way, the photograph embodies a character study of great complexity, one marked by double articulations and torn allegiances, and the dual, opposing nature of these qualities in the image hits the mark admirably. After all, as portrayed by Shakespeare and telegraphed throughout *Othello*, the character of Iago is meant to represent both honesty and duplicity; composure and disquiet; honourable trustworthiness and deceitful treacherousness. From the outset of the play, the audience is made aware of his scheming deception and disloyalty. Accordingly, the photograph's fixation on the model's face, the place where he expresses his torn loyalties and divided personality, enhances the intensity of Cameron's depiction of the character's opposing qualities.

Importantly, Cameron did not depict Iago in any one scene from the play, did not picture him uttering any specific lines, and did not represent her model expressing one of his many cunning attributes, as opposed to the many other qualities that comprise this complex character. By contrast, in 1865, Cameron made several compositions that portray specific scenes from Shakespeare's plays, like *Romeo and Juliet*. In the Herschel Album, for example, she included two versions of *Friar Laurence and Juliet*, in which she posed her models enacting lines from Act IV, scene 1 (Cox/Ford 1089; HA-84; and Cox/Ford 1090; HA-85). On 10 July 1867, Cameron sent for copyright protection yet another photograph also inspired by the same play, a version she titled simply *Romeo and Juliet* (Cox/Ford 1107; HA-65; fig. 101). Here, Cameron depicted her two models enacting a specific moment when the two characters embrace, a set-up much like the image included in the Herschel Album. On one of the prints of this image (Cox/Ford 1106), she made it clear that the photograph could all but illuminate the dramatic action itself, as she wrote lines of the play from Act II, scene 2, below the image: 'Yet I should kill thee with much cherishing / Good night good night parting is such sweet sorrow / That I could say good night until tomorrow'. The two versions of *Friar Laurence and Juliet* used models who were familiar with the photographer and her processes, notably her friend Henry Taylor and her maid Mary Ann Hillier. For *Romeo and Juliet*, she posed different models – Mary Ryan and Henry Cotton.

As we have seen in the example of Cox's interpretation of *Prospero*, above, historians have often used the identity of Cameron's models as a kind of index or guide to interpreting her imagery, as if Cameron's success demanded, or was dependent upon, an alignment of her model's personality and the allegorical subject of the photograph. Consequently, much has been made of Cameron's use of Ryan and Cotton because of their personal story. For example, historians have noted how Cameron was charmed by the mutual attraction Cotton and Ryan expressed for each other at the sitting and how the budding romance led to their taking marriage vows only several weeks later. Scholars have not only taken this story as evidence of Cameron's matchmaking skills, they have portrayed the union as if it were evidence that affirms the photographer's direct and honest approach towards her subjects and marks her influence over those in her domestic orbit, using these personal stories to demonstrate that she intentionally chose her models to align with the allegorical subjects she represented.

Unlike this composition, which depicts a specific scene in *Romeo and Juliet*, Cameron's photograph of Iago portrays an abstracted figure, an extreme close-up photograph of a man's face, one that provides no context and no reference point in the play. The image itself pushes the technology of photography to the maximum threshold of legibility by flattening the model's face against a shallow picture plane and by providing focus to the centre of the face while softly blurring the edges. Consequently, Cameron's portrait lacks virtually any kind of situational reference points whatsoever. Given this conspicuous lack of context, scholars have sought to assign meaning, once again, by identifying the model Cameron used in making the image. Noting that the photographer herself subtitled her photograph of Iago '*Study from an Italian*', the search for Cameron's model led investigators on a hunt, of sorts. After first examining paintings in Watts's studio, scholars identified the model for *Iago* as Alessandro Colorossi, and then, after further examination, determined his identity as belonging to Angelo Colarossi. Historians confirmed that this individual was not a professional stage actor, as one might assume, but rather a professional artist's model who was employed in this capacity by esteemed painters like Jean-Léon Gérôme, Lord Leighton, Frederick Sandys, John Everett Millais, and John Singer Sargent.[6] More recent scholarship has even thrown the Colarossi identification into doubt, as new documentation has emerged asserting that Alessandro di Marco, another professional studio model with a similar build and facial structure to Colarossi, was also popular among these artists.[7]

The use of professional models by painters, sculptors, and photographers during this era is indeed fascinating. And while these identifications have established interesting details about the ways that Royal Academy schools taught artists and how the same model was able to attract painters who were competing for similar commissions, they unfortunately do not bring us any closer to interpreting Cameron's photograph of Iago or

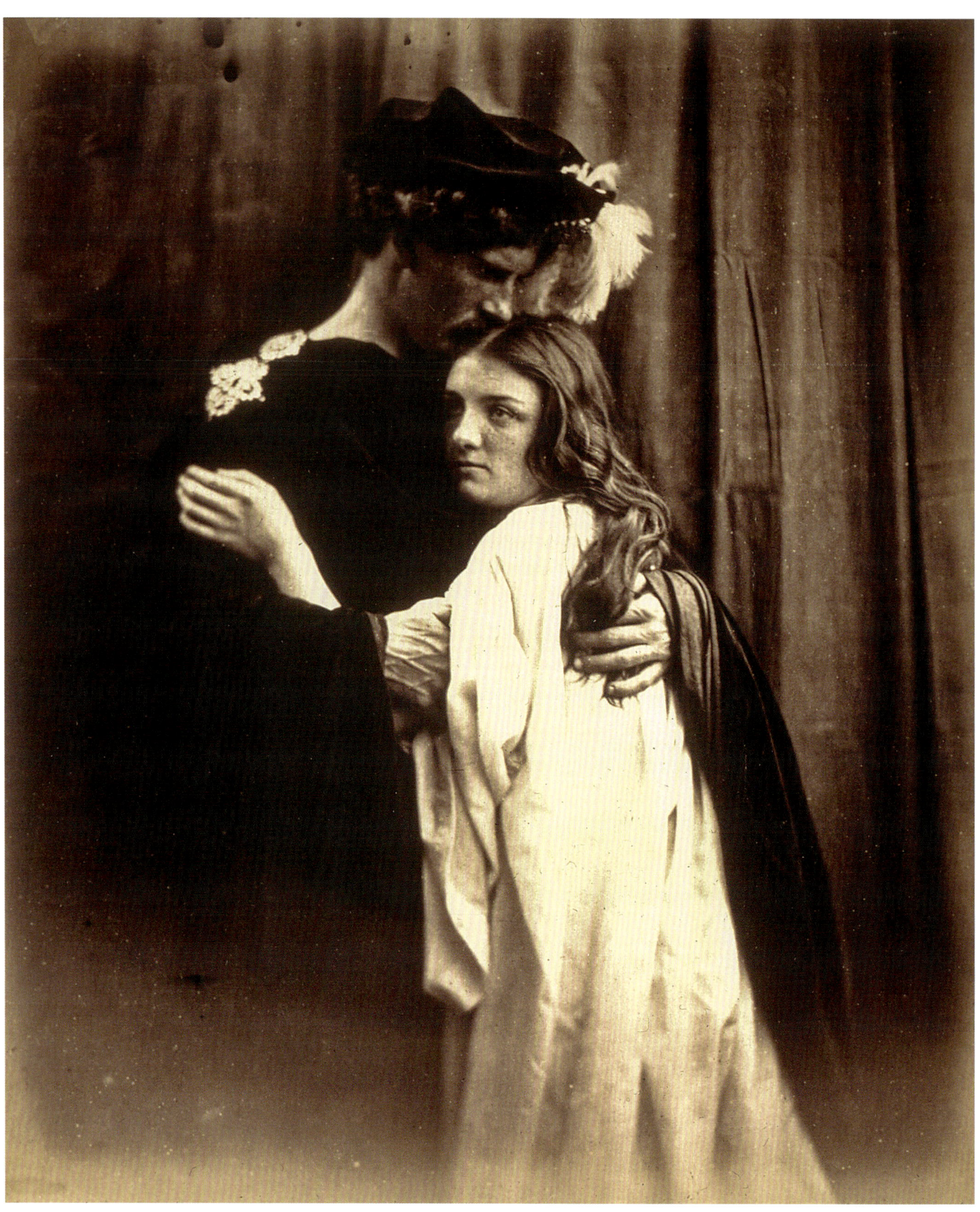

101 Julia Margaret Cameron, *Romeo and Juliet*, 1867, albumen print, 28.9 × 23.3 cm.
National Science & Media Museum / Science Museum Group. 10312785.

to explaining why she might have included it in Herschel's Album. Even if one were successful in identifying her Italian model conclusively, one would risk merging the personal attributes and appearance of Colarossi (or di Marco) with Shakespeare's character Iago, thereby placing a very high premium on the accurate identity of the model to assign meaning. But by over-investing in the model's personal traits or expression, this line of inquiry reduces photographic meaning into a peculiar kind of identity-blurring between the photographer's model and her intended subject.[8]

As I have established in my earlier study on Cameron, another of her models, Marie Spartali, was also widely admired for her physical appearance and, like Colarossi and di Marco, posed as a model for painters in Cameron's circle, notably Rossetti and Burne-Jones. But the diverse photographs that Cameron ultimately created from just one sitting with Spartali produced a wide range of discrete and disconnected allegorical subjects, including *Hypatia*, *The Spirit of the Vine*, *Memory*, *Mnemosyne*, *The Imperial Eleänore*, and *La Donna at her Devotions*.[9] Over the next several years, Cameron posed Spartali in no fewer than twenty additional sittings. Similarly, Henry Taylor posed for *Prospero*, but also as *Friar Laurence*, as *King David*, and as *Philip Van Artevelde*, and all appear in the Herschel Album. For some historians, Taylor radiated his unique, personal 'sage-like' character into his modelling for these literary figures. Even so, this still tells us nothing about how Cameron or her audience distinguished between these photographs as allegorical representations. The chief question, then, should not be whether Cameron drew upon the personal attributes or appearance of Taylor in relation to his personification of Friar Laurence or King David, but rather, to ask how and why Cameron used models like Taylor to create believable narrative imagery, and then, to ask what possible meanings these subjects held for her contemporaries.[10]

Nevertheless, the compelling physical features of Colarossi and di Marco have encouraged much speculation over time. Sally Barnden has noted that Cameron's photograph of Iago is unlike her other work in photography, chiefly because of its extreme close-up framing. In her analysis, Barnden shifted the emphasis away from portraiture to understand the photograph as an *academic study*, arguing that *Iago* should be placed in the discursive tradition of the 'fine arts study'. As she writes, the photograph's full title – *Iago, Study from an Italian*

> invokes the vocabulary of drawing and painting, claiming implicitly first that art is serious intellectual work and then that photography preserves the status of the artist in relation to that work.[11]

As an academic study, then, Barnden emphasizes that the model's status is primary, that he is represented as a photographic subject (as opposed to a portrait subject). This is accentuated by his anonymity and unreadable costume, tacit features of timeless academic studies since the Renaissance. By contrast, Taylor sports a beret as he takes on the guise of *Prospero*, which at a minimum associates him with Western costume in the modern period. Barnden also stresses how *Iago*'s extreme close-up differs significantly from longstanding conventions established to depict actors in a dramatic role, which historically have emphasized costume to convey the role played and used the representational format '[actor's name] as [character's name]'. As a result, Barnden argues that by using the term *Study* in her title, Cameron 'implies that the character in this case is *conjured in the act of photographing*; [the model's] face is the raw material from which Cameron produces her Iago' (my emphasis).[12]

Now redefined as photographic 'raw material', Barnden proposed that Cameron intentionally rendered Iago's face as an opaque mask, rather than as a transparent portrait of a Shakespearean character, as she did when portraying Taylor as *Prospero*. Unlike this photograph, in *Iago* Cameron directed her Italian model to gaze down, out of the line of sight; she then lit the contours of his face starkly, from above, casting deep shadows. To the extent that we might be able to divine the model's expressive intentions, we have only a paucity of visual clues, as his eyes are shielded by heavy lids, disguised in darkness, and obscured from view. As an academic 'Study', then, Cameron's photograph is emphatically *not* a representation of an actor in the role of 'Iago', portraying any one moment in the play, either on- or off-stage. As a result, Barnden regards this image as wholly foreign to the imagined portfolio we might construct of the many stage actors who portrayed Iago in commercial performances. When artists depicted these actors, they portrayed them in full costume and, in the caption, expressed their portrayals in the formula described above ('[actor's name] as [character's name]'). These images almost always represented a unique dramatic moment, depicting the actor *in media res*, that is, in the act of speaking or acting out specific lines.[13]

Although this formula predated the Victorian era, it was reinforced repeatedly during Cameron's day. In fact, the context of the specific play and performance of *Othello*, in particular, was considered especially important for positioning these visual representations, as histories of the actor's trade underscore how performers assigned to portray Othello and Iago on stage would agree to switch parts on designated nights. On the one hand, this practice allowed the performers to demonstrate their dramatic virtuosity; on the other, by switching roles on a regular schedule, the actors could avoid being stereotyped by negative associations connected to either role.[14] In addition, Iago's and Othello's stage performances were typically marked by differences in costume, defining one as Christian and the other as Muslim. Consequently, because no defining costume is evident in Cameron's photograph of Iago, she further obscured any clear identification of her subject.[15]

Iago's inscrutability as a portrait subject led Mike Weaver to draw new conclusions about the photograph. He first amplified upon the interconnected observations described above – that is, he extended the idea that Cameron used Colarossi or di Marco as a kind of 'raw material', he magnified Cameron's focus on the model's apparent opacity as a subject, and he emphasized the status of the 'academic study' alluded to in her title – and then connected these observations as if they revealed a cohesive strategy. Startlingly, Weaver proposed that Cameron never intended to depict 'Iago' after all. Following the logic of his own interpretive line of inquiry, which is based upon the belief that Cameron used Christian taxonomies as the chief iconographic foundation of her work, Weaver declared that Cameron represented Iago as a photographic interpretation of Jesus Christ as the Man of Sorrows. Weaver made this claim without any historical evidence to support his contention. In the process, he consciously erased Cameron's title *Iago* as it appeared in the Table of Contents to the Herschel Album, as if this were negotiable to begin with. Provocatively, he asked, 'could we not have here a preposterous and beautiful attempt to depict Christ?'[16] Weaver then looked for support for this idea and found it from Michel Frizot, who extended the impression that Cameron's photograph was untethered to any particular subject matter or historical grounding. Frizot claimed that Cameron used 'Iago' in an arbitrary way, as if the title were merely a cunning stratagem. Why would she do so? By drawing her title from Shakespeare, Frizot wrote, Cameron could deflect 'the ultimate taboo of depicting the Messiah naturalistically'.[17]

But in arguing to separate *Iago*'s title from her image, it must be said, Weaver and Frizot have proposed that we deny Cameron her very subject, that is, the character of Iago, and ignore the historical relevance of Shakespeare's play, *The Tragedy of Othello, the Moor of Venice*, for her Victorian audience. And yet, there is absolutely nothing from the nineteenth-century record to substantiate or support this idea, as much as a modernist notion might want to step aside from the subject and argue one way (or the other) for (or against) how much (or how little) Cameron's model Colarossi (or di Marco) actually resembled an idealized image of the Man of Sorrows.[18] The historical evidence, by contrast, argues that Victorians would have found a photographic representation of Christ as highly problematic. Nothing in Cameron's biography would have prepared her for knowingly creating an audacious representation of Christ and then deliberately using a Shakespearean character to hide or masquerade her efforts. In the wake of the 1865 publication of *Essays and Reviews*, moreover, which pitted clerics of the Broad Church against those of the High Church and led to the fierce public outcry against Benjamin Jowett for proposing that the Bible should be interpreted like 'any other book', any explicit effort to represent Christ in photographic form would have been regarded as dangerous and would have been met with explicit charges of blasphemy.[19] The religious prohibitions of the time therefore plainly argue against such a representation. And even if one wanted to engage in an obscure philological dispute that argues over Shakespeare's intention to represent Othello's actions in Act V as an allegorical shift from Christ to Judas, such a limited, text-based consideration involves the motivations and actions of Othello, and *not* Iago, and in any case, is an abstruse literary and historical debate that emerged only in the twentieth century.[20]

Moreover, there is no evidence to support the idea that Cameron regarded her devotional subjects, like the series of Madonnas she called *The Fruits of the Spirit*, as if they were physically imbued with sacred or reverential substance, as if these photographs were materially equivalent to holy icons. Rather, as we have seen, Cameron bisected her photograph representing the Madonna with Christ and St John (see fig. 82), then discarded the upper portion depicting the Virgin, in order to isolate the two children as primary subjects, ultimately settling on using that smaller fragment from the original print to create a version of Charles Kingsley's *Water Babies* (see fig. 83). Not only did Cameron refrain from investing sacred meaning in photographs like these, but she also valued their public display as accessible objects of study, sending them to the South Kensington Museum and the British Museum, mounting them for public display in the French or German Galleries, pasting them to the album page. 'Cult value', by contrast, depends upon *inaccessibility*, where sacred or holy relics or divine images like that of Christ would be entirely withdrawn from public view and available only to a very few.[21] In the Herschel Album, *Iago* is positioned only six album pages away from *Prospero*, and occupies a prominent spot amid portraits of Taylor and Tennyson.[22] In 1868, William Allingham observed Cameron in the act of posing one of the Tennysons' housemaids as a model for *Desdemona*.[23] Although she might never have produced such an image, and an extant print of this subject has never been found, Allingham's anecdote helps us establish that Cameron pursued at least some sustained interest in depicting characters from *Othello*.

Regrettably, Weaver's and Frizot's interpretations have endured, but not without the undesirable effect on Cameron scholarship that allows for a model's apparent opacity to replace its evident allegorical title, and in the process, erase its very subject matter, sanctifying the photograph as if it were a devotional object in the Christian tradition, and worse, detaching the entire analysis from history and politics. Rather than attempting to connect this photograph's evident ambiguities to a rigorously historical framework, Weaver and Frizot have instead proposed an ahistorical 'narrative free-for-all', one that allows 'almost any notion or narrative to sail under a Shakespearean flag and claim the legitimacy that bequeaths', as Barnden has conspicuously phrased it.[24] But this process of loosening the tether that anchors a Shakespearean text to a particular historical moment is not a phenomenon unique to the visual arts. In fact, as Adrian Poole has demonstrated, the process of assimilating the identity and history of Shakespeare's characters across different media had already begun to take place, even in Cameron's time: 'Once Shakespeare's characters are liberated from their dramatic contexts – into other media, into other words – there is no knowing what they may help to unleash'.[25] But Iago was not 'liberated' in this way, and certainly not by Cameron, who assigned 'Iago' to her print in the Herschel Album and sent the photograph to Kew for copyright protection on 4 July 1867, with the explicit notation: 'Male, bust, full face entitled "Iago".'[26]

Moreover, rather than deny Cameron her title *and* her subject matter, as Weaver and Frizot have endorsed, I want to reaffirm the importance of the original text in the Herschel Album (and restore the subject and its historical relevance in Cameron studies) by securely tying the photograph directly to a range of likely meanings for viewers of the image in 1867. Rather than invent sacred associations between Iago and Christ where none are present in Shakespeare's drama, where none were evident in Victorian staged productions of the play, and where none impelled the photographer to create an image of Christ masquerading as Iago, I want to examine what kind of political importance Iago had for British audiences, and in particular, among Cameron's circle. And rather than detach Iago from the narrative associations the character acquired for Victorian audiences, as if we could allow the image to accommodate virtually any range of possible alter-egos, or substitute Christ for Iago in a modernist turn where meaning is fluid and unreliable, I want to re-establish the historical significance of the text-based narrative structure that gave Iago his importance, to Shakespeare, to Cameron, and to the Victorians. In fact, evidence of Iago's importance to the Victorians is present in essays published by Cameron's closest circle.

This book has argued that Julia Margaret Cameron's interest in and exploration of an imperial rhetoric of power – one that was born in colonial India, seared by the convulsive British reactions to the Indian Uprising, and nurtured by the literary and artistic circles of Holland Park, Kensington, and Freshwater – provides us with an interconnected narrative structure and discursive model that together provides an essential context for key works in the Herschel Album and throughout her *oeuvre*. The same approach may be used to restore Cameron's photograph of Iago as an allegorical subject of historical and political importance to audiences in Victorian England.

THE STAGE DRAMA

Historical context and setting are important to Shakespearian dramas, not incidental colourful background. As Martin Orkin wrote about *Othello*, the play's setting in Venice and its relationship to the island colony of Cyprus was significant historically:

> Evidence suggests that the Venetian state and its island Cyprus, for at least the influential and powerful élite in early seventeenth-century audiences watching *Othello*, would have invited keen, pointed interest.[27]

Victorian audiences were similarly attached to Shakespeare's portrayal of established political institutions and the social status of the performers in those roles. As Samuel Taylor Coleridge wrote, Shakespeare

> should be styled a philosophical aristocrat, delighting in those hereditary institutions which have a tendency to bind one age to another, and in that distinction of ranks, of which, although few may be in possession all enjoy the advantages.[28]

A decade later, Charles Cameron's close friend Thomas Babington Macaulay distinguished between the two chief actors in *Othello*. He asserted that an Italian audience of the Renaissance would have viewed the character of Othello with 'nothing but detestation and contempt'. On the other hand, he argued that the same spectators would have regarded Iago with admiration. Macaulay wrote that the same sentiments accorded to both characters would also have been held by nineteenth-century audiences:

> The conduct of Iago they would assuredly have condemned; but they would have condemned it as we condemn that of his victim. Something of interest and respect would have mingled with their disapprobation. The readiness of the traitor's wit, the clearness of his judgment, the skill with which he penetrates the dispositions of others and conceals his own, would have insured to him a certain portion of their esteem.[29]

In his *Life and Letters of Lord Macaulay*, George Trevelyan noted that his uncle loved Shakespeare's plays. Macaulay possessed the twelve-volume edition produced in 1778 and, according to Trevelyan, annotated these volumes with his thoughts in ink.[30] 'Macaulay reckoned *Othello* the best play extant in any language', wrote Trevelyan, adding, 'It may well be that he had ceased reading it because he knew the whole of it by heart'.[31] In his comments above, Macaulay essentially describes Iago's role as that of the anti-hero, although he did not use that term. Nineteenth-century British audiences did not unilaterally brand Iago a villain, nor did Macaulay understand the character as defined solely by a one-dimensional trait, like evil. Rather, according to Macaulay, Iago was to be appreciated, even respected, not only for his command of narrative, of reason, and rhetorical vitality, but as I will demonstrate, because this character is unique for exerting a particular kind of imperial power: Iago sows chaos in order to restore order. Closely related, contemporary analyses have regarded Iago as the essential 'focusing agent' of the play; as Charles Baxter and Susan Neville have argued, his character is necessary to the unfolding of the drama.[32] But historically speaking, Iago focuses the action of the play only because he is the chief agent of imperial order.

The imperial context of the drama seized the imagination of Victorian audiences. Almost all of the action in *Othello* takes place in Cyprus, then a colony of Venice. But the context of the drama is set in an uncertain world because it is threatened by Ottoman expansion, during both the Renaissance and the Victorian era: 'Othello registers nascent English anxieties about cultural alterity and the looming threat of losing one's identity to the Islamic Ottoman Empire', wrote Debra Johanyak.[33] By emphasizing the setting in this way, we may reconsider how, for British audiences, the play would have represented a site of anxiety and concern over Ottoman influence in the Mediterranean, not only with respect to maritime commerce, but also in relation to the global conflict between East and West.

For Julia Margaret and Charles Cameron, the political stability of the Mediterranean was also of longstanding personal concern. Years earlier, in 1851, after having retired from his post in India, Charles had put in his name to be considered for a colonial governorship in the Mediterranean. He was most interested in ruling over the island of Malta or the confederacy called the Ionian Islands. Both colonial territories were associated with the shifting political control and conflict between rival empires in the region.[34] Prior to 1797, for example, Venice managed the Ionian Islands, when France and Russia then vied for their control. This power struggle was resolved in 1815, when the Treaty of Paris conferred control of the islands upon Britain. The Colonial Office then managed the island republic as a protectorate and took advantage of their natural seaports to shelter the Royal Navy.[35] When Disraeli finally ceded the Ionian Islands to Greece in 1864, so too did he end Charles's hopes to assume the post of colonial governor in the region.[36] And in nearby Cyprus, then under Turkish control, the return of the Ionian Islands was greeted with enthusiasm by Greek nationalists, who were hostile to Ottoman rule and desperately wanted to bring about a similar reunion of Cyprus to Greece.[37]

Therefore, while the governmental structure of Venice might seem incidental to the conflict between the characters in *Othello*, 'in fact it is indispensable for generating the basic dramatic situation, and it influences every personal relationship in the play', as Mark Matheson has persuasively argued.[38] Moreover, the island of Cyprus, as opposed to the governmental seat of Venice, must be read as the chief contested zone of conflict in *Othello*, as it was balanced uncomfortably in-between the Muslim, Ottoman East and the Christian, Venetian (read European) West.[39] Consequently, the second act of *Othello* is pivotal. As Colm MacCrossan summarized it, Cyprus

> has been on high alert for an invasion [from the Ottoman Turks]. A defence force has been sent out from Venice. There is a huge storm at sea, due to which the defenders might not make it over safely. Instead, however, news arrives that the enemy has been wiped out by the storm. As Othello puts it, 'Our wars are done, the Turks are drowned' (2.1.203).[40]

What follows is Iago's inexplicable embrace of chaos and discord: his intentional disruption of the peace, his insertion of a 'private and domestic quarrel' into the public affairs of the state, and his manipulation of others in his orbit to advance his own position. Othello takes charge to demand civility and get to the bottom of this manufactured fracas, to understand who began 'this barbarous brawl'. Yet after interrogating his men, Othello comes up empty. But he emerges nonetheless with an uncomfortable awareness that, while his ensign, Iago, professes to have told him the unvarnished truth, he is not entirely trustworthy.[41] As Stephen Greenblatt has convincingly argued, Iago's manipulations are revealed through his control of narrative storytelling.[42] Iago's mastery of narrative control is demonstrated here, first when he evades responsibility for undermining the peace, and later in the play, when he concocts a devastating and false story about Desdemona's behaviour as adulterous.

Victorians might have also noted the parallels with recent colonial wars. As Venetian commanders, Othello the general, and Iago his ensign, lead a contingent of soldiers on assignment to exert control over an island colony. They are accompanied by their wives, Desdemona and Emelia, much as British wives accompanied their soldier-husbands as 'camp followers' in the East India Company's wars in Afghanistan, the Punjab, and in Awadh during the 1857 Uprising in India. Moreover, Shakespeare's text makes clear that Othello's physical and cultural differences – that is, his Moorish identity as an outsider and his racial otherness as a dark-skinned man – define him more so than does his sober allegiance to the Venetian Duke, his pious commitment to the Christian religion, or his matrimonial bond to his wife. As Ania Loomba explains,

> Despite being a Christian soldier, Othello cannot shed either his blackness or his 'Turkish' attributes, and it is his sexual and emotional self, expressed through his relationship with Desdemona, which interrupts and finally disrupts his newly acquired Christian and Venetian identity. In the eyes of many Venetians, he

remains illegitimate as Desdemona's suitor; as her husband, he seems fated to play out the script of jealousy and wife-murder.[43]

Iago's scheming, outright lies, and half-truths are therefore undertaken to purge society of this illegitimacy, and by pushing Othello to take his own life in Act v, Iago simultaneously demonstrates his ability to purge the physical presence of 'the East' from his midst. Shakespeare therefore provides him with the tools, however underhanded and deceitful, to quash his two enemies in one blow by spreading racist innuendo and misogynistic trickery. In the end, he has restored the male-dominated status quo of Venetian military order. For the Victorians, the colonial imposition of 'despotic rule' as a governing strategy in the wake of the Indian Uprising is a tacit parallel to the trajectory of order replacing social anarchy in *Othello*.

In addition, with a name associated with Spain's patron saint, Tiago (Saint Tiago or Santiago), Iago has none of the 'Turkish attributes' that would have defined him as a Muslim or cultural outsider to British audiences.[44] Rather, he shares key attributes with European societies that valued duty and obligation through the ages. As several Shakespearean scholars have observed, Iago is defined structurally by his role in the Venetian army, where hierarchy is valued over cooperation and consultation.[45] Personally, Iago is driven by envy, by jealousy, by racial hatred, by an over-inflated self-regard, and by an interior world of secrets that is so deep it threatens to dissociate him from himself. That said, how could this complex character have won the esteem and respect of Victorian audiences, as Macaulay would have it?

One answer lies in the civil order that Othello and Iago have brought to Cyprus (even though that order is initially undermined by Iago's scheming). As Martin Orkin observed, 'the play remains mainly concerned not with the relationship between coloniser and colonised, but with the internal workings of the governing class itself'.[46] Another lies in Iago's reputed 'honesty', a quality whose measure is taken repeatedly throughout the play. In fact, Iago's reputed decency and trustworthiness is reiterated so often as to cast doubt upon its veracity as a true and verifiable attribute of the man. Consequently, what emerges despite this apparent contradiction is the character's commitment to his own autonomy and self-determination. Finally, by having achieved the death of Desdemona and Othello at the play's end, Iago has successfully dissipated the threat of miscegenation that Shakespeare embedded throughout *Othello*. Like the legend of Miss Wheeler in Charles Ball's *History of the Indian Mutiny* or the tangled tale of Alice and Ahmedoolah in Tom Taylor's play, *A Sister's Penance*, Victorians would have valued Iago as the chief agent who maintains racial and cultural separateness, a most reassuring message to Victorians after the restoration of British control following the Uprising. These intersecting attributes, I have been arguing, characterize Iago as a prototypical anti-hero to Cameron and her circle: Iago professes his loyalty to Othello even as he exposes him as 'the Other'; he 'cries a mutiny' – a manufactured conflict – only to quash the contrived skirmish himself; he spreads discord only to re-establish apparent calm. Iago, and not Othello, represents the established order, a model of social cohesion and the imperial status quo.

THE TERCENTENARY

Shakespeare was vividly alive for Cameron and her circle, especially during the years leading up to the three-hundredth anniversary of Shakespeare's birth, in 1864, an auspicious year marked for this national celebration. On the Isle of Wight, Tennyson discussed with Julia Margaret the diverse activities of the literary and social committees that had emerged to honour the occasion. In conversation, the two expressed hopefulness that the celebrations would exclude contemporary politics and be limited to Shakespeare's writings alone. As she wrote to Henry Taylor in 1862, Tennyson 'thanked God Almighty with his whole heart and soul that he knew nothing, and that the world knew nothing, of Shakespeare but his writings'.[47] Cameron's circle participated actively in these planning events: for example, Thackeray served on the committee of the Royal Dramatic College, one of the three different committees that was formed to honour Shakespeare. The college wanted to celebrate Shakespeare's legacy by underwriting the pensions of ageing actors and funding a school for their children. This committee competed for prominence (and funding) with two other camps. One, the Shakespeare Fund, was committed to renovating the Stratford properties. A second, the Urban Club, wanted to erect an elaborate stone monument to honour Shakespeare's greatness. Predictably, the three groups disagreed bitterly.[48] Ultimately, by 1864, two factions emerged: a Stratford Committee that was devoted to creating new productions of Shakespeare's plays in the city, to which Tennyson signed on as vice president, and the National Shakespeare Committee, which focused its activities in London.[49] In Stratford that year, *Othello* was performed 'to very large audiences' on the tenth day of the festival, with James Bennett in the role of Iago.[50]

The diverse political activities of the Tercentenary Committees leading up to and during the events of 1864 demonstrate how Victorian groups of various political persuasions attempted to colonize 'Shakespeare' as their own. As Antony Taylor put it, these debates 'illustrate the tensions between elite and plebeian radical readings of the national past, and of the literary landscape of England', when Shakespeare became associated with 'a crude nationalism, an anti-Gallican tendency, and a celebration of national greatness'.[51] During this time, religious scholars and clerics also drew Shakespeare into their own disciplinary controversies as well, especially in the debates about divine inspiration of the Bible.[52] But issues of British national identity preoccupied the class divisions that were exposed by the 1864 tercentenary celebrations. Representatives of the National Shakespeare Committee, for example, emphasized 'patriotism' in order to brand 'Shakespearean Englishness' in relation to the imagined cultural bond that united Britain's colonies from all across the empire; through Shakespeare, the colonial periphery was bonded to the imperial centre. In contrast, radical groups wanted to take advantage of Giuseppe Garibaldi's visit to England that same year by redirecting attention to his support for republican ideals. By focusing on the liberation of Italy from colonial rule, for example, they attempted to subvert the nationalistic and imperial message of the National Shakespeare Committee and reclaim Shakespeare as their own. As a final example, when the festival's organizers planted an oak tree that Queen Victoria had donated amid these political divisions, the clash of political symbolism that was attached to the tercentenary celebration was exposed in full view. As Taylor summarized it, for National Committee members, the oak tree symbolized the English naval fleet and therefore represented the nation's global power. Whereas, for radical groups, the oak was embraced as a symbol of liberty with its ancient roots in the Anglo-Saxon assemblies that united communities before they were disrupted by 'Norman invaders'.[53]

THE HERO AS POET

The tercentenary was important to both Charles and Julia Margaret Cameron, who shared with Tennyson and others in their circle a belief in the universalizing bond of Shakespeare and its cultural value as a foundation of British colonial rule because of the civilizing nature of his works. As Charles Trevelyan explained in his book *On the Education of the People of India* (1838), by bringing Shakespeare into the educational curriculum of India, a new era of enlightenment could be inaugurated in the colony. The 'languages of India will be assimilated to the languages of Europe, as far as the arts and sciences and general literature are concerned', which would thereby bring about the general uplift of society, he argued.[54] As we have seen, when Charles Cameron was a member of India's Supreme Council, he helped to install these ideas in policy and in practice.[55] Consequently, as Sushil Mukherjee explained,

> when the English came to Calcutta they brought with them the plays of Shakespeare. Early in the nineteenth century, Shakespeare was a subject of study in the Hindu College. Much before that Shakespeare's plays had begun to be staged in the theatres that local Englishmen had set up in the city for their entertainment and relaxation.[56]

The recorded performances of Shakespearean plays in Calcutta date to 1753, when 'The Playhouse' was erected right next to the East India Company's Writers' Building. Sudipto Chatterjee documented how the early Calcutta theatres were created to meet the entertainment needs of British expatriates, but also how these dramas soon attracted members of the élite indigenous Bengali community:

> Watchful of the cultural norms and practices of their English overlords, by the end of the eighteenth century the rich natives were gathering to witness the theatrical activities of the English.[57]

Othello was performed regularly. Chaterjee reported that by 1848,

> producer-manager James Barry, the umpteenth owner of the Sans Souci Theatre in white Calcutta, desperate to keep his theatre going, decided to try something new with his production of *Othello*: he cast a native gentleman for the title role, one 'Baboo Bustomchurn Addy'.[58]

But James Barry's staging of *Othello* in Calcutta was reviewed harshly by critics, as the Indian-cast Moor, 'despite his complexion, was not dark enough for the Bengali native to play. It was Shakespeare after all, and none but the white English could carry off Othello'.[59] Such were the limits of Indian mimicry, even in a profession defined by role-playing. Nevertheless, even as Indian theatre began to find its own footing after 1872, with staged productions of works like *Neeldarpan* [The Mirror of Indigo] by Dinabandhu Mitra, actors and production companies continued to seek inspiration from the London stage, consuming critical reviews of the famous performances of Sarah Siddons, for example, or newspaper reports on the costumes worn by Ellen Terry.[60] When the Camerons resided in Calcutta, they did not have to attend performances like James Barry's to understand how the East India Company intended to remake Indian society by making Shakespearian English the dominant language of the colony. The successful outcome of that policy was described some one hundred years later, at the quatercentenary of Shakespeare's birth, when the Indian critic C. D. Narasimhaiah remarked how for

> English education Indians, Shakespeare's characters, the situations in his plays, and those memorable lines of his have become almost as intimate a part of our lives as those of the best of our own writers. Shakespeare, more than the English monarch, seems to be the true and vital link between India and England.[61]

Among Cameron's contemporaries, Thomas Carlyle was another of Shakespeare's many enthusiasts. The essayist called him the 'greatest of Intellects' because he possessed an unconscious genius, one that was unbounded by external restrictions and in immediate touch with his creative gifts. In his 1840 lecture 'The Hero as Poet', Carlyle famously posed a revealing question-and-answer supposition that put the relationship of Shakespearean English to Indian colonization in high relief: 'If they asked us', he hypothesized, 'Will you give up your Indian Empire or your Shakespeare, you English', how would you answer? To which he replied in unambiguous terms:

> Should not we be forced to answer: Indian Empire, or no Indian Empire; we cannot do without Shakespeare! Indian Empire will go, at any rate, some day; but this Shakespeare does not go, he lasts for ever'.[62]

When he expressed these romantic and nationalist sentiments, Carlyle was intent to deny the material value of Britain's colonial possessions should the empire inexplicably be threatened with the loss of its home-grown national genius. And yet, several years later, when the 1857 Uprising in India was brand new, Carlyle expressed grave concerns in the national press that Britain itself was to blame for the revolt because it held fast to a permissive approach to governing the colony. To Carlyle, India was a most valuable possession, and the Indian Uprising represented a grave threat to the empire. At the same time, Carlyle regarded the governing policies of the East India Company as weak and ineffective, and its army lacking in rigorous military discipline and authority. In his mind, these two grave faults conspired to encourage the sepoys to revolt against their British commanders in the first place, which unleashed the anti-colonial rebellion. Carlyle learned first-hand of these apparent missteps in colonial governance and army discipline from a commanding soldier in the field – none other than Julia Margaret Cameron's brother-in-law, Colin Mackenzie. The two men met in 1843 at a gathering of the Highland Society after Mackenzie had returned to England.[63] The soldier and the philosopher saw eye to eye, and stayed in touch. On 6 July 1857, drawing upon Carlyle's personal assistance to place his letter to the editor in *The Times*, Mackenzie claimed the East India Company's policies led directly to the Uprising, alleging that 'system of centralisation' had 'deprived officers of all authority'.[64]

For Carlyle, Shakespeare was not incidental but rather *essential* to the British empire, no less important to managing the colonies than strict military control or authoritarian policies of colonial governance, which included the replacement of English for indigenous tongues in foreign lands. Shakespeare inspired troops in the field and those left behind: as we have seen, Queen Victoria was imagined providing comfort to widows and orphans of the Indian Uprising by uttering inspiring lines from Shakespeare's *Henry V* (see fig. 33). As Carlyle wrote in his book *On Heroes*, Shakespeare must be considered an effective instrument of empire because his gifts were such that they could unite colonial subjects from across the globe. Shakespeare's 'voice of genius' – which is to say, the language of his poetry and his drama – was able to bring together those diverse voices under a single emblem. For Carlyle, this flash of genius made Shakespeare a national treasure whose value was no less than that of a true sovereign:

> England, before long, this Island of ours, will hold but a small fraction of the English: in America, in New Holland, east and west to the very Antipodes, there will be a Saxondom covering the great spaces of the Globe. And now, what is it that can keep all these together into virtually one Nation, so that they do not fall-out and fight, but live at peace, in brotherlike intercourse, helping one another? … Here, I say, is an English King, whom no time or chance, Parliament or combination of Parliaments can dethrone! This King Shakespeare, does not he shine, in crowned sovereignty, over us all, as the noblest, gentlest, yet strongest of rallying-signs. … We can fancy him as radiant aloft over all the Nations of Englishmen, a thousand years hence.[65]

In the Herschel Album, Julia Margaret Cameron included two portraits of Carlyle, which she also made in 1867 with her new camera and lens (Cox/Ford 627, 629; HA-2, -4). Carlyle takes his place in the album alongside portraits of Tennyson and Herschel, here positioned in context as emblematic of the cultural authority these men represented for the photographer and her circle.

In the Herschel Album, Cameron also made Carlyle proud by including photographs that depict the two sides of what we might call the Janus head of British imperialism. Facing in one direction is Herschel's portrait, the heroic allegory of the *paterfamilias*, an emblem of the stable, aristocratic, patriarchal, and hereditary order. As Lord Lansdowne phrased it, Herschel's work in the Cape Colony advanced the aims of British imperialism by opening 'a new hemisphere to the eye of the scientific observer' by means of 'annexing' those discoveries 'to the empire of knowledge'. Facing in the opposite direction is 'Iago', Shakespeare's Western anti-hero. It is Iago who first exposes the disguised presence of 'the East' hiding invisibly within the Western colonial command and then vanquishes 'the Other' along with his female co-conspirator, whose offspring would have posed a grave threat to Britain's ideal of pure Anglo-Saxon heritage. Consequently, Iago's actions reassure his Western audience that civilization and the social order will be preserved for future generations. Cameron's photograph *Iago* therefore represents one half of the imperial glue that cements this image as a pendant to her portrait of *Sir John Herschel with Cap*, the emblem of the paterfamilias. Together, and supported by the other extraordinary photographs in this volume, the two images narrate an imperialist polemic that could only have taken shape in the wake of the Uprising in India.

Endnotes

Prologue

1. Thackeray did not sign the poem with his own name when he published it in *The Times*, but rather attributed its authorship to 'Thomas Newcome'. See pp. 98–9 below for the author's analysis and rationale for why Thackeray chose to use his nom-de-plume.

Introduction Narrating History

1. Mark Brown, 'Work by Pioneering Photographer to Leave UK unless Buyer Found', *Guardian*, 6 February 2018. The article identifies the photographic album as the 'Norman Album', a volume Cameron gave to her daughter, Julia Hay (Cameron) Norman, and her husband, Charles Norman, in 1869. See also Julian Cox and Colin Ford, *Julia Margaret Cameron: The Complete Photographs* (Los Angeles: J. Paul Getty Museum, 2013), 505.

2. Secretary of State for Digital Culture, Media, and Sport, 'Case 10: Images from the Life (The Norman Album) by Julia Margaret Cameron', *Export of Objects of Cultural Interest 2017–18, Annual Report to Parliament* (London: Crown Copyright, 2019), 37.

3. 'Opinion', *Creative Camera*, 130 (April 1975), 111. This album came to be known as the Herschel Album and was published in its entirety in Colin Ford, *The Cameron Collection: An Album of Photographs by Julia Margaret Cameron Presented to Sir John Herschel* (London: National Portrait Gallery, 1975). Its contents are summarized in Cox and Ford, *Julia Margaret Cameron*, 503–4.

4. Robert Dex, 'Duchess of Cambridge Turns Curator for National Portrait Gallery Photography Show', *Evening Standard*, 16 February 2018.

5. Malcolm Daniel, 'Friends of Photography Newsletter', Museum of Fine Arts, Houston, 29 July 2021.

6. For a selected bibliographic overview of publications on Cameron in 1975, Cox and Ford, *Julia Margaret Cameron*, 533.

7. *Camera Work*, 41 (January 1913). Stieglitz printed a total of nine photographs in the issue; five were Cameron's and four his own.

8. Cameron, like most contemporary Britons, considered the rebellion a treasonous act of defiance, and the word Mutiny reflected that Anglo-centric sensibility. The term was also used as coded shorthand to restrict the nature of the conflict to isolated Indian soldiers and downplay the geographical range or ferocity of the revolt. As a 'Mutiny', the term emphasized the behaviour of sepoys as disloyal in the face of what the British regarded as their legitimate rule, while it also narrowed the extent of the conflict to several princely states rather than to the colony's entire territory. Today's scholars, by contrast, have documented how the Uprising was more accurately understood at the time as an anti-colonial struggle, pointing out how indigenous accounts of the battles used terms like 'Muslim holy war', 'revolution', 'Brahmanical protest', and 'national movement'. As a result, because indigenous opposition to Britain's presence was supported widely across India, this book uses the term 'Indian Uprising' to convey that assessment, but I also preserve Cameron's use of the term 'Indian Mutiny' when it was used explicitly by her, the British press, and governmental officials, because it reflected their understanding of the nature of the rebellion. See Salahuddin Malik, 'Nineteenth Century Approaches to the Indian "Mutiny"', *Journal of Asian History*, 7:2 (1973), 95–6; the various terms used to describe the conflict are also discussed by Pramod Kumar Srivastava, who emphasizes that an 'Indian Nation' did not exist as such in 1857, in 'Nationalism Imagined? Hidden Impacts of the Uprising of 1857', *South Asia Research*, 38:3 (2018), 229–30. See also: Biswamoy Pati, ed., *The 1857 Rebellion* (New Delhi: Oxford University Press, 2007); Thomas R. Metcalf, *The Aftermath of Revolt: India, 1857–1870* (Princeton: Princeton University Press, 1964); Francis G. Hutchins, *The Illusion of Permanence: British Imperialism in India* (Princeton: Princeton University Press, 1967).

9. As Michel de Certeau has written, 'The approach to culture begins when the ordinary [person] becomes the narrator, when it is he [or she] who defines the (common) place of discourse and the (anonymous) space of its development', Michel de Certeau, *The Practice of Everyday Life*, trans. Steven Rendell (Berkeley: University of California Press, 1984), 5.

10. Unlike earlier resistance movements in India, which were largely fragmented, rebels in 1857 could envision the colony as a geographically coherent national space, largely because during the preceding decades Britain had extended its authority across numerous contiguous regions. In fact, the 1833 Charter that gave legal authority to the East India Company to conduct business and shape governance in the colony had united the territories of Bengal, Madras, and Bombay under a single administration that was overseen by a Governor-General. Manu Goswami, *Producing India: From Colonial Economy to National Space* (Chicago: University of Chicago Press, 2004).

11. Homi K. Bhabha, 'Interrogating Identities', in *The Location of Culture* (London and New York: Routledge, 1994), 44.

12. William Holman Hunt, *Pre-Raphaelitism and the Pre-Raphaelite*

Brotherhood, 2 vols (New York and London: Macmillan, 1906), 2:166.

13. 'The New Quarterly Army List', in *The Quarterly Army List of Her Majesty's British and Indian Forces on the Bengal Establishment, exhibiting the Rank, Standing, and Various Services of every Officer in the Army [...] Corrected to 5th July 1859* (Calcutta: P. M. Cranenburgh and R. C. Lepage and Co., British Library, *c.*1959), 100. Prinsep made his whole career in the Bengali Cavalry and attained the rank of Lieutenant-Colonel in 1885. See Marquess of Anglesey, *A History of the British Cavalry, 1816 to 1919, Volume 3: 1872–1898* (London: Leo Cooper in association with Secker and Warburg, 1982), 150.

14. On Cameron's allegorical works, see Jeff Rosen, *Julia Margaret Cameron's 'Fancy Subjects': Photographic Allegories of Victorian Identity and Empire* (Manchester: Manchester University Press, 2016).

15. Patrizia Di Bello, *Women's Albums and Photography in Victorian England: Ladies, Mothers, and Flirts* (New York: Routledge, 2016), 4.

16. Julia Margaret Cameron, *Annals of My Glass House* (1874), reprinted in Violet Hamilton, *Julia Margaret Cameron: Annals of My Glass House* (Seattle: University of Washington Press, 1996), 11–16. Cameron never finished writing her autobiography, and this fragment alone remains.

17. R. Derek Wood, ed., *Julia Margaret Cameron's Copyrighted Photographs* (London: privately published, May 1996), www.midley.co.uk/cameron/cameron.pdf.

18. In this book I preserve the historical spelling of place names from British periodicals and Cameron's own correspondence rather than adopt modern conventions: Calcutta and not Kolkata; Cawnpore and not Kanpur; Bombay and not Mumbai.

19. About the period of the Indian Uprising (1857–8), Helmut Gernsheim wrote, 'The next few years brought no events which greatly add to our portrait of Julia Margaret Cameron', in *Julia Margaret Cameron: Her Life and Photographic Work* (New York: Aperture, 1975), 23.

20. Brian Hill wrote, 'The Pattles seem to have travelled to and fro from India to England or France with hardly more fuss than a tourist today makes in taking a plane to Paris', in Brian Hill, *Julia Margaret Cameron: A Victorian Family Portrait* (New York: St Martin's Press, 1973), 31.

21. Victoria Olsen, *From Life: Julia Margaret Cameron and Victorian Photography* (New York: Palgrave Macmillan, 2003), 102.

22. Quoted in Colin Ford, *Julia Margaret Cameron: A Critical Biography* (Los Angeles: J. Paul Getty Museum, 2003), 25–6.

23. Charles Hay Cameron, *Two Essays. On the Sublime and Beautiful, and On Duelling* (London: Elotson [?] and Palmer, privately printed, 1835). Claims for the sympathy of this work to Julia Margaret's sensibilities have been advanced by: Mike Weaver, *Whisper of the Muse: The Overstone Album and Other Photographs by Julia Margaret Cameron* (Malibu: J. Paul Getty Museum, 1986), 23; Mike Weaver, *Julia Margaret Cameron, 1815–1879* (Southampton: John Hansard Gallery, 1984), 22; and Ford, *Julia Margaret Cameron: A Critical Biography*, 57.

24. Julia Margaret Cameron to Sir John Herschel, 26 February 1864, Herschel Correspondence, Royal Society, London, 5.159.

25. The two have been studied extensively: *'For My Best Beloved Sister, Mia': An Album of Photographs by Julia Margaret Cameron* (Albuquerque: University of New Mexico Art Museum, 1994); Mike Weaver, *Whisper of the Muse.*

26. Joanne Lukitsh, 'Before 1864: Julia Margaret Cameron's Early Work in Photography', in Cox and Ford, *Julia Margaret Cameron*, 95–105. See also Ford, *Julia Margaret Cameron: A Critical Biography*, 35–40.

27. Because no extant records exist for the albums' construction and any changes made to them over time, historians have had to speculate about additions; however, subtractions or lost imagery, of course, cannot be ascertained. Writing about the album given to Cameron's sister, Maria (Mia) Jackson, Colin Ford wrote, 'this album reads in two ways. Start from one end and you see only Cameron prints. Start from the other, and there are pictures by a number of mainly unknown and unidentifiable photographers', in Ford, *Julia Margaret Cameron: A Critical Biography*, 36.

28. On the 'undervalued and under-researched' quality of photographic albums produced by Victorian women, see Patrizia Di Bello, *Women's Albums*, 13.

29. Lucy Smith wrote that Cameron's albums 'reflect both Victorian modes of artistically constructed truth and prefigure the postmodern text of composite forms reflecting fractured multiple identities. ... Their meaning is formed from a specific ordering, as is the case with the traditional archive with its focus on arrangement and context. Moreover, the potential fluidity of the authorship of image arrangement here, demonstrates the creative mutability of the albums as an ever-shifting archive, which develops in material form to reflect alterations and accumulations of meaning in the images', in Lucy Christina Smith, 'Julia Margaret Cameron and Archival Creativity: Traces of Photographic Imagination from the Victorian Album to New-Victorian Fiction' (PhD diss., University of Portsmouth, 2017), 118.

30. See, for example: Patrick Brantlinger, *Rule of Darkness: British Literature and Imperialism, 1830–1914* (Ithaca: Cornell University Press, 1988); Jenny Scharpe, *Allegories of Empire: The Figure of the Woman in the Colonial Text* (Minneapolis: University of Minnesota, 1993); Christopher Herbert, *War of No Pity: The Indian Mutiny and Victorian Trauma* (Princeton: Princeton University Press, 2008).

31. Edward Said, *Orientalism* (New York: Vintage, 1978).

32. Important exceptions include: Julie F. Codell, ed., *Power and Resistance: The Delhi Coronation Durbars* (Delhi, 2012); Julie F. Codell, ed., *Imperial Co-Histories: National Identities and the British and Colonial Press* (Cranbrook, NJ: 2003); Julia Thomas, *Pictorial Victorians: The Inscription of Values in Word and Image* (Athens: Ohio University Press, 2004); Julie F. Codell and Dianne Sachko Macleod, eds, *Orientalism Transposed: The Impact of the Colonies on British*

Culture (Aldershot: Ashgate, 1998); and Tim Barringer and Tom Flynn, eds, *Colonialism and the Object: Empire, Material Culture and the Museum* (London: Routledge, 1998).

33. Christopher Pinney, *The Coming of Photography in India* (London: British Library, 2008), 22–30.

34. See, for example: James R. Ryan, *Picturing Empire: Photography and the Visualization of the British Empire* (Chicago: University of Chicago Press, 1997); Eleanor M. Hight and Gary D. Sampson, eds, *Colonialist Photography: Imag(in)ing Race and Place* (New York: Routledge, 2002); Zahid R. Chaudhary, *Afterimage of Empire: Photography in Nineteenth Century India* (Minneapolis: University of Minnesota Press, 2012); Ali Behdad and Luke Gartlan, eds, *Photography's Orientalism: New Essays on Colonial Representation* (Los Angeles: J. Paul Getty Trust, 2013); Ali Behdad, *Camera Orientalis: Reflections of Photography in the Middle East* (Chicago: University of Chicago Press, 2016); Rashmi Viswanathan, 'The Tressider Album: A Case Study of a Private "Ethnology"', *Self and Nation*, 7:1 (Fall 2016); Rosie Llewellyn-Jones, ed., *The Uprising of 1857* (Ahmedabad, India: Mapin Publishing, 2107); Sean Willcock, *Victorian Visions of War and Peace: Aesthetics, Sovereignty and Violence in the British Empire, c.1851–1900* (London: Paul Mellon Centre for Studies in British Art, 2021).

35. John Szarkowski, *The Photographer's Eye* (New York: MOMA, 1966), Introduction; also online at https://www.jnevins.com/szarkowskireading.htm.

36. Lady Elizabeth Eastlake, 'Photography', reprinted from *Quarterly Review*, 101 (April 1857), in Beaumont Newhall, ed., *Photography: Essays and Images* (New York: MOMA, 1980), 81–95.

37. Elizabeth Edwards, *Photographs and the Practice of History* (London: Bloomsbury Academic, 2022).

38. Woolf asserted a self-evident claim that by revealing an individual's character the photographer was also telling a story about the sitter, perhaps providing an essential insight about his or her uniqueness or revealing something unique about the relationship between photographer and subject. Indeed, from her great-aunt Woolf learned the camera could capture personality and expression and record narrative performance photographically. See Virginia Woolf and Roger Fry, *Victorian Photographs of Famous Men and Fair Women by Julia Margaret Cameron* (London: Chatto & Windus, 1992), 18. See also Jane Garrity, 'Virginia Woolf, Intellectual Harlotry, and 1920s British *Vogue*', in Pamela Caughie, ed., *Virginia Woolf in the Age of Mechanical Reproduction* (York and London: Garland, 2000), 185–218.

39. For a concise history of the debates surrounding the theory of indexicality in contemporary photography, see James Elkins, ed., *Photography Theory* (London: Routledge, 2007).

40. Woolf and Fry, *Victorian Photographs*, 18.

41. These techniques led Ian Jeffrey to summarize Cameron as a wilful 'transgressor against photographic naturalism', Ian Jeffrey, 'British Photography from Fox Talbot to E. O. Hoppé', in Arts Council of Great Britain, *The Real Thing: An Anthology of British Photographs, 1840–1950* (London: Hayward Gallery, 1975), 15.

42. Roger Fry, 'Mrs. Cameron's Photographs', in Woolf and Fry, *Victorian Photographs*, 23. White wrote: 'Historical *stories* trace the sequences of events that lead from inaugurations to (provisional) terminations of social and cultural processes in a way that *chronicles* are not required to do', in Hayden White, *Metahistory: The Historical Imagination in Nineteenth-Century Europe* (Baltimore and London: Johns Hopkins University Press, 1973), 6 (original emphasis).

43. Priya Satia, *Time's Monster: How History Makes History* (Cambridge, MA: Belknap, 2020), 261.

44. Ibid., 81.

45. Ibid., 55.

46. 'Introduction', in Homi K. Bhabha, ed., *Nation and Narration* (London: Routledge, 1990), 2.

47. Ibid., 3.

48. Kathryn Ledbetter, *Tennyson and Victorian Periodicals: Commodities in Context* (Aldershot: Ashgate, 2007), 121.

49. Satia, *Time's Monster*, 261, 271.

50. For much of the analysis that follows I am indebted to Laura Wexler, 'The Purloined Image', in Shawn Michelle Smith and Sharon Sliwinski, eds, *Photography and the Optical Unconscious* (Durham, NC, and London: Duke University Press, 2017), 264–79.

51. Carol Armstrong, 'Cupid's Pencil of Light: Julia Margaret Cameron and the Maternalization of Photography', *October*, 76 (Spring 1996), 131.

52. Ibid., 119.

53. Robin Kelsey, *Photography and the Art of Chance* (Cambridge, MA, and London: Belknap, 2015), 92.

54. Julian Cox, '"To … startle the eye with wonder and delight": The Photographs of Julia Margaret Cameron', in Cox and Ford, *Julia Margaret Cameron*, 70.

55. Ibid., 71; this inscription is unique to the print conserved by the Tennyson Research Centre, making it a highly prized document as it is inscribed by Cameron's own hand and likely given to Tennyson as a gift or memento, further contextualizing the image in relation to Tennyson's relationship to the girl as a neighbour in Freshwater. As Victoria Olsen noted, as the child lay dying Tennyson visited her in the presence of an American essayist, Thomas Wentworth Higginson, who described the scene in religious and painterly terms, like a picture by Jusepe de Ribera or Eduardo Zamacois y Zabala. Olsen, *From Life*, 188. For the first-hand account of Tennyson's reaction, see Thomas Wentworth Higginson, *Cheerful Yesterdays* (Boston and New York: Houghton, Mifflin and Co., 1898), 295–6.

56. Jordan Bear, *Disillusioned: Victorian Photography and the Discerning Subject* (University Park: Pennsylvania State University Press, 2015), 102.

57. Ibid.

58. Cameron's death-bed photograph has also been interpreted in relation to the nineteenth-century fad of spirit photography by Jesse Hoffman, 'Arthur Hallam's Spirit Photograph and Tennyson's Elegiac Trace', *Victorian*

Literature and Culture, 42:4 (2014), 611–36.

59. 'War Office, 21st October 1859', *London Gazette*, 3792.

60. Lara Kriegel, 'The Transforming Power of the Victoria Cross, 1856–2010', *SEL: Studies in English Literature, 1500–1900*, 56:4 (Autumn 2016), 871–93.

61. Peter Harrington and Michel Tomasek, *Queen Victoria's Army in Colour: The British Military Paintings of Orlando Norie* (Atglen, PA: Schiffer Military History), 9.

62. Joany Hichberger, 'Democratising Glory? The Victoria Cross Paintings of Louis Desanges', *Oxford Art Journal*, 7:2 (1984), 42–51.

63. London, National Army Museum, see notes to Acc. 2019–11–10–1 (watercolour painting) and Acc. 1961–05–8 (photograph).

64. The sheer volume of Norie's work and the scant remains of Ackermann's print-selling history in the mid-nineteenth century make it difficult to identify specific auctions and sales. A partial account is provided in R. G. Harris, 'Orlando Norie – Military Artist, Part II', *Journal of the Society for Army Historical Research*, 50:204 (Winter 1972), 193–9.

65. On the concept of anti-allegory, see: Gayatri Chakravorty Spivak, 'Thoughts on the Principle of Allegory', *Genre*, 4 (December 1972), 331, 348–9; and Eduardo Cadava, *Words of Light: Theses on the Philosophy of History* (Princeton: Princeton University Press, 1997), with specific emphasis on Mortification (7–11); Ghosts (11–13); Translations (15–18); Inscriptions (18–21); Eternal Return (31–42); Similarity (106–15).

66. Walter Benjamin, 'Theses on the Philosophy of History', in *Illuminations*, trans. Harry Zohn, ed. Hannah Arendt (New York: Schocken, 1969), 255.

67. On the *paterfamilias*, see Hannah Arendt, *The Human Condition*, 2nd edn (Chicago: University of Chicago Press, 2018), 27.

68. Walter Benjamin, 'Little History of Photography', in *Walter Benjamin: Selected Writings, Volume 2, 1927–1934*, ed. Michael Jennings, Howard Eiland, and Gary Smith (Cambridge, MA: Belknap, 1999), 510–12.

69. Mackenzie's life was described by his second wife, Helen Douglas Mackenzie, *Storms and Sunshine of a Soldier's Life: Lt.-General Colin Mackenzie, C.B., 1825–1881*, 2 vols (Edinburgh: David Douglas, 1884).

70. The painting is now conserved by the National Army Museum, Acc. 1961–10–61.

71. Tara Mayer, 'Cultural Cross-Dressing: Posing and Performance in Orientalist Portraits', *Journal of the Royal Asiatic Society* (third series), 22:2 (April 2012), 297.

72. William Dalrymple, *Return of a King: The Battle for Afghanistan, 1839–42* (New York: Vintage, 2013).

73. Astrid Erll, 'Remembering across Time, Space, and Cultures: Premediation, Remediation and the "Indian Mutiny"', in Astrid Erll and Ann Rigney, eds, *Mediation, Remediation, and the Dynamics of Cultural Memory* (Berlin and New York: Walter de Gruyter, 2009).

74. Thomas Babington Macaulay, *The History of England from the Accession of James the Second*, vol. 4 (Leipzig: Bernhard Tauchnitz, 1855), 239.

75. On the 'great man' theory of history, especially in relation to Britain's construction of Indian history, see Satia, *Time's Monster*.

76. See Lydia Murdoch, '"Suppressed Grief": Mourning the Death of British Children and the Memory of the 1857 Indian Rebellion', *Journal of British Studies*, 51:2 (April 2012), 364–92.

77. John Berger, 'Understanding a Photograph', in *The Look of Things*, ed. Nikos Stangos (New York: Viking, 1971), 181.

78. Laura Wexler, 'The Purloined Image', 276.

79. See Wolfgang Welsch, 'Transculturality: The Puzzling Form of Cultures Today', in Mike Featherstone and Scott Lash, eds, *Spaces of Cultures* (London: Sage, 1999), 196–7. See also: Julie F. Codell, 'The Art of Transculturation', in Julie F. Codell, *Transculturation in British Art, 1770–1930* (Farnham, Surrey: Ashgate, 2012), 1–20; and Michael H. Fisher, *Counterflows to Colonialism: Indian Travellers and Settlers in Britain, 1600–1857* (Ranikhet, India: Permanent Black and Ashoka University, 2019).

Chapter One Empire's Children

1. Steven Ruskin, *John Herschel's Cape Voyage* (Aldershot: Ashgate, 2004), 193. For Herschel's correspondence, see Adler Planetarium's 'Calendar of the Correspondence of Sir John Herschel Database', http://historydb.adlerplanetarium.org/herschel/?p=about.

2. Victoria C. Olsen, *From Life: Julia Margaret Cameron and Victorian Photography* (New York: Palgrave Macmillan, 2003), 50–1.

3. For Prinsep, Mackenzie, and Jackson, see Olsen, *From Life*, 28–34, 38–9; for Bayley, see Ernest Axon, *Family of Bayley of Manchester and Hope* (Manchester: printed for the author, 1894), 36.

4. Partha Chaterjee, *The Black Hole of Empire: History of a Global Practice of Power* (Princeton and Oxford: Princeton University Press, 2012), ch. 1.

5. Swati Chattopadhyay, 'Blurring Boundaries: The Limits of "White Town" in Colonial Calcutta', *Journal of the Society of Architectural Historians*, 59:2 (June 2000), 154–79.

6. For other printed views of Government House and the East India Company's administrative buildings, see James Baille Fraser, *View of Government House, from the Eastward*, coloured aquatint, from *Views of Calcutta and its Environs*, 1824, British Library, Shelfmark: X644(3); and William Wood, *Esplanade Row*, lithograph, 1833, from *Views of Calcutta*, British Library, Shelfmark: X630(2).

7. For key components of the Act, see 'Government of India Act, 1833', in Barbara Harlow and Mia Carter, eds, *Archives of Empire, Volume 1: From the East India Company to the Suez Canal* (Durham, NC, and London: Duke University Press, 2003), 49–53.

8. 'Great Britain. Commission to Examine Report upon the Present State of the Laws, Regulations, Usages in the Settlements at the Cape of Good Hope

[,] the Islands of Mauritius [and] Ceylon', *Ceylon: [Reports of Lieutenant-Colonel Colebrooke and Charles Hay Cameron, Esq.]* (London: 1832). On the Royal Commission of Eastern Inquiry to Ceylon, see Vijaya Samaraweera, 'Governor Sir Robert Wilmot Horton and the Reforms of 1833 in Ceylon', *Historical Journal*, 15:2 (1972), 209–28.

9. Elizabeth Green Musselman, 'Swords into Plowshares: John Herschel's Progressive View of Astronomical and Imperial Governance', *British Journal for the History of Science*, 31:4 (December 1998), 424–5; Ruskin, *John Herschel's Cape Voyage*, xv–xviii, 45–53.

10. David S. Evans, Terrence J. Deeming, Betty Hall Evans, and Stephen Goldfarb, eds, *Herschel at the Cape: Diaries and Correspondence of Sir John Herschel, 1834–1838* (Austin: University of Texas Press, 1969), 47.

11. Ibid., xxix.

12. Ibid., 42 n. 22.

13. John Herschel to John Philip, 2 June 1835, quoted in Musselman, 'Swords into Ploughshares', 429.

14. According to Herschel, 'In place of a painful and humiliating distinction between master and slave, we have no other line of demarcation among us than what must subsist in every community between the educated & uneducated classes – A distinction which, if maintained as it ought to be, not by depressing those below, but by raising those above to a continually higher and higher level, contains as little evil and as much good as belongs to any condition of Society'. W. T. Ferguson and R. F. M. Immelman, eds, *Sir John Herschel and Education at the Cape, 1834–1840* (Cape Town: Oxford University Press, 1961), 57.

15. Ibid., 6–7; as described in this text, from 1835 to 1841 Herschel corresponded with the Secretaries of State for the Colonies (Lord Glenelg, the Marquis of Normanby, Lord John Russell) regarding the selection of teachers for the Cape Colony, 59–77. The examination paper Herschel devised for potential new teachers contained sections on abstract science, political economy, Latin, Greek, German, history, and geography, 68–70. For Charles Cameron's role in establishing the system of education in Ceylon, see G. C. Mendis, ed., *The Colebrooke-Cameron Papers: Documents on British Colonial Policy in Ceylon, 1796–1833*, 2 vols (New York: Oxford University Press, 1957).

16. See the summary of this exchange analysed by Mark Tunick, 'Tolerant Imperialism: John Stuart Mill's Defense of British Rule in India', *Review of Politics*, 68:4 (2006), 17–18.

17. On Adeline Pattle Mackenzie's genealogy, see Deborah Spooner, profile manager, WikiTree, entry on Adeline Marie (Pattle) Mackenzie (1812–1836), https://www.wikitree.com/wiki/Pattle-11. A family genealogy may also be found in Ferdinand Mount, *The Tears of the Rajas: Mutiny, Money, and Marriage in India, 1805–1905* (London: Simon & Schuster, 2015), 732–3.

18. William Dalrymple, *Return of a King: The Battle for Afghanistan, 1839–42* (New York: Vintage, 2013), 99–100, 239–41.

19. Ibid., esp. chs 6, 7, and 8.

20. Helen Douglas Mackenzie, *Storms and Sunshine of a Soldier's Life: Lt.-General Colin Mackenzie, C.B., 1825–1881*, 2 vols (Edinburgh: David Douglas, 1884).

21. Louis Dupree, 'The First Anglo-Afghan War and the British Retreat of 1842: The Functions of History and Folklore', *East and West*, 26:3/4 (September–December 1976), 503–29.

22. Major W. Broadfoot, *The Career of Major George Broadfoot, C.B. in Afghanistan and the Punjab Compiled from his Papers and those of Lords Ellenborough and Hardinge* (London: John Murray, 1888), 106.

23. Ibid., 118.

24. Eden's letters to her sister Mary about this experience were published in 1866 as *Up the Country: Letters Written to her Sister from the Upper Provinces of India* (London: Virago, 1983).

25. Dupree, 'First Anglo-Afghan War', 507, 510.

26. Broadfoot, *Career of Major George Broadfoot*, 124.

27. Ibid., 118.

28. Eden to an unknown recipient, 21 March 1836, in Emily Eden, *Letters from India* (London: Richard Bentley and Son, 1872), 1:115 (available electronically via the University of Pennsylvania Digital Library), https://digital.library.upenn.edu/women/eden/letters/letters.html.

29. Ibid., 1:84–5.

30. Dupree, 'First Anglo-Afghan War', 510.

31. Priya Satia, *Time's Monster: How History Makes History* (Cambridge, MA: Belknap, 2020), 83. As Satia makes clear, John William Kaye's *History of the War in Afghanistan* (London: Richard Bentley, 1851), was a notable exception in criticizing British actions. Acknowledgement that multiple narratives of this period have yielded differing historical accounts is recorded in W. Broadfoot, 'The Defence of Jalalabad', *English Historical Review*, 8:29 (January 1893), 93–108, and in Sarah Ansari, 'The Sind Blue Books of 1843 and 1844: The Political "Laundering" of Historical Evidence', *English Historical Review*, 120 (February 2005), 35–65.

32. Mackenzie, *Storms and Sunshine*, 1:378.

33. *Portraits of the Kabul Prisoners* (London: John Murray, 1843).

34. Thomas Carlyle, *Heroes, Hero-Worship, and the Heroic in History* (New York: A. L. Burt Co., n.d.), 1.

35. Satia, *Time's Monster*, 77–83.

36. Tara Mayer, 'Cultural Cross-Dressing: Posing and Performance in Orientalist Portraits', *Journal of the Royal Asiatic Society*, 22:2 (April 2012), 294–6.

37. Mackenzie, *Storms and Sunshine*, 2:3–5.

38. Broadfoot, *Career of Major George Broadfoot*, 200.

39. S. S. Bal, 'Maharaja Dalip Singh's Cis-Sutlej Territories and the Sikh War', *Proceedings of the Indian History Congress*, 30 (1968), 235.

40. Broadfoot, *Career of Major George Broadfoot*, 230–1.

41. Diana Preston, *The Dark Defile: Britain's Catastrophic Invasion of Afghanistan, 1838–1842* (New York: Walker and Co., 2012).

42. Patwant Singh and Jyoti M. Rai, *Empire of the Sikhs: The Life and Times of Maharaja Ranjit Singh* (London: Peter Owen Publishers, 2008), 236–7.

43. Lionel James Trotter, *The History of the British Empire in India from the Appointment of Lord Hardinge to the Political Extinction of the East-India Company, 1844 to 1862, Volume 1* (London: Wm. H. Allen, 1866), 44.

44. Bawa Satinder Singh, 'Raja Gulab Singh's Role in the First Anglo-Sikh War', *Modern Asian Studies*, 5:1 (1971), 37.

45. Trotter, *History of the British Empire in India*, 48.

46. Amarpal S. Sidhu, *The First Anglo-Sikh War* (Stroud: Amberley Publishing, 2010).

47. Ibid., Part 1, 'The Campaign'; see also Walter Kokernot, '"Where Ignorant Armies Clash by Night" and the Sikh Rebellion: A Contemporary Source for Matthew Arnold's Night-Battle Imagery', *Victorian Poetry*, 43:1 (Spring 2005), 99–108.

48. 'The Indian War', *Illustrated London News*, 21 March 1846, 189.

49. Lawrence James, *Raj: The Making and Unmaking of British India* (New York: St Martin's Press, 1997), 111–13.

50. These anecdotes are repeated in virtually all of Cameron's modern biographies, most recently in Colin Ford, 'Geniuses, Poets and Painters: The World of Julia Margaret Cameron', in Julian Cox and Colin Ford, *Julia Margaret Cameron: The Complete Photographs* (Los Angeles: J. Paul Getty Museum, 2003), 15.

51. Upon her arrival in the Cape Colony, Lady Herschel also had to supervise 'something like ten servants' and oversee operations for the equivalent of 'a small hotel, usually with about twenty people in it'. Evans, Deeming, Hall Evans, and Goldfarb, *Herschel at the Cape*, xxiii–xxiv; see also Brian Warner, ed., *Lady Herschel: Letters from the Cape* (Cape Town: Friends of the South African Library, 1991), 12.

52. Thackeray wrote, 'Scarce a soldier goes to yonder shores but leaves a home and grief in it behind him. The lords of the subject province find wives there; but their children cannot live on the soil. The parents bring their children to the shore, and part from them. The family must be broken up – keep the flowers of your home beyond a certain time, and the sickening buds wither and die'. William Makepeace Thackeray, *The Newcomes* (1855) (Cambridge: Heritage Press, n.d.), ch. 5, 49–50.

53. For the Cameron children's travel to England, see Colin Ford, *Julia Margaret Cameron: A Critical Biography* (Los Angeles: J. Paul Getty Museum, 2003), 20, and Olsen, *From Life*, 64. For Julia Margaret's travel to France, see Hugh Orange, *The Chevalier de l'Etang (1757–1840) and his Descendants, the Pattles*, ed. John Beaumont (Isle of Wight: Julia Margaret Cameron Research Group, 2002).

54. Quoted in Olsen, *From Life*, 66. Another photographic image on paper of Julia Margaret's firstborn is in the Norman Album and annotated 'Julia Hay Norman as a Child in Calcutta', National Science and Media Museum, 10709668; Source No.: 2003–5054.

55. Sir John Herschel to Julia Margaret Cameron, 18 August 1846, Cameron Collection, Box 11, Getty Research Institute, J. Paul Getty Museum, Los Angeles.

56. Michel Foucault used the term 'governmentality' to describe the installation of an administrative bureaucracy to manage people and regulate civil society. Michel Foucault, 'Governmentality', in Graham Burchell, Colin Gordon, and Peter Miller, eds, *The Foucault Effect: Studies in Governmentality* (Chicago: University of Chicago Press, 1991), 87–104.

57. Satia, *Time's Monster*, 109.

58. Herschel wrote, 'The sentence of expulsion of a whole nation [of] men, women, and children – widows – orphans of men slain in the war, from the land which gave them birth, and where they have their homesteads, at a dash of the pen, to seek new domiciles, to dispossess others, to spread war and famine, under pain of what? to be treated as *enemies* i.e. to be shot down by any man calling himself a *friend*! *Here* is a '*facinus majoris abolle*' [A crime committed by those who should have known better].' Quoted in Musselman, 'Swords into Plowshares', 429.

59. Prinsep promised that Herschel's son (miswritten as 'nephew') would receive direct appointment when he came of age. Julia Margaret Cameron to Sir John Herschel, 15 January 1851, Harry Ransom Center, University of Texas at Austin, H/M-0133. Charles Cameron sent Herschel letters of introduction to use when his son William arrived in India. Charles Hay Cameron to Sir John Herschel, 10 January 1853, Royal Society, HS 5.147.

60. Chandak Sengoopta, *Imprint of the Raj: How Fingerprinting was Born in Colonial India* (London: Pan Books, 2004), 55.

61. William Makepeace Thackeray, *Vanity Fair: A Novel without a Hero* (1849) (New York: Heritage Press, 1940), ch. 3, 23.

62. For additional evidence of this enthusiasm, see Jeff Rosen, 'Julia Margaret Cameron's Railway Station Exhibition: A Private Gallery in the Public Sphere', in Camilla Murgia and Dominique Bauer, eds, *The Home, Nations and Empires, and Ephemeral Exhibition Spaces, 1750–1918* (Amsterdam: Amsterdam University Press, 2021).

63. Sir John Herschel to Julia Margaret Cameron, 18 August 1846.

64. Julia Margaret Cameron to Captain George Broadfoot, 11 September 1843, quoted in Broadfoot, *Career of Major George Broadfoot*, 201.

65. Colin Ford, *The Cameron Collection: An Album of Photographs by Julia Margaret Cameron Presented to Sir John Herschel* (London: National Portrait Gallery, 1975), 121, notation to plate 19.

66. A second child, Robert William Arnot, was born on 22 February 1860, before Baby 'Pictet' entered the world. Rose Mackenzie went on to have four additional children with Francis Pictet. For the extensive Wood Family History, on Arnot and his issue, see http://woodlloydfamilyhistory.com/fam2543.html and on Pictet and his issue, see http://woodlloydfamilyhistory.com/fam2544.html.

67. 'No. 67, Petition of Captain Francis Pictet', *Accounts and Papers; East India* (Session 5 February – 28 July 1863), 40 (London: House of Commons, 1863), 84–6.

68. Broadfoot, *Career of Major George Broadfoot*, 404–14.

69. Satia, *Time's Monster*, 83, 96.

70. Mackenzie himself promoted this idea in *Storms and Sunshine*, vol. 2, ch. 28, on 'the Great Mutiny'; for a more sober reflection about the rigorous British system of military control, see Kaushik Roy, 'The Construction of Regiments in the Indian Army: 1859–1913', *War in History*, 8:2 (2001), 127–48. Another mythology told in this regard is that the Madras army, especially the Native Infantry regiments led by British officers, adopted such policies in the wake of the so-called Vellore Mutiny of 1806. See Crispin Bates and Marina Carter, eds, 'The Vellore Mutiny from the Sepoys' Point of View', *Mutiny at the Margins, New Perspectives on the Indian Uprising of 1857, Volume 7: Documents of the Indian Uprising* (Los Angeles and New York: Sage, 2017), 7–11, and James Frey, 'The Sepoy Speaks: Discerning the Significance of the Vellore Mutiny', in G. Rand and C. Bates, eds, *Mutiny at the Margins, New Perspectives on the Indian Uprising of 1857, Volume 4: Military Aspects of the Indian Uprising* (New York: Sage, 2013), 1–23.

71. On the Great Trigonometric Survey's integration of scientific and military activities, see Simon Naylor and Simon Schaffer, eds, 'Nineteenth-Century Survey Sciences: Enterprises, Expeditions and Exhibitions', *Notes and Records: Royal Society Journal of the History of Science* (Royal Society Publishing), 73:2 (2019), 135–47.

72. R. H. Phillimore, ed., *Historical Records of the Survey of India: Volume 4, 1830–1843* (Delhi: Surveyor General of India, 1958), 50 n. 74; plate 2.

73. Ibid., 1.

74. B. S. Shylaja, 'John Herschel's Astronomical Observations from Bangalore', *Current Science – Bangalore*, 90:2 (25 January 2006).

75. The triumphal arch erected for Ellenborough's farewell dinner was illustrated in the *Illustrated London News*, 12 October 1844, 236. Bernard S. Cohn, 'Honor and Honors in Great Britain and India', *HAU: Journal of Ethnographic Theory*, 3:3 (2013), 457–67.

76. 'Grand Field Day in Calcutta – Arrival of the Captured Sikh Guns – From a Sketch Received by the last Overland Mail', *Illustrated London News*, 29 May 1847.

77. Mackenzie, *Storms and Sunshine*, 2:22–3.

78. Eden, *Up the Country*, 294.

79. J. L. Hilton, 'The Herschel Obelisk, Classics, and Egyptomania at the Cape', *Akroterion*, 51 (2006), 117.

80. Thomas Maclear, 'An Account of the Erection of the Herschel Obelisk at the Cape of Good Hope', *Journal of the Franklin Institute*, 8:4 (1 October 1844), 281.

81. Ibid.

82. Hilton, 'Herschel Obelisk', 118.

83. Maclear, 'An Account of the Erection of the Herschel Obelisk', 281.

84. John Bell, 'Some Remarks on the Application of Definite Proportions and the Conic Sections to Architecture, Illustrated Chiefly by the Obelisk, with some History of that Feature of Art', *Journal of the Society of Arts*, 340 (27 May 1859), 478.

85. Fekri A. Hassan, 'Imperialist Appropriations of Egyptian Obelisks', in David Jeffreys, ed., *Views of Ancient Egypt since Napoleon Bonaparte: Imperialism, Colonialism and Modern Appropriations* (London: UCL Press, 2003), ch. 2.

86. Bell, 'Some Remarks', 480.

87. Hilton, 'Herschel Obelisk', 123.

88. Sarah Stickney Ellis, *The Women of England* (1839) in *The Prose Works of Mrs. Ellis* (New York: Henry G. Langley, 1845), 1:59.

89. Lady Herschel to Julia Margaret Cameron, n.d., but probably shortly after 1840, Cameron Collection, Box 11, Getty Research Institute, J. Paul Getty Museum, Los Angeles.

90. Rosemary Marangoly George, 'Homes in the Empire, Empires in the Home', *Cultural Critique*, 26 (Winter 1993–4), 95–127. Ironically, as Mary A. Procida has argued, 'imperial wives' after this period were not tied to the nursery or to the kitchen, but they nevertheless paid lip service to the sanctity of motherhood while participating in the cultural work of empire. Mary A. Procida, *Married to the Empire: Gender, Politics, and Imperialism in India, 1883–1947* (Manchester: Manchester University Press, 2002), 47, 58.

91. Jenny Sharpe, *Allegories of Empire: The Figure of the Woman in the Colonial Text* (Minneapolis: University of Minnesota Press, 1993), 10.

92. Éadaoin Agnew, *Imperial Women Writers in Victorian India: Representing Colonial Life, 1850–1910* (Cham, Switzerland: Palgrave Macmillan, 2017). For the influence of Christian missionaries on Indian women, see Indrani Sen, *Gendered Transactions: The White Woman in Colonial India, c. 1820–1930* (Manchester: Manchester University Press, 2017).

93. Ellis, *The Women of England*, 5. On Ellis's complex role for nineteenth-century Britain, see Caroline Austin-Bolt, 'Sarah Ellis's *The Women of England*: Domestic Happiness and Gender Performance', *Nineteenth-Century Contexts*, 37:3 (2015), 183–95; Angela Poon, *Enacting Englishness in the Victorian Period: Colonialism and the Politics of Performance* (Aldershot: Ashgate, 2008); Daryl Ogden, 'Double Visions: Sarah Stickney Ellis, George Eliot, and the Politics of Domesticity', *Women's Studies*, 25:6 (1996), 585–602.

94. Ralph Crane and Anna Johnston, 'How to Dine in India: Flora Annie Steel's *The Complete Indian Housekeeper and Cook* and the Anglo-Indian Imagination', in Susmita Roye, ed., *Flora Annie Steel: A Critical Study of an Unconventional Memsahib* (Alberta: University of Alberta Press, 2017), 161–82.

95. Ibid., 6.

96. Karen Chase and Michael Levenson, *The Spectacle of Intimacy: A Public Life of the Victorian Family* (Princeton: Princeton University Press, 2000), 69; Arianne Chernock, 'Queen Victoria and the "Bloody Mary of Madagascar"', *Victorian Studies*, 55:3 (Spring 2013), 425–49.

97. Partha Chaterjee, *The Nation and its Fragments: Colonial and Postcolonial Histories* (Princeton: Princeton University Press, 1993), 116–34.

98. Betty Joseph, *Reading the East India Company, 1720–1840: Colonial Currencies of Gender, Women in Culture and Society* (Chicago: University of Chicago Press, 2004), 93.

99. Joanna Liddle and Rama Joshi, 'Gender and Imperialism in British India', *Economic and Political Weekly*, 20:43 (October 1985), WS72–WS78; Sukanya Banerjee, *Becoming Imperial Citizens: Indians in the Late-Victorian Empire* (Durham, NC, and London: Duke University Press, 2010), 117–19.

100. In an 1850 letter from Charles to Julia Margaret, he wrote, 'Col. Braybrook tells me that I am the largest proprietor of land in the Island and I feel no doubt that the boys will one day be very thankful to me for providing them with this resource against dependence and place hunting'. Charles Cameron to Julia Margaret Cameron, 8 November 1850, Cameron Collection, Box 11, Getty Research Institute, J. Paul Getty Museum, Los Angeles.

101. Julia Margaret Cameron to Juley Hay Cameron, 29 December 1858, Kent County Archives, U310_C75_65.

Chapter Two Enchanted Palace

1. Colesworthey Grant, *Lithographic Sketches of the Public Characters of Calcutta, Published In the 'India Review', 'India Medical' ... From 1833 to 1850* (Calcutta: n.d.). For Grant, see Tom Young, 'Art in India's "Age of Reform": Amateurs, Print Culture, and the Transformation of the East India Company, *c.*1813–1858' (PhD thesis, Cambridge University, 2019), https://doi.org/10.17863/CAM.33241.

2. Swati Chattopadhyay, *Representing Calcutta: Modernity, Nationalism, and the Colonial Uncanny* (London: Routledge, 2005), 42–8.

3. Mrinalini Sinha, 'Britishness, Clubbability, and the Colonial Public Sphere: The Genealogy of an Imperial Institution in Colonial India', *Journal of British Studies*, 40:4 (October 2001), 489–521.

4. Ranajit Guha, 'Not at Home in the Empire', *Critical Inquiry*, 23 (Spring 1997), 483–4.

5. John Kaye, *A History of the Sepoy War in India, 1857–1858*, 3 vols (London: W. H. Allen, 1864), 1:509.

6. Lawrence James, *Raj: The Making and Unmaking of British India* (New York: St Martins, 1997), 113–18; G. Khurana, 'Cunningham's History of the Sikhs and the Parliamentary Debate on the Second Anglo-Sikh War', *Proceedings of the Indian History Congress*, 52 (1991), 556–60.

7. Minute by Marquis of Dalhousie, 28 February 1856, *Parliamentary Papers*, 1856 (245), quoted in Mark Condos, *The Insecurity State: Punjab and the Making of Colonial Power in British India* (Cambridge: Cambridge University Press, 2017), 66.

8. Douglas M. Peers, '"Those Noble Exemplars of the True Military Tradition"; Constructions of the Indian Army in the Mid-Victorian Press', *Modern Asian Studies*, 31:1 (1977), 131–2. 'Despotic government' is often defined in relation to unabashed military control, or martial law. But at other times, despotism was theorized by Mill and Charles Hay Cameron in a philosophic sense to refer to rigid forms of external control, but which were not necessarily martial. This question is taken up in chapter 5.

9. William Dalrymple, *The Last Mughal, the Fall of a Dynasty: Delhi, 1857* (New York: Vintage, 2006), 118–24.

10. *The Times*, 4 March 1856, 8.

11. On the East India Company and its economic history, see Nick Robins, *The Corporation that Changed the World: How the East India Company Shaped the Modern Multinational*, 2nd edn (London: Pluto Press, 2012).

12. Henry T. Prinsep, *The India Question in 1853* (London: Wm. H. Allen and Co., 1853).

13. Charles Hay Cameron, *An Address to Parliament on the Duties of Great Britain to India, in Respect of the Education of the Natives, and their Official Employment* (London: Longman, Brown, Green, and Longmans, 1853), 23.

14. Cameron's photographs with their embedded signposts contradict Roland Barthes's belief that such images were powerless to convey complex narratives. Roland Barthes, *Camera Lucida: Reflections on Photography*, trans. Richard Howard (New York: Hill and Wang, 1981), 5.

15. Paul Barlow, 'The Imagined Hero as Incarnate Sign: Thomas Carlyle and the Mythology of the "National Portrait" in Victorian Britain', *Art History*, 17:4 (1994), 522–3.

16. Cameron included this signed print in the Thackeray Album. Harry Ransom Humanities Research Center, University of Texas at Austin, Acc. 964:0312:0007.

17. For an overview of the Orientalist position, see Deirdre David, *Rule Britannia: Women, Empire, and Victorian Writing* (Ithaca and London: Cornell University Press, 1995), 125–9.

18. My appreciation to Robert King, author of *Nehru and the Language Politics of India* (Oxford: Oxford University Press, 1997), who viewed this image with me at the Harry Ransom Humanities Research Center in Austin, Texas, in 2000, and confirmed this translation.

19. Cameron included this photograph in the Lindsay Album, no. 103 (Cox/Ford 594).

20. Rembrandt van Rijn, *Aristotle with a Bust of Homer* (1653), Metropolitan Museum of Art, 61.198.

21. Erik Gray, *Milton and the Victorians* (Ithaca: Cornell University Press, 2009).

22. Gauri Viswanathan, *Masks of Conquest: Literary Study and British Rule in India* (New Delhi: Oxford University Press, 1989), 85. See also Julie Cyzewski, 'Heroic Demons in "Paradise Lost" and Michael Madhusudan Datta's "Meghanadavadha kavya": The Reception of Milton's Satan in Colonial India', *Milton Quarterly*, 48:4 (December 2014), 207–24.

23. G. O. Trevelyan, *The Life and Letters of Lord Macaulay*, 2 vols (London: Oxford University Press, 1932), 1:391.

24. Ibid.

25. On Macaulay's 'Minute on Indian Education', see Mia Carter and Barbara Harlow, eds, *Archives of Empire, Volume 1: From the East India Company to the Suez Canal* (Durham, NC, and London: Duke University Press, 2003), 227–68.

26. Edward Said, *Culture and Imperialism* (New York: Vintage, 1993), 77.

27. Ibid.

28. For an overview of Holland's and Lansdowne's influence over politics

during the first half of the nineteenth century, see Lloyd Sanders, *The Holland House Circle* (New York: G. P. Putnam's Sons, 1908).

29. See, for example, Charles H. E. Brookfield and Frances M. Brookfield, *Mrs. Brookfield And Her Circle*, vol. 2 (1848–1874), 2nd edn (London: Sir Isaac Pitman and Sons, Ltd., 1905), 461, 481, 494, 510; Sir Henry Holland, *Recollections of a Past Life* (London: Longmans, Green and Co., 1872), 186, 222, 231.

30. Thomas Carlyle, *On Heroes, Hero-Worship, and the Heroic in History* (1841) (New York: A. L. Burt, n.d.), 48.

31. Janet McLean, Richard Pelter and Rupert Shepherd, '"Gazing, but not Copying": The Creation of G. F. Watts's Alfred Inciting the Saxons to Prevent the Landing of the Danes', *Apollo*, 158:501 (November 2003); T. S. R. Boase, 'The Decoration of the New Palace at Westminster, 1841–1863', *Journal of the Warburg and Courtauld Institutes*, 17:3/4 (1954), 319–58.

32. Boase, 'Decoration of the New Palace', 342.

33. Trevelyan, *Life and Letters of Lord Macaulay*, 1:317–20.

34. 'The Herschel Dinner', *Athenaeum*, #555 (16 June 1838), 426.

35. Ibid.

36. Trevelyan, *Life and Letters of Lord Macaulay*, 2:226–7.

37. The German Gallery was located at 168 New Bond Street. For an overview of this exhibition, see Jeff Rosen, 'Cameron's Photographic Double Takes', in Julie Codell and Diane Sachko Macleod, eds, *Orientalism Transposed: The Impact of the Colonies on British Culture* (Aldershot: Ashgate, 1998), 158–86.

38. William Holman Hunt, *Pre-Raphaelitism and the Pre-Raphaelite Brotherhood*, 2 vols (New York and London: Macmillan, 1906), 2:65.

39. Emily Tennyson to Alfred Tennyson, 26 March 1859, in *The Letters of Emily Lady Tennyson*, ed. James O. Hoge (University Park: Pennsylvania State University Press, 1974), 133.

40. Donald Hawes, '"Better and Worse Voices": Tennyson and Thackeray', *Tennyson Research Bulletin*, 6:3 (November 1994), 175.

41. Hugh Orange and John Beaumont, 'The Chevalier de l'Étang (1757–1840) and His Descendants, the Pattles', *Virginia Woolf Bulletin*, 7 (2001), 51–62; 8 (2001), 31–48; 9 (2002), 70–2. For the Anglo-Indian community of which Thackeray was a part, see John Beaumont, 'Thackeray in Pattledom' (Freshwater, Isle of Wight: private research paper for the Julia Margaret Cameron Museum, 2011), https://sites.google.com/site/thackerayinpattledom/.

42. Gordon N. Ray, *Thackeray: The Uses of Adversity, 1811–1846* (New York: McGraw-Hill, 1855), 67.

43. William Dalrymple, *White Mughals: Love and Betrayal in Eighteenth Century India* (New York: Penguin Press, 2002), xlv.

44. Sara Suleri, *The Rhetoric of English India* (Chicago: University of Chicago Press, 1992), 97. One other Pattle sister did not emigrate back to England: Louisa Pattle Bayley remained with her husband in India and died there in 1873.

45. William Makepeace Thackeray, *Vanity Fair: A Novel without a Hero* (1848), (New York: Heritage Press, 1940), ch. 60, 659.

46. Henry T. Prinsep, *Origins of the Sikh Power in the Punjab and Political Life of Muha-Raja Runjeet Singh* (Calcutta: G. H. Huttmann, Military Orphan Press, 1834).

47. Ibid., vi.

48. William Broadfoot, *The Career of Major George Broadfoot, C.B. in Afghanistan and the Punjab* (London: John Murray, 1888), 13–21.

49. Priya Satia, *Time's Monster: How History Makes History* (Cambridge, MA: Belknap, 2020), 105.

50. As an example, see Holman Hunt, *Pre-Raphaelitism*, 2:234; for an account of contrasting views over Marochetti's equestrian statue of *Richard Coeur de Lion*, see John Harrison, 'The Prince, the Baron and the Knight: Baron Carlo Marochetti and the "Black Prince"', *British Art Journal*, 5:2 (Autumn 2004), 62–8.

51. The Royal Academy of Arts Collection conserves George Frederic Watts's portrait study of Marochetti, 03/1148. For an overview of Marochetti's commissions during his transition from France to Great Britain, see Philip Ward-Jackson, 'Expiatory Monuments by Carlo Marochetti in Dorset and the Isle of Wight', *Journal of the Warburg and Courtauld Institutes*, 53 (1990), 266–80. Despite Marochetti's close association with British royalty, his connection to Layard was marked by friction, as described by Philip Ward-Jackson, 'Austen Henry Layard (1817–1894), Reluctant Nemesis of Carlo Marochetti (1805–1867)', *British Art Journal*, 17:3 (Spring 2017), 64–73.

52. Pollock is often confused with his father, Lord Chief Baron of the Exchequer and Fellow of the Royal Society. An overview of the son's life can be found in Frank G. Madsen, 'The Wren Library Pollock Collection: A Victorian Dante Scholar', *Dante: Rivista internazionale de studi su Dante Alighieri*, 8 (2011), 23–42. See also Virginia C. Olsen, *From Life: Julia Margaret Cameron and Victorian Photography* (New York and Hampshire: Palgrave Macmillan, 2003), 161–2.

53. *Personal Remembrances of Sir Frederick Pollock*, 2 vols (London: Macmillan and Co., 1887), 1:14, 91. This contract, however, ultimately went to Woolner, although Lord Lansdowne facilitated the commission.

54. Ibid., 1:68.

55. Ibid., 2:35, 60, 107. In Cameron's letters to her daughter Juley, she referenced several of those dinner parties with the Spring Rices present. See the letters conserved by the Kent County Archives dated 9 February 1859 (U310_C75_68) and an undated letter of 1859 or 1860 (U310_C75_70). Thackeray and Spring Rice were at the centre of many of these gatherings as described in John Beaumont, *Thackeray in Pattledom* (Freshwater, Isle of Wight: Julia Margaret Cameron Museum, 2011), n.p.

56. For example, Cameron was present for Brookfield's sermons on 29 April 1860 (Kent County Archives, U310_C75_79) and with Anne Thackeray in 1864 (Hester Thackeray Fuller and Violet Hammersley, eds, *Thackeray's Daughter* (London: Guernsey Press, 1951), 111), and attended the public exhibition of Rosa Bonheur's *The Horse Fair* at the French Gallery on

Pall Mall with Mrs Brookfield and William Makepeace Thackeray on 5 September 1855 (Charles and Frances Brookfield, *Mrs Brookfield and Her Circle* (London: Pitman, 1905), 2:419).

57. See Fiona MacCarthy, *The Last Pre-Raphaelite: Edward Burne-Jones and the Victorian Imagination* (Cambridge, MA: Harvard University Press, 2012), ch. 5, 86–97. On Watts, see Barbara Bryant, *G. F. Watts in Kensington: Little Holland House and Gallery* (Compton, Surrey: Watts Gallery, 2009).

58. Caroline Dakers, *The Holland Park Circle: Artists and Victorian Society* (New Haven: Yale University Press, 1999), 39–40.

59. There are numerous accounts, but the most discreet is by Kathleen Fitzpatrick, *Lady Henry Somerset* (Boston: Little, Brown and Co., 1923), 7–8. For Henry Taylor's account, along with his poetic elegy to Lady Somers, see *Autobiography of Henry Taylor, Volume 2, 1844–1875* (London: Harrison and Co., 1877), 39–41.

60. See W. J. Lottie, *Kensington, Picturesque and Historical* (London: Field and Tuer, the Leadenhall Press, 1888), 217–18.

61. Carolyn Dakers, *Holland Park Circle*, 72–3. On the relationship of the artists and writers associated with the journal *Punch*, see Patrick Leary, *The Punch Brotherhood: Table Talk and Print Culture in Mid-Victorian London* (London: British Library, 2010), 10–56.

62. Marquis of Lansdowne to the Countess Somers, 31 May 1855, reprinted in Fitzpatrick, *Lady Henry Somerset*, 30–1.

63. See Caroline Hedengren-Dillon, 'Monument to Princess Elizabeth by Baron Marochetti (1805–1867)', in www.victorianweb.org/sculpture/Marochetti/34.html.

64. Scholars have not disputed the identity of Julia Jackson in this photograph, but several have thought the older child pictured, here identified by Cameron as 'May' (a common family nickname among the Pattle sisters, also used for the elder Maria Pattle Jackson) was inscribed under this print for a different family relation altogether. Julia Jackson, youngest of the Jackson sisters, was born in 1846, and her older sisters were five years older (Mary Jackson was born in 1841) and nine years older (Adeline Jackson was born in 1837), whereas only two years separated Julia Jackson from her older cousin, Alice Maria Prinsep, born in 1844, making her the most likely candidate because these dates align with Cameron's distribution of ages. Accordingly, we should discount two other possibilities for the identity of 'May' from the line of Charles Robert Prinsep, Thoby Prinsep's brother, who died in 1864: Anne Mary Prinsep was born in 1848, making her two years *younger* than Julia Jackson, and Mary ('May') Emily Prinsep was born in 1853, seven years *younger* than Julia Jackson. Therefore, assuming the correct identity of Julia Jackson at age eleven in the photograph, the only plausible family relation two years older is Alice Maria Prinsep, who perhaps was referred to also as 'May', as this image was taken some seven years *before* Julia Margaret and Charles Cameron adopted Charles Robert Prinsep's daughter, Mary 'May' Prinsep. See Wood Family History, family of Henry Thoby Prinsep and Sarah Monckton Pattle, family of John Jackson and Maria Theodesia Pattle, family of Charles Robert Prinsep and Louisa Anne White, http://woodlloydfamilyhistory.com/.

65. Email correspondence dated 13 October 2021 to the author from Dr Cathryn Spence, Curator/Archivist at Bowood House, Wiltshire. See also letter from Henry Petty Fitzmaurice to William Henry Fox Talbot, 4 January 1855, Document 7112, and letter from Constance Talbot to William Henry Fox Talbot, 5 January 1855, Document 7116, in *The Correspondence of William Henry Fox Talbot*, http://foxtalbot.dmu.ac.uk/index.html.

66. William Henry Fox Talbot to Henry Petty Fitzmaurice, 5 January 1855, private collection; reprinted in *Correspondence of William Henry Fox Talbot* (Document 7114).

67. In 1855, Lansdowne, accompanied by Lady Shelburne, Earl Somers, and Virginia Somers, visited Talbot at his estate, Lacock Abbey. See Constance Talbot to William Henry Fox Talbot, 5 January 1855, British Library, Manuscripts, Fox Talbot Collection, and http://foxtalbot.dmu.ac.uk/ (Document 7116). On the connection between Talbot and Lansdowne, see also Graham Smith, 'Talbot at Bowood', *History of Photography*, 21:4 (1997), 333–4.

68. Watts Gallery – Artists' Village, Compton, UK. Acc. # COMWG 137, oil on canvas, 231.1 cm × 144.8 cm.

69. Collection of William Dalrymple and Hew Dalrymple, UK.

70. Joanne Lukitsh, 'Before 1864: Julia Margaret Cameron's Early Work in Photography', in Julian Cox and Colin Ford, *Julia Margaret Cameron: The Complete Photographs* (Los Angeles: J. Paul Getty Museum, 2003), 95–105. The album contains two different portraits of Tennyson, both taken in 1861 by James Mudd, and both are conserved by the National Portrait Gallery, London: NPG P34 and NPG Ax18237.

71. In 'Julia Margaret Cameron and Archival Creativity: Traces of Photographic Imagination from the Victorian Album to New-Victorian Fiction' (PhD diss., University of Portsmouth, September 2017), Lucy Christina Smith wrote of the albums given to Lansdowne and others as 'composite forms reflecting fractured multiple identities' (118).

72. Patrizia Di Bello, *Women's Albums and Photography in Victorian England: Ladies, Mothers, and Flirts* (New York: Routledge, 2016), 3.

73. Ibid., 24–5.

74. Roland Barthes, 'The Death of the Author', in *Image – Music – Text*, trans. Stephen Heath (New York: Hill and Wang, 1977), 148.

75. 'John Stewart, photographer', 'The Bronte Sisters – a True Likeness?', online commentary: https://brontesisters.co.uk/John-Stewart,-Photographer.html.

76. See the work conserved by the National Portrait Gallery, London: George Frederic Watts, *Thomas Wright*, chalk, *c.*1850–1851, 24 in. × 20 in. (61 × 50.8 cm), Given by George Frederic Watts, 1895. NPG 1016. I thank the Curator at Bowood House, Dr Cathryn Spence, for her assistance in identifying Cameron's image and its source.

77. 'The Photographic Album for the Year 1856' [*sic*], *Illustrated London News*, 3 May 1856, 475.

78. Di Bello, *Women's Albums*, 26.

79. Marta Weiss, 'The Page as Stage', in Elizabeth Siegel, ed., *Playing with Pictures: The Art of Victorian Photo-Collage* (Chicago: Art Institute of Chicago, 2009), 40–1.

80. Elizabeth Edwards, 'Photographs as Objects of Memory', in Marius Kwint, Christopher Breward, and Jeremy Aynsley, eds, *Material Memories* (Oxford and New York: Bloomsbury Academic, 1999), 221–36.

81. Di Bello, *Women's Albums*, 145.

82. Scottish National Portrait Gallery, accession number: EP VI 12.2, https://www.nationalgalleries.org/art-and-artists/31753?search=Pickersgill&search_set_offset=31. For an overview of Herschel's celebrity as a portrait subject, see Steven Russell, *John Herschel's Cape Voyage* (Aldershot: Ashgate, 2004), 194–201.

83. Sir John Frederick William Herschel, 1st Bt, by Maull & Co., albumen *carte-de-visite*, 1860s, NPG Ax18331.

84. Sarah Stickney Ellis, *The Women of England* (1839) in *The Prose Works of Mrs. Ellis*, vol. 1 (New York: Henry G. Langley, 1845), ch. 13.

85. This domestic history has informed a large part of Cameron's place in photographic history; as Carol Armstrong has written, it was 'Cameron, the good mother and grandmother, who has left us with the ... record of a fascination with the allure of childish bodies', uniquely because of her motherly identity, describing Cameron's representations of eroticized children as celebrations of 'that pseudononchalant, crossed-foot pose, that slightly sullen, almost sultry look, that sliding slip, and its revelation of plumped baby flesh'. Carol Armstrong, 'Cupid's Pencil of Light: Julia Margaret Cameron and the Maternalization of Photography', *October*, 76 (Spring 1996), 115. For a more nuanced take on similar ideas, see Anne McCauley, 'Brides of Men and Brides of Art: The "Woman Question" of the 1860s and the Photographs of Julia Margaret Cameron', *Études photographiques*, 28 November 2011, http://journals.openedition.org/etudesphotographiques/3469.

86. These cares involved her family's health and well-being, including her husband's persistent gastric distress, parasites contracted by two of her young sons, eye vision problems with yet another son, her own self-described 'giddiness', a term she used to describe feelings of light-headedness experienced during times of stress. While tending to the needs of young boys at home, she corresponded almost daily with her eldest child, Julia, whom she affectionately called Juley, Jules, and Doodie in her letters, and who lived apart from the family while preparing for her pending marriage to Charles Norman, the son of her father's close friend, George Norman. For an extensive family biography, see Olsen, *From Life*.

87. In September 1857 the Camerons lived in Bromley, by the end of the year in Putney Heath, and by the end of the following year in a house at 7 Park Street, Westminster, London. See Kent County Archives, letters of 26 September 1857 (U310_C75_56), 24 July 1858 (U310_C75_61), and 29 December 1858 (U310_C75_65) from Julia Margaret Cameron to her daughter Julie Hay Cameron. In successive years, the family seemed almost nomadic. In the summer of 1861, the Camerons stayed in a cottage on Colwell Bay on the Isle of Wight (U310_C75_85); then moved back to Putney Heath in winter 1862 (U310_C75_88); then in 1863 settled into their cottage in Freshwater.

88. The intersection of family drama and public culture that took place in Sara Prinsep's salon therefore also describes the years when Julia Margaret emerged as a self-conscious producer of imagery, not exclusively as a consumer of photographs. See Michel de Certeau, *The Practice of Everyday Life*, trans. Steven Rendell (Berkeley: University of California Press, 1984), 30–42. Drawing upon the example and support of this literary, political, and artistic circle, she crafted a distinctive narrative voice using photography to engage with the public, determined to participate in an emergent public sphere in which women increasingly participated. See Jürgen Habermas, *The Structural Transformation of the Public Sphere: An Inquiry into a Category of Bourgeois Society*, trans. Thomas Burger (Cambridge, MA, and London: MIT Press, 1989), 141–51. Cameron had stories she wanted to tell and did not let gender become an obstacle in moving from the domestic to the public sphere; as a narrator of historical events on her own terms, she became a full contributor to the culture of her day. As Michel de Certeau wrote, 'The approach to culture begins when the ordinary man becomes the narrator, when it is he who defines the (common) place of discourse and the (anonymous) space of its development', de Certeau, *Practice of Everyday Life*, 5.

Chapter Three
Letters to Juley

1. Sir John Herschel to Charles Hay Cameron, 1 May 1850, Cameron Collection, Box 11, Getty Research Institute, J. Paul Getty Museum, Los Angeles.

2. 'The Mutiny in India', *Illustrated London News*, 13 June 1857.

3. Julia Margaret Cameron to Sir Henry Cole, 20 May 1865, National Art Library, Victoria and Albert Museum.

4. Julia Margaret Cameron to Julia Hay Cameron, 10 August 1857, Kent County Archives, U310_C75_54.

5. Julia Margaret Cameron to Julia Hay Cameron, 31 July 1857, Kent County Archives, U310_C75_53. Throughout her extensive correspondence, Cameron frequently abbreviated words and used various shorthand terms and symbols. For example, she shortened the word 'about' to 'abt.', and compressed the word 'your' to 'yr.' Similarly, she used a variety of symbols to represent the word 'and', including the plus sign (+), the Greek letter alpha (α), and the ampersand (&). To conform with earlier published transcriptions of Cameron's correspondence, this book also transcribes her letters using the ampersand where her intention was unambiguously to connote the word 'and'.

6. Dan Randall, 'Autumn 1857: The Making of the Indian "Mutiny"', *Victorian Literature and Culture*, 31:1 (2003), 6–7; Douglas M. Peers, 'The Blind, Brutal,

British Public's Bestial Thirst for Blood: Archive, Memory and W. H. Russell's (Re) making of the Indian Mutiny', in Kaushik Roy and Gavin Rand, eds, *Culture, Conflict and the Military in Colonial South Asia* (London: Routledge, 2018), 113. The extent to which the battle for Cawnpore was experienced by native Indians as an anticolonial struggle is well explained in Rudrangshu Mukherjee, '"Satan Let Loose upon Earth": The Kanpur Massacres in India in the Revolt of 1857', *Past and Present*, 128 (August 1990), 92–116.

7. Thomas de Quincey, 'Europeans', *Titan* (October 1857), reprinted in: 'The Letters and Writings of Thomas de Quincey', in Crispin Bates and Marina Carter, eds, *Mutiny at the Margins, New Perspectives on the Indian Uprising of 1857, Volume 7: Documents of the Indian Uprising* (Los Angeles: Sage, 2017), 159–60.

8. Rajat Kanta Ray, 'The Mentality of the Mutiny: Conceptions of the Alternative Order', in Biswamoy Pati, ed., *The 1857 Rebellion* (New Delhi: Oxford University Press, 2007), 282. Mary Amelia Vansittart, the wife of a civil servant, wrote the contemporaneous account: 'This mutiny has been planned since the taking of Oudh [in 1856]. It was settled about 20 May that every cantonment all down the country was to rise and murder all the Europeans, seize forts, magazines, treasure. But the confining of the 80 troopers of the 3rd Cavalry at Meerut, and putting them under the guard of their own brethren in arms, caused the plot to explode ten days too soon'. Quoted in Ferdinand Mount, *The Tears of the Rajas: Mutiny, Money and Marriage in India, 1805–1905* (London: Simon & Schuster, 2015), 566.

9. Mukherjee, 'Satan Let Loose upon Earth', 99.

10. John Stuart Mill, *Memorandum of the Improvements of the Administration of India during the Last Thirty Years, and the Petition of the East-India Company to Parliament* (London: William H. Allen, 1858).

11. John Stuart Mill, 'On Liberty', in *Utilitarianism, On Liberty, and Considerations of Representative Government*, ed. H. B. Acton (London: J. M. Dent & Sons, Ltd., 1972), 140, 141.

12. Eric Stokes, *The English Utilitarians and India* (Oxford: Oxford University Press, 1959).

13. Disraeli's speech in the House of Commons was reported on in *The Times*, 27 July 1857 and 28 July 1857, and was the subject of Karl Marx's contemporaneous letters about the 'Indian Mutiny' to the *New York Daily Tribune* that were published between 17 July 1857 and 14 May 1858.

14. Linda Colley has written about the rise of British nationalism in its relationship to Europe and to colonial identities in *Britons: Forging the Nation, 1707–1837* (New Haven: Yale University Press, 1992). However, the effort to distinguish between the emergence of 'British national consciousness' and British history as a part of a 'common European heritage' has been and continues to be problematic from many points of view. Although not the object of this study, the point here is to contextualize the shift in British nationalism and its identity formation in relation to its imperial approach to India.

15. For the Anglo-Indian community of which Thackeray was a part, see John Beaumont, 'Thackeray in Pattledom' (Freshwater, Isle of Wight: private research paper for the Julia Margaret Cameron Museum, 2011), https://sites.google.com/site/thackerayinpattledom/. For a more contemporary account, see Robyn Andrews, 'Quitting India: The Anglo-Indian Culture of Migration', *Sites: A Journal of Social Anthropology and Cultural Studies*, 4:2 (2007), 32–56.

16. Mount, *Tears of the Rajas*, 465.

17. Gordon N. Ray, *Thackeray: The Uses of Adversity, 1811–1846* (New York: McGraw-Hill, 1955), 170; Victoria C. Olsen, *From Life: Julia Margaret Cameron and Victorian Photography* (Hampshire: Palgrave Macmillan, 2003), 28; Beaumont, 'Thackeray in Pattledom'.

18. Patrick Cadell, 'The Outbreak of the Indian Mutiny', *Journal of the Society for Army Historical Research*, 33:135 (1955), 118–22.

19. *The Quarterly Army List of Her Majesty's British and Indian Forces on the Bengal Establishment, Exhibiting the Rank, Standing, and Various Services of every Officer in the Army* (Calcutta: P. M. Cranenburgh; London: R. C. LePage and Co., British Library), 100.

20. Olsen, *From Life*, 102.

21. *Quarterly Army List*, 'List of Civil Servants in the Presidency of Fort William, corrected up to the 19th July 1859', 12.

22. See Wood Family History, family of David Arnot and Rose Prinsep Mackenzie, https://woodlloydfamilyhistory.com/fam2543.html.

23. Julia Margaret Cameron to Julia Hay Cameron, 10 August 1857, Kent County Archives, U310_C75_54.

24. Julia Margaret Cameron to Julia Hay Cameron, 12 August 1857, Kent County Archives, U310_C75_55.

25. William Holman Hunt, *Pre-Raphaelitism and the Pre-Raphaelite Brotherhood*, 2nd edn, 2 vols (New York: E. P. Dutton and Co., 1914), 2:166–7.

26. Jenny Sharpe, *Allegories of Empire: The Figure of the Woman in the Colonial Text* (Minneapolis: University of Minnesota Press, 1993).

27. See http://www.rossettiarchive.org/docs/sa265.raw.html.

28. Rossetti appended a footnote to her poem: 'I retain this little poem, not as historically accurate, but as written and published before I heard the suggested facts of the first verse contradicted'. Mount, *Tears of the Rajas*, 713 n. 45.

29. Mukherjee, 'Satan Let Loose upon Earth', 108.

30. See Andrew Ward, *Our Bones are Scattered: The Cawnpore Massacres and the Indian Mutiny of 1857* (New York: Henry Holt, 1996); Mukherjee, 'Satan Let Loose upon Earth', 92–116; B. English, 'Debate: The Kanpur Massacres in India and the Revolt of 1857', *Past and Present*, 142 (1994), 169–78, 178–89.

31. Mukherjee, 'Satan Let Loose upon Earth', 114.

32. Quoted in Peter Harrington, 'Inflammatory Visions: Charles Wade Crump's Cawnpore Massacre Prints', *Print Quarterly*, 30:2 (June 2013), 179.

33. For an analysis of the role of *The Times* reports of these events from W. H. Russell, see Peers, 'The Blind, Brutal, British

Public's'; see also Brian Wallace, 'Nana Sahib in British Culture and Memory', *Historical Journal*, 58:2 (June 2015), 589–613.

34. 'Nana Sahib', *Illustrated London News*, 26 September 1857, 326; Nana Sahib's engraved portrait appeared on p. 328 by an anonymous hand. For a historical and cultural analysis, see Brian Wallace, 'Nana Sahib in British Culture and Memory', *Historical Journal*, 58:2 (June 2015), 589–613.

35. George Trevelyan, *Cawnpore* (London: Macmillan, 1865), 57.

36. Michel Foucault, 'Of Other Spaces', trans. Jay Miskowiec, *Diacritics* 16:1 (Spring 1986), 22–7.

37. See Rebecca M. Brown, 'Inscribing Monumentality: A Case Study of the 1763 Patna Massacre Memorial', *Journal of Asian Studies*, 65:1 (February 2006), 91–113.

38. See Partha Chaterjee, *The Black Hole of Empire: History of a Global Practice of Power* (Princeton: Princeton University Press, 2012), ch. 4, 160–7. For the story of the Black Hole in relation to the long arc of East India Company control in India, see William Dalrymple, *The Anarchy: The Relentless Rise of the East India Company* (New York: Bloomsbury, 2019), 99–106.

39. In *The Location of Culture* (London and New York: Routledge, 1994), Homi K. Bhabha reminds us that 'Blasphemy is not merely a misrepresentation of the sacred by the secular; it is a moment when the subject-matter or the content of a cultural tradition is being overwhelmed, or alienated, in the act of translation' (225); the symbolic transformation of the 'well-as-mass tomb' generates that dissonance, alienation, horror, and panic, especially when we substitute 'well' for 'chapati' in the following observation: 'The semiotic condition of uncertainty and panic is generated when an old and familiar symbol (chapati) develops an unfamiliar social significance as sign through a transformation of the temporality of its representation' (202).

40. Patrick Brantlinger, *Rule of Darkness: British Literature and Imperialism, 1830–1914* (Ithaca: Cornell University Press, 1988), 204.

41. As quoted in Mukherjee, 'Satan Let Loose upon Earth', 107.

42. For an extensive analysis, see Sharpe, *Allegories of Empire*, 57–84; as an inspiration for fiction, see Nancy L. Paxton, 'Mobilizing Chivalry: Rape in British Novels about the Indian Uprising of 1857', *Victorian Studies*, 36:1 (Autumn 1992), 5–30, and Alison Blunt, 'Embodying War: British Women and Domestic Defilement in the Indian "Mutiny", 1857–8', *Journal of Historical Geography*, 26:3 (June 2000), 403–28. In 'Satan Let Loose upon Earth', Mukherjee agrees that there is no evidence that women were dishonoured by the rebels (116).

43. George Otto Trevelyan, *Cawnpore*, 3rd edn (London: Macmillan, 1866); for Christopher Herbert's analysis of Trevelyan's emphasis on earlier notions of chivalry, see his *War of No Pity: The Indian Mutiny and Victorian Trauma* (Princeton: Princeton University Press, 2008), 182–94.

44. Julia Margaret Cameron to Julia Hay Cameron, 31 July 1857, Kent County Archives, U310_C75_53, and this quote, from 12 August 1857, U310_C75_55.

45. Olsen, *From Life*, 102.

46. Julia Margaret Cameron to Julia Hay Cameron, 10 August 1857, Kent County Archives, U310_C75_54.

47. Julia Margaret Cameron to Julia Hay Cameron, 26 September 1857, Kent County Archives, U310_C75_56.

48. Julia Margaret Cameron to Julia Hay Cameron, 1 October 1857, Kent County Archives, U310_C75_58.

49. Arthur Prinsep to his mother, Sara Princep, n.d., enclosed with Julia Margaret Cameron's letter to her daughter Juley Hay Cameron, 1 October 1857, Kent County Archives, U310_C75_58.

50. Ibid.

51. Ibid.

52. Ibid.

53. William Dalrymple, *The Last Mughal, the Fall of a Dynasty: Delhi, 1857* (New York: Vintage, 2006), 13.

54. On the Siege of Delhi and the creation of memorials to the dead in the aftermath of the Uprising, see Nayanjot Lahiri, 'Commemorating and Remembering 1857: The Revolt in Delhi and its Afterlife', *World Archaeology*, 35:1 (June 2003), 35–60.

55. Dalrymple, *The Last Mughal*, ch. 10; Mount, *Tears of the Rajas*, 504–10.

56. Olsen, *From Life*, 237.

57. Herbert, *War of No Pity*, 102.

58. Malcolm Allbrook, '"Imperial Family": The Prinseps, Empire and Colonial Government in India and Australia' (PhD diss., Griffith University, Queensland, Australia, 2008), 143–8.

59. Augusta Emily Prinsep Becher, *Personal Reminiscences in India and Europe, 1830–1888, of Augusta Becher*, ed. H. G. Rawlinson (London: Constable and Co., Ltd., 1930), 139–40.

60. Harriet Tytler, *An Englishwoman in India: The Memoirs of Harriet Tytler, 1828–1858*, ed. Anthony Sattin (New York: Oxford University Press, 1986), 169, 219 n. 65.

61. Ibid., 144.

62. Becher, *Personal Reminiscences*, xiii.

63. Julia Margaret Cameron to Juley Hay Cameron, 1 October 1857, Kent County Archives, U310_C75_58.

64. On the spread of panic during the Indian Mutiny, see Bhabha, 'By Bread Alone', in *The Location of Culture*, 202–3.

65. Ranajit Guha, 'Not at Home in Empire', *Critical Inquiry*, 23 (Spring 1997), 486–7.

66. Sir John Herschel to Julia Margaret Cameron, n.d., Cameron Collection, Box 11, Getty Research Institute, J. Paul Getty Museum, Los Angeles.

67. Sir John Herschel to Julia Margaret Cameron, 18 August 1846, Cameron Collection, Box 11, Getty Research Institute.

68. Sir John Herschel to Charles Hay Cameron, 1 May 1850, Cameron Collection, Box 11, Getty Research Institute,.

69. Bhabha, 'Conclusion', in *The Location of Culture*, 244, 243.

70. Ibid., 242.

71. Hunt, *Pre-Raphaelitism*, 2:5.

72. Bhabha expounds on this idea: 'Modernity, I suggest, is about the historical construction of a specific position of historical enunciation and address. It privileges those who "bear witness", those who are "subjected", or [those who are] historically displaced. It gives them a representative position through the spatial distance, or the *time-lag* between the Great event and its circulation as a historical sign of the "people" or an "epoch", that constitutes the memory and the moral of the event *as a narrative*, a disposition to cultural communality, a form of social and psychic identification' (original emphasis). *Location of Culture*, 243.

73. For an analysis of the subterfuge of Palgrave, Layard, and Burton, and the concealed violence of their infiltration into other lands, as well as the context of Cameron's German Gallery exhibition, at 168 New Bond Street, that displayed this imagery, see Jeff Rosen, *Julia Margaret Cameron's 'Fancy Subjects': Photographic Allegories of Victorian Identity and Empire* (Manchester: University of Manchester Press, 2016), 218–21.

74. Julia Margaret Cameron to Juley Hay Cameron, 29 September 1857; envelope dated 1 October 1857, Kent County Archives, U310_C75_57.

75. *The Times*, 28 September 1857, 4.

76. *Punch*, 10 October 1857, facing page 150.

77. Randall, 'Autumn 1857', 13–14.

78. Bates and Carter, *Mutiny at the Margins*, 7:137–40.

79. C. H. Spurgeon, *Spurgeon's Fast-Day Sermon* (New York: Sheldon, Blakeman and Co., 1857), 43.

80. Ibid., 17.

81. 'The Rev. C. H. Spurgeon', *Illustrated London News*, 17 October 1857, 400.

82. R. S. Sugirtharajah, *The Bible and India: Postcolonial Explorations* (Cambridge: Cambridge University Press, 2005), 64–7.

83. George Otto Trevelyan, *The Life and Letters of Lord Macaulay*, vol. 2 (Oxford: Oxford University Press, 1978), quoted in Bates and Carter, *Mutiny at the Margins*, 7:150.

Chapter Four
Galahad's Homecoming

1. Julia Margaret Cameron to Julia Hay Cameron, 29 December 1858, Kent County Archives, U310_C75_65.

2. Charles Cameron to Sir John Herschel, 10 January 1853, Royal Society Collection, HS 5.147.

3. Chandak Sengoopta, *Imprint of the Raj: How Fingerprinting was Born in Colonial India* (London: Macmillan, 2003), 55–7.

4. See the Correspondence of Sir John Herschel, http://historydb.adlerplanetarium.org/herschel/. For example, in August 1857, Herschel sent a letter to his son John communicating 'extensive comments on the fighting and restructuring of the colonial system in India' (Letter ID: 885). Augustus de Moran wrote in October 1857 assuring Herschel about recent news in the Indian mails (Letter ID: 7071); John Bullar wrote to Herschel in November 1857 that hostilities had abated and expressed hopes that his anxieties should prove groundless (Letter ID: 5860).

5. Sir John to his wife, Margaret Brodie Herschel, *c.*1859. Correspondence of Sir John Herschel, http://historydb.adlerplanetarium.org/herschel/ (Letter ID: 878).

6. Hunt described the outdoor setting of Little Holland House: 'In the season the company was received out of doors, played bowls and croquet on the lawn at hand, and tables with tea, at which Mrs. Prinsep presided, were placed under shady elms, where in the summer time the dinner table was occasionally brought out, many artists were present, and literary stars shone in brilliant scintillation'. *Pre-Raphaelitism and the Pre-Raphaelite Brotherhood*, 2 vols (New York and London: Macmillan, 1906), 2:165.

7. William Dalrymple, descendant of Julia Margaret's sister Sophia Dalrymple, understood that Sophia and her husband John exchanged daily letters during the rebellion, but that these no longer survive, having been destroyed by his great-grandfather. Email correspondence with the author, 21 October 2021.

8. Mrs Colin Mackenzie, *Six Years in India: Delhi: The City of the Great Mogul* (London: Richard Bentley, 1857), and Helen Douglas Mackenzie, *Storms and Sunshine of a Soldier's Life: Lt.-General Colin Mackenzie, C.B., 1825–1881*, 2 vols (Edinburgh: David Douglas, 1884).

9. Ferdinand Mount, *The Tears of the Rajas: Mutiny, Money and Marriage in India, 1805–1905* (London: Simon & Schuster, 2015), 631–3.

10. Ibid., 632.

11. Ibid.

12. See Victoria C. Olsen, *From Life: Julia Margaret Cameron and Victorian Photography* (New York: Palgrave Macmillan, 2003), 188, 244.

13. Mount, *Tears of the Rajas*, 633.

14. Laura Peters, *Orphan Texts: Victorian Orphans, Culture and Empire* (Manchester: Manchester University Press, 2000), 5.

15. The evocation of such emotion was for many an explicit goal of narrative painting. See Pamela Fletcher, '"To Wipe a Manly Tear": The Aesthetics of Emotion in Victorian Narrative Painting', *Victorian Studies*, 51:3 (2009), 457–69.

16. William Makepeace Thackeray, *Vanity Fair: A Novel without a Hero* (1848), (New York: Heritage Press, 1940), ch. 6, 56.

17. See Cornelia D. J. Pearsall, 'Burying the Duke: Victorian Mourning and the Funeral of the Duke of Wellington', *Victorian Literature and Culture*, 27:2 (1999), 365–93.

18. William Holman Hunt, *Pre-Raphaelitism and the Pre-Raphaelite Brotherhood*, 2nd edn, 2 vols (New York: E. P. Dutton, 1914), 2:130. Hunt reprinted Thackeray's poem in full on pp. 129–30. Note that this edition carries the full poem, whereas the 1906 edition printed by Macmillan does not. Also of note is that in the 1914 edition, a photograph of Henry Taylor by Julia Margaret Cameron accompanies the poem on p. 130.

19. Christopher Herbert, *War of No Pity: The Indian Mutiny and Victorian Trauma* (Princeton: Princeton University Press, 2008), 34.

20. Priya Satia, *Time's Monster: How History Makes History* (Cambridge, MA: Belknap, 2020), 104.

21. Ibid., 35.

22. Thomas Hobbes's (1843) first Greek–English translation was reprinted five times during this era and no fewer than six full or partial re-translations of the work (by others) were made between 1829 and 1881. For an overview, see Henry Jones, 'Jowett's Thucydides: A Corpus-Based Analysis of Translation as Political Intervention', *Translation Studies*, 13:3 (March 2020), 333–51.

23. Thackeray, *Vanity Fair*, ch. 5, 42.

24. Julia Margaret Cameron to Juley Hay Cameron, 26 September 1857, Kent County Archives, U310_C75_56.

25. See Patrick Leary, *The Punch Brotherhood: Table Talk and Print Culture in Mid-Victorian London* (London: British Library, 2010).

26. *Justice*, *Punch*, 12 September 1857. Not all of British India believed in executing such retribution; in fact, Governor-General Canning wanted to distinguish between those sepoys who had rebelled from those who were 'loyal' to British authority. After enacting a clemency resolution in July 1857, Canning was dubbed 'Clemency Canning'. See Michael Maclagan, *'Clemency' Canning: Charles John, 1st Earl Canning, Governor-General and Viceroy of India, 1856–1862* (London: Macmillan, 1962); and Herbert, *War of No Pity*, 106.

27. Arthur Prager, *The Mahogany Tree: An Informal History of Punch* (New York: Hawthorn Books, 1979), 14–17; Lewis Melville, in *The Life of William Makepeace Thackeray*, 2 vols (London: Hutchinson, 1890), 2:175, points out that Thackeray contributed more than 400 drawings to *Punch* over the years he contributed to the magazine.

28. The brutality of this practice and the sense of revulsion experienced by British troops who inflicted it under orders is vividly described in Mount, *Tears of the Rajas*, 465, 647 n. 65. Following Bhabha, one could argue that, symbolically, the cannons brought into view by the British spread panic among the Indians, much as the distribution of *chapati* functioned to spread fear among the British. See Homi K. Bhabha, 'By Bread Alone', in *The Location of Culture* (London and New York: Routledge, 1994), 200–4.

29. Kathryn Ledbetter, *Tennyson and Victorian Periodicals* (Aldershot: Ashgate, 2007), 114.

30. Hallam Tennyson, *Alfred Lord Tennyson, a Memoir by His Son*, 2 vols (New York: Macmillan, 1898), 1:423–4.

31. On the Havelock myth, see Projit Bihari Mukharji, 'Ambiguous Imperialisms: British Subaltern Attitudes towards the "Indian War"', in Andrea Major and Crispin Bates, eds, *Mutiny at the Margins, New Perspectives on the Indian Uprising of 1857, Volume 2: Britain and the Indian Uprising* (New Delhi: Sage, 2013), 124–9.

32. Matthew Bevis, 'Tennyson's Civil Tongue', *Tennyson Research Bulletin*, 7:3 (November 1999), 121.

33. Victor Kiernan, 'Tennyson, King Arthur and Imperialism', in Raphael Samuel and Gareth Stedman Jones, eds, *Culture, Ideology and Politics* (London: Routledge & Kegan Paul, 1982), 131.

34. Ibid., 145.

35. Lieutenant-Colonel D. G. Crawford, *Roll of the Indian Medical Service 1615–1930*, 2 vols (Luton: Andrews, 2012), 2:338. Jowett's pain at the loss of his brother is described in Evelyn Abbott and Lewis Campbell, *The Life and Letters of Benjamin Jowett, M.A., Master of Balliol*, 2 vols (London: John Murray, 1897), 1:252.

36. Benjamin Jowett to Emily Tennyson, 12 December 1858, in Hallam Tennyson, *Alfred Lord Tennyson*, 1:435.

37. For the theatrical dramas, see Wendy C. Nielsen, 'Boadicea Onstage before 1800, a Theatrical and Colonial History', *SEL: Studies in English Literature, 1500–1900*, 49:3 (Summer 2009), 595–614; for the Palace at Westminster, see T. S. R. Boase, 'The Decoration of the New Palace at Westminster, 1843–1863', *Journal of the Warburg and Courtauld Institutes*, 17:3/4 (1954), 330.

38. On Thornycroft, see Martha Vandrei, 'A Victorian Invention? Thomas Thornycroft's "Boadicea Group" and the Idea of Historical Culture in Britain', *Historical Journal*, 57:2 (June 2014), 485–508; Walter L. Arnstein, 'The Warrior Queen: Reflections on Victoria and Her World', *Albion: A Quarterly Journal Concerned with British Studies*, 30:1 (Spring 1998), 1–28; and Stephanie Lawson, 'Nationalism and Biographical Transformation: The Case of Boudicca', *Humanities Research*, 19:1 (2013), 101–19.

39. For the inception of the poem in 1858, see Christopher B. Ricks, *The Poems of Tennyson in Three Volumes* (London: Longman, 1987), 3:36; James Hoge records that Thomas Woolner sent the poet an engraving of *Boädicea* by Thomas Stothard on 12 February 1859. *The Letters of Emily Lady Tennyson*, ed. James O. Hoge (University Park: Pennsylvania State University Press, 1974), 131.This image is reprinted as Figure 7 in Martha Vandrei, *Queen Boudica and Historical Culture in Britain* (Oxford: Oxford University Press, 2018), 142. According to Vandrei, p. 141, Woolner also urged the poet to write an epic poem based upon the Indian Uprising.

40. *Letters of Emily Lady Tennyson*, 147; Hallam Tennyson, *Alfred Lord Tennyson*, 1:436, 459, 473.

41. Deirdre David, *Rule Britannia: Women, Empire, and Victorian Writing* (Ithaca: Cornell University Press, 1995), 173–5.

42. Cecil Lang and Edgar Shannon, eds, *The Letters of Alfred Lord Tennyson, Volume 2: 1851–1870* (Cambridge, MA: Harvard University Press, 1987), 415–16.

43. Hallam Tennyson, *Alfred Lord Tennyson*, 1:426.

44. Donald Hawes, '"Better and Worse Voices": Tennyson and Thackeray', *Tennyson Research Bulletin*, 6:3 (November 1994), 174–82; Hédi Abdel-Jaouad, 'The Sands of Rhyme: Thackeray and Abd al Qadir', *Research in African Literatures*, 30:3 (Autumn 1999), 194–206.

45. Thackeray, *Vanity Fair*, ch. 32, 356.

46. Julia Margaret Cameron to George Frederic Watts, 3 December 1860, National Portrait Gallery, NPG 1014.

47. National Portrait Gallery, *G. F. Watts: 'The Hall of Fame': Portraits of his Famous Contemporaries* (London: Her Majesty's Stationery Office, 1975), 6.

48. Charlotte Boyce, '"She Shall Be Made Immortal": Julia Margaret Cameron's Photography and the Construction of Celebrity', in Charlotte Boyce, Páraic Finnerty, and Anne-Marie Millim, eds,

Victorian Celebrity Culture and Tennyson's Circle (Hampshire: Palgrave Macmillan, 2013), 97–135.

49. 'Love to Val, tell him & the Signor to write'. Arthur Prinsep to his mother, n.d., enclosed in a letter from Julia Margaret Cameron to her daughter Julia Hay Cameron, 1 October 1857, Kent County Archives, U310_C75_58.

50. George Frederic Watts to Julia Margaret Cameron, 21 June 1865, National Portrait Gallery, NPG P125.

51. Hallam Tennyson, *Alfred Lord Tennyson*, 1:443–4.

52. In addition, 'the story of his quest for the Grail could be seen as part of a national legend stretching back into the mists of time, something with a specifically British identity, hallowed by ancient tradition'. Christine Poulson, 'Galahad and War Memorial Imagery of the Nineteenth and Early Twentieth Centuries', *Nineteenth-Century Contexts*, 21:4 (2000), 493–512.

53. Marilynn Lincoln Board, 'Art's Moral Mission: Reading G. F. Watts's *Sir Galahad*', in Debra Mancoff, ed., *The Arthurian Revival: Essays on Form, Tradition, and Transformation* (London: Taylor & Francis, 2014), 132.

54. See Wilfrid Blunt, 'Watts and Ellen Terry', *Burlington Magazine*, 106:730 (January 1964), 43.

55. See Jeff Rosen, *Julia Margaret Cameron's 'Fancy Subjects': Photographic Allegories of Victorian Identity and Empire* (Manchester: Manchester University Press, 2016), ch. 6.

56. Virginia Woolf, *Freshwater: A Comedy* (San Diego: Harcourt, Brace, Jovanovich, 1976), 66.

57. Virginia Woolf, *The Diary of Virginia Woolf, Volume 1, 1915–1919*, ed. Anne Olivier Bell (San Diego: Harcourt Brace & Co., 1977), 108.

58. On the temporal break ('caesura') in representation made possible by a cultural time-lag, such as the one I am identifying here for Cameron, as interpreted through Woolf's eyes, see Bhabha, *Location of Culture*, 144, 237.

Chapter Five
An Indian Prince in London

1. As Priya Satia has written, 'The very idea of "civilization" depended on the racist notion of barbarism. Liberal ideas of colonial tutelage, the very structuring of the so-called "rule of law", were founded on race'. Priya Satia, *Time's Monster: How History Makes History* (Cambridge, MA: Belknap, 2020), 119.

2. For questions of Indian sovereignty prior to 1857, see: Sudipta Sen, *Distant Sovereignty: National Imperialism and the Origins of British India* (New York: Routledge, 2002); and, after 1857, Pramod Kumar Srivastava, 'Nationalism Imagined? Hidden Impacts of the Uprising of 1857', *South Asia Research*, 38:3 (November 2018), 229–46; Suparna Sengupta, 'The Sovereign Exception: Interpreting "British Subjects" in the Queen's Amnesty of 1858', *Social Scientist*, 46:5–6 (May–June 2018), 21–38.

3. For a useful overview, see Thomas R. Metcalf, *The Aftermath of Revolt, India, 1857–1870* (Princeton: Princeton University Press, 1964), 46–91. Sen points out that 'India was not destined to become a settler colony, and military operations seldom resulted in the direct annexation of the territory of subjugated native rulers. Rather, the defeated were made signatories to uneven treaties'. Sudipta Sen, 'Unfinished Conquest: Residual Sovereignty and the Legal Foundations of the British Empire in India', *Law, Culture and the Humanities*, 9:2 (2012), 238.

4. Lord Clive established this policy in 1765; see Sen, *Distant Sovereignty*, xv; Sengupta, 'Sovereign Exception', 28.

5. Katherine Porter, Lance Brennan, and Robin Haines, 'Bad Language: The Role of English, Persian, and Other Esoteric Tongues in the Dismissal of Sir Edward Colebrooke as Resident of Delhi in 1829', *Modern Asian Studies*, 35:1 (February 2001), 75–112.

6. Michael H. Fisher, 'Indirect Rule in the British Empire: The Foundations of the Residency System in India (1764–1858)', *Modern Asian Studies*, 18:3 (1984), 393–428; See also Karuna Mantena, *Alibis of Empire: Henry Maine and the Ends of Liberal Imperialism* (Princeton: Princeton University Press, 2010). On British diplomacy and the ceremonial expectations of their Indian hosts, see Bernard Cohn, 'Representing Authority in Victorian India', and 'Cloth, Clothes, and Colonialism: India in the Nineteenth Century', in *The Bernard Cohn Omnibus* (New Delhi: Oxford University Press, 2004), 633–82, 106–62.

7. House of Commons, *Parliamentary Papers*, Draft of the Indian Penal Code prepared by the Indian Law Commissioners (1838), 86 (quoted in Sengupta, 'Sovereign Exception', 25).

8. Sen, 'Unfinished Conquest', 228.

9. Partha Chaterjee, *The Black Hole of Empire: History of a Global Practice of Power* (Princeton: Princeton University Press, 2012), 191.

10. Mahmood Mamdani called this division one 'between a *racialized* rights-bearing citizenry and an *ethnicized* subject population' in 'Historicizing Power and Responses to Power: Indirect Rule and Its Reform', *Social Research*, 66:3 (Fall 1999), 859–86, quoted with original emphasis 867. The lack of resolution to this question encouraged Indians with grievances to take their appeals directly to London. See Michael H. Fisher, 'Multiple Meanings of 1857 for Indians in Britain', *Economic and Political Weekly*, 42:19 (12–18 May 2007), 1703–9; Michael H. Fisher, *Counterflows to Colonialism: Indian Travellers and Settlers in Britain, 1600–1857* (Ranikhet, India: Permanent Black, 2004).

11. 'Iqbal al-Daula' is a phonetic rendering of the prince's name and is adopted here as a convention. Other spellings in newspaper reports, government documents, letters to the editor, and privately published materials include: Newab Ekbaloo-dowlah, Ak bal od dowlah, Akbaloddowla, Ekbal-Ood-Dowlah Bahador, and Nawáb Ikbál Ud Daulah Bahádur.

12. Sukanya Banerjee, *Becoming Imperial Citizens: Indians in the Late-Victorian Empire* (Durham, NC, and London: Duke University Press, 2010), 7.

13. Sen, 'Unfinished Conquest', 233.

14. The new Council of India also preserved recalcitrant members from the East India Company's two boards, which diminished its overall effectiveness. See

Donovan Williams, 'The Council of India and the Relationship between the Home and Supreme Governments, 1858–1870', *English Historical Review*, 81:318 (January 1966), 56–73.

15. J. B. Conacher, *The Aberdeen Coalition, 1852–1855: A Study in Mid-Nineteenth-Century Party Politics* (Cambridge: Cambridge University Press, 1968), ch. 4, 'The India Act of 1853'.

16. William Walker, after Sir John Gilbert, *The Coalition Ministry* (oil on canvas, 1854), reproductive engraving, 1857 (527 × 721 mm), National Portrait Gallery, London, NPG-1125a.

17. Cameron: *Hansard Parliamentary Debates*, 3rd series, 7 April 1853, vol. 125, 698; Cameron also published his own pamphlet, Charles Hay Cameron, *An Address to Parliament on the Duties of Great Britain to India, in Respect of the Education of the Natives* (London: Longman, Brown, Green and Longmans, 1853). Cameron's brother-in-law and former associate on the Council of India, Henry Thoby Prinsep, wrote his own tract arguing to extend the East India Company's monopoly: H. T. Prinsep, *The India Question in 1853* (London: Wm. H. Allen & Co., 1853).

18. Conacher, *Aberdeen Coalition*, 137ff.

19. 'The Peace Fete at the Crystal Palace', *Illustrated London News*, 17 May 1856, 524–5.

20. The event was also covered with an engraving on 17 May 1856 in the *Illustrated Times*. Frith's 'Universal Series' can be found in numerous collections; these topographic views are albumen prints, approximately 6" × 8", mounted on brown card stock.

21. Marquis of Lansdowne to Countess Somers, 31 May 1855, reprinted in Kathleen Fitzpatrick, *Lady Henry Somerset* (Boston: Little, Brown and Co., 1923), 31. For Lord Panmure in Parliament, see *Hansard Parliamentary Debates*, 3rd series, 8 July 1856, vol. 143, 493–5. On the Scutari monument, see *Hansard*, 8 July 1856, vol. 143, 493–5; and Kaan Sag, 'The Scutari Monument in Istanbul: The Introduction of Victorian Monumental Language to Ottoman Society', *Sculpture Journal*, 23:3 (2014), 279–92.

22. The public indecisiveness about the statue's ultimate destination was lampooned in *Punch*: 'A resting-place for Richard Cœur de Lion', *Punch*, 29 August 1857, 91. See also John Harrison, 'The Prince, the Baron and the Knight: Baron Carlo Marochetti and the "Black Prince"', *British Art Journal*, 5:2 (Autumn 2004), 62–8.

23. Julia Margaret Cameron to Julia Hay Cameron, 29 September 1857, Kent County Archives, U310_C75_57.

24. 'Havelock Memorial Fund', *The Times*, 20 March 1858, 7.

25. John Kaye and George Bruce Malleson, *A History of the Indian Mutiny, 1857–1858*, 3 vols (London: Allen and Co., 1892), 2:298–303. See Christopher Herbert's analysis of Kaye's narrative in his book, *War of No Pity: The Indian Mutiny and Victorian Trauma* (Princeton: Princeton University Press, 2008), 194–204.

26. The Havelock commission ultimately went to William Behnes, an academician who had taught sculpture to both Watts and Woolner, and Behnes's bronze was dedicated before a large crowd, but not until 1861.

27. British Governors-General who ruled different colonies of the empire discussed the exile of the deposed Mughal emperor and worked together to find a suitable place of exile. See Donovan Williams, 'An Echo of the Indian Mutiny: The Proposed Banishment of Bahadur Shah II to the Cape Colony, 1857', *Historia Archive*, 17:4 (1972), 265–8. On the fate of the Mughal imperial family, see William Dalrymple, *The Last Mughal: The Fall of a Dynasty: Delhi, 1857* (New York: Vintage, 2006).

28. See *Illustrated London News*, 10 October 1857 (ex-King of Delhi) and 28 November 1857 (ex-King of Oude).

29. Ranajit Guha, 'The Prose of Counter-Insurgency', in Ranajit Guha and Gayatri Chakravorty Spivak, eds, *Selected Subaltern Studies* (New York: Oxford University Press, 1988), 71.

30. Quoted in Srivastava, 'Nationalism Imagined', 232.

31. 'Banquet at the Royal Academy of Arts', *The Times*, 3 May 1858, 7.

32. The critic for the *Illustrated London News* called it 'horrible' and 'revolting', 'The Exhibition at the Royal Academy', *Illustrated London News*, 15 May 1858, 498.

33. John Ruskin, *Notes on Some of the Principal Pictures Exhibited in the Rooms of the Royal Academy: The Old and New Societies of Painters in Water Colours, the Society of British Artists, and the French Exhibition*, No. IV (London: Smith, Elder and Co., 1858), 14.

34. Julia Thomas, *Painted Victorians: The Inscription of Values in Word and Image* (Athens: Ohio University Press, 2004), 129.

35. Many of these ideas were summarized in a protest recorded by Lord Monteagle in the House of Lords, the 'Protest of Lord Monteagle', in James Silk Buckingham, *Plan for the Future Government of India*, 2nd edn (London: Partridge and Oakey, 1853), 65–8; and by John William Kaye, who complained of the postponement of the enactment of Cameron's Penal Code, in *The Administration of The East India Company: A History of Indian Progress*, 2nd edn (London: Richard Bentley, 1853), 105–6, 596–7.

36. [Walter Bagehot], 'Principles of Indian Government', *National Review*, 6 (January 1858), 1–37.

37. Ibid., 9. The essay was unsigned, yet Bagehot had assumed large responsibilities for writing and editing such significant pieces in the new journal, according to James Grant, *Bagehot: The Life and Times of the Greatest Victorian* (London: W. W. Norton, 2019), 90–9; also see Robert Tener, 'R. H. Hutton's Editorial Career, II. "The Prospective" and "National Review"', *Victorian Periodicals Newsletter*, 7:4 (December 1974), 6–13.

38. [Bagehot], 'Principles of Indian Government', 15.

39. Nadia Urbanati, 'The Many Heads of the Hydra: J. S. Mill on Despotism', in Nadia Urbanati and Alex Zakaras, eds, *J. S. Mill's Political Thought: A Bicentennial Reassessment* (Cambridge: Cambridge University Press, 2007), 66–97.

40. [Bagehot], 'Principles of Indian Government'; Urbanati, 'Many Heads of the Hydra', 21. On the desire to keep India a permanent colony, see Francis G. Hutchins, *On the Illusion of Permanence:*

British Imperialism in India (Princeton: Princeton University Press, 1967).

41. Chaterjee, *Black Hole of Empire*, 181.

42. John Stuart Mill, 'On Liberty', in *'Utilitarianism', 'On Liberty', and 'Considerations of Representative Government'*, ed. H. B. Acton (London: J. M. Dent and Sons, 1972), 79.

43. Satia, *Time's Monster*, 128.

44. Charles Cameron, as quoted in [Bagehot], 'Principles of Indian Government', 22.

45. Michel Foucault, 'Governmentality', in Graham Burchell, Colin Gordon, and Peter Miller, eds, *The Foucault Effect: Studies in Governmentality* (Chicago: University of Chicago Press, 1991), 87–104.

46. R. J. Moore, *Sir Charles Wood's Indian Policy, 1853–66* (Manchester: Manchester University Press, 1966); Metcalf, *Aftermath of Revolt*.

47. Williams, 'Council of India', 72–3.

48. R. J. Moore, 'John Stuart Mill at East India House', *Historical Studies*, 20:81 (1983), 497–519; information provided here informs this brief overview of Mill's intersection with the administration and rule of Awadh.

49. Ibid.

50. The question of the 'rightful succession' of the Awadh line of kings (i.e. Wajid Ali Shah's line or Iqbal al-Daula's line) was considered by Captain W. White, *Mirzas Kaiwan Jah, or the Dethroned King of Oude, In Chains!!!* (London: William Strange, 1838); this also informs the collection of 'Papers Relating to Oude' printed in 1856 by Parliament. These questions may be separated from questions of governance and corruption, for example, which form the basis of Malcolm Lewin, *Has Oude been Worse Governed by its Native Princes than our Indian Territories by Leadenhall Street?* (London: James Ridgway, 1857). Governance continued to dominate the Oude discussion in the public forum into the 1870s, as summarized in Thomas Carlyle, 'The Indian Deficit', *Fraser's Magazine*, new series, 3:13 (January 1871), 14–27. But the issue of royal succession also seems to have never abated. See Ellen Barry, 'The Jungle Prince of Delhi', *New York Times*, Special Section, 22 November 2019.

51. Fisher, *Counterflows to Colonialism*, chs 7 and 8.

52. Captain W. White, *The Prince of Oude; or, The Claim of the Nawaub Ekbal-ood-Dowlah Bahador to the Throne of Oude* (London: William Strange, 1838).

53. Quoted in Fisher, *Counterflows to Colonialism*, 272–4.

54. Michael H. Fisher, 'Conflicting Meanings of Persianate Culture, an Intimate Example from Colonial India and Britain', in Nile Green, ed., *The Persianate World: The Frontiers of a Eurasian Lingua Franca* (Oakland: University of California Press, 2019), 236.

55. Reporting in 1858 for the *New-York Daily Tribune* to make sense of the Uprising, Karl Marx interpreted the events in this way, noting that as early as 1831, Lord Palmerston, then Foreign Secretary, gave orders to Governor-General Bentinck to annex Oude, an act Marx called an attempted *coup d'état*. For Marx, this action was among the first of a long list of double-dealing and treachery inflicted by the British occupiers on the indigenous population. Karl Marx, 'The Annexation of Oude', *New-York Daily Tribune*, 28 May 1858, https://www.marxists.org/archive/marx/works/1858/05/28.htm.

56. Captain W. White, *The Prince of Oude*, Appendices A and B.

57. *The King of Oude, his Brother, and Attendants: Sketched while on their Visit to England, by a Lady* [H. T.] (London: Ackermann and Co, *c.*1840).

58. Smart's painting is now in the British Library, Foster 575:1838.

59. Fisher, *Counterflows to Colonialism*, 274. Iqbal al-Daula's legal status to travel internationally is discussed by Julia Stephens, 'An Uncertain Inheritance: The Imperial Travels of Legal Migrants, from British India to Ottoman Iraq', *Law and History Review*, 32:4 (November 2014), 749–72. Iqbal al-Daula was knighted Grand Commander of the Star of India in the India Office in London on 23 May 1882. *London Gazette*, 23 May 1882, 2409.

60. *Illustrated London News*, 14 March 1857, 246.

61. *Illustrated London News*, 1 August 1857, 121.

62. 'The Princes of Oude', *Illustrated London News*, 1 August 1857, 118.

63. Fisher, *Counterflows to Colonialism*, 243–98.

64. Additional stories of Asian rulers appealing to Britain for the restitution of their stripped titles are found in Robert Aldrich, *Banished Potentates: Dethroning and Exiling Indigenous Monarchs under British and French Colonial Rule, 1815–1955* (Manchester: Manchester University Press, 2018), 75–116.

65. Sudipta Sen, 'Imperial Subjects on Trial: On the Legal Identity of Britons in Late Eighteenth Century India', *Journal of British Studies*, 45:3 (July 2006), 532–55; see also Sengupta, 'Sovereign Exception', 32.

66. Chaterjee, *Black Hole of Empire*, 201. The same period is examined by Dalrymple, *The Last Mughal*, 118–23.

67. Metcalf, *Aftermath of Revolt*, 31–6. For the 'Proclamation to the People of Oude on its Annexation', delivered in February 1856, see Barbara Harlow and Mia Carter, eds, *Archives of Empire, Volume 1: From the East India Company to the Suez Canal* (Durham, NC, and London: Duke University Press, 2003), 404–9.

68. Williams, 'Council of India', 72.

69. John Stuart Mill, 'A Few Words on Non-Intervention' (1859), in *Dissertations and Discussions: Political, Philosophical, and Historical, Volume 3* (Boston, MA: William V. Spencer, 1865), 238–63.

70. Quoted in Julia Stephens, 'An Uncertain Inheritance: The Imperial Travels of Legal Migrants, from British India to Ottoman Iraq', in Lâle Can, Michael Christopher Lowe, Kent F. Schull, and Robert Zens, eds, *The Subjects of Ottoman International Law* (Bloomington: Indiana University Press, 2020), 132.

71. A. Major, 'British Humanitarian Political Economy and Famine in India, 1838–42', *Journal of British Studies* (2019), 19, http://eprints.whiterose.ac.uk/148482/.

72. Meir Litvak, 'Money, Religion, and Politics: The Oudh Bequest in Najaf and Karbala, 1850–1903', *International Journal*

of Middle East Studies, 33:1 (February 2001), 1–21.

73. Ibid., 6.

74. *Lady Layard's Diary*, entry for 19 January 1865 (Armstrong Browning Library: Baylor University, TX, 2001–4), http://www.browningguide.org/browningscircle.php.

75. Julia Margaret Cameron wrote about the beautiful Mrs Hambro some ten years earlier, in 1855, in a letter to Alfred Tennyson: 'Amongst the young Wives "the Queen of Beauty" is Mrs. Hambro (one month younger than my Juley), frolicsome and graceful as a kitten and having the form and eye of an antelope. She is tall and slender, not stately, and not seventeen – but quite able to make all daisies rosy and the ground she treads seem proud of her'. Quoted in Anne Thackeray, 'From Friend to Friend', in *Cornhill Magazine*, new series, 41 (1916), 27.

76. Laura Troubridge, *Memories and Remembrances* (London: Heinemann, 1925), 10. Troubridge was one of Alice Prinsep Gurney's two daughters.

77. For a deeper analysis of Cameron's relation to the story of *Paul and Virginia*, see Jeff Rosen, *Julia Margaret Cameron's 'Fancy Subjects': Photographic Allegories of Victorian Identity and Empire* (Manchester: Manchester University Press, 2016), 30–65.

78. The Julia Hay Norman Album is housed in the National Science Museum, London, and the photograph of Alice Prinsep Gurney is 10709672.

79. Samuel Bourne, 'Photography in the East: Simla, Himalayas, May 5th, 1863', *British Journal of Photography*, 1 July 1863, reprinted in Samuel Bourne, *Photographic Journeys in the Himalayas*, ed. Hugh Ashley Rayner (Bath: Pagoda Tree Press, 2014), 1.

80. Ariella Aïsha Azoulay, *Potential History: Unlearning Imperialism* (London: Verso, 2019).

81. John Falconer, '"A Pure Labor of Love": A Publishing History of The People of India', in Eleanor M. Hight and Gary D. Sampson, eds, *Colonialist Photography: Imag(in)ing Race and Place* (London: Routledge, 2002), 51–83, and James R. Ryan, *Picturing Empire: Photography and the Visualization of the British Empire* (Chicago: University of Chicago Press, 1997), 155–8.

82. On the *carte-de-visite* fad in England, see Annie Rudd, 'Victorians Living in Public: *Cartes-de-Visite* as 19th-Century Social Media', *Photography and Culture*, 9:3 (2016), 195–217; and on celebrity portraiture, see Charlotte Boyce, '"She Shall be Made Immortal": Julia Margaret Cameron's Photography and the Construction of Celebrity', in Charlotte Boyce, Paraic Finnerly, and Anne-Marie Millim, eds, *Victorian Celebrity Culture and Tennyson's Circle* (London: Palgrave Macmillan, 2013), 97–135.

83. See Hellis and Sons, Photographers, London: *Carte-de-visite* portrait photograph, reverse, *c.*1865, https://www.alamy.com/victorian-advertising-cdv-carte-de-visite-showing-the-illustration-and-calligraphy-from-hellis-sons-head-studios-211-213-regent-street-london-image244933384.html?imageid=FD380B8F-68D3-4044-9659-FCC2E9D167A0&p=818036&pn=1&searchId=0ea0319e2e25b050791f61ca50925489&searchtype=0.

84. John Plunkett, 'Celebrity and Community: The Poetics of the Carte-de-visite', *Journal of Victorian Culture*, 8:1 (2003), 55–79; Lara Perry, 'The Carte de Visite in the 1860s and the Serial Dynamic of Photographic Likeness', *Art History*, 35:4 (September 2012), 728–49.

85. Banerjee, *Becoming Imperial Citizens*, 5.

86. Christopher Pinney, *The Coming of Photography in India* (London: British Library, 2008), 44–6.

87. Julie F. Codell, 'Victorian Portraits: Re-Tailoring Identities', *Nineteenth-Century Contexts*, 34:5 (December 2012), 513.

88. Julian Cox and Colin Ford, 'Appendix B: Inscriptions, Stamps, and the Business of Photography', in *Julia Margaret Cameron: The Complete Photographs* (Los Angeles: J. Paul Getty Museum, 2003), 498–501.

89. *List of Members of the Royal Asiatic Society of Great Britain and Ireland* (London: 1861), 3, 10.

90. bell hooks, 'Representing the Black Male Body', *Art on My Mind: Visual Politics* (New York: New Press, 1995), 205.

91. bell hooks, 'Feminism as a Persistent Critique of History: What's Love Got to Do with It?', in Alan Read, ed., *The Fact of Blackness: Frantz Fanon and Visual Representation* (Seattle: Bay Press, 1996), 82–3.

92. For additional case studies of travellers from the colonies to London, see Fisher, *Counterflows to Colonialism*; Catherine Hall, *Civilizing Subjects: Metropole and Colony in the English Imagination, 1830–1867* (Cambridge: Polity Press, 2002); Robert Aldrich, *Banished Potentates: Dethroning and Exiling Indigenous Monarchs under British and French Colonial Rule, 1815–1955* (Manchester: Manchester University Press, 2018); and Thomas R. Metcalf, *Imperial Connections: India in the Indian Ocean Arena, 1860–1920* (Berkeley: University of California Press, 2007).

93. hooks, 'Feminism', 85.

94. Christopher Herbert wrote that 'the eroded cultural supremacy of the retributive principle' motivated British soldiers like her nephew, Arthur Prinsep, to participate in the massacre of native Indians of Delhi, see *War of No Pity*, 102. This double sense of trauma inflicted on 'both sides' of the colonizer/colonized divide was described earlier by Ashis Nandy, 'The Psychology of Colonialism: Sex, Age, and Ideology in British India', in *The Intimate Enemy: Loss and Recovery of Self Under Colonialism* (New York: Oxford University Press, 1983), later published in Ashis Nandy, *Exiled at Home* (New Delhi: Oxford University Press, 2005), 2–63.

95. Homi K. Bhabha, 'Of Mimicry and Man: The Ambivalence of Colonial Discourse', in *The Location of Culture* (London and New York: Routledge, 1994), 85–92.

96. Judith Butler, *Frames of War: When is Life Grievable?* (2009) (London: Verso, 2016), 139–40. The dialogical nature and status of colonial identity and citizenship has also been taken up recently by Gabrielle Moser, *Projecting Citizenship: Photography and Belonging in the British Empire* (University Park: Pennsylvania State University Press, 2019).

97. Banerjee recently argued that such photography provides visible evidence that citizenship is not so much defined 'in the realm of statutory enactment as in the cultural, imaginative, and affective fields that both engender it and are constituted by it', in *Becoming Imperial Citizens*, 5.

98. Homi Bhabha's notions of the time-lag that stages 'the past as symbol, myth, memory, history, the ancestral' and that also reinscribes the lessons of the past 'into the very textuality of the present' seem inadequate to account for the evident ambiguity described here, a consequence of the indeterminacy of Iqbal al-Daula's legal and social status. See Bhabha's 'Conclusion' in *Location of Culture*, 247.

Chapter Six Blood of the Fathers

1. Sarah Stickney Ellis, *The Women of England: Their Social Duties and Domestic Habits* (London: Fisher, Son and Co., 1839), 83, 161–2.

2. Janice Fiamengo, 'Forms of Suffering in Charlotte Yonge's *The Clever Woman of the Family*', *Victorian Review*, 25:2 (Winter 2000), 80–105; Kate Lawson, 'Indian Mutiny/English Mutiny: National Governance in Charlotte Yonge's *The Clever Woman of the Family*', *Victorian Literature and Culture*, 42:3 (2014), 439–55; Tamara S. Wagner, *Victorian Narratives of Failed Emigration: Settlers, Returnees, and Nineteenth-Century Literature in English* (London and New York: Routledge, 2016), ch. 4, 'No Exotic Ends in Charlotte Yonge', 158–210.

3. Here I part company with the scholarship of Mike Weaver, who wrote about Cameron's Tractarian tendencies as if she were a prototypical 'Anglo-Catholic' in his *Julia Margaret Cameron, 1815–1879* (Southampton: John Hansard Gallery, 1984). For an alternative interpretation of the role of Anglican religious debates in Cameron's allegories, see Jeff Rosen, *Julia Margaret Cameron's 'Fancy Subjects': Photographic Allegories of Victorian Identity and Empire* (Manchester: Manchester University Press, 2016), ch. 2, 66–104.

4. Here I borrow the term used by Mary A. Procida in *Married to the Empire: Gender, Politics, and Imperialism in India, 1883–1947* (Manchester: Manchester University Press, 2017), esp. ch. 4, 'Re-writing the Mutiny'.

5. Éadaoin Agnew, *Imperial Women Writers in Victorian India: Representing Colonial Life, 1850–1910* (Cham, Switzerland: Palgrave Macmillan, 2017), 92.

6. Julia Margaret Cameron to Juley Hay Norman and Charles Norman, 9 February 1859, Kent County Archives, U310_C75_68.

7. On these two paintings, see: Stefanie Markovits, *The Crimean War in the British Imagination* (Cambridge: Cambridge University Press, 2009); Paul Barlow, *Time Present and Time Past: The Art of John Everett Millais* (Farnham, Surrey: Ashgate, 2005); and Michael Hancher, '"Urgent Private Affairs": Millais's "Peace Concluded, 1856"', *Burlington Magazine*, 133:1061 (August 1991), 499–506. See also Kate Flint, 'Feeling, Affect, Melancholy, Loss: Millais's *Autumn Leaves* and the Siege of Sebastopol', *19: Interdisciplinary Studies in the Long Nineteenth Century*, #23 (2016), 9–12.

8. M. H. Spielmann, *Millais and his Works, with Special Reference to the Exhibition at the Royal Academy, 1898* (Edinburgh and London: William Blackburn, 1898), 72.

9. On the Patriotic Fund, see 'The Patriotic Fund', *Illustrated London News*, 21 October 1854, 381. See also: Janis Lomas, 'Delicate Duties: Issues of Class and Respectability in Government Policy towards the Wives and Widows of British Soldiers in the Era of the Great War', *Women's History Review*, 9:1 (2000), 123–40; Jessica A. Sheetz-Nguyen, 'Lloyd's Patriotic Fund, 1791–1841: "To the Heroes of Trafalgar"', in Marilyn D. Button and Jessica A. Sheetz-Nguyen, eds, *Victorians and the Case for Charity: Essays on Responses to British Poverty by the State, the Church, and the Literati* (Jefferson, NC: McFarland and Co., 2014), 58–76.

10. Orlando Figes, *The Crimean War: A History* (New York: Metropolitan Books/Henry Holt, 2011).

11. The extremes of the count of war dead defy any close scrutiny: for example, using British sources alone, the website 'FindMyPast' records some 2,400 names (https://www.search.findmypast.com), which seems an extremely low count, given that some contemporaneous accounts listed that many dead in one battle alone (cf. John William Kaye, *A History of the Sepoy War in India, 1857–58*, 3 vols (London: Allen, 1877); whereas, more recently, Amaresh Misra, in *War of Civilizations: India AD 1857* (New Delhi: Rupa and Co., 2008), estimates almost 10 million dead Indians over the ten-year span of 1857–67.

12. Ferdinand Mount, *The Tears of the Rajas: Mutiny, Money and Marriage in India, 1805–1905* (London: Simon and Schuster, 2015), 590.

13. Rosie Llewellyn-Jones, 'Marginalised Victims of 1857', in Andrea Major and Crispin Bates, eds, *Mutiny at the Margins: New Perspectives on the Indian Uprising of 1857, Volume 2, Britain and the Indian Uprising* (New Delhi: Sage, 2013), 160–3.

14. See Durba Ghosh, 'Making and Un-making Loyal Subjects: Pensioning Widows and Educating Orphans in Early Colonial India', *Journal of Imperial & Commonwealth History*, 31:1 (2003), 1–28; and Judith Edna Hinshaw, 'Imperialism and Widowhood: British Widows of the 1857 "Indian Mutiny"' (PhD diss., University of Calgary, July 2011), 175–6.

15. 'Sufferers of the Indian Mutiny', *Examiner*, 29 August 1857, 555.

16. Judith Edna Hinshaw, 'Imperialism and Widowhood', 149, 152.

17. 'The India Relief Fund', in Crispin Bates and Marina Carter, eds, *Mutiny at the Margins, New Perspectives on the Indian Uprising of 1857, Volume 7: Documents of the Indian Uprising* (Los Angeles: Sage, 2017), 229–35.

18. See Kelly Hager, 'Chipping Away at Coverture: The Matrimonial Causes Act of 1857', *BRANCH: Britain, Representation and Nineteenth-Century History*, ed. Dino Franco Felluga, https://www.branchcollective.org/?ps_articles=kelly-hager-chipping-away-at-coverture-the-matrimonial-causes-act-of-1857.

19. See the history of the Royal Victoria Patriotic Asylum at http://www.childrenshomes.org.uk/WandsworthVictoriaGirls/.

20. Arthur N. Birch and William Robinson, *The Colonial Office List for 1867* (London: Harrison, 1867), 18.

21. Julia Margaret Cameron to Julia Hay Norman, 7 November 1861, Kent County Archives, U310_C75_87.

22. Olive Anderson, 'Warfare in the Crimean War', *Economic History Review*, new series, 14:1 (1961), 34–47; Manuel Díaz-Ordóñez, 'European Imperialism, War, Strategic Commodities and Ecological Limits: The Diffusion of Hemp in Spanish South America and its Ghost Fibers', in Bartolomé Yun-Casalilla, Ilaria Berti, and Omar Svriz-Wucherer, eds, *American Globalization: Trans-Cultural Consumption in Spanish Latin America* (New York and London: Routledge, 2022), 56–77.

23. For extracts of reports from *The Times* promoting this display, see 'The Victorian Royal Navy' website, https://www.pdavis.nl/Times.php?id=507.

24. Emily Tennyson to Thomas Woolner, 28 April 1856, in *The Letters of Emily Lady Tennyson*, ed. James O. Hoge (University Park: Pennsylvania State University Press, 1974), 96–7.

25. As quoted in 'The Victorian Royal Navy' website, https://www.pdavis.nl/ILN_260456.htm.

26. 'The Soldier's Dream', *Punch*, 1 April 1854, 130 (ll. 23–4). On the works of Thomas Campbell in relation to this poem, see Tai-Chun Ho, 'The Afterlife of Thomas Campbell and "The Soldier's Dream" in the Crimean War', *19: Interdisciplinary Studies in the Long Nineteenth Century*, #20 (2015), 1–18.

27. P. G. Scott, *Tennyson's* Enoch Arden*: A Victorian Best Seller* (Lincoln: Tennyson Research Society, 1970); Marion Shaw, 'Tennyson's Dark Continent', *Victorian Poetry*, 32:2 (Summer 1994), 157–69; Alison Chapman, '"A Poet Never Sees a Ghost": Photography and Trance in Tennyson's *Enoch Arden* and Julia Margaret Cameron's Photography', *Victorian Poetry*, 41:1 (Spring 2003), 47–72; Anne Humpherys, '*Enoch Arden*, the Fatal Return, and the Silence of Annie', *Victorian Poetry*, 30:3/4 (Autumn–Winter 1992), 331–42; Roger Ebbatson, 'Enoch Arden's Other Island', *Tennyson Research Bulletin*, 6:4 (November 1995), 240–53; Marion Shaw, 'Elizabeth Gaskell, Tennyson and the Fatal Return: *Sylvia's Lovers* and *Enoch Arden*', *Gaskell Society Journal*, 9 (1995), 43–54.

28. This episode was described by Victoria C. Olsen, *From Life: Julia Margaret Cameron and Victorian Photography* (New York: Palgrave Macmillan, 2003), 125.

29. Scott, '*Tennyson's* Enoch Arden', 15.

30. As Anne Humpherys wrote, 'the central act in this story is betrayal, and the central emotions anxiety, jealousy, and anger'. Humpherys, '*Enoch Arden*, the Fatal Return, and the Silence of Annie', 332. On the sensation novel, see Mariaconcetta Constantini, 'Sensation, Class and the Rising Professionals', in Andrew Mangham, ed., *The Cambridge Companion to Sensation Fiction* (Cambridge: Cambridge University Press, 2013), 99–112; 'Sensation Novels', *Blackwood's Edinburgh Magazine*, 91 (May 1862), 568; 'Our Female Sensation Authors', *Christian Remembrancer*, 46 (1864), 209–36.

31. Scott, '*Tennyson's* Enoch Arden', 1.

32. A print of *Philip Ray, Annie Lee, and Enoch Arden* is in the Henry Taylor album, for example. The photographer returned to the theme once more in 1872 with '*This is My House, This is My Little Wife*' (Getty Museum), explicitly portraying a line from 'Enoch Arden'.

33. Rosen, *Julia Margaret Cameron's 'Fancy Subjects'*, ch. 1.

34. Shaw, 'Tennyson's Dark Continent', 162.

35. As Fredric Jameson writes, 'it is in detecting the traces of that uninterrupted narrative, in restoring to the surface of the text the repressed and buried reality of this fundamental history, that the doctrine of a political unconscious finds its function and its necessity'. *The Political Unconscious: Narrative as a Socially Symbolic Act* (Ithaca: Cornell University Press, 1981), 20.

36. Humpherys, '*Enoch Arden*, the Fatal Return, and the Silence of Annie', 337.

37. Derrida referred to this kind of voyeurism by the term 'the visor effect', in Jacques Derrida, *Specters of Marx: The State of the Debt, the Work of Mourning, & the New International*, trans. Peggy Kamuf (New York: Routledge, 1994), 4–11.

38. Julia Margaret Cameron, 'Annals of My Glass House' (1874), reprinted in Violet Hamilton, *Annals of My Glass House: Photographs by Julia Margaret Cameron* (Claremont, CA: Scripps College, 1996), 12.

39. Rosen, *Julia Margaret Cameron's 'Fancy Subjects'*, 15–19.

40. Although Watts's letter is undated, scholars surmise these examples functioned like 'working prints' rather than 'finished pieces', and correspond to Watts's request that Cameron send him only 'defective unmounted impressions' to evaluate in order to provide critical feedback to help improve her artistic process; see G. F. Watts to Julia Margaret Cameron, n.d., National Portrait Gallery, NPG P215.

41. R. Derek Wood, ed., *Julia Margaret Cameron's Copyrighted Photographs* (London: privately published, May 1996), copy archived by the Royal Photographic Society and online at www.midley.co.uk/cameron/cameron.pdf.

42. In addition, during this period she also often used photographs of very young children as if they were 'raw materials', that is, by deliberately cutting out fragments of heads from larger works, or by joining photographic fragments together with other pieces to fashion wholly new compositions.

43. David Albert Jones, *Angels: A Very Short Introduction* (Oxford: Oxford University Press, 2011), 23–8.

44. On putti, see Charles Dempsey, *Inventing the Renaissance Putto* (Chapel Hill: University of North Carolina Press, 2001), and Alexandra M. Korey, 'Putti, Pleasure, and Pedagogy in Sixteenth-Century Italian Prints and Decorative Arts' (PhD diss., University of Chicago, 2007); for their use in grave-markers, see Adam R. Heinrich, 'Cherubs or Putti? Gravemarkers Demonstrating Conspicuous Consumption and the Rococo Fashion in the Eighteenth Century', *International Journal of Historical Archaeology*, 18:1 (March 2014), 37–64.

45. On the technical reproducibility of Raphael's work, see Brigid Doherty,

'Between the Artwork and its "Actualization": A Footnote to Art History in Benjamin's "Work of Art" Essay', *Paragraph*, 32:3 (November 2009), 331–58. On the infatuation of Cameron's circle, particularly Austen Henry Layard, Lord Lindsay, John Ruskin, George Scharf, Sir William Gregory, and others, with chromolithographic reproductions of Renaissance artworks, see ch. 1, and Tanya Ledger, 'A Study of the Arundel Society 1848–1897' (DPhil thesis, University of Oxford, 1978).

46. On Prince Albert's project, see Anthony Hamber, *'A Higher Branch of the Art': Photographing the Fine Arts in England, 1839–1880* (London: Gordon and Breach, 1996), 220–3; E. Becker and C. Ruland, 'The "Raphael Collection" of H.R.H. the Prince Consort', in *Fine Arts Quarterly Review*, 1 (1863), 27–40; J. Montagu, 'The Ruland / Raphael Collection', *Visual Resources*, 3 (1986), 167–83. In the Royal Collection at Windsor Castle, one can find multiple images of the *Sistine Madonna* in different sizes and media types, including: an engraving by Agostino Capelli from *c.*1800 (RCIN 851068); an engraving and etching by Eduard Mandel from *c.*1830–70 (RCIN 851067); a lithograph from *c.*1800 by Ludwig Theodor Zoellner (RCIN 851065); and a reproduction photograph in carbon by Adolphe Braun from *c.*1860 (RCIN 851062).

47. On Caldesi's and Cameron's images, see Rosen, *Julia Margaret Cameron's 'Fancy Subjects'*, 56–62.

48. For example, see Weaver, *Julia Margaret Cameron, 1815–1879*, 18–63.

49. Cameron recorded her familiarity with the East India House in 1859 in a letter to her daughter Juley, in which she told her of visiting Thoby Prinsep in India House: Julia Margaret Cameron to Juley Hay Norman, dated 28 Leo St Paul Friday 1859 (possibly the feast day of St Leo), Kent County Archives, U310_C75_67. In 1858, Prinsep was appointed to one of the seven directorships of the Council of India, following the Uprising. *Dictionary of National Biography, 1885–1900*, vol. 36, https://en.wikisource.org/wiki/Dictionary_of_National_Biography,_1885-1900/Prinsep,_Henry_Thoby.

50. Putti also accompany *Britannia Receiving the Riches of the East*, a similar representation in sculpture by John Michael Rysbrack (1728); see Barbara Groseclose, *British Sculpture and the Raj: Church Monuments and Public Statuary in Madras, Calcutta, and Bombay to 1858* (Cranbury, NJ: Associated University Presses, 1995), 49. Roma's painting was moved to the Foreign and Commonwealth Office prior to 1861, when the East India Company building was demolished.

51. This image is known by a number of titles, including: 'Night in Town', 'Night in London', 'Poor Jo', 'Homeless', and 'A Night on the Streets of London'.

52. Robert Mallet, *Record of the International Exhibition, 1862* (London: William Mackenzie, 1862), 576.

53. For Edwards, photography's 'allotropic qualities' meant that it was impossible to disentangle the grit of industrial production from the visual image because photographic narratives were always enmeshed with their physical properties; consequently, photographers could not create a faultless separation of artistic ideas from the manual labour associated with industrial production; see *The Making of English Photography* (University Park: Pennsylvania State University Press, 2006), 190–3.

54. Joanne Lukitsh, 'Before 1864', in Julian Cox and Colin Ford, *Julia Margaret Cameron: The Complete Photographs* (Los Angeles: J. Paul Getty Museum, 2003), 101–4; Victoria Olsen, *From Life,* 137–9; Colin Ford, *Julia Margaret Cameron, A Critical Biography* (Los Angeles: J. Paul Getty Museum, 2003), 36.

55. Stephanie Spencer, 'O. G. Rejlander's Photographs of Street Urchins', *Oxford Art Journal*, 7:2 (1984), 17–24.

56. Charles Dickens, *Bleak House*, ed. Stephen Gill (Oxford: Oxford World Classics, 1996), 669.

57. See Malcolm Daniel, 'Darkroom vs. Greenroom: Victorian Art Photography and Popular Theatrical Entertainment', *Image*, 33:1–2 (Fall 1990), 13–20.

58. For the case of India, see: Mary Isbell, 'When Ditchers and Jack Tars Collide: Benefit Theatricals at the Calcutta Lyric Theatre in the Wake of the Indian Mutiny', *Victorian Literature and Culture*, 42:3 (2014), 407–23; Tobias Becker, 'Entertaining the Empire: Theatrical Touring Companies and Amateur Dramatics in Colonial India', *Historical Journal*, 57:3 (September 2014), 699–725; Derek Forbes, 'Simla: Amateur Theatrical Capital of the Raj', *Theatre Notebook: A Journal of History and Technique of the British Theatre*, 62:2 (2008), 76–120.

59. Becker, 'Entertaining the Empire', 701.

60. Patrick Leary, *The Punch Brotherhood: Table-Talk and Print Culture in Mid-Victorian London* (London: British Library, 2010), 61.

61. Tom Taylor, *Payable on Demand, an Original Domestic Drama in Two Acts* (London: Thomas Hailes Lacy, 1859).

62. The domestic context seems to have keenly interested earlier scholars, see Winton Tolles, *Tom Taylor and the Victorian Drama* (New York: Columbia University Press, 1940), 144–7.

63. On Robson, see Craven Makie, Frederick Robson and the Evolution of Realistic Acting', *Educational Theatre Journal*, 23:2 (May 1971), 160–70.

64. 'The Theatres', *Spectator*, vol. 32, 16 July 1859, 743.

65. See Alison Chapman, 'The Drama of Capital: Risk, Belief, and Liability on the Victorian Stage', in Francis O'Gorman, ed., *Victorian Literature and Finance* (New York and Oxford: Oxford University Press, 2007), ch. 5.

66. 'The Theatres', 744.

67. 'Payable on Demand', *Illustrated London News*, 6 August 1859, 131. Tamar Garb has written how, 'in British imperial discourse, the Jew could be embraced in the construction of a Judeo-Christian "common culture" whose mission it was to civilize the world and, simultaneously, could be figured as its dark other, the savage within European consciousness'. See: 'Introduction' to Tamar Garb, *The Jew in the Text: Modernity and the Construction of Jewish Identity*, ed. Linda Nochlin and Tamar Garb (London: Thames and Hudson, 1995), 25; and Reina Lewis, *Gendering Orientalism: Race, Femininity, and Representation* (London: Routledge, 1996), 212–20.

68. For the importance of understanding the relationship of specific Victorian

audiences to dramatic performances created especially for them, see Jim Davis and Victor Emeljanow, *Reflecting the Audience: London Theatregoing, 1840–1880* (Iowa City: University of Iowa Press, 2001).

69. Tom Taylor, *A Tale of Two Cities, a Drama in Two Acts and a Prologue, Adapted from the Story of that Name by Charles Dickens* (London: Thomas Hailes Lacy, 1860).

70. On Taylor's adaptation of Dickens's novel, see: Priti Joshi, 'Mutiny Echoes: India, Britons, and Charles Dickens's "A Tale of Two Cities"', *Nineteenth-Century Literature*, 62:1 (2007), 48–87; Philip V. Allingham, 'A Discussion of Fox Cooper's July 1860 Adaptation of Dickens's *A Tale of Two Cities*', *The Victorian Web*, https://victorianweb.org/authors/dickens/2cities/pva227.html; and John McBratney, 'The Return and Rescue of the Émigré in *A Tale of Two Cities*', in Tamara S. Wagner, ed., *Victorian Settler Narratives: Emigrants, Cosmopolitans and Returnees in Nineteenth-Century Literature* (London: Pickering & Chatto, 2011), 99–109.

71. The inscription '*The Private Theatricals of the Cameron's Thatched House*' also appears on the reverse side of another of Cameron's portraits of Lionel Tennyson in the role of the Marquis de St Cast, Cox/Ford 1032.

72. Taylor, *Payable on Demand*, Act II, 48.

73. Sukanya Banerjee, *Becoming Imperial Citizens: Indians in the Late-Victorian Empire* (Durham, NC, and London: Duke University Press, 2010), 17.

74. John Berger writes, 'A photograph is already a message about the event it records. The urgency of this message is not entirely dependent on the urgency of the event but neither can it be entirely independent from it'. See 'Understanding a Photograph', in *The Look of Things: Essays by John Berger*, ed. Nikos Stangos (New York: Viking, 1971), 179.

Chapter Seven
Triumph and Mourning

1. Many of these accounts inform the history of Cawnpore written by Andrew Ward, *Our Bones are Scattered: The Cawnpore Massacres and the Indian Mutiny of 1857* (New York: Henry Holt, 1996) and Rosie Llewellyn-Jones, ed., *The Uprising of 1857* (New Delhi: Alkazi Collection of Photography, 2017).

2. Stephen Heathorn, 'The Cawnpore Memorial Well as a British Site of Imperial Remembrance', *Journal of Colonialism and Colonial History*, 8:3 (Winter 2007), 1–21; Stephen Heathorn, 'The Absent Site of Memory: The Kanpur Memorial Well and the 1957 Centenary Commemoration of the Indian "Mutiny"', *German Historical Institute, London, Bulletin Supplement*, Bd. 1 (2009), 73–116; Ward, *Our Bones are Scattered*, 539–54; Gary D. Sampson, 'Unmasking the Colonial Picturesque', in Eleanor M. Hight and Gary D. Sampson, eds, *Colonialist Photography: Imag(in)ing Race and Place* (New York: Routledge, 2002), 93–102; Zahid R. Chaudhary, *Afterimage of Empire: Photography in Nineteenth Century India* (Minneapolis: University of Minnesota Press, 2012), 12–35.

3. See Alison Blunt, 'Embodying War: British Women and Domestic Defilement in the Indian "Mutiny", 1857–8', *Journal of Historical Geography*, 26:3 (2000), 403–28.

4. Andreas Huyssen, 'Monumental Seduction', in Mieke Bal, Jonathan Crewe, and Leo Spitzer, eds, *Acts of Memory: Cultural Recall in the Present* (Hanover, CT: University Press of New England, 1999), 200.

5. Kaan Sag, 'The Scutari Monument in Istanbul: The Introduction of Victorian Monumental Language to Ottoman Society', *Sculpture Journal*, 23:3 (2014), 279–92.

6. It is striking that, from the earliest verbal descriptions of Marochetti's angel sculpture, the figure of the angel was gendered female. Harriot Dufferin's journal entry from 1886 is emblematic: Hariot Dufferin, *Our Viceregal Life in India: Selections from my Journal, 1884–1888*, 2 vols (London: John Murray, 1889), 2:23.

7. For an analysis of the role of 'imperial women' in spreading British culture in India during these years, see Éadaoin Agnew, *Imperial Women Writers in Victorian India: Representing Colonial Life, 1850–1910* (Cham, Switzerland: Palgrave Macmillan, 2017).

8. Fredric Jameson, *The Political Unconscious: Narrative as a Socially Symbolic Act* (Ithaca: Cornell University Press, 1981).

9. The Resolution was first promulgated in Parliament on 31 July 1857; see Michael Maclagan, *'Clemency' Canning: Charles John, 1st Earl Canning, Governor-General and Viceroy of India, 1856–1862* (London: Macmillan, 1962), Appendix 2, 324–7. For the dispatch of the proclamation to General Outram, see John Kaye and G. B. Malleson, *History of the Indian Mutiny of 1857–8*, 6 vols (1897), vol. 5. Book 15, ch. 1, 'Lord Canning's Oudh Proclamation', 173–4, https://www.ibiblio.org/britishraj/KayeMalleson5/index.html.

10. Quoted in Thomas R. Metcalf, *The Aftermath of Revolt, 1857–1870* (Princeton: Princeton University Press, 1964), 147.

11. Maclagan, '*Clemency Canning*', 132–65; on the continuing controversy of the annexation of Awadh and its claim that Britain had dislodged its rightful royal lineage, see Anon., *Dacoitee in Excelsis; or, the Spoilation of Oude, by the East India Company* (London: J. R. Taylor, 1857).

12. Metcalf, *Aftermath of Revolt*, 170–3.

13. James Grant, *Bagehot: The Life and Times of the Greatest Victorian* (New York: W.W. Norton, 2019), 107–11.

14. Metcalf, *Aftermath of Revolt*, 170.

15. Partha Chaterjee, *The Black Hole of Empire: History of a Global Practice of Power* (Princeton: Princeton University Press, 2012), 215.

16. Virginia Surtees, *Charlotte Canning: Lady-in-Waiting to Queen Victoria and Wife of the First Viceroy of India, 1817–1861* (London: J. Murray, 1975), 233–5.

17. Virginia Surtees, ed., *Sublime and Instructive: Letters from John Ruskin to Louisa, Marchioness of Waterford, Anna Blunden and Ellen Heaton* (London: Michael Joseph, 1972), 3–5.

18. Augustus J. C. Hare, *The Story of Two Noble Lives, Being Memorials of Charlotte, Countess Canning, and Louisa, Marchioness of Waterford*, 3 vols (New York: Anson D. F. Randolph and Co., 1893), 3:59–62, 76–9.

19. *Illustrated London News*, 27 March 1858, 332.

20. Christopher Pinney, *The Coming of Photography to India* (London: British Library, 2008), 125–6.

21. The Royal Photographic Society took notice of Murray's contributions in a brief notice in the *Photographic Journal*, 21 May 1858, 210.

22. C. Beaton to John Murray, 22 January 1858, quoted in Roger Taylor, *Impressed by Light: British Photographs from Paper Negatives, 1840–1860* (New York: Metropolitan Museum of Art, 2007), 125.

23. Extract from the report of the meeting of the Photographic Society of Bengal, held in the CE College Library and published in the *Englishman* of 31 March 1859: 'The collection included views of most places rendered notable during the mutiny, and were taken at Delhi, Mussoorie, Landour, Meerut, Roorkie, Cawnpore, Lucknow, Benares and Agra, in all nearly five hundred negatives. Major Tytler took occasion to express how much he was indebted for assistance to the kindness of Dr. Murray and M. Beato'. Additional notices appeared in the *Bengal Hurkaru and India Gazette* and the *Englishman*, both of 28 May 1859. Luminous-Lint Website: http://www.luminous-lint.com/app/photographer/Robert_Christopher__Tytler/A/.

24. Christopher Pinney memorably called the barrenness depicted by Murray and the Tytlers 'the banality of place'; Pinney, *Coming of Photography to India*, 84–6.

25. Photographic Exhibitions in Britain, 1839–1865, http://peib.dmu.ac.uk/index.php.

26. *Journal and Transactions of the Photographic Society of Great Britain*, 5:79 (22 February 1859), 185.

27. Murray's photographs exhibited in December 1857 at the London Photographic Society's exhibition displayed well-worn conventions of the picturesque landscape tradition that presented the horizon at the frame's vertical mid-point and the chief subject of the image at the dead-centre of the picture plane. *Art Journal*, 19 (December 1857), 386.

28. John Tagg analysed the incongruity of Murray's picturesque scenes of the Suttee Ghat in Cawnpore, the site where British officers were murdered on the Ganges, with the violence that made this view worthy of picturing: 'The Mute Testimony of the Picture: British Paper Photography and India', in Ali Behdad and Luke Gartlan, eds, *Photography's Orientalism* (Los Angeles: J. Paul Getty Trust, 2013), 185–99.

29. Henry Christopherson, 'The Well at Cawnpore', *The Times*, 14 January 1860, 12.

30. Ibid.

31. C. M., 'The Well at Cawnpore', *The Times*, 17 January 1860, 8.

32. Carmichael, 'The 32nd Regiment', *The Times*, 19 January 1860, 12.

33. 'The Well at Cawnpore', *The Times*, 29 March 1861, 4.

34. John Nicholas Tressider, Photographic Album, Alkazi Collection of Photography, two albumen prints posted vertically to the page, ACP: 97.15.0002(26), depicting the Well near the Slaughter House and the Monument over the Well, Cawnpore. For a reproduction and analysis, see fig. 11 in Rashmi Viswanathan, 'The Tressider Album: A Case Study of a Private "Ethnography"', *Self and Nation*, 7:1 (Fall 2016). Another analysis of Tressider's album is provided by Sean Robert Willcock, 'Insurgent Citizenship: Dr John Nicholas Tressider's Photographs of War and Peace in British India', *British Art Studies*, #4 (28 November 2016).

35. These words are barely legible from fig. 11, Viswanathan, 'The Tressider Album', but they are quite explicit from the report in *The Times*: 'The Well at Cawnpore', *The Times*, 29 March 1861, 4.

36. Lord Canning to Lord Granville, 3 March 1861, in Fitzmaurice, Edmond George Petty-Fitzmaurice, 1st Baron, *The Life of Granville, George Leveson Gower, Second Earl Granville, K.G., 1815–1891*, 2 vols, 3rd edn (London: Longmans, Green, 1905), 1:395.

37. Hare, *Story of Two Noble Lives*, 3:60 n. 2.

38. George O. Trevelyan, *Cawnpore* (London: Macmillan, 1865), 304.

39. Louisa Anne Beresford, *Scrap Book*, Victoria and Albert Museum, E.1615–1966.

40. Hare, *Story of Two Noble Lives*, 3:42 n. 1.

41. 'The Signor 1857 Album', auction catalogue, Sotheby's, 12 December 2012, http://www.sothebys.com/en/auctions/ecatalogue/2012/english-literature.

42. Julia Margaret Cameron to Juley Hay Norman, 11 August 1861, Kent County Archives, U310_C75_85.

43. John Lewis Bradley, 'Ruskin's Advice to an Amateur Artist: Some New Letters to Louisa, Marchioness of Waterford', *Studies in English Literature, 1500–1900*, 1:4 (Autumn 1961), 101–22.

44. Pinney, *Coming of Photography to India*, 23, 30, 93.

45. See Julian Cox and Colin Ford, *Julia Margaret Cameron: The Complete Photographs* (Los Angeles: J. Paul Getty Museum, 2003), 17.

46. Lord Canning to Lord Granville, 17 June 1861, in Fitzmaurice, *Life of Earl Granville*, 396.

47. James Anthony Froude to Thomas Woolner, 2 July 1861, in Amy Woolner, *Thomas Woolner, R.A., Sculptor and Poet. His Life in Letters* (New York: E. P. Dutton, 1917), 204.

48. Lord Granville to Lord Canning, 10 July 1861, in Fitzmaurice, *Life of Earl Granville*, 398.

49. Lord Canning to Lord Granville, 21 July 1861, in Fitzmaurice, *Life of Earl Granville*, 398.

50. Lord Granville to Lord Canning, 16 January 1862, in Fitzmaurice, *Life of Earl Granville*, 402.

51. 'The International Exhibition', *The Times*, 10 July 1862, 9.

52. 'India', *The Times*, 24 March 1863, 6.

53. Ibid.

54. See Gary D. Sampson, 'The Success of Samuel Bourne in India', *History of Photography*, 16:4 (Winter 1992), 336–471, and Hugh Rayner, ed., *Photographic Journeys in the Himalayas, 1863–1866 by Samuel Bourne*, 4th edn (Bath: Pagoda Tree Press, 2014).

55. In contemporary terms: 'The reality is that professional historians do not control the present or the past. Their production of history flows into a vast lake of historical production to which politicians,

"popular historians," museums, novels, films, TV dramas, activists, and countless members of the public contribute. The narratives of empire that the public consumes are not those produced by academic historians but nostalgic TV series, great-man histories, and other pageants of empire'. Priya Satia, *Time's Monster: How History Makes History* (Cambridge, MA: Belknap, 2020), 282–3.

56. Narrative repetition also discloses its opposite, marking and informing the ambivalence of the process of writing the nation, unwittingly emphasizing that meaning is constructed alongside counter-knowledge: 'In the production of the nation as narration there is a split between the continuist, accumulative temporality of the pedagogical, and the repetitious, recursive strategy of the performative'. Homi K. Bhabha, 'Dissemination: Time, Narrative and the Margins of the Modern Nation', in Homi K. Bhabha, *The Location of Culture* (London and New York: Routledge, 1994), 145.

57. Satia, *Time's Monster*, 81.

58. Gilles Deleuze, *Difference and Repetition*, trans. Paul Patton (New York: Columbia University Press, 1994), 103–5.

59. The Freudian notion of the 'return of the repressed' relies upon the idea that narratives are repeated to control buried dreams and fantasies or disturbing images and memories (*Beyond the Pleasure Principle*). Turning Freud on his head, Deleuze writes: 'it is because repetition is necessarily disguised, by virtue of the characteristic displacement of its determinant principle, that repression occurs in the form of a consequence in regard to the representation of presents. ... We do not repeat because we repress, we repress because we repeat'. Ibid., 105.

60. Don Randall, 'Post-Mutiny Allegories of Empire in Rudyard Kipling's Jungle Books', *Texas Studies in Literature and Language*, 40:1 (Spring 1998), 118.

61. Jenny Sharpe, *Allegories of Empire: The Figure of the Woman in the Colonial Text* (Minneapolis: University of Minnesota Press, 1993), 7.

62. According to W. H. Russell, who wrote a first-hand account of the Uprising, 'the peculiar aggravation of the Cawnpore massacres was this, that the deed was done by a subject race – by black men who dared to shed the blood of their masters, and that of poor helpless ladies and children'. Quoted in Rudrangshu Mukherjee, '"Satan Let Loose upon Earth": The Kanpur Massacres in India in the Revolt of 1857', *Past and Present*, 128 (August 1990), 92.

63. Jacques Derrida, *Specters of Marx*, trans. Peggy Kamuf (New York: Routledge, 1994), 10–11, 41.

64. For the financial and political underpinnings of the exhibition, see Henry Trueman Wood, *A History of the Royal Society of Arts* (London: John Murray, 1913), 417–24. On the construction of the exhibition, see 'The Exhibition Building of 1862', in *Survey of London: Volume 38, South Kensington Museums Area,* ed. F. H. W. Sheppard (London: London County Council, 1975), 137–47. British History Online, http://www.british-history.ac.uk/survey-london/vol38/pp137–147. Cameron wrote numerous letters to Juley and her husband, Charles Norman, at 1 Cromwell Place, on 20 May 1861 (U310_C75_82), 7 June 1861 (U310_C75_83), and 18 August 1861 (U310_C75_86), Kent County Archives.

65. *The Letters of Emily Lady Tennyson*, ed. James O. Hoge (University Park: Pennsylvania State University Press, 1974), 167.

66. Francis Turner Palgrave, *Handbook to the Fine Art Collections of the International Exhibition* (London: Macmillan, 1862), 46, 91; William Holman Hunt, *Pre-Raphaelitism and the Pre-Raphaelite Brotherhood*, 2nd edn, 2 vols (New York: E. P. Dutton, 1914), 2:178.

67. Mike Weaver, *Julia Margaret Cameron, 1815–1879* (Southampton: John Hansard Gallery, 1984), 66.

68. Joanne Lukitsh, 'Before 1864', in Cox and Ford, *Julia Margaret Cameron*, 101–4; Victoria C. Olsen, *From Life: Julia Margaret Cameron and Victorian Photography* (New York: Palgrave Macmillan, 2003), 137–9; Colin Ford, *Julia Margaret Cameron, A Critical Biography* (Los Angeles: J. Paul Getty Museum, 2003), 36.

69. *The Letters of Lewis Carroll, Volume 1, ca. 1837–1885*, ed. Morton N. Cohen, and Roger Lancelyn Green (London: Macmillan, 1979), 66–7.

70. One cannot determine whether these images were present in the album when Julia Margaret dedicated it to her sister, or whether they were sent separately for Mia to paste in.

71. See R. Derek Wood, *Julia Margaret Cameron's Copyrighted Photographs* (London: privately published, May 1996), #30: 'Mary Ryan as Maid with Pitcher in hand, head drooping' [30 June 1864], and #50: 'Miss[es] Aldersons at the Well, one girl full face one arm on wood work of Well the other arm holding pail. Other girl profile with jug in right hand' [10 October 1864].

72. Colin Ford first identified these individuals as Mary Catherine Alderson, later Lady Humphrey, or her sister; see Colin Ford, *The Cameron Collection: An Album of Photographs by Julia Margaret Cameron Presented to Sir John Herschel* (London: National Portrait Gallery, 1975), 139, and these identities are confirmed in the PRO copyright registries. As Baron Alderson and his family were close family friends with the Frederick Pollocks, it is possible, though not documented, that the Aldersons accompanied the Pollocks on a visit to Freshwater that summer.

73. Roland Barthes, *Camera Lucida: Reflections on Photography*, trans. Richard Howard (New York: Hill and Wang, 1981), 5.

74. Ibid. For a similar reason, photographs that are intended to convey 'horror' seldom do so effectively because they hold no meaning, context, or history for the viewer; Barthes wrote that viewers of such photographs are held aloof from their own genuine response to such imagery because the photographer has already intervened and translated them first, thereby 'overconstructing' the horror she or he has represented. Roland Barthes, 'Shock-Photos', in *The Eiffel Tower and Other Mythologies*, trans. Richard Howard (New York: Hill and Wang, 1979), 71. As much as Cameron's photographs might have been motivated by controlling the panic and horror she *felt* for the victims at Cawnpore, these images were not designed to *evoke* horror but rather to use the language of symbolism to memorialize the horrible event.

75. Cox and Ford linked this image to the copyright registry (Wood, *Cameron's Copyrighted Photographs*, #50), but its verbal description does not exactly conform to the placement of models within the photograph. However, the photograph that Cameron called *At the Well, A Farewell* might be an enlarged segment of another image in which the Alderson sisters served as models. For example, #52, also registered on 10 October 1864, reads, 'Two Miss Aldersons, one hand on shoulder of the other, the other hand of each with the others, one profile the other ¾ face, Striped skirt on one, broad belts & buckles on both'.

76. Ford, *Julia Margaret Cameron*, 36.

77. See Karen Bloom Gevirtz, *Life After Death: Widows in the English Novel, Defoe to Austen* (Newark, DE: University of Delaware Press, 2005), 43. In Charlotte Yonge's novels, the convention of wearing mourning is typically spread across the entire household. See Alethea Hayter, 'Mourning and Funeral Customs in Charlotte Yonge's Novels', *Journal (Charlotte M. Yonge Fellowship)*, 2 (1997), 17–27.

78. Pat Jalland, *Death in the Victorian Family* (Oxford: Oxford University Press, 1996), 301; Lou Taylor, *Mourning Dress: A Costume and Social History* (1983), (Oxford: Routledge Revivals, 2009), 45, 88, 94.

79. In 1858, William Henry Fox Talbot read the book and shared a copy with his sister, Caroline. Caroline Augusta Edgcumbe to William Henry Fox Talbot, 8 May 1858, Fox Talbot Collection, British Library, viewable online as Document 7626, *The Correspondence of William Henry Fox Talbot*, https://foxtalbot.dmu.ac.uk/project/project.html.

80. G. Harris, *A Lady's Diary of the Siege of Lucknow* (London: John Murray, 1858), 192; see also Katherine Mary Bartram, *A Widow's Reminiscences of the Siege of Lucknow* (London: James Nisbet and Co., 1858), 50.

81. Lydia Murdoch, '"Suppressed Grief": Mourning the Death of British Children and the Memory of the 1857 Indian Rebellion', *Journal of British Studies*, 51:2 (April 2012), 388.

82. On the white widow's cap favoured by Queen Victoria, see Kay Staniland, *In Royal Fashion: The Clothes of Princess Charlotte and Queen Victoria, 1796–1901* (London: Museum of London, 1997), 157. See also Elizabeth Jane Timms, 'Queen Victoria's Widow's Cap', *Royal Central* (2018), https://royalcentral.co.uk/features/queen-victorias-widows-cap-111104/. In his *History of Mourning* (1889), Richard Davey noted that after Prince Albert's passing, Queen Victoria 'slightly modified the conventional English widow's cap, by indenting it over the forehead *à la* Marie Stuart, thereby imparting to it a certain picturesqueness which was quite lacking in the former head-dress. This coiffure has been not only adopted by her subjects, but also by royal widows abroad'. Project Gutenberg, https://www.gutenberg.org/files/44379/44379-h/44379-h.htm. The same is confirmed in Taylor, *Mourning Dress*, 157–8.

83. During the second half of the nineteenth century, according to Julia Baird, one in three women aged fifty-five to sixty-four was widowed, but only one in seven men. Julia Baird, *Victoria the Queen: An Intimate Biography of the Woman who Ruled an Empire* (New York: Random House, 2017), 337.

84. Susan P. Casteras, *The Substance or the Shadow: Images of Victorian Womanhood* (New Haven: Yale University Press, 1988), 35.

85. Rebecca N. Mitchell, 'Death Becomes Her: On the Progressive Potential of Victorian Mourning', *Victorian Literature and Culture*, 41:4 (2013), 595–620.

86. Anthony Trollope, *Can You Forgive Her?* (1864) (Oxford: Oxford University Press, 1973), Book 1, 70, 92.

87. Kaelin B. C. Alexander, 'Turning Mourning: Trollope's Ambivalent Widows', *Victorian Literature and Culture*, 43:3 (2015), 611.

88. 'Petition to Parliament in Defence of the Regulation Prohibiting the Practice of Suttee (1830–31)', quoted in Barbara Harlow and Mia Carter, eds, *Archives of Empire, Volume 1: From the East India Company to the Suez Canal* (Durham, NC, and London: Duke University Press, 2003), 372–4.

89. Lucy Carroll, 'Law, Custom, and Statutory Social Reform: The Hindu Widows' Remarriage Act of 1856', *Indian Economic & Social History Review*, 20:4 (1983), 363–88.

90. Gayatri Chakravorty Spivak, 'The Rani of Sirmur: An Essay in Reading the Archives', *History and Theory*, 24:3 (1985), 267.

91. 'Fine Arts', *Illustrated London News*, 13 August 1862, 178.

Chapter Eight
Betrayal and Atonement

1. Christopher Herbert, *War of No Pity: The Indian Mutiny and Victorian Trauma* (Princeton: Princeton University Press, 2008), 273.

2. Gautam Chakravarty, *The Indian Mutiny and the British Imagination* (New Delhi: Cambridge University Press, 2006), 113.

3. Patrick Brantlinger, *Rule of Darkness: British Literature and Imperialism, 1830–1914* (Ithaca: Cornell University Press, 1988), 204. For the essential work of denying privileged status to 'the historical archive', see Gayatri Chakravorty Spivak, 'The Rani of Simur: An Essay on Reading the Archives', *History and Theory*, 24:3 (October 1985), 247–72.

4. 'The Canterbury Week', in *The Journal of the Household Brigade for the Year 1864*, ed. I. E. A. Dolby (London: W. Clowes and Sons, 1864), 217.

5. William Allingham, *A Diary* (London: Macmillan, 1907), 84.

6. Colin Ford, 'Geniuses, Poets, and Painters: The World of Julia Margaret Cameron', in Julian Cox and Colin Ford, *Julia Margaret Cameron: The Complete Photographs* (Los Angeles: J. Paul Getty Museum, 2003), 25.

7. Ibid., 147.

8. Ellen Terry, *The Story of My Life: Recollections and Reflections* (New York: Doubleday, Page & Co., 1908), ch. 3, 'Rossetti, Bernhardt, Irving, 1865–67'.

9. Marion Shaw, 'Elizabeth Gaskell, Tennyson and the Fatal Return: *Sylvia's Lovers* and *Enoch Arden*', *Gaskell*

Society Journal, 9 (1995), 43–54; Anne Humpherys, '*Enoch Arden*, the Fatal Return, and the Silence of Annie', *Victorian Poetry*, 30:3/4 (Autumn–Winter 1992), 331–42; Deborah Wynne, 'Two Audley Courts: Tennyson and M. E. Braddon', *Notes and Queries*, 44:3 (September 1997), 344–5.

10. Sonakshi Goyle, 'Tracing a Cultural Memory: Commemoration of 1857 in the Delhi Durbars, 1877, 1903, and 1911', *Historical Journal*, 59:3 (2016), 799–815; Astrid Erll, 'Re-Writing as Re-Visioning: Modes of Representing the "Indian Mutiny" in British Novels, 1857–2000', *European Journal of English Studies*, 10:2 (August 2006), 163–85.

11. Andrew Ward, *Our Bones are Scattered: The Cawnpore Massacres and the India Mutiny of 1857* (New York: Henry Holt, 1996), 47; Michael H. Fischer, *Counterflows to Colonialism: Indian Travellers and Settlers in Britain, 1600–1857* (Ranikhet: Permanent Black, 2004), 295–6.

12. Tom Taylor, *A Sister's Penance* (London: Thomas Hailes Lacy, 1865), Act I, 8.

13. Ibid., Act II, 39.

14. Quoted in *The Adelphi Theatre Calendar for 1866–1867: A Record of Dramatic Performances at a Leading Victorian Theatre*, https://www.umass.edu/AdelphiTheatreCalendar/, 4.

15. 'A Penance Made Pleasant', *Punch*, 52–3 (5 January 1867), 3.

16. 'The Theatres', *Illustrated London News*, vol. 49, 1 December 1866, 535.

17. 'Adelphi', *Athenaeum*, no. 2040 (1 December 1866), 723.

18. Herbert, *War of No Pity*, 274.

19. On the importance of these signs and countersigns to the insurrection, see Homi K. Bhabha, 'By Bread Alone: Signs of Violence in the Mid-Nineteenth Century', in *The Location of Culture* (London and New York: Routledge, 1994), 198–211.

20. Taylor, *A Sister's Penance*, Act II, 34–5. For Ellis's views in relation to Britain's missionary role in India, see Alison Twells, 'Missionary Domesticity, Global Reform and "Women's Sphere" in Early Nineteenth-Century England', *Gender & History*, 18:2 (August 2006), 266–84.

21. Allingham, *Diary*. On Carlyle, see the entry for 14 November 1867, 166; on the Fenians, see the entries for 25 November 1867 and 24 December 1867, 166–7.

22. Ibid., 9 November 1872, 217.

23. Charles Ball, *The History of the Indian Mutiny*, 2 vols (London: London Printing and Publishing, n.d. [1858]), 1:340–80. For an analysis of this scene in Ball's text, see Herbert, *War of No Pity*, 147–49.

24. Taylor, *A Sister's Penance*, Act II, 42.

25. Brantlinger, *Rule of Darkness*, 206.

26. Taylor, *A Sister's Penance*, Act II, 24, 25, 29.

27. Brantlinger, *Rule of Darkness*, 204–5.

28. For the complexities of this story, see Herbert, *War of No Pity*, 148–51, and Jenny Sharpe, *Allegories of Empire: The Figure of the Woman in the Colonial Text* (Minneapolis: University of Minnesota Press, 1993), 84–110.

29. Ahmedoolah's dispossession is made clear in Act I, as one character disparages the Raharajah of Hazareepore as 'an old rogue as ever abused the longsuffering of Government; [and who] ought to have been annexed thirty years ago' … 'and would have been', rejoins another, 'but for that long headed old wuzeer of his, Ahmedoolah's father'. Taylor, *A Sister's Penance*, Act I, 19.

30. Sigmund Freud, 'The Dissection of the Psychical Personality', New Introductory Lectures on Psycho-Analysis, *The Standard Edition of the Complete Psychological Works of Sigmund Freud* (1932), (London: Hogarth Press, 1933), 22:74.

31. Herbert, *War of No Pity*, 55.

32. Lydia Murdoch, '"Suppressed Grief:" Mourning the Death of British Children and the Memory of the 1857 Indian Rebellion', *Journal of British Studies*, 51:2 (April 2012), 364–92; Alison Blunt, 'Embodying War: British Women and Domestic Defilement in the Indian "Mutiny", 1857–8', *Journal of Historical Geography*, 26:3 (2000), 403–28; Rebecca N. Mitchell, 'Death Becomes Her: On the Progressive Potential of Victorian Mourning', *Victorian Literature and Culture*, 41:4 (2013), 595–620.

33. On the relevance of anniversaries to key moments in historical memory, see Benjamin Zachariah, 'Histories and National Memory: 1857', in Crispin Bates, ed., *Mutiny at the Margins, New Perspectives on the Indian Uprising of 1857, Volume 6: Perception, Narration and Reinvention: The Pedagogy and Historiography of the Indian Uprising* (New Delhi: Sage, 2014), 84–112. On the importance of historical memory to the narratives of the 1857 Indian Uprising, see Astrid Erll, 'Re-Writing as Re-Visioning', 163–85; Astrid Erll, 'Remembering across Time, Space, and Cultures: Premeditation, Remediation and the "Indian Mutiny"', in Astrid Erll and Ann Rigney, eds, *Mediation, Remediation and the Dynamics of Cultural Memory* (Berlin: Walter de Gruyter, 2009), 109–38. Larger questions of memory in relation to constructing narratives of culture and national identity are also explored in Edward W. Said, 'Invention, Memory and Place', *Critical Inquiry*, 26:2 (Winter 2000), 175–92; and Pierre Lora, 'Between Memory and History: Les Lieux de Mémoire', *Representations*, 26 (Spring 1989), 7–24. Interestingly, the extent to which memory and history are determined by geography and site-specific place is essential to each of these essays; this would seem to exclude heterotopias of the kind described by Foucault, in which symbolic, iconographic, and narrative histories have taken the place of accounts that are exclusively site-specific.

34. See Homi K. Bhabha, 'Interrogating Identity', in *The Location of Culture*, 44–5.

35. Jacques Derrida, *Specters of Marx*, trans. Peggy Kamuf (New York and London: Routledge, 1994), 21.

36. Allingham, *Diary*, 17 January 1864, 96.

37. Ibid., 23 August 1868, 186. On Prince Alamayou and his representation by Cameron, see Jeff Rosen, *Julia Margaret Cameron's 'Fancy Subjects': Photographic Allegories of Victorian Identity and Empire* (Manchester: Manchester University Press, 2016), ch. 5, 196–229.

38. Ibid., 15 October 1868, 188. Allingham's story was not unique or unprecedented; see Kim A Wagner, *The Skull of Alum Bheg: The Life and Death of a Rebel of 1857* (Oxford and New York: Oxford University Press, 2018).

39. Julia Margaret Cameron to Sir John Herschel, 31 December 1864, National Portrait Gallery, London, NPG-P201; see also Rosen, *Julia Margaret Cameron's 'Fancy Subjects'*, ch. 2.

40. See Julian Cox, '"To Startle the Eye with Wonder & Delight": The Photographs of Julia Margaret Cameron', in Cox and Ford, *Julia Margaret Cameron*, 58–9, 76 n. 102.

41. The persistence of this perspective that limits photographic experimentation to in-the-camera or in-the-darkroom activities is epitomized by recent arguments related to the performative aspects of Cameron's art: 'By welcoming both the inadvertent detail and the glitch into her photographs, Cameron made them complex registers of chance.' Robin Kelsey, *Photography and the Art of Chance* (Cambridge, MA, and London: Belknap, 2015), 82. But by privileging the negative in this way we constrain how we understand Cameron's creative process, because this approach prioritizes darkroom processing where haphazard accidents may take place prior to the making of the final print, which may mistakenly privilege Cameron's ultimate goal of producing 'final prints'.

42. Elizabeth Siegel, *Playing with Pictures: The Art of Victorian Photocollage* (Chicago: Art Institute of Chicago, 2009).

43. The Overstone Album contains the whole suite of 'Water Babies': *The bereaved Babes* (67r); *Water Babies* (89r), *The Water Babies* (27r), and *Water Babies again* (55r). These photographs are accompanied in the album by numerous other similar images of two infants or young children, including: *The Double Star* (55r); *The Infant Bridal* (18r); *The Red and White Roses* (10r), and *Paul and Virginia* (10r). Mike Weaver, *Whisper of the Muse: The Overstone Album and Other Photographs by Julia Margaret Cameron* (Malibu: J. Paul Getty Museum, 1986).

44. Henry Taylor Album, Bodleian Library, Shelfmark: Arch. K b.12; photograph 44v. The entire album may be viewed online at https://digital.bodleian.ox.ac.uk/.

45. Henry Cole, unpublished correspondence, National Art Library, Box 8, Victoria and Albert Museum; Cameron's letter is also excerpted in Mark Haworth-Booth, *Photography: An Independent Art: Photographs from the Victoria and Albert Museum, 1839–1996* (London: Victoria and Albert Museum, 1996), 80.

46. Ibid., 81. The Museum later acquired a plaster cast of a child and a photograph by the Alinari brothers depicting one of Desiderio's well-known wall tombs from the Church of S. Croce in Florence, as well as a plaster cast of the sculpture itself. See Victoria and Albert Museum, REPRO 1891–129 (cast) and PH.4366–1890 (photograph).

47. In Sir John Soane's Museum he described his 'pasticcio' (or pastiche) of architectural fragments in his published Description to his Museum: 'in the centre of this court is an architectural Pasticcio of about thirty feet high. This Pasticcio is composed of the pedestal upon which the Cast of the Belvidere [*sic*] Apollo, now in the Museum, was charged: a marble Capital of Hindu architecture; a Capital in stone, like those of the Temple at Tivoli, and of the same dimensions; and another Captial of Gothic invension [*sic*]. These are surmounted by architectural Groups of varied forms, composed of fragments from different works, chiefly in cast iron, placed one upon the other; the whole terminated with a Pine Apple.' Quoted in Sir John Soane's Museum Collection Online: the 'pasticcio', a column of fragments including marble, stone, and cast iron elements, erected by Soane at the heart of his Museum in the Monument Court. See: http://collections.soane.org/object-mc26. On the guidebook to the house museum itself, see Danielle S. Willkens, 'Reading Words and Images in the *Description(s)* of Sir John Soane's Museum', *Architectural Histories*, 4(1):5, 1–22. On the many drawings of the Museum produced to convey theatrical affects upon the viewer and the intersection of different design elements, see Thomais Kordonouri, 'Picturesque Features in Sir John Soane's Museum', *Studies in History and Theory of Architecture* (2020), 185–96.

48. Andrew Butterfield, 'Social Structure and the Typology of Funerary Monuments in Early Renaissance Florence', *RES: Anthropology and Aesthetics*, 26 (Autumn 1994), 47–67.

49. Barbara Groseclose, *British Sculpture and the Company Raj: Church Monuments and Public Statuary in Madras, Calcutta, and Bombay to 1858* (Cranbury, NJ: Associated University Presses, 1995).

50. Ibid., 126.

51. Ibid., 37–8.

52. Ibid., 71; on this page is a contemporary photograph taken of Broadfoot's monument in St George's Cathedral in Madras.

53. Walter Benjamin, 'The Storyteller', in *Illuminations*, trans. Harry Zohn, ed. Hannah Arendt (New York: Schocken, 1969), 94.

54. J. C. Robinson, *South Kensington Museum. Italian Sculpture of the Middle Ages and Period of the Revival of Art* (London: Chapman and Hall, 1862). The publication was made for the 'Science and Art Department of the Committee of Council on Education', an early proponent of using historical works as models for teaching design principles to art students. On the influence of Robinson and his conflicts with Cole, see Helen Davies, 'John Charles Robinson's work at the South Kensington Museum, Part II, From 1863 to 1867: Consolidation and Conflict', *Journal of the History of Collections*, 11:1 (1999), 95–115. See also: Louise Purbrick, 'The South Kensington Museum: The Building of the House of Henry Cole', in Marcia Pointon, ed., *Art Apart: Art Institutions and Ideology across England and North America* (Manchester: Manchester University Press, 1994), 69–88; and Tim Barringer, 'Re-presenting the Imperial Archive: South Kensington and its Museums', *Journal of Victorian Culture*, 3:2 (Spring 1998), 357–73.

55. Helen Davies, 'John Charles Robinson's work at the South Kensington Museum, Part I', *Journal of the History of Collections,* 10:2 (1998), 169–88; and Davies, 'John Charles Robinson's work at the South Kensington Museum, Part II', 95–115.

56. John Ruskin, *The Two Paths: Being Lectures on Art, and its Applications to Decoration and Manufacture, Delivered in 1858–9* (New York: John Wiley, 1859), 25.

57. The plaster cast was moved with the Crystal Palace from Hyde Park to Sydenham and remained there until the disastrous fire of 1936, when the cast was transferred to the South Kensington Museum and installed in 1938. See Victoria and Albert Museum, REPRO.A.1938–12.

58. Cornelia D. J. Pearsall, 'Burying the Duke: Victorian Mourning and the Funeral of the Duke of Wellington', *Victorian Literature and Culture*, 27:2 (1999), 385ff.

59. Wm. M. Rossetti, 'Fine Arts Correspondence', *Crayon*, 3:6 (June 1856), 183.

60. 'The Wellington Monument', *Punch*, 13 June 1857, 234; 'A Peep into Westminster Hall', *Punch*, 15 August 1857, 68–9.

61. Ibid., 68.

62. For this lengthy history see J. Physick, *The Wellington Monument* (London: Victoria and Albert Museum, 1970), 51–80.

63. Cameron was listed as a subscriber in 1859 and again in 1866; see Mike Weaver, *Julia Margaret Cameron, 1815–1879* (Southampton: John Hansard Gallery, 1984), 38. On the Arundel Society, see Tanya Ledger, 'A Study of the Arundel Society, 1848–1897' (DPhil thesis, University of Oxford, 1978), and Robyn Cooper, 'The Popularization of Renaissance Art in Victorian England: The Arundel Society', *Art History*, 1:3 (1978), 263–96.

64. Inscribed 7 February 1859; the album is in the collection of the Earl and Countess of Shelburne, Bowood House, Wiltshire. See Joanne Lukitsh, 'Before 1864: Julia Margaret Cameron's Early Work in Photography', in Cox and Ford, *Julia Margaret Cameron*, 95–105.

65. 'Publications of the Arundel Society', *Quarterly Review*, 104:208 (1858), 277–325. Women members of the Arundel Society numbered only one-tenth of the club's total membership. Although small, this was a significant improvement over the composition of the Fine Arts Club, a similar organization that developed around the same time but that was devoted to developing personal collections, where women members numbered fewer than four per cent. For the Arundel Society, see Lucina Ward, 'A Translation of a Translation: Dissemination of the Arundel Society's Chromolithographs' (PhD diss., Australian National University, 2016). For the Fine Arts Club, see Ann Eatwell, 'The Collector's or Fine Arts Club 1857–1874. The First Society for Collectors of the Decorative Arts', *Journal of the Decorative Arts Society 1850–Present*, 18 (1994), 25–30.

66. 'Fresco Painting', *Quarterly Review*, 104 (October 1858), 309.

67. Letter to the Editor, *The Times*, 31 December 1859, 10.

68. John Ruskin, *The Two Paths*, 23–6.

69. Ibid., 14–15.

70. Ibid., 18–19.

71. Ibid., 15–16.

72. 'The New Museum at the East India House', *Illustrated London News*, 6 March 1858, 228.

73. Thomas R. Metcalf, *An Imperial Vision: Indian Architecture and Britain's Raj* (London: Faber and Faber, 1989), 144.

74. *A Guide to the Art Collections of the South Kensington Museum: Illustrated with Plans and Wood Engravings* (London: South Kensington Museum, *c.*1868), 62.

75. For a study of the popularity of these types throughout Renaissance Italy, see Charles Dempsey, *Inventing the Renaissance Putto* (Chapel Hill and London: University of North Carolina Press, 2001), and Alexandra M. Korey, 'Putti, Pleasure, and Pedagogy in Sixteenth-Century Italian Prints and Decorative Arts' (PhD diss., University of Chicago, 2007).

76. Helen Davies, 'John Charles Robinson's Work, Part 1', *Journal of the History of Collections* (1998), 186–7.

77. Colin Ford, *The Cameron Collection: An Album of Photographs by Julia Margaret Cameron Presented to Sir John Herschel* (London: National Portrait Gallery, 1975), 137.

78. Cameron scholars have long insisted that the photographer was motivated solely by the drive to make photography a form of 'high art'. For example, see the three essays by Joanne Lukitsh, Patrizia Di Bello, and Marta Weiss in Juliet Hacking and Joanne Lukitsh, eds, *Photography and the Arts: Essays on Nineteenth-Century Practices and Debates* (London: Bloomsbury, 2020). These ideas are not incompatible with my analysis here, although I contend the impulse that informed Cameron's 'fine art activities' as expressed through the Arundel Society and South Kensington Museum was informed by the evident political associations of the iconography in relation to the historical rhetoric of imperial power associated with these fine art forms, especially as they were connected to funerary practices following the Indian Uprising of 1857, as described by Groseclose and others.

79. Roland Barthes, *Camera Lucida: Reflections on Photography*, trans. Richard Howard (New York: Hill and Wang, 1981), 6.

80. As Walter Benjamin realized, the 'mechanical reproducibility' and ephemeral qualities of the paper-based photograph denied its cult value', like the fixed wall tombs of church interiors, making them exclusively susceptible to the 'exchange value' of commodities. See 'The Work of Art in the Age of Mechanical Reproduction', in *Illuminations*, 217–51.

81. Benedict Anderson, *Imagined Communities: Reflections on the Origin and Spread of Nationalism*, rev. edn (London: Verso, 1991), 9.

82. Michel Foucault, 'Of Other Spaces', trans. Jay Miskowiec, *Diacritics*, 16:1 (Spring 1986), 24, 26.

83. Anderson, *Imagined Communities*, 10.

Chapter Nine
Paterfamilias

1. See Helmut Gernsheim, *Julia Margaret Cameron: Her Life and Photographic Work* (New York: Aperture, 1975), 70–1.

2. Peter Henry Emerson, 'Mrs Julia Margaret Cameron', *Sun Artists*, #3, ed. W. Arthur Boord (London: Kegan Paul, 1891; reprinted New York, 1973), 36–7. Mirjam Brusius rightly notes that terms like 'depth of field' or 'depth of focus' had not yet been coined or formalized as creative photographic techniques; nevertheless, the terms used are not important, as the effect of larger aperture settings was well known and predictable in practice. See 'Impreciseness in Julia Margaret

Cameron's Portrait Photographs', *History of Photography*, 34:4 (2010), 342–55.

3. Geoffrey Batchen has written how the London Photographic Society 'sought to maintain a clear division between those "in trade" and those "in society"'. 'Photography: Latent History', *Art in America* (February 2008), 57.

4. On cultivating photographic 'glitches', see Robin Kelsey, *Photography and the Art of Chance* (Cambridge, MA, and London: Belknap, 2015), 66–101; on multiple printing for artistic effect, see Sylvia Wolf, *Julia Margaret Cameron's Women* (Chicago: Art Institute of Chicago, 1998), 66–75; on the 'politics of gender' and Cameron's soft-focus approach, see Lindsay Smith, 'The Politics of Focus: Feminism and Photographic Theory', in Isobel Armstrong, ed., *New Feminist Discourses* (London: Routledge, 1992), 238–62, and Lindsay Smith, 'Further Thoughts on the Politics of Focus', in David Oliphant, ed., *Gendered Territories: Photographs of Women by Julia Margaret Cameron* (Austin, TX: Harry Ransom Center, 1996), 13–31.

5. Julia Margaret Cameron to Sir John Herschel, 31 December 1864, reprinted in Colin Ford, *The Cameron Collection: An Album of Photographs by Julia Margaret Cameron Presented to Sir John Herschel* (London: National Portrait Gallery, 1975), 140–1.

6. Gernsheim, *Julia Margaret Cameron*, 70–1.

7. Julian Cox, '"To ... startle the eye with wonder and delight": The Photographs of Julia Margaret Cameron', in Julian Cox and Colin Ford, *Julia Margaret Cameron: The Complete Photographs* (Los Angeles: J. Paul Getty Museum, 2003), 63.

8. Sir John Herschel to Julia Margaret Cameron, 25 September 1866, reprinted in Ford, *The Cameron Collection*, 142.

9. The image of Carlyle is Cox/Ford 627 and HA-2. Photographs inspired by Greek statuary include *Teachings from the Elgin Marbles* (Cox/Ford 1110 and HA-45) and *Elgin Marbles 2nd Version* (Cox/Ford 1111 and HA-52).

10. Sir John Herschel to Julia Margaret Cameron, 5 February 1866, Herschel Correspondence, Royal Society, London.

11. Robin Kelsey looks past Herschel's reference to Cameron's sculptural effect in photography, wishing to see instead 'Cameron's habit of playacting to her colonial past'. He understands colonialism as a 'performance of culture', a form of theatre essentially disconnected from the cares or concerns of the larger world. For Kelsey, colonialism is either performed 'for the natives' or penetrates into the dominant culture by means of exotic infiltration. By reducing the complexity of colonialism to a simplified and artificial artistic strategy, Kelsey erases Cameron's practice from politics and history while denying her embrace of an iconography of racial and cultural superiority or its connection to the imperial project. See Kelsey, *Photography and the Art of Chance*, 92–4, 348–9 n. 114.

12. Julia Margaret Cameron to Sir Henry Cole, 22 February 1866, National Art Library, Victoria and Albert Museum, Cole Correspondence, Box 8.

13. For an exploration of Thompson's contributions to reproducing works of art through photography, see Anthony Hamber, *'A Higher Branch of the Art': Photographing the Fine Arts in England, 1839–1880* (Amsterdam: Overseas Publishers Association via Gordon and Breach, 1996).

14. Alicia Craig Faxon, 'Rossetti's Reputation: A Study of the Dissemination of His Art through Photographs', *Visual Resources*, 8:3 (1992), 223–4.

15. David Mattison, 'Arthur Vipond's Certificate of Competency in Photography', *History of Photography*, 13:3 (July–September 1989), 224.

16. See Royal Collection Trust, RCIN 2906105.

17. Julia Margaret Cameron to Lady Herschel, 17 March 1867, Royal Society, London; quoted in Colin Ford, *Julia Margaret Cameron: A Critical Biography* (Los Angeles: J. Paul Getty Museum, 2003), 46.

18. Inscribed on the reverse of this photograph in the Science Museum (Herschel Album): 1984–5017/1, and quoted in Ford, *Julia Margaret Cameron: A Critical Biography*, 46.

19. Ibid.

20. Ibid.

21. Quoted in Cox and Ford, *Julia Margaret Cameron*, 500.

22. For an extensive discussion on the existential confrontation between the self and the other, with particular reference to the theories of Barthes, see Laura Wexler, 'The Purloined Image', in Shawn Michelle Smith and Sharon Sliwinski, eds, *Photography and the Optical Unconscious* (Durham, NC, and London: Duke University Press, 2017), 264–79.

23. Julia Margaret Cameron to Sir John Herschel, 31 December 1864, quoted and printed in Ford, *The Cameron Collection*, 140–1.

24. Leon Battista Alberti, *The Family in Renaissance Florence: A Translation of I libri della famiglia*, trans. Renée Watkins (Columbia, SC: University of South Carolina Press, 1969), 153–4.

25. Julia Margaret Cameron to Sir John Herschel, 31 December 1864, quoted and printed in Ford, *The Cameron Collection*, 140–1.

26. Sir John Herschel to Julia Margaret Cameron, 1 June 1867, Smithsonian Institution, 68.1, Acc. # 274.157.

27. Arnold Victor Coonin, 'Portrait Busts of Children in Quattrocento Florence', *Metropolitan Museum Journal*, 30 (1995), 66.

28. Alberti, *Family in Renaissance Florence*, 58.

29. Troy Boone, *Youth of Darkest England: Working-Class Children at the Heart of Victorian Empire* (New York: Routledge, 2005); James Kinkaid, *Child-Loving: The Erotic Child and Victorian Culture* (New York: Routledge, 1992); Carolyn Steedman, *Strange Dislocations: Childhood and the Idea of Human Interiority, 1780–1930* (Cambridge, MA: Harvard University Press, 1995); James Walvin, *A Child's Worth: A Social History of English Childhood, 1800–1914* (New York: Penguin, 1982).

30. 'The British Association for the Advancement of Science', *Illustrated London News*, vol. 6, 28 June 1845, 404.

31. As early as 1835, Herschel urged Latin to be included in 'a good practical system of public education' in the colonies, with particular reference to the curriculum

of the South African College. Sir John Herschel to the Rev. Dr J. Adamson, 21 November 1835, reprinted in W. T. Ferguson and R. F. M. Immelman, eds, *Sir John Herschel and Education at the Cape, 1834–1840* (Cape Town: Oxford University Press, 1961), 40–51.

32. Hannah Arendt, *The Human Condition*, 2nd edn (Chicago: University of Chicago Press, 2018), 27–8.

33. David Roberts, 'The Paterfamilias of the Victorian Governing Classes', in Anthony S. Wohl, ed., *The Victorian Family: Structure and Stresses* (New York: St Martin's Press, 1978), 76.

34. Claudia Nelson, 'Deconstructing the Paterfamilias: British Magazines and the Imagining of the Maternal Father, 1850–1910', *Journal of Men's Studies*, 11:3 (Spring 2003), 293–308; Henrietta Twycross-Martin, 'The Drunkard, the Brute, and the Paterfamilias: The Temperance Fiction of Sarah Stickney Ellis', in A. Hogan and A. Bradstock, eds, *Women of Faith in Victorian Culture* (London: Palgrave Macmillan, 1988), 6–30.

35. See reviews of her 1864 exhibition in Scotland in the *Scotsman* of 20 December 1864 and the *Edinburgh Daily Review* of 21 December 1864, quoted in Roddy Simpson, 'Julia Margaret Cameron and the Photographic Society of Scotland', *History of Photography*, 28:1 (2004), 85–6.

36. Richard Dyer, *White* (London: Routledge, 1997), 118.

37. Ibid.

38. Homi K. Bhabha, 'Remembering Fanon: Self, Psyche, and the Colonial Condition', in Barbara Kruger and Phil Mariani, eds, *Remaking History* (Seattle: Bay Press, 1989), 140.

39. Gayatri Chakravorty Spivak, 'The Rani of Sirmur: An Essay in Reading the Archives', *History and Theory*, 24:3 (October 1985), 247–72.

40. Edward Said, 'Reflections on Exile', in Russell Ferguson, Martha Gever, Trinh T. Minh-ha, and Cornel West, eds, *Out There: Marginalization and Contemporary Cultures* (New York: New Museum of Contemporary Art, 1990), 362.

41. Christopher Pinney, *The Coming of Photography in India* (London: British Library, 2008), 110.

42. bell hooks, *Talking Back: Thinking Feminist, Thinking Black* (New York and London: Routledge, 2015). These points are reinforced in *Talking Back: The Idea of Civilization in the Indian National Discourse*, where Sabyasachi Bhattachararya observes that during most of the colonial era in India, authentic records of indigenous Indians 'talking back' to the British simply do not exist (Oxford: Oxford University Press, 2011), 1.

43. Nor could anyone else literally or metaphorically 'speak for' Iqbal al-Daula and represent the subaltern condition into which he was objectified by Cameron's camera: Gayatri Chakravorty Spivak, 'Can the Subaltern Speak?', in C. Nelson and L. Grossberg, eds, *Marxism and the Interpretation of Culture* (Basingstoke: Macmillan Education, 1988), 271–313.

44. Roland Barthes, *Camera Lucida: Reflections on Photography*, trans. Richard Howard (New York: Hill and Wang, 1981), 51–3, 90–1. For a useful analysis of the concept of performativity versus indexicality in Barthes's thought, see Margaret Olin, 'Touching Photographs: Roland Barthes's "Mistaken" Identification', *Representations*, 80 (Fall 2002), 114–15.

45. Barthes, *Camera Lucida*, 10.

46. On exile vs nationalism, see Timothy Brennan, 'The National Longing for Form', in Homi K. Bhabha, ed., *Nation and Narration* (London: Routledge, 1990), 60.

47. See Arendt, *The Human Condition*, 9, 115, 137, 187–8, and Ariella Aïsha Azoulay, *Potential History: Unlearning Imperialism* (London: Verso, 2019), 20, 303, 306–20, 389–92, 460.

48. For contemporary expressions of this ambivalence, see Ajay Sinha, 'Response: Modernism in India: A Short History of a Blush', *Art Bulletin*, 90:4 (2008), 561–8.

49. Edward Said, 'The Voice of a Palestinian in Exile', *Third Text*, 3/4 (Spring–Summer 1988), 48.

Conclusion
Reclaiming 'Iago'

1. 'India', *The Times*, 24 December 1867, 8. The arrangement the British government made with the princes of India after the British restored order in the colony is described by Thomas R. Metcalf, *The Aftermath of Revolt: India, 1857–1870* (Princeton: Princeton University Press, 1964), 219–48. Photographs of the event are conserved in the Gramstorff Collection, National Gallery of Art (USA), Photo ID# 6277; Barcode 1900137730.

2. On the coronation *durbars*, see Julie F. Codell, 'Photography and the Delhi Coronation Durbars, 1877, 1903, 1911', in *Power and Resistance: The Delhi Coronation Durbars* (Ahmedabad: Mapin, 2012), and Val C. Prinsep, *Imperial India: An Artist's Journals* (London: Chapman and Hall, 1879).

3. 'India', *The Times*, 24 December 1867, 8.

4. Roland Barthes, *Mythologies*, trans. Annette Lavers (New York: Hill and Wang, 1972), 143.

5. Julian Cox, *Julia Margaret Cameron, In Focus: From the J. Paul Getty Museum* (Los Angeles: J. Paul Getty Museum, 1996), 44.

6. Colin Ford, '"Mountain Nymph" and "Damnèd Villain"', *History of Photography*, 27:1 (2003), 60–5.

7. Scott Thomas Buckle, 'Is this the Face of Alessandro di Marco? The Forgotten Features of a Well-Known Italian Model', *British Art Journal*, 13:2 (Autumn 2012), 67–75.

8. For an argument that Cameron's sitters merge their identities with the characters they perform in an uncanny 'ghostly' or 'haunted' way, both in performance and in photography, see Peter Holland, 'Haunting Shakespeare, or King Lear meets Alice', in Mary Luckhurst and Emilie Morin, eds, *Theatre and Ghosts: Materiality, Performance and Modernity* (Basingstoke: Palgrave Macmillan, 2014), 197–216.

9. Jeff Rosen, *Julia Margaret Cameron's 'Fancy Subjects': Photographic Allegories of Victorian Identity and Empire* (Manchester: Manchester University Press, 2016), 15–18.

10. For another example of the biographical interpretation of Cameron's models as an index of their manifestation of complex identity formations within the imagery itself, see Kirsten Hoving, '"Flashing Thro' the Gloom": Julia

Margaret Cameron's "Eccentricity"', *History of Photography*, 27:1 (2003), 45–59.

11. Sally Barnden, *Still Shakespeare and the Photography of Performance* (Cambridge: Cambridge University Press, 2020), 131.

12. Ibid., 134.

13. Consequently, it is not particularly useful to compare Cameron's photograph of Iago to Pre-Raphaelite illustrations or earlier British paintings. See: Christine Paulson, 'A Checklist of Pre-Raphaelite Illustrations of Shakespeare's Plays', *Burlington Magazine*, 122:925 (April 1980), 244–50; T. S. R. Boase, 'Illustrations of Shakespeare's Plays in the Seventeenth and Eighteenth Centuries', *Journal of the Warburg and Courtauld Institutes*, 10 (1947), 83–108.

14. See the various discussions and analyses about the individual performances of Gustavus Vaughan Brooke, Charles Fechter, William Macready, Frederick Robson, and later, Edwin Booth and Henry Irving, in: Marvin Rosenberg, *The Masks of Othello: The Search for the Identity of Othello, Iago, and Desdemona by Three Centuries of Actors and Critics* (Berkeley and Los Angeles: University of California Press, 1961); George Taylor, *Players and Performances in the Victorian Theatre* (Manchester: Manchester University Press, 1989); John Glavin, '"To Make the Situation Natural": *Othello* at Mid-Century', in Gail Marshall and Adrian Poole, eds, *Victorian Shakespeare, Volume 2: Literature and Culture* (Hampshire and New York: Palgrave Macmillan, 2003), 30–45; Craven Mackie, 'Frederick Robson and the Evolution of Realistic Acting', *Educational Theatre Journal*, 23:2 (May 1971), 160–70.

15. Nancy Rose Marshall, 'The Many Shades of Shakespeare: Representations of Othello and Desdemona in Victorian Visual Culture', in Julie F. Codell, ed., *Transculturation in British Art, 1770–1930* (Surrey: Ashgate, 2012), 86.

16. Mike Weaver, *Julia Margaret Cameron, 1815–1879* (London: John Hansard Gallery, 1984), 26.

17. Michel Frizot, *The New History of Photography*, trans. Susan Bennett, Liz Clegg, John Crook, and Caroline Higgitt (Cologne: Könemann Verlagsgesellschaft, 1998), 194.

18. As I wrote earlier with regard to historians' differing interpretations of assessing Cameron's degree of 'success' in choosing the 'right model' for her Madonna pictures, 'The question ... is not how convincingly one thinks Cameron managed to represent her living models as idealized forms in art or whether a particular photograph of the Madonna is more or less sacred than another, since subjective assessments might reasonably change over time and differ in relation to one's taste, education, culture, religion, or gender'. The same is true for Cameron's photograph of Iago. See Rosen, *Julia Margaret Cameron's 'Fancy Subjects'*, 71–2.

19. On Cameron's production of imagery in relation to this religious controversy, see ibid., 83–99.

20. The debate stems from differing readings of Shakespeare's Quarto and Folio editions regarding the possible meanings behind a typo or printer's error to the lines 'Like the base Indian, threw a pearle away, / Richer than all his tribe' (Act v, scene 2, ll. 345–6). See Grace Hunter, 'Notes on Othello's "Base Indian"', *The Shakespeare Association Bulletin*, 19:1 (January 1944), 26–8; Barnden, *Still Shakespeare*, 140.

21. Walter Benjamin, 'The Work of Art in the Age of Mechanical Reproduction', in *Illuminations*, trans. Harry Zohn, ed. Hannah Arendt (New York: Schocken, 1969), 224–5.

22. The close proximity of the two images in the Herschel Album and their visual similarity suggests it is likely that Cameron envisioned both of these photographs in relation to British colonialism. For example, in *The Tempest*, Prospero exerts power over both Miranda and Caliban, 'displaying the psychology of colonials' as weapons of power and 'who projected their disowned traits onto New World natives'. Meredith Anne Skura, 'Discourse and the Individual: The Case of Colonialism in The Tempest', *Shakespeare Quarterly*, 40:1 (Spring 1989), 42–69. There is a vast bibliography on the subject, the scope of which is beyond this project.

23. William Allingham, *A Diary* (London: Macmillan, 1907), 186.

24. Barnden, *Still Shakespeare*, 145.

25. Adrian Poole, *Shakespeare and the Victorians* (London: Arden, 2004), 79.

26. R. Derek Wood, ed., *Julia Margaret Cameron's Copyrighted Photographs* (London: privately published, May 1996), #307.

27. Martin Orkin, 'Civility and the English Colonial Enterprise: Notes on Shakespeare's Othello', *Theoria: A Journal of Social and Political Theory*, 68 (December 1986), 1.

28. Quoted in: William Greenslade, 'Shakespeare and Politics', in Gail Marshall, ed., *Shakespeare and the Nineteenth Century* (Cambridge: Cambridge University Press, 2012), 231.

29. Thomas Babington Macaulay, 'Machiavelli', *Edinburgh Review*, March 1827, https://oll.libertyfund.org/title/macaulay-critical-and-historical-essays-vol-1.

30. George Otto Trevelyan, *The Life and Letters of Lord Macaulay*, vol. 2 (1876) (London: Oxford University Press, 1932), 408–9.

31. Ibid., vol. 2, 417.

32. Charles Baxter, 'Captain Happen: Some Notes on Narrative Urgency', in *Wonderlands: Essays on the Life of Literature* (Minneapolis: Graywolf Press, 2022), 69; Susan Neville, 'Where's Iago?', in Charles Baxter and Peter Turchi, eds, *Bringing the Devil to His Knees: The Craft of Fiction and the Writing Life* (Ann Arbor: University of Michigan Press, 2001), 31–44.

33. Debra Johanyak, '"Turning Turk," Modern English Orientalism, and *Othello*', in Debra Johanyak and Walter S. H. Lim, eds, *The English Renaissance, Orientalism, and the Idea of Asia* (Hampshire and New York: Palgrave Macmillan, 2009), 81.

34. Charles Cameron to Julia Margaret Cameron, 28 July 1851, Cameron Collection, Box 1, Getty Research Institute, J. Paul Getty Museum, Los Angeles.

35. The Ionian Islands comprised Corfu, Paxo, Cephalonia, Ithaca, Santa Maura, Zante, and Cerigo. For the tangled history of colonial control, see C. C. Eldridge, 'The Myth of Victorian "Separatism": The Cession of the Bay Islands and the Ionian

Islands in the Early 1860s', *Victorian Studies*, 12:3 (1969), 331–46.

36. Nevertheless, even into the year 1864, Charles Cameron apparently kept putting his name forward for such a post. In a letter of 11 June 1864, Sir Henry Taylor responded to a formal inquiry about Charles Cameron's 'fitness for Colonial Government', which broadly supported Cameron for his intelligence, literary knowledge, and clear writing, but wrote that his advanced age of sixty-six years old was a liability. Taylor indicated he discouraged Cameron from competing for the governorship of the Cape Colony, although it was expressed to him as a post of keen interest. Sir Henry Taylor to E.D.E., 11 June 1864, Bodleian Library, Acc. # [MS Eng lett d 12 ff17].

37. Britain did not establish formal colonial control of Cyprus until the 1878 Cyprus Convention, which maintained Turkish sovereignty but gave governance to Britain. See Nancy Crenshaw, *The Cyprus Revolt: An Account of the Struggle for Union with Greece* (London: Routledge, 1978).

38. Mark Matheson, 'Venetian Culture and the Politics of *Othello*', in Catherine M. S. Alexander, ed., *Shakespeare and Politics* (Cambridge: Cambridge University Press, 2004), 171.

39. R. M. Christofides, *Othello's Secret: The Cyprus Problem* (London and New York: Bloomsbury Arden Shakespeare, 2016). See also R. M. Christofides, '*Othello*, Cyprus and the Greater Middle East: Past, Present, and Future', *Shakespeare*, 16:3 (2020), 225–38.

40. Colm MacCrossan, '"What, in a Town of War ... to Manage Private and Domestic Quarrel?": *Othello* and the Tragedy of Cyprus', *Shakespeare*, 16:3 (2020), 242.

41. See Cory Stockwell, '*Othello*, the Secret of the Political', in Leonidas Donskis and J. D. Mininger, eds, *Politics Otherwise: Shakespeare as Social and Political Critique* (Amsterdam and New York: Rodopi, 2012), 56–9.

42. Stephen Greenblatt, *Renaissance Self-Fashioning: From More to Shakespeare* (Chicago: University of Chicago Press, 1980), 222–54.

43. Ania Loomba, *Shakespeare, Race, and Colonialism* (Oxford and New York: Oxford University Press, 2002), 97.

44. Stockwell, '*Othello*, the Secret of the Political', 61. Michael Neill has suggested Iago is an Iberian version of James, connected culturally to 'Saint James, the Moor-Slayer'. Michael Neill, '*Othello* and Race', in Peter Ericson and Maurice Hunt, eds, *Approaches to Teaching Shakespeare's Othello* (New York: MLA, 2005), 47.

45. Matheson, 'Venetian Culture and the Politics of *Othello*', 177.

46. Orkin, 'Civility and the English Colonial Enterprise', 6–7. The same point is also made by Matthew Steggle, 'Where Iago Lies: Home, Honesty and the Turk in *Othello*', *Early Modern Literary Studies*, 14:3 (January 2009), 1–27.

47. Julia Margaret Cameron to Sir Henry Taylor, 29 November 1862, in Cecil Lang and Edgar Shannon, eds, *The Letters of Alfred, Lord Tennyson, Volume 2: 1851–1870* (Cambridge, MA: Harvard University Press, 1987), 319.

48. Tom Taylor and his compatriots at *Punch* memorably mocked the sculpture committee in a large-cut graphic called 'Shakespeare and the Pigmies', published in the issue of 30 January 1864.

49. Richard Foulkes, *The Shakespeare Tercentenary of 1864* (London: Society for Theatre Research, 1984), 7–8, 11–21. For the list of vice presidents of the Stratford Committee, see Robert E. Hunter, *Shakespeare and Stratford-Upon-Avon, A 'Chronicle of the Time'* (London: Whittaker and Co., 1864), 135–7.

50. Hunter, *Shakespeare and Stratford-upon-Avon*, 237–8.

51. Antony Taylor, 'Shakespeare and Radicalism: The Uses and Abuses of Shakespeare in Nineteenth-Century Popular Politics', *Historical Journal*, 45:2 (2002), 358, 362.

52. Charles Laporte, 'The Bard, the Bible, and the Victorian Shakespeare Question', *ELH*, 74 (2007), 609–28; Richard Foulkes, '"Every Good Gift from Above": Archbishop Trench's Tercentenary Sermon', *Shakespeare Survey*, 54 (2001), 80–8.

53. Taylor, 'Shakespeare and Radicalism', 373–7.

54. Charles Trevelyan, *On the Education of the People of India* (London: Orient Longman, 1838), 124.

55. On the formal introduction of Shakespeare and Milton into the curriculum of colonial India, and the role of Charles Cameron in helping accomplish this goal, see: Guari Vishwanathan, *Masks of Conquest: Literary Study and British Rule in India* (New York: Columbia University Press, 1989), 1–54; and Jyotsna G. Singh, *Colonial Narratives, Cultural Dialogues: 'Discoveries' of India in the Language of Colonialism* (London and New York: Routledge, 1996).

56. Sushil Kumar Mukherjee, *The Story of the Calcutta Theatres, 1753–1980* (Calcutta and New Delhi: K. P. Bagchi and Co., 1982), 1; Singh, *Colonial Narratives, Cultural Dialogues*, 128.

57. Sudipto Chatterjee, *The Colonial Staged: Theatre in Colonial Calcutta* (Oxford, New York, Calcutta: Seagull Books, 2007), 24.

58. Ibid., 58.

59. Ibid., 66.

60. Ibid., 140, 160.

61. Quoted in Singh, *Colonial Narratives, Cultural Dialogues*, 133–4.

62. Thomas Carlyle, *On Heroes, Hero-Worship, and the Heroic in History* (New York: A. L. Burt Company, n.d.), 133.

63. Helen Douglas Mackenzie, *Storms and Sunshine of a Soldier's Life: Lt.-General Colin Mackenzie, C.B., 1825–1881, Volume 2* (Edinburgh: David Douglas, 1884), 3–5.

64. Thomas Carlyle to Lord Ashburton, 18 August 1857, in *The Carlyle Letters Online*, https://carlyleletters.dukeupress.edu/volume/33/lt-18570818-TC-LOA-01.

65. Carlyle, *On Heroes*, 133–4.

Acknowledgements

This book builds upon the publications of numerous scholars and museum professionals who have preceded me and upon whose analyses my own depends, especially seminal works of Julian Cox and Colin Ford, Helmut Gernsheim, Mike Weaver, Mark Haworth-Booth, Victoria Olsen, Marta Weiss, and Joanne Lukitsh. For access to Cameron's photographs I thank the following: the J. Paul Getty Museum, Los Angeles; the Bodleian Library, Oxford; in London, the Victoria and Albert Museum, the Science and Media Museum, the British Library, the National Army Museum, the British Museum, and the National Portrait Gallery; the George Eastman House Museum, Rochester, New York; the Art Institute of Chicago; and the Harry Ransom Humanities Research Center at the University of Texas, Austin.

I am also grateful for the generosity of collectors and curators who provided access to archival documents in their collections: Charles, Marquis of Lansdowne, and Cathryn Spence, Curator/Archivist, Bowood House & Gardens, Wiltshire; Hew Dalrymple (UK) and William Dalrymple (India); Colin Ford, London; Liz Siegel, Milwaukee; Jonathan Barker, Archives Collections Officer, Kent History and Library Centre, Maidstone; Michael Mattis and Judy Hochberg, New York; Richard Fattorini, Sotheby's; Lauren Richman, Sidney and Lois Eskenazi Museum of Art, Bloomington, Indiana; Kathryn Jones, Lincolnshire Archives, Lincoln, and Malcolm Daniel, Museum of Fine Arts, Houston.

I would also like to thank Catherine de Zegher and Griselda Pollock, organizers of the 2015 Cameron symposium at the Museum voor Schone Kunsten, Ghent; and Martina Droth, who organized the 2016 symposium 'Photography and Britishness' at the Yale Center for British Art, New Haven, Connecticut. George Dimock and John Leary read early versions of the manuscript and provided valuable insights, as did anonymous readers for the Paul Mellon Centre for Studies in British Art. It has been an absolute joy working with the Paul Mellon Centre's editorial and production team, assembled under the extraordinary direction of Emily Lees. Christine Considine provided wise and insightful copy-editing and Robert Dalrymple produced a beautiful and thoughtful book design. For their meticulous work proofreading and indexing this book, I would also like to thank Jacquie Meredith and Jane Horton. Their contributions have made this a stunning volume, and I am extremely thankful to them all. Finally, I am heartened each day by the loving support of my wife, Lynn Sloan, who provided steadfast encouragement and love throughout the process of writing this book.

Index

NOTE: Page numbers in *italics* refer to illustrations.
JMC = Julia Margaret Cameron